Photo
scapes

Edited by Frédéric Pousin

The Nexus between Photography and Landscape Design

Photo scapes

Birkhäuser
Basel

Photographers' Portfolios:

Acknowledgments

This book is the result of a research program funded by the French National Research Agency, entitled "Photography and Landscape: knowledges, practices, projects" (ANR 13-BSH3-0008-01). Its publication was made possible through the financial support awarded by the research unit AUSser CNRS, the Department of Culture and Communication, the IPRAUS – National School of Architecture Paris-Belleville and the LAREP – National Landscape School of Versailles, each of which deserves my sincere thanks.

I also want to thank the institutions which have hosted the various study days of this program: the University of New Mexico in Albuquerque, and especially the vice president in charge of international relations, Virginia Joy Scharff, the Potager du Roi in Versailles, its director Antoine Jacobsohn, Nathalie Lancret, the director of the research unit (UMR) AUSser, the National School of Architecture in Nancy and the landscape teaching unit headed by Marie-José Canonica.

Our perspective, which was to interweave landscape architects' and photographers' approaches to landscape, was challenging in its arrangement. May the authors, landscape architects, and photographers who lent themselves to this demanding exercise find here the expression of my gratitude. I also wish to express my thanks to each and every person who has contributed to this intellectual adventure and has pushed it forward through their advice and encouragements during the three years it took: Henri Bava, Elizabeth Barlow Rogers, Claire Lise Benaud, Emmanuelle Blanc, Gilles Clément, Matthew Coolidge, Katya Crawford, Denis Delbaere, Sabine Delcour, Sabine Ehrmann, Miguel Gandert, Brian Goldstein, Jérôme Goze, Paul Groth, Laura Harjo, Helen L. Horowitz, Aurélien Humm, Andreas Kofler, Lin Chi-Ming, Lucy Lippard, Richard Longstreth, Chester Liebs, Caroline Maniaque, Aude Mathé, Kymberly Pinder.

Special thanks to those who spared no effort and tremendously helped the accomplishment of this work: Sylvie Archaimbault, Cristina Ros Ballester, Morgane Hamon, Sonia Keravel, Marie-Hélène Loze, Chris Wilson.

Finally, I wish to express my gratitude towards my editors, Françoise Arnold and Valérie Thouard, who have dared to create something that adapted itself wonderfully around the never-ending motion of this work. The touch of Line Celo and Clémence Michon, graphic designers, must also be applauded.

The texts have been translated from French to English by Christopher Hinton and Nicolas Carter: I wish to thank them for their great efficiency and professionalism.

Frédéric Pousin

Milestones for an Intercultural Approach

Frédéric Pousin

The aim of this book is to explore the subtle links woven between photography and landscape projects. Following on from a three-year joint research project, it attempts to consider the role that photography plays in the management and transformation of landscapes and in the debates that may ensue. Changes to the countryside often reflect changes in society, be they economic, social or cultural. For Augustin Berque, geographer and expert on Japan, landscape expresses the relationship between a society and its environment.[1] Yet perception of a landscape is also an eminently subjective reality, often emotionally charged: whether we think of familiar, political or even wartime landscapes. And finally, it is a living reality that continuously evolves and changes. Landscape projects are the result of foresight, of a vision that guides action so as to meet a need or a desire for transformation. Historically speaking, they were rooted in garden design and then in urbanism, with parks becoming urban and public. Park projects were major levers for town development, as can be seen from the exemplary works of Olmsted: his first plans for a park system for the city of Buffalo in 1868 or the creation of Jackson Park on the shores of Lake Michigan in Chicago[2] inspired the thinking and projects of numerous French landscape architects, from yesteryear's Jean Claude Nicolas Forestier to Michel Desvigne today. Closely linked to town and country planning, the scale of landscaping projects has grown – in France, to that of a communauté de communes (a grouping of local authorities), a nature park or a *département* (county). But a landscaping project is characterized by the overall vision and coherency that it channels, and by the convergence of opportunities for action that it organizes within a region. The objectives that it sets itself are developed and discussed at length; landscape projects thus generate argument and debate – a debate that has many different forms of expression and in which photography is taking an ever-increasing part.

The role of photography is of course eminently variable, depending on the cultural context and the historical period. From its very beginnings, photography was solicited for regional planning purposes. Was the purpose of the first aerial pictures taken by Nadar not to help in the creation of a land registry?[3] In the United States, photography was used in geological and geographical missions commissioned by the Government, to take account of the progress in prospection and exploration during the second half of the 19th century. The role that photographers played in the creation of natural parks is well known,[4] particularly that of Carleton Watkins, who was the first person to arouse national interest in the Yosemite Valley. Photographic reportages proved crucial in the promotion of conservation policies. The same was true of William Henry Jackson's pictures with regard to the creation of Yellowstone Park in 1872, and the emblematic works of Ansel Adams in the 1930s. Photography also accompanied the construction of railways and roads, and parkways[5] in particular.

1
See Augustin Berque, *Les raisons du paysage. De la Chine antique aux environnements de synthèse*, Hazan, Paris, 1995.

2
See Charles E. Beveridge and Paul Rocheleau, *Frederic Law Olmsted, Designing the American Landscape*, Universe Publishing, New York, 1998.

3
Stephen Bann, "La vue aérienne de Nadar", in Mark Dorrian and Frédéric Pousin (eds.), *Vues aériennes. Seize études pour une histoire culturelle*, MétisPresses, Geneva, 2008, p. 69–78.

4
See Jamie M. Allen, *Picturing America's National Parks*, George Eastman Museum, Rochester, New York, 2016.

5
See Timothy Davis, *National Park Roads. A Legacy in the American Landscape*, The University of Virginia Press, Charlottesville, 2016.

At the turn of the 20th century in France, photographers were also involved in a context of defending and preserving sites and landscapes – urban in particular – as can be seen in the *Casier archéologique et artistique de Paris et du département de la Seine*, implemented by the *Commission historique du vieux Paris* between 1916 and 1928.[6] With a dual objective of study and preservation, several thousand photographs were taken to document buildings or complexes under threat. The dossiers compiled in this way were used to develop plans for the future expansion of Paris. The inventory of all of the city's components, landscapes included, covered not only Paris but also the municipalities that made up the Greater Paris of the future.

In such situations, photography participates in the development of an archive that serves to create inventories which in turn serve heritage policies. The archive is not, however, the sole objective of these commissions. In France, after the Second World War, public commissions were intended to serve a national land policy. Ensuring the promotion of the reconstruction and modernization of the country, photography found itself being integrated into modes of communication targeting the general public – such as the *Salon des arts ménagers* (houseware exhibition) in Paris.

These various photographic productions related to various commissioning situations, which should not be confused with one another. The initiative of a photographer such as Eugène Atget – who sells his pictures to a private clientele, to municipal institutions and to museums – is different from a public commission – such as that of the *Commission des Monuments Historiques*, which in 1851 asked five well-known photographers to document an inventory of the country's architectural and artistic heritage.[7] And this mission undertaken by artist-photographers, which remains famous under the name of *Mission héliographique*, cannot be equated to the case of technician-operators working for an institution – such as the *Eaux et Forêts* engineers in the *Service de restauration des terrains de montagne* (department for the restoration of mountain lands) – who between 1866 and 1940 took series of photos which were essentially intended for professional use in the field of landscape management.[8]

In a comparative study of photographic missions in France and the United States, Raphaële Bertho established a dividing line between commissions that call upon technicians and those that appeal to creative artists for their unique perspective and viewpoint.[9] However enlightening it may be, this dividing line nonetheless merits close examination, in terms of the historical and social acceptation of the notion of creative artist. In France in the 1980s, the *Mission photographique de la DATAR* (DATAR Photographic Mission) called upon highly renowned photographers in a cultural context who were endeavoring to gain artistic recognition. Two historical antecedents were used: DATAR's prestigious Heliographic Mission and the no less famous commission from the Farm Security Administration (FSA), which had come into being in the late 1930s in the United States, at the time of the Great Depression when photographers were struggling to achieve artist status. In inaugurating a commission for artist-photographers, DATAR triggered numerous initiatives, including that of the landscape photography observatories in France, most of which were implemented within regional nature parks.

We have chosen to explore certain historical moments and representative processes of the role that photography has played in the manufacture of landscapes: above and beyond viewpoint or the production of documents, it is a question of a photography expanded to include commissions, the photographer's perspective, and vectors of dissemination.

American national parks are an excellent laboratory for observing the diversity of photography's functions and uses, as well as the status of the photographers themselves. Timothy Davis explores an underappreciated period between the discovery of the national parks (the creation of the NPS) and the growing influence of Ansel Adams during the 1930s – that particular moment when the parks' commercial and salaried photographers were endeavoring to express a popular perception of nature that would henceforth become the official perception. The NPS's strategy for disseminating pictures made use of various media so as to create a symbol proper to America's national parks.

In the history of photography and landscape, photography has often been solicited to accompany and promote projects. But its value cannot be limited to this instrumental function, because the pictures also help to develop – or challenge – cultural norms. Public commissions have fueled a debate on these norms. Taking a cross-section of commissions from 1994, Raphaële Bertho analyzes the policies behind these photographic projects. 1994 proved to be a landmark year, both for France and internationally, with numerous commissions being placed simultaneously by institutions in charge of town and country planning. The author presents both the moment at which thinking about landscape became established in France – principally in the 1990s – and the institutional background for these commissions, via the DATAR Photographic Mission. She finds an evolution in commissioning that forsakes land planning issues and shifts more towards the cultural stakes of regional valorization.

Geographer and landscape theorist J. B. Jackson provides a strong link between the essays in this book, which discuss different geographical, institutional and artistic contexts. Indeed, John Brinckerhoff Jackson's thinking constitutes both a cultural reference and a theoretical foundation for articulating the photography of cultural, natural or inhabited landscapes with the role that photography plays in landscape, management or transformation projects pursued by professionals and activists.[10] With the journal *Landscape*, which he created in 1951, J. B. Jackson was one of the leading promoters of the notion of cultural landscape in the United States. But he was also able to link reflection on the cultural landscape to the culture of urbanism and planning.

In his essay, Chris Wilson shows how, depending on the period of his life, J. B. Jackson developed several different understandings of photography. As a publisher, his initial approach was utilitarian – to his eyes a print was merely a document – which made him less than open to the emerging world of fine-art photography. It was in a later period, when the success of his conception of the cultural landscape allowed him to give lectures and teach courses, that Jackson, using thousands of color slides, turned to photography as a means of documenting the cultural landscape of North America as he encountered it during his travels. Finally, his contact in universities with the counterculture generation and new artistic trends further modified his perception of photography.

Bruno Notteboom's careful reading of the journal *Landscape* shows that Jackson relies on a conception of landscape that is both complex and ambiguous, being based on actual examples. To this end he analyzes the construction of a discourse made up of interwoven text, images and intertextuality. It was Jackson's responsibility as editor to assemble the texts and pictures for each issue and this allowed him to have a discourse parallel to the text. Notteboom's analysis focuses mainly on articles relating to the urban landscape; he shows that by widening the field to include the urban sphere, i.e. to disciplines other than geography, Jackson offered, through his journal, a non-hegemonic view of landscape that was open to emerging theories and practices.

This book contains several contributions that focus on the circulation of ideas between different cultural milieus, via publications, exhibitions and conferences – three forms of mediation that make use of photography.

Laurie Olin looks back at the post-war period in the United States, where the broad dissemination of landscape projects in specialist and general publications defined a veritable "photographic landscape". Indeed, the manner in which these forms of media "framed" the projects contained therein shaped the "perceptive apparatus" of an American public keen on design and landscape architecture. As a landscape architect active throughout the 1960s, he also attests to photography's impact on his work. He describes the methods employed within his own agency, Olin Studio, to classify and archive the photographic documentation of projects, prior to

6
See, Laurence Bassière, "Prémisses d'un urbanisme patrimonial. L'épisode du Casier archéologique et artistique de Paris et du département de la Seine, 1916–1928", in Actes du colloque des 5 et 6 décembre 2013, Cité de l'architecture et du patrimoine, http://www.inventer-legrandparis.fr/panoramas-historiques/1911-1919/

7
See Anne de Mondenard, *La mission Héliographique. Cinq photographes parcourent la France en 1851*, Monum, Éditions du patrimoine, Paris, 2002.

8
See Luce Lebart, "La restauration des montagnes. Photographies de l'Administration des forêts au XIXe siècle", *Études photographiques*, no. 3, Revue de la Société française de photographie, p. 82–101, 1997. http://etudesphotographiques.revues.org/96

9
See Raphaële Bertho, "From the American Survey to the French Mission, What Photographic Landscape Policy?" talk given at the *PhotoPaysage/Landscape Representation* conference, 15–17 October 2015. http://photopaysage.huma-num.fr/from-the-american-survey-to-the-french-mission-what-photographic-landscape-policy/

10
See the *PhotoPaysage/Landscape Representation* conference, *op.cit.* See also, Janet Mendelsohn, Christopher Wilson, *Drawn to Landscape. The Pioneering Work of J. B. Jackson*, The University of Virginia Press, Charlottesville, VA, 2015.

the advent of digital photography. Finally, establishing a link between the post-war "photographic landscape" and the current period, Olin underlines the veritable "photographic utopia" that is now available through the internet.

Representations of projects through photography form a structural theme of the book. Culturalist theories of landscape have stressed the role that representations play in constructing the fact of landscape – whether they consider artistic expression to be a prerequisite for the manifestation of landscape or as the translation of a physical reality into a society's collective imaginary.[11] Both reality and representation, landscape is conducive to the coming together of professional and artistic practices whose boundaries are becoming increasingly porous.

Frédéric Pousin posits that photography is an instrument of choice for transforming a project into fragments of discourse. He examines the uses that Gilles Clément makes of the slide, which is more of a tool for communicating about project experiences than a project instrument. It is by studying Clément's conferences that we can see the extent to which photography contributes to the theoretical discourse of the landscape architect. Indeed, in an original fashion and in terms that differ from publication or exhibition, the conference as a medium touches on the interplay between word and image. As a channel for disseminating landscape culture, it also raises the issue of the relationship with the audience.

Marie-Madeleine Ozdoba's close reading of landscape projects reveals novel ways of using photography in landscape design; ordinarily, the latter tends to see photography as a means of recording, from the documentation of the site through to that of the completed project. She examines the approach used by Bas Smets, a landscape architect in Brussels, who on the contrary considers photography to be a field of creation and expression in its own right. He develops a relationship between photography and reality, following a culturalist conception of landscape as a constructed representation, the relevance of which is supported by the critical apparatus of contemporary theories of photography.

Nowadays, landscape design is an increasingly complex task that involves numerous professions, photographers included, which participate in the process of land transformation. Their practices vary, combining the creative stance with participation in public debate. We know that the construction of a field, be it professional or artistic, is founded on veritable media strategies.[12] Interaction between photographers and landscape architects has proved fruitful and we are able to see how a landscape is built within this interaction. It therefore makes sense to examine the way in which one field – landscape design – shakes up the other – photography – and vice versa.

For Sonia Keravel, project photographers have long been confined to the role of technician. The inventive aspect of their work has until now been overlooked. Yet more often than not, in books and exhibitions, it is through the photographer's eye that we learn about landscaping projects. Keravel studies the relationships between photographers and landscape architects who work together on town and country planning projects. Duos are formed, with complex attachments often interwoven with friendship. In examining the partnership between Alain Marguerit and Gérard Dufresne, she finds a veritable coproduction of the landscape project.

Franck Michel makes a detailed analysis of Bertrand Carrière's *Après Strand* photographic project, which is both an encounter with a leading figure of photographic history and an examination of a region that is dear to the author – the Gaspésie. This photographic project looks at both the human and geographical experience of appropriating a region and at a voyage through the historical depth of places and perspectives. The project moves beyond the photographs and their idiosyncrasies, into the strategies developed to share, exhibit and publish. Bertrand Carrière's project is a self-commission that caught the attention of a cultural institution, that of the *Musée regional de Rimouski*. It differs from an institutional project designed to valorize a region, by offering a critical perspective that uses only the levers of photography.

The relevance of a fresh debate on landscape and photographic projects – a debate that this book hopes to reflect and nurture – was confirmed by a round table with photographers, landscape architects and researchers. The discussions were organized around the various forms of media coverage that a project might have triggered. Publication was found to be the most shared form, with exhibition relating more to photographers and conferences relating more to landscape architects. The round table was an opportunity to talk about collaborations between these professionals and, above all, to clarify the reciprocal expectations. Photography was felt to be a flexible medium that can create pictures with different statuses. Because ultimately it is the use of photography – the integration of the document into a process of design or communication, or into artistic projects that may take different forms – that allows the document to exist in an environment that goes beyond the mere world of images. Photography nevertheless has its own distinctive characteristics which, according to Catherine Mosbach, constitute its value to landscape architects. As Geoffroy Mathieu points out, a photograph is a fixed image that invites consideration and leaves no one indifferent. Its limits are its strength. For Pascale Hannetel, the landscape project calls for a photographic eye capable of revealing its hitherto unnoticed aspects, and of mobilizing people around how best to manage it. The numerous actors involved are invited to discuss it on the basis of representations (mainly maps and photos), as Valérie Kauffmann notes, with the expectation that they will then sign off on it collectively. The photographic project is inevitably framed in very different terms, in light of the "creative photography" approach that Raphaële Bertho sees as being so pervasive nowadays, leading her to dissociate the photographic project from photographic practice. With Édith Roux, visual forms tend towards a performativity which, precisely, does not relate to regional actors. The articulation around the region's social and political reality is of course variable, with the photographic project also acting within the imaginary – an imaginary that is just as much photographic as it is territory and landscape oriented. By the end of the round table, we find permeabilities emerging, first and foremost of which is the need to question the very terms used in discourses relating to professional practices. The modalities through which photographic images exist – archives, the revelation of the non-visible, interdiscursivity – are widely shared.

Finally, through visual discourse, a certain number of image portfolios, accompanied by brief argumentation, shed light on the encounter between photographic project and landscape transformation.

11
See Alain Roger (ed.), *La Théorie du paysage en France*, 1974, 1994, Champ Vallon, Seyssel, 1995.

12
See Beatriz Colomina, *Privacy and Publicity: Modern Architecture as Mass Media*, MIT Press, Cambridge, MA, 1994.

Filling in the Picture: A Broader Perspective on National Park Photography

Timothy Davis

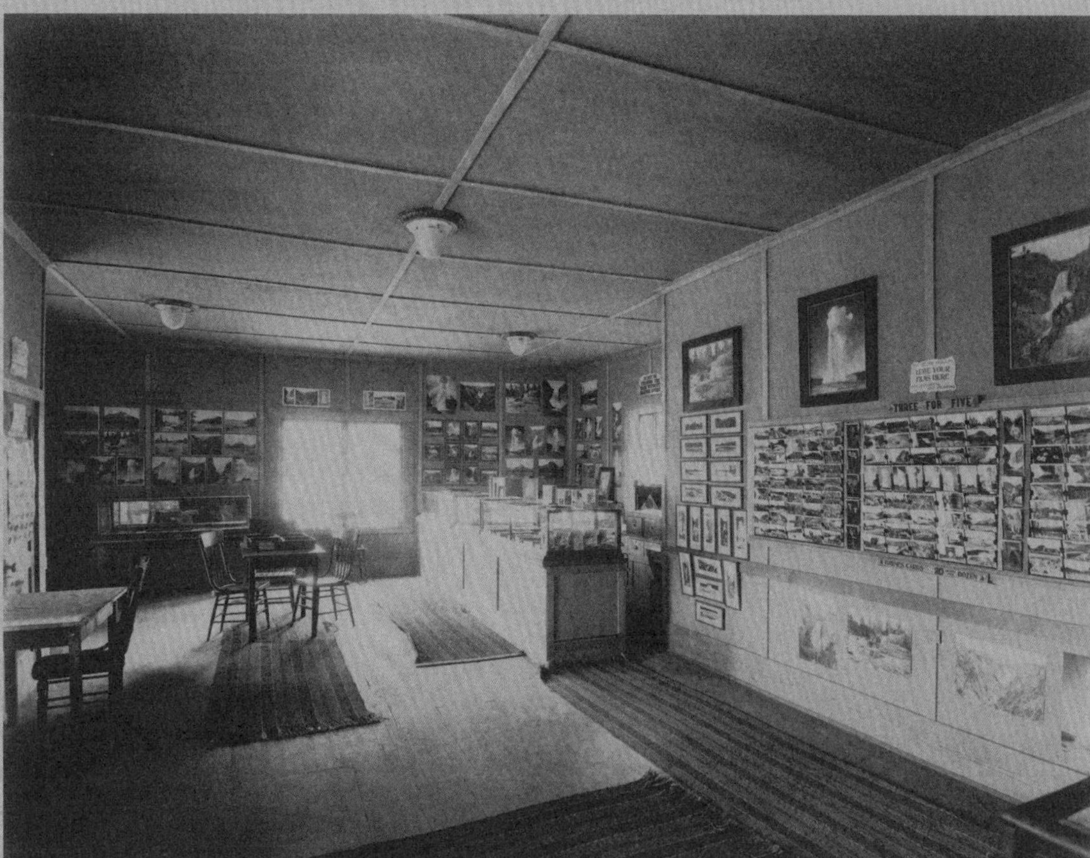

National park photography is such a well-known genre that the topic would seem to be thoroughly exhausted. From Carleton Watkins' emblematic Yosemite images and William Henry Jackson's role in the establishment of Yellowstone to Ansel Adams' monumental oeuvre, the masterworks of national park photography have generated a wealth of academic interest and popular acclaim. The emphasis on prominent artists and pioneering practitioners is understandable, but this narrow focus provides a limited perspective on national park photography. Much can be gained by examining the undervalued interlude between the discovery era and Adams' ascendancy, when commercial photographers and government employees played prominent roles in shaping popular and official perceptions of the nature and meaning of America's national parks. Eschewing the traditional filter of aesthetic evaluation to focus on the ways in which the federal government employed photographs to promote national parks and advance institutional agendas illuminates the broader role of photography in the construction of landscape values and social relations. Informal collaborations between federal officials, commercial interests, and professional image-makers gave way to more structured arrangements after 1916 as the newly formed National Park Service (NPS) relied heavily on photographic imagery to cultivate support, expand its influence, and celebrate its achievements.

The influence of Jackson's photographs on the establishment of Yellowstone National Park is one of the most celebrated episodes in the annals of both photography and conservation, but the role of photography in the authorization and popularization of the more broadly conceived U.S. National Park System has been largely overlooked, at least by chroniclers of the photographic medium. Several contributors have attracted interest from park historians and regional institutions, but technical factors have combined with scholarly and critical biases to marginalize an important aspect of the relationship between photography and America's national parks. Initial efforts relied heavily on commercial photographers, who were more intent on pleasing popular tastes than acquiring artistic accolades. Along with employing conventional compositional strategies that did little to advance the aesthetic aspects of the genre, they focused on marketable commodities such as post cards, stereo views, souvenir albums, and other items that were considered beneath the dignity of artistic consideration. Not only did their mercantile orientation detract from efforts to define photography as a fine art, but they exhibited little enthusiasm for the soft-focused fancies of the contemporary photographic avant-garde.

The National Park Service (NPS) photographers who succeeded them combined traditional landscape imagery with depictions of tourist activities and even more prosaic documentation of capital improvements, natural specimens, and historical artifacts. While the NPS displayed photographs in visitor facilities and temporary exhibitions, the images were primarily seen in government publications and popular periodicals, where the reproduction quality was marginal at best. Another common method of dissemination – public lectures illustrated by glass lantern slides – has been overlooked due to the ephemerality of the performances and the challenges of storing, viewing and reproducing the medium. Contemporary social reform photographers such as Jacob Riis and Lewis Hine[1] faced similar impediments, but their sensational imagery and humanitarian agendas appealed more strongly to historians of photography and American culture. Similar biases shaped the reception of work produced during the 1930s. Overshadowed by the Farm Security Administration's chronicle of the social and environmental costs of the Great Depression, the efforts of NPS photographers have gone largely unremarked. While these momentous events inspired memorable images by mesmerizing artists such as Walker Evans, Ben Shahn and Dorothea Lange, scholarly and critical preferences for social documentary over landscape photography also came into play.[2] Despite Ansel Adams' popular appeal, landscape was regarded as a less significant genre throughout most of the 20th century, especially when portrayed in the straightforward mode favored by park photographers. Scholars have become increasingly attuned to the ideological implications of landscape representation, however, and are interrogating the ways in which even the most seemingly benign images serve to construct or contest cultural norms and values. Coupled with growing interest in the ways in which the production and dissem-

1
See: Maren Stange, *Symbols of Ideal Life: Social Documentary Photography in America, 1890–1950*, Cambridge University Press, New York, 1989.

2
See: F. Jack Hurley, *Portrait of a Decade: Roy Stryker and the Development of Documentary Photography in the Thirties*, University of Louisiana Press, Baton Rouge, 1972; Alan Trachtenberg, *Reading America Photographs: Images as History, Matthew Brady to Walker Evans*, Hill & Wang, New York, 1989.

ination of photographic imagery influences its cultural impact, this emphasis on looking beyond aesthetic filters and outdated perceptions affords an opportunity to examine National Park Service photography in an illuminating new light. The 100th anniversary of the establishment of the National Park Service provides additional incentive for reflection on this pivotal period in the relationship between parks, people and the photographic medium.

Prior to 1916 national parks were technically under the control of the U.S. Department of the Interior, but administered by military officers and politically appointed private citizens with widely varying aims and abilities. With no comprehensive management policies or unified leadership, they were often poorly managed and subject to threats from mining, grazing, and water development interests. They were also seen as under-utilized and elitist. Not only did the expense of traveling in the pre-automotive era restrict visiting to those who could afford lengthy vacations, but it created the impression that national parks were of limited value to the broader public. Tourists typically traveled cross-country by train and spent a week or more staying at park hotels that offered similar service to private resorts and charged accordingly. Yellowstone and Yosemite were by far the most popular destinations, along with the Grand Canyon, which was not a national park but a national monument under the jurisdiction of the Department of Agriculture. Many viewed the parks as individual resorts operated by and for the railroad companies and concessionaires rather than as national institutions "for the benefit and enjoyment of the people," as Yellowstone's founding legislation proclaimed.

Park advocates believed the best way to protect existing parks and create new ones was to establish a fully-fledged government agency to oversee them and expand the constituency of park supporters by emphasizing their appeal to the growing ranks of middle-class Americans seeking to enjoy modest vacations along with the increased mobility afforded by the proliferation of automobiles. They also sought to underscore the broader value of national parks as economic assets and cultural institutions. During a series of conferences leading up to agency's creation, park advocates emphasized the need for improvements in three key areas: transportation, accommodation, and public relations. While everyone from the Sierra Club to the Secretary of the Interior agreed that automobiles were the wave of the future, existing roads would require significant upgrades to accommodate automobile traffic. Newly established parks such as Glacier had hardly any roads at all. Park hotels, meanwhile, charged exorbitant rates and were too few and far between to accommodate significant increases in patronage. Proponents lamented that American national parks possessed the finest scenery in the world, but inadequate infrastructure prevented these fantastic sights from being seen. The drive to improve the physical infrastructure of national parks has been amply documented by historians of landscape architecture and engineering, but park advocates understood that constructing a conceptual infrastructure for understanding and appreciating national parks was equally important – and that photography would play an indispensable role.[3]

Federal officials realized that they were ill-equipped for the task. While William H. Jackson, Timothy O'Sullivan and other pioneering expositors of park landscapes conducted their most famous work for official geologic surveys, the government exhibited little interest in funding ongoing photographic activity in national parks. Private photographers filled the void, but the nature of the imagery and relationships between photographers and their audiences evolved as well. Instead of authenticating the existence of supreme spectacles in need of federal protection, photographers sought to emphasize their touristic appeal. Eye-catching images of geysers, cliffs and waterfalls remained popular, but as emblems of touristic experiences ranging from the ridiculous to the sublime. Exotic attractions such as Yosemite's Tunnel Trees and Yellowstone's bears joined the mix, while images showing visitors enjoying park landscapes began to proliferate.

Many photographers developed long-time associations with individual parks, either visiting frequently or setting up concessions that catered to tourists' demands for film developing and ready-made souvenirs. F. J. Haynes established the first official national park photographic concession in Yellowstone in 1884. By the turn of the 20th century Haynes was operating "picture shops" in multiple locations in conjunction with his son Jack, who succeeded him in 1916 | **FIG. 1** |. Along with catering to tourists' demands, the Haynes supplied promotional imagery to magazines, railroads, and other park concessionaires. They also worked closely with park officials, photographing roads, bridges and other improvements, along with special events and notable visitors. While it was clearly in the Haynes's interest to amplify their customer base, both father and son were genuinely committed to popularizing the park. They were also highly conscious of their role as the primary creators and curators of Yellowstone's visual history. During their 60 year reign as the dominant purveyors of Yellowstone photography, they produced thousands of negatives chronicling the transition from trackless wilderness to bustling resort, the birth of the National Park Service, and the dawn of the automobile age. Both the military officers who oversaw the park prior to 1916 and the National Park Service officials who succeeded them recognized the crucial role played by the Haynes operation, routinely characterizing father and son as "the park photographer" or "the official park photographer". There was no legal basis for the designation, but it reflected the Haynes's status as Yellowstone's primary photographic concessionaire and their willingness to perform the duties a federally employed photographer would normally fulfill, if park authorities had the means to engage one.[4]

Similar relationships existed between photographers and federal officials in other parks. Yosemite's most noted practitioners in the post-Carleton Watkins era were George Fiske, Julius Boysen, Harry Best and Arthur Pillsbury | **FIG. 2** |. Pillsbury was the most active during the early decades of the 20th century, taking an energetic role in promoting Yosemite and national parks in general. Lindley Eddy was Sequoia's primary photographic concessionaire, while Fred Kiser played a similar role at Crater Lake. Kiser's photographs had been instrumental in the authorization of both Crater Lake and Glacier National Parks. His Glacier work was funded by the Great Northern Railway, whose president Louis Hill was the driving force behind the park's authorization and the popularization of the See America First movement, whose argument that Americans should spend their tourist dollars at home rather than abroad played a key role in the establishment of the National Park Service. Asahel Curtis was not only Mount Rainier's primary photographer, but its most ardent booster, serving as chairman of the organization that promoted the park's interests in Congress and advertised its attractions to the public at large. Federal officials freely admitted that railroads, concessionaires and local boosters bore the brunt of the effort to popularize national parks. They also agreed it was time for the government to take a more prominent role,

3
The development of national park infrastructure is detailed in Ethan Carr, *Wilderness by Design: Landscape Architecture and the National Park Service*, University of Nebraska Press, Lincoln, NE, 1998; Linda McClelland, *Building the National Parks: Historic Landscape Design and Construction*, Johns Hopkins University Press, Baltimore, MD, 1998; and Timothy Davis, *National Park Roads: A Legacy in the American Landscape*, University of Virginia Press, Charlottesville, VA, 2016.

4
Haynes's interactions with park officials can be traced in National Archives and Records Administration (NARA), Record Group 79, NPS Central Files, Yellowstone, Boxes 225–26, 490–500, 1780; the NPS holdings in NARA's Still Pictures Branch contains an extensive collection of Haynes photographs. The Montana Historical Society is the primary repository of Haynes material. See: Aubrey Haines, *The Yellowstone Story*, vol. 1, Yellowstone Library and Museum Association in cooperation with Colorado Associated University Press, Yellowstone National Park, WY, 1977; Montana Historical Society, *F. J. Haynes, Photographer*, Montana Historical Society Press, Helena, MT, 1981; Carl Schreier (ed.), *Yellowstone: Selected Photographs 1870–1960*, Homestead Publishing Company, Moose, WY, 1989.

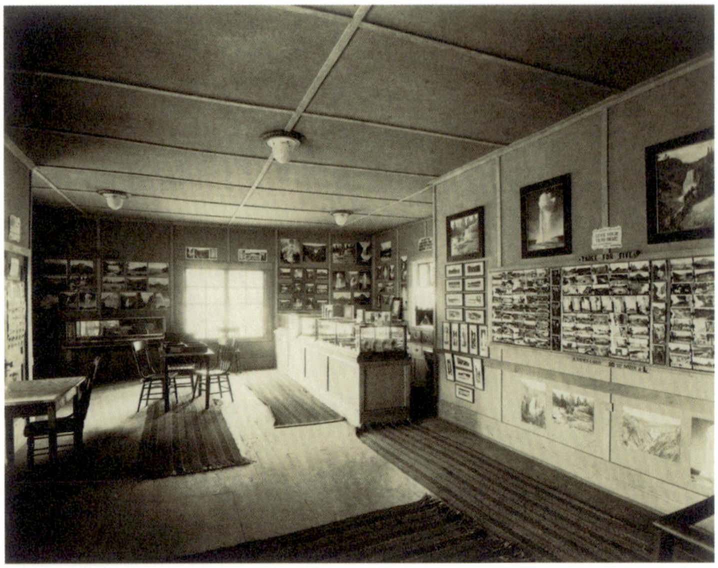

| FIG. 1 |

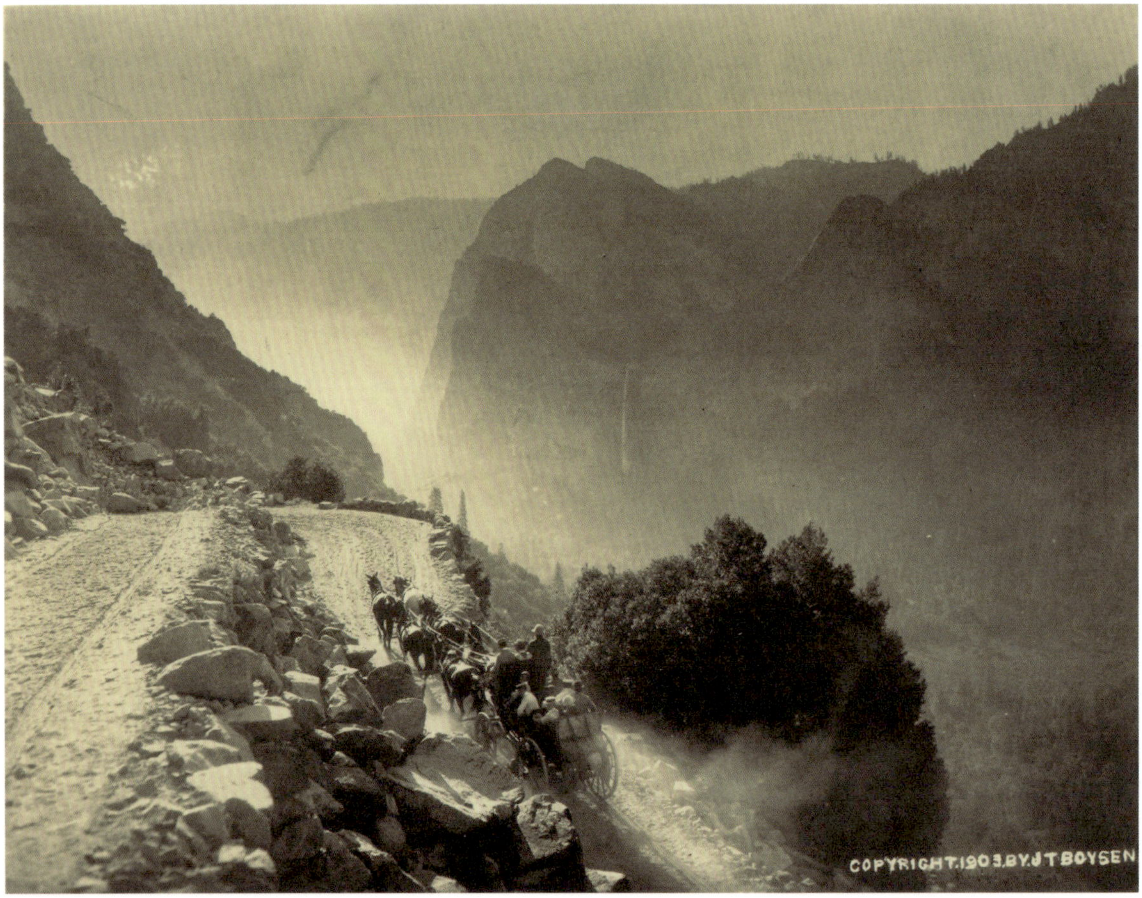

| FIG. 2 |

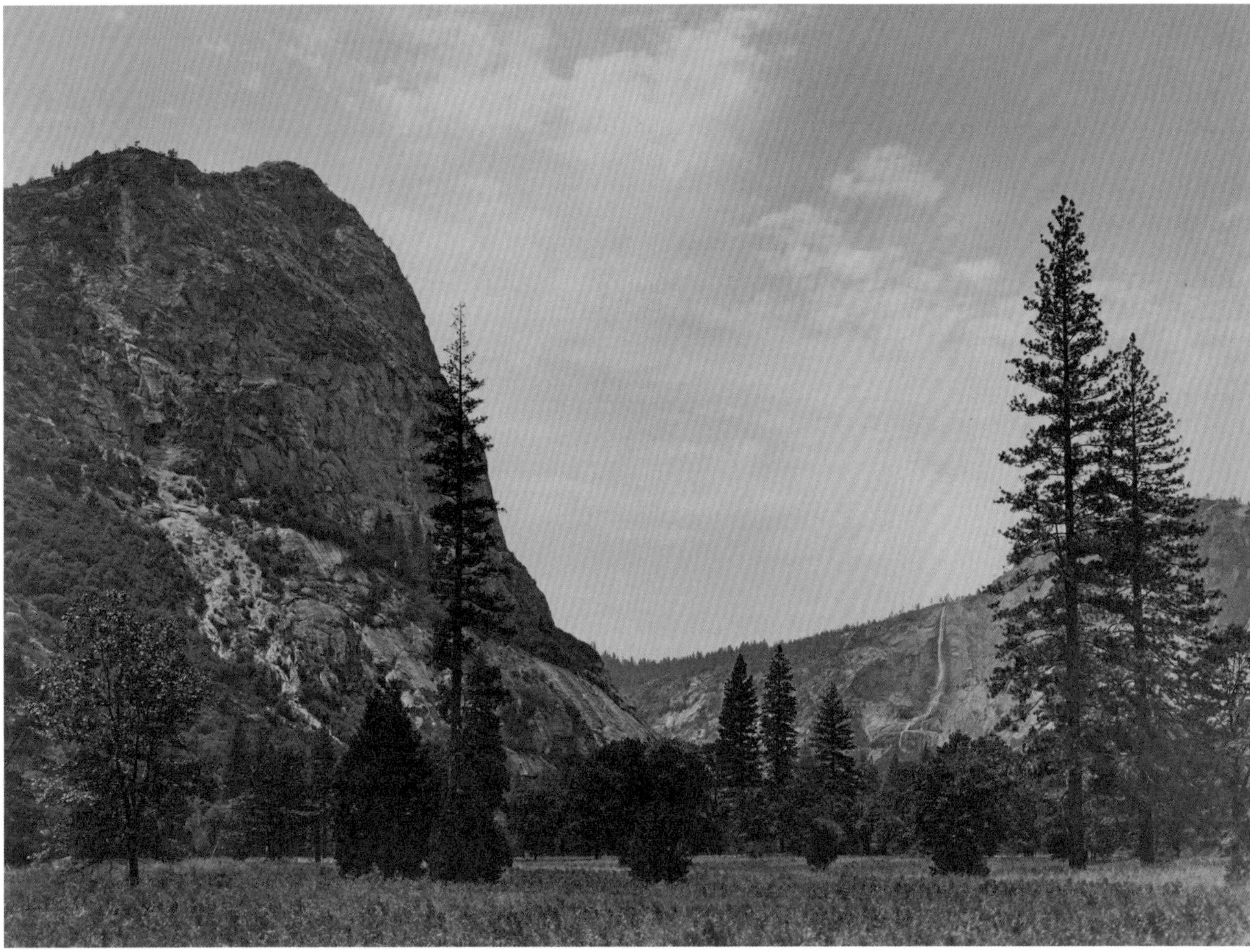

| FIG. 3 |

| FIG. 1 |
Jack Haynes, Haynes Picture Shop, Yellowstone National Park, c. 1920.

| FIG. 2 |
Julius T. Boysen, Stagecoach on Big Oak Flat Road, Yosemite National Park, 1903.

| FIG. 3 |
Herbert W. Gleason, Hetch Hetchy Valley, Yosemite National Park, published in *Sierra Club Bulletin* 7, June 1910, plate LXXXV.

emphasizing that they were national assets and instruments of civic betterment, educational improvement, and spiritual uplift.[5]

The initial effort to employ photography in this vein was undertaken by the Department of the Interior's Clerk in Charge of Publications, Laurence F. Schmeckebier.[6] At the first national park conference in 1911, Schmeckebier observed that the annual reports submitted by park superintendents reached such a small audience and were so dry and technical that they did little to advance the cause. He urged park officials to ply the press with news releases aimed at raising public awareness of park activities, whether it be the completion of a bridge or information about natural features or fishing opportunities. Illustrated Sunday supplements were to be especially targeted. Noting that the government had relied on the tourist industry to provide guidebooks, which were often self-serving and outdated, he called on the assembled superintendents to provide information from which the department could produce more authoritative and up-to-date circulars. He also advocated issuing illustrated handbooks highlighting the attractions of individual parks. Finally, he emphasized the importance of promoting the parks by means of photographic exhibitions, lantern slides, and moving pictures.

By the end of the year Schmeckebier had compiled a modest exhibition that the department made available to interested institutions. The program was so successful that a second set was created the following year. To reach an even broader audience, he produced a heavily illustrated article for *National Geographic Magazine*.[7] While a number of photographs were credited to the U.S. Geological Survey, most came from independent sources. Haynes contributed to the Yellowstone section; Best and Boysen provided Yosemite images; Kiser and the Great Northern Railroad were co-credited for Glacier; Asahel Curtis sent some of his signature Mount Rainier shots; the Southern Pacific Railroad supplied additional Yosemite images along with several of Sequoia. The series concluded with photographs of the newly designated Petrified Forest and Devil's Postpile National Monuments, the latter taken by Sierra Club member Walter Huber. Along with presenting eye-catching images of soaring cliffs, spouting geysers and towering trees, Schmeckebier emphasized that America's natural beauty was not meant to be marveled at from afar but enjoyed in person. The classic format of foreground spectators admiring distant views was augmented with images of hikers, climbers, horseback riders, a stagecoach passing through a tunnel tree (automobiles were not yet allowed in Yosemite when the article appeared in 1912), and, in a sign of things to come, automobile tourists winding their way to Mount Rainier. A photograph of Yosemite's cavalry troop arrayed along a fallen Sequoia underscored the magnitude of the marvels visitors would encounter and while assuring them that they could view them in peace and safety. Lest anyone doubt the article's underlying intent, Schmeckebier noted that Congress was considering a bill to authorize a dedicated national park bureau, quoting President William Howard Taft's endorsement of the proposal.

Despite Taft's exhortations, Congress declined to move forward on the park bill. Momentum was building, however, driven in part by widespread disappointment over a 1913 ruling to allow the damming of Yosemite's Hetch Hetchy Valley in order to create a reservoir for the city of San Francisco. John Muir and other conservationists fought the measure, enlisting the Boston-based photographer Herbert Gleason to give supportive slide lectures and illustrate articles and pamphlets decrying the desecration of this little-known region, which rivaled Yosemite Valley in scenic splendor **| FIG. 3 |**. Gleason illustrated handsomely published volumes of writings by Muir and Henry David Thoreau, but his primary medium was the lantern slide lecture. This engaging blend of education and entertainment was employed by social reformers, educators and other professional speakers to reach middle- and upper-class audiences in search of edifying diversions. Women's clubs, civic associations, and social organizations were popular targets. Gleason and his contemporary George Peabody crisscrossed the country offering uplifting presentations on national parks, nature appreciation, and the patriotic and educational value of American scenery. Both men employed hand-colored slides for more compelling and realistic effects. Gleason's wife Lulie Rounds Gleason was his principal colorist, accompanying him on travels and taking meticulous notes to guide her application of watercolor tints. Muir, Gleason and their allies were unable to prevent the inundation of Hetch Hetchy Valley. The campaign broadened the base of the park movement, however, with photographs by Gleason and others testifying to the paradise lost through inadequate protection for America's national parks.[8]

While Taft did not win reelection, Woodrow Wilson's Secretary of the Interior Franklin K. Lane embraced the cause. His choice to lead the push for a national parks bureau was Stephen Mather, an ardent park supporter who had made a fortune in the borax industry and was looking for new outlets for his prodigious energy and promotional talents. Arriving in early 1915, he threw himself into the effort, lobbying Congress and currying favor with journalists, businessmen, automobile enthusiasts and other potential supporters. *National Geographic Magazine* publisher Gilbert Grosvenor was an early convert. Grosvenor published an entire issue on American scenery while the bill to establish the park service was being debated, devoting considerable space to national parks and monuments. Haynes, Kiser, Curtis, Pillsbury and Eddy were again featured, along with several photographs by Grosvenor himself. Rather than directly press the case for the park service bill, the text combined broader See America First rhetoric with descriptions of existing parks and proposed additions. Grosvenor continued to feature park-related subjects and gave an extended lecture on the use of photography to increase public appreciation at the 1917 National Parks Conference.[9]

Mather enlisted veteran journalist Robert Sterling Yard to bolster the publicity effort. An old friend from Mather's days as a journalist for the *New York Sun*, Yard had gone on to edit *Century Magazine* and the *Sunday New York Herald*, where he honed his facility for combining compelling photographs with engaging prose.[10] Building on Schmeckebier's handbook concept, Yard put together a series of pamphlets showcasing individual parks, devoting 20 to 30 photographs to each area. Gathered together in an attractive wrapper and introduced by effusive testimonials from Mather and Lane, the full set was dubbed the *National Parks Portfolio* **| FIG. 4 |** and distributed to politicians, chambers of commerce, women's clubs, professional organizations, prominent businessmen and anyone else deemed likely to support the national park bill or promote national parks in general.[11] Since there was no allowance in the Department of the Interior's budget for publications of this kind, Mather paid the $5,000 cost of the initial plates himself and cajoled railroad companies into contributing $43,000 to have 275,000 copies printed by an independent publishing house.[12] While this was hailed as a grand patriotic gesture, the

5
Horace Albright and Margaret Albright Schenk, "Photographers in the National Parks", unpublished manuscript, NPS Historic Photograph Collection; Fred H. Kiser file, NPS Historic Photograph Collection NARA RG 79, NPS Central Files, Yosemite Privileges: A.C. Pillsbury; NARA RG 79, NPS Central Files, General Records, Publicity. U.S. Department of the Interior [USDOI], *Proceedings of the National Park Conference Held at the Yellowstone National Park, September 11 and 12, 1911*, Government Printing Office, Washington, DC, 1911.

6
Laurence F. Schmeckebier, "Our National Parks", *National Geographic Magazine*, 23, 1912, p. 532–79; Robert Shankland, Steve Mather of the National Parks, 3rd edition, Alfred Knopf, New York, 1970; Margaret Shaffer, *See America First: Tourism and National Identity, 1880–1940*, Smithsonian Institution, Washington, DC, 2002.

7
Laurence F. Schmeckebier, *op. cit.*

8
The NPS eventually acquired Peabody's glass slides, which are housed in the NPS photographs collection at NARA. See: Sierra Club, "Hetch Hetchy Hearing", *Sierra Club Bulletin*, 7, 1910, p. 260–63; Herbert Gleason, *The Western Wilderness of North America*, introduction by George Crosette, Barre Publishers, Barre, MA, 1972; Leslie Perrin Wilson, "Herbert Wendell Gleason's Negatives in the Concord Public Library: Odyssey of a Collection", *The Concord Saunterer*, 7, 1999, p. 174–99; Finis Dunaway, *Natural Visions: The Power of Images in American Environmental Reform*, University of Chicago Press, Chicago, IL, 2005.

9
Gilbert Grosvenor, "The Land of the Best", *National Geographic Magazine*, 24, 4, 1916, p. 327–430; U.S. National Park Service, *Proceedings of the National Parks Conference, Held in the Auditorium of the New National Museum, Washington, DC, January 2, 3, 4, 5 and 6, 1917*, Government Printing Office, Washington, DC, 1917, p. 130.

10
Robert Shankland, *op. cit.*

11
U.S. Department of the Interior, *National Parks Portfolio*, Charles Scribner's Sons, New York, NY, 1916.

12
U.S. National Park Service [NPS], *National Parks Portfolio, by Robert Sterling Yard*, Government Printing Office, Washington, DC, 1917.

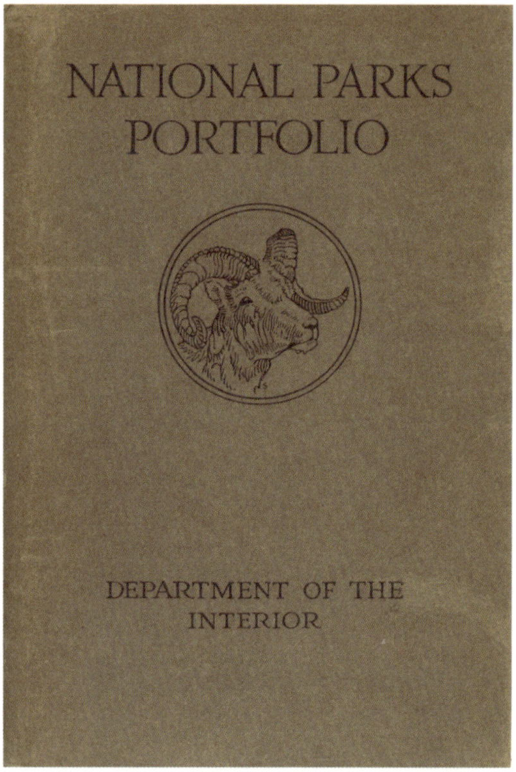

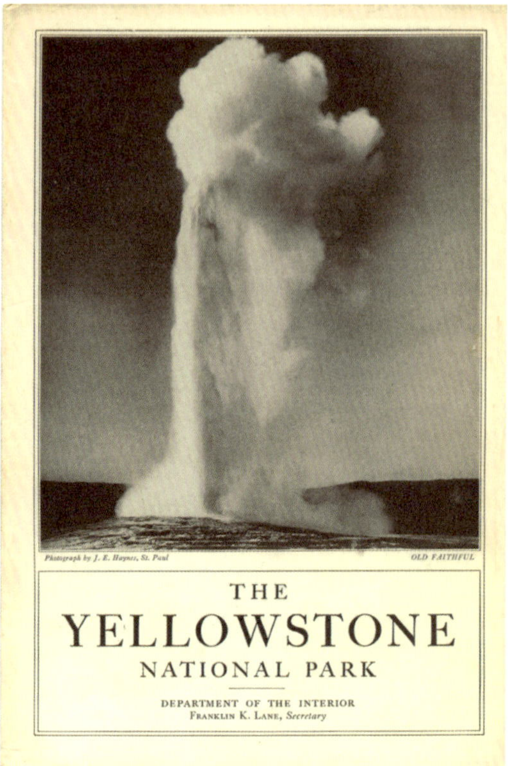

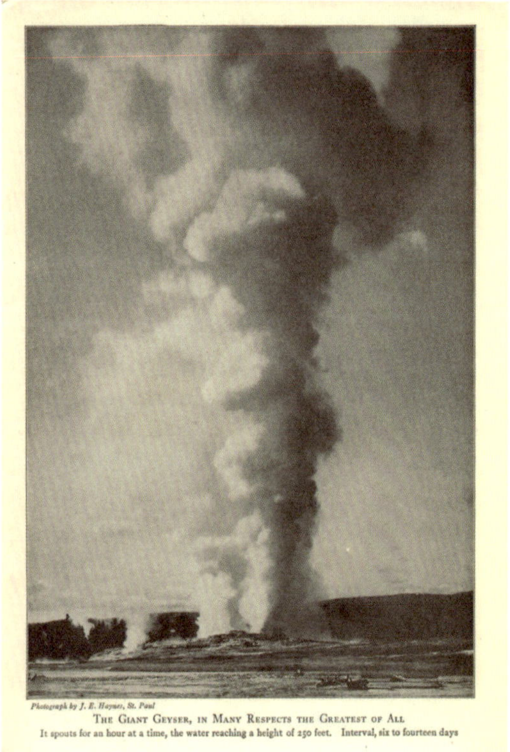

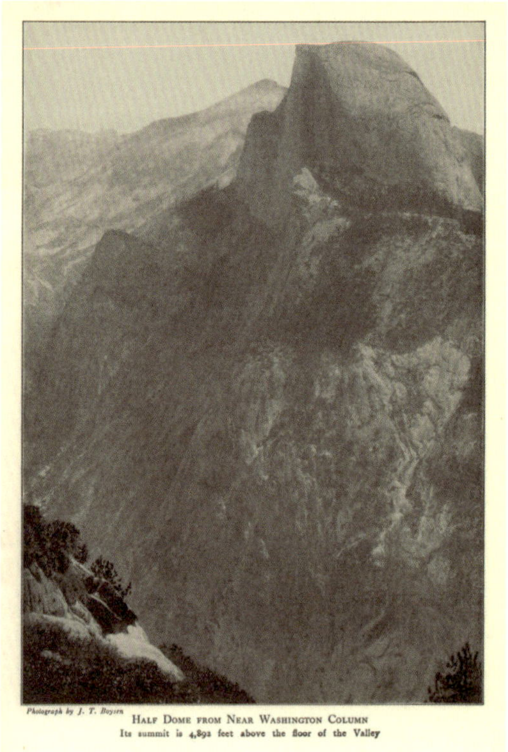

| FIG. 4 |
National Parks Porfolio,
U.S. Department of the Interior, 1916.

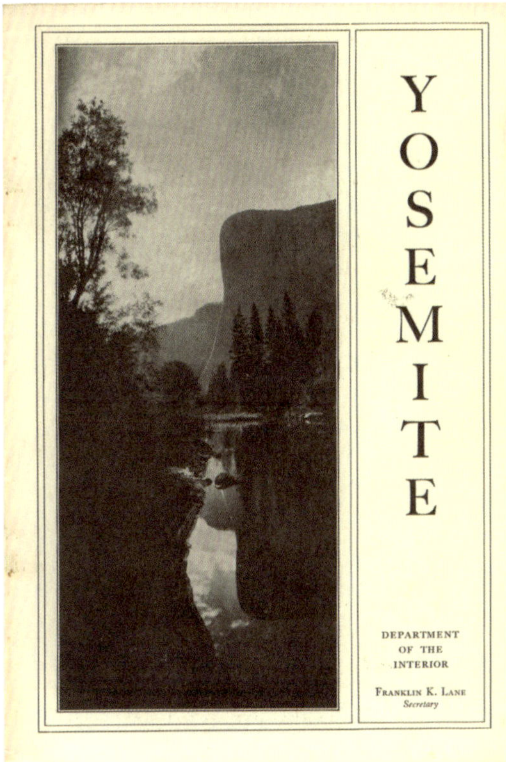
YOSEMITE
DEPARTMENT OF THE INTERIOR
FRANKLIN K. LANE
Secretary

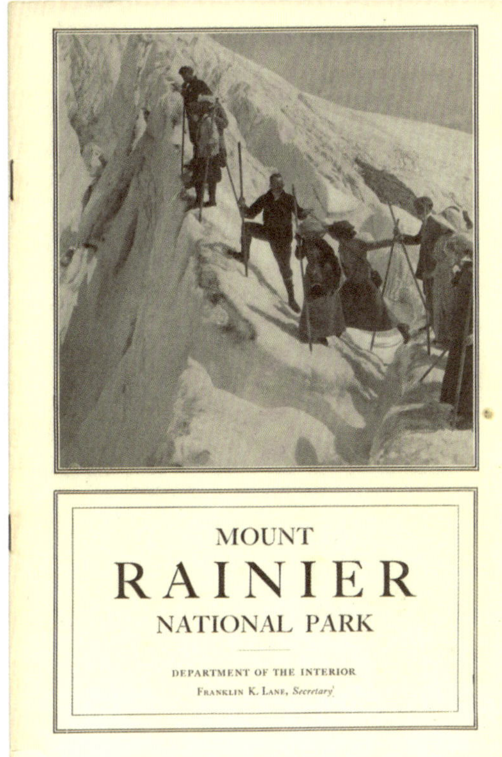
MOUNT
RAINIER
NATIONAL PARK
DEPARTMENT OF THE INTERIOR
FRANKLIN K. LANE, Secretary

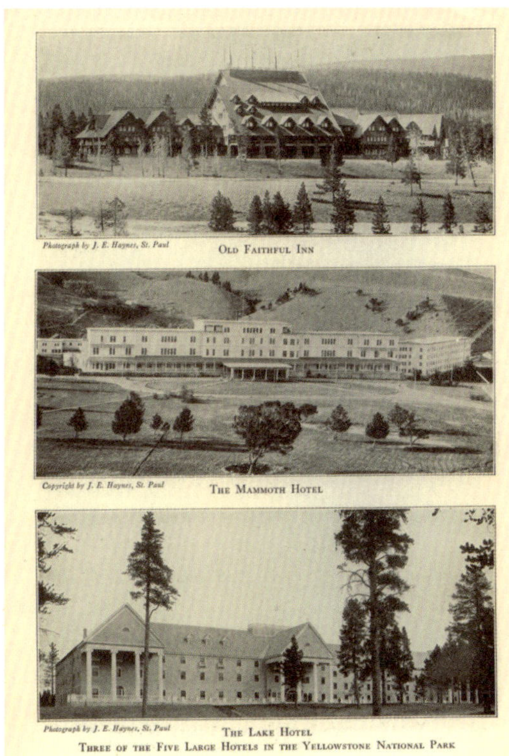
Photograph by J. E. Haynes, St. Paul
OLD FAITHFUL INN
Copyright by J. E. Haynes, St. Paul
THE MAMMOTH HOTEL
Photograph by J. E. Haynes, St. Paul
THE LAKE HOTEL
THREE OF THE FIVE LARGE HOTELS IN THE YELLOWSTONE NATIONAL PARK

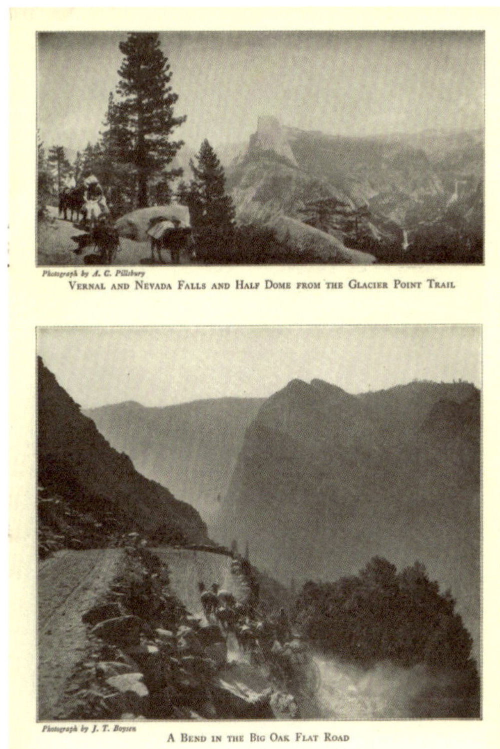
Photograph by A. C. Pillsbury
VERNAL AND NEVADA FALLS AND HALF DOME FROM THE GLACIER POINT TRAIL
Photograph by J. T. Boysen
A BEND IN THE BIG OAK FLAT ROAD

railroads had a long history of supporting park-based photography to increase ridership on their western lines. The back cover of each pamphlet provided a map showing the relationship between the parks and the railroad lines that served them. The introductions by Mather and Lane combined See America First domestic travel promotion with expansive rhetoric about the aesthetic, recreational and educational value of America's national parks. Mather lamented that the American people failed to realize that they possessed more impressive scenic and recreational resources than any country in the world. Casting the portfolio as "the first really representative presentation of American Scenery of grandeur ever published", he proclaimed that the panoramic presentation was destined to transform public perception of the nature and value of America's national parks.[13]

The *National Parks Portfolio* was so well received that the NPS put out a second edition in 1917, this time as an official publication through the Government Printing Office.[14] Yard also produced a cheaply printed and less generously illustrated one-volume compendium, *Glimpses of Our National Parks*.[15] *Glimpses* was provided for free and *National Parks Portfolio* made available for a nominal cost. With no budget or staff allotted to photographic work, these publications relied heavily on images provided by the railroads and private photographers. Haynes was once again the primary source for the Yellowstone. Boysen and Pillsbury contributed classic Yosemite images and Pillsbury joined Eddy in supplying Sequoia scenes. Curtis single-handedly covered Mount Rainier while Kiser provided photographs of Crater Lake and Glacier. Grand Canyon concessionaire Fred Harvey was happy to provide views, while Southern Pacific Railroad photographer H.C. Tibbets contributed scenes of Yosemite, Sequoia and the Kings Canyon and Mount Whitney area, which the NPS was lobbying to obtain from the U.S. Forest Service. The Grand Canyon pamphlet constituted to an even more conspicuous act of photographic appropriation, since it was officially a national monument under Forest Service control. Yard also prevailed on private individuals with national park ties such as western author Emerson Hough, Rocky Mountain National Park founder Enos Mills, and Sierra Club members Walter Huber and Joseph N. LeConte.

Since the U.S. Reclamation Service was also under the Department of the Interior, Mather was also able to "borrow" reclamation photographer H.T. Cowling for a brief but critical period.[16] Cowling spent the summer and fall of 1915 on an extended tour of national parks, producing photographs and films at Mather's behest. Cowling's films were circulated to promote park travel and Yard employed many of his photographs to illustrate the portfolio's sections on Rocky Mountain, Crater Lake, Grand Canyon, and Glacier National Parks.[17] In addition to producing striking scenic views, Cowling filled a crucial need by supplying images of visitors engaging in park-related pastimes such as fishing, camping and horseback riding | **FIG. 5** |. These artistically unremarkable photographs helped promote the perception that national parks were not just elite retreats for scenic contemplation but engaging environments for ordinary people to enjoy wholesome outdoor activities. Commercial photographers had long produced postcards of park visitors, but they were infrequently updated so the subjects often wore conspicuously outdated clothes. Underscoring the transitional nature of the period, the first edition of the portfolio included photographs of visitors traveling by both stagecoaches and automobiles. Both publications received frequent updates. Spectacular landscapes continued to predominate, but automobiles eclipsed equine transportation and there was increasing

13
U.S. Department of the Interior, *National Parks Portfolio*, Charles Scribner's Sons, New York, 1916, n. p.

14
U.S. National Park Service [NPS], *National Parks Portfolio, by Robert Sterling Yard*, Government Printing Office, Washington, DC, 1917.

15
U.S. Department of the Interior, *Glimpses of Our National Parks*, Government Printing Office, Washington, DC, 1916.

16
The Hereford T. Cowling file, NPS Historic Photograph Collection, contains additional information on Cowling's career. See: Robert Shankland, *op. cit.*

17
U.S. National Park Service [NPS], *National Parks Portfolio, by Robert Sterling Yard, op. cit.*

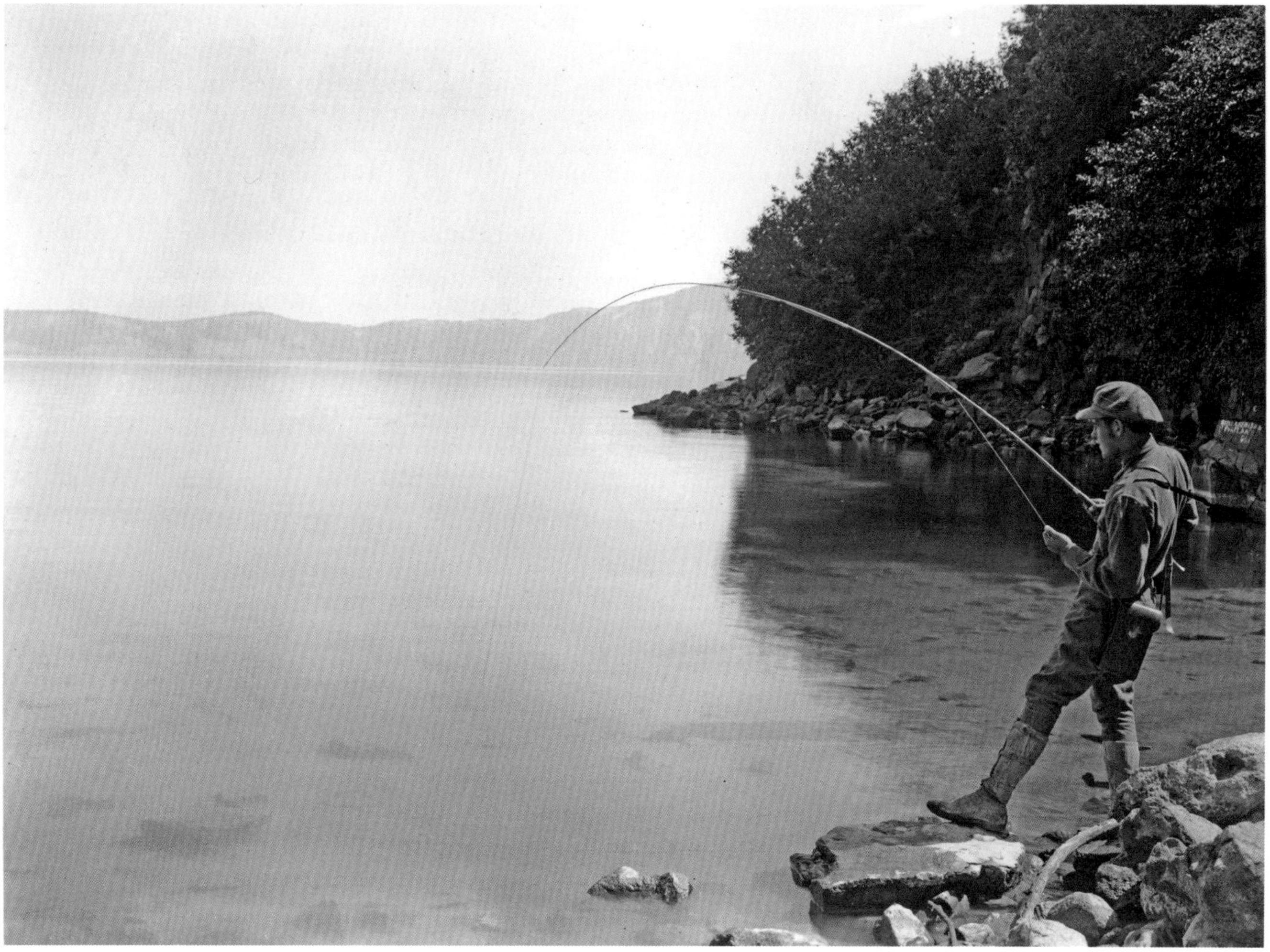

| FIG. 5 |

| FIG. 5 |
Hereford T. Cowling, Fly Fisherman,
Crater Lake National Park, 1915.

emphasis on visitor activities along with images of newly created amenities such as public campgrounds, budget-priced lodgings, and motor roads.

Mather reprised the idea of a traveling exhibit of national park photographs, again relying on images provided by private photographers and railroads. The NPS also instituted a lantern slide lending program for universities, public schools, churches and other organizations. Mather chafed at the budget constraints that prevented the service from providing enough of these materials to satisfy the demand, much less hire staff photographers to expand and update the collection. Maintaining that early exposure to national park images would not just increase visits but promote patriotism among the native born and help Americanize immigrants, he called for the placement of photographs of park scenery in classrooms and school books. America's entry into First World War bolstered the argument for such inspiration but further constrained federal funding. It also reduced the railroad's ability to supply new images and made it harder for private lecturers such as Peabody and Gleason to attract audiences for their park-related performances. The war's end reinvigorated demand without a commensurate increase in funding for what the NPS was increasingly characterizing as "education" rather than outright promotion.[18]

In December 1918 Mather finally secured a temporary appointment for Gleason to serve as an "inspector" for the Department of the Interior. As a genteel Bostonian with a national reputation for employing landscape photography to promote conservation and scenic appreciation, Gleason was just the sort of man Mather was looking for to advance the NPS agenda. Along with photographing existing parks, Gleason was charged with investigating areas under consideration for park designation, for which he prepared illustrated reports of their potential for recreational development. He also gave the NPS access to his earlier slides and negatives and printed photographs taken by other NPS personnel.[19]

Gleason covered an imposing amount of terrain during his short but productive appointment. In December 1918 he accompanied Mather on a trip to Yosemite and Mount Rainer to fill a gap in the collection by taking photographs of the parks in winter. Unwilling to relocate for a temporary appointment, he spent the spring in Boston, tending to his own affairs and printing photographs for

an exhibition of national park photographs the agency was mounting to convince Congress of the need for increased support. Mather requested additional enlargements to bestow on key representatives and invited him to give one of his signature slide lectures. Gleason spent the first part of the summer of 1919 in New Mexico, Arizona, southern Utah, and southwestern Colorado reconnoitering existing and proposed parks and monuments including Grand Canyon, Mesa Verde, Natural Bridges, Zion, Bryce, Capitol Reef and Bandelier. The second half of the summer was devoted to California, highlighted by a week-long horseback trip along the partially constructed John Muir Trail, which traversed the backbone of the Sierra Nevada from Mount Whitney to Yosemite | **FIG. 6** |. A second swing through the Southwest included Inscription Rock and Petrified Forest and culminated in a presentation at the September 1919 national park conference in Denver.[20]

Gleason returned to Boston with an impressive array of images and valuable insights about the characteristics and development potential of areas the NPS was considering for park designation. Several, including Bryce, and the sweep of Sierra scenery between Sequoia and Yosemite that the NPS sought to transform into a national park were controlled by the U.S. Forest Service, which strongly resisted efforts to diminish its holding. Since both regions were remote and rarely visited, the NPS believed Gleason's photographs could play important roles in the campaign for park designation. His colored slides and prints of Bryce were particularly compelling, authenticating the remote area's other-worldly splendor in the same way that Thomas Moran's paintings of Yellowstone helped convince congressional skeptics. Along with using Gleason's photographs to promote park legislation, the NPS made them available to publications such as the *Saturday Evening Post* and *National Geographic Magazine*, which were eager to support the park cause while slaking the public thirst for engaging views.[21] Yard also used several images of the proposed Sierra park expansion in his commercially published *Book of the National Parks,* which combined advocacy with more detailed information on individual parks.[22]

Gleason occasionally included automobiles and other evidence of tourist activities, but his preference for scenes of unadulterated nature was more suited to advancing park legislation than the equally important goal of celebrating visitation. Both aesthetically and philosophically, Gleason's Thoreauvian sensibilities were at odds with Mather's vision of national parks as playgrounds for the American people. Gleason's unwillingness to relocate posed additional problems. Not only did this increase the time and expense of ordering reproductions, but the challenges of sharing limited quantities of hand-colored lantern slides created further complications. Mather was unable to extend his employment in any event, as changes in administration made the departmental inspector appointments unavailable. Gleason continued to supply prints and slides and assist the NPS whenever possible. To help combat proposed reservoir development in Yellowstone's southwest corner, he joined Albright, Appalachian Mountain Club president Harlan Kelsey, and landscape architect Frederick Law Olmsted, Jr. on a horseback excursion through the seldom-visited region during July 1921, photographing the myriad waterfalls threatened with inundation. When disputes arose about proposed road developments in Acadia in 1924, he gave a supportive slide lecture in advance of congressional hearings. Gleason continued to lecture and photograph, with the latter activities focusing on New England nature, until his death in 1937.[23]

Mather continued to emphasize the value of photography throughout the 1920s, both for publicity purposes and to fulfill his vision of incorporating national park imagery into the American educational system. He was so eager to promote this agenda that he personally paid for a trial program employing national park photographs at an elite New York City private school. The NPS also worked with universities to provide images for courses on natural history and recreational landscape architecture, a new subfield the agency had a vested interest in promoting given the stunning increase in visitation arising from the rapid increase in automobile ownership and the impacts of the agency's capital improvement and public relations programs. The number of people entering national parks rose from 356,000 in 1916 to 1 million in 1921 and continued on the same trajectory throughout the decade.[24]

While the surge in popularity was just what the NPS hoped for, it produced even greater demand for photographs. The NPS needed to document improvements and lobby for additional funds, other park agencies and conservation organizations sought examples and inspiration, and magazines and newspapers reported on the trend and touted its local and national impacts. Demand for photographs and lantern slides poured in from across the country and around the world. Not only did the NPS have insufficient quantities to keep up with requests, but by the mid-1920s the photographs they had were literally wearing out, since contemporary reproduction technologies required prints to be sent to the publisher and then returned, with inevitable wear and tear. Since most of the images had been acquired from private sources, copyright concerns caused additional hurdles and delays. Not coincidently, the greatest problems revolved around the most

18 U.S. National Park Service [NPS AR], *Annual Report of the Director of the National Park Service*, Government Printing Office, Washington, DC, 1917–1921.

19 Gleason's NPS-related activities are detailed in NARA RG 79, NPS Central Files, Pictures, Herbert W. Gleason and in the NPS Historic Photograph Collection's Herbert Gleason file. The NPS Historic Photograph Collection has contact prints of his government photographs and some previous work. The majority of Gleason's surviving work is archived at the Concord, Massachusetts public library.

20 NARA RG 79, NPS Central Files, Pictures, Herbert W. Gleason.

21 NARA RG 79, NPS Central Files, General Records, Publicity.

22 Robert Sterling Yard, *The Book of the National Parks*, Charles Scribner's Sons, New York, 1921.

23 NARA RG 79, NPS Central Files, Pictures, Herbert W. Gleason.

24 U.S. National Park Service [NPS AR], *Annual Report of the Director of the National Park Service*, Government Printing Office, Washington, DC, 1919–1929.

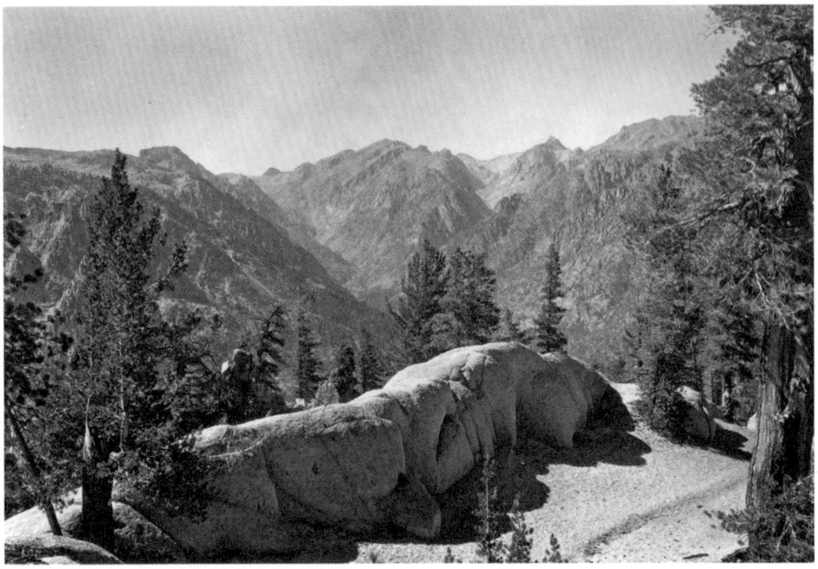

| FIG. 6 |

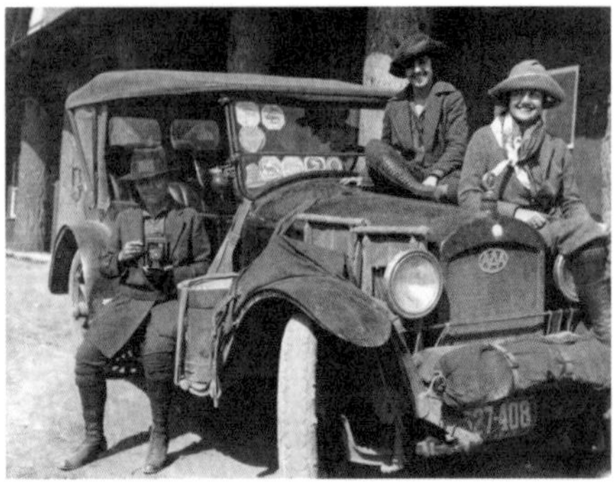

| FIG. 7 |

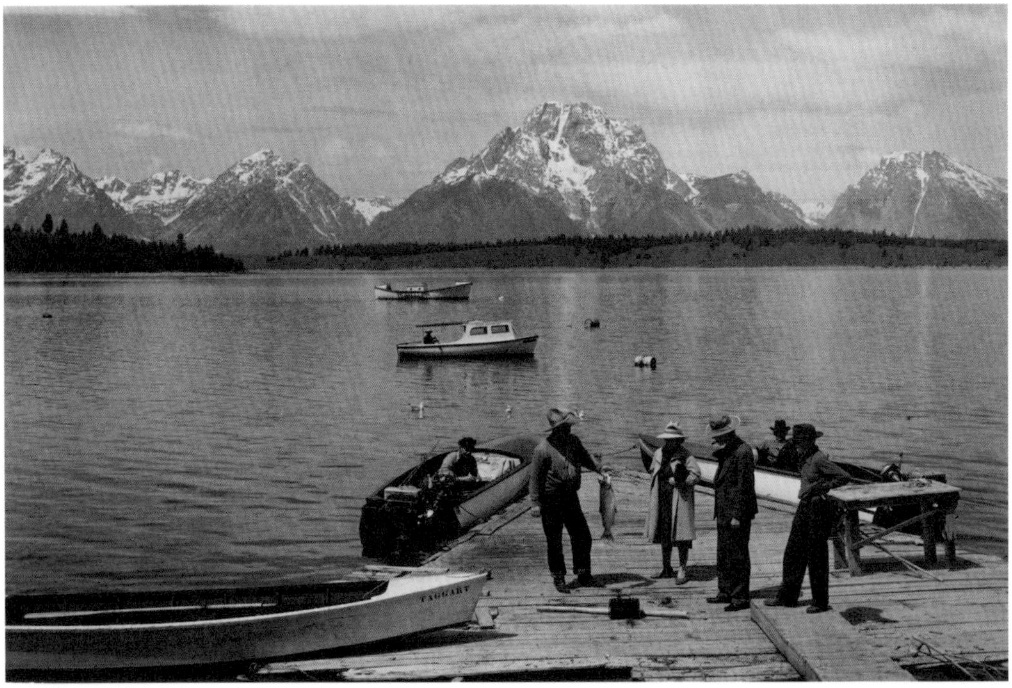

| FIG. 8 |

| FIG. 6 |
Herbert W. Gleason, View from John Muir Trail in future Kings Canyon National Park, 1919.

| FIG. 7 |
George Alexander Grant, Mary Crehore Bedell and daughters, Yellowstone National Park, 1922.

| FIG. 8 |
George Alexander Grant, Skipper Displaying Prize Cutthroat Trout, Grand Teton National Park, 1941.

compelling images, whose creators sought recognition and in some cases compensation. There was also a need to update the collection. Pure landscape and wildlife images were timeless, but images of visitors were rendered obsolete by changing clothing styles and vehicles. Mather repeatedly bemoaned the situation and pleaded for dedicated photographic funds, but to no avail.[25]

Yard's replacement as NPS publications specialist and editor-in-chief, Isabelle Storey, managed to pull together 92 new images for a major revision of the *National Parks Portfolio* in 1928, but she was again forced to rely heavily on private photographers and other government agencies.[26] The additions provided ample evidence that the NPS was succeeding in its goal of transforming parks into playgrounds for the American people. There were photographs of road improvements, free public campgrounds, and visitors enjoying not just camping and fishing but winter sports such as skiing, tobogganing and dog sledding. The NPS's educational mission was emphasized in photographs of guided nature study groups and expanded coverage of archeological sites. Storey also updated *Glimpses* and improved the photographic component of the agency's annual reports with a mixture of unprepossessing images by NPS staff and more accomplished views from private providers including newcomers such as Glacier-based T.J. Hileman and Ansel Adams, whose photograph of a high alpine lake in the proposed Minarets addition to Yosemite appeared in Mather's 1924 submission.[27]

Adams had higher aspirations than providing fodder for government reports, but another budding photographer whose work first appeared in the 1922 annual was lobbying hard for the then non-existent position of official NPS photographer. Born in 1891, George Alexander Grant was eleven years older than Adams and from a much less privileged background. Where Adams was raised amid cultured surroundings in California's Bay Area, harboring visions of being a concert pianist and first encountering Yosemite on a family outing in 1916, Grant grew up in central Pennsylvania and worked in garages and machine shops before securing a position as a metal worker at the Roycroft Community in East Aurora, New York. Roycroft was an American offshoot of the British Arts and Crafts Movement, which emphasized the dignity of craftsmanship and elevated anonymous artisanship over individual artistic pretensions. Grant's five-year stint with the Roycrofters undoubtedly ingrained this mentality, along with painstaking attention to detail and appreciation for elegant but unassuming design. His lifelong fascination with the American West took hold in 1917, when he was stationed at Fort D.A. Russell near Cheyenne, Wyoming, after enlisting in the U.S. Army. Grant returned to Pennsylvania after being discharged and found work managing the printing department of a textile mill while angling for a way to return the West. Adams, at this point, was spending summers caretaking the Sierra Club's lodge in Yosemite Valley, developing his nascent photography skills and courting Virginia Best, whose father owned one of the park's long-time photographic concessions.[28]

Grant's military experience was influential in securing a seasonal ranger position in Yellowstone for the summer of 1922. While he appears to have had no significant photographic experience, he augmented his largely clerical duties taking photographs with camera equipment the park had on hand. Horace Albright, who had served as Mather's right-hand man during the NPS authorization drive, was serving as superintendent and encouraged Grant's efforts, bringing him along on inspection trips and instructing him to take photographs of visitors enjoying the park. These initial efforts were somewhat crude, both in terms of technique and composition, but Albright was more concerned with public relations than artistic expression. When an eastern authoress and

25
NARA RG 79, NPS Central Files, General, Publicity. See: U.S. National Park Service [NPS AR], *Annual Report of the Director of the National Park Service*, Government Printing Office, Washington, DC, 1919–1929.

26
U.S. National Park Service, *National Parks Portfolio, by Robert Sterling Yard*, 5th edition, Isabelle Storey (ed.), Government Printing Office, Washington, DC, 1928.

27
U.S. National Park Service, *Glimpses of Our National Parks*, Government Printing Office, Washington, DC, 1931.

28
Mark Sawyer, *The Early Days: Photographer George Alexander and the Western National Parks*, Northland Press, Flagstaff, AZ, 1986; Jonathan Spaulding, *Ansel Adams and the American Landscape: A Biography*, University of California Press, Berkeley, CA, 1995; Ren and Helen Davis, *Landscapes for the People: Photographs by George Alexander Grant, First Chief Photographer of the National Park Service*, University of Georgia Press, Athens, GA, 2015.

her two daughters pulled up to park headquarters with their windshield covered with the colorful entrance stickers the NPS was employing to encourage visitation, he had Grant take a series of photographs | **FIG. 7** | testifying not just to the success of the program, but to the fact that park travel had become so safe and easy that three women could complete the circuit on their own.[29] Abbott tried to enlist Grant as a full-time ranger so that he could continue to take photographs on the side, but he proved ill-suited to the more rigorous aspects of the task, which included frequent backcountry travel on horseback. Grant decided he would be better served by returning east and honing his photographic skills, while Mather and Albright pressed the case for a dedicated photography position. After taking courses in New York City he secured a position as a technical photographer at Pennsylvania State College, which provided him with a modest salary, access to photographic equipment, and valuable experience. He kept in close contact with Albright over the next few years, inquiring about job prospects and building goodwill by making prints and lantern slides from NPS negatives at nominal cost.[30]

Grant's patience was rewarded in April 1929, when Abbott instructed him to report to the NPS Educational Division offices at the University of California to serve as the NPS's first official photographer. Mather and Yosemite Chief Naturalist Ansel Hall had worked hard to build up this aspect of the agency's operations, collaborating with universities and other organizations to strengthen the argument that national parks were not just recreational outlets but educational institutions. Mather suffered a severe stroke that forced him to retire in January 1929, but Hall pressed on, developing a comprehensive educational program that received considerable support from the Laura Spellman Rockefeller Foundation, which initially funded Grant's position. Hall overcame the Interior Department's reluctance to authorize the position by maintaining that the division needed its own photographer because park-based commercial photographers had no interest in making the sort of technical photographs required for museum exhibits and scientific cataloguing. Albright, who succeeded Mather as director, wholeheartedly supported the move, recognizing that the Educational Division's photographer could also address the ongoing need to document improvements and update visitor photographs. Employing a staff photographer would also eliminate copyright issues and allow the NPS to avoid paying commercial rates for reproductions from the agency's negative collection. Grant was considered an ideal fit for the position. His Penn State experience would stand him in good stead for the more technical assignments, while his presence in the parks would alleviate the need to rely on commercial photographers for landscape views and public use pictures. Abbott was also impressed with Grant's commitment to NPS ideals and eagerness to do whatever he could to support them. During the long wait for approval Grant repeatedly offered to work for free, though his entreaties were respectfully declined. Accepting the NPS position entailed a significant pay cut from his Penn State position, where he had risen to become head of the university's darkroom operations, but Grant insisted that he cared little for material rewards.[31]

In a pattern that would be repeated with minor variation until the outbreak of the Second World War, Grant spent the summer of 1930 traveling from park to park, taking photographs of landscapes, capital improvements, visitor activities, and scientific specimens. He also took photographs of historic buildings and sites as the NPS increased that aspect of its holdings, and accompanied NPS employees on surveys of proposed additions to the park system.[32] Grant quickly demonstrated his improved compositional skills and technical mastery. Working primarily with a 5 × 7 inch view camera equipped with a wide-angle lens, he produced restrained but graceful images with finely textured details and an extended range of warm middle tones that brought to mind to the work of 19th-century survey photographers rather than the bold tonalities and operatic compositions Ansel Adams was bringing to the fore. During the winter Grant would return to the office to print photographs and coordinate the next year's travel in consultation with Storey, Hall, and other NPS officials. Like Gleason, Grant preferred to make classically composed photographs of unadulterated natural landscapes, but he dutifully acquiesced to official urgings to chronicle improvements and celebrate the parks' ever-increasing popularity | **FIG. 8** |. These images appeared in both NPS publications and journalistic media, where the human interest aspect was considered especially important.

Grant rapidly developed a reputation for his ability to marshal technical and aesthetic skills in support of the agency's agendas. In some cases the results were just enticing images of happy campers or well-composed illustrations of visitor facilities, road projects, and scientific specimens; in others, he subsumed new constructions within broader scenic tableaux, satisfying his artistic aspirations while attesting to the agency's ability to fulfill its mission of balancing preservation and access in iconic American landscapes. The passage of time has imbued Grant's photographs with nostalgic allure, but it also makes these embedded messages harder to decode. Beyond the obvious celebration of Mount Rainier's majestic beauty, Grant's photograph of a newly completed overlook attested to the NPS's success in making such views accessible to the motoring public while minimizing the impact of development | **FIG. 9** | This message had broad implications as the agency grappled with unprecedented popularity, but was particularly relevant to Mount Rainier, where NPS officials sought to calm conservationists' fears by insisting that construction would impact a minute portion of the park – the same proportion, in fact, that Grant allotted to the picturesque parking area. His photograph of a mounted ranger overlooking an unbroken expanse of mountainous terrain | **FIG. 10** | was not simply a picturesque platitude, but an affirmation of the NPS's commitment to preserving the wilderness quality of Olympic National Park,[33] which had been a key condition of the authorization process. On a deeper level, it evoked contemporary sentiments about the frontier's impact on the formation of American character and the need for national parks to instill similar values.

As the National Park System expanded dramatically in the 1930s, it became apparent that Grant could not meet all the agency's needs. The NPS was able to hire two additional photographers, resulting in Grant's transfer to Washington and elevation to the position of Chief Photographer. Grant chafed at the additional managerial responsibilities and maneuvered to spend as much time in the field as possible. Another reorganization in 1937 consolidated the Department of the Interior's photographic activities within a centralized Department of Information. While this enabled Grant to expand his activities to encompass non-NPS subjects such as the construction of Boulder Dam, it meant the NPS had to compete for his time, leading to additional work for younger NPS photographers such as Ralph Anderson and Alan Rinehart. Grant was very supportive of these efforts. The Yosemite-based Anderson's forte was action photographs of recreational activities in the increasingly popular 35 mm format, while Rinehart photographed primarily in the East, which held less attraction for the western-focused Grant. Top NPS officials continued to view Grant as their premier photographer, but his prominence began to wane. Not only did the ease and superior color rendition of 35 mm Kodachrome slides reduce the need for expertise with large-format cameras and cumbersome lantern slides, but Interior Secretary Ickes had identified another photographer to serve as the organization's ultimate image maker.

In January 1936 the Sierra Club sent Ansel Adams to Washington to promote the long-sought goal of establishing a national park encompassing the sweep of Sierra scenery centered on Kings Canyon. Ickes was charmed by Adams demeanor and so impressed with the photographs he brought with him to underscore the area's appeal that he ordered a mural-sized photographic screen to display in his office. Two years later Adams sent his sumptuously printed monograph *Sierra Nevada: The John Muir Trail* to NPS director

29
Mary Crehore Bedell, *Modern Gypsies*, Brentano's, New York, 1924.

30
Documentation for Grant can be found in NARA RG 79, NPS Central Files, Employment, George A. Grant; NARA RG 79, NPS Central Files, Pictures, General; and in the NPS Historic Photograph Collection's George Grant file. The NPS Historic Photograph Collection contains hundreds of Grants photographs. Additional photographs by Grant can be found in the NPS photographs collection at NARA and in many individual park archives. See: Mark Sawyer, *op. cit.*; Ren and Helen Davis, *op. cit.*

31
U.S. National Park Service [NPS AR], *Annual Report of the Director of the National Park Service*, Government Printing Office, Washington, DC, 1924–1930; Mark Sawyer, *op. cit.*; Ren and Helen Davis, *op. cit.*

32
U.S. National Park Service, *Glimpses of Historical Areas East of the Mississippi River Administered by the National Park Service*, Government Printing Office, Washington, DC, 1937; U.S. Congress, Senate, *Natchez Trace Parkway Survey*, 76th Cong., 3rd sess., February 26, 1940, S. Doc. 148.

33
About debates over creation of Olympic NP, see: Timothy Davis, *National Park Roads: A Legacy in the American Landscape*, University of Virginia Press, Charlottesville, VA, 2016, p. 154–85.

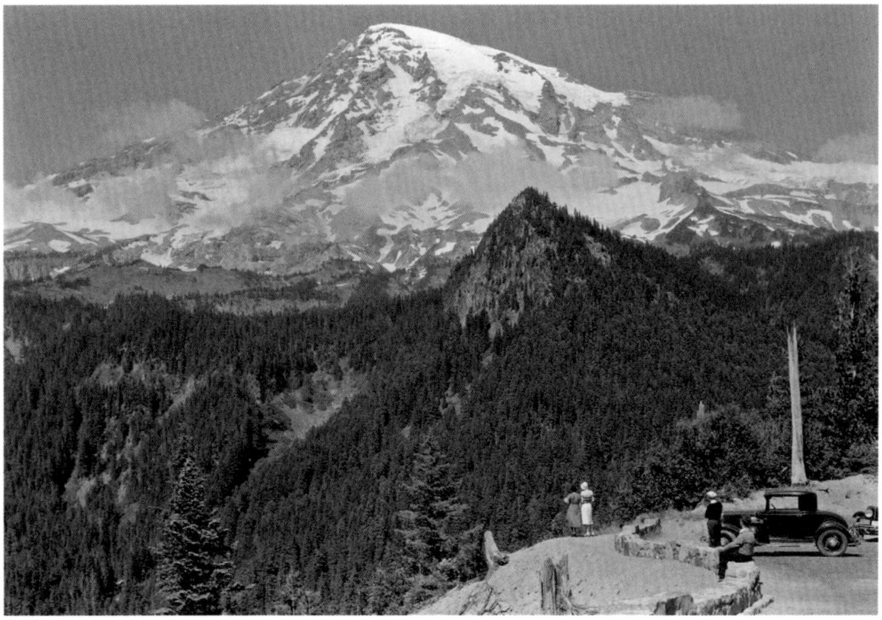

| FIG. 9 |

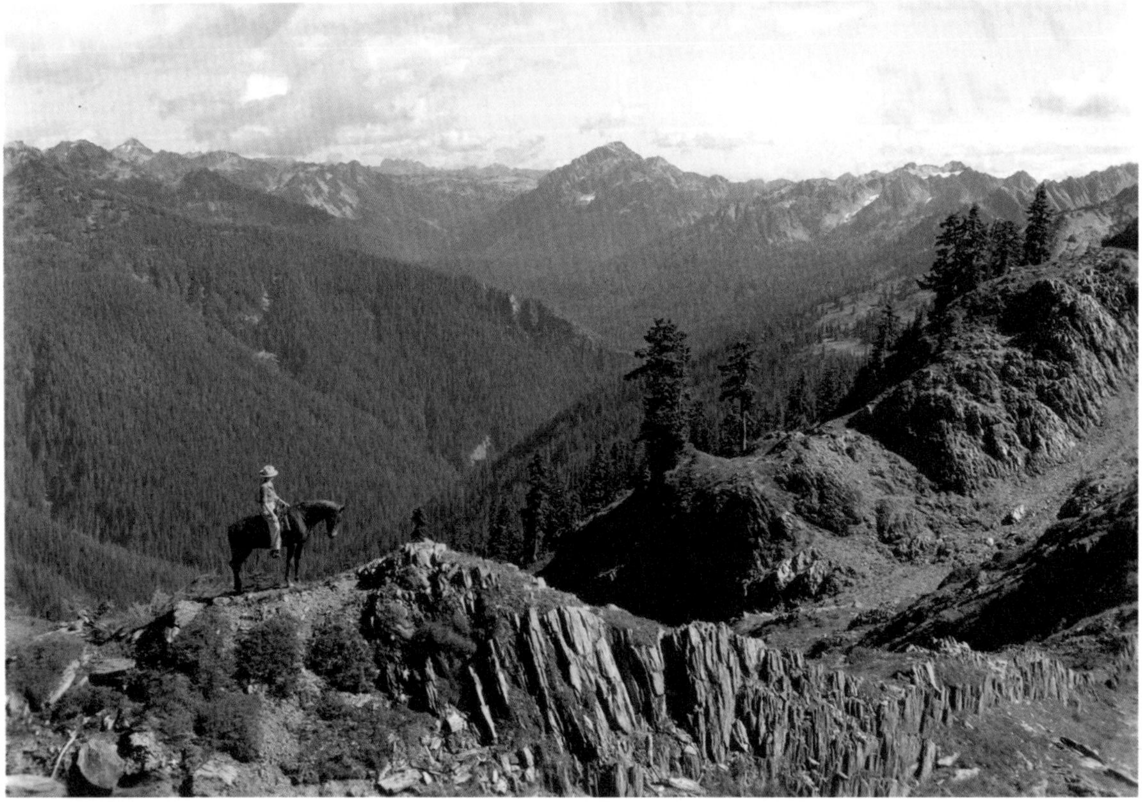

| FIG. 10 |

| FIG. 9 |
George Alexander Grant, Tourists Enjoying View from Ricksecker Point, Mount Rainier National Park, 1932.

| FIG. 10 |
George Alexander Grant, View from High Divide, proposed Olympic National Park, 1934.

| FIG. 11 |
Ansel Adams, Clouds, White Pass, Kings River Canyon, proposed National Park, California, 1936.

| FIG. 12 |
Ansel Adams, The Tetons, Snake River, Grand Teton National Park, 1942, U.S. Department of the Interior, Building Mural Project.

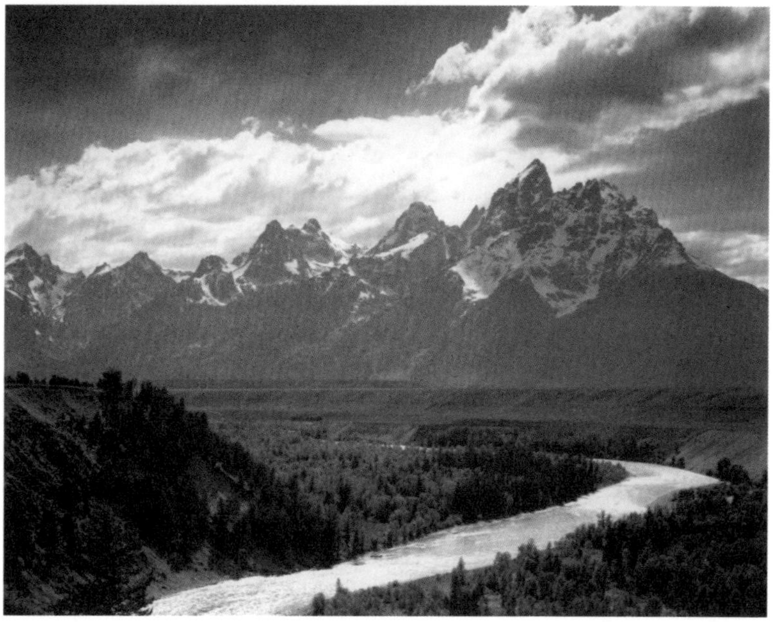

| FIG. 12 |

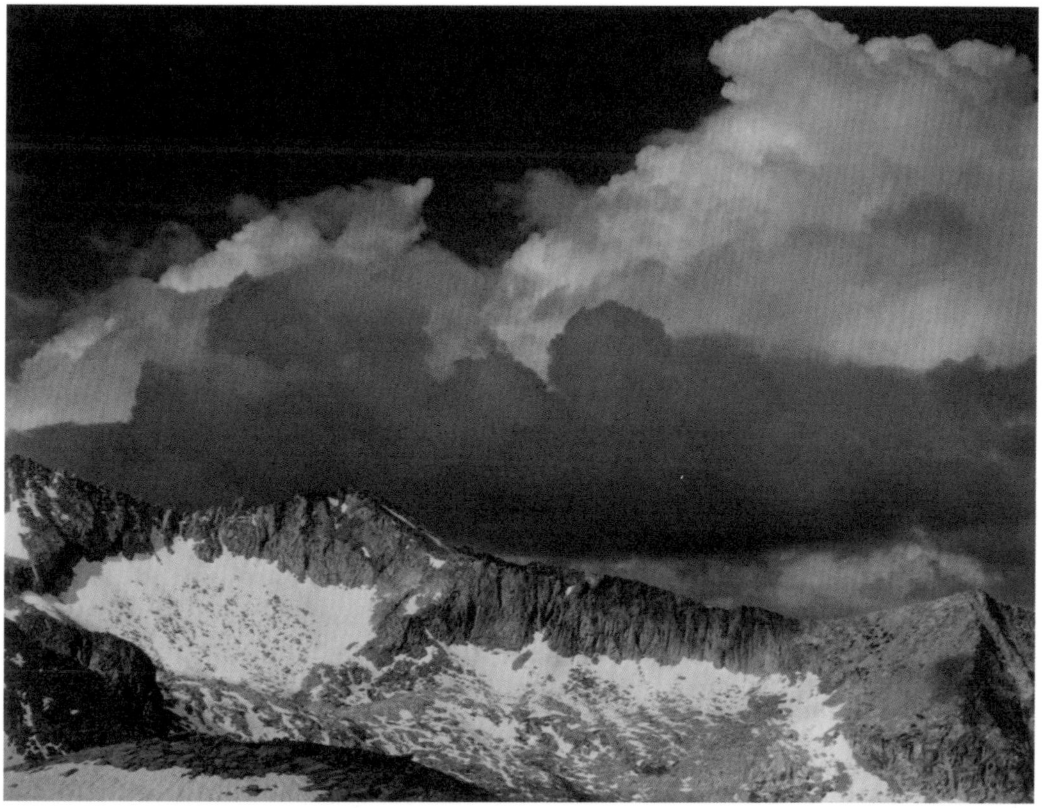

| FIG. 11 |

Arthur Demaray to further advance the cause. Demaray passed the book on to Ickes, who showed it to President Roosevelt. Roosevelt was equally taken by the publication and appropriated it for himself. Along with requesting a replacement copy, Ickes began making plans to hire Adams to produce a series of photographic murals of Interior Department landscapes to decorate the hallways of the newly completed headquarters building.[34] While this would seemingly be a task for Grant and relying on the ever-expanding NPS photography collection would save both time and money, Ickes was so enamored of Adams that he appears to have never considered the option. Ickes arranged for Adams to do the work on a short-term appointment, instructing NPS officials to do everything possible to facilitate the effort. Adams produced several hundred impressive views before America's escalating participation in the Second World War curtailed his activities in July 1942. Unlike Grant, he was under no obligation to clutter his scenes with cloying tourists or promote automobile-oriented development policies that conservationists were already beginning to question. He also had the luxury of experimenting with multiple versions of promising subjects, which Grant's efficiency-minded superiors discouraged. Adams images often sacrificed informational content for artistic intent, ruminating on cloud patterns or employing creative cropping to make abstract patterns out of natural features **| FIG. 11 |**. While Grant employed his skills to enhance the message rather than call attention to the messenger, an Adams photograph was as much about its maker as the nominal subject at hand. The mural program was not resumed after the war, but Adams secured a Guggenheim fellowship to continue the project on his own, which culminated in *My Camera in the National Parks*, an impeccably produced monograph that played a major role in cementing his reputation as America's premier landscape photographer **| FIG. 12 |**.[35]

Grant, meanwhile, had been relegated to taking photographs for the Interior Department's flood control projects in the Missouri River Basin. While NPS officials hoped he would be able to do double duty updating the agency's photo collection, Grant spent most of his time producing images of historic structures and archeological sites destined for inundation, working primarily in 35 mm format. Cutbacks in the Department of the Interior's budget lead to his retirement in October 1955. Looking back over a career during which he traveled more than 500,000 miles and produced over 30,000 images, Grant appeared unconcerned about his failure to achieve art-world approbation, though he was undoubtedly gratified by the Meritorious Service Award he received upon retirement. Praising the quality of his work and noting the exposure his photographs received through reproduction in government publications and popular media, the certificate lauded his contributions to the national park cause. Grant's images played a dominate role in NPS publications for decades and continue to appear today.[36] He has recently received greater acknowledgement, but his photographs have often been reproduced without attribution or credited simply to "National Park Service." This could be perceived as a personal slight, but it was also a testament to the extent to which his meticulously crafted oeuvre dominated the photographic representation of the U.S. National Park System during a key period in its development during which the agency transformed itself from a disparate collection of elite retreats into a central component of American life.

Focusing on photography's role in shaping perceptions of America's national parks underscores that landscape production is as much a conceptual process as a physical act. While the agency went to great lengths to upgrade roads and other accommodations, agency officials recognized that physical improvements alone would not transform public perceptions of the nature and purpose of America's national parks, nor would additional photographs in the W.H. Jackson or Carleton Watkins mode, portraying parks as inviolate wilderness or exotic arenas for aesthetic contemplation. The public had to be enticed by park attractions, but they also had to be assured they could reach them without undue effort and experience them in ways that were familiar, affordable and socially appealing. Beginning with the *National Parks Portfolio*, agency officials collaborated with private and public sector photographers to construct a new vision of the national park landscape, wherein middle-class Americans made use of newly created improvements to enjoy themselves in accessible natural and historic settings. Their beneficial influence on American families was strongly emphasized, as was their civic value as educational institutions and social landscapes, where groups of strangers came together in campgrounds and other informal settings. Automobiles were ubiquitous: in campgrounds, on newly constructed roads, and participating in widely popular "auto nature caravans". While these photographs may not have constituted high art, they exemplified the agency's emphasis on increasing public access to national parks. The next generation of national park photographers played an equally transformative role. By the 1950s NPS management policies were being challenged by environmentalists and wilderness advocates, who accused the agency of over-developing the parks. The national park landscape portrayed by Ansel Adams, Eliot Porter and other Sierra Club-aligned photographers was devoid of roads, cars and other visitor facilities. Humans themselves were largely absent, embodying the sentiment that national parks should prize wilderness values over recreational imperatives. This perspective remains dominant today – at least in terms of elite and middle-brow opinion – but perusal of Flickr or Instagram will underscore the extent to which popular taste continues to embrace images of visitors enjoying the social landscape of America's national parks.

34
NARA RG 79, NPS Central Files, Pictures, Photographs by Ansel Adams, 1941–47; NARA's NPS photography collection includes photographs taken by Adams for this assignment and along with images of the future Kings Canyon National Park taken in 1936.

35
Ansel Adams, *Sierra Nevada: The John Muir Trail*, Archetype Press, Berkeley, CA, 1938.

36
Along with their appearance in NPS-related publications, Grant's photographs have been highlighted in three books over the past 30 years. Two were relatively low-circulation volumes (Mark Sawyer, *op. cit.*; George A. Grant, *Trains, Trails & Tin Lizzies: Glacier National Park, 1932–1934: photographic plates from the George A. Grant Collection*, Glacier Natural History Association, West Glacier, Mont., 1987). A more recent and well-publicized monograph (Ren and Helen Davis, *op. cit.*) provided an excellent overview of Grant's life and work, though many of the images were printed in bolder, more Adams-like tones than they originally appeared, underscoring the latter's influence on landscape photography sensibilities.

1994

A Decade of Photographic Missions in Town and Country Planning Institutions

Raphaële Bertho

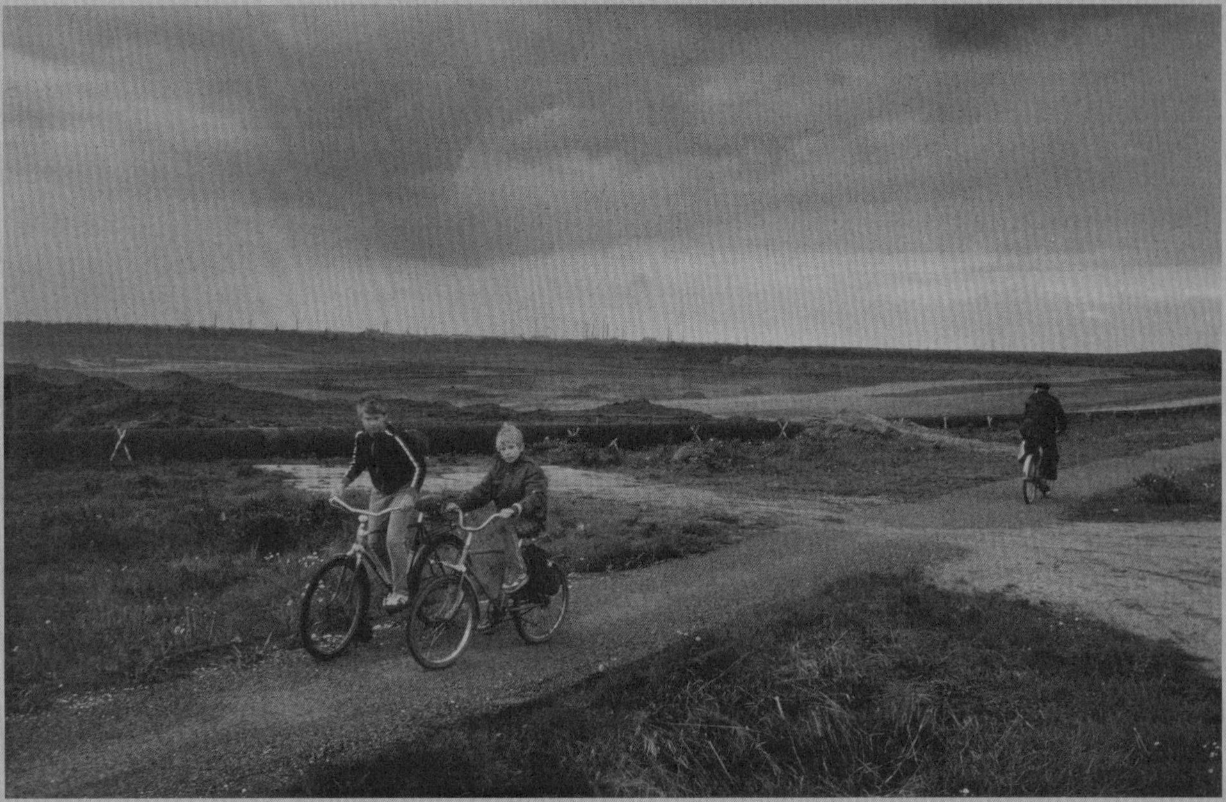

1
A reduced version of this exhibition later toured France; its full version, with local additions, was also shown at the Bazacle (EDF space) in Toulouse.
2
"Paysages pour demain. Actes du colloque du mercredi 2 novembre 1994, Cité des sciences et de l'industrie – Paris", *Environnement magazine*, no. 2720, 1995.
3
Christian Leyrit and Bernard Lassus (eds.), *Autoroute et paysages*, Editions du Demi-Cercle, Paris, 1994.
4
Law no. 93-24 of January 8, 1993 on protecting and valuing landscapes, amending certain provisions with regard to public inquiries.
5
Augustin Berque et al., *Cinq propositions pour une théorie du paysage*, Champ Vallon, Seyssel, 1994.
6
Alain Roger, *La Théorie du paysage en France (1974–1994)*, Champ Vallon, Seyssel, 1995.
7
See Mark Rice, *Through the Lens of the City, NEA Photography Surveys of the 1970s*, University Press of Mississippi, Jackson, MS, 2005.
8
John Brinckerhoff Jackson, one of the leading cultural geography theorists in the United States, created and ran the *Landscape* journal from 1951 to 1970. See also Chris Wilson's article in this book, p. 52.
9
Luigi Ghirri, Gianni Leone, Enzo Velati (eds.), *Viaggio in Italia*, Il Quadrante, Alessandria, 1984. The book offers a compilation of photographs taken between 1974 and 1983 by Olivo Barbieri, Gabriele Basilico, Giannantonio Battistella, Vincenzo Castella, Andrea Cavazzuti, Giovanni Chiaramonte, Mario Cresci, Vittore Fossati, Carlo Garzia, Guido Guidi, Luigi Ghirri, Shelley Hill, Mimmo Jodice, Gianni Leone, Claude Nori, Umberto Sartorello, Mario Tinelli, Ernesto Tuliozi, Fulvio Ventura and Cuchi White.

In 1994, it would appear that the institutions responsible for town and country planning were taking photography wholeheartedly on board. From the picture rails of the *Rencontres d'Arles* international photography festival, and later those of the *Musée des Beaux-Arts* in Caen, hung works from the *Conservatoire du littoral*'s photographic mission | FIG. 1 |. In Paris, the Fnac's photo galleries exhibited works on rural Europe commissioned by the French Ministry of Agriculture and Fisheries; the latter was also behind the initiative for the *D'Est en Ouest, chemins de terre et d'Europe* exhibition held at the Pompidou Center's Public Information Library. The first series by the *Observatoire photographique national du paysage* initiated by the Ministry of the Environment's *Bureau des paysages* could be seen at the *Cité des sciences et de l'industrie* | FIG. 2 |.[1] At the same time, the *Paysages pour demain*[2] conference provided the opportunity to take another look at these experiments and to broaden reflection to include other departments such as the French Ministry for Infrastructure's Roads Directorate, which published *Autoroute et paysages*.[3] This profusion of photographic projects, led by the institutions in charge of town and country planning, marked the essentially cultural approach to landscaping in France at that time.

By no means accidental, this examination resulted in several converging dynamics. After the so-called "Landscape Law" (Loi Paysage) was passed in January 1993,[4] 1994 would seem to have been a waypoint in the history of landscape thinking, with the publication of the *Cinq propositions pour une théorie du paysage* manifesto that brought together the leading actors in the field, namely Augustin Berque, Michel Conan, Pierre Donadieu, Bernard Lassus and Alain Roger.[5] This collegiate synthesis was the fruit of 20 or so years of research and was echoed in the anthology *La Théorie du paysage en France (1974–1994)*.[6] The essentially cultural understanding upon which the conception of landscape was then based asserted itself through the following notions: Alain Roger's "artialization" and Augustin Berque's "intermediation" and "trajectivity". The very existence of an idea of landscape was thus related to that of representation which, by placing the eye at the center of the landscape perception process, opened the way for a renaissance of the landscape genre in the visual arts.

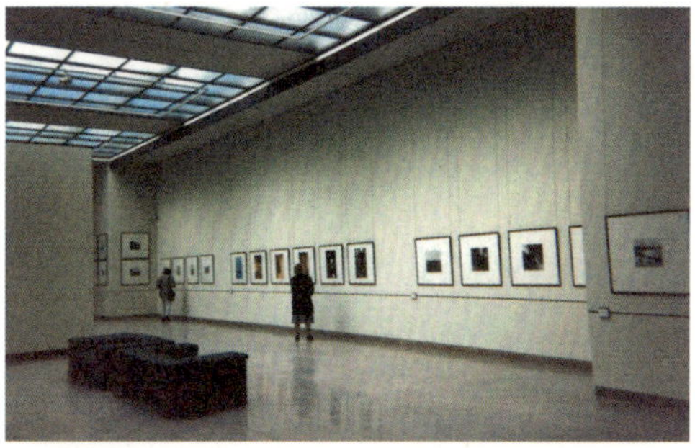

| FIG. 1 | *Figures du littoral* exhibition presented in 1994 for the reopening of the *Musée des Beaux-Arts* in Caen.

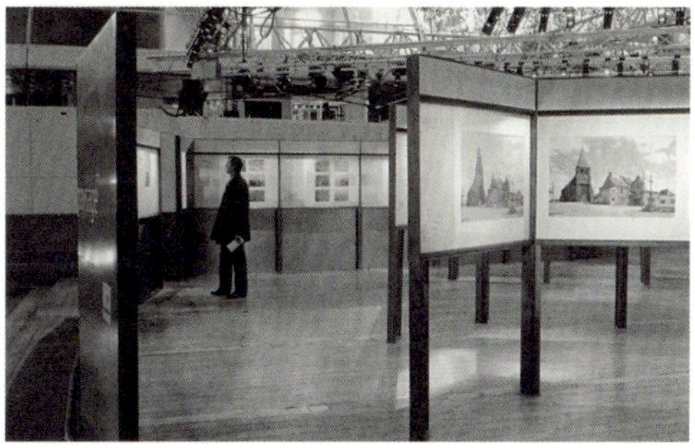

| FIG. 2 | Daniel Quesney, exhibition at the *Cité des sciences et de l'industrie*, 1994.

Indeed, this process was not specific to France; other works and projects were carried out in an international context. Between 1976 and 1982 in the United States, the National Endowment for the Arts funded a dozen photography surveys. The latter systematically linked photographers, solicited as authors, to local institutions so as to produce a territorial representation informed by historical and social issues.[7] This visual research intersects with the contemporary landscape questions that were being explored during that period by the geographer and historian John B. Jackson.[8] In Europe, this type of artistic public commission, linking territorial and photographic considerations, did not emerge until later on. In Italy in 1984, the *Viaggio in Italia* project set the foundations for this productive dialogue;[9] it introduced a dynamic for public commissions, among which we might mention the *Archivio dello spazio* undertaken by the province of Milan between 1987 and 1997[10] or the *Linea di confine* organized as from 1990 in the Emilia-Romagna region.[11] We might also cite Sweden's *Ekodok-90* project, which from 1990 to 1994 brought together 25 authors around an environmental theme,[12] the *Vinex Photo Project* initiated in Holland by the *Rijksplanologische Dienst* (a division of the Dutch Ministry of Housing, Town & Country Planning and the Environment) in relation to the construction of new residential districts between 1993 and 1994,[13] the 1990 to 1991 photographic mission in Brussels,[14] or the projects launched in the wake of Germany's reunification in regions of the former DDR, such as *Fotografie und Gedächtnis* from 1992 to 1996[15] and *East* as from 1992.[16] Crossing national boundaries, the *Mission transmanche* (1998–2005)[17] and the Cross Channel Photographic Mission (1987–1994)[18] observed the changes caused by the implementation of the "project of the century", the Channel Tunnel. From the late 1970s through to the 1990s, all Western societies seemed to share the same need to question and reappropriate their regions, turning to photography as a means to achieving this end.

In order to understand the genesis of the association between photography, landscape and public institutions in France, we need to go back to the *Mission photographique* initiated in 1984 by DATAR.[19] This project consciously displaced the standard framework for photography commissioned by public institutions of non-cultural vocation. For the directors Bernard Latarjet and François Hers this meant soliciting photographers as authors and artists, thereby conferring upon the photographs taken the status of works of art. This decision stemmed from the realization that the age-old balance between "the physical experience necessary to survival and imaginary experience"[20] had been lost. Faced with the omnipresence of "specialists" and "professionals" serving to manufacture and disseminate mass-produced representations, Bernard Latarjet felt that creators "undoubtedly remain the only ones (...) to formulate, clearly and with the boundless complexity of symbolic expression, the meaning of our relationship with the world and with our destiny".[21] Convinced of the role that photographers played in this recreation of a "landscape culture", the two directors wanted to make their pioneering experience an example to be followed. Faithful to the policy of initiation proper to DATAR, throughout the duration of the four-year project they committed themselves to a pedagogy of public commissioning. This stance is clearly evident in the first edition of *Paysages Photographies, travaux en cours, 1984–1985*,[22] which pretty much constitutes a "manual" on how to set up a photographic mission. It was a case of initiating a movement "to approach town and country planning issues in cultural terms and no longer simply from administrative and technical standpoints".[23] In this sense, with its plethora of photographic events initiated by public institutions responsible for town and country planning, 1994 stands out as the year in which this aspect of the project first came under the spotlight.

However, photography was not entirely foreign to 1994's commissioning institutions, such as the ministries and the *Conservatoire du littoral*. As far back as 1859 the *École Nationale des Ponts et Chaussées* had introduced a course on the photographic process and as from 1886 engineers from the *Service de restauration des terrains de montagne* pioneered the systematic use of the medium in their fieldwork. It came into general use after 1945, with the introduction of photographic libraries in all government departments with a view to developing "modern governance".[24] Photographs for these libraries were supplied by departmental employees, salaried photographers and occasionally via *ad hoc* commissions.[25] The use of the photographic medium was nevertheless based on the postulate of the objectivity of the image, providing information that was supposedly neutral and transparent.[26] The rupture proposed by the *Mission photographique de la DATAR* (DATAR Photographic Mission) lay in emancipation from this exclusively documentary or illustrative status, and in photography stating its claim as an art form.

An examination of the various projects initiated in 1994 will allow us to see how institutions appropriated the 1984's Mission program on new uses of photography, in conjunction with a renewed focus on contemporary landscapes, midway between the continuance and transformation of professional cultures.[27]

THE *CONSERVATOIRE DU LITTORAL* AND THE HERITAGE OBJECTIVE

At first glance, the relationship between the *Conservatoire du littoral* and the *DATAR* photographic mission would seem to be evident. Indeed, in 1986[28] the first campaigns were managed as partnerships between the two institutions, in line with DATAR's own "initiation" policy. This interministerial institution, created in 1963 and placed under the direct authority of the Prime Minister, operated in accordance with a horizontal rationale, by space and not by sector, with the aim of ensuring territorial balance at national level whilst at the same time injecting "new ways of thinking".[29] The *Conservatoire du littoral* mission objective was more directly operational, in the sense that it was a case of promoting its action among the general public: "The Conservatoire (...) might play a useful role by better defining its action and by better explaining to the general public its role in protecting natural spaces and the collective heritage, and, as a priority, basing itself on the cultural values of the landscape and of the environment".[30]

1996 was a watershed for this administrative governmental institution which had been created in 1975 for the purpose of "leading a land policy to preserve coastal space and to ensure that natural sites and ecological balance are respected".[31] Indeed, paradoxically, the so-called "Coastal" law, which extended its prerogatives, was passed during a period of "public disenchantment with 'ecological discourse'."[32] The *Conservatoire's* action therefore needed to find legitimacy not just among the inhabitants and elected officials of the sites concerned, but also more broadly. As a first step, the *Conservatoire* entrusted the task of preparing reports on these protected sites to civil servants within the institution, or else called upon local photographers. However, the "highly uneven"[33] quality of the photographs made it impossible to use them

10
See the website of the Museo fotografia contemporanea: https://www.mufoco.org/en/collections/archivio-dello-spazio/

11
See the website of *Linea di confine*: http://www.lineadiconfine.org/

12
Annette Rosengren (ed.), *I människans hand.Fotografier kring det ekologiska landskapet. Ekodok-90 / In the hand of mankind. Photographies around the ecological landscape*, Nordiska Museet, Stockholm, 1994.

13
See in particular Frits Gierstberg (ed.), *SubUrban Options. Photography Commissions and the Urbanization of the Landscape*, Nederlands Foto Instituut, Rotterdam, 1998.

14
04° 50° La Mission photographique à Bruxelles, Contretype, Brussels, 1991.

15
Diethart Kerbs and Sophie Schleussner, *Fotografie und Gedächtnis, eine Bilddokumentation*, 3 vol., be.bra Verlag, Berlin, 1997.

16
See in particular Raphaële Bertho, "East, L'histoire d'un mécénat, l'histoire d'un territoire", *Études photographiques*, no. 24, November 2009, p. 118–149.

17
See the website of the *Centre régional de la photographie Nord-Pas-de-Calais*: http://www.crp.photo/page-collection/

18
Jane Alison and Brigitte Lardinois (eds.), *Soundings*, Cross Channel Photographic Mission, 1994.

19
Délégation interministérielle à l'aménagement du territoire et à l'attractivité régionale (Interministerial delegation for town and country planning and regional attractiveness). See Raphaële Bertho, *La Mission photographique de la DATAR. Un laboratoire du paysage contemporain*, La documentation française, Paris, 2013.

20
Bernard Latarjet, in Gabriele Basilico, *Bord de mer*, Arte, Milan, 1990, p. 15.

21
Ibid., p. 16.

22
Mission photographique de la DATAR (ed.), *Paysages Photographies, travaux en cours, 1984-1985*, Hazan, Paris, 1985.

23
Patrick Roegiers, "Douce France", interview with Bernard Latarjet, *Révolution*, no. 266, April 5–11, 1985, p. 40.

24
Véronique Figini-Veron, "Effort de la France (1946–1960). De la propagande à l'information, la photographie industrielle à la Documentation française ou le document à l'œuvre", in Martine Dancer-Mourès and Danièle Méaux (eds.), *Les Photographes et la commande industrielle. Autour des éditions Paul Martial, Musée d'art moderne et contemporain/* Université Jean Monnet, Saint-Étienne, 2014, p. 40–51.

25
Raphaële Bertho, "Une première approche de la photographie institutionnelle, *Pour mémoire*, no. 16, winter 2015, p. 9-11.

26
Véronique Figini-Veron, *op. cit.*

27
An aspiration that can be found during that period in other projects such as *Les quatre saisons* from the *Territoire de Belfort* (1987 and 1991) or *Trwa kartié* in Reunion Island (1990–1994). For analytical purposes and in order to ensure the coherency of the corpora, only projects of national scope were selected.

28
Agreement between the *Conservatoire du littoral* and the *Fondation nationale de la photographie*, summer 1986 (AN 20040212/01).

29
Jérôme Monod and Philippe de Castelbajac, *L'Aménagement du territoire*, Presses universitaires de France, Paris, 2001, p. 29.

30
"Compte rendu de la réunion entre la Mission photographique de la DATAR et le *Conservatoire du littoral* du 21 octobre 1986", 1986 (AN 20040212/01).

31
Law no. 2005-157 dated February 23, 2005, art. 133-I and II, *Journal officiel* of February 24, 2005.

32
Bernard Latarjet and Francois Hers, "L´expérience du paysage", *Paysages Photographies, En France les années quatre-vingt*, DATAR's photographic mission/ Hazan, Paris, 1989, p. 14.

33
According to the brochure presenting the *Figures du littoral* exhibition to the French General Assembly between May 4 and 27, 2005, setting out the *Conservatoire du littoral's* photographic collection, compiled with the support of the Fondation Gaz de France.

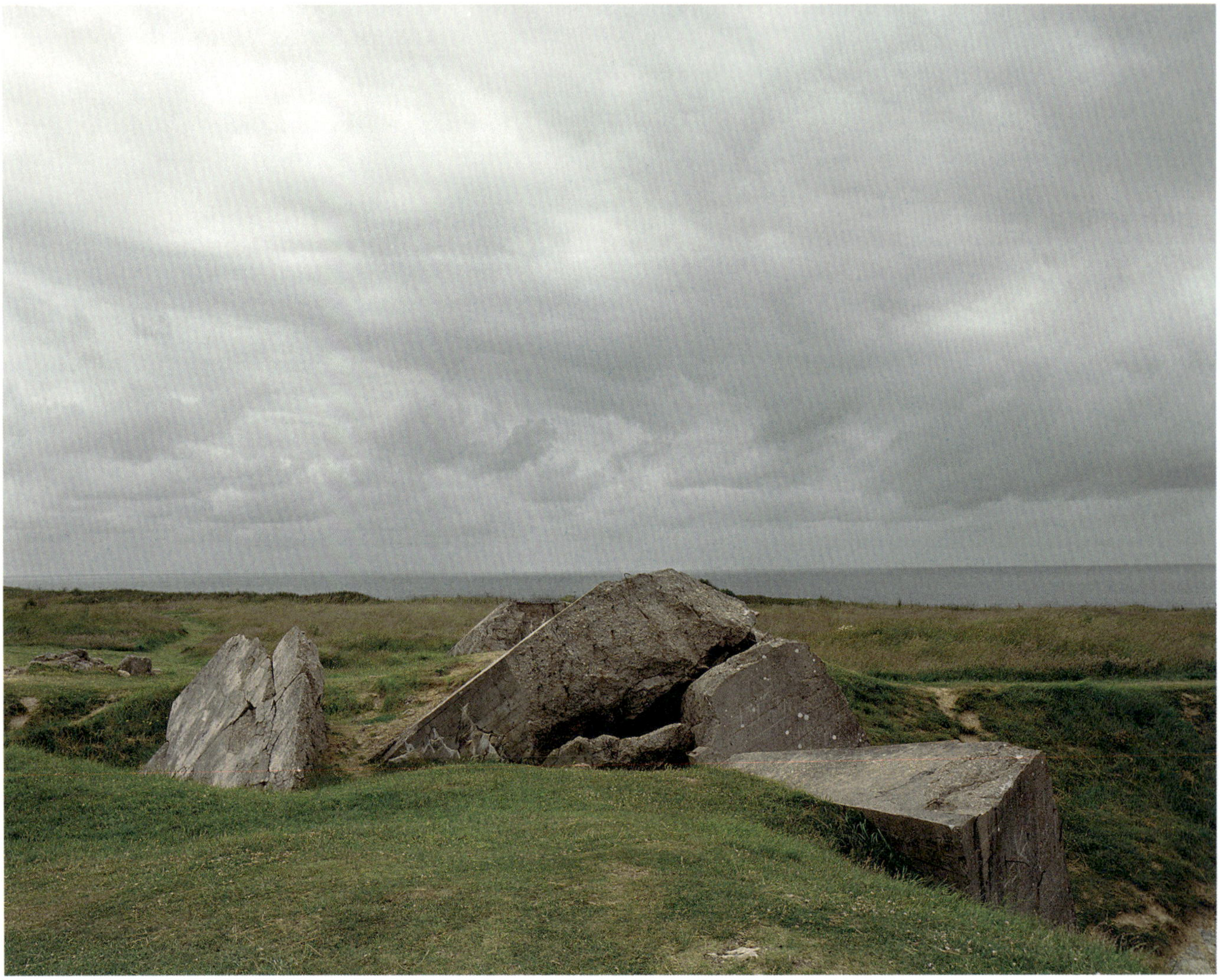

| FIG. 3 |

| FIG. 3 |
Alain Ceccaroli, 2008.
Conservatoire du littoral's
photographic mission.

as part of an awareness campaign. It was felt that the artistic dimension of the pictures taken by the photographers was more likely to show the sites to their best advantage.

Photography was not therefore used for its descriptive capacities, but as a format that offered a singular vision enhanced by an aesthetic quality. It was not a question of convincing through demonstration, but of gaining support through a form of sublimation. So as Odile Marcel points out, the institution's action was not confined to acquiring land; it had a landscaping aspect to it, by developing spaces "in harmony with their geography, their natural resources, their history and their contemporary uses".[34] These landscapes, developed under the aegis of public authority, were enhanced with the works of recognized artists. The pictures – of the dunes in the Pas-de-Calais by Vincent Monthiers, of the Domaine de Certes by Suzanne Lafont, of the Agriates and the Normandy landing sites by Alain Ceccaroli and of the Vendée marshes by Werner Hannapel – do not show the geographical situation or geological particularities of the sites | **FIG. 3** |. Each of these four photographers solicited as part of the partnership with DATAR chose a formal and sometimes radical perspective that reveals an atmosphere, a light, a substance. They "artialize" the landscapes, following the process described by Alain Roger, emphasizing an atemporal approach to sites that were already considered "remarkable" (to use the legal terminology).[35] This dynamic endured beyond the variety of styles and approaches proposed by the photographers, be they John Batho's refined color compositions of the Ploumanac'h rocks or Bernard Plossu's grainy photos of the Riou archipelago. These pictures provide a visual transcription of the conception that governs the *Conservatoire*'s activity, that of a heritagized landscape, henceforth protected from the ravages of time and use.

The photographic commissioning activity became perennial as from 1991, with the patronage of the Fondation Gaz de France. Unlike the DATAR model, the *Conservatoire* did not finance the photography campaign but engaged in the acquisition of works *a posteriori* – a choice that allowed the institution to reduce risks taken within the framework of an artistic commission: by definition, the latter remained open and the photographer could work without any specific directives or obligation to produce. 1994 marked a new step forward, with the creation of a collection comprising 72 original prints. The collection was presented as part of the official program of the *Rencontres internationales de la photographie* in Caen, at the inaugural exhibition of the Museum of Fine Art in Coimbra, Portugal, during the *Encontros de fotografia*, as well as in Paris at the *Maison de l'Amérique Latine*, in Nantes, Bordeaux, Montpellier, Lyon, Marseille and Tunis. Finally, two large books entitled *Littoral* were brought out in 1994 and 1995 by Marval,[36] who had regularly published the results of photographic campaigns since 1991. The schism between the documentary photograph collection and the *Conservatoire*'s collection, entrusted to independent artistic director Line Lavesque (from *À travers le paysage*), was thus complete: the pictures henceforth had a distinct status and visibility. The archive was linked to the agents in the field and to their specific iconographic needs; the collection presented the long-term task of valorizing sites, one that fitted in with the *Conservatoire*'s landscape concerns. As such, the images in the collection constituted not just a tool for cultural distinction, in the manner of a classic patronage strategy; they also helped to establish the legitimacy of the *Conservatoire*'s action: they were an attempt to use the presentation of gratifying images to gain acceptance for the benefits of its action.

The *Conservatoire du littoral*'s approach was heritage oriented in two ways: through the creation of a collection of photographic works and through a protection of the landscape that was *a priori* exceptional. From this standpoint, the project shifted away from one of DATAR's announced objectives, that of moving towards renewed

34 Odile Marcel, *Littoral. Les aventures du Conservatoire du littoral*, Champ Vallon, Seyssel, 2013, p. 303.

35 "Paysage" law dated January 8, 1993, article 1.

36 *Littoral*, vol. 1, Marval, Paris, 1994, 319 pages and *Littoral*, vol. 2, Marval, Paris, 1995, 287 p.

representations of landscapes, instead favoring the reiteration of landscape models, especially those that were sublime or picturesque.[37]

THE ROADS DIRECTORATE AND THE INVENTION OF A LANDSCAPE

The partnership that the French Ministry for Infrastructure's Roads Directorate established with the DATAR Mission in 1986 was an integral part of a visual policy which differed from that of the *Conservatoire du littoral*. Far removed from the heritage oriented bias, the project of the 1980s and 1990s followed an original approach designed to accompany the invention of a highway landscape in France.

Whilst this partnership with the DATAR Mission would appear to have been in keeping with the cultural direction of the policy pursued by the Roads Directorate in the late 1980s,[38] the works carried out by François Hers, Sophie Ristelhueber and Jean-Louis Garnell have a unique status **| FIG. 4 |**.[39] The pictures were not placed in the photographic library's documentary archive created within the department in 1986, the year which began with another commission for photographer Albert Bérenguier relating to civil engineering structures, cofinanced with Sétra (department for research on transport, roads and their planning). These initiatives demonstrated the desire to refresh the way in which the government's highways were viewed, and departed from usual practice in terms of the visual and photographic documentation of this type of construction work. Indeed, the engineer training program at the *École Nationale des Ponts et Chaussées* included a photography course and students were accustomed to taking pictures of work sites and engineering structures. The Roads Directorate also had access to the ministry's photography department.[40] Such a sidestep in relation to the institution's customs was justified by a desire to elicit a point of view that was "artistic" and not merely technical – an attitude that was confirmed in the explicitly named book published by Albert Bérenguier in 1989: *L'Art et l'autoroute*.[41] The project was thus presented as the accomplishment of a cultural program that had been initiated in the middle of the decade, based on showcasing the engineer, with, in particular, Director of Roads Jean Berthier's creation of the "Road and culture" work group in 1984 and the scaling up of historical and heritage exhibitions.

The turn of the decade was marked by a shift in the direction of the communication policy towards a discourse that focused on the landscape value of major highway works. Convinced that "in the 21st century European motorists will discover France solely from its highways,"[42] as soon as he took up his post at the end of 1989, the new Director of Roads, Christian Leyrit, decided to bring in a panel of "landscape and environment" experts made up of architects, urban planners, geographers, historians, philosophers, landscape architects and sociologists, coordinated by Bernard Lassus. The group's work received particular media attention over the course of 1994, as part of the "Paysages pour demain" conference and following publication of *Autoroute et paysage*, edited by Christian Leyrit and Bernard Lassus.[43] It is worth noting that this work came out at the same time as two other books – *Trois regards sur le paysage français*[44] and *Cinq propositions pour une théorie du paysage*[45] – bringing together geographer Pierre Donadieu and philosopher Alain Roger – who were working during that period with Bernard Lassus on the "Jardin, paysages, territoires" postgraduate degree (DEA) – John Dixon Hunt, Director of Studies in landscape architecture at the University of Pennsylvania and Yoshio Nakamura, doctor of engineering and landscape specialist at the Tokyo Institute of Technology. The partnership between the authors of the Roads Directorate work was thus not merely a one-off event; it was part of a more general research dynamic relating to the issue of landscape.

37
Yves Luginbühl, *La Mise en scène du monde. Construction du paysage européen*, CNRS Éditions, Paris, p. 142.

38
See Raphaële Bertho, "Le paysage autoroutier, une invention photographique ?", *Pour mémoire*, no. 16, winter 2015, p. 16–29.

39
The portfolios of these three artists were deposited at the *Maison européenne de la photographie* in 1996 at the time of the exhibition *Qu'est-ce qu'une route ?*

40
Didier Mouchel and Danièle Voldman, *Photographies à l'œuvre. Enquêtes et chantiers de la Reconstruction 1945–1958*, Jeu de paume/Le point du jour, Paris, 2011.

41
Albert Bérenguier, *L'Art et l'autoroute*, Belfond, Paris, 1989.

42
Interview with Christian Leyrit, "Techniques et politiques d'équipement", *Revue des ingénieurs des travaux publics de l'État*, no. 105, July 1991, p. 9; Christian Leyrit, "Le paysage n'est pas l'environnement", minutes of the "Paysages pour demain" conference (1994), published in *L'Environnement magazine*, special edition, March 1995, p. 82; Christian Leyrit, "L'autoroute, le paysage et l'environnement", in Christian Leyrit and Bernard Lassus (eds.), *Autoroute et paysages, op. cit.*, p. 176.

43
Christian Leyrit and Bernard Lassus (eds.), *op. cit.*

44
Yoshio Nakamura, John Dixon Hunt and Dirk Frieling, *Trois regards sur le paysage français*, Champ Vallon, Seyssel, 1993.

45
Pierre Donadieu et al., *op. cit.*

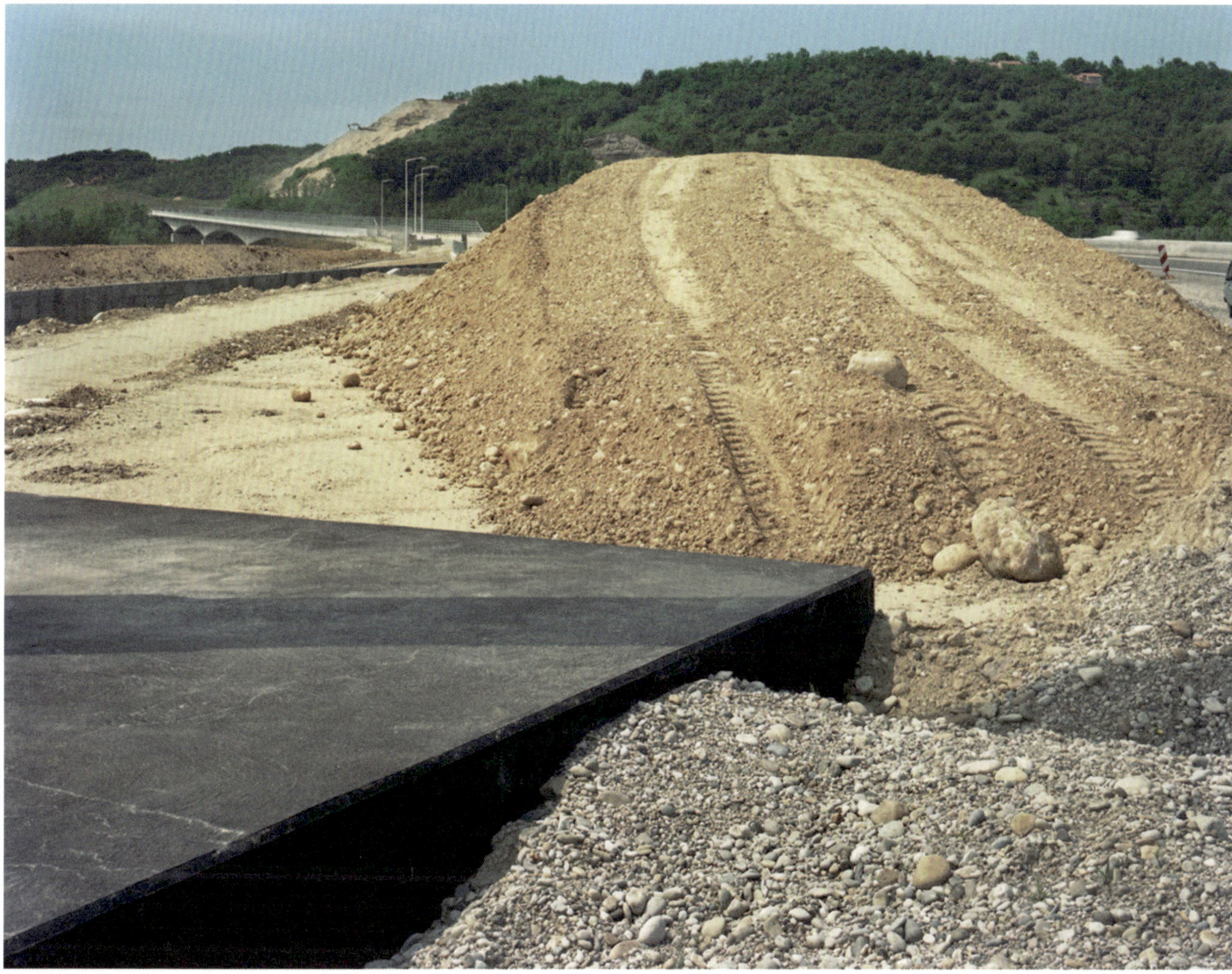

| FIG. 4 |

| FIG. 4 |
Jean-Louis Garnell, *Routes*, 1986. Photographic mission for DATAR/French Ministry for Infrastructure's Roads Directorate.

| FIG. 5 |
Éric Bénard, A20 Haute-Vienne:
Intégration dans le paysage avant Pierre-Buffière, 1990.
French Ministry for Infrastructure's
Roads Directorate.

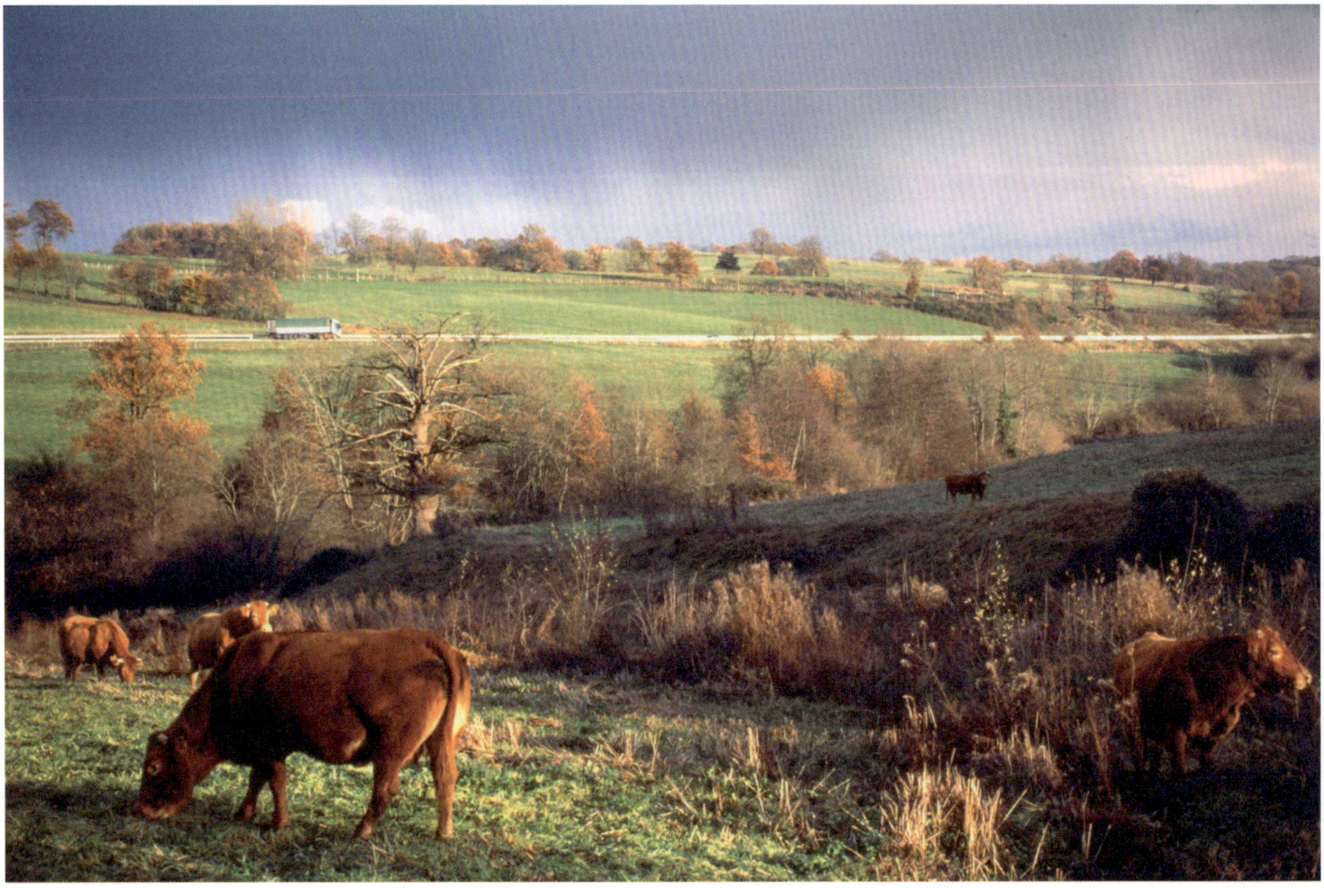

| FIG. 5 |

All of the above contributed to a desire to "invent" a highway landscape,[46] which was developed in practice through the continuation of highway programs, in discourses and in images. The development of the photographic library thus followed the various institutional stages of a process to showcase the landscapes surrounding road and highway infrastructures. Photographer activity nevertheless remained on the fringes of the reflections put forward by the group of experts, with their pictures essentially serving a communication strategy that remained within the visual tradition of representations of engineering structures. Although Bernard Lassus was promoting the notion of a highway considered as a piece of "kinetic art"[47] in which "the perceived objects evolve in a ballet of contradictory movements, swirling in the foreground, slowly drifting to the horizon",[48] transforming the cars into veritable "mobile viewing platforms".[49] None of the photographic library's photo campaigns develop this proposition. On the contrary, flowing landscapes seemed to be giving way to sedentary landscapes. The landscape seen from the highway was rapidly being replaced by a valorization of roadside landscapes. The two white papers produced in the context of the construction of two toll-free highways – the Méridienne (A75) and the Occitane (A20)[50] – so as to promote the implementation of the "1% landscape and development" policy as from 1989, thus combined traditional iconographic representations with national landscape depictions inherited from the 19th century,[51] with verdant hills, peasant farmers working the fields, and old stone buildings. These two projects, presented as exemplary, were not however places of visual experimentation, far from it | **FIG. 5** |.

The same goes for the Ruban d'Or competition, which spearheaded the Roads Directorate's communication policy in the 1990s. Presented as "the symbol of road-landscape communication",[52] its objective was to counter the "scar complex"[53] that systematically equated highways with visual pollution. The competition took place every two years between 1991 and 2003, recognizing public and private developers for the landscaping qualities of their infrastructures and linking the engineering world to that of the arts. The photographic dimension of the competition was unusual, in that the jury, working together in Paris, used only slides to judge the various works. Yet far from a cultural valorization of the infrastructures, the images ultimately proved to be the most effective medium for dissimulating the works of art within a bucolic frame. Highways, with their bridge, rest area and toll booth avatars, were "integrated" into compositions modeled on the picturesque. Spring bouquets, autumn leaves and sunflowers frequently appeared in the photographic foreground, ultimately identifying elements of vegetation with the landscape in a visual shortcut that ran contrary to the idea put forward by the commissioning institution.

The photographic image thus remained confined to documentary and illustrative use, designed to bear witness or to convince. The highway did not invent its photographic landscape, it did not shift one's gaze or perception as the roads or railways of previous centuries had done.[54] At best, the tons of concrete sought to discreetly integrate the standard representation of the French countryside.

THE MINISTRY OF AGRICULTURE AND FISHERIES' AUDIOVISUAL BUREAU AND THE CREATIVE PHOTO ESSAY

The photographic missions initiated by the French Ministry of Agriculture and Fisheries were also directly set in the tradition of the *Mission photographique de la DATAR*, even though there was no institutional partnership. At that time, the example put forward by the *Mission photographique de la DATAR* was seen as a veritable "trigger"[55] and

46 Pierre Donadieu et al., *op. cit.*, p. 7.

47 Bernard Lassus "Découvrir, s'arrêter", in Christian Leyrit and Bernard Lassus (eds.), *Autoroute et paysages*, *op. cit.*, p. 56.

48 *Ibid.*, p. 43.

49 *Ibid.*, p. 37–56.

50 The photographic library's activity is devoted entirely to the valorization of these two major projects in 1989 and 1990, with commissions placed with Albert Bérenguier, Richard Nespoulos and Éric Bénard. The white papers were issued in 1992.

51 See Françoise Cachin, "Le paysage du peintre", Pierre Nora (ed.), *La Nation II. Les lieux de mémoire*, Gallimard, Paris, 1986, p. 982–992.

52 *Le Paysage et la route*, booklets published by the Roads Directorate, July 2003.

53 Alain Roger "Paysage et environnement : pour une théorie de la dissociation", in *Autoroute et paysages*, *op. cit.*, p. 33.

54 Marc Desportes, *Paysages en mouvement. Perception de l'espace et transports (XVIIIe–XXe siècle)*, Gallimard, Paris, 2005.

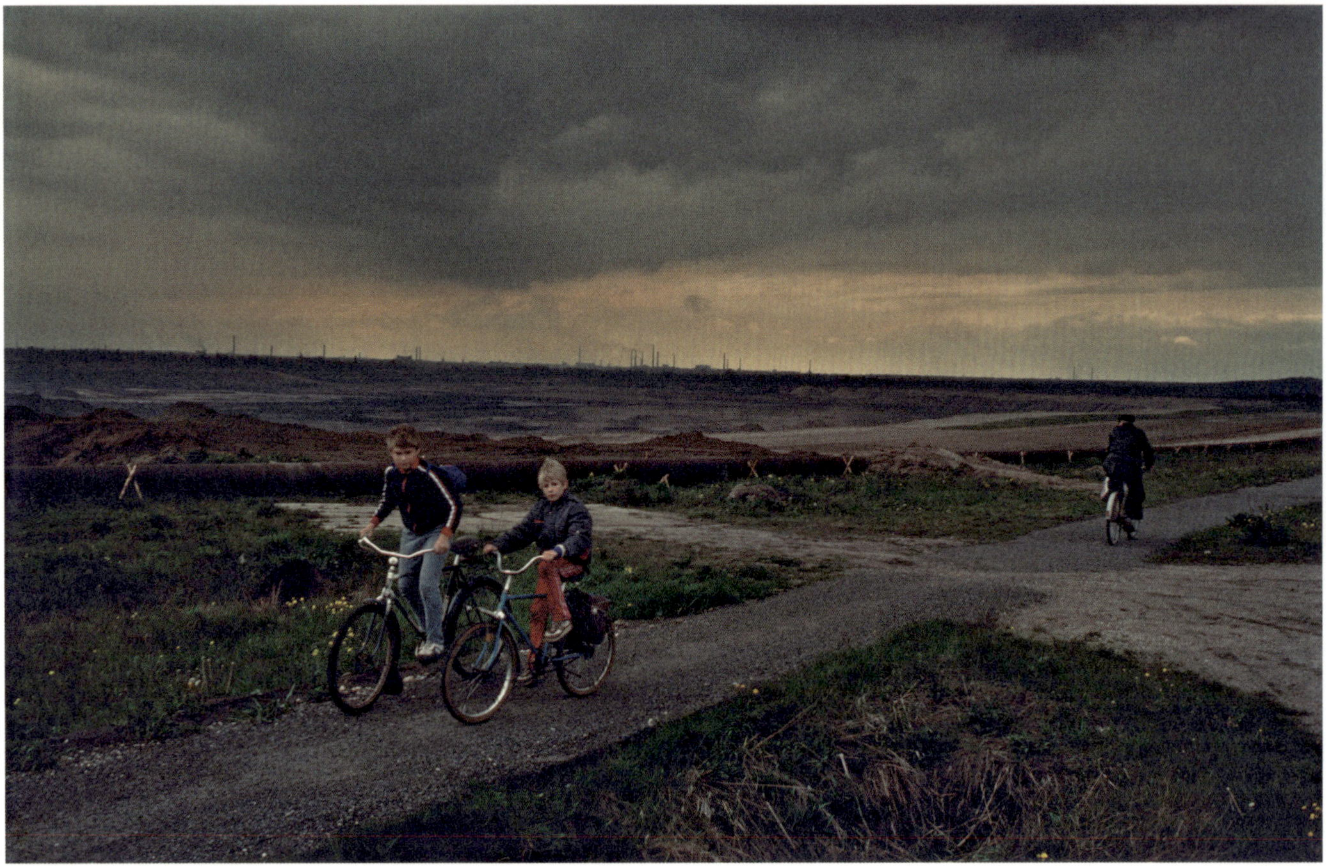

| FIG. 6 |

| FIG. 6 |
Stéphane Duroy, *RFA et ex-RDA 1989/1990, Europe rurale. Regards hors des villes.* Audiovisual Office of the French Ministry of Agriculture and Fisheries.

was part of the renewal of a visual policy that was already very much established.

The Ministry had taken a very early interest in photographic and cinematographic images. In particular we might mention the systemized use of photography in the work done by the Reforestation Department,[56] whose collection became a "remarkable example" of photographic archives used "for administrative and pedagogical purposes, based on the practice of civil servants".[57] Similarly, as from the beginning of the century, cinematographic images had been appreciated for their didactic value, at a time when illiteracy was still rife, and the *"Cinématographe agricole"* was created in 1923 on the initiative of Minister Henri Queuille.[58] After becoming the *Service du cinéma du ministère de l'Agriculture* (SCMA) in 1947, during the post-war period it accompanied the profound upheavals affecting rural society, due in part to agricultural modernization. When it was created, the department was equipped with a photographic library for the purposes of documenting the Ministry's activity, supporting the film-making teams and making documentaries.[59] In addition to these photographic campaigns, many pictures were either purchased or simply donated by actors from the farming world. The photographic library also trained correspondents from among the engineers in outside departments, as well as agricultural and home economics teachers.[60] These photographs were used internally, but were also solicited by other organizations; in the 1980s, access to this archive of approximately 100,000 photographs and slides was facilitated for a broad public (journalists, researchers, teachers, students) by the creation of the Resapho computerized image network.[61]

Photography was thus very much present at the French Ministry of Agriculture, though it was considered from a documentary or pedagogical standpoint alone. In no part of the audiovisual archive was any mention made of the photographers; the images were valued solely for their subject matter or for the event they illustrated. As from the late 1980s the example of the *Mission photographique de la DATAR* helped to evolve these practices and the commissioning policy introduced in 1988 under Éric Perrot's direction represented a marked shift away from the practices in force, by highlighting the artistic quality of the photographs and the status of those who took them. The ways in which images were disseminated changed too, with works published by a specialist publisher, Filigranes, and exhibitions at cultural venues. 1994 was to become the climax of this policy, with the exposition of two major projects: *Europe rurale. Regards hors des villes* and *D'Est en Ouest. Chemins de terre et d'Europe*.

Europe rurale might be regarded as the "linchpin" project of the renewal of the photographic library's visual policy **| FIG. 6 |**. Launched in 1988, this commission lasted six years; it led to the creation of 250 photographs[62] by 17 photographers[63] and in 1994 was the object of a series of exhibitions in the Fnac's photo galleries[64] and of a book.[65] In the preface to the latter, Minister Jean Puech stressed both the pedagogical and heritage purposes of the project, the aesthetic quality of the images serving a "personal and collective reflection on the identity of the European rural world". The project was a perfect example of Éric Perrot's determination (he was then in charge of the photographic library and artistic coordinator of these projects) to work with photographers over the long term, in a spirit of partnership and innovation. As with the DATAR Mission, among those chosen there was a mixture of well-known

55 Interview with Éric Perrot, formerly in charge of the Ministry of Agriculture's photographic library.

56 See in particular Luce Lebart, "La 'restauration' des montagnes", *Études photographiques,* no. 3, November 1997, online: http://etudesphotographiques.revues.org/96

57 Charles-André Buffet and Anne-Gaël Noussan, "Le fonds photographique de la restauration des terrains en montagne conservé par le ministère de l'Alimentation, de l'Agriculture et de la Pêche: une illustration de la sauvegarde et de la domestication du paysage", in Cécile Souchon (ed.), *Les Outils de représentation du paysage*, CTHS, Paris, 2012, p. 175.

58 See in particular Valérie Vignaux, *Jean Benoît-Lévy ou le corps comme utopie, une histoire du cinéma éducateur dans l'entre-deux-guerres en France,* AFRHC, Paris, 2007.

59 Decree dated December 11, 1946.

60 The photographic library organized four courses in 1961. See SCMA's activity report, 1961, AN 19800403/2.

61 Numerous public photographic libraries belong to the "automatisation des photothèques" commission (photographic library automatization). For example, the photographic libraries of: the Albert Kahn museum, the CNRS, the SNCF, the BNF, ECPA, the CNDP's media library, the CCI's slide library, the Ministry of Agriculture, the BPI, the *Musée de l'Armée,* the *École Polytechnique,* Inalco, the *Musée national d'art moderne*, the RMN, the *Centre de recherches sur l'urbanisme, La Documentation française*, etc. See AN 19940034/48.

62 This is the exhibited image (and hence selected image) count.

63 Carl de Keyzer, Louise Oligny, Didier Hubert, Luc Choquer, Martine Voyeux, Marie-Paule Nègre, Xavier Lambours, Bernard Molins, Jean-Pierre Favreau, Dominique Cros, Gilles Peress, Fouad Elkoury, Marie-France Dublé, Roger Wagner, Paul den Hollander, Georges Dussaud, Stéphane Duroy.

64 Exhibition May–June 1994 in the Fnac Forum's photo galleries at Montparnasse, La Défense and Étoile.

65 *Europe rurale 1994. Regards hors des villes*, Filigranes, Trézélan, 1994.

photographers and upcoming youngsters. They were accompanied by the artistic director throughout the entire creative process, from shooting to developing (the photographic library had its own laboratory) and onwards to dissemination and the organization of exhibitions and publication.

Also in 1994, the *Centre Georges-Pompidou's* BPI Gallery hosted the *D'Est en Ouest. Chemins de terre et d'Europe*[66] exhibition – the result of a joint commission by the two institutions. More modest in appearance, the project brought together the works of six photographers on eleven East European regions.[67] It had a similar ambition, that of offering a "representation above and beyond visual expectations" so as to allow a "better appreciation of this [rural] reality" and to "give it meaning".[68] So the challenge was no longer to simply to attest to the facts, but to bring out a representation in the literal and symbolic sense. This "responsibility"[69] explains the space given to the photographers in the exhibition's press file. Formerly invisible and unnamed, they were now praised for the "pertinence of their perspective".[70] The first deviation from the DATAR model was the profile of the photographers solicited. The latter were affiliated with agencies (Métis, Rapho, Magnum and Vu) and demanded a *"photoreportage d'auteur"* (to use the term employed during the debate at that time). This conception, inherited from a legitimization process initiated, among others, by Christian Caujolle, photographic director of the newspaper *Libération*, was endorsed by the government's cultural policy in the 1980s. The figure of the *auteur* was thus clearly embedded in the field of photography; it differed from the artist status claimed by other photographers, which conveyed the wish to belong to the world of contemporary art.[71] Terminological distinctions aside, distance was also created in forms of writing. While the DATAR Mission's productions were marked by a conceptual dimension and by a move away from the representation of the figure,[72] the majority of *Europe rurale*'s photographers remained committed to the visual codes of the photo essay, with the wide angle, the "on-the-spot" photo, and landscape views in which human beings feature prominently.

The development of this "carte blanche" policy for photographers opened up the status of photographic images within the ministry's photographic library. Already a documentary and pedagogical tool, it also became an element of cultural distinction, this time without any direct link to operability. Promotion of the European theme was of course linked to the implementation of a common agricultural policy, resonating with the enactment of the 1993 Maastricht treaty and the prospect of a single market;[73] it had no links, however, with any specific political or institutional agenda. It related more to a *zeitgeist*, that of rapidly expanding European construction and the opening up of East European countries following the fall of the Berlin wall in 1989. In going beyond the national framework propounded by DATAR, these works questioned the identity of the rural world through the representation of an inhabited land, revealing the faces of a vernacular landscape, in the sense of J. B. Jackson,[74] on a continental scale.

THE OPNP AND THE RECOURSE TO PROTOCOL

Despite their obvious differences, it would appear that the *Observatoire photographique national du paysage* (OPNP – national landscape photography observatory) project launched in 1989 shared the same goals as those of the DATAR Mission, regularly cited as an "important reference in landscape representation".[75] Run by the Ministry of the Environment's Landscape Bureau, the *Observatoire* had very similar methods and ambitions, whilst at the same time having different recommended methods.[76]

In both cases it was a question of soliciting the eye of photographic artists in order to give direction to those in charge of town and country planning.[77] The two projects were run by the same small team of three: Caroline Stefulesco, *chargée de mission* at the Ministry of the Environment; Véronique Ristelhueber, freelance documentalist; and Daniel Quesney, project manager at the *Cité des sciences et de l'industrie*. Finally, it was a matter, using the same methods, of creating a blueprint for action and of accompanying its development throughout France via a policy of partnership with local institutions – in this case essentially the *Conseils d'architecture d'urbanisme et de l'environnement* (CAUE – urban and environmental architecture committees) and the *Parcs naturels régionaux* (PNR – national regional parks).[78]

However, the place and role that the OPNP allowed photographers – for both their vision and their photographs – was radically different to that of DATAR ten years earlier. Whereas DATAR established and demanded creative freedom, the *Observatoire* insisted that the work be subject to strict control: from the qualitative standpoint, with the creation of a board of experts to identify territorial themes and to monitor and validate the work, and from a quantitative point of view, with photographers being obliged to produce a predetermined number of photographs and to follow a strict protocol of annual recurring shoots. The "right to fail" demanded by Bernard Latarjet and François Hers had given way to a strict instruction, and the photographers' free wanderings had become itineraries with geolocated waypoints. Finally, the fixed-term campaign turned into a partnership between the actors – local sponsors and photographers – for an initial duration of three years, with scope for renewal over the long term.

In so doing, and far from denaturing the DATAR legacy, at the heart of their project the observatories established a dual status for photography, "the documentary and artistic values of which are mutually reinforcing",[79] here taking up the program announced for the first mission. On the one hand, the image is deemed to be a transparent reflection of reality, expressing a precise coextensivity with its object; it depicts a state of affairs, a spatial and physical configuration. It is on this condition that it may be considered to be a management tool, with the protocol here guaranteeing its operability. On the other hand, photography is perceived in its opacity, as a representation that expresses the photographer's view of a region.[80] This duality of use, which allowed photographs to be seen both as archives and as tools of communication and awareness-raising, both as documents and as works of art, proved to be fruitful given the subsequent developments in this approach, but also a source of ambiguity with regard to the status of the images.[81]

66
D'Est en Ouest. Chemins de terre et d'Europe, Filigranes, Trézélan, 1994.

67
Stéphane Duroy in the Czech Republic and Slovakia; Graciela Iturbide in Hungary; Yvon Lambert in Romania; Paulo Nozolino in Poland; Klavdij Sluban in Croatia, Kosovo, Macedonia, Slovenia and Albania; Anthony Suau in Bulgaria.

68
D'Est en Ouest. Chemins de terre et d'Europe, exhibition press file.

69
Ibid.

70
Ibid.

71
See in particular Gaëlle Morel, *Le Photoreportage d'auteur. L'institution culturelle de la photographie en France depuis les années 1970*, CNRS Éditions, Paris, 2006.

72
With the exception of the portraits by Despatin & Gobeli and the series by Dominique Auerbacher and Holger Trülsch.

73
Europe rurale 1993. Premiers travaux, Ministère de l'Agriculture et de la Forêt, 1993. This catalogue was published for the exhibition shown at the *Cité des sciences et de l'industrie* as part of the Eurocité think tank, from March to June 1991.

74
See John Brinckerhoff Jackson, *Discovering the Vernacular Landscape*, Yale University Press, New Haven, CT, 1984.

75
Daniel Quesney, Caroline Stefulesco and Véronique Ristelhueber-Guilloteau, *L'Observatoire photographique du paysage*, ministère de l'Environnement/Cité des sciences et de l'industrie, Paris, 1994, p. 6.

76
On this point, see in particular Raphaële Bertho, "Du territoire au paysage, la Mission photographique de la DATAR et l'Observatoire photographique du paysage", in *Photographier le territoire*, Somogy, Paris, 2009, p. 109–117.

77
In 1994 several photographers from the DATAR Photographic Mission were solicited for the OPNP: Sophie Ristelhueber (1992), Raymond Depardon (1992), Alain Ceccarolli (1993) and Dominique Auerbacher (1993); Gilbert Fastenaekens would work for the Observatory in 1997.

78
Of the OPNP's 20 itineraries, six were conducted in PNRs and three with CAUEs. More broadly, a census of the "local" observatories that were based on the OPNP's method counted 24 projects in PNRs and eight in the CAUEs. See Monique Chauvin and Pascal Chevallier, *Observatoires photographiques du paysage "locaux", Recensement et typologie*, Ministère de l'Environnement, de l'Énergie et de la Mer, Bureau des paysages, report, 2015.

79
Bernard Latarjet and Francois Hers, "L'expérience du paysage", in *Paysages Photographies, travaux en cours, 1984–1985, Mission photographique de la DATAR*/ Hazan, Paris, 1985, p. 32.

80
See Louis Marin, *Opacité de la peinture, essais sur la représentation au Quattrocento*, EHESS, Paris (1989), 2006.

81
See in particular Raphaële Bertho and Frédéric Pousin, "L'Observatoire photographique du paysage du PNR des Vosges du Nord: de l'œuvre à l'action", thematic dossier, *Projets de paysage*, no. 15, 2017, online: http://www.projetsdepaysage.fr/l_observatoire_photographique_du_paysage_du_pnr_des_vosges_du_nord_de_l_u0153uvre_l_action

On another note, this entire approach was in keeping with a revised conception of the landscape itself. Over a period of ten or so years, the direction of government policies had shifted towards a consideration of landscapes not just as "remarkable" but also as "everyday", in line with rising environmental concerns. The exhibition of the OPNP's works followed on from the national *Mon paysage, nos paysages* photographic competition in 1992.[82] An analysis of contributions reveals a high level of commitment by participants to this question of landscape, with comments ranging from virulent criticism of town and country planning to pleas for the protection of biodiversity. Sociologist Françoise Dubost nevertheless notes that the selected landscapes matched the visual archetypes relating to the countryside or to vacation areas such as the mountains and coasts, even though a decade earlier the DATAR Mission had attempted to update these representations by promoting prosaic and contemporary landscapes showing factories, housing developments and commercial zones. The OPNP was located at the crossroads of these two philosophies, seeking to establish strong regional identities around recognizable landscape markers, whilst at the same time paying attention to landscapes of modernity, to the roadsides and village entrances that do not belong to the heritage pantheon. Between confirmation and renewal, each of the itineraries thus sketches a contrasting portrait of the territories photographed, in an original synthesis of landscapes that are both "political", in other words managed and organized by the State, and "vernacular", i.e. essentially usage-driven, to here take up the distinction suggested by American geographer John B. Jackson.[83]

POLITICAL LANDSCAPES AND VISUAL POLICIES

1994 was a clear milestone in the history of public photography commissions: it marked the shift from town and country planning challenges which acted as a channel for projects, to the cultural challenges of regional valorization. Returning after almost 30 years to the *Mission photographique de la DATAR* project, Bernard Latarjet esteemed that people's "confidence that art could clarify policies, or change them, was excessive"[84] at the time. The desire to give photographic creation a veritable social role by encouraging a fruitful dialogue between planners, elected officials and artists did not seem to be working. Furthermore, over the long term, the increasing number of artistic projects backed by non-cultural institutions raised the question of the sustainability of the works. Indeed, whilst the majority of these institutions had photographic libraries, they had no vocation to preserve the photographs, which required specific conditions for physical storage and archive management. This difficulty led to the photographs being deposited in suitable institutions or to the creation of suitable structures: DATAR deposited the Mission's archive with the *Bibliothèque nationale de France* in 1988, the *Observatoire photographique national du paysage* stored its photographs in the National Archives, the Roads Directorate gave some of its works to the *Maison européenne de la photographie* in 1996 and the *Conservatoire du littoral* founded a collection that was managed independently.

These mixed results led to photographic missions being reconfigured, and as from 1990 they were essentially backed by cultural institutions.

The link with territorial issues was not broken, but took a valorizing form, with the creation of collections. This was particularly the case with missions initiated in Corsica by the *Centre Méditerranée de la photographie* (also in 1994) and by the *Pôle image Haute-Normandie* as from 2001, and with residencies in Clermont-Ferrand as from 2004. This shift in sponsors was also visible at a European level, with the soberly entitled *De l'Europe* project backed by the *Centre national de l'audiovisuel* in Luxembourg between 1996 and 2003[85] or *Photoworks*, founded in 1996, which pursued a commissioning policy in southeast England.[86]

More fundamentally, it can be argued that the landscape issue was appropriated by the world of photography: the prescriptive commissioning system gave way to the creation of spaces for experimenting with the photographic medium. For example, the "Des territoires" seminar, founded by historian Jean-François Chevrier in 1994 at the *École Nationale Supérieure des Beaux-Arts* in Paris, suggested replacing the landscape perspective marked by the visual paradigm with a relationship with regions that was both physical and imaginary. More broadly, we see the shift from a modern conception of the landscape, operating a strict distinction between the perceiving subject and the perceived object, to a phenomenological conception, based on an experience that embeds the observer in the region, the landscape being the result of this forever singular relationship.[87] Moving from the paradigm of description to that of inscription, photographic creation thus deployed a series of conceptual propositions, no longer based solely on visual representation as its objective, but also on protocols as instruments of these experiences of place.

These shifts do not mean that town and country planning institutions have abandoned the idea of developing a visual landscape policy. In this respect the *Observatoire photographique national du paysage*, which has been active since the 1990s, has been encouraging numerous initiatives in France.[88] The very principle behind the *Observatoire*, which indeed links a political landscape, managed by the State, with a vernacular landscape born of use, is located at the crossroads of public policy, between the preservation of remarkable landscapes and the valorization of everyday landscapes. The evolution in photographic postures over the years offers new potentialities for the operability of representations. Initially solicited for documentation purposes, photographs have demonstrated their aptitude for revealing little-known landscapes; finally, they come across as instruments for mediating between different publics, inhabitants, elected officials and experts.[89] This dynamic was in line with that found in projects backed by photographers themselves as part of an activist and artistic engagement. We might mention here the collective projects that have been initiated since the 2000s with a view to painting a shared picture of a national territory: *France14* (2006–2010),[90] *France(s) territoire liquide* (2011–2014)[91] and *La France vue d'ici* (2014–2017),[92] as well as participatory propositions such as *Paysages usagés* launched in 2012 by photographers Geoffroy Mathieu and Bertrand Stofleth.[93] The dialogue between art and landscape thus remains lively and fruitful, adopting a variable geometry in response to the way photographic and landscape issues are reconfigured.

82
In February 1993, the competition winners were shown at the *Maison de la radio*; Lucien Clergue and Françoise Dubost's work, *Mon paysage: le paysage préféré des Français*, was published in 1995 (Marval, Paris).

83
John Brinckerhoff Jackson, *op. cit.*

84
Bernard Latarjet, "1983", in Christian Milovanoff, *Bureaux*, Nouvelles Éditions Scala, Lyon, 2015, n.p.

85
De l'Europe. Photographies, essais, histoires, Filigranes, Trézélan, 2007.

86
See the *Photoworks* website: http://www.photoworks.org.ok

87
See in particular Michel Collot, *La Pensée-paysage. Philosophie, arts, littérature*, Actes Sud, Arles, 2011.

88
These were projects that were based on the OPNP protocol whilst at the same time offering methodological innovations. They were listed under the heading of "local observatories" in the censuses conducted by the *Bureau des paysages* in 2015. See Monique Chauvin and Pascal Chevallier, *op. cit.* no. 78.

89
See in particular Raphaële Bertho and Frédéric Pousin, "L'observatoire photographique du paysage du PNR des Vosges du Nord: de l'œuvre à l'action", *op. cit.*

90
France 14, Trans Photographic Press, Paris, 2010.

91
See mission website http://www.francesterritoireliquide.fr/

92
See mission website http://www.lafrancevuedici.fr/

93
See project website http://www.opp-gr2013.com/

J. B. Jackson, Photography and the Quickening of Cultural Landscape Studies

Chris Wilson

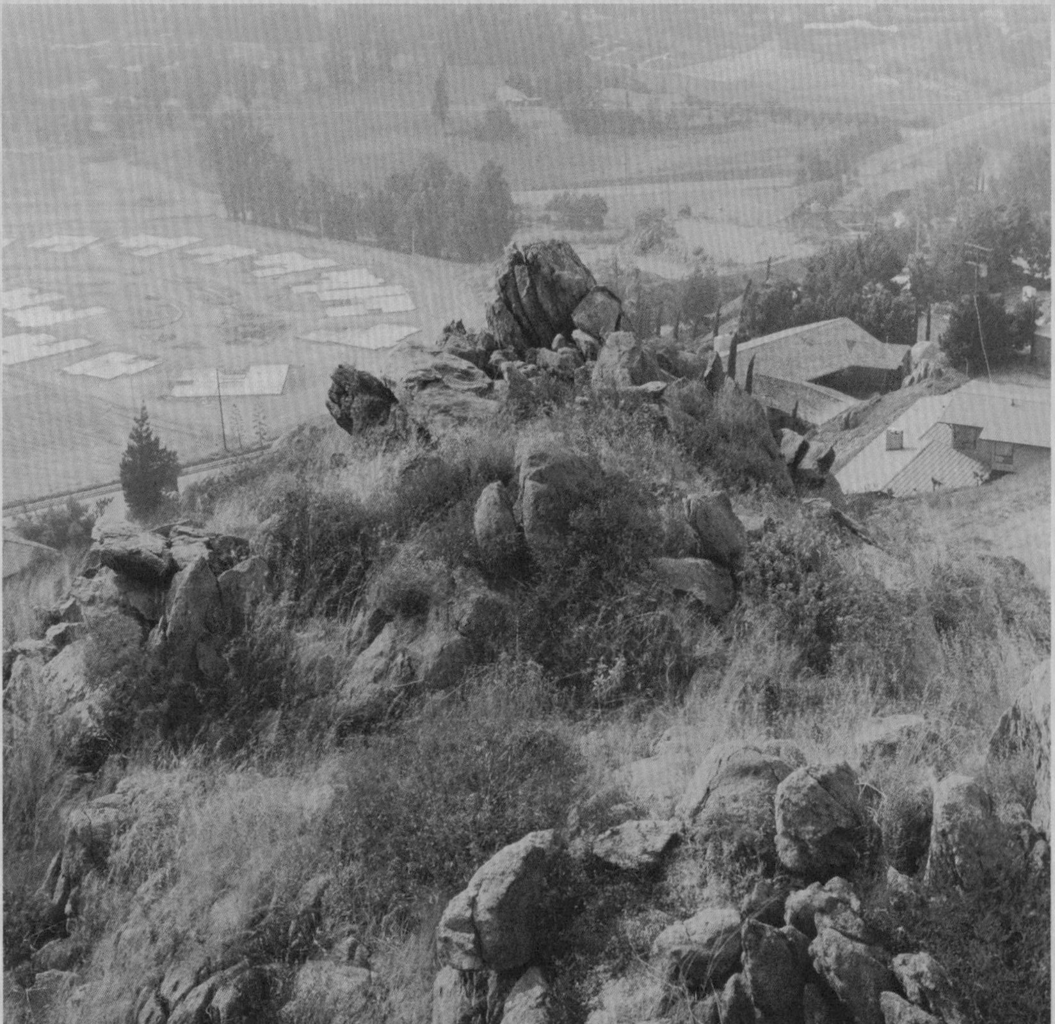

For 35 years starting with the founding of his magazine, *Landscape,* in 1951, J. B. Jackson was the leading proponent of the idea of *cultural landscape* in the United States. Best known for his elegant, incisive essays, which taught people to read history and culture in the everyday landscape, he also lectured widely at universities and conferences. Teaching large lecture courses annually in the late 1960s and the 1970s at Berkeley and Harvard – long centers of landscape thinking on the east and west coasts of the United States – Jackson connected the antiauthoritarianism of the counterculture generation to an appreciation of vernacular landscapes.

While spoken and written words were his main vehicles, his graphic design and use of images in *Landscape* added a visual component to this discourse. In addition, the 5500 slides he took while traversing the country during his teaching years put his analysis into photographic form and today provide a valuable window onto his thinking. From Timothy O'Sullivan and Mark Twain to Ed Ruscha and Joan Didion, American artists and thinkers have repeatedly returned to the everyday American landscape. Academic geographers similarly developed the concept of cultural landscape between the World Wars. But while Jackson was far from the first person to take up the subject, he played a pivotal role in the quickening of cultural landscape thinking in the U.S. following the Second World War.

THE DEVELOPMENT OF A LANDSCAPE EYE

Born in Dinard, France, to American parents in 1909, Jackson began his education in Washington DC, but regularly accompanied his mother, a buyer for a New York department store, on trips to Paris. An infatuation with Charles Dickens' novel of social conditions at age eleven suggests an early interest in vernacular culture. Starting in 1921, at twelve, he spent two years at the premier Swiss boarding school, Le Rosey, followed by an addition school year in Paris. This left Jackson fluent in French, with a conversational command of German. Back in the U.S. he attended Choate prep school, then transferred to and graduated from the Deerfield Academy. Summers he traveled with his uncle, New York lawyer Percy Jackson, to his uncle's New Mexico cattle ranch, and mixed in the nearby Santa Fe art colony.[1]

Because of his artistic abilities, at the suggestion of the Deerfield headmaster, Jackson entered the new University of Wisconsin Experimental College, a great books program linking art, literature and society in the study of civilization. He was particularly taken with the sweeping historical and cultural analysis of Oswald Spengler's just published *The Decline of the West,* although Jackson would challenge Spengler's interpretations in print within a few years. Leading public intellectual Lewis Mumford, a regular visitor at the experimental college, opened Jackson's mind to architecture, urbanism and regional planning.[2]

After an unhappy year at Wisconsin, Jackson transferred to Harvard, where he entered the undergraduate history and literature program chaired by F. O. Matthiessen, best known for celebrating the emergence of a distinctly American literary tradition in the mid-19th century works of Ralph Waldo Emerson, Henry David Thoreau, Herman Melville and Walt Whitman. A voracious reader, Jackson almost certainly encountered Alexis de Tocqueville's celebration of the American popular democratic spirit, as well as Melville and Whitman's hymns to the rough vitality of vernacular culture. The natural wonders of the West, styled as America's own cathedrals, and enshrined in national parks starting in 1872, provided another focus for American identity. Jackson may have seen the monumental paintings of the Yellowstone and the Grand Canyon by the likes of Albert Bierstadt and Thomas Moran. But

1
See Helen Lefkowitz Horowitz, "J.B. Jackson and the Discovery of the American Landscape", in Horowitz (ed.), *Landscape in Sight: Looking at America,* Yale University Press, New Haven, CT, 1997, p. x–xi; Paul Groth and Chris Wilson, "The Polyphony of Cultural Landscape Studies", in Wilson and Groth, *Everyday America: Cultural Landscape Studies after J. B. Jackson*, University of California Press, Berkeley, CA, 2003, p. 6–7; Helen Lefkowitz Horowitz, "The Writer's Path: J. B. Jackson and Cultural Geography as a Literary Genre", *Site/Lines,* fall 2015, p. 3–4; Wilson, Chris, "A Life on the Stranger's Path", in Janet Mendelsohn, and Chris Wilson, *Drawn to Landscape: The Pioneering Work of J. B. Jackson*, University of Virginia Press, Charlottesville, VA, 2015, p. 19–20 [originally published in *Designer/Builder*, November 1996].

2
Helen Lefkowitz Horowitz, "J. B. Jackson and the Discovery of the American Landscape", *op. cit.,* p. xi–xii; Paul Groth and Chris Wilson, *op. cit.,* p. 7; Jackson, John Brinckerhoff, "Prussianism or Hitlerism", *The American Review* 3, April–October 1934, p. 469.

whether he would have read the reports of the great Federal topographic surveys of the West, much less seen the companion photographs by Timothy O'Sullivan and William Henry Jackson, then buried in archives, seems less likely. Derwett Whittlesey's geography courses did introduce Jackson to the role of economic conditions and cultural values in shaping the physical landscape. Among the pieces he contributed to the *Harvard Advocate* as a writer and editorial board member was an extended critique of modernist architecture for its links to the relentless profit motive in business culture – an interpretation influenced by another of his professors, conservative cultural critic Irving Babbitt.[3]

Following graduation from Harvard in 1933, he spent a year in the architecture program at MIT, then six months as a reporter on a New England newspaper. Jackson returned to Europe, where he took a commercial illustration course in Vienna. Travel throughout central Europe by motorcycle in 1934 and 1935 gave him first-hand exposure to the rise of fascism, and material for two magazine articles and a novel. His drawings from those years reveal his training in the conventions of perspective and the picturesque, that is to say, balanced, asymmetric composition. One pen and watercolor drawing, for instance, adopts the conventional sense of landscape as a pleasing view **| FIG. 1 |**. The setting is rural: a mountain off-center in the background, foothills of varying colors and textures balancing on either side, and an expanse of lake in the foreground stretching to a small village.[4]

In contrast to such romantic visual aesthetics are the penetrating historic and cultural analysis, punctuated by bursts of dry humor, of his 1934 article in *The American Review*, "Prussianism or Hitlerism." Jackson finds the acceptance by many Americans of the Nazi coopting of the Prussian tradition naive:

> *Prussianism according to Goebbels is Comradeship, Discipline, Honour, Courage; solid virtues all of them, and the basis for a new social order, revolutionary in themselves; but Goebbels and his friends do not stop here; Prussianism is more than these; it is Nationalism, Race Pride, Intolerance, Provincialism, and a hatred of Liberal ideals. The western world has never been prone to take Germany at her own appraisal, but it has taken Prussianized Germany at her own appraisal. We do not believe Germany when she is sane but only believe her when she boasts of having sold herself to the Devil; we believe in the Devil as well; we believe in Hitler's Prussianism.*[5]

What a clear eyed passage, written by a 25-year-old, the year after National Socialism gained power in Germany, and appearing alongside other *American Review* contributors sympathetic to Fascism.

While his novel landed him on the cover of *The Saturday Review of Literature*, the premier U.S. literary journal of those days, Jackson chose to return to New Mexico and to adopt the life of a cowboy. He may have intended to gather experiences for further writing, say, for a sequel to Mark Twain's *Roughing It*. But this tough new life – always in the saddle, sleeping on the range or in bunkhouses packed with cowboys – captivated Jackson. As he recalled years later, "I took it and I loved it," and discovered, "a streak of commonness in me." He took up rodeo and suffered a first serious injury.[6]

Then in 1940, with the specter of world war looming, Jackson, like other cowboys across the American West, enlisted in the U.S. Calvary. While he found that he enjoyed the discipline of taking orders, he also passed an officers' training correspondence course. Because of his language abilities, the army sent him to the Military Intelligence Training Center at Camp Ritchie, Maryland. Nearly half of his fellow students were recent refugees from Austria and Germany – the majority Jews fleeing Hitler. Jackson knew far better than most Americans what they had faced, and what the U.S. would soon face. The curriculum at Camp Ritchie emphasized map reading and a thorough study of the German military, its organization, munitions and strategy.[7]

Jackson fought in North Africa, was wounded in the invasion of Sicily, and landed on the beaches of Normandy on D-Day Plus 2. When the Allied advance bogged down in the Huertgen Forest in the fall of 1944, Jackson found himself stationed for five months at the Ninth Infantry Division headquarters in a local chateau. As Jackson poured over the chateau library (and later scoured the bookstores of Paris while on leave), he was taken by geography books, especially those by Deffontaines, Vidal de La Blanche and Demangeon. These suggested to him an important limitation of traditional military intelligence. At Camp Ritchie, he later wrote, they taught us "to collect, evaluate and disseminate information about the enemy and his capabilities. We did not speculate about the environment and its psychological impact nor about the relationship between the environment and man."[8] He found that popular regional geographies in the library helped him answer such practical questions as "would our half-tracks bog down in the naked winter fields," and "if barns were large enough to accommodate trucks and whether there were orchards where guns [artillery] could be concealed."[9] The aerial photos used by military intelligence certainly helped him form a mental image of the terrain ahead, but Jackson also turned to guidebooks, tourist maps and postcards. Interrogations of German prisoners added information as did Jackson own field sketches locating German positions in relation to the landscape.[10]

That winter a popular biography of Frederick the Great, the 18th-century king of Prussia, also made a lasting impression on Jackson: "What impressed me was the description of Frederick as an old man, through with war, traveling about his impoverished and ruined country in a carriage, stopping to talk to villagers and farmers. 'How much do you pay for bread?' 'What rent do you pay?' 'What crops are you planting?'"[11] It is striking both that Jackson would adopt a similar tone in his impromptu interrogations of those he met in his later travels across America, and that a similar concern for how common people make their lives and living would animate his later essays.[12]

Discharged in 1946 after six years in the army, Jackson purchased a surplus jeep and drove cross country. His fresh interest in the everyday landscape – nurtured during his *in extremis* study of French geography – is evident in one of his field sketches. In place of a village nestled beside an Alpine lake, the man-made now predominates in the form of a two-lane highway, raised railroad tracks and both phone and power lines | **FIG. 2** |. Where renaissance painters often used architecture to set up a disappearing one-point perspective, here Jackson deploys the typical infrastructure of the American West, set as it was on the Cartesian survey grid. Only sun-raked sagebrush and distant mountains peaking above the rail roadbed conform to picturesque stereotypes.[13]

3
Helen Lefkowitz Horowitz, "J.B. Jackson and the Discovery of the American Landscape", *op. cit.*, pp. xii–xiv; Paul Groth and Chris Wilson, *op. cit.*, p. 7; Helen Lefkowitz Horowitz, "The Writer's Path: J.B. Jackson and Cultural Geography as a Literary Genre", *Site/Lines*, Fall 2015, p. 4; "Matthiessen, F. O.", *Wikipedia*, accessed 4-13-17: https://en.wikipedia.org/wiki/F._O._Matthiessen.

4
Helen Lefkowitz Horowitz, "J.B. Jackson and the Discovery of the American Landscape", *op. cit.*, p. xiv-xvi; Paul Groth and Chris Wilson, *op. cit.*, p. 7; Helen Lefkowitz Horowitz, "The Writer's Path...", *op. cit.*, p. 4.

5
John Brinckerhoff Jackson, "Prussianism or Hitlerism", *op. cit.*, p. 456.

6
Helen Lefkowitz Horowitz, "J.B. Jackson and the Discovery of the American Landscape", *op. cit.*, p. xvi; Paul Groth and Chris Wilson, *op. cit.*, p. 7; Helen Lefkowitz Horowitz, "The Writer's Path...", *op. cit.*, p. 4.

7
John Brinckerhoff Jackson, *Discovering the Vernacular Landscape*, Yale University Press, New Haven, CT, 1984, p. 133; Helen Lefkowitz Horowitz, "J.B. Jackson and the Discovery of the American Landscape", *op. cit.*, p. xvii; Paul Groth and Chris Wilson, *op. cit.*, p. 7–8; Helen Lefkowitz Horowitz, "The Writer's Path...", *op. cit.*, p. 4; "Ritchie Boys", *Wikipedia*, accessed 10-21-16: https://en.wikipedia.org/wiki/Ritchie_Boys; F. Douglas Adams, "J.B. Jackson: Drawn to Intelligence" and "Notes on the Drawings and Watercolors", in Mendelsohn and Wilson, *op. cit.*, p. 36–39.

8
John Brinckerhoff Jackson, *op. cit.*, p. 133.

9
Idem, p. 134.

10
Idem, p. 133–137 ; Helen Lefkowitz Horowitz, "J.B. Jackson and the Discovery of the American Landscape", *op. cit.*, p. xvi; Helen Lefkowitz Horowitz, "The Writer's Path...", *op. cit.*, p. 4–5.

11
John Brinckerhoff Jackson, *op. cit.*, p. 135.

12
Bob Calo, "The Love of Everyday Places", 58 video, San Francisco: KQED-TV, 1989; reissued on DVD, Documentary Educational Resources (www.der.org), Watertown, MA, 2016; and included with the hardback edition of Mendelsohn and Wilson, *op. cit.*; Chris Wilson, "A Life on the Stranger's Path", *op. cit.*, p. 28 and 30.

13
Helen Lefkowitz Horowitz, "J.B. Jackson and the Discovery of the American Landscape", *op. cit.*, p. xix; Paul Groth and Chris Wilson, "The Polyphony of Cultural Landscape Studies", *op. cit.*, p. 9; Helen Lefkowitz Horowitz, "The Writer's Path...", *op. cit.*, p. 5; Chris Wilson, *op. cit.*, p. 25–26.

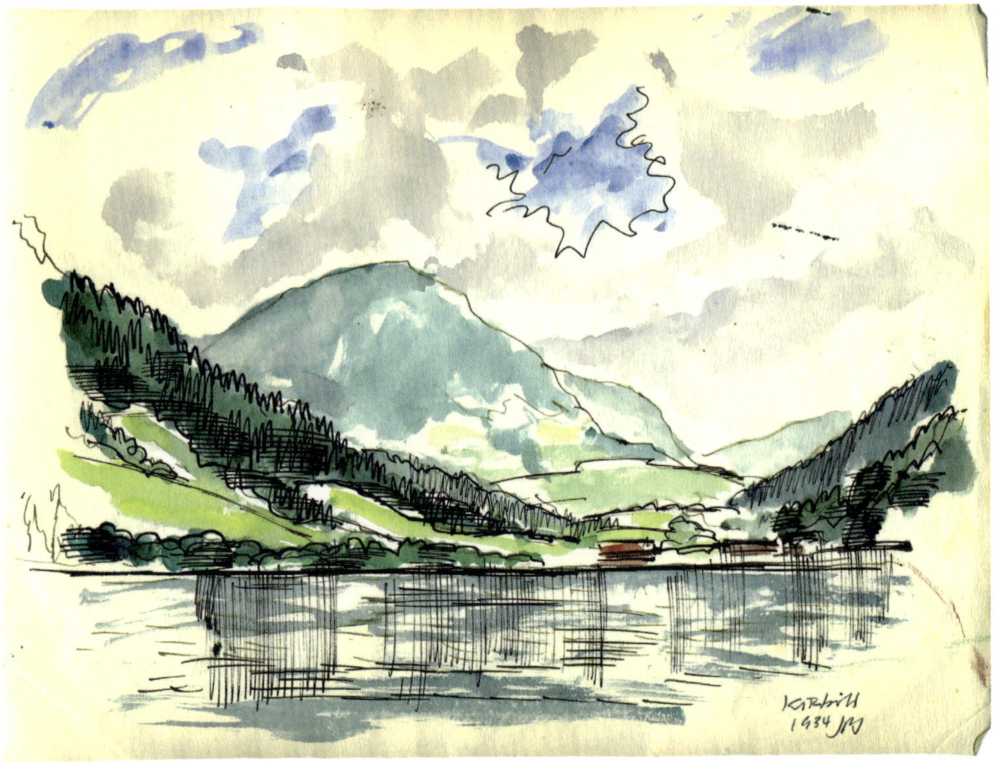

| FIG. 1 |

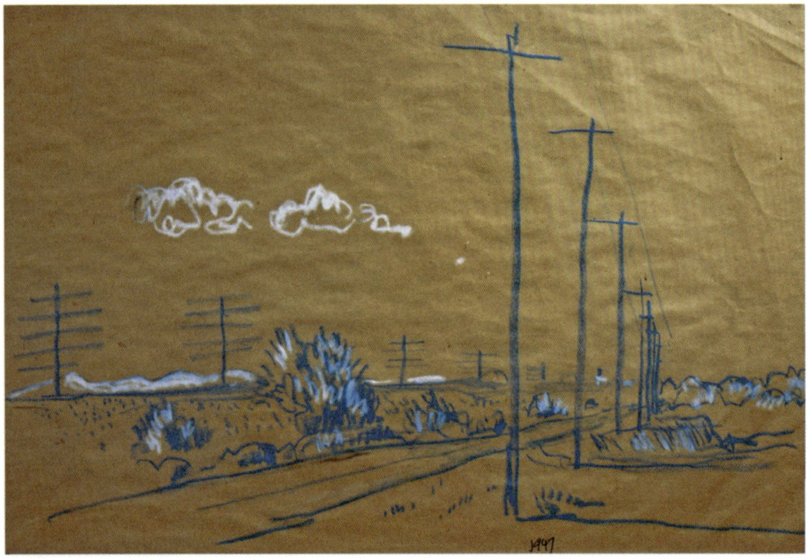

| FIG. 2 |

| FIG. 1 |
J. B. Jackson, Kirbild, 1934.

| FIG. 2 |
J.B. Jackson,
Telephone poles, road, and railroad in the American Southwest, 1947.

LANDSCAPE MAGAZINE AND ART PHOTOGRAPHY

Jackson took up the management of a ranch in east central New Mexico. Thrown and dragged by a horse, he spent eighteen months in hospital and convalescing at a ranch. In the interval, he nurtured the idea of founding a magazine to bring the spirit of popular French geography books to an American audience.[14] In March of 1951, having settled in Santa Fe, and gathering images for the launch his magazine, he paid a call on Laura Gilpin, known nationally for her photographs of western landscapes and Native Americans.[15] As he wrote to his mother and brother in Washington, DC, he hoped, to buy if possible an aerial photograph for the magazine:

> *She had a very handsome one of the Rio Grande Valle north of Espanola which she will let me have for twenty dollars, though her usual price is 50. She considers her pictures works of art, which is perhaps the case, though I wouldn't have thought so myself; and she is curious to know whether they are going to be cut or altered in any way. I couldn't give her much assurance, since I don't know how this reproduction process is. She is a very pleasant and intelligent woman, busy at present on a book of pictures of the Navajo. If she would only let me take the pictures for her she would be finished in two weeks or less; as it is she has been working for more than a year.*[16]

Most Americans in those days shared his skepticism about photography being art, if they thought about the question at all. Despite the self-deprecating hyperbole of his last sentence, Jackson clearly viewed photographs in instrumental terms, a point underlined by his happiness when he soon discovered that he could secure good aerials of cultural landscapes from the local U.S. Soil Conservation Service (SCS) office for $6 a piece.[17] He used Gilpin's photograph uncropped on the first cover of *Landscape*, Spring, 1951, and repeated it, cropped with full bleeds, on his final issue as editor and publisher, Spring, 1967.

The Federal government had embraced photography for instrumental purposes in the 1930s through the Information Division of the Farm Security Administration (later renamed the Office of War Information). Starting in 1934, such FSA photographers as Walker Evans, Dorothea Lange, Russell Lee, Arthur Rothstein and Gordon Parks worked to create a catalogue of the full range of activities in the cities, villages and countryside of every region. Prints distributed to newspapers, magazines and publishers were intended first to show the dire conditions of the Great Depression to rally support for Franklin Roosevelt's New Deal, then to demonstrate the positive impacts of government programs, and, finally, to rally support for the war effort. In retrospect we see the collection as an invaluable, comprehensive record of the American cultural landscape.[18]

Beyond the instrumental use of the collection as a news photo service in the 1930s and 1940s, many of the photographers aspired to recognition as artists. Walker Evans, for instance, received the first solo photographic exhibit at the New York's Museum of Modern Art in 1938. Lincoln Steffens text accompanying the companion catalogue, *American Photographs*, and that of James Agee in his collaboration with Evans the following year, *Let Us Now Praise Famous Men*, both argue explicitly for photography as art. That Evans' work is presented as uncaptioned portfolios at the beginning of both books emphasizes that they stand alone as works of art rather than illustrations to the text.[19]

Evans' fascination with the American vernacular closely parallels the topics Jackson would soon explore in *Landscape*. Evans published and exhibited prints of row houses, factories and rail yards; classical mansions, worker cottages and sharecropper cabins; vegetable gardens, cemeteries and construction sites; parlors, bedrooms and barber shops, shop windows, main streets, and country stores; sidewalk scenes, parades and picnics; war monuments, business signs and bill-

14
Helen Lefkowitz Horowitz, "J. B. Jackson and the Discovery of the American Landscape", *op. cit.*, p. xx; Paul Groth and Chris Wilson, "The Polyphony of Cultural Landscape Studies", *op. cit.*, p. 9; Helen Lefkowitz Horowitz, "The Writer's Path...", *op. cit.*, p. 5; Chris Wilson, *op. cit.*, p. 21–22.

15
Martha A. Sandweiss, "Laura Gilpin and the Tradition of American Landscape Photography", in Vera Norwood and Janice Monk (eds.), *The Desert is No Lady: Southwestern Landscapes in Women's Writing and Art*, Yale University Press, New Haven, CT, 1987.

16
J. B. Jackson, to Wiebe [his mother] and Boo [his brother, Wayne], Washington, DC, 1951, probably March 5. Private collection.

17
J. B. Jackson to Wiebe, Washington, DC, March 22, 1951. Private collection.

18
While it is easily accessible today on the American Memory website, the collection was little known and in the process of being catalogued at the Library of Congress in the early 1950s. See: Britt Salvesen (ed.), *New Topographics: Robert Adams et al.*, Center for Creative Photography, University of Arizona, Tucson, AZ, 2009, especially, Salvesen, "New Topographics", p. 11–67.

19
James Agee and Walker Evans, *Let Us Now Praise Famous Men*, Houghton Mifflin, New York, 1939; Britt Salvesen, "New Topographics", *op. cit.*, p. 3–16.

boards; filling stations, roadside stands, and junk car lots.[20] Working primarily with a large-format camera set on a tripod, his photos are straightforward, sharply focused and carefully composed. He approaches the everyday with an unsentimental, clear-eyed reserve, a sensibility the Germans called *Neue Sachlichkeit*, the New Objectivity, and that became known in the U.S. as the documentary style. If earlier photographers employed soft-focus painterly effects in their quest to gain admittance to art museums, documentarians instead created sharp focus, straightforward images, imbued with their individual perspectives, often by drawing attention to everyday contemporary subjects.

Evans' photos dignify vernacular people and places: both the self-composed, unblinking gazes of his sharecroppers portraits, and the façade of the two-story country store in Sprott, Alabama. To gain neighborhood overviews Evans climbed hills and sought the upper floors of buildings. His view of the boulevarded main street of Macon, Georgia **| FIG. 3 |**, for instance, captures the building façades, display windows and awnings, the sidewalks and parked cars on one side, and just enough of the cars, sidewalk, and building shadows on the other side to contain the space. The standardized street furniture that were the signs of a prosperous, progressive city are all there: streetlights, fire hydrants, mailboxes, park benches, accenting bushes, and a traffic signal (bottom left). The diagonal thrust of Evans' angled view adds dynamism to a formal, repetitive space. The capacity parking and throngs of shoppers dressed in their going-to-town clothes, packages tucked under their arms, suggest a Saturday afternoon. The long shadows cast by people in their winter coats, socializing in threes and fours, adds a melancholy finish to a long-anticipated day downtown.

Jackson's comments about Gilpin's print suggests he had little knowledge of (or, perhaps, sympathy with) the emerging world of art photography. His own mode was the essay; his topic, the everyday American landscape. In sixteen years of publishing *Landscape* he would popularize the concept of cultural landscape and valorize all manner of landscapes: historic and contemporary; rural and urban; domestic, public and commercial. But by launching a self-published magazine from a provincial capital, Jackson was leftto be his own image editor and graphic designer. The Gilpin and SCS photos initiated a graphics morgue including aerial and landscape photographs; village and town plans; loose pages from books and magazines; and a collection of 16th- to 19th-century prints of landscapes, cityscapes and bird's eye views.[21] While he did not take photographs himself for the magazine, Jackson continued to draw in the field throughout the 1950s and 1960s. Only occasionally did he include a half-tone of one of his field drawings in the magazine. More frequently he created new line drawings to fill out the illustrations for articles. Some were redrawn from photographs for legibility. Others showed simplified views of the key characteristics of a landscape type. Still others provided abstract visualizations of landscape experiences, especially that of speeding through the new automobile landscape. But for Jackson and his contributors, the essay was the thing. Images were supplementary at best, illustrating the topic at a variety of scales, but never rising to the level of an independent visual narrative.

The best design magazines in this period embraced a Bauhaus-inspired, Modernist aesthetic. But academic journals and even some leading architecture magazines retained a conventional two-column layout. Jackson adopted such a traditional graphic language.[22] Starting with the first issue of the second year and greatly escalating at the beginning of the fifth year, he introduced modern type faces and asymmetric layouts especially on the cover, the contents page and the title page of major articles, but reverted to a two-column format on subsequent pages. Article titles sometimes playfully mixed serif and sans serif with 19th-century engraved specialty typefaces. Contemporary dingbats of a house, hand, eye,

20
Walker Evans, *Walker Evans: Photographs for the Farm Security Administration, 1935–1938*, Library of Congress, Washington, DC, Prints and Photographs Division, 1973; *Walker Evans* (Clément Chéroux, ed.), Éditions du Centre Pompidou, Paris, 2017.

21
"Jackson Graphics Portfolio", Jackson Collection, Center for Southwest Research, University of New Mexico.

22
For examples of his magazine designs, see Bruno Notteboom's article in this book, p. 72.

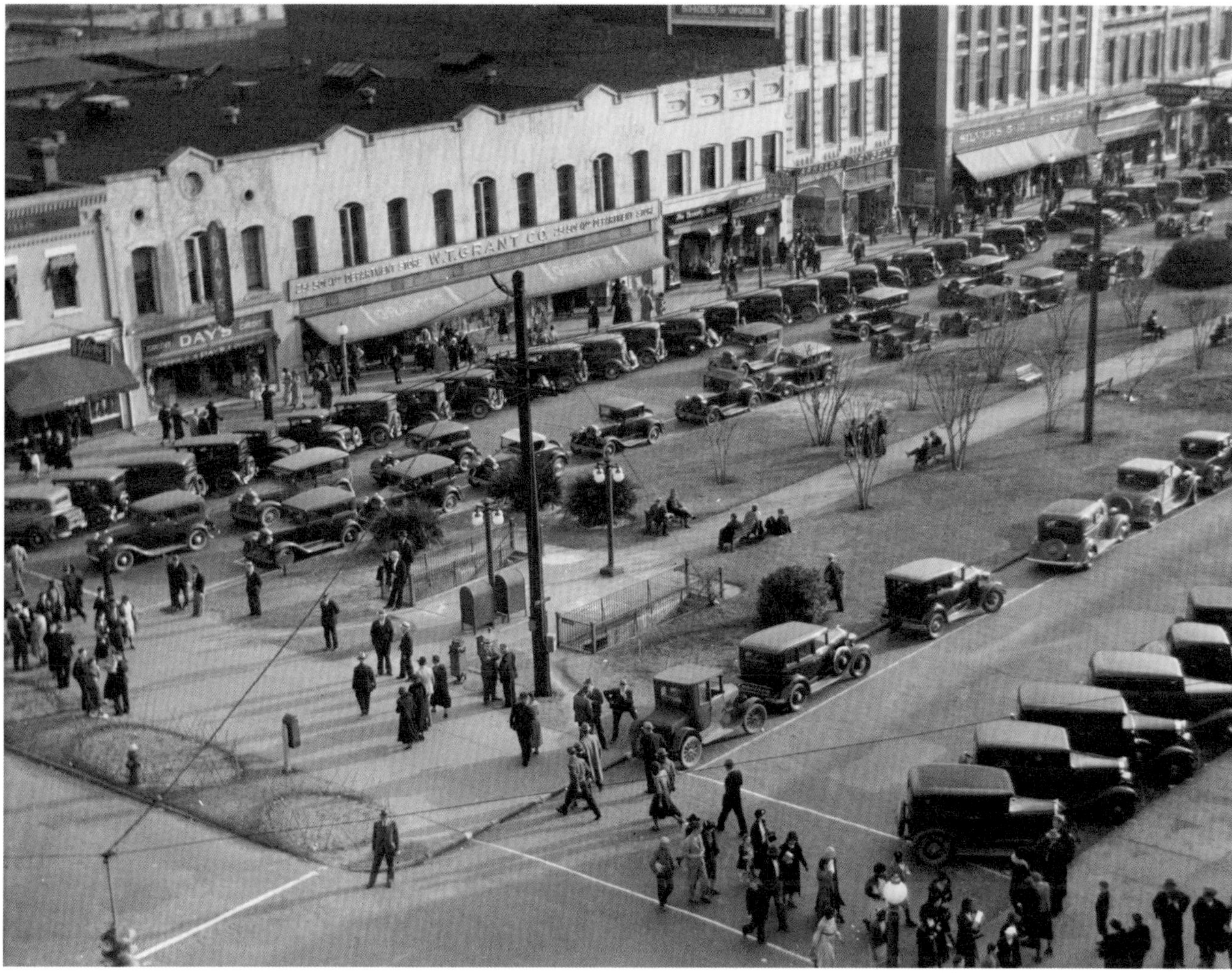

| FIG. 3 |

| FIG. 3 |
Walker Evans,
Main Street. Macon, Georgia,
March, 1934.

road intersection, fort, setting sun, and globe scattered throughout the magazine underlined his focus on landscape archetypes. Overall, the design became playful, yet still conventional; the images plentiful, yet primarily illustrative.[23]

TEACHING SLIDES

The stimulating conception of cultural landscape advanced by Jackson's magazine soon attracted correspondence and written contributions from such leading figures as botanist Edgar Anderson, geographers Carl O. Sauer, D. W. Meinig and Fred Kniffen, journalist Grady Clay, anthropologist Edward T. Hall, landscape architects Garrett Eckbo and Lawrence Halprin, and critics Lewis Mumford and Christopher Tunnard. Invitations to speak at conferences and universities soon followed. Jackson formed lasting ties to the geography, landscape architecture and architecture departments at Berkeley, where he taught a guest seminar in 1963. In 1967, Jackson began to teach a seminar and a large lecture course, "The History of the American Cultural Landscape",[24] each spring in the College of Environmental Design, a role he also took up at the Graduate School of Design at Harvard in fall 1969. Over the next ten years he took an annual motorcycle tour from his home in New Mexico to Harvard in the fall, then to Berkeley for the spring term, and finally home for the summer. Varying his routes allowed him to assemble a collection of slides covering the full range of American landscapes. Over ten years, Jackson reached upwards of 4,000 inquisitive students drawn primarily from architecture, landscape, planning, and geography departments, but also from history, photography and journalism.[25]

Paul Groth, who would take over Jackson's courses when he retired from teaching, remembers the lecture course in spring 1977, when he sat in the front row along with Peirce Lewis from Penn State and Reuben Rainey from the University of Virginia, visiting professors auditing the course.[26] "The course is designed," explained Jackson's syllabus that year, "to familiarize the student with the origins of some of the common features of the American built environment and with the social, economic, technological and aesthetic influences which brought them into being." Jackson later elaborated on his approach to teaching the course: "It dealt with such commonplace things as fences and roads and barns, the design of factories and office buildings, the layout of towns and farms and graveyards and parks and houses, and toward the end of the course I talked about the superhighway and certain kinds of sports I referred to as psychedelic."[27]

Jackson laid out the history and primary influences shaping a particular era and landscape type during the first 40 to 45 minutes of each 50-minute class. "This was followed," he writes, "by the display of a few slides illustrating change in certain familiar places. Slide shows are popular in the classroom and though my slides were poor in quality, they were of familiar, everyday objects and places, and that, I suspect, was the principal reason for the success of the course."[28] (A typical bit of self-deprecation perhaps, for needless to say, not everyone who included a few slides at the end of their lectures could attract 200–300 students to their course.) Typically organized in chronological order, Jackson identified each of the three to nine slides per class, and added a point or two about each. Women's and environmental historian Virginia Scharff, who was in the same class as Groth, for instance, noted Jackson's comments on a slide of San Juan Pueblo offered as a contrast to New England villages, "Tewa cosmic circle – dance pattern reproducing movement of cosmos. Sacred center."[29]

Groth recorded nine slides at the end of Jackson's lecture on "The Factory" that year:

Tennessee Grist Mill
1809 – *Crown & Eagle Mill* – one of the handsomest, a national landmark (burned recently); was in the *Blackstone Valley Whitneyville* destroyed. New Haven owns most of the site
Yale: Am Studies [did a book on it?]
Whitensville [?] (also caught fire)
Pennycook, N.H. – looks like a Roman [?] monastery
1820-50 – (Arkwright houses in a New England Mill town) not in Maine, NH, Vermont
Manchester, NH – *Amoskeag mill,* ... an image [of] tower + elevator last image of ...
Fall River Mass.
1873 – low almost flat roof – granite;
larger windows 1890 – Broud
1st factory after 1887 – reinforced=cd conc. – Adams
Lawrence, Mass. – huge "Alternate" [?] mill of 1890s type[30]

By first discussing landscape and building types without images, Jackson introduced underlying generic patterns that student could visualize from their own experience, and subsequently apply to any landscape. Rather than establishing a hierarchy of monuments and elite architects, and charting the spread of their influence – as architectural historians did in those days – Jackson used his slides "of familiar, everyday objects and places",[31] to illustrate variation and change within widespread vernacular landscape patterns.[32]

A number of two-to-four image assemblages that Jackson created from his collection of historic prints suggests how he visualized landscape categories **| FIG. 4 |**. One collage juxtaposes a 17th-century French engraving of a fort, cliff-edged harbor and classical ruins with an 1867 German engraving of the Bay of Fundy on the Maine coast; and a page from the December 4, 1869 issue of the popular *Frank Leslie's Illustrated Newspaper* showing "Sunday in the Rocky Mountains".[33] The balanced, asymmetric composition of each image, and the variety and texture of details – especially the rugged rocks – are typical Romantic devices. Tranquil fisher folk and travelers pausing to view the fort enhance the picturesque qualities of the French view. The foreboding cliffs, angry sea, and foundering ship in Fundy Bay shift over into a dread-inspiring sublime. The minister under a rock overhang preaching to a motley congregation of miners, Chinamen and proper young ladies demonstrate how the Romantic tropes of nature and the vernacular were deployed in the mid-19th century search to define a distinctive American character.

In his writing, his teaching and the slides he took on his motorcycle circuits of the country, Jackson sought nothing less that to catalogue and interpret the entire American landscape.[34] His analysis rested on

23
This discussion is based on a review of *Landscape* magazine, 1951–1966, as well as *Geographical Review, National Geographic, Progressive Architecture, Journal of the AIA* and *Landscape Architecture*, 1952.

24
Janet Mendelsohn and Claire Marino's 1988 film, "Figure in a Landscape," gives a good sense of the typological approach, themes and lecture style of Jackson's History of the American Cultural Landscape class. See: Janet Mendelsohn and Claire Marino, 1988, "Figure in a Landscape", 47 minute film, Santa Monica: Direct Cinema Limited; reissued on DVD, Watertown, MA, 2016, Documentary Educational Resources (www.der.org); and included with the hardback edition of Mendelsohn and Wilson, *op. cit.*

25
Helen Lefkowitz Hotowitz, "J. B. Jackson and the Discovery of the American Landscape", *op. cit.*, pp. xxvi-xxvii; Paul Groth and Chris Wilson, "The Polyphony of Cultural Landscape Studies", *op. cit.*, p. 11; F. Douglas Adams, *op. cit.*, p. 33; Paul Groth, "J. B. Jackson's Slides", in Mendelsohn and Wilson, *op. cit.*, p. 121.

26
Paul Groth, email interview by Chris Wilson, September 30 to October 10, 2016.

27
Course Syllabus, p. 1, "Environmental Design 169B [actually 169A] winter 1977," MSS 866 BC, box 1, folder 12, Jackson Collection.

28
John Brinckerhoff Jackson, *The Necessity for Ruins*, The University of Massachusetts Press, Amherst, MA, 1980, p. 114, 115.

29
Virginia Scharff, course notes, January 12, 1977, "Notes for ED 169a, The History of the American Cultural Landscape," MSS 866 BC, Jackson Collection.

30
Paul Groth, course notes, February 11, 1977. "Environmental Design 169B [actually 169A] winter 1977," MSS 866 BC, box 1, folder 12, Jackson Collection. This quotation is based on a transcription of the original notes edited by Paul Groth for clarity.

31
John Brinckerhoff Jackson, *The Necessity for Ruins*, *op. cit.*, p. 113.

32
Groth also worked with Bob Calo to recreate a typical Jackson teaching slide sequence for his 1989 film about Jackson: Calo, 45:45 – 46:15 (see note 12)

33
"Jackson Graphics Portfolio", MSS 866 BC, Jackson Collection. Captions of the three images: "Inventé et gravé par Perelle, Avec privil. du Roy. A Paris chez Pierre Mariette. Rue St. Jacques, a l'Espérance." (The Perelles, a family of engravers, were active in Paris in the second half of the 17th century, while Mariette was a renowned connoisseur of prints in the middle of the following century. Remaining penciled dimension notes on this panel show the preparation of this image for use as the wraparound, front-and-back cover image of *Landscape*, 5/2, winter 1955–1956.) "Die Bai von Fundi, P. Wurster, 1867." "Sunday in the Rocky Mountains," *Frank Leslie's Illustrated Newspaper*, December 4, 1869.

34
This discussion of Jackson's photography is based on a study of the 5500 slides in the J. B. Jackson Pictorial Materials Collection, 000-866, Center for Southwest Research, University of New Mexico, Albuquerque. See also: Paul Groth, "J. B. Jackson's Slides", in Mendelsohn and Wilson, *op. cit.*, especially p. 121–22.

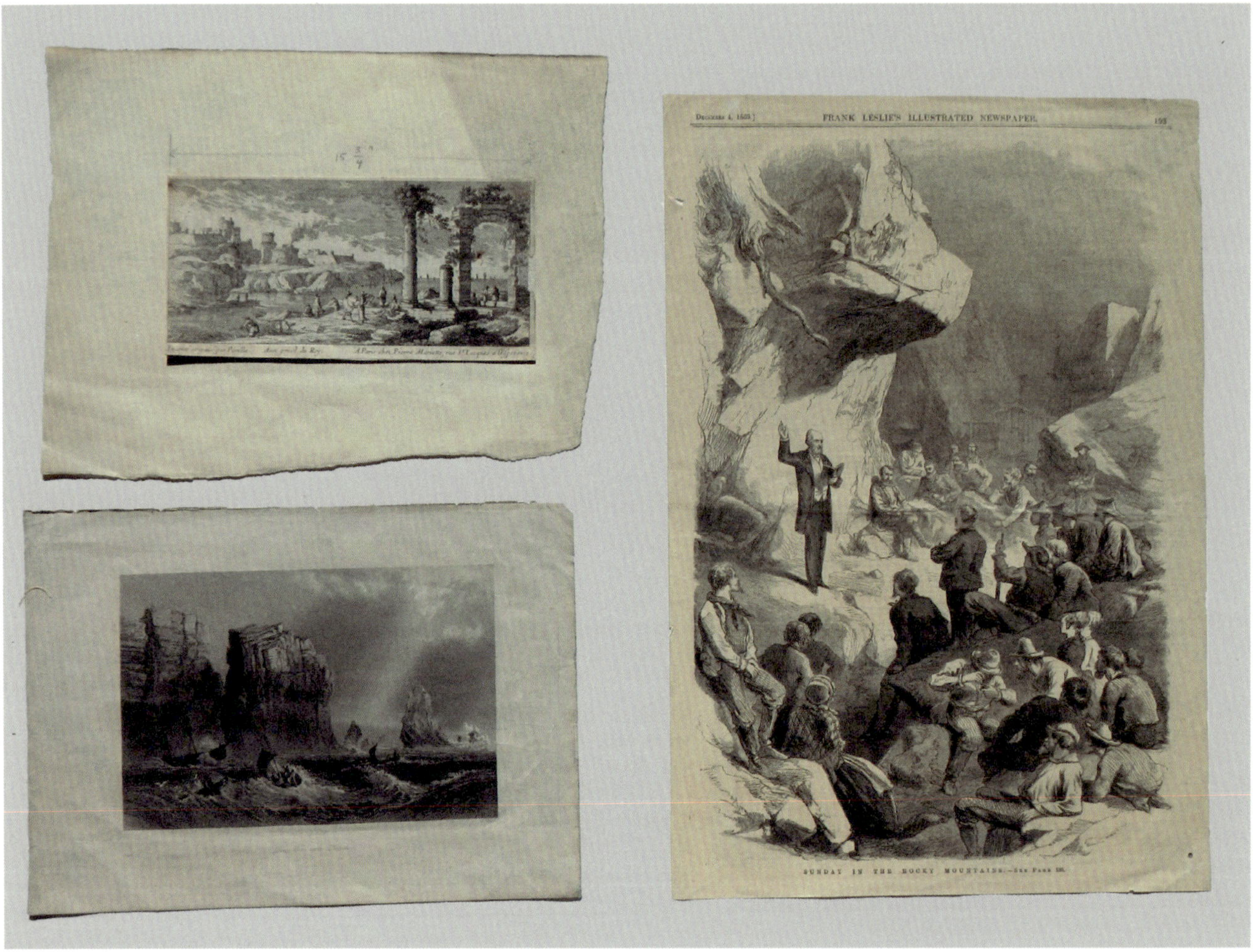

| FIG. 4 |

| FIG. 4 |
J. B. Jackson, Historic Prints Assemblage, date unknown.

a principal he first formulated in the waning days of the Second World War: "Every landscape of any size or age has a style of its own, a period style such as we discern or try to discern in music or architecture or painting, and a landscape true to its style, containing enough of the diagnostic trait, whether it is in Appalachia or Southern California, can give an almost aesthetic satisfaction."[35] This meant both that he sought to photograph all of the diagnostic traits of each period, regional or cultural style, and that he often worked to capture all of the characteristics of a particular landscape type in a single image. This is one reason he took and collected so many aerial photographs: they showed the organization and key components of a landscape at a glance. One of his own aerial photographs, for instance, captures the walled perimeter of a regimented mobile home park with a community building at its middle, surrounded by bits of arterial streets, a drive-in movie theater, leveled pads awaiting the construction of single-family houses and a channelized arroyo emptying into a golf course – which together give a good sense of the raw, ad hoc development of Southwestern cities **| FIG. 5 |**.

Or he might seek a slightly elevated vantage point to assemble the telling features of a landscape. In rural, preindustrial settings, he often settled on balanced asymmetric compositions similar to his Swiss mountain watercolor, but now emphasizing roads, buildings, fences and the other human marks on the land. Indeed, such a pairing of romantic aesthetic and subject matter underpinned earlier conceptions of the cultural landscape. But in viewing the American landscape since industrialization, Jackson suggested, "we tend to see it not as it is, with its own unique character, but as a degenerate version of a traditional landscape. [...] But a more sensible approach, it seems to me, is to try to discover when some of its characteristics first made their appearance, rather than to dwell on the disappearance of the old."[36] And so Jackson was always on the lookout for new features in the landscape, stopping to photograph them, and to question local residents on the reasons for their appearance. The emergence of temporary storage facilities, people jogging for exercise, car washes, motorcycle rallies and similar extreme sports, political bumper stickers, suburban houses with two car garages hiding the front door, and all manner of construction sites attracted his attention. Where the car had taken over the landscape, Jackson uses the road to compose his photos, for instance, a white-striped highway leading away from a new Interstate interchange, flanked by service stations with monumental signs readable at 65 miles an hour **| FIG. 6 |**.

While Jackson viewed all human traces on the land as significant, he took a particular interest in monuments, signage and other literal inscriptions, and was alert to the humor in many of these more overt signifiers. For instance, the congregation that erected the turn-off sign for their revival meeting grounds next to an official road sign, yielding "Do Not Pass/Holy Ghost Grounds." Or Jackson might stop to photograph a "No Parking" sign poking up from the surface of a lake, or "Black Earth 5, Spring Green 24," or "339th Ave Exit" leading to parched desert, or, hand-lettered on the back of a mobile home, "End Time Revival Crusade for Jesus / Thank you Jesus for our Trailer." Or more poignantly, a granite public drinking fountain inscribed "Presented by the Japanese of Hanford and vicinity November 10, 1915." Of course, Hanford, Washington's Japanese Americans would be transported to concentration camps by the U.S. government at the outset of the Second World War, and the hamlet leveled to make way for a nuclear weapons plant. Another photo ironically contrasts the solidity of a 19th-century courthouse square with its bronze and granite Civil

35
John Brinckerhoff Jackson, *Discovering the Vernacular Landscape*, *op. cit.*, p. 136.

36
John Brinckerhoff Jackson, *The Necessity for Ruins*, *op. cit.*, p. 120.

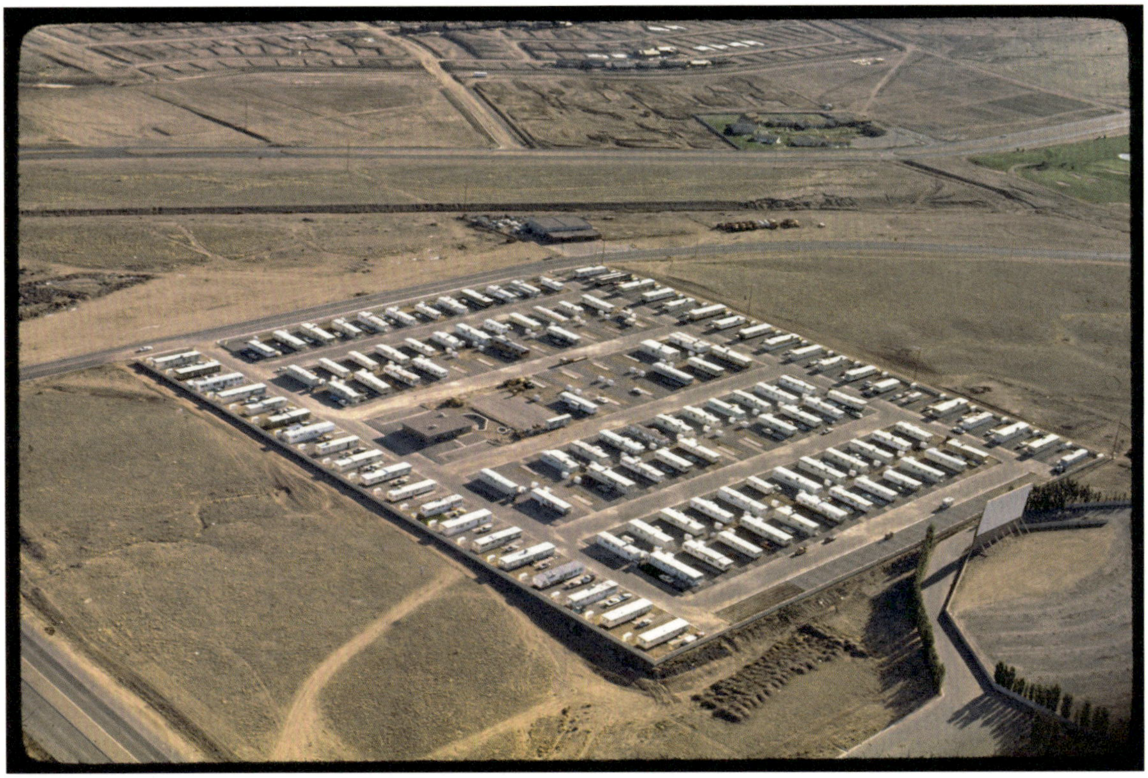

| FIG. 5 |

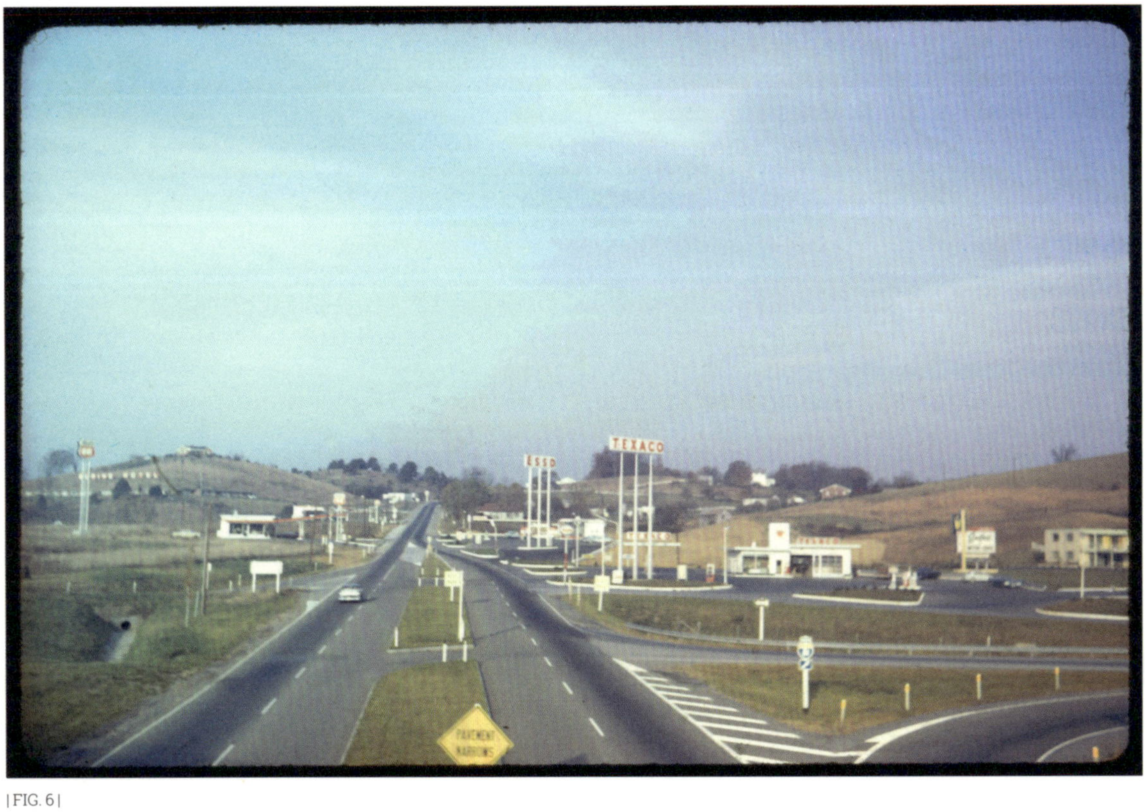

| FIG. 6 |

| FIG. 5 |
J. B. Jackson,
Trailer Village, New Mexico,
about 1970.

| FIG. 6 |
J. B. Jackson,
Interstate interchange,
Kentucky Tennessee,
December, 1965.

| FIG. 7 |
J. B. Jackson,
Monument, Fall River,
Massachusetts,
about 1970.

| FIG. 8 |
J. B. Jackson,
Fremont Street, Downtown
Las Vegas, Nevada,
about 1970.

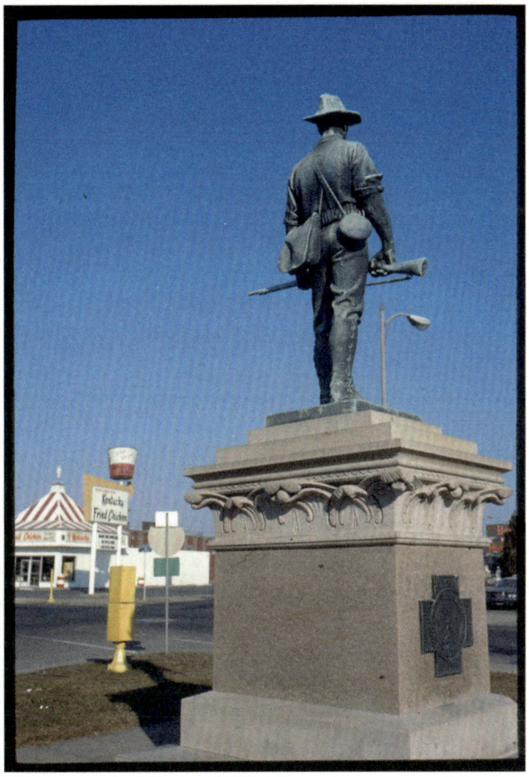

| FIG. 7 |

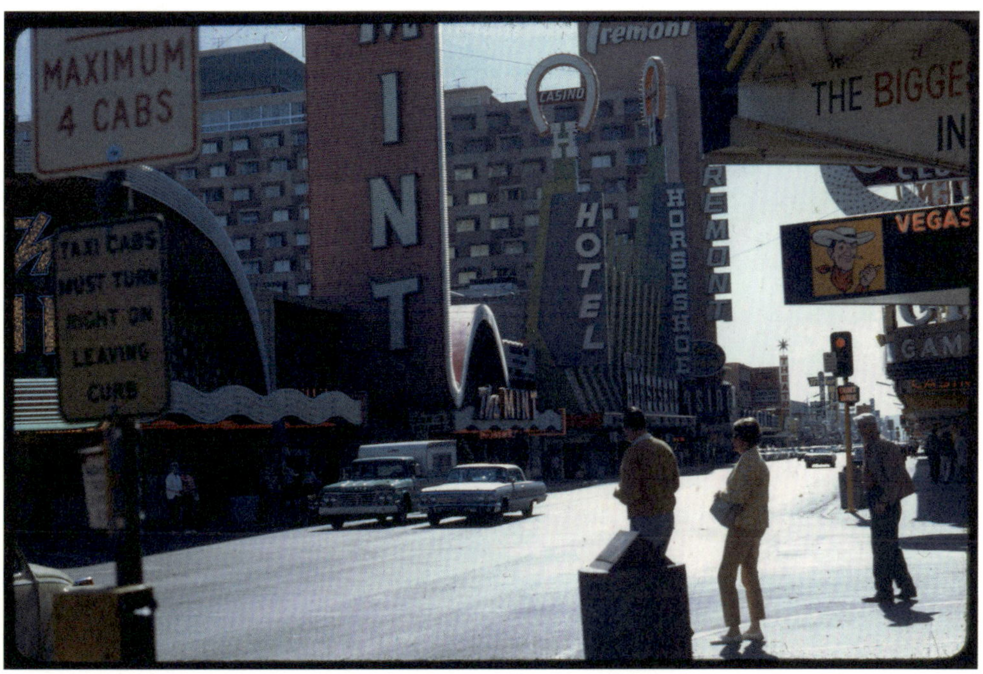

| FIG. 8 |

War monument to a 20th-century commercial strip in the background featuring the circus tent stripped roof of a restaurant with a giant bucket of Kentucky Fried Chicken atop its sign | **FIG. 7** |.

Jackson first sang the praises of the American roadside, and of its garish flashing and neon signs, in a 1956 essay. What would a Baroque architect do with such theatrical means, he wondered. Rather than denigrate the commercial roadside, he counseled civic reformers to instead pause to appreciate its raw vitality. Like the Pop Artists of the day, he exulted in the super graphics and saturated colors of this new commercial landscape | **FIG. 8** |. In another vein, his photos of the concrete bumpers and stripped spaces of parking lots, or of crisp patches of yellow and white paint on black asphalt take on an abstract Minimalist character. His eye for modern infrastructure – a curving highway slicing a neat V through a hillside, for instance – paralleled the sensibility of contemporary Land Artists.

The pieces of art he copied into his teaching slide collection embraced anyone interested in the vernacular cultural landscape: schoolyard games and working cowboys by Winslow Homer and Frederic Remington; twilight mansions and roadside stands by Edward Hopper and Walker Evans; mist-shrouded skyscrapers and gigantic factor gears by Hugh Ferris and Charlie Chaplin; stock tank baptisms and Dust Bowl ghost towns by John Steuart Curry and by Alexandre Hogue; monumental grain elevators and Ford factories by Charles Demuth and Charles Sheeler; Standard Stations and U.S. Highway 1 by Ed Ruscha and Allan D'Arcangelo; earth pyramids and spiral jetties by Michael Heizer and Robert Smithson; even a family sitting in front of their open garage by one of his former students, Bill Owens.

CULTURAL FERMENT AND THE NEW TOPOGRAPHICS

The anti-Vietnam War movement and the rise of the hippie counter culture typified the cultural ferment of the late 1960s, when Jackson began teaching at Berkeley and Harvard. Although born 35 years before the oldest of the post-war baby boomers (and himself a wartime comrade of the commander of U.S. forces in Vietnam, General William Westmoreland), Jackson's perspective on the world nevertheless resonated with his young students. Amid the anti-authoritarian *zeitgeist* of those years, Jackson's valorization of the vernacular offered an alternative to establishment cultural hierarchies (even as his black leather blazers and lack of a graduate education set him apart from most professors). The counterculture bible of tools and ideas, *The Whole Earth Catalogue*, edited in San Francisco, profiled Jackson's first book of essays, *Landscapes*, in its 1971 edition (on the same page with Ian McHarg's environmental planning classic, *Design with Nature*). Jackson "isn't another moralistic planner," began the *WEC* review. "Rather [he] is more like a rural historian, who is philosophical, talking about suburbs, highways, shopping centers, neon signs, and poverty, not as enemies, but for what they are: 'They are us.'"[37]

In contrast to this attitude, Peter Blake's 1963 book, *God's Own Junkyard,* featured unflattering telephoto shots of business signs and tract houses to denigrate the commercial roadside and suburbia. Ansel Adams' sentimental landscapes typically included a rustic cabin or dispensed with the man-made entirely. But other photographers such as Robert Frank and Lee Friedlander extended the tradition of Evans and the FSA when they toured America, eyes wide open to contemporary culture and landscape. Still others such as Edward Ruscha engaged Pop and Conceptual Art currents, for instance, in his deadpan survey of a roadside building type in *Twentysix*

Gasoline Stations (1963) or in the hopes and delusions implied by For Sale signs standing in forlorn vacant lots in *Real Estate Opportunities* (1970). Exhibitions and monographs in this period also revealed such little-known work as Timothy O'Sullivan's 19th-century topographic survey photographs of the American West, and Eugène Atget's reverential views of historic Paris. Brought together in new art photography programs across America, these currents fostered greater historical consciousness among a new generation of photographers.[38]

A 1975 group show of eight young Americans and the German duo of Bernd and Hilla Becher surveyed a fresh photographic genre that dispassionately documented overlooked industrial and suburban landscapes, while also giving the movement its name, New Topographics. One photographer in the exhibit, Joe Deal, noted in an interview two years later, "We found out the we were really interested in a kind of attitude that came through Atget, Walker Evans and Ed Ruscha and was just being done by a lot of young photographers."[39] (All but one of the Americans in the show were 28 to 33 years old at the time.) Deal and others in the exhibit were also taken with Jackson's essays. Even those who had not read Jackson directly found a similar appreciation of the contemporary vernacular in *Learning from Las Vegas* (1972) by Jackson's friend and Berkeley colleague, Denise Scott Brown, her husband, Robert Venturi, and collaborator, Steven Izenour.[40]

Like Jackson, the New Topographic photographers went on road trips to conduct surveys of the everyday landscape. Just as Jackson had broadened the conception of the cultural landscape from the rural and historic to encompass all manner of urban and contemporary settings, so too these photographers critiqued the nostalgia of nature photography by training a dispassionate eye on industrial, suburban and roadside landscapes. If architectural historians and historic preservationists in those days carefully framed their images to exclude telephone and utility poles – the better to ennoble isolated masterworks – Jackson and the New Topographic photographers stepped back or climbed to higher vantage points to encompass a larger, meaningful context. And both took particular interest in construction sites – the signs of new landscapes in the making.

While the first two collections of Jackson's essays published in 1970 and 1980 lacked any images, the next two volumes included a sampling of historic prints complemented by photographs drawn from commercial, corporate and government archives.[41] That *A Sense of Place, A Sense of Time* (1994) includes ten recent photographs of the vernacular landscape and subterranean economy of Hispanic Northern New Mexico by Jackson (the topic of two essays in the volume) demonstrates that he continued to take slides as part of his field research after retiring from teaching in 1978. An image from Ruscha's *Twenty-four Parking Lots in Los Angeles* (1967), in this same volume, along with two from Owens' book, *Suburbia* (1972), also suggests his growing familiarity with contemporary photography. Jackson's collaboration with the New Mexico Photographic Survey in the 1985 book, *The Essential Landscape,* exposed him to the work of twelve photographers. While some of these worked in the photo documentary vein pioneered by the FSA, others showed clear sympathies with the conceptualist and deadpan sensibilities of the New Topographics.

An invitation to write the foreword for a 1992 monograph of Joe Deal's work elicited Jackson's fullest discussion of photography. "[M]ost of us, regardless of our degree of education or aesthetic sensibility, use our camera in a very specific way: less as a means of self-expression or creativity than as a means of recording, as objectively, as rapidly, as precisely as possible, some object, some person, some event we want to register."[42]

37
The Last Whole Earth Catalog, Portola Institute, Menlo Park, CA, 1971, p. 82 [distributed by Random House, New York].

38
Peter Blake, *God's Own Junkyard: The Planned Deterioration of America's Landscape*, Holt Rinehart Winston, New York, 1963; Britt Salvesen (ed.), *New Topographics: Robert Adams* et al., Center for Creative Photography, University of Arizona, Tucson, AZ, 2009, p. 13, 15, 17, 19, 26–27, 37; Jeffery David Blankenship, "Reading *Landscape*: Mid-Century Modernism and the Landscape Idea," Dissertation, University of Massachusetts, Amherst, MA, 2011, p. 72–74.

39
Salvesen, Britt (ed.), *New Topographics, op. cit.*, p. 39.

40
Idem, p. 20–21, 25–26, 29; Robert Venturi, Denise Scott Brown, Steven Izenour, *Learning from Las Vegas,* The MIT Press, Cambridge, MA, London, 1972.

41
John Brinckerhoff Jackson, *Landscapes: Selected Writings of J. B. Jackson*, Ervin Zube (ed.), University of Massachusetts Press, Amherst, MA, 1970; Jackson, John Brinckerhoff, *The Necessity for Ruins, op. cit.;* John Brinckerhoff Jackson, *Discovering the Vernacular Landscape, op. cit.*

42
John Brinckerhoff Jackson, "Joe Deal and the Vernacular", in *Joe Deal, Southern California Photographs, 1976–86*, University of New Mexico Press, Albuquerque, NM, 1992, p. 6.

This was not only the way that Jackson and most amateurs used the camera, but also the transparent way that Jackson had long assumed that everyone used the camera (judging by his earlier skepticism about Gilpin's photographs being art). Yet, he acknowledges, photography had been "enriched and given structure by university patronage, and transformed into what is now surely the most innovative and promising study of how to perceive the world in a fresh manner and how to reinterpret our own relationship to the world."[43]

This new approach, as Jackson understood it, "signifies more than seeing and recording [...] it signifies an interaction between the artist and the world with the camera playing a subordinate part. The interaction results in modifying both the vision of the photographer and the image itself: a synthesis of the two makes for a highly individual work of art." Perhaps it was the degree of uncritical romanticism in Gilpin and Adams' landscapes (and his limited familiarity with Evans' work) that prevented Jackson from seeing photography as art earlier. For Jackson, Deal's undeniable artistic consciousness was something else entirely:

> *Deal introduces his camera into a world where no artist ever had been before: a world of ravaged vegetation and bulldozed landforms, of frame tract houses being built in a confusion of scrap lumber and chicken wire and bits of styrofoam floating in the air. He shows us things we have seen and rejected: the tight rows of trailers, the crowded beaches, the streets reaching across empty expanses of desert scrub. Without the help of myth or icon or archetype, without sentimentality or easy indignation, he shows us the beginnings of a landscape, the first groupings for form and permanence.*[44]

Every exuberant descriptive detail here betrays Jackson's love of the vernacular landscape. Indeed, he could have been describing his own earlier essays in this passage or when he adds, "Deal's contribution is a very simple one, easy to accept: he shows us that there is a much wider and much more stimulating choice of subjects in the everyday urban world than we had ever suspected."[45] That the vernacular landscapes of the New Topographic photographers could appear so fresh and riveting in the late 1970s is a testament to the prescience of Jackson's 1950s *Landscape* magazine essays. (Indeed, Jackson played a similar role in the quickening of cultural landscape studies in a half dozen other fields.)

If the themes of Jackson's earliest essays were original, expansive and influential, the aesthetics of his subsequent handheld 35 mm slides were often haphazard. Deal's images, by comparison – taken, like the 19th-century expeditionary photographers before him, with a tripod-mounted large format camera using expensive sheet film – are as carefully selected as Jackson's subjects, but more deliberately framed, and capable of capturing greater detail and depth of focus.

In the photograph selected as the portfolio frontispiece in his 1992 monograph **| FIG. 9 |**, Deal has climbed a hill to gain his favorite vantage point: a sort of aerial close-up with the virtues of a landscape overview but with more detail than an aerial shot from a moving airplane. The rocky hillside dominating the foreground has all the crisp detail, even in its shadowy clefts, of the best nature photography. The background samples an edge of suburbia: the utility poles and rows of trees lining roads and property boundaries, the house rooftops and freshly poured concrete pads around a future cul-de-sac – a temporary Readymade Land Art piece. The contrast between the saturated foreground and the hazy aerial perspective of the background suggests a complementary jin-jang of nature and the man-made. If hazy mountains stood in the distant background of picturesque landscape paintings and photographs, the artist has now climbed into the mountains and gazes back down on the new picturesque of suburbia. An environmental activist would have

43 *Idem*, p. 4.
44 *Idem*, p. 5.
45 *Idem*.

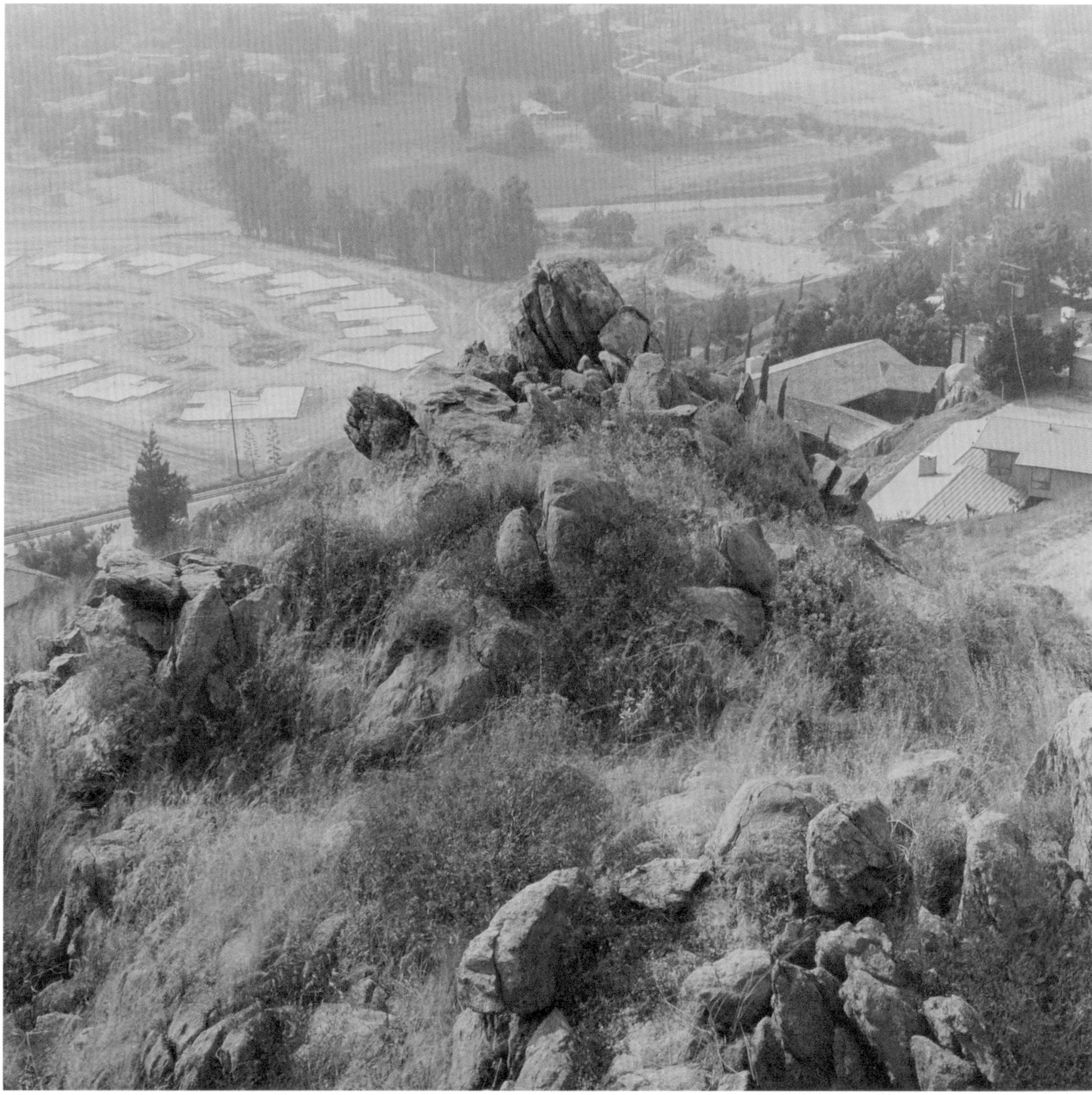

| FIG. 9 |

| FIG. 9 |
Joe Deal, Colton, California, 1978.

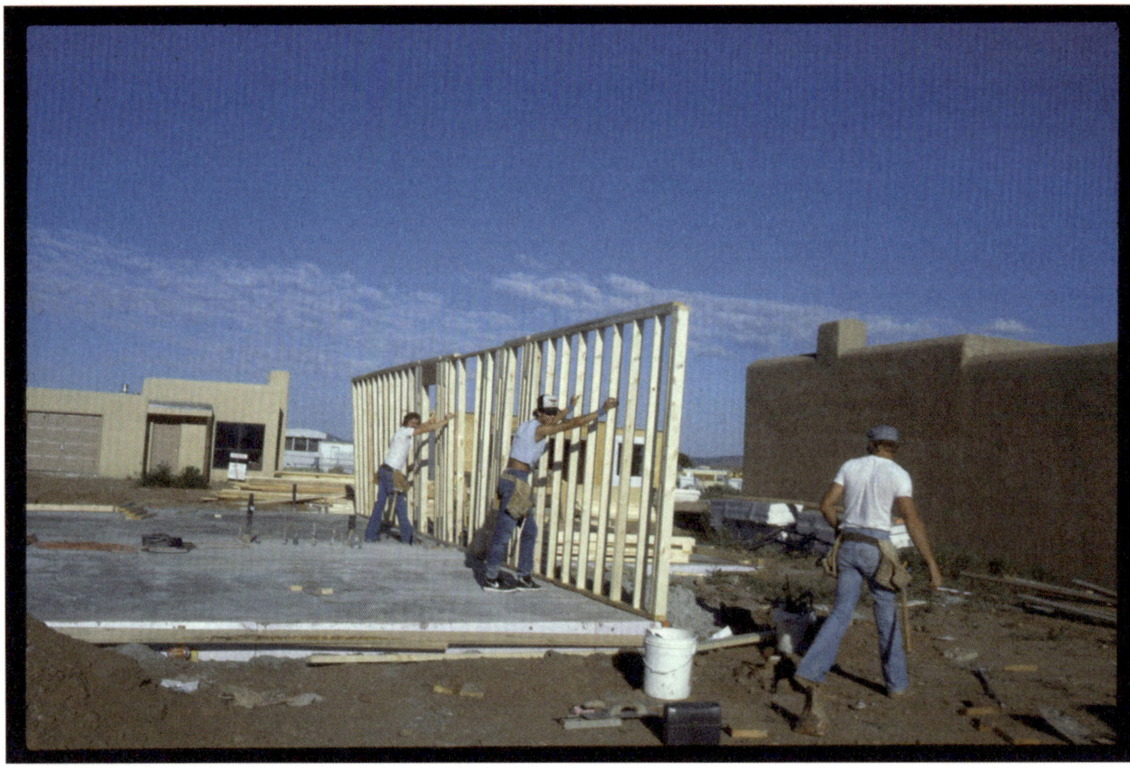

| FIG. 10 |
J. B. Jackson, House Construction, near Santa Fe, New Mexico, March, 1985.

foregrounded some unsightly man-made detail to drive home a man-versus-nature critique. But the calm, reverential light of Deal's photography instead signals respect for the natural *and* the man-made.

GRAPHIC LEGACY

In the years after Jackson stopped teaching full time in 1978, he distributed his slides to scholars at Harvard, Smith, Berkeley and New Mexico.[46] He continued to accept invitations to lecture around the country and to contribute essays to design and planning journals. He also gave up his annual cross-country motorcycle tour, and, after being injured in an accident in the early 1980s, replaced his motorcycle with a mini-pickup truck fitted out with a tool rack. Although he was independently wealthy, and continued to reserve his afternoons for writing, he took a series of menial cleaning jobs during his final decade at a small private post office, an auto repair shop and various construction sites amid the "confusion of scrap lumber and chicken wire and bits of styrofoam floating in the air." This work kept him out and in touch with the working poor striving to make their way in the world – a culture and a landscape he engaged with in his new photos and essays in *A Sense of Place*. As Jackson took fewer slides in retirement, he drew more, especially in an annual field drawing trip in the Southwest with architect, F. Douglas Adams[47] **| FIG. 10 |**.

Jackson had always been adept at striking up conversations with people, but never comfortable photographing them up close. So in 1985 he engaged social documentary photographer Miguel Gandert, a veteran of the New Mexico Photographic Survey, to take slides for an upcoming lecture. Jackson pointed him toward the subterranean economy and hardscrabble landscape, and Gandert found trailer homes, roadside stands, and mechanics working out of the trunks of their cars. But where photographer Jackson stayed back at a respectful distance, Gandert inserted himself into the immediate social circle.[48]

Only in his last year, 1996, did Jackson's drawings begin to attract wider attention. A well-received exhibition at the Municipal Art Society of New York led *New York Times* architecture critic Herbert Muschamp to call Jackson "America's greatest living writer on the cultural forces that have shaped the land this nation occupies." "No one familiar with the writings," Muschamp continued, "needs further proof that Jackson has an eye. But like Ruskin's drawings, Jackson's graphic work shows that the man has a hand as well. Jackson has always insisted that we look at the environment in other than pictorial terms, [...] For Jackson, it seems, drawing is not primarily a way of depicting things. It is a tool for framing things, a technique for fixing or loosening the boundaries around the object on view."[49] A way to make the context around a monumental building visible, or to notice that a road and row of telephone poles extend out into infinite space. A way, in fact, that Jackson "extended the borders of landscape over the entire land and everything built on it."

In his final years, historian Helen Lefkowitz Horowitz also worked with Jackson on a selection of his best writing, *Landscape in Sight*, which appeared in print the year after his death. Horowitz proposed and Jackson agreed to the inclusion of his drawing and photographs. He also approved but did not participate in Horowitz's selection and sequencing of 25 drawings and 24 photographs.[50] What Muschamp writes about the ability of his drawings to extend the mind and eye into the larger landscape context applies equally to his comprehensive photographic survey of America. With the reassembly of the four fragments of his slide collection into the Jackson Pictorial Collection at the University of New Mexico, and their availability on line, a recent wave of publications have begun the evaluation of the role of his graphic works in the quickening of cultural landscape studies following the Second World War.[51]

J. B. Jackson would likely have been amused to think that anyone would treat his photographs as art. His carefully crafted essays and some of his drawings, perhaps. But his photographs were merely a direct instrumental extension of his ability to see the everyday landscape with fresh eyes. They aided his analysis and his campaign to get others to appreciate the vernacular landscape.

Admittedly, many of his slides were poorly framed, others out of focus. Yet his ability to array the key components of a landscape in a single image, or to perceive ironic juxtapositions in the everyday, on occasion approach the symbolic compression of art. The power of his photographs comes primarily from the presence of an original mind behind the camera reading the record of history, culture and human aspirations in the landscape. For him, photography was a useful tool. But near the end of his life, Jackson also belatedly understood the artistic potential of photography. Indeed, he was delighted to encounter a younger generation of like-minded photographers who applied their art to the very landscapes he loved.

I would like to thank Audra Bellmore and Erin Fussel at the Center for Southwest Research, University of New Mexico, U.S.A., for their stewardship of the Jackson Collections; Peter Goin, Paul Groth, Helen Lefkowitz Horowitz, Virginia Scharff and Paul Starrs for sharing research information and leads; and Goin, Groth and Horowitz for reviewing and making valuable comments on a draft of this essay.

46
In addition to John Stilgoe at Harvard, Paul Groth and Marc Treib at Berkeley and Chris Wilson at New Mexico, all discussed by Paul Groth (*op. cit.*, p. 122–23), Helen Lefkowitz Horowitz at Smith also received slides from Jackson, which she later conveyed to the University of New Mexico for inclusion in the Jackson Pictorial Collection.

47
Helen Lefkowitz Horowitz, "J. B. Jackson and the Discovery of the American Landscape", *op. cit.*, p. xxvii; Paul Groth and Chris Wilson, "The Polyphony of Cultural Landscape Studies", *op. cit.*, p. 11–12; F. Douglas Adams, *op. cit.*, p. 34, 39–40; Paul Groth, "J. B. Jackson's Slides", in Mendelsohn and Wilson, *op. cit.*, p. 121.

48
Miguel Gandert, interview by Chris Wilson, August 22, 2013, Jackson Collection; Paul Groth, "J. B. Jackson's Slides", in Mendelsohn and Wilson, *op. cit.*, p. 122.

49
Herbert Muschamp, "Eloquent Champion of the Vernacular Landscape", *New York Times*, April 21, 1996.

50
Helen Lefkowitz Horowitz, telephone interview by Chris Wilson, October 10, 2016.

51
Paul Groth, *op. cit.*, p. 122–124; Mendelsohn, Janet and Chris Wilson, *op. cit.*; Jordi Ballesta, "Le vernaculaire selon John Brinckerhoff Jackson" and "Parmi les archives textuelles et visuelles de John Brinckerhoff Jackson", in "John Brinckerhoff Jackson", *Les Carnets du paysage*, no. 30, Actes Sud/ENSP, Arles, Versailles, 2016.

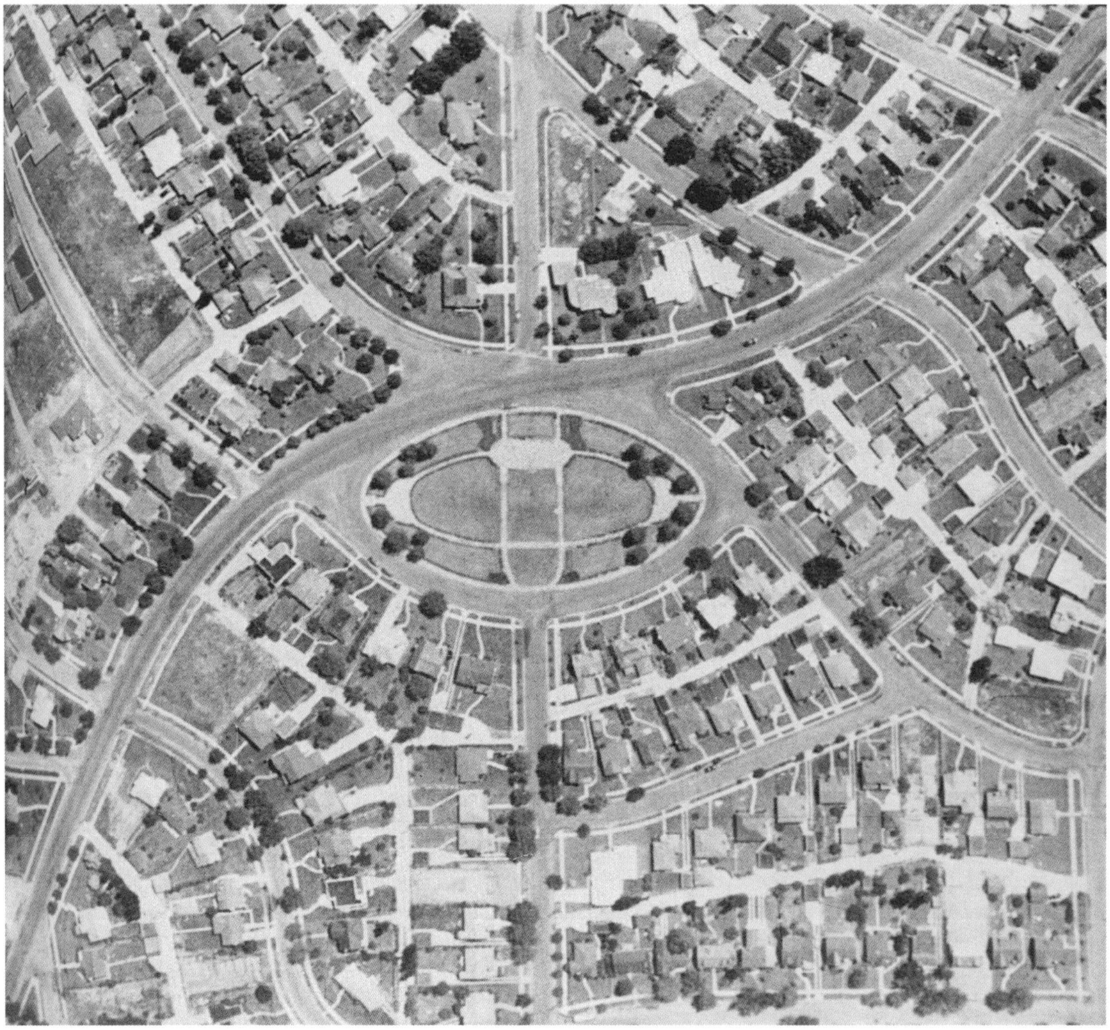

Order and Ambiguity

The Urban Landscape in J. B. Jackson's Magazine *Landscape*

Bruno Notteboom

"Landscape is a rich and beautiful book, we have but to learn to read it."[1] This much-cited phrase concludes the editorial of the first issue of *Landscape*, the magazine for human geography founded by John Brinckerhoff Jackson in 1951. For Jackson, who is described by some of his biographers as a "maverick writer, philosopher and publisher"[2], the magazine was an intellectual but in a sense also a pedagogical project on landscape: "We have become, in the course of the last few decades, a nation of city-dwellers," he writes, man has become ignorant of the "lie of the land" and therefore the magazine aims at the professional as well as "the intelligent layman".[3] Teaching in the field of cultural landscape studies at Harvard in the 1960s and 1970s, Jackson allegedly favored a Socratic way of teaching, encouraging students to speculate and try out a wide range of ideas.[4]

If Jackson's work can be considered as pedagogical, it is based on a conception of (urban) landscape that does not shy away from complexity and even ambiguity, as it is informed by particularity, experience and example.[5] While Jackson's life and writings have been discussed extensively,[6] one aspect of his work has been less examined: the way Jackson's discourse is constructed in text and image (and the combination of both), and in relation to the work of other authors in the magazine *Landscape*.[7] Looking at the period of Jackson's editorship of *Landscape* (1951–1968), I mainly will focus on articles that deal with the urban landscape, an interest that became increasingly thematized from the mid-1950s onwards. By including the urban realm, *Landscape* expanded its initial focus on geography to other disciplines (such as urban planning, urban sociology, architecture and visual studies), creating a unique forum for emerging theory and practices related to the notion of urban landscape. Reading *Landscape* as a mouthpiece for multiple voices, my intention is to shed a light on how text and image were used by Jackson as ways of developing his non-hegemonic approach to landscape. Landscape and its representation have a long history of being related to power relations, and visuality can be understood as a historically variable envisioning of authority.[8] Parallel to the discourse on townscape developed around *Architectural Review* in the UK in the 1950s and 1960s,[9] Jackson and the authors publishing in *Landscape* developed in their own way a counterdiscourse and – to a certain extent – a "countervisuality"[10] that supported a critical attitude toward rational and quantitative methods of modern urban planning.

DISTANCE AND PROXIMITY

By choosing "Human Geography of the Southwest" as subtitle for the first issue, Jackson anchored the magazine not only in a specific geographical region, but also in a specific field of knowledge. Citing Maurice Le Lannou – who closed the first issue with an excerpt from his *Géographie humaine*,[11] Jackson explicitly referred to the influence of French geography he encountered during his studies

1
John Brinckerhoff Jackson, "The Need of Being Versed in Country Things", *Landscape* 1/1, spring 1951, p. 1–5, here p. 5.

2
Paul Groth and Chris Wilson, "The Polyphony of Landscape Study: An Introduction", in Paul Groth and Chris Wilson (eds.), *Everyday America. Cultural Landscape Studies after J. B. Jackson*, University of California Press, Berkeley, Los Angeles, London, 2003, p. vii–x, here p. x.

3
John Brinckerhoff Jackson, "The Need of Being Versed in Country Things", *op. cit.*, p. 1.

4
Jeffrey W. Limerick, "Basic 'Brinckmanship'. Impressions Left in a Youthful Mind", *in* Groth, Paul and Chris Wilson (eds.), *Everyday America*, *op. cit.*, p. 130–141.

5
For that reason Jackson generally avoided the question of pedagogy. See Peirce Lewis, "The Monument and the Bungalow. The Intellectual Legacy of J. B. Jackson", in Paul Groth and Chris Wilson (eds.), *op. cit.*, p. 85–108.

6
See, among others, Helen Lefkowitz Horowitz, *Landscape in sight: looking at America / John Brinckerhoff Jackson*, Yale University Press, New Haven, CT, 1997; Paul Groth and Chris Wilson (eds.), *op. cit.*; Marc Treib, "The Measure of Wisdom: John Brinckerhoff Jackson", in Marc Treib, *Settings and Stray Paths. Writings on Landscapes and Gardens*, Routledge, London, 2003, p. 198; Bruno Notteboom, 2016, "The Westward-Moving House and other stories. J.B Jackson reading and writing the landscape", in Klaske Havik, Jorge Mejia Hernández, Mike Schäfer, Mark Proosten, Susana Oliveira (eds.), *Writingplace. Investigations in Architecture and Literature*, nai010 Publishers, Rotterdam, 2017; Janet Mendelsohn and Chris Wilson (eds.), *Drawn to Landscape. The Pioneering Work of J. B. Jackson*, George F. Thompson Publishing, Staunton, VA, 2015. For essays on J.B. Jackson and a translation of some of his texts into French, see the theme issues of *Le Visiteur* (5, 2000), *Les Carnets du Paysage* (30, 2006) and *L'Espace géographique* (3, 2016).

7
An exception is: Paul F. Starrs and Peter Goin, "In the Beginning Was *Landscape*", in Janet Mendelsohn and Chris Wilson (eds.), *op. cit.*, p. 92–104.

8
Guzman, Alicia Inez and Marr, Alexander Brier, "Introduction. Making Sense of Visual Culture", *InVisible Culture*, 18, 2013.

9
Frédéric Pousin, "Visuality as Politics: the Example of Urban Landscape", in Mark Dorrian and Gillian Rose (eds.), *Deterritorialisations… Revisioning Landscapes and Politics*, Black Dog Publishing, London, New York, 2003.

10
This term is coined in Mirzoeff, Nicholas, *The Right To Look. A Counter-history of Visuality*, Duke University Press Books, Durham, NC, 2011.

11
Maurice Le Lannou, "The vocation of human geography", *Landscape* 1/1, spring 1951, p. 41.

at Harvard University and, more importantly, during his service for the U.S. army as an intelligence officer during the Second World War.[12]

In his analysis of the Jacksonian approach to human geography, which was deeply influenced by French geographers such as Le Lannou, Pierre Deffontaines and Vidal de La Blache, Jean-Marc Besse observes that human geography, the study of "marks, tracings and imprints on the ground of man's most diverse actions"[13] found an ally in aerial photography. The enthusiasm of French geographers for aerial photography was shared by Jackson: "It is from the air that the true relationship between the natural and the human landscape is first clearly revealed (...) No one who has experienced this spectacle (...) can have failed to be fascinated by it, nor wonder at the variety of men's ways of coming to terms with nature."[14] However, in *Landscape* it was the combination of different media – maps, perpendicular views, oblique views and sketches on the terrain – that allowed Jackson to fully explore the complexities of the relationship between "man the inhabitant" and the earth, a "mixed strategy" that can be considered as part of an epistemological project inherent to geography since aerial photography made its entry.[15] Through a succession of images, the reader is subjected to different viewpoints, alternating details and the larger context, displaying the landscape from close by and from a distance.

While the visual strategy of these first issues of *Landscape* is not exceptional – geographical publication had used this juxtaposition of different types of images for much longer – his texts added a degree of complexity that made the magazine quite unique. Before the war, Jackson had majored in history and literature at Harvard and had written a well-received novel on the effects of the political changes of the 1930s on a rural community in Eastern Europe.[16] This background was echoed in *Landscape* in the use of narrative techniques and an essayistic, almost literary writing in Jackson's texts on cultural landscape history. A well-known example is *The Westward-Moving House*, in which he describes the lives of three generations of farmers from the 19th-century to the 1950s, and the way they interact with the landscape.[17] By placing his analysis in the context of an intergenerational family history, Jackson develops an understanding of the mutually constitutive relationship between cultural ideas and the physical environment. Throughout the text, the perspective of the reader goes back and forth between that of the protagonists – as in a literary story – and the meta-narrative of the socioeconomic and architectural history. Both in this more "literary" story, and in his "geographical" articles, Jackson alternates perspectives in text as well as images to explain the interaction between humans and their environment: from above and from below, determined by large-scale geographical context or by local conditions, as an effect of large-scale sociopolitical and economic evolutions and as the result of individual aspirations and decisions.

URBAN LANDSCAPE

During the first years of its existence, *Landscape* went through a gradual programmatic shift to the urban, which was reflected in the text as well as in the imagery. Jackson announced in 1952 that the magazine would widen its regional focus beyond the Southwest,[18] and in the issue of winter 1954–1955 the urban landscape was for the first time visually thematized by putting an urban landscape on the cover: an aerial photo of a suburb of Denver | **FIG. 1** |. The issue also featured an article by the French geographer Max Sorre, which is a condensed version of the last volume of his work *Les Fondements de la géographie humaine*.[19] Referring to Sorre, Jackson argued that that the methods of human geography can also be used in the context of the city, however it also allowed him to point at the specificity of the American territory. In the same issue, he observes that, in contrast to Europe, the boundaries between city, suburb and countryside in the US are quite blurred, especially because of rising automobility and telecommunication.[20]

Jackson had used the image of a suburb on the cover before, to illustrate an article by Christopher Tunnard of Spring 1952, "Fire on the prairie", which was a prepublication of *The City of Man*.[21] This article dealt with the specific condition of the American grid as a tool both for territorial and city planning. His awareness of the differences between the European and the American city was paired with his interest in new and inherently American forms of urbanity such as the highway strip or the shopping mall that would characterize *Landscape* throughout the 1950s and 1960s.[22]

Nevertheless, Jackson's discourse on the urban landscape was in tune with an increasing number of European architects and urban planners,[23] in the sense that he criticized the alienating effects of a top-down *tabula-rasa* planning and a pleaded for a way of reading and designing the city from a perspective of the observing subject moving through it on the ground. The winter 1958–1959 issue ("The urban scene") tied in with what could be considered this experiential approach of the city by putting a street scene in Naples on the cover **| FIG. 2 |**. A new visual paradigm – street photography – entered *Landscape*, reminiscent, for example, of the photos of Nigel Henderson that were presented by Alison and Peter Smithson at the 1953 CIAM conference as part of a critique on the abstract viewpoint of modern city planning.[24]

However, although it is tempting to stress the similarities to what was happening in the architecture scene in Europe, Jackson's references were mainly American, and were rooted in a respect for "the lie of the land", both urban and natural. His critique on modern architecture was in the first place rooted in his appreciation of the site-specificity and adaptability of pueblo architecture of the Southwest.[25] One of the contributors to the "Urban scene" issue, with an essay titled "The city watcher" was botanist Edgar Anderson, whose literary stylistic qualities equaled those of Jackson.[26] In the essay, the botanist's observant eye observes the city as a natural phenomenon, claiming that humans are part of nature, even in the city. Two issues later, in an essay titled "The Imitation of Nature", Jackson built further on this line of reasoning, stating that there is nothing "unnatural" about the city – preluding David Harvey's famous quote "there is nothing unnatural about New York city" by a couple of decades.[27] By coining the term "subjective nature" for the sensory experiences nature offers us, Jackson transfers this concept to the city, as he describes Grand Central Terminal as the summum of "a rich and almost completely satisfactory sensory experience",[28] and he summons professionals to develop research and design methods to analyze and shape the American city from this sensory characteristics.

From the end of the 1950s onwards, *Landscape* provided a forum for (mainly American) research on a sensorial and experiential analysis of the urban environment, and it is no surprise that Kevin Lynch published one of his first articles in the magazine: "A walk

12
On the relationship between Jackson and French geography, see Jean-Marc Besse, "J. B. Jackson and human geography", *Le Visiteur*, 5, 2000, p. 44–53; Jean-Marc Besse, "Fonder l'étude des paysages: John Brinckerhoff Jackson face à la géographie humaine française", *L'Espace géographique*, 45/3, 2016, p. 195–210.

13
Jean-Marc Besse, 2016, *op. cit.*, p. 50.

14
John Brinckerhoff Jackson, 1951, *op. cit.*, p. 4–5.

15
Marie-Claire Robic, "From the sky to the ground: the aerial view and the ideal of the vue raisonnée in geography during the 1920s", in Mark Dorrian and Frédéric Pousin, *The aerial view in visual culture*, I.B. Tauris, London, New York, 2013, p. 163–187.

16
Helen Lefkowitz Horowitz, 1997; *op. cit.*, p. xvii–xii.

17
John Brinckerhoff Jackson, "The Westward-Moving House. Three American Houses and the People Who Lived in Them", *Landscape* 2/3, spring 1953, p. 8–21. See also Bruno Notteboom, *op. cit.*, and Marc Treib, *op. cit.*

18
John Brinckerhoff Jackson, "Human, all too human, geography", *Landscape*, 2/2, fall 1952, p. 2–7. See also Helen Lefkowitz Horowitz, *op. cit.*, p. xxii.

19
Max Sorre, "The structure of cities", *Landscape*, 4/2, winter 1954–1955, p. 5–15.

20
John Brinckerhoff Jackson, "Town and Country", *Landscape*, 4/2, 1954–1955, p. 2–3.

21
Christopher Tunnard, "Fire on the prairie", *Landscape*, 2/1, 1952, p. 9–12.

22
In *A sense of place. A sense of time*, Jackson writes that pre-war (European) geography did not provide the right categories to describe the evolution of the American vernacular landscape. See Jean-Marc Besse, *op. cit.*, p. 208.

23
For example, the younger generation of CIAM, or the architects publishing in *Architectural Review*. See Frédéric Pousin, *op. cit.*, 2003.

24
Claude Lichtenstein and Thomas Schregenberger, *As Found: The Discovery of the Ordinary*, Lars Müller Publishers, Zurich, 2006, p. 23.

25
John Brinckerhoff Jackson, "Pueblo architecture and our own", *Landscape*, 3/2, winter 1953–1954, p. 20–25.

26
Edgar Anderson, "The city watcher", *Landscape*, 8/2, winter 1958–1959, p. 7–8. See also Paul F. Starrs and Peter Goins, 2015, *op. cit.*, p. 96.

27
John Brinckerhoff Jackson, "The Imitation of Nature", 9/1, fall 1959, p. 9–12. On the quote of Harvey: Nik Heynen, Maria Kaika and Erik Swyngedouw (eds.), *In the Nature of Cities: Urban Political Ecology and the Politics of Urban Metabolism*, Routledge, London, 2006.

28
John Brinckerhoff Jackson, 1959, *op. cit.*, p. 11.

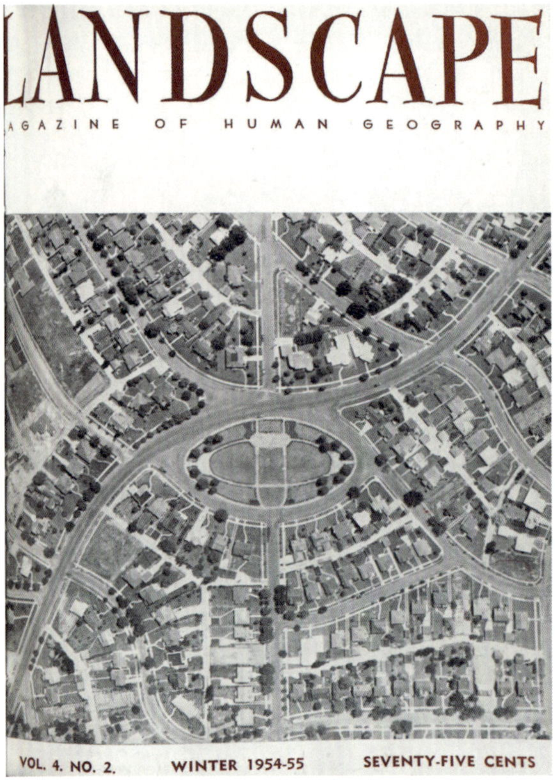

| FIG. 1 |

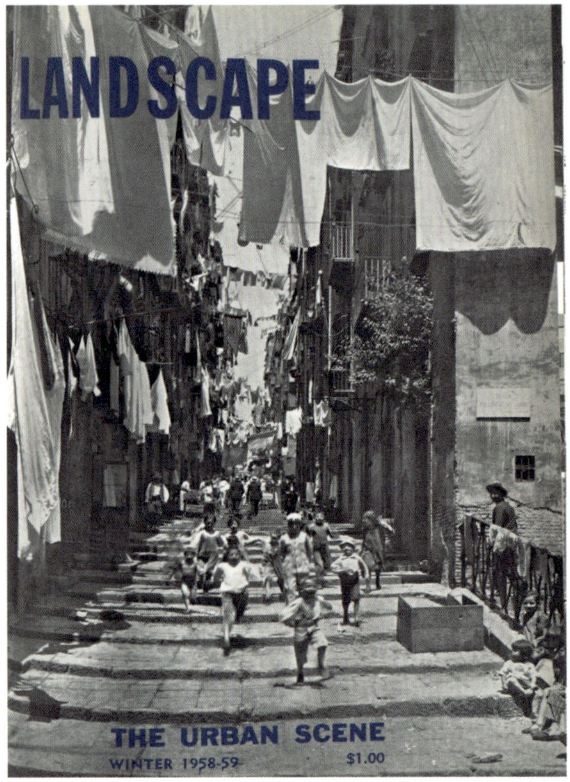

| FIG. 2 |

| FIG. 3 |

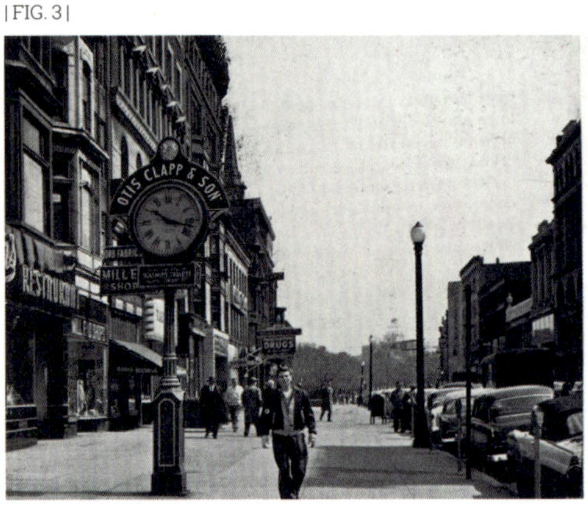

WHAT THEY SAW:

(left) looking down Boylston Street to the Public Gardens; the spire of the Arlington Street Church is visible above the clock;

(below) Arlington Street; the church, the brick pavement, the Public Gardens to the right; the Ritz is the tall building in the background;

(opposite) Newberry Street with the Ritz parking lot and the spire of the Church of the Covenant.

| FIG. 1 |
Suburb of Denver.
Cover, *Landscape* 4/2,
winter 1954–1955.

| FIG. 2 |
Cover of "The urban scene" issue.
Landscape 8/2, winter 1958–1959.

| FIG. 3 |
Kevin Lynch and Malcolm Rivkin,
"A Walk Around the Block".
Landscape 8/3, spring 1959.

| FIG. 4 |
Grady Clay, "Remembered Landscapes".
Landscape 7/2,
winter 1957–1958.

| FIG. 5 |
Philip Langley, "Urban Sequence',
Landscape 10/1, fall 1960.

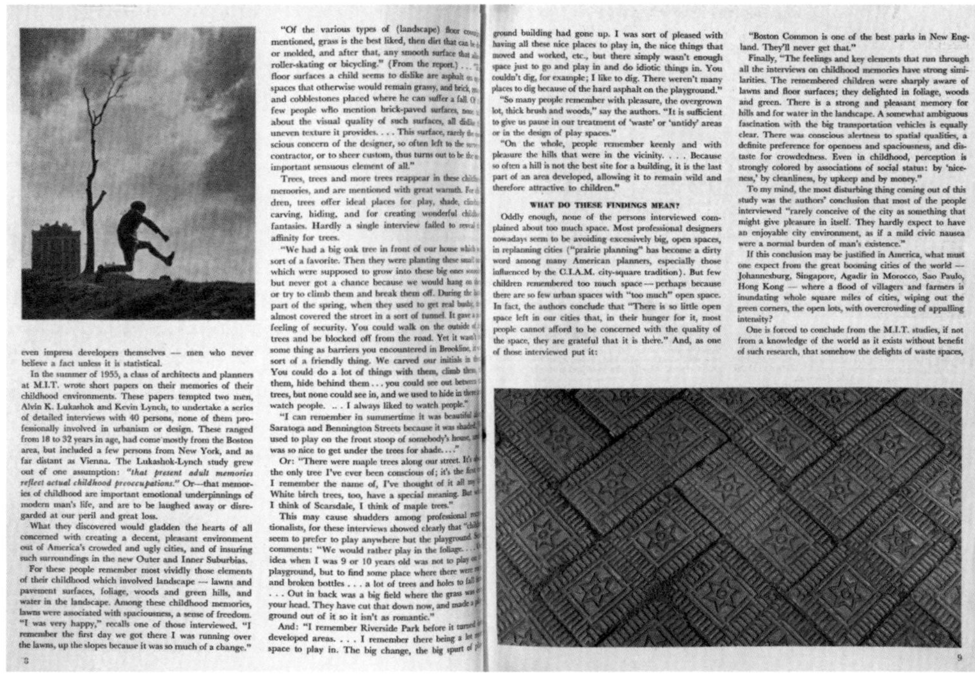

even impress developers themselves — men who never believe a fact unless it is statistical.

In the summer of 1955, a class of architects and planners at M.I.T. wrote short papers on their memories of their childhood environments. These papers tempted two men, Alvin K. Lukashok and Kevin Lynch, to undertake a series of detailed interviews with 40 persons, none of them professionally involved in urbanism or design. These ranged from 18 to 32 years in age, had come mostly from the Boston area, but included a few persons from New York, and as far distant as Vienna. The Lukashok-Lynch study grew out of one assumption: *"that present adult memories reflect actual childhood preoccupations."* Or—that memories of childhood are important emotional underpinnings of modern man's life, and are to be laughed away or disregarded at our peril and great loss.

What they discovered would gladden the hearts of all concerned with creating a decent, pleasant environment out of America's crowded and ugly cities, and of insuring such surroundings in the new Outer and Inner Suburbias.

For these people remember most vividly those elements of their childhood which involved landscape — lawns and pavement surfaces, foliage, woods and green hills, and water in the landscape. Among these childhood memories, lawns were associated with spaciousness, a sense of freedom. "I was very happy," recalls one of those interviewed. "I remember the first day we got there I was running over the lawns, up the slopes because it was so much of a change."

"Of the various types of (landscape) floor ... mentioned, grass is the best liked, then dirt that can be ... or molded, and after that, any smooth surface that ... roller-skating or bicycling." (From the report.) ... floor surfaces a child seems to dislike are asphalt ... spaces that otherwise would remain grassy, and brick ... and cobblestones placed where he can suffer a fall. ... few people who mention brick-paved surfaces, ... about the visual quality of such surfaces, all dislike ... uneven texture it provides. ... This surface, rarely the ... scious concern of the designer, so often left to the ... contractor, or to sheer custom, thus turns out to be the ... important sensuous element of all."

Trees, trees and more trees reappear in these childhood memories, and are mentioned with great warmth. For children, trees offer ideal places for play, shade, climbing, carving, hiding, and for creating wonderful childish fantasies. Hardly a single interview failed to reveal ... affinity for trees.

"We had a big oak tree in front of our house which ... sort of a favorite. Then they were planting these small ... which were supposed to grow into these big ones ... but never got a chance because we would hang on ... or try to climb them and break them off. During the ... part of the spring, when they used to get real bushy ... almost covered the street in a sort of tunnel. It gave a ... feeling of security. You could walk on the outside of ... trees and be blocked off from the road. Yet it wasn't ... some thing as barriers you encountered in Brookline, ... sort of a friendly thing. We carved our initials in ... You could do a lot of things with them, climb them, ... them, hide behind them ... you could see out between ... trees, but none could see in, and we used to hide in there ... watch people. ... I always liked to watch people."

"I can remember in summertime it was beautiful ... Saratoga and Bennington Streets because it was shaded. ... used to play on the front stoop of somebody's house, ... was so nice to get under the trees for shade. ..."

Or: "There were maple trees along our street. It's ... the only tree I've ever been conscious of; it's the first ... I remember the name of, I've thought of it all ... White birch trees, too, have a special meaning. But ... I think of Scarsdale, I think of maple trees."

This may cause shudders among professional ... tionalists, for these interviews showed clearly that "children ... seem to prefer to play anywhere but the playground. ... comments: "We would rather play in the foliage. ... idea when I was 9 or 10 years old was not to play on ... playground, but to find some place where there were ... and broken bottles ... a lot of trees and holes to fall ... ... Out in back was a big field where the grass was ... your head. They have cut that down now, and made a ... ground out of it so it isn't as romantic."

And: "I remember Riverside Park before it turned ... developed areas. ... I remember there being a lot ... space to play in. The big change, the big spurt of ... ground building had gone up. I was sort of pleased with having all these nice places to play in, the nice things that moved and worked, etc., but there simply wasn't enough space just to go and play in and do idiotic things in. You couldn't dig, for example; I like to dig. There weren't many places to dig because of the hard asphalt on the playground."

"So many people remember with pleasure, the overgrown lot, thick brush and woods," say the authors. "It is sufficient to give us pause in our treatment of 'waste' or 'untidy' areas or in the design of play spaces."

"On the whole, people remember keenly and with pleasure the hills that were in the vicinity. ... Because so often a hill is not the best site for a building, it is the last part of an area developed, allowing it to remain wild and therefore attractive to children."

WHAT DO THESE FINDINGS MEAN?

Oddly enough, none of the persons interviewed complained about too much space. Most professional designers nowadays seem to be avoiding excessively big, open spaces, in replanning cities ("prairie planning" has become a dirty word among many American planners, especially those influenced by the C.I.A.M. city-square tradition). But few children remembered too much space — perhaps because there are so few urban spaces with "too much" open space. In fact, the authors conclude that "There is so little open space left in our cities that, in their hunger for it, most people cannot afford to be concerned with the quality of the space, they are grateful that it is there." And, as one of those interviewed put it:

"Boston Common is one of the best parks in New England. They'll never get that."

Finally, "The feelings and key elements that run through all the interviews on childhood memories have strong similarities. The remembered children were sharply aware of lawns and floor surfaces; they delighted in foliage, woods and green. There is a strong and pleasant memory for hills and for water in the landscape. A somewhat ambiguous fascination with the big transportation vehicles is equally clear. There was conscious alertness to spatial qualities, a definite preference for openness and spaciousness, and distaste for crowdedness. Even in childhood, perception is strongly colored by associations of social status: by 'niceness,' by cleanliness, by upkeep and by money."

To my mind, the most disturbing thing coming out of this study was the authors' conclusion that most of the people interviewed "rarely conceive of the city as something that might give pleasure in itself. They hardly expect to have an enjoyable city environment, as if a mild civic nausea were a normal burden of man's existence."

If this conclusion may be justified in America, what must one expect from the great booming cities of the world — Johannesburg, Singapore, Agadir in Morocco, Sao Paulo, Hong Kong — where a flood of villagers and farmers is inundating whole square miles of cities, wiping out the green corners, the open lots, with overcrowding of appalling intensity?

One is forced to conclude from the M.I.T. studies, if not from a knowledge of the world as it exists without benefit of such research, that somehow the delights of waste spaces,

8 9

| FIG. 4 |

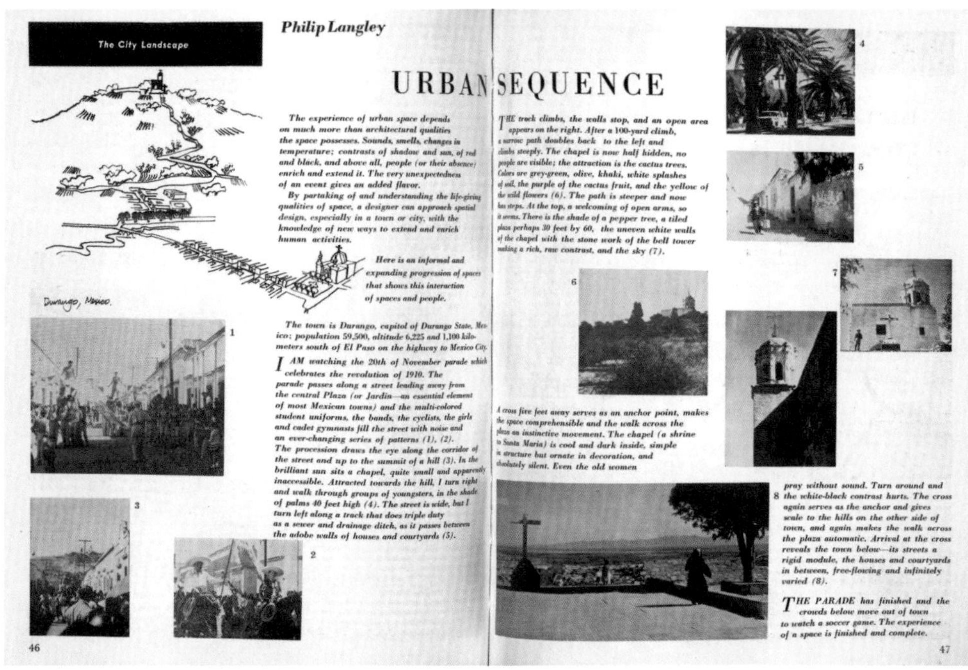

The City Landscape

Philip Langley

URBAN SEQUENCE

The experience of urban space depends on much more than architectural qualities the space possesses. Sounds, smells, changes in temperature; contrasts of shadow and sun, of red and black, and above all, people (or their absence) enrich and extend it. The very unexpectedness of an event gives an added flavor.

By partaking of and understanding the life-giving qualities of space, a designer can approach spatial design, especially in a town or city, with the knowledge of new ways to extend and enrich human activities.

Here is an informal and expanding progression of spaces that shows this interaction of spaces and people.

Durango, Mexico.

The town is Durango, capitol of Durango State, Mexico; population 59,500, altitude 6,225 and 1,100 kilometers south of El Paso on the highway to Mexico City.

I AM watching the 20th of November parade which celebrates the revolution of 1910. The parade passes along a street leading away from the central Plaza (or Jardin—an essential element of most Mexican towns) and the multi-colored student uniforms, the bands, the cyclists, the girls and cadet gymnasts fill the street with noise and an ever-changing series of patterns (1), (2). The procession draws the eye along the corridor of the street and up to the summit of a hill (3). In the brilliant sun sits a chapel, quite small and apparently inaccessible. Attracted towards the hill, I turn right and walk through groups of youngsters, in the shade of palms 40 feet high (4). The street is wide, but I turn left along a track that does triple duty as a sewer and drainage ditch, as it passes between the adobe walls of houses and courtyards (5).

THE track climbs, the walls stop, and an open area appears on the right. After a 100-yard climb, a narrow path doubles back to the left and climbs steeply. The chapel is now half hidden, no people are visible; the attraction is the cactus trees. Colors are grey-green, olive, khaki, white splashes of soil, the purple of the cactus fruit, and the yellow of the wild flowers (6). The path is steeper and now has steps. At the top, a welcoming of open arms, so it seems. There is the shade of a pepper tree, a tiled plaza perhaps 30 feet by 60, the uneven white walls of the chapel with the stone work of the bell tower making a rich, raw contrast, and the sky (7).

A cross five feet away serves as an anchor point, makes the space comprehensible and the walk across the plaza an instinctive movement. The chapel (a shrine to Santa Maria) is cool and dark inside, simple in structure but ornate in decoration, and absolutely silent. Even the old women pray without sound. Turn around and the white-black contrast hurts. The cross again serves as the anchor and gives scale to the hills on the other side of town, and again makes the walk across the plaza automatic. Arrival at the cross reveals the town below—its streets a rigid module, the houses and courtyards in between, free-flowing and infinitely varied (8).

THE PARADE has finished and the crowds below move out of town to watch a soccer game. The experience of a space is finished and complete.

1 2 3 4 5 6 7 8

46 47

| FIG. 5 |

around the block" in the issue following the "Urban Scene" issue | **FIG. 3** |.[29] The article focuses on research Lynch carried out at MIT while working on *The Image of the City*.[30] It was a record of the impressions of 27 "subjects" walking round a street block in Boston, illustrated by schemes depicting orientation signs, the (lack of) relations between streets, blocks, buildings and open spaces as well as photos of pedestrians walking on the sidewalk. However, this was not Lynch's first appearance in *Landscape*. In the winter issue of 1957–1958, in an article called "Remembered Landscapes", journalist Grady Clay (who would become the editor of *Landscape Architecture* magazine from 1960 onwards) refers to the research on childhood memories that Lynch had done at MIT in 1955 in order to "prove" that trees and open spaces are an essential element in good city design.[31] The article was illustrated with Robert Doisneau's "La Poterne des peupliers", shot in Paris in 1934, an image that displayed the silhouette of a child, jumping in what appears to be a kind of wasteland at the edge of the city, and an image of a paved surface, as seen through the eyes of someone walking through the city[32] | **FIG. 4** |. Note the difference in visual language between these images and the ones illustrating the "A walk around the block" article. The unique moment – or the "decisive moment" – of Doisneau's image expresses the feeling associated of the individual, sensory experience of the city, while the pedestrians in "A walk around the block" are "subjects" in an experiment that is looking for a system behind these individual experiences, in order to "search for order in the environment".[33]

SEQUENCING AND JUXTAPOSING

The visual language of *Landscape* magazine is far less experimental than contemporary architectural urbanism journals as *Architectural Review* or the myriad of experimental "little magazines", as Denise Scott Brown called them, from the 1960s and 1970s.[34] However, the images in the magazine are not merely an illustration of the text, but in many cases form a narrative in themselves, and visual strategies as sequencing and juxtaposing images play an important role in the construction of such a narrative. The imagery accompanying Lynch and Rivkin's article, forms an obvious example. The visual sequence presented in this article not only expresses the systematic character of the researcher's exploration of the city block, it also introduces a sense of movement and the notion of time. Each photo stages a main character, a "protagonist" in the form of a pedestrian, seen from the front, from close by, from afar. Such sequences would become quite current in the course of the 1960s in order to generate a sense of movement, for example in Cullen's *Townscape* (1961) and Edmund Bacon's *Design of Cities* (1967). In an analysis of Bacon's book, Andrew Shanken points at the ambiguity of such photo series and the relationship between the viewer and the protagonist.[35] The "embedded" researcher/architect/urbanist identifies with both the observer behind the camera and with the city dweller observed walking through the city, and as a viewer we are at once inside and outside the image (and the city).

This combination of on the one hand a systematic observation of the city from an outsider's perspective, and on the other hand an immersive point of view in which the perspective of the researcher/designer coincides with that of the city dweller of Lynch and Rivkin's article, can also be found in several other articles in *Landscape*. A telling example, textually as well as visually, is "Urban Sequence", published by landscape architect Philip Langley in the 10th anniversary issue of fall 1960 | **FIG. 5** |.[36] The narration, told in the first person, evokes the experience of Langley walking through the Mexican city of Durango, experiencing an urban space that "depends on much more than architectural qualities the space possesses. Sounds, smells, changes in temperature: contrasts of shadow and sun, of red and black, and above all, people (or their absence) enrich and extend it."[37] The narrator follows a parade through the city, after which he climbs up a hill to arrive at a church square offering a view back over the city, illustrated by photos looking up and down, left and right, and eventually, overlooking the city.

Also here the (landscape) architect, whose narrative is clearly meant to inspire fellow professionals, takes on a double perspective: the one mingling in the crowd, and the one observing it from a distance: "The parade has finished and the crowds below move out of town to watch a soccer game. The experience of a space is finished and complete."[38] This combination of an immersive and a synthetic gaze is further expressed by the sketch made by the landscape architect, evoking the path zigzagging its way up the hill.

In the tenth anniversary issue the urban landscape and its visualization are explicitly thematized. Moreover, in the issue Jackson expands the notion of urban landscape and its experiential approach from the city to a territorial scale. Doing so, a new visual paradigm, based on a more distant viewpoint and the (auto)mobile viewer, enters the journal. Jackson illustrates an article on the Oklahoma Panhandle with two sets of images that visualize this shifting paradigm.[39] A first series of images consists of vernacular landscapes that seem to be shot from the window of a car and the organization of the images seems to suggest the movement of a car traveler, looking left and right through the window **| FIG. 6 |**. The next page displays a composition of photos of grain elevators, a kind of "archive" of agro-industrial installations that are typical for the Oklahoman rural landscape **| FIG. 7 |**. The two images series seem to prefigure different visual strategies that would pervade artists (such as Ed Ruscha and the "New Topographics") as well as architects and urban planners (such as Donald Appleyard, Robert Venturi and Denise Scott Brown).[40]

It is hard to trace the exact lineage of concepts and ideas – all the more since very little on *Landscape* and its network of contributors is left in Jackson's archive. However, judging by the many appraisal letters printed in the 10th anniversary issue from academics and practitioners in different fields (such as Ansel Adams, Louis Kahn, David Lowenthal, Ian Mc Harg, Lewis Mumford, Carl Sauer etc.) Jackson and *Landscape* were quite influential and capable of putting on the agenda a field of investigation, a mode of analysis, design and reflection in the theme of "urban landscape" for the decade to come. In this sense, the cover of the 10th anniversary issue can be considered as a kind of visual program statement **| FIG. 8 |**. Apart from the names of all who praised the journal, it consisted of a composition of text and images. The text bands – white letters on a black background, exactly as used in the interior pages of the issue – indicated the different types of landscapes and themes that are discussed in the journal ("the designed landscape", "the city landscape", "the architectural landscape", "the rural landscape", "geographer's landscape", "gardens", "landscape and dwelling"), while the images provided a selection of illustrations.

The cover not only represents the content of the 10th anniversary issue, it also reframes images and text to give them a new meaning, and to construct a visual argument on what *Landscape* is about. The cover constructs a categorization of the different types of landscapes *Landscape* deals with, but at the same time it creates a deliberate confusion between these categories: "The City Landscape" is placed below the images of Durango, but closer to the images of the Oklahoma grain elevator; "Geographer's Landscape" in between the Durango town square, a truck with oil pipeline and an aerial photo; "Landscape and Dwelling" above a hydroelectric dam. Jackson shows a landscape that essentially "humanized", as he writes in the introduction

29
Kevin Lynch and Malcolm Rivkin, "A walk around the block", *Landscape*, 8/3, spring 1959, p. 24–33.

30
Tridib Banerjee and Michael Southworth (eds.), *City Sense and City Design. Writings and Projects of Kevin Lynch*, The MIT Press, Cambridge, MA, 1995, p. 99.

31
Grady Clay, "Remembered Landscapes", *Landscape*, 7/2, winter 1957–1958, p. 7–10.

32
Although the picture credits mention the origins of most of the images in *Landscape*, it is not always clear whether Jackson or the authors chose the images.

33
Kevin Lynch and Malcolm Rivkin, 1959, *op. cit.*, p. 24.

34
Beatriz Colomina (ed.), *Clip, stamp, fold: the radical architecture of little magazines, 196X to 197X*, Actar, Barcelona, London, 2010, p. 8.

35
Andrew Shanken, "Plot Lines: A Story about Edmund Bacon", *OASE*, 98, 2017.

36
Philip Langley, "Urban Sequence", *Landscape* 10/1, fall 1960, p. 46–47.

37
Philip Langley, 1960, *op. cit.*, p. 46.

38
Philip Langley, 1960, *op. cit.*, p. 47.

39
Arthur H. Doerr and John W. Morris, "Oklahoma Panhandle", *Landscape*, 10/1, fall 1960, p. 32–35.

40
See, for example, Donald Appleyard, Kevin Lynch and John Meyer's, *The View From the Road* (1964), translating the phenomenological approach from the pedestrian in the city to the automobile in the road landscape, as well as the 'inventorization' of the landscape by Ed Ruscha in amongst others *Twentysix Gasoline Stations* (1963) and *Every building on the Sunset Strip* (1966) – or, later on, the work on industrial installations by Bernd and Hilla Becher and the American photographers of the "New Topographics" exhibition of 1975, and Robert Venturi, Denise Scott Brown and Steve Izenour's *Learning from Las Vegas* of 1972.

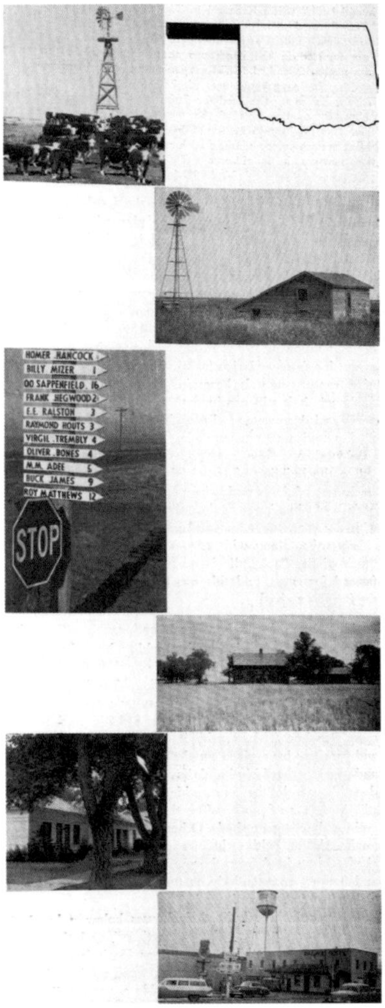

| FIG. 6 |

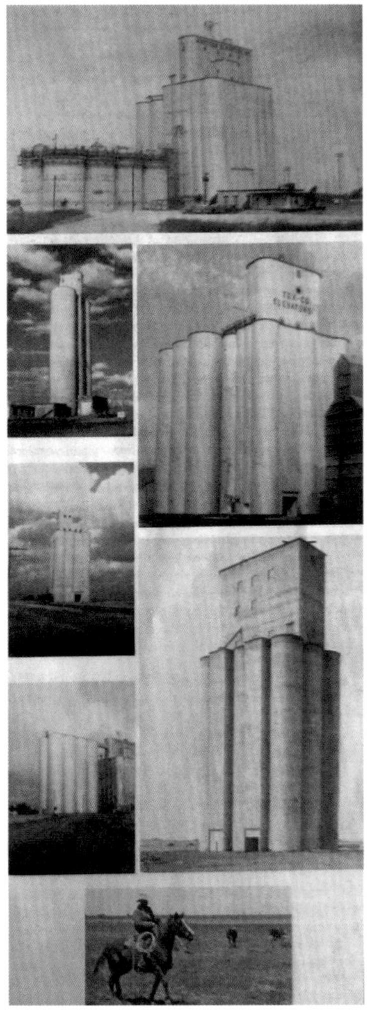

| FIG. 7 |

| FIG. 6 |

Arthur H. Doerr & John W. Morris, "Oklahoma Panhandle". Record of a road trip in a series of images. *Landscape* 10/1, fall 1960.

| FIG. 7 |

Arthur H. Doerr & John W. Morris, "Oklahoma Panhandle". Series of grain elevators (and one cowboy). *Landscape* 10/1, fall 1960.

| FIG. 8 |

Cover of tenth anniversary issue. *Landscape* 10/1, fall 1960.

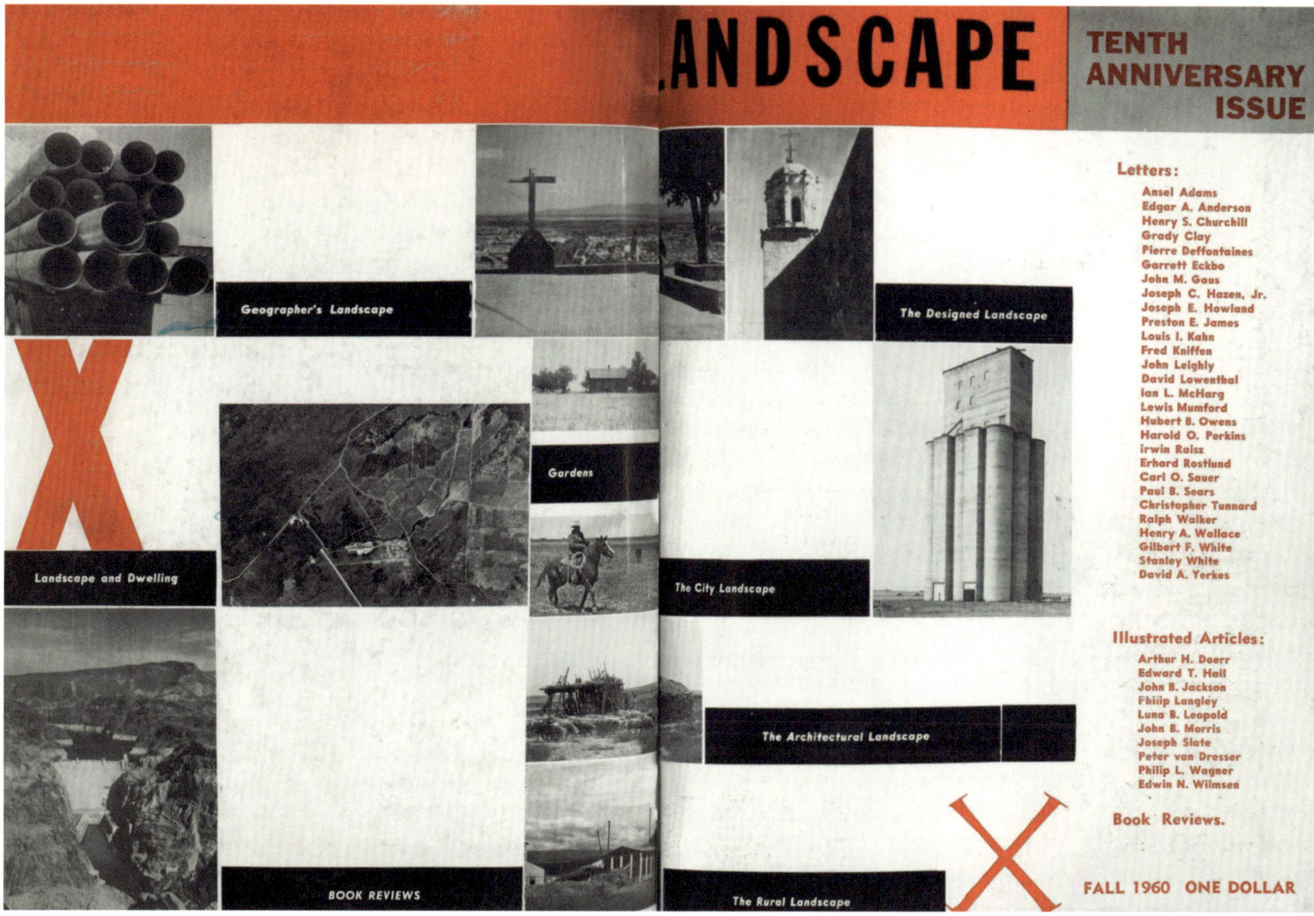
LANDSCAPE
TENTH ANNIVERSARY ISSUE
Geographer's Landscape
The Designed Landscape
Gardens
Landscape and Dwelling
The City Landscape
The Architectural Landscape
BOOK REVIEWS
The Rural Landscape
Letters:
Ansel Adams
Edgar A. Anderson
Henry S. Churchill
Grady Clay
Pierre Deffontaines
Garrett Eckbo
John M. Gaus
Joseph C. Hazen, Jr.
Joseph E. Howland
Preston E. James
Louis I. Kahn
Fred Kniffen
John Leighly
David Lowenthal
Ian L. McHarg
Lewis Mumford
Hubert B. Owens
Harold O. Perkins
Irwin Raisz
Erhard Rostlund
Carl O. Sauer
Paul B. Sears
Christopher Tunnard
Ralph Walker
Henry A. Wallace
Gilbert F. White
Stanley White
David A. Yerkes
Illustrated Articles:
Arthur H. Doerr
Edward T. Hall
John B. Jackson
Philip Langley
Luna B. Leopold
John B. Morris
Joseph Slate
Peter van Dresser
Philip L. Wagner
Edwin N. Wilmsen
Book Reviews.
FALL 1960 ONE DOLLAR

| FIG. 8 |

of the issue, but also a landscape in which the categories between what is urban, rural or industrial become blurred: the silo is as much a landmark as the church tower.[41]

UGLINESS, ORDER AND SOCIOPOLITICS

The introduction of a new type of aesthetics of roadside landscapes, as well as his preoccupation with a vernacular landscape that is open for multiple readings, sets Jackson somehow apart from some of the contributors to *Landscape*. Especially the discussion on ugliness and disorder is quite present in the magazine in the 1960s, and it allows Jackson's position to sharpen vis-à-vis contemporaries as Cullen and Lynch. In the introduction to the fall issue of 1962, an editorial entitled "The Hazards of Uglitudinizing", he reacts to the proliferation of books and articles in both the popular and the professional press on the decline of the post-war American landscape, all revolving around a single term: "ugly; ugliness, uglification and (ugliest derivative of all) de-uglification".[42] The term, Jackson states, is undoubtedly imported from England and he explicitly blames the *Architectural Review's* "crusade" against the desecration of England, in its special issues *Outrage* (1955) and *Counter Attack* (1956), in which Gordon Cullen and his colleagues developed the idea of visual planning.[43]

Rather than "prettifiying" the landscape and aiming for a "the preservation of beauty", Jackson argued, we should strive for "the preservation of life". Jackson points at the "surrogate" use of the term which is "nothing but a euphemism" that allows us to avoid talking about "poverty, disease, greed, laziness, corruption" and "polluted air and water, fire traps, dust bowls, poorly designed expressways, uncontrolled advertising, slums". "The aesthetic judgement is the easiest one", he continues, and what we need instead of "freezing" the landscape is "not an imposed or a carefully tended beauty, but cities and coutrysides which are healthy and self supporting and optimistic."[44] In many of his texts in *Landscape* in the course of the 1960s Jackson criticized nature preservation organizations, such as the Sierra Club, which gained widespread popularity in times of rising environmental awareness, denouncing them as being part of an elitist establishment that tended to reduce societal questions to aesthetic ones.

A prominent example is his polemic with the Garden Club in 1965–1966 about a speech of President Johnson, claiming that "beauty-destroying junkyards" were damaging the outlook of urban open spaces.[45] Johnson, and especially his wife Lady Bird Johnson, were supporters of the famous Highway Beautification act of 1965, the kind of government intervention Jackson feared would result in nothing more than an embellishment operation, turning the cities in "Potemkin villages for the delight of passing tourists".[46] Jackson's aversion to an environmental policy that focused solely on embellishment operations and the establishment of nature reservations was anchored in his above-mentioned conviction that the human and the non-human world were inextricably intertwined, and that nature was not a separate realm from the urban, the social and the political, claims that have in recent decades again come to the fore in disciplines such as urban political ecology.[47]

In an equally didactic and ingenious way, Jackson uncovered the core of an essential American dilemma by a comparison of the "anti-urbanist" attitudes of Thomas Jefferson and Henry David Thoreau in his essay "Jefferson, Thoreau & After" in the winter 1965–1966 issue.[48] In Jefferson's model of a rural society, Jackson argues that, the "natural" has little to do with wilderness – a natural man was inevitably a social or, more precisely, a political creature. To Thoreau, on the other hand, the essential distinction between town and country/wilderness, was that between society and nature, a distinction that was rooted in a Romantic conception of landscape that was "fragmented, highly self-conscious, and from the beginning identified with an urban middle-class point of view."[49]

Jackson thus grounded discussions on ugliness and culture/nature relationships in a sociopolitical discourse, instead of treating them solely as a question of aesthetics. As Pierre Bourdieu argued at the end of the 1970s, taste is a category that is inextricably linked with social mobility, in the sense of social emancipation or social distinction.[50] Many texts and images in *Landscape* can be read against the backdrop of this discussion on taste, linked to the concept of "good conduct".[51]

A good example of such a polemic can be found in an article entitled "The Drive for Beauty and the Popular Taste" in the fall 1965 issue. Douglas Haskell – former editor of *Architectural Forum* – reacts to Peter Blake's *God's Own Junkyard*. Blake's book had appeared a year earlier as a virulent plea against the deterioration of the American landscape by, among others, junkyards and roadside landscapes and was largely based on a visual discourse of confronting photos of "good" and "bad" landscapes.[52] Similarly to the way in which Venturi, Scott Brown and Izenour would use imagery in *Learning from Las Vegas*, Haskell reversed the argument of Blake. Venturi & Co. turned in their book the image of the duck-shaped building – for Blake an example of bad taste – into a new paradigm: the building as a symbol.[53] Haskell also pleaded for a positive appreciation of popu-lar taste: the images of a junkyard, a billboard-filled streetscape and a gas station – similar to those in *God's Own Junkyard* – acted as an antidote to the "snobbery" and "scorn" of the "politically guided drive for beauty".[54]

41 A similar act of "categorizing", and naming and renaming the landscape would also take place in Jackson's image archive.

42 John Brinckerhoff Jackson, "The Hasards of Uglitudinizing", *Landscape*, 12/1, fall 1962, p. 1–2, here p. 2.

43 Frédéric Pousin, *op. cit.*, 2003, p. 162.

44 John Brinckerhoff Jackson, 1962, *op. cit.*

45 John Brinckerhoff Jackson, "Message on Natural Beauty", *Landscape*, 14/3, spring 1965, p. 1.

46 John Brinckerhoff Jackson, *ibid.* On the "beautification" campaigns of President Johnson and his wife: Christoph Mauch and Thomas Zeller, *The world beyond the windshield. Roads and landscapes in the United States and Europe*, Ohio University Press, Athens, OH, 2008.

47 See Heynen, Kaika and Swyngedouw, 2006.

48 John Brinckerhoff Jackson, "Jefferson, Thoreau & After", *Landscape*, 15/2, winter 1965–1966, p. 25–26.

49 *Ibid.* p. 26.

50 Pierre Bourdieu, *La Distinction. Critique sociale du jugement*, Minuit, Paris, 1979.

51 The role of social formation by means of producing and consuming landscape images, as well as the way of exploring the actual, physical landscape has been explored in the literature on social identity and nation-building. See, for example, Denis E. Cosgrove, (orig. 1980), *Social formation and symbolic landscape*, University of Wisconsin Press, Madison, WI, 1998; David Matless, *Landscape and Englishness*, Reaktion Books, London, 1998.

52 Peter Blake, *God's own junkyard: the planned deterioration of America's landscape*, Holt, Rinehart & Winston, New York, NY, 1964.

53 Robert Venturi, Denise Scott Brown and Steven Izenour, *Learning from Las Vegas*, The MIT Press, Cambridge, MA, 1972. See also Aron Vinegar and Michael J. Golec (eds.), *Relearning from Las Vegas*, University of Minnesota Press, Minneapolis, MN, London, 2009.

54 Douglas Haskell, "The Drive for Beauty and the Popular Taste", *Landscape*, 15/1, fall 1965, p. 2–5. The argument for the appreciation of the junkyard is threefold: first, aesthetic – referring to the aesthetics of pop art: "the one kind of place where a Campbell's soup can look really good and almost like a part of nature", secondly, environmental "the junkyard gives physical materials resurrection as well as decent burial" and thirdly, socio- economical: "It is impractical to put the responsibility upon the consumer, for obviously the last consumer of used goods is the poorest one."

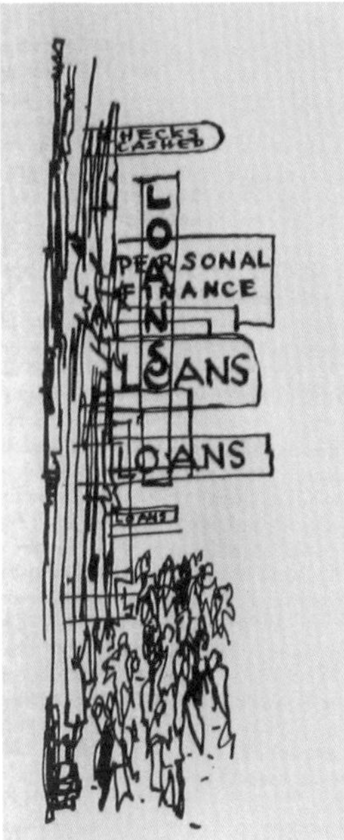

| FIG. 11 |

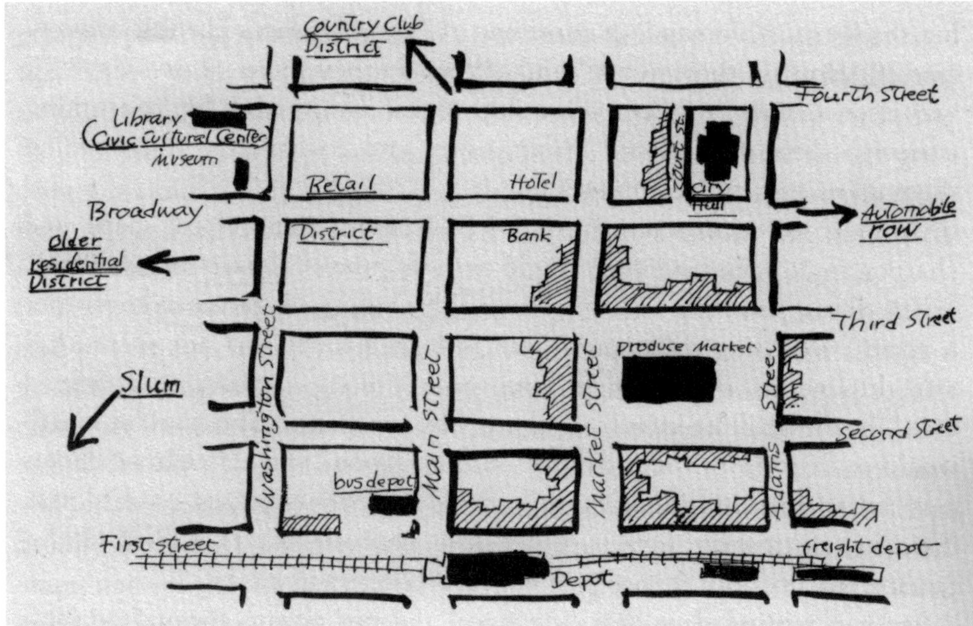

| FIG. 10 |

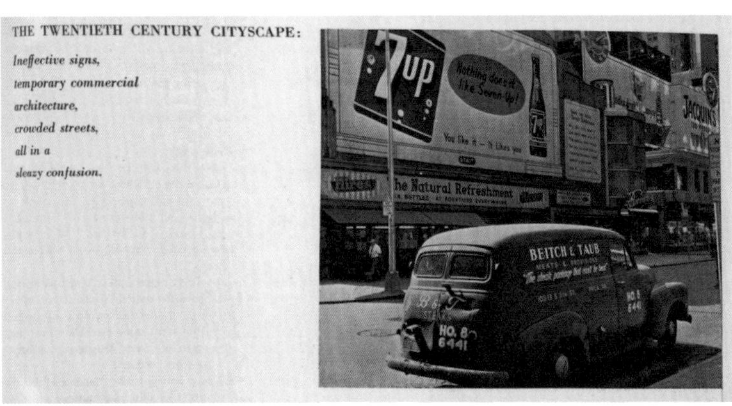
THE TWENTIETH CENTURY CITYSCAPE:

Ineffective signs, temporary commercial architecture, crowded streets, all in a sleazy confusion.

| FIG. 9 |

| FIG. 9 |
John Maass, "Images and Letters". *Landscape* 8/2, winter 1958–1959.

| FIG. 10 |
J. B. Jackson, "The Stranger's Path". *Landscape* 7/1, fall 1957.

| FIG. 11 |
J. B. Jackson, "The Stranger's Path". *Landscape* 7/1, fall 1957.

ORDER, LEGIBILITY AND AMBIGUITY

Haskell's conception of the junkyard – and that of many authors who wrote in *Landscape* about vernacular (roadside) landscapes, including Jackson himself – however surpassed the stage of mere acceptance and fascination, supported by sociopolitical arguments, and tried to decipher the possibilities of a new architectural and visual language: Haskell discerns in the "junking procedure" "its own kind of order" which can help to "achieve a new setting".[55] Order is the keyword in many of the articles on the visual aspects of the urban landscape, and it is interpreted in a variety of ways. In the "Urban Scene" issue for example, Jackson invites John Maass, the "Visual Presentation Director" of the city of Philadelphia to write an article on the use of images and letters in the city.[56] Maass equates visual pollution with the lack of *legibility*: the problem of the proliferation of signs, symbols and letters is not a problem as such, however the chaos it provokes is, as it leads to "crazy clutter" and "sleazy confusion" in comparison with the "bold craftmanship"' of 19th-century signage | FIG. 9 |.

The "need for order" in connection with legibility was also, as I already mentioned, a central concern in Lynch and Rivkin's "A walk around the block" The authors' search for – spatial as well as social – mechanisms of ordering the city can be read as a normative lens: in their drawings they not only effaced parts of the streetscape in order to illuminate orientation points and omit distracting information, they also seem to prefer some parts of the city over others – a critique that will later be formulated on Lynch's work in general. While a certain degree of chaos is tolerable for Lynch and Rivkin in for example a shopping district, where "intensive use and association have satisfactorily overcome physical confusion, there is 'no satisfaction in the fringe' of that shopping district", only leading to "discomfort".[57] Moreover, the quest for visual/spatial legibility and order dominates the social considerations of the text. Although Lynch and Rivkin expose the normative middle-class conceptions of some of their subjects as they walk into a back alley – "Do we have to walk down here? There is no place to walk. Oh, this is awful ... if they did have a fire people would come down here and land on the garbage and they'd be killed for sure ..."[58] – the concern is more about "good city form" than about a "just city".[59]

In contrast to Lynch's analysis, Jackson's seminal text "The Stranger's Path" published two years before, shows a much more ambiguous position towards the need of a visual order of the urban landscape, and it exemplifies Jackson's position standing midway between the idea of clarity and legibility on the one hand, and fascination for disorder and the bodily experience of a proliferation of sensory stimuli on the other. In Jackson's essayistic text, the "subject" is "the stranger" – both referring to Jackson himself as a traveler/storyteller and to "the outsider, the transient, not only (the) tourist, (...) not very prosperous, often with no money at all."[60] The article is illustrated with two images. The first one is a map which evokes a city that is legible as it reveals a certain inherent configuration that is proper to any American city, an order that is discovered by Jackson in an inductive manner, based on Jackson's observations of many American cities during his travels[61] | FIG. 10 |. The second drawing visualizes his fascination with the chaos of publicity, heraldry and neon lights found along the Stranger's Path, in the "seedy" part of town | FIG. 11 |, which is also evoked in the text:

> *The Path bursts into a luxuriance of colored and lighted signs: Chiliburgers. Red Hots. Unborn Calf Oxfords: They're new! They're smart! They're Ivy! Double Feature: Bride Of The Gorilla-Monster From Outer Space. Gospel Evangelical Mission. Checks Cashed. Snooker Parlor. The Best ShineIn Town! Dr. Logan and His Amazing Europathic Method. Coney Islands. Fortune Told; Madame LaFay.*[62]

55 Douglas Haskell, 1965, *op. cit.*, p. 5.

56 John Maass, "Images and letters", *Landscape*, 8/2, winter 1958–1959, p. 1–5.

57 Kevin Lynch and Malcolm Rivkin, 1959, *op. cit.*, p. 28.

58 *Idem*, p. 29.

59 I borrow the terms "feel good city" and "just city" from a lecture by Margaret Crawford on Jane Jacobs' *The death and life of Great American Cities* (1961), in which she observes that the street life she observes in the village consists of exclusively white, working-class Irish and Italians, but no black people. See Margaret Crawford, "From the Feel good City to the Just City", lecture at USC Bedrosian Center, October 2, 2015.

60 John Brinckerhoff Jackson, "The Stranger's Path", *Landscape*, 7/1, fall 1957, p. 12.

61 Bruno Notteboom, *The Westward-Moving House and other stories. J. B. Jackson reading and writing the landscape*, *op. cit.*; Jordi Ballesta, "John Brinckerhoff Jackson, au sein des paysages ordinaires. Recherches de terrain et pratiques photographiques amateurs", *L'Espace géographique*, 45/3, 2016, p. 211–224.

62 John Brinckerhoff Jackson, *op. cit.*, 1957, p. 12.

The same kind of image that a year later in the John Maass article in the "Urban Scene" issue would be commented as "crazy clutter", and the visual overload that in Lynch and Rivkin's sketches was wiped away in order to create an unambiguously legible urban landscape, was staged by Jackson as an essential element of the American urban landscape and in his critique of modern urban planning and planners' attempts to clean up the urban landscape, the spatial and the social argument were inextricably intertwined: "their emphasis on convenience, cleanliness, and safety, their distrust of everything vulgar and small and poor is symptomatic of a very lopsided view of urban culture."[63]

Throughout the 1950s and 1960s and especially by the end of the 1960s, the tone in *Landscape* became more outspokenly political. In two virulent texts in the fall 1967 issue, "Non-Environment" and "To Pity the Plumage and to forget the Dying Bird", situated against the backdrop of the riots and racial tensions in many U.S. cities, Jackson states that "before we set out to redesign the slums", we should realize that it is actually economic poverty and political inertia, that the problems that should be addressed, instead of beautification.[64] Jackson's indignation came to the fore in a period in which the discipline of architecture and urban planning became more "scientific", and in a way more apolitical.

At the end of the 1960s the rise of the notion of "environmental" design was an equal source of criticism for Jackson as the lack of societal concern of policy makers and designers: he did not feel at home in the rising interest in computers and systems theory, and its belief in a possibility of designing an environment generated by data and feedback loops, even if it trickled through to the pages of *Landscape*.[65] In "Pretentions and Delusions" in the spring 1967 issue, Jackson warned that the tense expectations of behavioral sciences and the idea that psychological and sociological information can be processed in statistical data in order to make a better world. Although by then far less outspoken on a sociopolitical level than Jackson, Lynch was invoked as a good example of urban analysis for its empirical quality and the "alert, unbiased, informal observation of what actually happens around us" that contributed "far more to our knowledge on the urban scene than the many more scientific studies being publicized."[66]

AGAINST HEGEMONY

In the winter 1969 issue, Jackson writes his last editorial as a kind of postscript. In the editorial, he looks back on his years as an editor and describes his work as an attempt to judge landscape in terms other than ecological or aesthetic ones. His approach was "explorative and speculative", he adds, an approach that did not fit the "boom" of environmental studies in the late 1970s. As an editor of *Landscape*, Jackson brought together multiple voices, through which he constructed a counterdiscourse and, to a certain extent, a "countervisuality", in Nicholas Mirzoeff's term,[67] which opposed a hegemonic approach to landscape. This counterdiscourse allowed him to formulate a critique of several evolutions that occurred during the 1950s: the alienating effects and lack of site-specificity of modern planning and architecture; the "elitist" quest for beauty and, by the end of his editorship; the "scientific" take on environmental design.

Jackson's goal was pedagogical, but it was a pedagogy that left room for multiplicity, experience and ambiguity. Combining a synthetic gaze with immersive experience, in text as well as image, Jackson drew a line from pre-Second World War French human geography to the experiential and sensory approach of the urban landscape in the work of American architects and urban planners of the 1960s, assisted by insights and methods from a large array of disciplines such as biology, anthropology and sociology. These alternating viewpoints also characterized Jackson's eclectic education and his position in the academic world, being at once an insider and an outsider. As the editor of his own magazine,

Jackson constructed a discourse through the words and images of others, but his own voice was actually the most dissident one in many discussions on urban landscape, textually as well as visually. As his archives give very little clues to Jackson's work process many questions however remain open on how he exactly worked as an editor, and what his relationship with the authors was in terms of content and image choice.

I have argued that Jackson at once supported and undermined the quest for order and legibility that was at the heart of any discussion of the urban landscape. Jackson's work was in a sense closer to that of Venturi and Scott Brown's work from the 1970s, than it was to that of contemporaries as Lynch. Upon her discovery of "Other-Directed Houses" (winter 1956–1957), one of the first text to summon designers not to turn away from the highway landscape, Denise Scott Brown wrote a letter to Jackson, saying "years before we wrote, you wrote and you wrote better".[68] Although Venturi and Scott Brown approached the sociopolitical aspect of the urban landscape differently[69] and they flirted with systems theory, their acceptance of the vernacular landscape in all its aspects is thoroughly "Jacksonian" and they would take the visual expression of the complexity and the contradictory nature of the contemporary urban landscape to the next level in the 1970s and 1980s.

However, Jackson had already introduced the idea of "urban semantics"[70] in a more modest way in the layout concept of the magazine itself, by developing a whole set of dingbats that acted as an aid to orientation in the magazine, while creating a proliferation of signs the meaning of which is often ambiguous.[71] Learning to read the landscape was for Jackson not a disciplinary action, following a strict method, but a way of opening the eyes of his audience in all its complexity. *Landscape*'s visual and textual discourse was not monolithic and hegemonic, but open to multiple interpretations, and it was up to the reader to find his or her own way.

63
Idem, p. 15.

64
John Brinckerhoff Jackson, "Non-environment", *Landscape* 17/1, fall 1967, p. 1, and John Brinckerhoff Jackson, 'To Pity the Plumage and to Forget the Dying Bird', *idem*, p. 1–4.

65
See, for example, Warren M. Brodey, "The Design of Intelligent Environments. Soft Architecture", *Landscape*, 17/1, fall 1967, p. 8–12. On the evolution of Edmund Bacon towards a systems approach. See Andrew Shanken, *op. cit.*, 2016.

66
John Brinckerhoff Jackson, "Pretensions and Delusions", *Landscape*, 17/2, winter 1967–1968, p. 2–3, here p. 3.

67
Nicholas Mirzoeff, *The Right to Look. A Counterhistory of Visuality, op. cit.*

68
Denise Scott Brown, "Learning from Brinck', in Chris Wilson and Paul Groth, 2003, *op. cit.*, p. 49–61.

69
This was a topic of a discussion with Kenneth Frampton in the early 1970s. See Aron Vinegar and Michael J. Golec, 2009, *op. cit.*, p. 36–38.

70
A term that was on the cover of the issue of winter 1966–1967.

71
For example, the pictogram of the house was used for articles that dealt with the subject of domestic culture, or the globe in the hand for pieces on environmental subjects, or the man and the globe when dealing with geography. This use of dingbats shows some similarities with *The Image of the City*, with its small drawings in the margins of the text. However, in Lynch's book these drawings are schemes that have a one-on-one relationship with the text, while in *Landscape* the meaning of these dingbats is much looser. Sometimes their meaning is not clear at all, or he uses the same dingbats for different kinds of subjects in two issues, resulting in a kind of proliferation of signs the meaning of which is often ambiguous, a theme that would be prominent in the work of Venturi and Scott Brown.

Seeing is Believing/ Looks are Deceiving

Photography in American Landscape Architecture Practice, 1950–2000

Laurie Olin

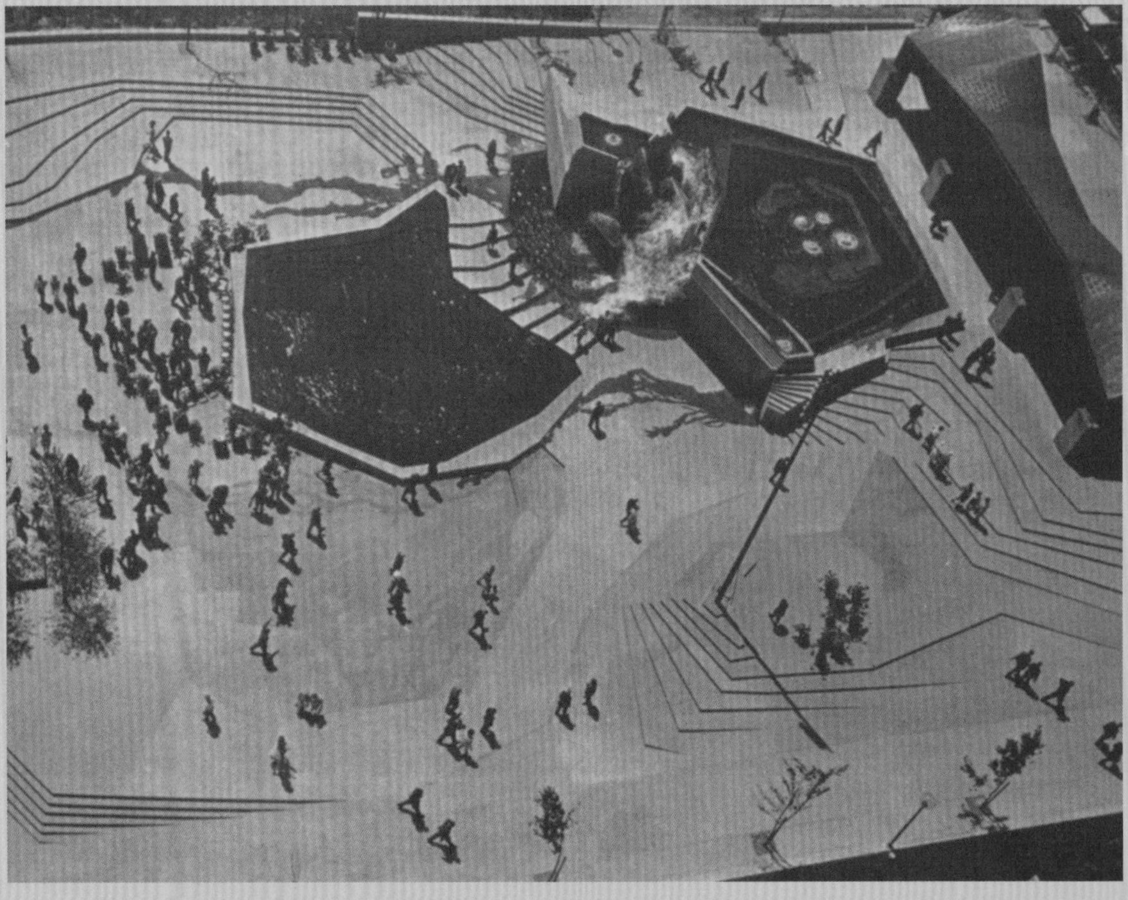

As with so much else with landscape architecture in America, the story of the use of photography begins with the Olmsted office, where such images were used extensively to document site conditions prior to and during the construction of numerous projects between the end of our Civil War and the 20th century. Small, handheld cameras became readily available for amateurs and professionals alike following the First World War. By the late 1930s cameras were widely in use throughout the western world for a variety of purposes and had been employed extensively by members of the Bauhaus in Germany, by Le Corbusier and others in France, and a number of modernists in Britain, most notably Christopher Tunnard. Interest in the use of photography by such Modernists was closely followed in America, and with the outbreak of the Second World War a diaspora of designers led to the arrival of prominent exponents of photography, a number of whom were welcomed into prominent university architecture design schools. Prominent examples included Walter Gropius, Ludwig Mies van der Rohe, László Moholy-Nagy, and Serge Chermayeff. Another of these figures, György Kepes, published an influential book, *Language of Vision*, in 1944[1] promoting the use of photography and cinema for design study and as a communication tool.

Christopher Tunnard, a British expatriate, brought to Harvard by its Dean Joseph Hudnut, filled a book he published in 1939, *Gardens in the Modern Landscape*,[2] now seen as a landmark in landscape design history and theory, with numerous photos of his own work, models of student planning projects, and images of gardens by his own contemporaries, such as Thomas Church in California. Earlier in September of 1937 one of his students, Garrett Eckbo, published photos of a set of townhouse garden studies in the architectural magazine *Pencil Points*.[3] After graduating from Harvard and beginning practice on the west coast, Eckbo and others adopted Tunnard's journalistic use of photos extensively in presenting the design projects of their California practices. Church, another Californian, and others had been publishing photographs of completed garden designs in professional and popular magazines such as *Architectural Forum*, *House Beautiful*, and *Sunset Magazine* from the late 1930s onward.

In 1950, five years after the end of the Second World War with his landscape practice flourishing, Eckbo published *Landscapes for Living*,[4] a book on garden design that offered advice regarding the nature of landscape design, employing ample photographic documentation using his own work depicting a new casual environment for post-war family life **| FIG. 1 |**.

Scooped by his younger rival, Thomas Church, who had become a highly influential landscape architect in the San Francisco Bay region and whose office nurtured a number of young designers that were to become prominent later – Robert Royston, Peter Walker and Richard Haag, among others – published his own book, *Gardens Are for People*,[5] five years later. Like Eckbo's earlier book, it was profusely illustrated with his own built designs, some of which, such as the Donnell garden pool and terrace in Sonoma, was to become truly iconic and highly influential, in large part because of these particular images. Studying pages from Church's book one can see how he used and reused portions of his projects, particularly the Donnell pool and cabana that he and a young employee, Lawrence Halprin, had recently built just north of San Francisco, to advertise his practice to a wide audience – offering design advice to new homeowners and prospective clients, while simultaneously influencing young designers across the country.

By the 1950s, in addition to professional journals such as *Architectural Forum*, *Architectural Record*, *Landscape Architecture* and *Progressive Architecture*, a wide variety of magazines appeared monthly and weekly across America featuring quantities of large photographs of the American and international scene: *Life; Look; Colliers; Arizona Highways; Holiday; National Geographic*. All employed high-quality imagery, often by professional photographers now considered legendary, with improved

1
György Kepes, *Language of vision*, P. Theobald, Chicago, 1944.

2
Christopher Tunnard, *Gardens in the Modern Landscape*, Michigan University, The Architectural Press, London, 1938.

3
Garrett Eckbo, "Small Gardens in the City", *Pencil Points*, September 1937, p. 573–586.

4
Garrett Eckbo, *Landscape for Living*, University of Massachussets Press, Amherst, MA, 1950.

5
Thomas Church, *Gardens Are For People*, Reinhold, New York, NY, 1955.

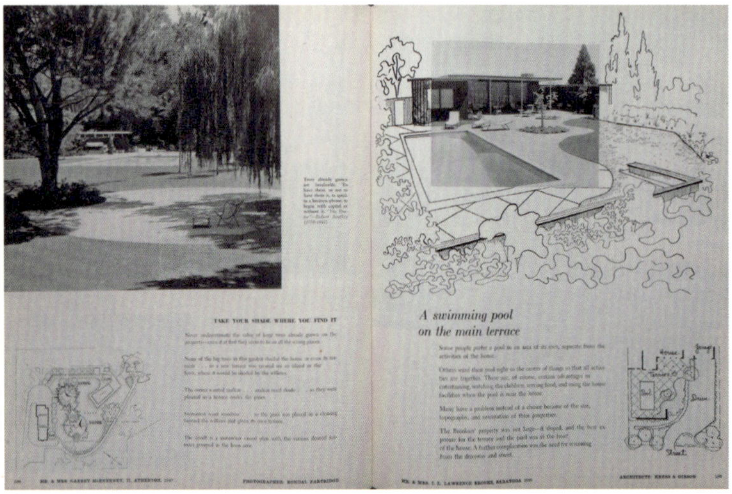
TAKE YOUR SHADE WHERE YOU FIND IT

A swimming pool on the main terrace

| FIG. 1 |

| FIG. 1 |
Garrett Eckbo, *Landscapes for Living*, University of Massachussets Press, 1950, p. 106–107.

| FIG. 2 |
35 mm SLR cameras, usually used for black and white and slides.

| FIG. 3 |
35 mm Kodak carousel slide projectors, frequently used by teachers and professionnals.

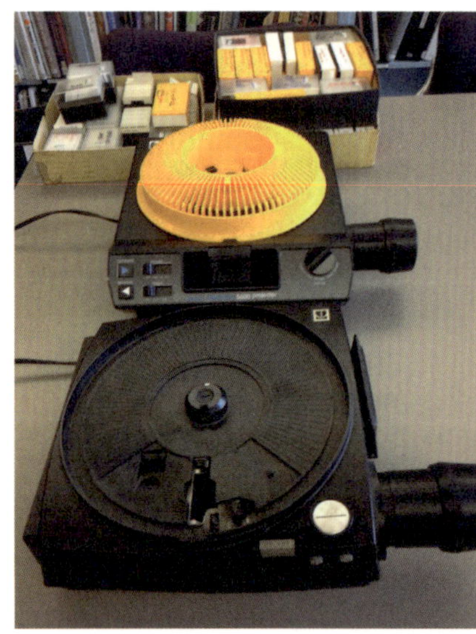

| FIG. 3 |

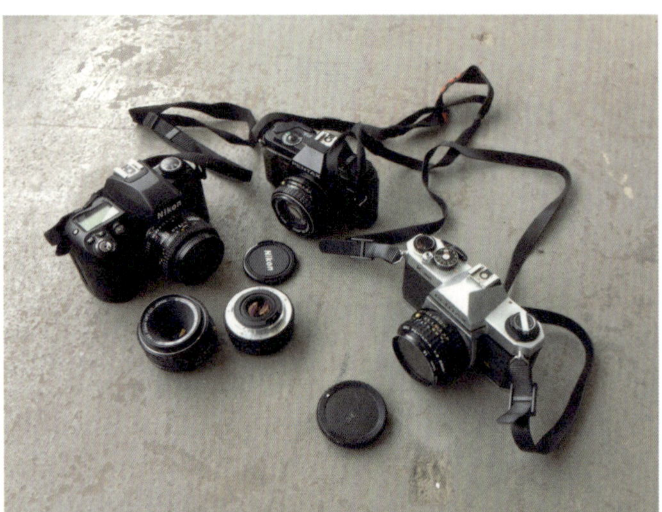

| FIG. 2 |

high-quality paper and printing, bringing edited and curated images of both the vernacular and designed world into homes and offices across the country on a regular basis. Museums began exhibiting photography as art. Journals regarding photography appeared for both professionals and amateurs, with the work of photographers such as Edward Weston and Ansel Adams setting high visual standards regarding landscape perception and an aesthetic regarding composition and views, which became pervasive and continues today in the art market. An original print of an image of Yosemite Valley from a now famous series taken by Ansel Adams in 1944 that was printed and published in 1958 was recently estimated by Christie's auction house to sell at a price between $25,000 and $30,000.

Throughout the post-war years Church and Eckbo exhibited photographs of their work in museum and professional exhibitions. In addition to appearing in popular journals such as *House Beautiful* and *Sunset*, photographs of their work were frequently published in *Arts & Architecture*, a magazine published on the west coast that was avidly read by leading architects and designers across the country. This publication was highly influential in part because of its innovative Case Study houses, a series of commissioned Modernist works that began in 1945, coinciding with the emergence of avant-garde landscape designs.

This work by a handful of professionals coincided with another phenomenon at the end of the Second World War. Several million American men returned from overseas to a new life and the subsequent prosperity of the Truman and Eisenhower era. Many brought cameras from Europe and Asia or of popular American manufacturers: Leica, Rolliflex, Kodak, Argus, Nikon, Pentax. These were light, handheld, relatively inexpensive and easy to use. Veterans attending college on the GI Bill who enrolled in architecture and landscape architecture programs brought skills they had acquired in the service along with experience and interests developed abroad. Throughout the 1950s, books on foreign design appeared in America. As early as 1943, G. E. Kidder Smith, who served in the Navy during the war as a photographic specialist, published his first book *Brazil Builds*[6] in conjunction with an exhibition at the Museum of Modern Art in New York, which along with the work of Roberto Burle Marx and Oscar Niemeyer caught the attention of west coast designers. After the war he continued to publish influential photographs in *Italy Builds: Its Modern Architecture & Native Inheritance* in 1956,[7] and *Sweden Builds* in 1957.[8] In 1955 Norman Carver, another Second World War veteran, published a remarkable collection of photographs taken while on a subsequent Fulbright Fellowship to Japan, entitled *Form and Space in Japanese Architecture*.[9] These books, with their presentation of attractive designs of landscape, architecture and urban design in photographic images, along with an invasion of professional design magazines that included *Domus, Casabella, Rassegna, L'Architecture d'Aujourd'hui, Architecture Review*, and *Japan Architect (JA)* – were studied assiduously by American architects, landscape architects, and their students through the 1950s, 1960s and early 1970s. Their influence and transmission of design ideas, form and content, was achieved more through their photographic images than the often skimpy texts and captions. Highly edited, selectively cropped for visual imagery and Modernist formal composition, and focused upon particular details and forms, these publications had a marked impact upon my generation and our design vocabulary, methods and aesthetic biases.

Relatively inexpensive and ubiquitous small, handheld cameras were taken up by nearly every person in architecture and landscape architecture during the next three decades **| FIG. 2 |**. 35 mm single lens reflex cameras – Nikon, Pentax, Olympus, Leica, Kodak models – 2×2 Rolliflexes, and the more expensive 4×4 Hasselblads were universally employed by professional offices and

6 Philip Lippincott Goodwin, G. E. Kidder Smith, *Brazil Builds: Architecture New and Old 1652–1942*, Museum of Modern Art, New York, NY, 1943.

7 G. E. Kidder Smith, *Italy Builds: Its Modern Architecture & Native Inheritance*, The Architectural Press, London, 1956.

8 G. E. Kidder Smith, *Sweden builds. Extensively revised, with 130 recent illustrations*, Reinhold Publishing Corporation, New York, NY, 1957.

9 Norman F. Carver, *Form and space of Japanese architecture*, Shokokusha, Tokyo, 1955.

practitioners across the country. Thousands upon thousands of black and white photographs and color transparencies were taken. Every successful office I know took them, used them, and stored them, in boxes, in folders, in sleeves, in binders and portfolios. Slide projectors became the principal means of delivering these images to clients and students. At first in the 1950s they were used singly, and then by the mid-1960s in pairs or even more (four simultaneously!) to project more and more images | **FIG. 3** |. Marshall McLuhan, famous for his remark, "The medium is the message", wrote and lectured about this development as part of a broader phenomenon in the period regarding the use of photographic imagery for persuasion (commonly for commerce) in contemporary society, most notably in *The Mechanical Bride: Folklore of Industrial Man*, 1951 and *Understanding Media: The Extensions of Man*, 1964.[10]

Each office developed its own methods of filing, a necessity with the proliferation of thousands of 35 mm slides. In my office, green folders were used for preexisting sites, the "before" images; blue was for design studies, drawings, models and presentations; orange was for construction photos, yellow was for "after", or completed work; and red folders were for the best slides, which also had prominent red dots on their mounts, and had been selected for use in lectures and presentations. There were light tables at the office for use in sorting, study, and working with slides and transparencies. Many practitioners and teachers also had light tables and slide storage at their homes and academic offices. Many university schools of design and architecture such as Harvard, the University of Pennsylvania, and the University of California at Berkeley often had slide and photographic collections as a part of their libraries. These images were used by professors teaching history and theory, but could be viewed and checked out like books by faculty and students alike.

The next step was the employment of 16 mm film with the development and marketing of light handheld devices, and eventually the use of video for field research, the documentation of sites intended for design projects, and for presentations to clients, public meetings and workshops. In addition to the wholesale adoption of film as a medium for recording and presentation, another direct result of wartime technology was the development of aerial reconnaissance and its migration into planning and design. Others have commented upon the use of photography by J. B. Jackson, an influential author, critic, editor and exponent of the appreciation and study of the American landscape. Jackson himself has written about his experiences in army intelligence during the Second World War, when he frequently worked with photography and was deeply involved in the interpretation of visual materials such as maps, plans and photographs. Aerial photographs were seen as being far superior to traditional maps because of the amount of detail information. After the war this technology became widely available for civilian use, and planners and designers found they could purchase aerial photographs from commercial firms and government agencies. They had a beguiling graphic quality that appealed to many designers. Luis Barragán, for example, prepared a plan study for the suburban development of El Pedregal near Mexico City over an air photo of the site, which he blew up and mounted, filling one of the walls of his office. Like Church and Eckbo – or prominent architects such as Saarinen, SOM, Aalto and Mies van der Rohe – Barragán's work became rapidly known around the world through a set of carefully edited black and white images that were widely published.

An international market for images of advanced design had been created. I purchased a bilingual issue of *Rassegna* devoted to Frank Lloyd Wright's Fallingwater residence, edited by Bruno Zevi and Edgar Kauffman Jr., consisting almost entirely of color photographs, in Seattle, Washington in 1962. The publication of beguiling and carefully composed images by a handful of gifted professional photographers such as Ezra Stoller and Julius Shulman of select works set standards for visual composition and design motifs throughout the post-war era. Examples of this are Stoller's photos of the Miller Residence in Columbus, Indiana, by Eero Saarinen and Dan Kiley, and a number of images of Richard Neutra's Kauffman residence in Palm Springs, which became a touchstone of modernity.

Handsome black and white photos by Alan Ward, a partner in the landscape architecture and planning firm Sasaki, of Kiley's design at the Miller residence | **FIG. 4** |, in their studied and loving presentation were in some ways the antithesis of J. B. Jackson's equally studied and loving presentation of the vernacular made at the same time. While ogling both – images of high style design and vernacular landscapes – my generation was also reading Jack Kerouac's *On the Road*, listening to folksongs from the Dust Bowl, and beginning to read Jackson's little magazine, *Landscape*, while looking at his versions of anonymous landscape across the country.

In 1964 Elizabeth Kassler curated an exhibition at the Museum of Modern Art in New York, *Modern Gardens and the Landscape*,[11] which had a catalogue by her consisting of photographs bestowing status and wide visibility to a series of now famous projects producing a canon of modern landscape design imagery: here can be found unforgettable photos of Asplund and Lewerentz's Forest Crematorium in Sweden; Barragán's horse trough in a eucalyptus grove at Las Pedregal in Mexico; Burle Marx's Copacabana beach promenade in Rio; and Ted Osmundson's landmark garden on the roof of the Kaiser Aluminum Co. headquarters in Oakland, California (notably an aerial view), among dozens of other sites. While these were photographs of real projects, the careful and highly scenographic presentation of a number of them conjured a dreamy utopian new landscape that beguiled and inspired a generation of students and practitioners. Opposite an image from Stockholm and a rare drawing of a design by Ian McHarg is one of many photographs of a model made during the collaboration between Louis Kahn and Isamu Noguchi for a playground in Riverside Park, New York, that gained wide circulation, admiration, envy and emulation. I do not know a designer of my generation who doesn't know the images from this book of Hideo Sasaki's pastoral masterpiece done in collaboration with Saarinen for the John Deer Company, while almost none of us have ever been to Moline, Illinois | **FIG. 5** |.

Landscape architect and educator Ian McHarg, the most famous promulgator of ecological planning and design, profusely employed photographs in his lectures and historic book, *Design with Nature* | **FIG. 6** |.[12] A veteran of the Second World War imbued with contemporary science and technology, he employed aerial photographs with a wide regional perspective throughout his career. Subsequently a generation of American students and professionals produced natural-factor maps for planning and design projects derived from their study of aerial photographs, which they

10
Herbert Marshall McLuhan: *The Mechanical Bride: Folklore of Industrial Man*, The Vanguard Press, New York, NY, 1951; *Understanding Media: The Extensions of Man*, McGraw-Hill, New York, NY, 1964.

11
Elizabeth Bauer Kassler, *Modern Gardens and the Landscape*, Museum of Modern Art, New York, NY, 1964.

12
Ian L. McHarg, *Design with nature*, American Museum of Natural History, The Natural History Press, Garden City, New York, NY, 1969.

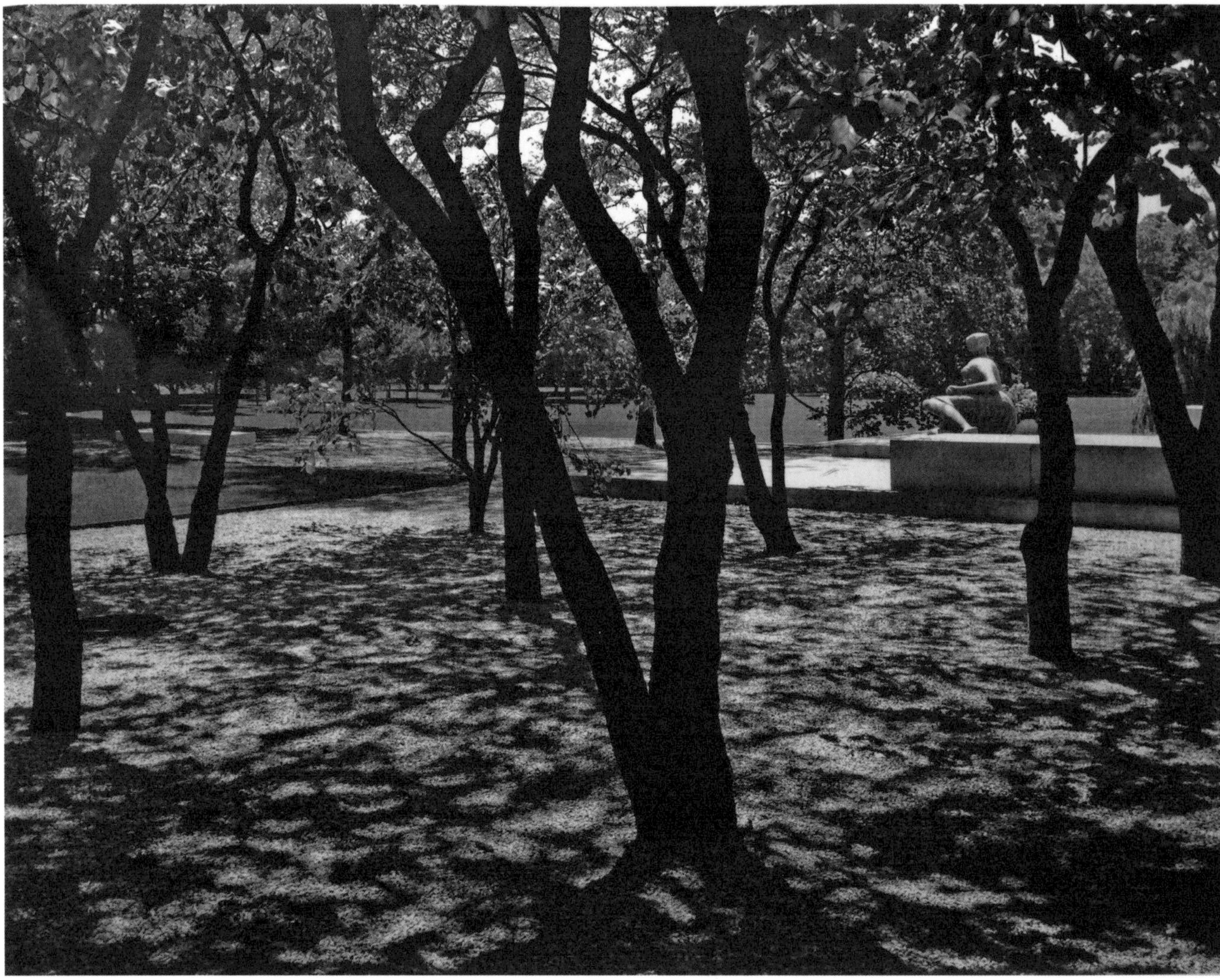

| FIG. 4 |

| FIG. 4 |
Alan Ward, Irwin Miller's residency, Columbus, Indiana; Daniel Urban Kiley, landscape architect, and Eero Saarinen, architect.

| FIG. 5 |
Ezra Stoller, John Deere Headquarters, Moline, Illinois; Hideo Sasaki, landscape architect and Eero Saarinen architect; published in Elizabeth Kassler, *Modern Gardens in the Landscape*, Museum of Modern Art, New York, 1964.

| FIG. 6 |
Ian McHarg, double page illustrated of *Design with Nature*, 1969.

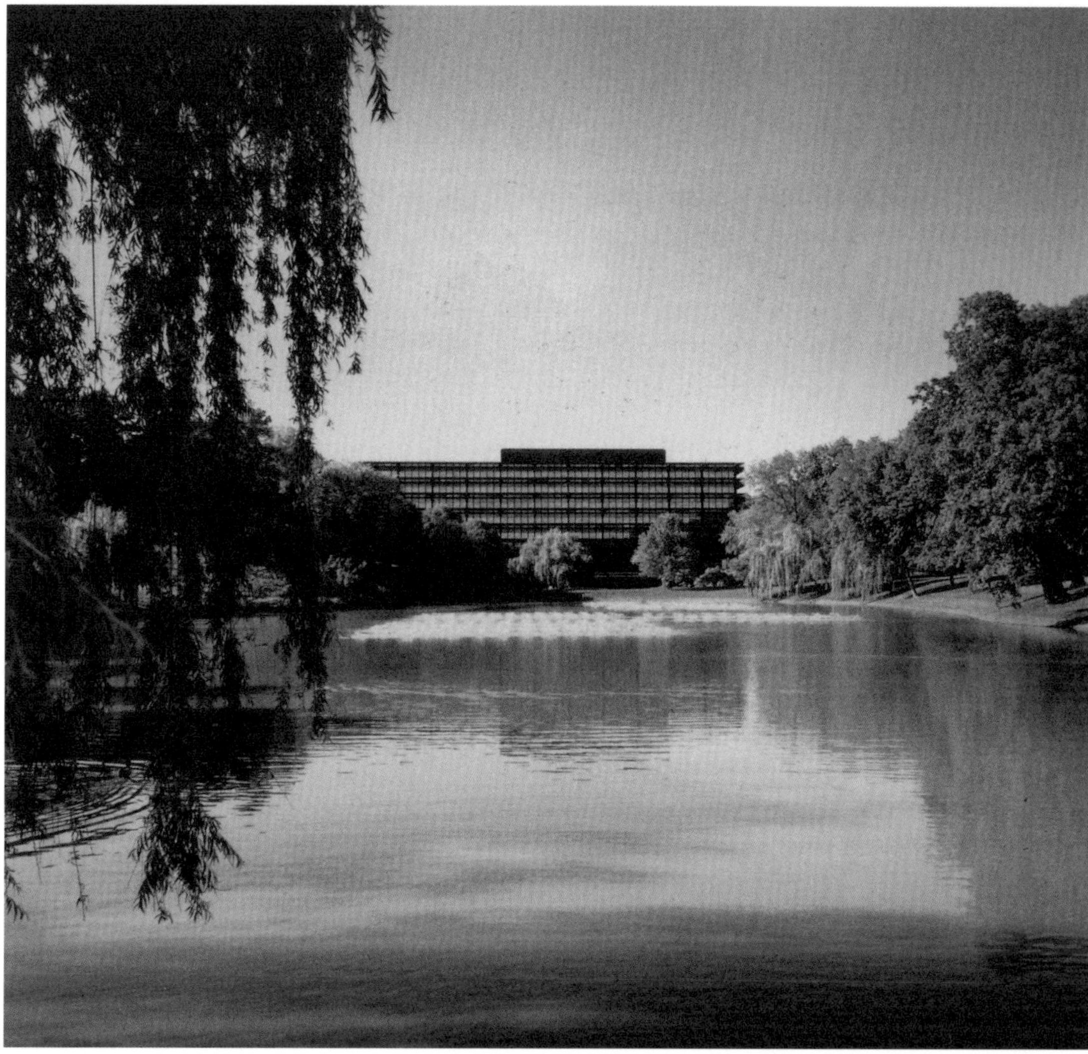

| FIG. 5 |

| FIG. 6 |

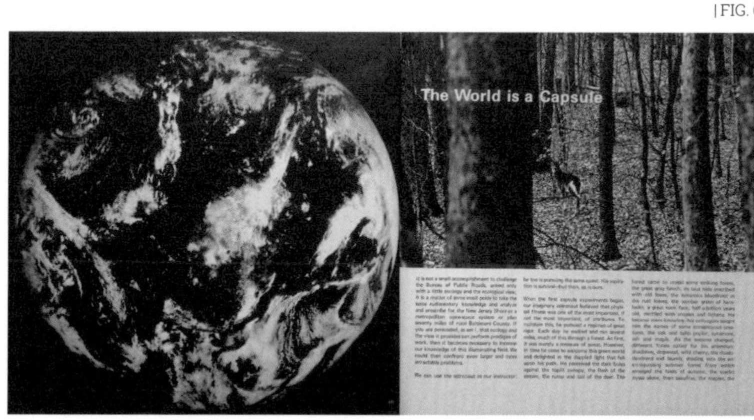

combined with topographic and geologic maps.

No longer exclusively reserved for the military, by the late 1960s stereo-pair photographs had come into relatively common use for those doing large-scale planning and design. Public agencies and private offices employed aerial photos heavily for resource planning, management of public land, and commercial development. *Terrain Analysis: A Guide to Site Selection Using Aerial Photographic Interpretation*,[13] a fundamental text for the field, was published in 1973 by Doug Way, who was on the faculty in the Graduate School of Design at Harvard in the early 1980s, prior to his becoming the chairman of the Department of Landscape Architecture at Ohio State University.

A cross-pollination of influences and fields occurred throughout the 1960s and 1970s. Photographs taken by sculptor Isamu Noguchi of an 18th century observatory in India were widely known in the profession, having been published in *Perspecta*[14] by Yale Architecture students, and subsequently included in an exhibition at the Walker Museum in Minneapolis[15] and published in a double edition of their *Design Quarterly*.

Noguchi's own sculpture and design work was particularly suited to architectural photography, in part because it tended to be composed of objects in bounded or coherent image-able situations, not of disparate ensembles in an extended field as is common with so much actual landscape.

No American landscape architect in the period between 1950 and 2000 better exemplifies the use of photography in his work than Lawrence Halprin and the several offices he created during his career. Like many of his contemporaries, a few years after returning to the states from military service in the Second World War and starting a practice, he took an extended and deeply influential trip to Europe, which he documented extensively in his publication of *Cities*[16] soon thereafter in 1963 with his own photographs. Intended in part to be an urban design primer for Americans it is a compendium of his encyclopedic survey of European public space, and a plethora of its diverse forms and elements presented in black and white photographs. Following the publication of *Cities*, Halprin produced *Freeways*,[17] 1966; *New York, New York*,[18] 1968; and *RSVP Cycles: Creative Processes in the Human Environment*,[19] 1970, the latter a survey at the time of his recent work, especially documenting a number of workshops he had developed as part of his working process. All these publications were filled with photographs, taken by him and others. Like Church and Eckbo earlier, he attempted to teach and proselytize while promoting himself through the publication of photographs of his work.

Throughout his career Halprin documented all of his work photographically, the extensive files of which reside in the Architectural archives at the University of Pennsylvania. There in box after box, one finds a photographic record of all of his projects carefully dated and labeled **| FIG. 7 |**. Not only did he take pictures of the final work, but he also carefully – one might even say obsessively – recorded his design process and key studies, drawings, models, mock-ups and sites through construction at every step photographically **| FIG. 8 |**. But then we all did. It was the definitive way to save and record things. Things such as models were not just recorded, but were *studied* through the lens. All of his famous projects: the Sea Ranch, the urban fountains, squares, and parks in Portland, Seattle, San Francisco, Denver, and elsewhere, along with his numerous commercial and residential projects. Looking through this extensive archive one finds examples of how his office used aerial photographs for instance to study the ridges and watersheds of an area near San José for a development, tracing directly over the photos, transferring information onto tracing paper overlays **| FIG. 9 |**.

Like those who use drawing as a means to see, which he also did admirably, Halprin used the camera well to help him isolate particular visions and to show them to others, as with the photos

13
Doug Way, *Terrain Analysis: A Guide to Site Selection Using Aerial Photographic Interpretation*, Dowden, Hutchinson & Ross, Stroudsburg, PA, 1973.

14
Perspecta, The Yale Architectural Journal, School of Art and Architecture at Yale University, no. 6, New Haven, CT, 1960.

15
Noguchi's imaginary landscapes, exhibition curated by Martin Friedman, held at the Walker Art Center, *Design Quarterly*, 106–107, Walker Art Center, Minneapolis, MN, 1978.

16
Lawrence Halprin, *Cities*, Reinhold, New York, NY, 1963.

17
Lawrence Halprin, *Freeways*, Reinhold, New York, NY, 1966.

18
Lawrence Halprin, *New York, New York: a study of the quality, character, and meaning of open space in urban design*, Department of Housing and Urban Development, Washington, DC, 1968.

19
Lawrence Halprin, *RSVP Cycles: Creative Processes in the Human Environment*, George Braziller, New York, NY, 1970.

| FIG. 7 |
Lawrence Halprin,
contact sheets and prints from black and white 35 mm movies from site visits.

| FIG. 8 |
Lawrence Halprin, photographs of the Seattle Freeway Park model.

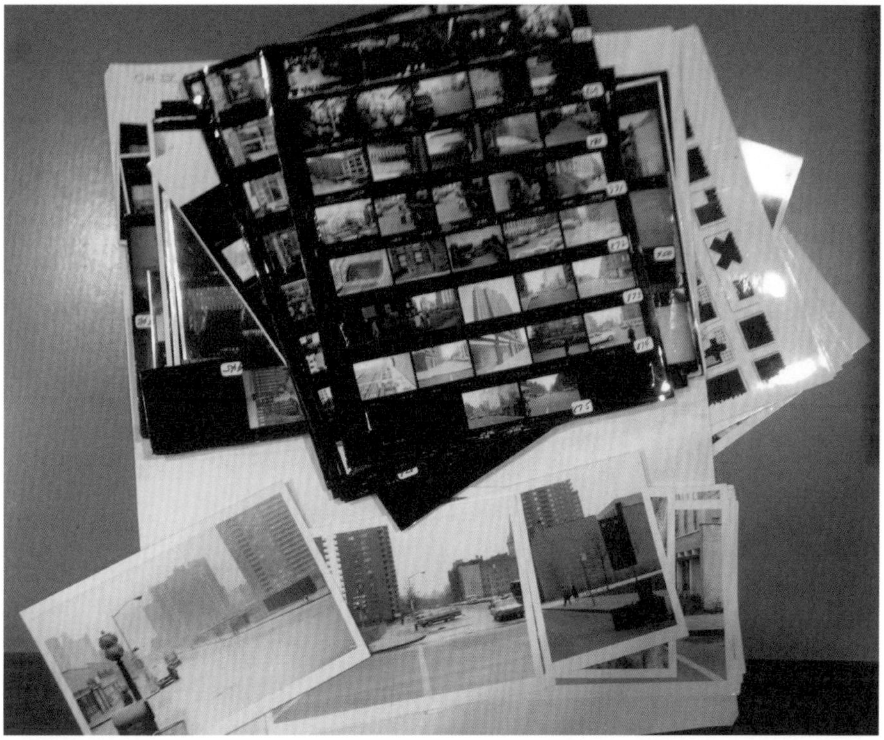

| FIG. 7 |

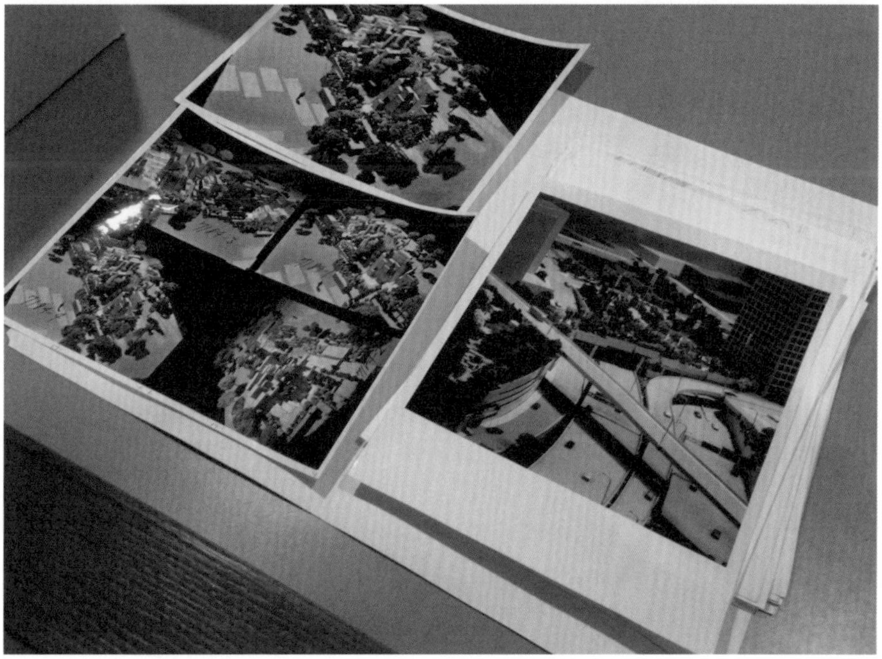

| FIG. 8 |

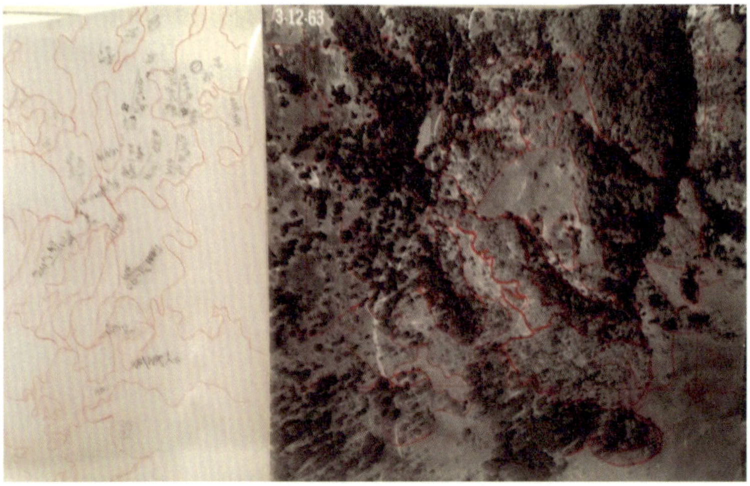

| FIG. 9 |

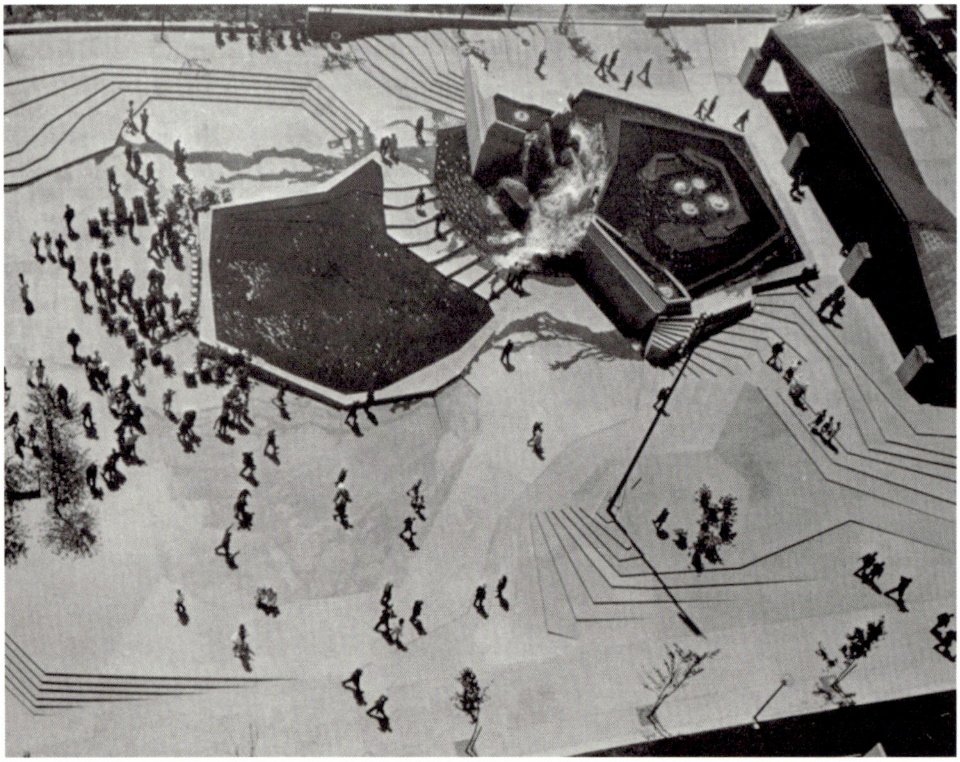

| FIG. 10 |

| FIG. 9 |
Lawrence Halprin,
aerial photography with tracing for a site analysis of a construction layout near San José, California.

| FIG. 10 |
Lawrence Halprin,
aerial photograph of Lovejoy Fountain, published in Elizabeth Kassler, *Modern Gardens and the Landscape*, Museum of Modern Art, New York, 1964.

of water and stone from the John Muir Trail in Yosemite that he published in an article in *Landscape* in 1961, "The Gardens of the High Sierra".[20] He admitted that these were a source of inspiration for him in the design of his fountains later in the 1960s and early 1970s in Portland, Seattle, Denver, Rochester and San Francisco **| FIG. 10 |**. The collection of his office photographs in the University of Pennsylvania Architectural Archive contains many boxes of photos of completed work intended for publication and publicity, many of which are stunning and dramatic images. Some such as those for Skyline Park that he built in Denver, Colorado, now form the historic record following its unfortunate demolition.

Since this era of landscape practice and photographic use the world has entered an age of digital information and records. Today we are deluged with a cascade of images and new methods of manipulation of photography and images. Another generation, raised on techniques developed by the previous one, frequently combines and incorporates the graphic inventions of the Bauhaus, Surrealism, film and advertising with the scientific apparatus of remote and analytic sensing in a cornucopia of new visualization. Professionals and students of landscape architecture around the world today employ photography in numerous ways, from working directly upon aerial surveys to having encyclopedic photographic collections of plants and other environmental elements and design through history at their fingertips.

In a recent student presentation from a University of Pennsylvania graduate studio involving the Navajo Reservation in New Mexico there were straightforward photographs of the site and others that had drawings inserted into them. A number of the students rendered perspectival drawings included photographic elements skillfully inserted into them. Typically today such Photoshop presentation renderings consist of images constructed almost entirely from a library of photo information and are done by young landscape architects in offices across the country today.

The second half of the 20th century was a period in which landscape architects employed photography extensively in a number of ways: to document sites prior to design as part of fact-finding exploration and recording; they used aerial photography as it evolved to improve mapping and planning for large site planning and design; it was used to study and present design models and drawings, and in presentations to clients; they recorded completed work to promote their personal careers and business practices and proselytize for the field in popular and professional journals as well as self-authored books. Photographs of landscape design became a subject for exhibitions, particularly since, like architecture, the work could not be brought from the field into galleries and museums – anticipating the phenomenon of later "site art". Also, it would appear that photographic images, especially as framed by 35 mm film, had a pronounced effect upon the education, imagination, conception, development, of a generation of landscape architects and the production of a significant portion of designed landscapes in America in the five decades between 1950 and 2000.

20
Lawrence Halprin, "The Gardens of the High Sierra", *Landscape*, winter 1961, p. 26–28.

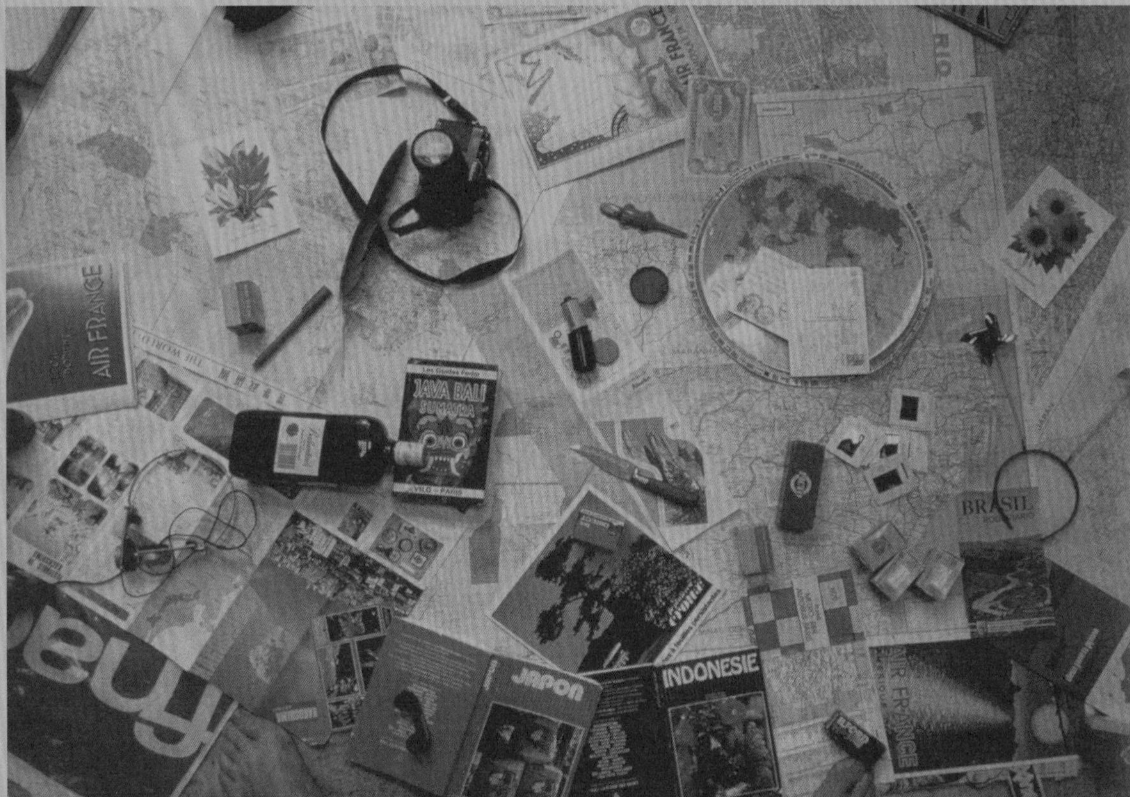

The Photographic Discourses of Gilles Clément

Frédéric Pousin

The gardener and landscape architect Gilles Clément is a well-known figure in France. He speaks readily of his work, his ideas, and the projects that embody them, about which much has already been written. His theoretical thinking is rich and complex, but at the same time very accessible. It has developed over time around now familiar notions such as the Garden in Movement, the Planetary Garden, or the Third Landscape (*le tiers paysage*).[1] Photography is a still relatively little-studied aspect of his work. And yet, even if it does not strictly amount to an *oeuvre* as such, it is a practice that irrigates his entire output, from garden and landscape projects through to publications, lectures and exhibitions.

If we were to try and define the status of photography in Gilles Clément's work, we might compare it to an amateur practice, insofar as he does not see himself as a professional photographer or as an *auteur*. Nor is he an operator acting within an institution that might decide to commission work or engage a photographic mission. His is a photography that emanates from a designer who adopts an artistic stance in his approach, but without laying claim to any artistic recognition. Clément is neither a photographic artist, nor a photographic technician: he comes to photography as a landscape designer. This explains why this original object, even if it belongs to the canonical category of "landscape photography", does not automatically hold our attention.[2] Besides, the term "amateur" is hardly a satisfactory description of this singular photographic practice, as the landscape designer is acting in a professional context, related to the projects he is commissioned to design and execute. From this angle, it could be described as a vernacular photography, inasmuch as it has a utilitarian dimension.[3]

For landscape architects, photography plays multiple roles. It is primarily a powerful communication tool for showcasing their work in professional publications and in the press. But it is also, as a representation, an instrument of the project. It has many different uses, as an observation or recording tool, or as a means of prefiguration, as the articles in this volume show. Photography enables landscape designers to formulate a discourse on their own practice, as well as a theoretical discourse on the landscape, based on the experience of their projects. It is therefore clearly an instrument of choice for transforming a project into an object, or even into an element of discourse.

Clément assigns great importance to photography. He has developed an intense practice of photography related to his travels. Photography is a powerful presence in his exhibitions, and thereby helps to shape the different discourses that they convey. But it is above all in his lectures that photography underpins the landscape designer's theoretical discourse. Lectures are a very particular channel for putting the practice of the project into words. They touch – in an original way, unlike any printed work – on the question of how words and images interact.[4] They are one of the places where thoughts are formalized that help to structure and sustain the practitioner's approach. Lectures also raise the question of the relationship with the audience, as do exhibitions, teaching and publication, which are the main vectors for the dissemination of the landscaping culture.

The photographs Clément takes are color slides, which often end up being projected. Projection is a primordial dimension in the discursivization of the project, which articulates the spoken word with the projected image. By studying the different forms of expression employed by Clément – while giving priority to the lecture,

1
See: www.gillesclement.com

2
Particularly within the framework of a history of photography that focuses on interactions with the artistic domain. The integration of photography into cultural institutions and its legitimation in the art market took place, in France, in the 1970s, with the acclamation of a new figure, that of the creative photographer, sought after for major public commissions from the 1980s to the present day. See Gaëlle Morel, *Le Photoreportage d'auteur. L'institution culturelle de la photographie en France depuis les années 1970*, CNRS Éditions, Paris, 2006. On public commissions, see Raphaële Bertho's article in this volume, p. 36.

3
For a definition of vernacular photography, see Clément Chéroux, "Introducing Werner Kühler. Prolégomènes personnalisés", in *Vernaculaires. Essais d'histoire de la photographie*, Le Point du Jour, Cherbourg, 2013, and "L'art de l'oxymore. Le style vernaculaire de Walker Evans," in *Walker Evans* (Clément Chéroux, ed.), Éditions du Centre Pompidou, Paris, 2017, p. 9–14.

4
On this topic, see Bruno Notteboom's article in this volume, p. 72.

which embodies something original and particularly accomplished – we can reveal something of the discursive uses of photography by landscape architects.

TRAVEL AND THE COLOR SLIDE

For Gilles Clément, photography is bound up with the exercise of perception, with a way of seeing, feeling, and talking about the landscape. Ever since buying a Nikon F, his first camera, while on national voluntary service in Nicaragua, he has kept images of the place where he lived for almost two years, as well as of a six-month voyage around South America.[5]

Consequently, his practice of photography continues to be linked to the experience of travel | **FIG. 1** | and to a comparative approach: "I still say today – it hasn't changed – that traveling is about knowing where you live once you get back. That's when you understand where you are; otherwise, you don't know. You don't need a camera for that, but it's better if you do have one, because you can produce proof of the comparison."[6]

Like drawing or writing, photography is, for the landscape architect, as much a means of exploration as a mode of expression.[7] In the novel he published in 1997, *Thomas et le voyageur*, the two protagonists devise a plan to represent the world by painting the Planetary Garden. Among the instruments serving this ambitious project is the camera: "I wanted it [the room where the image was produced] to be clear, reserved solely for the painting, but objects, books, various sources of information kept creeping in, coming on top of the pigments, the brushes, different maps of the world, and a whole panoply of photographic equipment, which is very new here. Sometimes I project images of distant horizons…".[8] Note that, in this excerpt, photography is associated with projection; it is very much slides that he has in mind.[9]

It was at a "slide evening" organized on his return to France – an obligatory cultural habitus of the time – that Clément became aware of the merits of classifying photos | **FIG. 2** |, a kind of overture to the cognitive act of juxtaposition and comparison:

> *When I came back I organized a sort of slide evening. Usually, they're deadly, but I had been asked to do it. I did it using themes, and that was where the classification of photos started. For example, I used means of transport: I showed how rivers were crossed in boats, how buses operated in Colombia, in a completely different way to Nicaragua, and so on. […] I had placed elements in comparison.*[10]

Though indissociable from travel, the slide also connotes a "middlebrow practice" of photography – to borrow Pierre Bourdieu's term[11] – that of the family cell: that symbol of mass consumption and the target of Kodak's marketing department. Witness the iconic status attained by the round slide tray known as a "carousel" that used to be employed for projecting slides. An installation by Janet Cardiff and George Bures Miller for *Le mois de la photo* in Montreal in the fall of 2015[12] subtly underlined the link between the slide and the cultural context of emerging mass consumption. The artists had set up a slide show, with slides from their family collections, on an old Kodak carousel. The projected images documented a journey across Canada to New York, and the dialogues

5
See Frédérique Basset, *Les Quatre Saisons de Gilles Clément. Biographie*, Rue de l'échiquier, Paris, 2014.

6
Interview with Gilles Clément, December 9, 2014. Unless otherwise indicated, all interviews were conducted by the author, and all translations are our own.

7
See the analysis of the role assigned to photography in the making of the landscape atlas of the Val de Marne by the Folléa-Gauthier landscape bureau, in Frédéric Pousin, "Photographier le paysage urbain", *Ethnologie française*, no. 4, 2010, p. 673–684.

8
Gilles Clément, *Thomas et le voyageur*, Albin Michel, Paris, 1997, p. 40.

9
Up to the end of the 1930s, the projector was sometimes assimilated to the magic lantern, an instrument for projecting photographic plates that was, in some ways, the ancestor of the slide projector. See Olivier Lugon, "La conférence. Parole, dessin et projection chez Le Corbusier", *Les Cahiers du MNAM*, no. 103, spring 2008, p. 47–65, and Ariane Pollet, "The Cavalcade of Color", *Études photographiques* [online], 30| 2012, uploaded May 6, 2014, accessed February 9, 2017: http://etudesphotographiques.revues.org/3339 and Tim Davis' article in this volume, p. 14.

10
Interview with Gilles Clément, December 9, 2014.

11
Pierre Bourdieu, *Un art moyen. Essai sur les usages sociaux de la photographie*, Minuit, Paris, 1965.

12
Janet Cardiff and Georges Bures Miller, *La Condition post-photographique*, exhibition at the Parisian Laundry Art Gallery, for the 14th edition of *Le mois de la photo*, Montreal, September 10 – October 11, 2015.

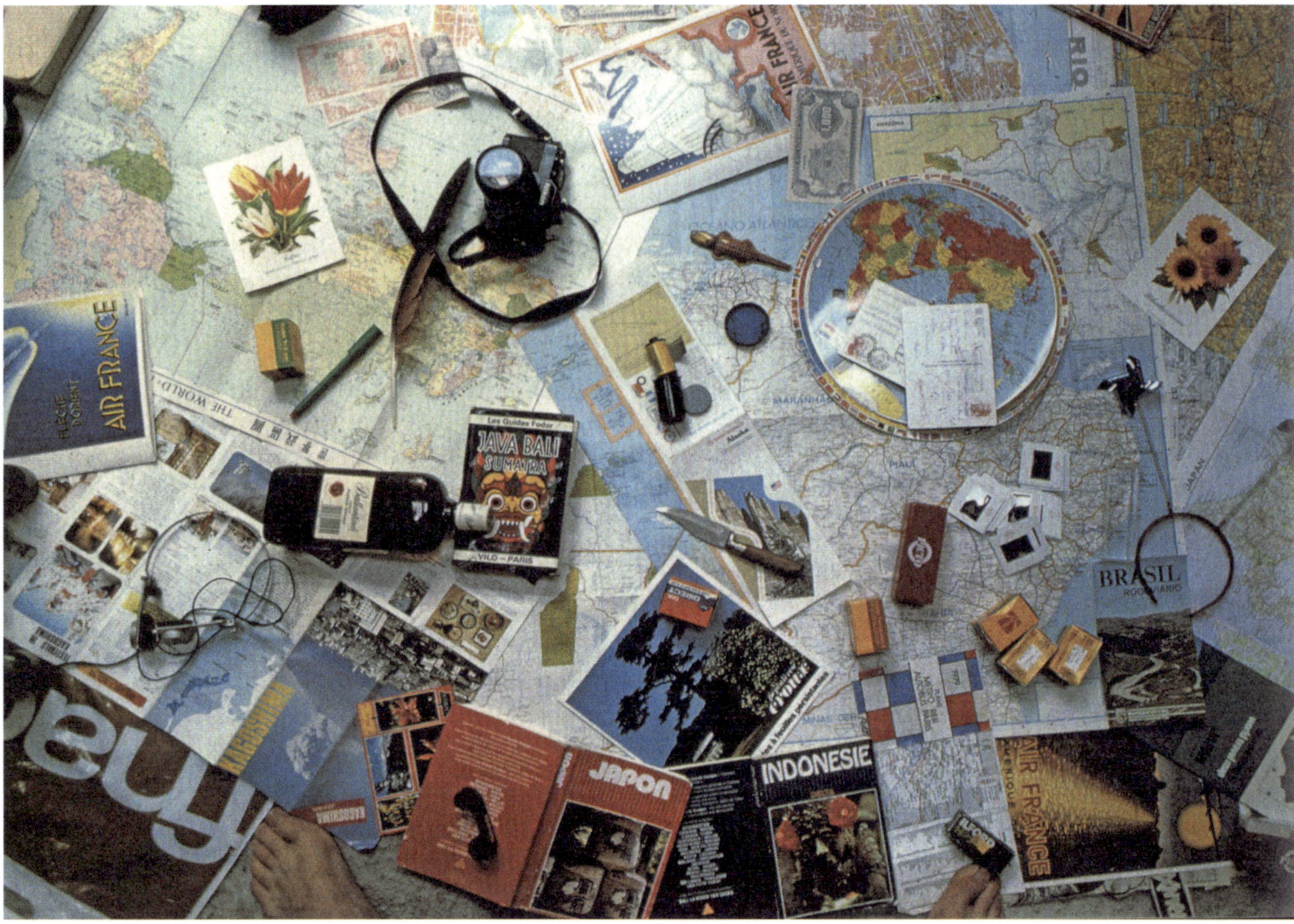

| FIG. 1 |

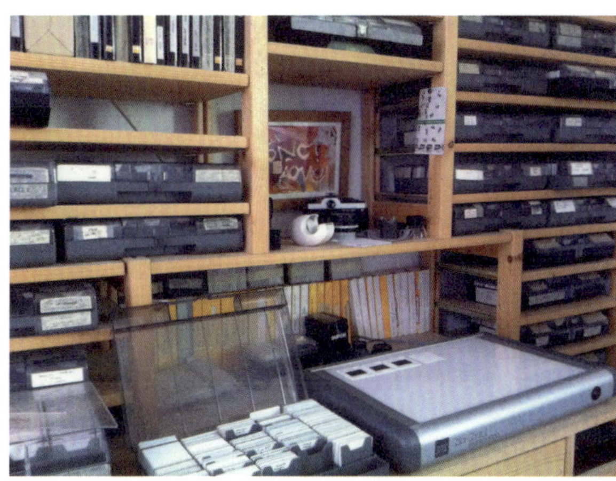

| FIG. 2 |

| FIG. 1 |
Gilles Clément, *L'équipement du voyageur*, 1997.

| FIG. 2 |
Sandra Parvu, Slide collection, Gilles Clément's workshop, 2013.

accompanying the projection centered around what order to place the photos in so as to reconstitute the itinerary taken. This reconstitution was punctuated with hesitations and second thoughts, reflected by the machine backtracking. Through the cross country journey, what was actually being placed center stage was the reasons that drive people to take photographs, reasons that stem from people's individual, emotional and family histories.[13]

For Clément, aesthetic emotion is an integral part of the projection: "I find the quality of slide projections extraordinary; the light is magnificent. We have completely lost all that."[14] This dual dimension – emotional and aesthetic – that slide shows distill within them is worth closer attention, particularly now that the color slide is an object of research in the history of art and in cultural history.

A BRIEF HISTORY OF THE COLOR SLIDE

Because it is connected to color and needs to be projected, the color slide is, for the historian of photography, strongly associated with the amateur world. It began to be used on a massive scale in the 1960s by the public, but also by the press and a range of professional circles, including architecture and landscape agencies. The ease of use of 35 mm single lens cameras, their affordability, the low cost of development, and the release of Kodachrome favored intensive use of the slide from the 1970s[15] through to the advent of digital in the 2000s.

At the start of the 20th century, autochrome plates were recognized as a new medium full of undeniable potential, and yet it was not until the late 1970s that color photography would receive recognition in the art world. The Eggelston exhibition at MoMA in 1976 was the institutional event that finally secured its consecration,[16] and while this belated recognition was partly due to the technical complexity of the development process,[17] the social and cultural reasons should not be underestimated. Color technologies saw the use of color spread to cinema and television in the 1960s, while the press was flooded with color photographs.[18] Color consequently came to be associated with mass media and mass culture. The reader may recall the damning judgment pronounced on color photography by Walker Evans (despite having experimented with it in commissions for *Fortune* magazine):[19] "Color tends to corrupt photography and absolute color corrupts it absolutely. Consider the way color film usually renders blue sky, green foliage, lipstick red, and the kiddies' playsuit. There are four simple words for the matter, which must be whispered: color photography is vulgar."[20] This judgment reflects the institutionalization of creative photography and the distance it seeks to establish between itself and photojournalism. And it was under the influence of the press, independently of the disputed field of artistic photography, that the color slide rose to prominence. As with any new medium, and despite – or rather because of – the connotations attached to it, it offered a potential that certain artists were quick to seize upon, often developing a critical and political discourse on landscape and the environment. The work of Robert Smithson and Dan Graham[21] was seminal in this respect. The documentary use of photography to support a critical perspective on the environment was a piece of cultural baggage that landscape architects, foremost among them Jacques Simon in France, were happy to carry. Gilles Clément also associated the image with an explicit political discourse.

Slides were also very popular among professional agencies in the 1970s and 1980s, as projection has a place in the history of architecture, towns and landscapes. It provides a powerful channel for the propagation of ideas, which Le Corbusier put to exemplary use in the period between the wars to present his work. More than other modes of exhibition, it allowed – as he saw it – for substantial and objective explanations.[22] Olivier Lugon attributes this interest in slide projections to several factors.[23] Firstly, it enables diverse productions, on different scales, to be included in a homogeneous discourse; in so doing, it underlines the coherence of the architect's work, as the projection format and its immateriality help to smooth out the dissimilarities. Secondly, when the speaker operates the device and accompanies the images with a commentary, he introduces an element of spontaneity that is absent from the printed word. He can calibrate his arguments and control his interactions with the public. Finally and most importantly, the luminous image holds a power of fascination that is linked to its ephemeral, event-bound character. Slide projections hold tried and tested discursive potential for land development professionals.

THE ROLE OF THE SLIDE IN THE CONSTRUCTION OF LECTURES

Gilles Clément builds his lectures on images. For a long time, he used a set of slides; nowadays he uses digital images. In his own personal history, images have often served to convey his ideas, especially those of the "Garden in Movement":

> *[...] when it came to the Garden in Movement, for Parc André Citroën, it was a real struggle to get it accepted! I had all the City of Paris engineers, and the politicians, against me. I did several photography shows drawing on the eight-year experience of my own garden at La Vallée,*[24] *explaining how it moved, what it meant, how I did it, and so on. And that constituted my power of persuasion.*[25]

13
This is further underlined by the reference to the cult TV series *Mad Men,* which relates, in fictional mode, the advertising launch of the carousel by Kodak. In her paper on the Kodak pavilion at the Universal Exhibition of 1939, Ariane Pollet analyzes the centerpiece of the pavilion, a color slide show with sound, made up of enlarged Kodachromes projected onto a large semicircular screen. See Ariane Pollet, "The Cavalcade of Color", *op. cit.* The episode of *Mad Men* featuring the Kodak carousel can be viewed on YouTube: https://www.youtube.com/watch?v=suRDUFpsHus

14
Interview with Gilles Clément, December 9, 2014.

15
See Laurie Olin's article in this volume, p. 88.

16
William Eggleston: Color Photography; see Nathalie Boulouch, "Couleur versus noir et blanc", *Études photographiques* [online], no. 16, May 2005, uploaded September 17, 2008, accessed February 9, 2017: http://etudesphotographiques.revues.org/726

17
See Thomas Weski, "From Memphis With Love", in *William Eggleston. From Black and White to Color,* exhibition catalogue, *Musée de l'Élysée,* Lausanne/Fondation Cartier-Bresson, Paris, Steidl, Göttingen, 2015, p. 192–193.

18
See Jason Hill, Vanessa R. Schwartz (ed.), Getting the Picture: The Visual Culture of the News, Bloomsbury Publishing, London, New York, NY, 2015.

19
See David Campany, *Walker Evans: The Magazine Work,* Steidl, Göttingen, 2014.

20
Cited by Nathalie Boulouch, "The (In)Visible Public Life of Colour Photography", in Thierry Gervais (ed.), *The Public Life of Photographs,* RIC Books, Toronto/MIT Press, Cambridge, MA, 2016, p. 184.

21
The first formulation of Graham's famous series *Homes for America* was presented in the form of a slide show at the *Projected Art* exhibition at Finch College Museum of Art, New York, December 8, 1966 – January 8, 1966; cited by Nathalie Boulouch, *ibid.*

22
Le Corbusier equipped his workshop with a projection room, which held a professional projector; see Tim Benton, *The Rhetoric of Modernism: Le Corbusier as a Lecturer*, Birkhäuser, Basel, 2009.

23
Olivier Lugon, "La conférence. Parole, dessin et projection chez Le Corbusier", *op. cit.*, p. 49.

24
Clément's property in the Creuse, south-central France.

25
Interview with Gilles Clément, December 9, 2014.

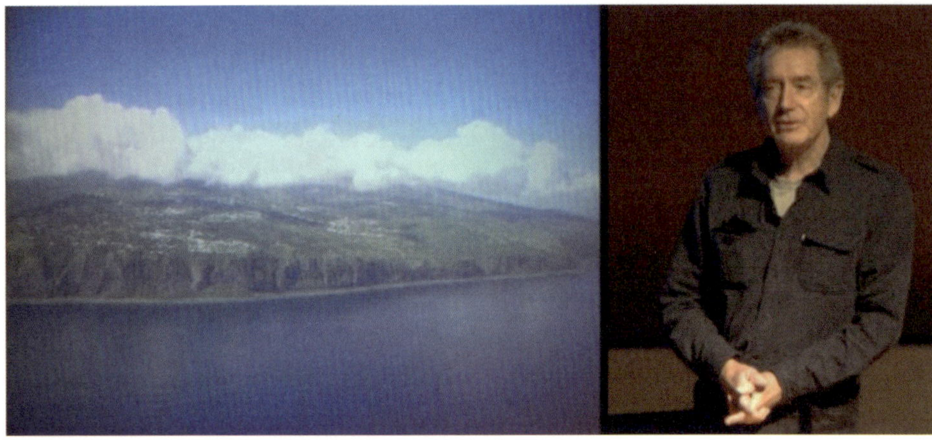

| FIG. 3 |

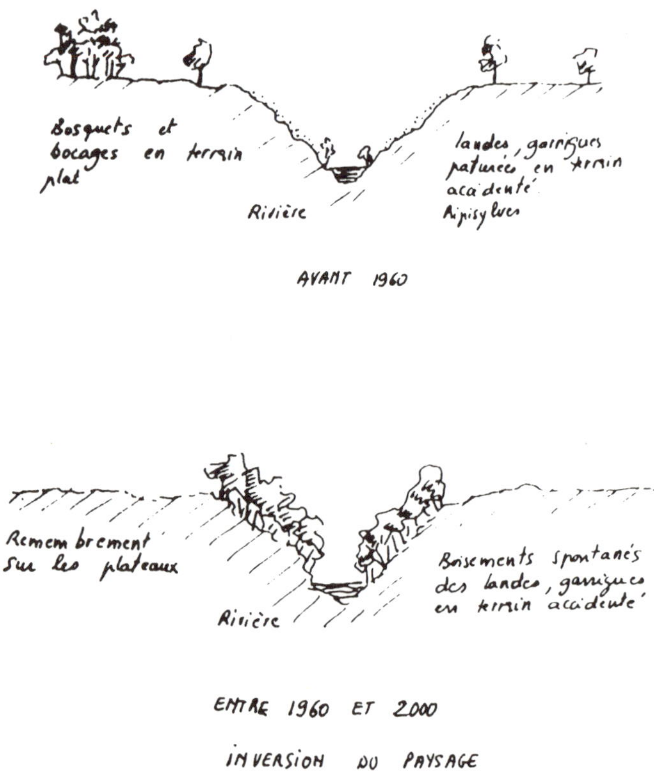

| FIG. 4 |

| FIG. 3 |
Lee waves over Reunion Island, *Collège de France* lecture on "The Planetary Garden", December 15, 2011.

| FIG. 4 |
Gilles Clément, Diagram of landscape inversion in Ardèche, exhibition *Toujours la vie invente*, 2014.

In a photographic *exposé*, the image has demonstrative value, illustrating the phenomena that underlie the argument: "I don't talk about what I haven't seen, because I don't believe what I can't see – I am an unbeliever! So I show what is there – and don't let anybody tell me otherwise! That's just the way it is; I don't tell stories."[26]

Every *exposé* is constructed with a particular situation in mind and mobilizes a set of deliberately chosen images. Clément never repeats himself, as the *exposé* belongs to the register of interpersonal exchange; it is a living dialogue that takes place with the viewers. He constructs his *exposés* for a given audience, and develops one or other aspect of his favorite topics. His goal is not to convince people at any price – unlike Le Corbusier, for example – but rather to get his ideas across, and share them. Each *exposé* nonetheless takes place in an enunciative setting[27] that regulates the nature of the discourse. One cannot lump together lectures given as part of occupational training courses with those given in places of knowledge transmission such as conferences, prestigious venues such as the *Collège de France*, or the media spaces in museums. Each space defines its own expectations and possibilities of enunciation, as well as its own requirements and impossibilities. An unsupported claim, for example, is unlikely to be accepted in academic circles, whereas a poetic discourse will be looked upon favorably in an artistic environment.

The cycle of lectures Clément gave at the *Collège de France* in 2012 was part of the teaching requirement of the Chair in Artistic Creation that was conferred upon him following his nomination by Philippe Descola. The two men met at a cycle of lectures at the Pompidou Center in Paris entitled *Le monde selon* ... (The world according to...), which Clément had been tasked with organizing two years earlier.[28] The teaching dispensed in this professorial role took a number of forms: in addition to the inaugural lecture, *Jardins, paysage et génie naturel*[29] (Gardens, landscape and natural genius)[30] – from which the overall cycle took its title – eight public lectures were scheduled,[31] along with two seminars including guest speakers, and two extramural lectures for the personnel of the *Collège de France*. According to the program, the lectures consisted of "[...] a series of projected images following a plan that presents the topic of study, asking key questions, expounding on experiments relating to these questions, sketching the outlines of a response, and touching on other questions that will lead us to the next lecture."[32]

When asked how he designs his lectures and *exposés*, Clément insists that he always proceeds in the same way, by putting together a plan rather than a text to read out: "I never read. There is no text, but there is a plan. Every paragraph is reduced to a single word. However, there are lots of images inside it. That's equivalent to having sentences. When I put together the exposé, I say to myself: 'That is what I'm going to say about this image'."[33]

The discourse, then, is constructed around the material in the slides, between 120 and 150 for a one-hour *exposé*. Each slide depicts a content, whose meaning is not unique: some images can be used to support different arguments. Notes are then taken, corresponding to the discourse constructed by the images. The writing therefore comes afterwards, not before.[34] From these notes, a detailed plan is defined, like those for the *Collège de France* program. The notes can also be used in other contexts.

Within the program, the lecture entitled "The Planetary Garden" (*Le jardin planétaire*) is the one that best expresses Clément's theoretical thinking, and in its image-based argumentation it employs processes that converge on a fully-fledged visual rhetoric.

THE DEVELOPMENT OF A VISUAL RHETORIC: ALLUSIONS, ASSOCIATIONS, EXAMPLES, EMBLEMS

The notion of the Planetary Garden, explored in the first part of the lecture, is constructed from elements presented in earlier lectures. At this point, Clément turns to the slides **| FIG. 3 |**. The

26
Idem.

27
On the notion of "enunciative setting" (*scène énonciative*), see Michel Foucault, *L'Archéologie du savoir* [The Archeology of Knowledge], Gallimard, Paris, 1969. On the analysis of architectural representation in enunciative settings, see Frédéric Pousin, *L'Architecture mise en scène*, Arguments, Paris, 1995.

28
"*Le monde selon* ...", lecture cycle organized by Gilles Clément at the Pompidou Center from October to December 2010. Session of October 13: "Nature à lire", with the anthropologist Philippe Descola and the geographer Éric Julien.

29
Gilles Clément, *Jardins, paysage et génie naturel*, "Leçons inaugurales du Collège de France", *Collège de France*/Fayard, Paris, 2012.

30
"Natural genius" is the translation that seems to have "stuck", but the term *génie naturel* plays cleverly on two meanings: "the genius of nature" and "natural engineering" – (translators' note).

31
For the lecture program, see the *Collège de France* website: http://www.college-de-france.fr/site/gilles-clement/course-2011-2012.htm

32
Ibid.

33
Interview with Gilles Clément, December 9, 2014.

34
Ibid.

selected images express ideas or concepts: Reunion Island, the Panama canal, stratus clouds over Milan, melting sea ice, etc. – none of these images is chosen for its situation or composition, but because it alludes to the idea of evaporation and the water cycle. Allusion, according to the philosopher of language Nelson Goodman,[35] is an indirect mode of reference consisting of a chain of elementary references, and the transition from an aerial image of Reunion Island to the idea of the water cycle is indeed not a direct one. Several of the assembled examples show that a key concept can be embodied in fundamentally different landscapes. It only remains to discover the point of commonality shared by the deep structure of these images and landscapes. With regard to the water cycle, Clément introduces the idea of the vertical garden: the relationship between top and bottom, the concept of evaporation, the water we drink, which has evaporated from plants and, indeed, humans; humans are thus included in the vast array of living things. The goal of the demonstration has been met: Clément has elicited the idea of a finite space, that of the planet, in which mankind is included and has responsibility for life on earth. The association of images entails the association of ideas.

This association of images and ideas crops up again in his lecture on the Garden in Movement. A series of images is used to build up an expanded argument around a single topic, and to convey the idea that one can start out from personal experience to explore other, more general situations. To approach the concept of the Garden in Movement, for example, Clément speaks of his experience in his own garden at La Vallée; he then extends the argument to the practices of others who have displayed inventiveness in addressing similar issues, such as in the garden of the *École Normale Supérieure* in Lyon or at Jules-Rieffel agricultural college in Loire-Atlantique. The multiplication of examples serves his argument and makes his case more compelling: it is all part of the business of persuasion.

The art of discourse echoes the visual rhetoric developed through the selection and assembly of images. Nor is it solely about landscape photographs. Just as in practice of landscape design, where several modes of representation – drawings, maps, diagrams, photographs – collaborate with each other, Clément is happy to make use of drawings to develop an argument:

> *It sometimes happens that I don't have an image that fits the idea I have for demonstrating something or for talking about something. In that case, I do a drawing, and I photograph the drawing, which I then show* **| FIG. 4 |**.
> *We don't have any images of the biosphere; it is impossible to take a photo of the biosphere. So I did a drawing to speak about that, or about the fact that we are in water, we are swimming in water.*[36]

The images may also be drawings borrowed from other fields, or photographs of maps. For example, a picture from the Argentinian cartoon strip by Quino, *Mafalda,* is used to introduce the political dimension of the nord-south divide – a reading of the world that is central to the fundamentally unitary planetary garden. The relation of image to idea is complex, and would seem to be a case of allusion, in terms of the logical categories established by Goodman. But some images have an ability to act mainly as a starting point for more abstract forms of discourse. A map of Australia, for example, reframed into a multiplicity of images, serves to decenter our representations of the world by revealing a myriad of small islands. These pictures provide the keys to understanding the diversity of species engendered by geographic isolation. Political discourse becomes intermeshed with scientific discourse, with the emergence of the idea of planetary mingling. The argument in this case is conveyed more by words than by the image of a multitude of islands, which serves mainly to denote the concept of isolation. Some of the images gathered together in this first part of the lecture act as emblems. The image of *Mafalda* for political discourse, as we saw, but also a drawing of a dragonfly, whose aquatic larva mutates into a flying insect, symbolizing vertical exchange, or a photo of *Welwitschia mirabilis* in the Namib desert, to signify the singularity that emerges from isolation **| FIG. 5 |**. These emblematic images may have a real referent, or they may have a fictional one, like the "diagrammatic" image of the theoretical "average continent" devised by the geographer Carl Troll in 1948, depicting a biological reality that has no

35
Nelson Goodman, *Of Mind and Other Matters*, Harvard University Press, Cambridge, MA, 1984, p. 65–66.

36
Interview with Gilles Clément, December 9, 2014.

| FIG. 5 |
Gilles Clément, *Welwitschia mirabilis*, Namib desert, 1986.

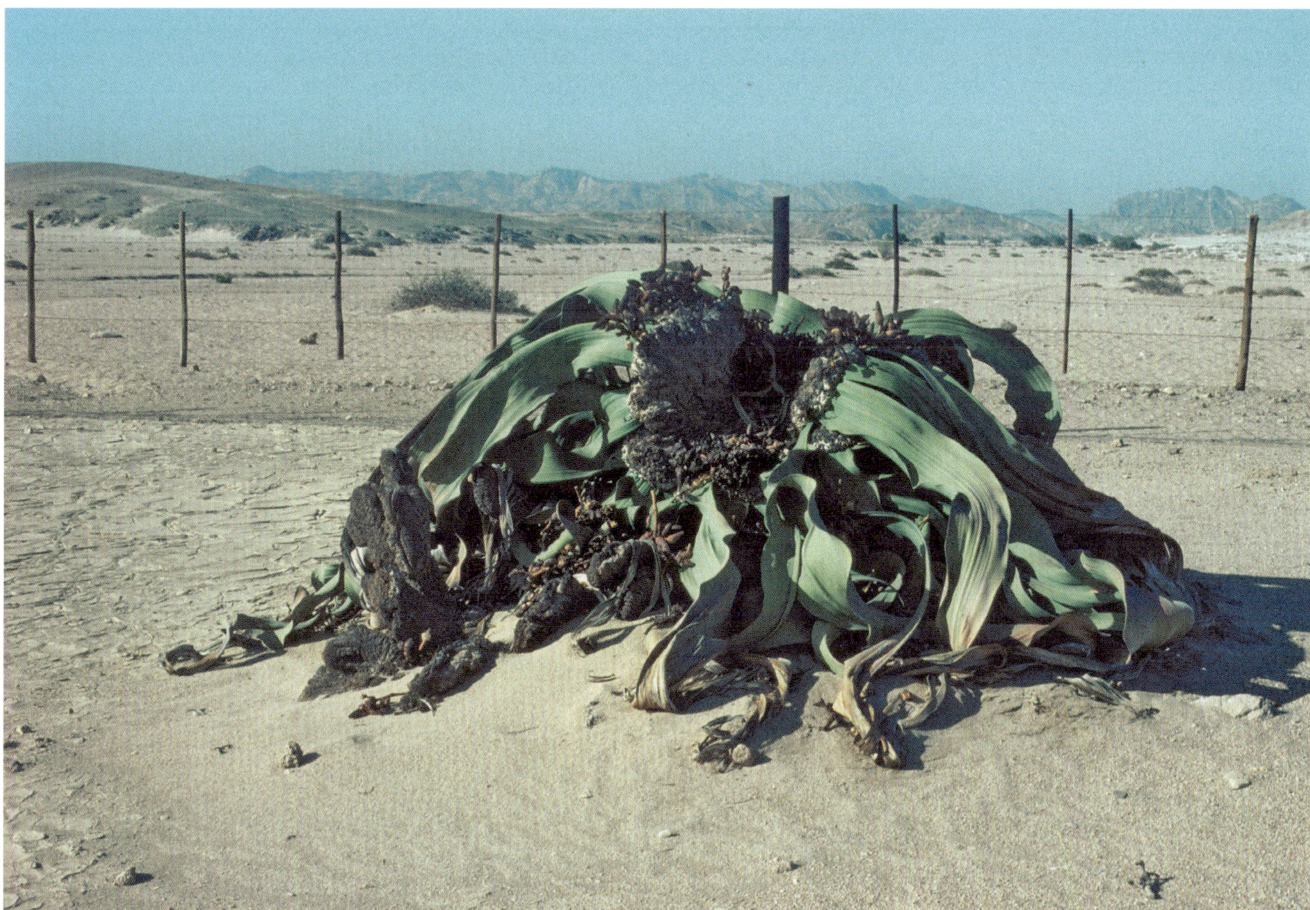

| FIG. 5 |

physical reality, namely the aggregated biomes (a set of compatibilities between life forms in the same climate) along the north-south axis of the hemispheres. This theoretical continent unites different biological realities into a single figure.

THE PROJECT AS THE STUFF OF DISCOURSE: PARALLELS, COMPARISONS, DEMONSTRATIONS

With the images of the garden at the Domaine du Rayol, we are confronted with the physical realities of the biome. It is also at this point that the part of the lecture dedicated to past or future projects begins. These embody the ideas developed by Gilles Clément, and are quite often the source of those ideas, as can be seen from the chronology: work on the garden at Le Rayol began in 1989,[37] which means that the practical application of the notion of biome preceded its theoretical exposition at the Planetary Garden exhibition in 2000. In the structure of the lecture, by contrast, the theoretical explanation precedes the example for reasons of clarity: knowledge is expounded before it is exemplified. This rhetorical order, though appropriate to the context of the *Collège de France*, does little justice to the theoretical value contained in the landscape designer's projects.

Nevertheless, the lecture performs a crucial operation: thanks to the slides, and to certain processes made possible by photographic imagery, the completed project becomes material for discourse. The logical relationship between symbol and referent, as analyzed by Goodman,[38] explains how the photographic image, as a symbolic representation, articulates around a referent, given that photography is basically an operation that extracts samples of reality. By virtue of the photographic image, the project is transformed into an element of discourse, a visual discourse that is not autonomous, but is articulated around a verbal discourse.

All discourse presupposes an enunciative framework, constituted in this case by an *exposé*, lecture or conference. It also presupposes an enunciator, who addresses one or more interlocutors in an enunciative interplay. Gilles Clément, garden and landscape designer, often enters into a dialogue with scientists specializing in ecology or life sciences; he accompanies them in their work, without actually performing any strictly scientific work himself. In the context of the Chair in Artistic Creation at the *Collège de France*, he contributes his knowledge on "natural genius": how landscapes and gardens are created. His discourse, while voluntarily poetic, is also critical, and sometimes has real political implications. His aim is to realize projects that will anchor political positions in the concrete space of the landscape, used and lived in by all.

The enunciative framework is also a temporal framework, and the photographic image, as we know, is frozen in time. How does this time capture reintegrate into a different timeframe? The "long time" of the project, firstly, which requires us to step back from its implementation; and secondly, the timeframe of the discourse, which is enunciated in the here and now; but also the timeframe of a universal present – that of the laws of nature. And what role does time play in the development of political awareness and action? To find elements of answers to these questions we must decipher both the uses of the photographic image and the actual process of projection. Because they are projected, slides must be analyzed by exploring the associations, linkages, rhythms and sequences induced by the projection process. The visual space of projection might be compared, as a space of representation, to that of an "atlas" in which heterogeneous objects are assembled, and legends and comments added to them.[39] But unlike such a collection, the projection space is fundamentally dynamic and ephemeral, and the discourse associated with the images it contains is a highly specific verbal discourse.

The lecture sequence on the garden at Le Rayol gives the general impression of summoning up a multitude of visual examples. But what exactly do we mean here by "example"? Exemplification, according to Goodman, is a logical relationship that associates a referent with a symbol, starting out from the former. It assumes that the referent has properties that function as labels.[40] The slide, which can be assimilated to a visual symbol, can therefore exemplify the dominant idea of the garden at Le Rayol, which was designed not as a botanical collection but as an assembly of landscapes. Just as the photograph of a landscape carpeted in cistus exemplifies a typically European territory, or one of shrub ferns exemplifies a much more humid New Zealand landscape. The idea of an assembly of landscapes is expressed visually by a series of eloquent examples **| FIG. 6 |**.

During the projection, the images are associated with each other by means of processes that reward closer examination. These include the time-parallel, which establishes a relationship between one or more situations that belong to distinct times. Because photography bears witness to different states of the project and its transformations, the projection can easily place them in parallel: for example, an early stage of the garden, at the beginning, where the Australian part runs alongside the South African part, and a recent picture, showing how the South African plants have spread massively, starting with the aloes. However, this process is not systematic, unlike the protocols adopted by the photographic landscape observatories **| FIG. 7 |**.[41]

The use of parallel can also apply to space, as illustrated by two photographs of fire in South Africa: a view of the Cape of Good Hope and another of Sandy Bay, just to the north, where the fire burns itself out in the sea **| FIG. 8 |**. Other photographs, taken during subsequent trips, then construct a time-parallel to act as an introduction to the behavior of pyrophytic plants and the concept of management by fire, which appeals to Clément. Pyrophytic plants depend on fire for their germination, in response to thermal shock or chemical phenomena such as smoke **| FIG. 9 |**. The fires that break out regularly in South Africa are an example of the natural management of an environment by fire. In speaking of "natural genius", Clément suggests, a tad provocatively, using fire as a gardening tool at Le Rayol, stressing that small winter fires were long used as a traditional form of management in the Mediterranean.

Comparison – that fundamental operation in the production of knowledge – places two objects side by side to bring out their similarities and differences. The paired association of slides in this case allows us to compare an original landscape, from a site in New Zealand coated in silky expanses of sedge, with the patch of grassland in the New Zealand garden at Le Rayol **| FIG. 10 |**. The comparison between the artifact and the original model is designed to establish the visual identity of the landscape motif, that of the desert landscapes of the center of the island, which must not only be installed in the context of the garden, but also maintained by managing it. Here, the nature of the comparison takes us on to the construction of the garden.

In the first part of the lecture, Clément compares two macro photos: a maple seed and a dragon-fly wing, to introduce the phenomenon of homoplasy (convergence of form). The same process of juxtaposing objects with shared characteristics in visual space is employed again later. Three photographs of plants displaying a formal analogy – they all look like rushes – are shown together in the projection space although they belong to different botanical families and are of diverse geographical origins. Nonetheless, under the same climate, they assume the same shape **| FIG. 11 |**. Through these three photographs, Clément explains the phenomenon of vicariance, which applies to geographically separate species that display similar behaviors. The immediately apparent visual resemblance elicits the theoretical explanation, which leads on to plant behavior, and beyond, to the domain of the unseen.

The concept of Third Landscape,[42] essential to the theoretical discourse on landscape, concerns a particular category of spaces that belong to the Planetary Garden: leftover spaces (*délaissés*). It

37
This garden, situated on the Corniche des Maures, between Le Rayol and Cavalaire on the French Riviera, takes up just 5 hectares of a 25-hectare domain acquired by the *Conservatoire du littoral* coastal protection agency thanks to a determined team: Jean-Philippe Grillet, followed by Christian Desplats, and now Olivier Arnaud; see Gilles Clément, Philippe Deliau, Christian Desplats, *Carnet de mission. Domaine du Rayol: 1989–2009, Conservatoire du littoral*, Doublevébé Récup, Vals-le-Chatel, 2009, and Gilles Clément & Dominique Mansion, *Les Jardins du Rayol*, Actes Sud/ *Conservatoire du littoral*, Arles, 2005.

38
Nelson Goodman, *Languages of Art*, Bobbs-Merrill, Indianapolis, IN, 1968.

39
See Georges Didi-Huberman, *Atlas ou le gai savoir inquiet. L'œil de l'histoire 3*, Minuit, Paris, 2011.

40
Nelson Goodman, *op. cit.*

41
On the principle of long-term time-lapse photography as practiced by the National Photographic Landscape Observatory (OPNP) and adapted to multiple local situations, see "Méthode de l'Observatoire photographique du paysage", Meeddm, 2008: http://www.developpement-durable.gouv.fr/IMG/DGALN_methodeOPP.pdf. See also Raphaële Bertho's article in this volume, p. 36.

42
Gilles Clément, *Manifeste pour le Tiers paysage*, Sujet/Objet, Paris, 2004.

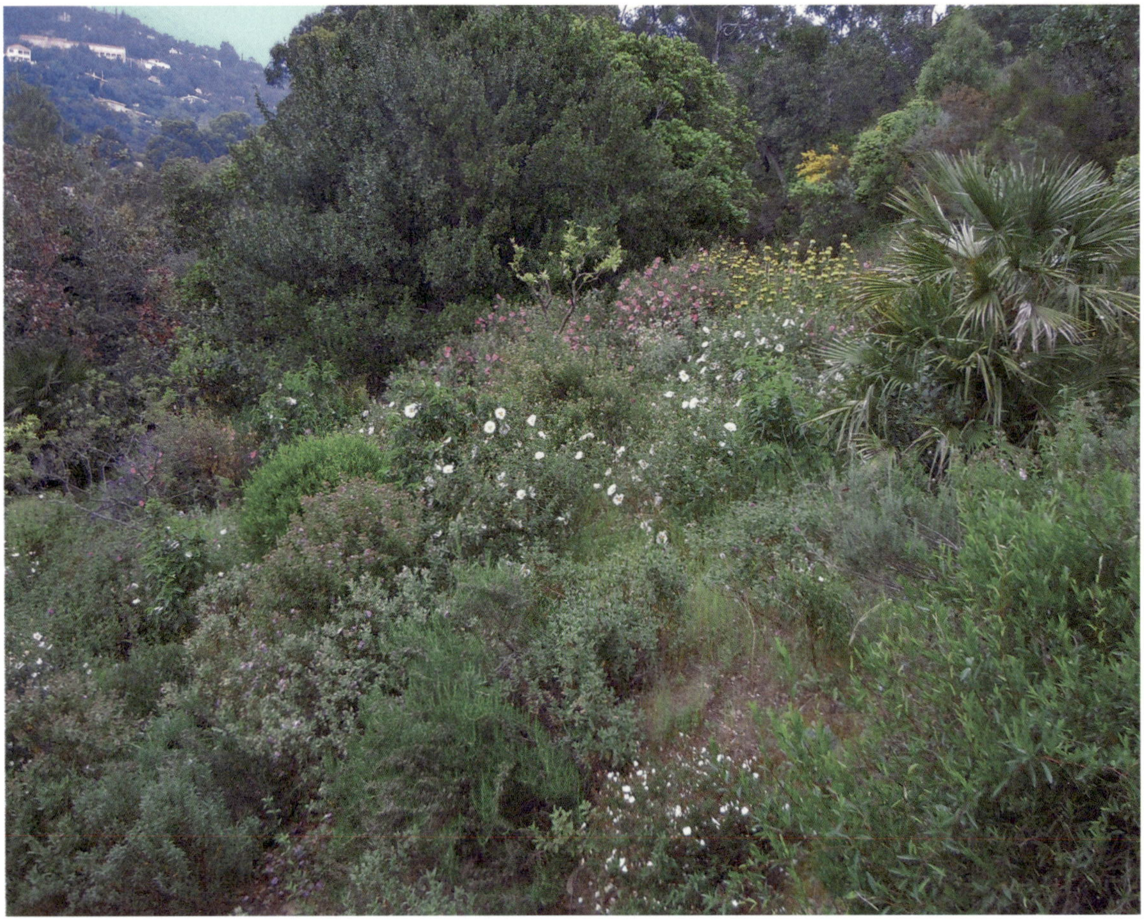

| FIG. 6 |

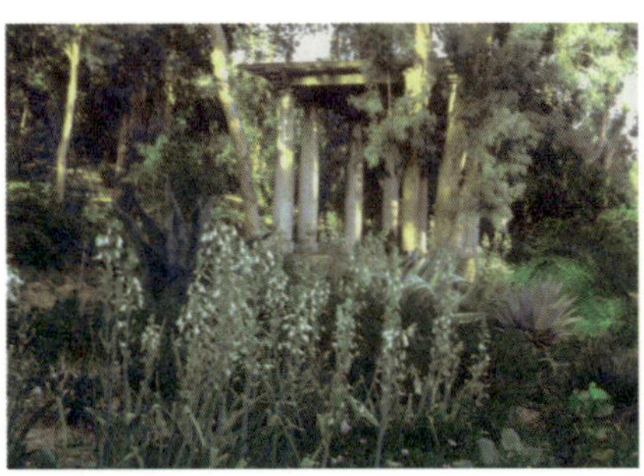

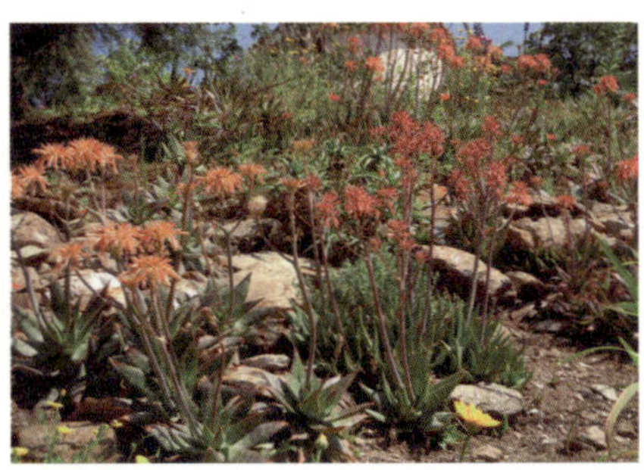

| FIG. 7 |

| FIG. 6 |
Gilles Clément, Garden at Le Rayol, the cistus corridor, exemplification of a European landscape, 1999.

| FIG. 7 |
Gilles Clément, Garden at Le Rayol, two states of the South Africa garden: the galtonias and the aloes, 1993.

| FIG. 8 |
Gilles Clément, Fire at the Cape of Good Hope and at Sandy Bay, South Africa, 1992.

| FIG. 9 |
Gilles Clément, Pyrophytic plants (fire lilies), South Africa, 1993.

| FIG. 10 |
Gilles Clément, Center of North Island, New Zealand, carpeted in blonde fields of sedge (Cyperaceae), 1983. This, the original landscape, is compared with the expanse of Stipa grasses in the New Zealand garden at Le Rayol, 1992.

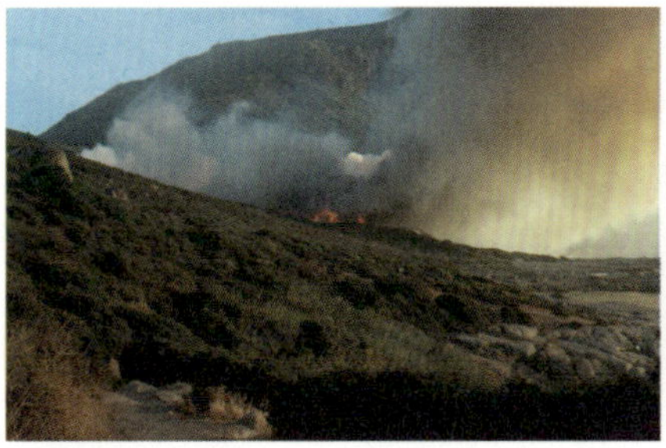

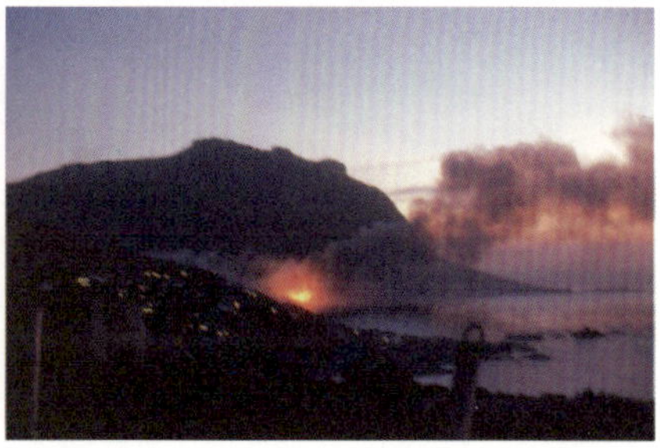

| FIG. 8 |

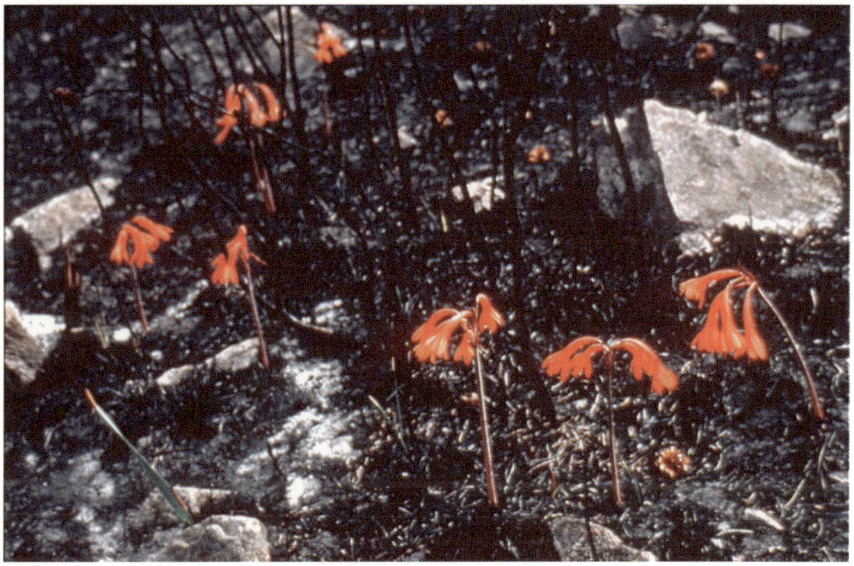

| FIG. 9 |

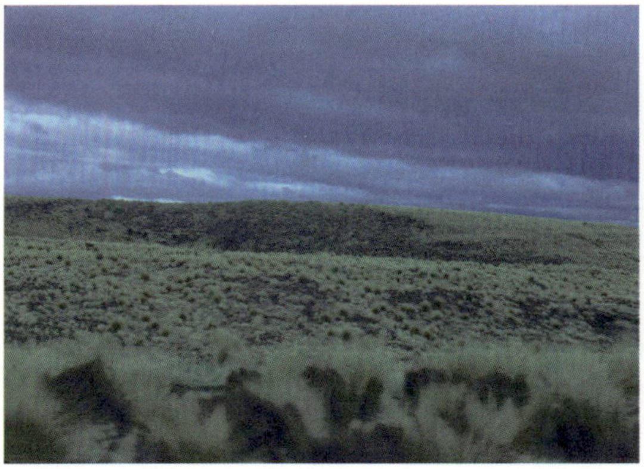

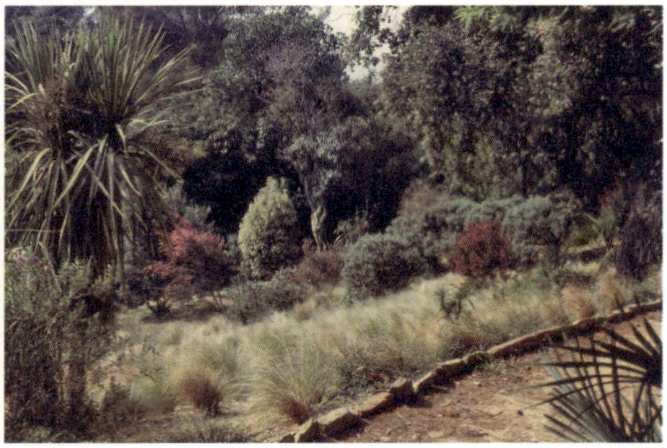

| FIG. 10 |

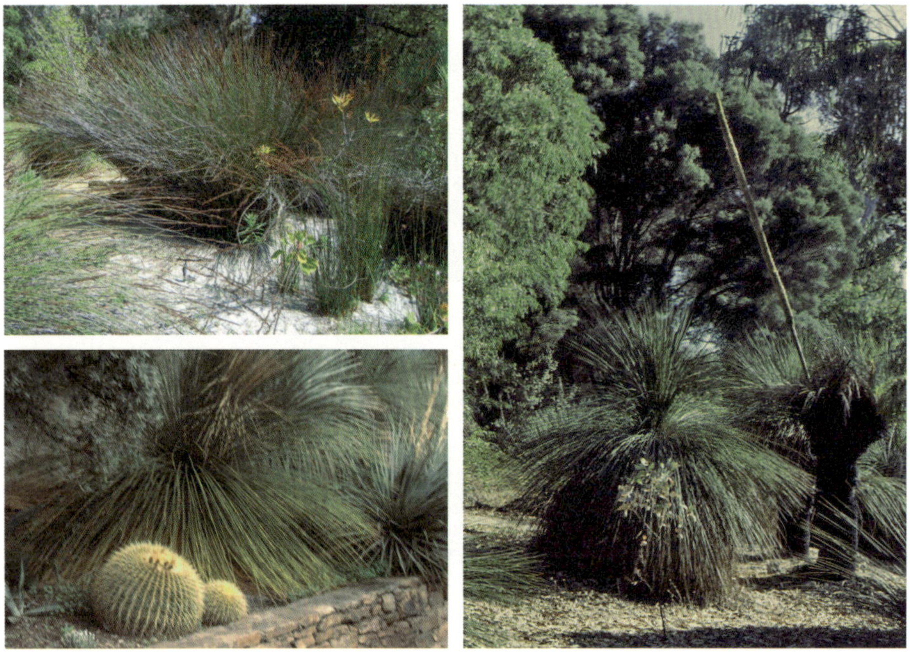

| FIG. 11 |

| FIG. 11 |

Gilles Clément, Xanthorrhoea "Black-boy" (Asphodelaceae) from Australia, Dasylirion (Liliaceae) from Mexico and Chondropetalum (Restionaceae) from South Africa: three "vicariant" plants that look very similar despite their different geographic origins, 2005.

| FIG. 12 |

Gilles Clément, Derborence Island and the lawn, Parc Henri Matisse, Lille, 2008.

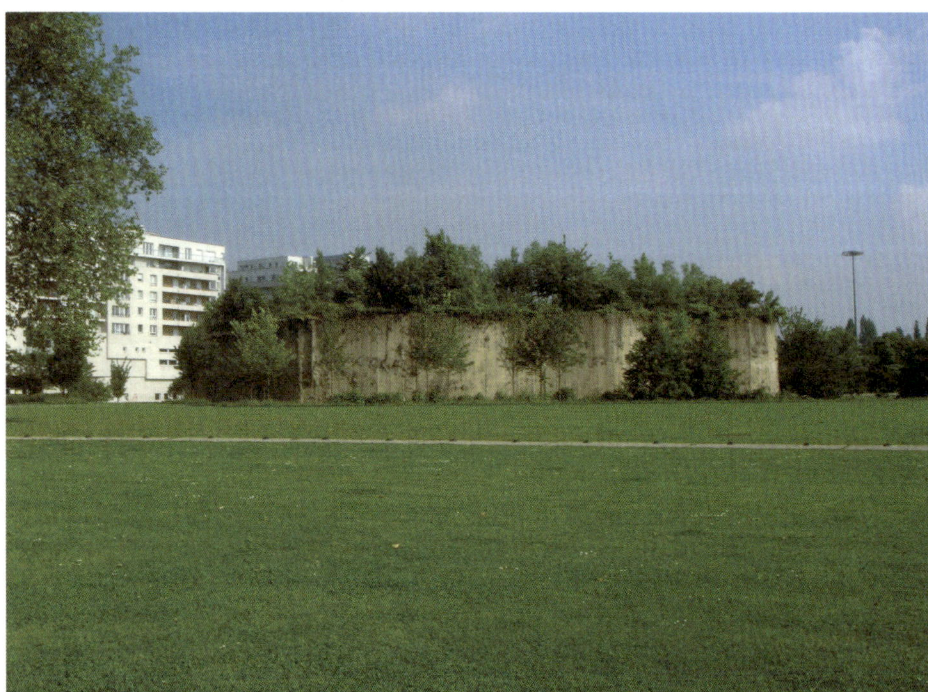

| FIG. 12 |

seeks to endow them with a political representation. Usually ignored and unmentioned, these leftover spaces are nonetheless rich in implications for biological diversity. The lecture on the Third Landscape sheds light on their mechanisms of creation: the slides show examples of the abandonment of strips or plots of land, the subtraction of fragments of space from cultivated or urbanized land, and the development of infrastructures that fence off inaccessible spaces. But are these three mechanisms – abandonment, subtraction, development – deduced *a posteriori* from a reading of the landscape, of which the photo is a recording, a material trace of observed examples? Or is the image an *a priori* representation of a type of mechanism easily illustrated by various examples? It is this latter hypothesis that is supported by Clément, for whom any act of development has the ability to generate leftover spaces. Ultimately, the value of the image lies in its contextualization alone: here, each slide functions as a representation of one of the mechanisms by which leftover spaces are generated, rather than as a simple example of their diversity. In this lecture, the projects listed as examples of required actions include mapping exercises, such as the "forest of leftover spaces" – since cartography can become a political landscape management tool, as advocated by Coloco, a team of landscape design partners – or exhibition projects, like those of the Canadian Centre for Architecture (CCA) in Montreal and the Melle Biennale, or development projects such as that of a wasteland in Nanterre, on the historic Paris axis, or that of Derborence Island in Parc Henri Matisse in Lille | **FIG. 12** |, or that of the submarine base at Saint Nazaire. In each of these projects, the slides identify the elements or properties that link them, like labels, to the Third Landscape. In so doing, they inscribe the projects in a clearly identified register of discourse, one that could be described as "militant" or "political". For Clément, photography plays an important role in political advocacy, as for example when denouncing the deterioration or confiscation of landscapes:

> *It is, precisely, the demonstration of something. When I want to talk about the Third Landscape, I have aerial views that are totally demonstrative. They touch on the economic model and, depending on how you address it, they can also touch on political thinking – it depends very much on the talk that accompanies the slides. Mostly, it gives you something to base yourself on, and that is very valuable.*[43]

THE DYNAMICS OF PROJECTION

The slide unifies the visual material that Clément draws upon for his demonstrations. Sketches, maps, drawings, exhibition photos, project photos, diagrams... all of these heterogeneous formats are homogenized by the act of projection. As we have seen, new relations between these representations can emerge from the copresence of images and their association. But, more fundamentally, photography takes samples from the world and rearranges them within the space of representation.

The sequencing of the images also structures the discourse, weaving arguments together. It sets in motion a chain of ideas: ideas that lead on to the use of other images, and so on. Clément describes this process when talking about the construction of his speech on the Garden in Movement:

> *For the Garden in Movement, which is the thing I'm asked to do most often, I speak about the plant that triggered the idea: hogweed.*[44] *I explain that it was here, and that it arrived in that patch of land over there, and I show the corresponding photo. I explain that it happened two years later. Then I say that this physical movement gives this type of gardening its name: the Garden in Movement. In fact, the plants that behave like that are*

43 Interview with Gilles Clément, December 9, 2014.

44 Hogweed is a wild plant from the Apiaceae (formerly Umbelliferae) family.

all short-cycle plants, and I show others that have nothing in common with this one. However, there is a logical sequence. Finally, I say that I've learnt to live with this physical displacement. But can I not also live with the mole, which is an animal? When I was a lad, I was taught to kill mullein plants that spread across the garden... and moles too! Now I realize that mullein is good, it's interesting. And what if moles were interesting? So there is a sort of sequence, and each image is connected to that."[45]

With projection, the rhythm and temporality of enunciation come into their own. Hesitation becomes possible; even the reorientation or interruption of the talk by skipping a picture or going back to a previous one. Hesitations in the image sequence give the speaker a degree of freedom with regard to the inexorable flow of time of his speech. The juxtaposition of utterances specific to verbal expression makes for a good fit with the organization of images into series, and this particular pairing integrates seamlessly into a discourse which is, overall, perfectly articulated. The underlying verbal structure becomes apparent through signs such as digressions, or the sudden emergence of a secondary narrative, which is quickly interrupted.

Projection creates a particular relationship of proximity to the lecturer's audience. As in the day of the Kodak carousel, projecting slides – or, today, digital images from a video projector (but the technology is incidental) – is an easy way to share experiences. It calls for commentary, makes allowance for digressions and shortcuts in a preestablished script, sometimes imposes varied rhythms. It gives the present moment its full value; it constitutes an extraordinary medium of exchange. The projected image has the power to capture the attention of audience and speaker alike. This focusing of attention on a shared object is a key factor in the quality of the procedure. A genuinely shared attention is created, and the spoken word is listened to in a different way.

Additionally, projection taps into a ritual: that of lowering the lights, to create a subdued atmosphere that is also conducive to sharing. A sense of familiarity sets in, one that was already associated with the Kodak carousel and which endures in the ritual of projection; it relegates strangeness to the background, it assumes that the unknown has been tamed.[46] Slide shows differ in this respect from their ancestor the magic lantern, which projected photographic plates. The attendant aura of magic predisposed it to serve its intended purpose of convincing the audience above all else, like the one used by Le Corbusier, who took advantage of its technical prowess and the element of surprise.[47] Slide shows speak more to the imagination, being associated with travel, with journeys through space and through life and, indeed, with the emotions.

Lectures and conferences, however, are embedded in institutional contexts, and thus in formats. In the field of urban and rural planning, as in that of landscape architecture, they are often paired with exhibitions, in a general effort to disseminate ideas and reach out to, or even mobilize, a particular audience. Every such event is a key moment in the sharing of issues between specialists on the one hand and the public on the other, and in these contexts, photography plays a prime role in the transmission of experience.[48]

FROM PROJECT TO DISCOURSE: THE EFFICACY OF PHOTOGRAPHY

For the designers of gardens and landscapes, these two fora – the lecture (or conference, de-

pending on the context) and the exhibition – are, along with the printed media, the main channels for disseminating their work; in Clément's case, that work is constructed, but also written and, indeed, drawn.[49] In the various exhibitions he has staged, the projects do not all have the same prominence. In the exhibition presented at the Espace Électra in 1997 – *Gilles Clément, une école buissonnière*[50] – theoretical discourse and projects are clearly distinct. The part devoted to the projects is presented more as an exhibition of a designer's output, following
a chronological sequence. The exhibition *The Planetary Garden* in the Grande Halle at La Villette, in 2000, adopted a very different angle: entirely oriented towards, and structured by, a particular discourse, it put the accent on direct contact with objects, in the tradition of the universal exhibitions. The landscape projects were not really displayed, with the exception of the "forest of leftover spaces", a project to map neglected areas in the Paris region and their forestation, developed by Clément in association with Patrick Bouchain, and the garden of the Sítio Roberto Burle Marx, southwest of Rio de Janeiro, named for its architect. The projects presented in the "Garden of Experiences" part are projects for green manufacturing or urban governance sites such as those in Stockholm, Curitiba or Porto Alegre.[51] They nonetheless provide the material on which the discourse is built, while the photography has a mainly illustrative function.

It is a distinguishing feature of lectures and conferences, as we have seen, to bind theory and practice closely together, each reinforcing the other. The project, thanks to photography, becomes the stuff of discourse. Through imagery, it takes on the status of a rhetorical argument. And by sampling a fragment of the designed or completed project, photography elevates the image of the garden or landscape project into a symbol that can be articulated with a line of discursive reasoning. These images, organized around the projection, give rise to a verbalization which, in Clément's case, develops into an exposition that is both theoretical and political, a practice that originates in the teaching he dispenses, notably at the National School of Landscape Architecture (ENSP) in Versailles.

In the exhibition *Toujours la vie invente*,[52] photographs of projects, whether completed or otherwise, are displayed on the same level as the photographs brought back from travel or field trips. Here, the garden and landscape projects are the supporting material for a discourse on the living world, a discourse that is at once artistic and scientific. The exhibition spatializes this discourse, in which theoretical reflection is combined with concrete action. It showcases a creative stance that is expressed both in landscape creations and in manifestations of "involuntary art" collected from around the world. This exhibition is a new step in Gilles Clément's unfinished project to represent the multidimensional work of a planetary gardener.

I would like to thank Gilles Clément for his generosity and helpfulness, as well as Sylvie Archaimbault for her ever-relevant advice.

45 Interview with Gilles Clément, December 9, 2014.

46 See Bruce Bégout, *La Découverte du quotidien*, Allia, Paris, 2005.

47 See Tim Benton, *op. cit.*, especially Ch. 1, "Le Corbusier's logic".

48 A detailed analysis of the status of the images conveyed at these events has already been outlined but requires more in-depth investigation. See Olivier Lugon (ed.), *Exposition et médias. Photographie, cinéma, télévision*, L'Âge d'homme, Lausanne, 2012, and the round table discussion in this volume, p. 173.

49 Gilles Clément publishes widely in parallel to his activity as a designer. In addition to his many articles, a list of his published books can be found in Frédérique Basset, *op. cit.*, p. 179–180.

50 *Gilles Clément. Une école buissonnière*, published to accompany the exhibition of the same name, held at the Espace Électra (September 17 – November 23, 1997), Hazan, Paris, 1997.

51 See *Gilles Clément. Le jardin Planétaire. Réconcilier l'homme avec la nature*, published to accompany the exhibition *The Planetary Garden* at the Grande Halle, La Villette, September 1999 – January 2000, Albin Michel, Paris, 1999. *English translation*: Clément, Gilles, et al. "The Planetary Garden: Reconciling Man and Nature." *The Planetary Garden and Other Writings*, University of Pennsylvania Press, Philadelphia, PA, 2015, p. 1–64.

52 *Toujours la vie invente*, exhibition staged for the Melle Biennale of Contemporary Art, and presented at Saint-Benoît-du-Sault (Creuse) and at ENSA Paris-La Seine, September 30 – October 25, 2014.

From Photorealism to Post-Photography: The Imagined Landscapes of Bureau Bas Smets

Marie-Madeleine Ozdoba

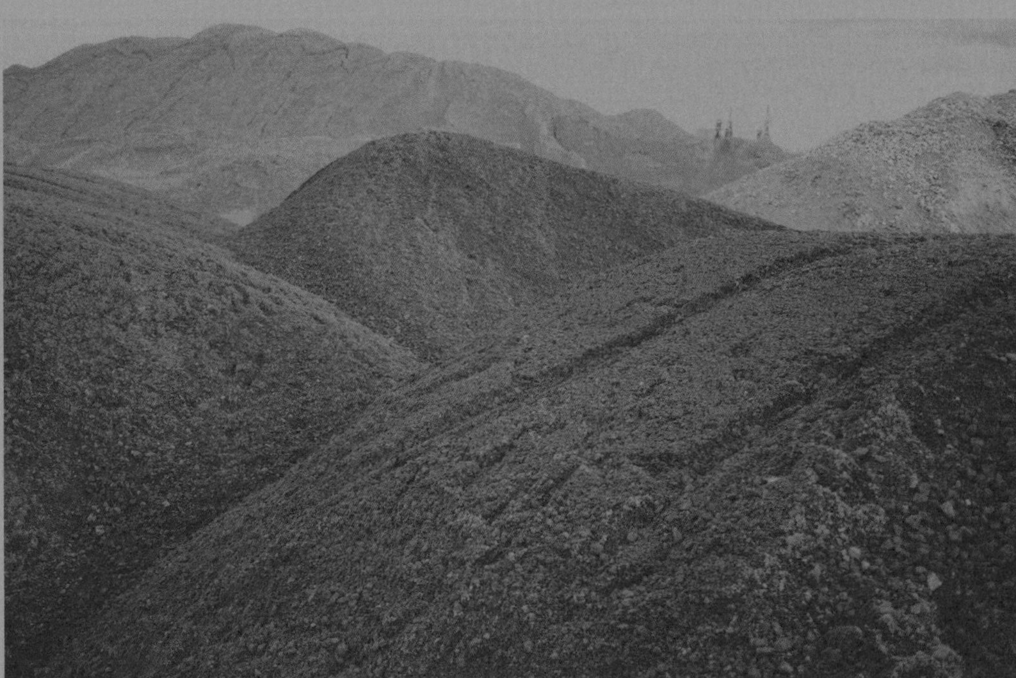

A landscape is a cultural image, a pictorial way of representing, structuring or symbolizing surroundings [...], a landscape park is more palpable, but no more real, nor less imaginary, than a landscape painting or a poem.[1]

Whereas painting and drawing are widely recognized as fields where landscape architects can produce "artworks",[2] photographs – from photos of the site to those that document the completed project – still tend to be assimilated, in the trade, to mere recording instruments. The case of Bas Smets, a young landscape architect based in Brussels, paves the way for a reassessment of photography in the practice of landscape architecture, as a field of creation and expression in its own right.

Bas Smets leverages the photographic medium in the broadest sense (3D renderings, photography, cinema) to represent "imagined landscapes"; through this unique visual practice, the landscaper builds up a complex relationship between photography and reality.

THE INSTRUMENTAL USE OF PHOTOGRAPHY IN THE PRACTICE OF LANDSCAPE ARCHITECTURE

In the project-led disciplines of architecture and landscape architecture, photography is usually expected to pass a kind of truth test – this applies as much to the photographic documentation of a site or a finished landscape as it does to the photo-realistic visualization of the project (whether 3D renderings or digital collage).[3] In this respect, the 2000s were a real turning point, when the performance of digital tools, particularly when it came to rendering vegetation, made it possible to produce photo-realistic views of landscape projects: the landscape architect's "touch" – characterized by graphic styles that are distinctive, if not necessarily realistic – gave way, in major French and international agencies, to images that were chiefly concerned with creating an illusion or, in other words, showing the project "like in a photo". Landscape architects such Agence Ter or Michel Desvigne, for example, began to call on the services of 3D visualization firms formerly used only by architects.[4] Though alternatives exist, and despite the resistance that it inevitably arouses in the profession, the photo-realistic standard in project representation has been gaining ground among landscape architects ever since.[5]

The Bureau Bas Smets, founded in Brussels in 2007, is no exception to the trend: the agency produces photo-realistic views of projects when the client so requests, which is the case increasingly often, in particular for public contracts. For example, the image used to advertise the project for the Tour & Taxis park – a landscape park on a piece of former industrial wasteland in the center of Brussels – was a semi-aerial photo-realistic view that combined a photograph of the site with a 3D rendering | **FIG. 1** |. Displayed on the site during the works, the picture, according to the landscape architect, corresponded to what has now become a standard requirement in the representation and mediatization of a landscape project: show-

1
Denis Cosgrove and Stephen Daniels, *The Iconography of Landscape*, Cambridge University Press, Cambridge (UK), 1988, p. 1.

2
The paintings of Roberto Burle Marx and the drawings of Gilles Clément are examples of graphic works that emanate from landscaping practice.

3
On a theoretical level, the "indexical" thesis (the photograph as a luminous trace, thus possessing a special bond with reality) was defended by Rosalind Krauss (*Le Photographique. Pour une théorie des écarts*, transl. Marc Bloch, Ann Hindry, Jean Kempf, Macula, Paris, 1990). It has since been widely challenged: see in particular the special report Que dit la théorie de la photographie?, *Études photographiques*, no. 34, spring 2016.

4
The latest 3D vegetation modeling techniques, derived from videogames, do not yet offer a satisfactory alternative to drawing or collage. Great skill is still required when it comes to working with graphic effects involving plants. In France, Luxigon, Labtop and Lou Kat are among the perspective specialists much sought after by the major landscaping agencies. See Marie-Madeleine Ozdoba, "Du déluge à l'écoquartier : projections urbaines à l'époque du réchauffement climatique", *picturingarchitecture.wordpress.com*, 2013.

5
Despite the current trend for photo-realistic images, many landscape architects continue to develop very free rendering styles. The project teaching approach at the ENSP school for landscape architecture in Versailles, for example, encourages the development of alternative representation strategies. On contemporary issues in landscape project representation, see Nadia Amoroso, *Representing Landscapes: A Visual Collection of Landscape Architectural Drawings*, Routledge, London, New York, 2012 and *Representing Landscapes: Digital*, Routledge, London, New York, 2015.

ing "what the real thing will look like". But it is only reluctantly that he consents to such demands: "There is absolutely no point: we'll see soon enough, once it has been built. The image ought to take you somewhere else. This is a major sticking point with clients."[6]

The increasingly widespread use of photo-realistic renderings to represent landscape projects is driven by the idea that the photographic image is merely a "transparent window" onto the future development. The belief that what we see is indeed real is *implicit*: "when we look at photographs, we assume – unless otherwise indicated – that they haven't been reworked."[7] For that reason, in its most widespread usage, the photo-realistic project rendering is tantamount to a promise.[8]

As Yves Michaud has shown, belief in the truth of the photographic image is deeply culturally engrained: "We all know that images are manufactured. What I mean by that is, we are well aware that they are not mere emanations of reality, simulacra, or little pictures emitted by things, like films that peel off them, as the Epicureans claimed, but constructed objects that relate to reality in complicated ways. [...] And yet, we don't want to believe that; we are all too eager to take them at face value..."[9] Overriding our initial intuition, we must remember that rather than its visual content, what actually determines the degree of "truth" of an image is the information that accompanies it (particularly its caption and its publication context): according to the context, the very same image, photographic or otherwise, can be either "honest" or "fake".[10]

Rather than being criticized, as Michaud would wish, the alleged "transparency" of the photographic image is often copiously exploited, especially – as in the example of the display for the Tour & Taxis park project – when it comes to gaining public buy-in. In the absence of contextual information to put its promise into perspective, the photo-realistic image is perceived as a reliable reflection of the future, endowed with a special bond to reality. In landscaping practice, photography is therefore used most often in an instrumental role; in the framework of the design or communication of a project, its role is to "stick" as closely as possible to reality, rather than to be appreciated as an image. Consequently, for landscape architects, photographic practice can never be an outlet for creation and expression, nor can it result in an autonomous visual work: the photo-realistic images produced in landscape architecture practice – from photography to computer graphics – are ascribed low cultural and heritage value.[11]

An analysis of the *expressive uses* of the medium, inspired by three original projects by Bas Smets, will be useful in probing whether – and how – in the world of landscape architecture, photography can lay claim to the status of a visual practice in its own right. A brief outline of contemporary theories of photography, and in particular the notion of the "post-photographic" image, will help us break away from the conception of the photograph as a supposedly "transparent" image.

HOW THE LANDSCAPE PROJECT CAN REFRAME PHOTOGRAPHY: THE "POST-PHOTOGRAPHIC" APPROACH

Questioning the instrumental use of photography in landscape architecture practice is an important critical step if we are to go beyond the sterile "true or fake" debates about photo-realistic images that have tended to plague the discipline.[12] Long preoccupied by the complex relationship between reality and its representations, theories of photography have developed a tool that is particularly useful for addressing the issue: the notion of the "post-photographic" image, which applies to photo-realistic images characterized by having been constructed and/or manipulated – mainly through the use of photo editing software – with the consequence that their photographic truth is understood as contextual information (and not as an intrinsic quality of the image). This contrasts with the so-called "indexical" thesis.[13]

As a representation of a *future* development, the photo-realistic representation of a landscape project (using 3D renderings and digital collage) is essentially the result of a construction: it corresponds, in this respect, to the definition recently formulated by Philippe Dubois: "A photograph devoid of all trace: a simple piece of visual material, designed to be contextualized at a later date."[14] Conceived of as a fictional world, made possible by the latest rendering and photo editing software, the photo-realistic representation of the landscape project "is no longer defined 'absolutely', in its 'original' principle, as a way of capturing reality, as its identity is no longer bound up with a simple 'sampling' of a fragment of the world, but with something that turns it into a representation that might not correspond to a real thing, a representation that may (may, not must) have been invented (in whole or in part) by an image-making machine."[15]

Can landscape architects break free from the instrumental use of the photographic image, in the same way that, in post-photographic mode, photography is breaking away from its "indexical" relationship to reality? Can the contextual information around the image become a field of creation and expression for landscape architects, to endow the photograph with meanings and imaginaries transcending its "objective" content? These questions are central to Bureau Bas Smets's visual practice.

In 2007, after seven years at the agency of Michel Desvigne, Bas Smets set up his own agency in Brussels, specializing in "the conception of *landscape strategies* and the construction of public space."[16] In his practice, the questioning of the relationship between image and reality emerges as the driving force behind a design approach that combines theory and practice to form the substance of the landscape project. This is reflected in the text accompanying an exhibition of the agency's projects, staged at three venues – Antwerp, Charleroi and Bordeaux – during the course of 2014. The text introduces a clear duality between "imagined landscape" and "realized landscape":

> *This exhibition explores the relationship between image and reality in the landscape projects of Bas Smets. Starting out from a precise reading of the territory, his projects transform 'land' into 'landscape'. The land can only become landscape through a cultural process. Land is the existing condition of physical reality and the landscape is the perception of this reality that can be comprehended and represented trough images [...]. These images pave the way for theactual transformation of the site, culminating in the 'realized landscape'. The transformed reality itself produces new perceptions or landscapes, creating an intimate and infinite feedback loop between image and reality.*[17]

With his agency, Smets develops projects happily blending landscape architecture with exhibition design, photography, cinema and visual arts. Beyond the instrumental uses of the image – inherent to the practice of landscape architecture – the photographic representation of the landscape project is, for Smets, a pretext for continual research, which he sees as a field of production in its own right. The "imagined landscapes" that result from this research entertain a complex relationship with reality – a stance that makes the landscape architect an inventor of "possible worlds". As Philippe

6
Bas Smets in an interview with Marie-Madeleine Ozdoba, Brussels, June 13, 2014. All translations are our own unless otherwise stated.

7
André Gunthert, "Sans retouche", *Études photographiques,* no. 22, 2008, p. 56–77.

8
On the implications of the "transparency" of the image in the representation of urban projects, see Marie-Madeleine Ozdoba, *La mise en paysage du Front de Seine: de la ville du futur à la ville durable (1960–2010);* (Landscapes of the Front de Seine. Staging the Urban Project, from the City of the Future to the Sustainable City (1960–2010)), *Articulo – Journal of Urban Research,* no. 4, 2013.

9
Yves Michaud, "Critiques de la crédulité", *Études photographiques*, no. 12, November 2012, p. 110–125.

10
On the question of the "fakeness" of images as contextual information independent from their degree of realism, see Marie-Madeleine Ozdoba, "Des usages et réalismes de l'image d'architecture", *picturingarchitecture. wordpress.com*, 2013: http://picturingarchitecture.wordpress.com/2013/06/25/sur-le-realisme-de-limage-darchitecture-et-son-rapport-a-lobjectivite.

11
There is a clear contrast here between the treatment reserved for the photographic output of landscape architects as part of a project and that granted to landscape photography as an artistic practice (contemporary art, commissions, photographic observatories, etc.).

12
For a survey of the main notions derived from culturalist theories of photographs as constructed representations in the field of landscaping, see Marc Treib, "Photographic landscapes: Time stilled, place transposed", in *Representing Landscape Architecture*, Marc Treib (ed.), Taylor & Francis, New York, 2007, p. 188–203.

13
On the notion of the post-photographic image, see Philippe Dubois, "De l'image-trace à l'image-fiction. Le mouvement des théories de la photographie de 1980 à nos jours", *Études photographiques*, no. 34, 2016, p. 52–69. See also: William J. Mitchell, *The Reconfigured Eye: Visual Truth in the Post-Photographic Era*, MIT Press, Cambridge, MA, 1992; Martha Langford and Vincent Lavoie (ed.), dossier "Post-photographie?", *Captures. Figures, théories et pratiques de l'imaginaire*, vol. 1, no. 1, 2016; Joan Fontcuberta, *The Post-Photographic Condition*, Kerber/Le mois de la photo à Montréal, Montreal, 2015.

14
Philippe Dubois, *op. cit.*

15
Philippe Dubois, *op. cit.*

16
Ten years on, Bureau Bas Smets employs 15 architects and landscapers and executes projects at every scale, from infrastructure to regional development, and from gardens to city centers (http://www.bassmets.be).

17
From the catalogue of the exhibition *Paysages* at the Palais des Beaux-Arts in Charleroi in 2014.

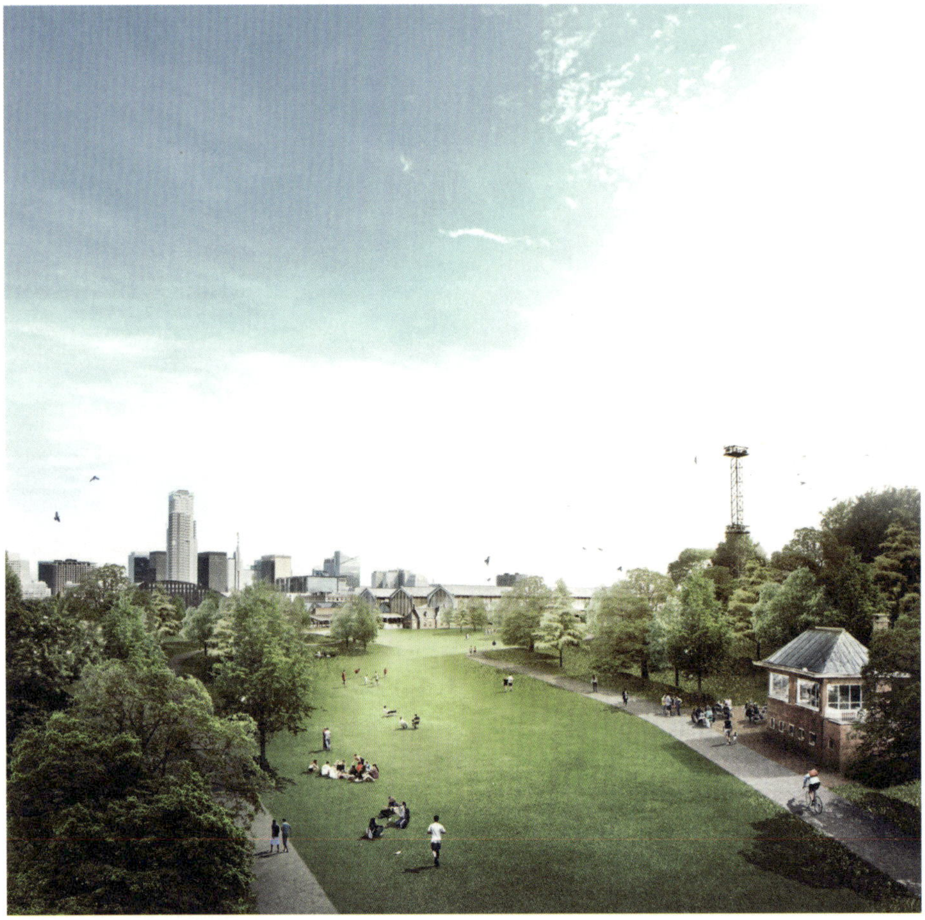

|FIG. 1|

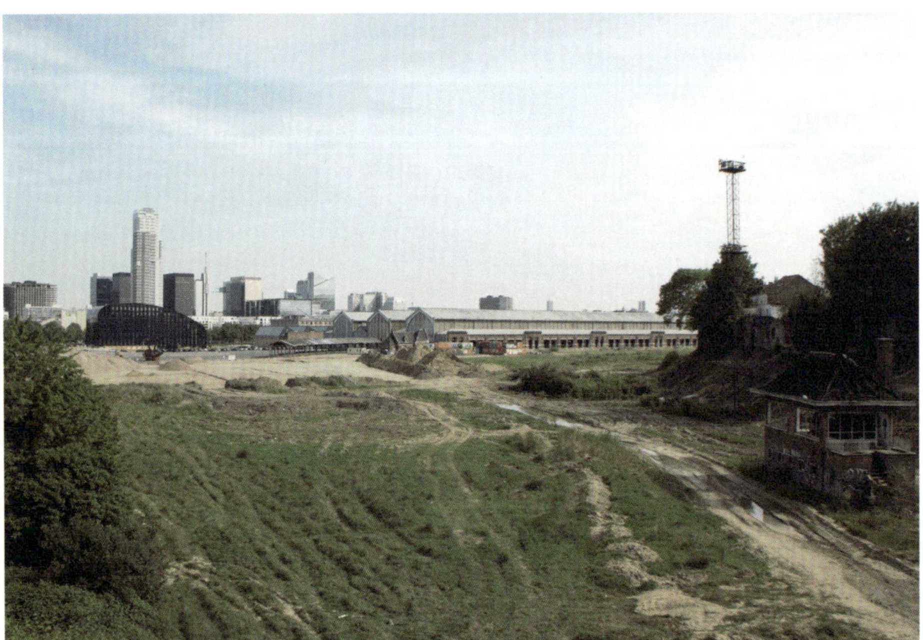

|FIG. 2|

|FIG. 1|
Rendering of the Tour & Taxis park project in Brussels.

|FIG. 2|
Photograph of the existing site used as a basis for the renderingof the project.

Dubois puts it: "theories of possible worlds seem to me to be the best way to approach, at the theoretical level, the status of the contemporary photographic image: no longer something 'that was (there)' in the real world but something 'that is (here)', in front of us, something we can accept (or reject), not as the trace of something that was, but for what it is, or more exactly for what it shows itself to be: a 'possible world' [...] An image conceived as a 'world of fiction' rather than as a 'world of reference'."[18]

Several of Smets's propositions explore the interplay "between image and reality" which, according to Dubois, characterizes the contemporary photographic image: the way he contextualizes the photo-realistic rendering of the Brussels Tour & Taxis park project, mentioned earlier, within the history of landscape painting; the design for an exhibition of the agency's projects, based on "snapshots" assembled into photographic walls, which Smets calls *atlases;* and finally, *Continuously Habitable Zones*, a hybrid object, half-film, half-landscape, produced in collaboration with the visual artist Philippe Parreno. From this analysis, Bas Smets's experimental approach – combining photographic theory and landscape architecture practice in an unprecedented way – emerges as a symptomatic, and particularly eloquent, illustration of "how the landscape project can reframe photography".

COMPUTER IMAGES AS IMAGINED LANDSCAPES

The *instrumental use* of the photo-realistic image resides in the possibility of measuring its conformity with the completed project. It leads, for some people, to a heightened distrust of renderings that idealize the project, but also, for others, to a blind faith in images that present themselves as actual photographs of the future: "If I can see it in 'the photo', it must be true." In opposition to this kind of instrumental use of 3D renderings, Bas Smets confronts the "imagined landscape" – the "post-photographic" image, whose frame of reference he locates in the field of landscape painting – with the project in its phenomenological (experienced) dimension, from worksite to completion, which, he claims, escapes any attempt at representation.

18
Philippe Dubois, *op. cit.* On the topic of "possible worlds" in logic and analytical philosophy, see Patrick Peccatte, "Fictions et mondes possibles", *Déjà vu*, August 28, 2012, http://dejavu.hypotheses.org/1188.

Thus, the official photo-realistic rendering of the Tour & Taxis park project **| FIG. 1 |** clearly belongs to the "paradigm of the contractual image": a representation aimed at an audience to whom it is presented as a promise. Produced in-house by the agency's landscape architects, the image was displayed on a billboard on the building site **| FIG. 3 |**, but it was also circulated to the press and presented at the Bureau's exhibitions. Starting from a photograph of the existing site **| FIG. 2 |**,

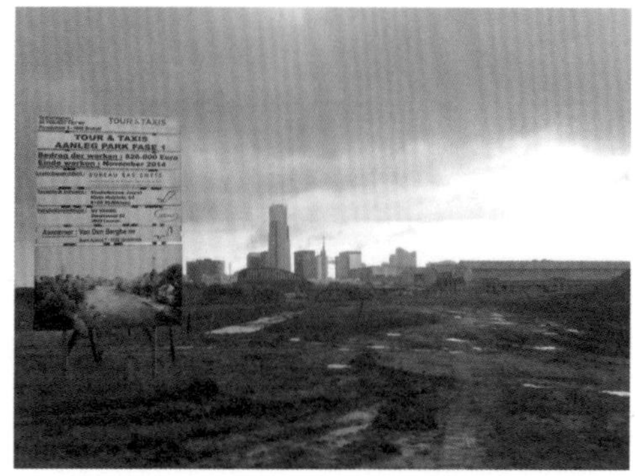

| FIG. 3 | Photo of the building site with billboard, September 2014.

the landscape architects used 3D rendering and digital editing software to integrate the new features – paths, plantations, urban furniture – as well as a series of elements to breathe life into the scene, from birds circling in the blue sky to people using the play areas in the foreground. All of which was then put through some "idealizing" graphic processing (erasing inconvenient elements; photoshopping a shabby-looking house in the foreground to "renovate" it; correcting colors and contrasts, etc.). The treetops, much fuller in the rendering than in the initial site photograph – touched up like a celebrity photo – have the perfection of an advertising picture. This view of the project is a "post-photographic image" *par excellence*: it has no more than the appearance of being a photograph... almost no part of it could be described as a "luminous trace" of reality.

In terms of its implicit meanings, the image is notable for a chromatic scale of blues and greens – colors, needless to say, with positive associations that are exploited relentlessly by the advertising world in this ecologically aware age – while the Brussels skyline, visible at the top of the picture, evokes, with its skyscrapers, the urban silhouettes that have become such a familiar feature of movie posters. And the choice of a semi-aerial perspective, a genuine "bird's eye view", is a standard of contemporary landscape project representation: a familiar *way of seeing* any urban park project.

The square format and the graphic style of the image, with its "smooth" texture and saturated colors, recall the aesthetics of the filters of Instagram, the famous photo-sharing network. The photo-realistic image of the project echoes contemporary tastes and fashions; the visual culture of urban developments is influenced by the graphic standards of advertising, video games and, most recently, popular applications.

In the absence of any further contextual details, the narrative register of the photo-realistic project rendering is that of the "true story": the publication of project renderings in informational media (the press, public announcements, exhibitions) suggests that what they represent is truthful, or at least plausible. In other words, the photo-realistic representation of the project implies a *contrat de lecture* or reading pact that assumes it to be honest, or even "transparent".[19] Thus it was with the image displayed at the worksite of the Tour & Taxis park. This presupposition of honesty in the image is strongly linked to the concrete impact of landscape projects on the appearance and/or uses of a place: in line with a legitimate public expectation of information, the image is not perceived *a priori* as a fiction, but as a document that reliably reflects a future reality.[20] And so, quite naturally, the image carries part of the factual information on the project, despite all the ambiguities and margins of interpretation inherent to visual media. It is up to the landscape architect and/or the PR team to provide all the details required for a proper understanding of the project, rather than taking advantage of the presupposition of "transparency" to gloss over the potential downsides: this misuse of the photo-realistic image in project communication is a major cause of the accusations of dishonesty frequently leveled against it.

Well aware of this danger, Smets focuses his critical approach on the enunciative context of the rendering: though he may comply with a request for a photo-realistic representation of the project, he develops a discourse that runs counter to the belief in an "honest" or "transparent" representation. And when he presents it at interviews, conferences, or indeed exhibitions, he invariably places the rendering of the park in the continuity of the pictorial tradition of the 15th-century Flemish artists, with whom the very concept of landscape originated[21] **| FIG. 4 |**. By contextualizing the image in this way, he makes it "reappear" for what it is.

In particular, Smets develops a parallel between contemporary photo-realistic landscape renderings and the landscape paintings of Joachim Patinir, which drew their inspiration from religious and mythological texts.[22] When he presents a rendering and a landscape painting side by side, what Smets is saying is this: *this image doesn't tell "the truth", it tells a story.* The view of the Tour & Taxis park project is very much a fiction, hidden under an outward appearance of realism. Rather than a promise, Smets presents the image as a fictional landscape, which explicitly and deliberately takes the landscapes of the Flemish painters as its visual frame of reference.

Taking this approach still further, in the context of a project to develop a freeway that blends in with the polders in Western Flanders, Belgium (the Autoroute A11), Smets commissioned the 3D artists at the firm Luxigon (Paris) to come up with renderings "that depict the landscape of the freeway as if it were in a 17th-century painting by Salomon van Ruisdael". Once again, Smets is distancing himself from a purely instrumental usage of the photo-realistic image, being careful to uphold the distinction between *imagined landscape* and realized landscape. When highlighted in this way, the contextual information ("this is an image!") guides the reception of the image and fundamentally alters people's expectations of it: it is no longer about the "reality of the project", but about the *landscape imaginary*.

Smets contrasts the imagined landscape of the picture (whether a painting or a computer rendering) with the landscape project in its phenomenological – i.e. experienced – dimension, in which time and change are key elements of the narrative. It is this realized landscape, to use his expression, which I was able to experience for myself on my first visit to the Tour & Taxis park worksite in 2014. I was struck by the way the users had already taken hold of the space, thanks notably to a temporary building erected in the middle of the earthworks,

19
Louis Marin, *Opacités de la peinture*, Éditions de l'EHESS, Paris, 2006.

20
On the social context of the image and the "naturalization of fiction" that can occur under certain conditions, see Howard Becker, "Visual sociology, documentary photography, and photojournalism: It's (almost) all a matter of context", *Visual Studies*, 10:1, 1995, p. 5–14.

21
Bas Smets is referring particularly to the theory of Alain Roger, *Court traité du paysage*, Gallimard, Paris, 1997. See also John D. Wylie, *Landscape*, Routledge, London, New York, 2007.

22
On landscape painting and its relationship to the representation of reality, see Svetlana Alpers, *The Art of Describing: Dutch Art in the Seventeenth Century*, John Murray, London; University of Chicago Press, Chicago, IL, 1983.

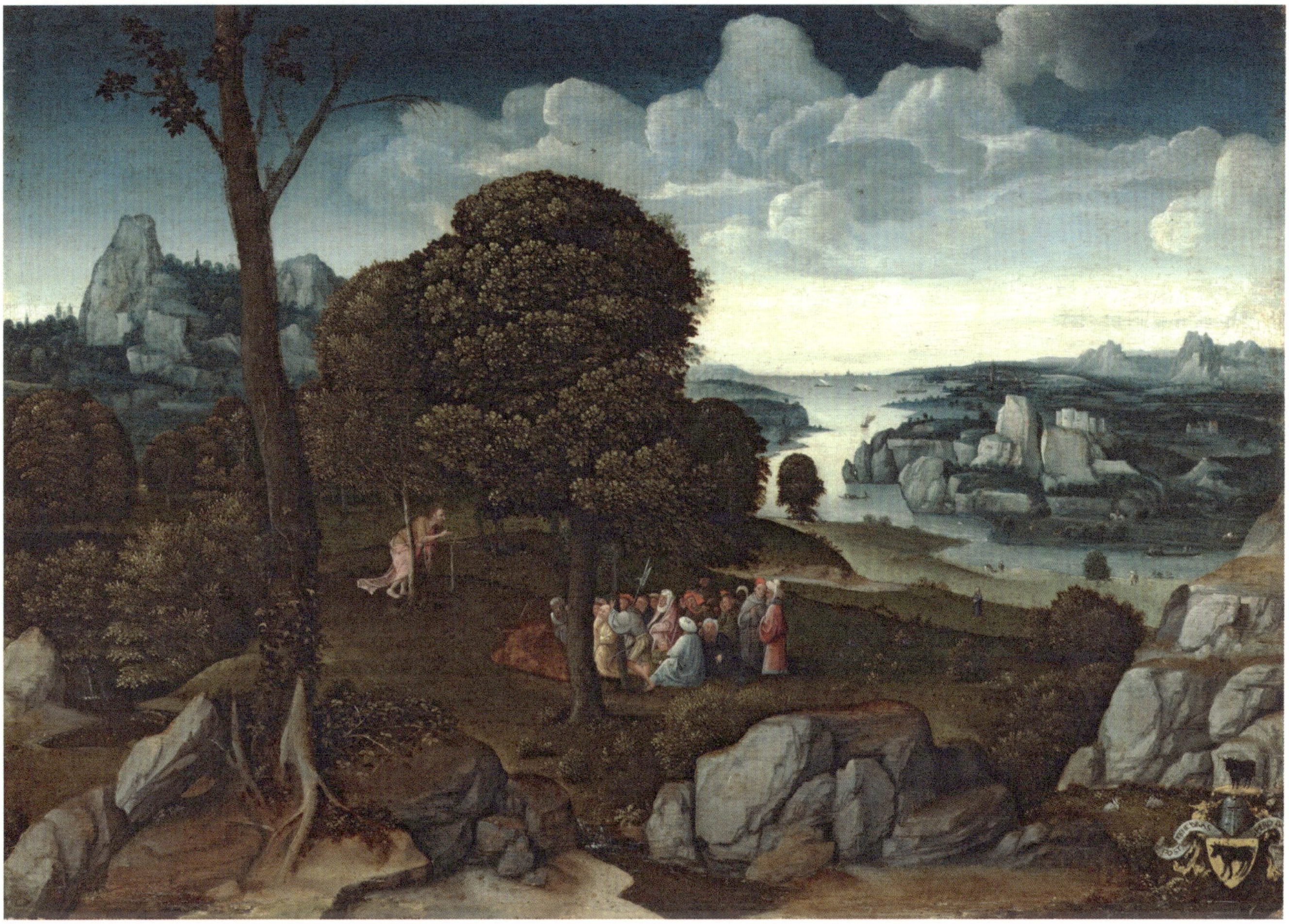

| FIG. 4 |

| FIG. 4 |
Studio of Joachim Patinir,
Landscape with St John the Baptist Preaching, c. 1515–1518, oil on oak,
37.5 × 50.8 cm,
Philadelphia Museum of Art,
inv. 1944-9-2.

where cooking and other collective activities were organized, which carried on outside the building using improvised-looking pine furniture: the people who lived near the park were using – in the landscape architect's words – an *intermediate stage* of the project.[23] This fundamentally transitory and unfinished quality of the landscape is at the heart of Smets's approach with the Tour & Taxis project, "saying that there is a form of transformation that nature proposes, by invading the wasteland, and designing the project to follow on from that transformation… […] It isn't very clear what was there and what wasn't. This isn't a 'before/after', it's a 'during'. […] It may not be spectacular, but you can feel the movement of the project; and that is where its quality lies." To illustrate his approach, Smets mentions the example of the process he developed for planting a lawn in the absence of viable topsoil on the site, which amounts to a genuine strategy for a "project in progress": clover was planted in order to create humus, which in turn will enrich the soil. At the end of this process, the landscape architect predicts, nature itself will provide a lawn of some kind. "You have to accept that it will evolve bit by bit. […] It's experimental, we don't know exactly what it will look like, but we think it's worth trying it out…"

For Smets, the photo-realistic image creates expectations, whereas this type of "landscape in progress" arouses curiosity: "People didn't say: 'this isn't what I was expecting'. They asked: 'what are you making?'" The project becomes very much a timeframe of invention with undefined limits, where non-standard strategies and uses are developed, which Smets contrasts with the idea that it is possible to present an image of the park that exactly resembles the finalized project:

We are often asked to do an 'official' or 'accurate' image, but I don't believe in that. […] I think that the rendering is a way of seeing things. If, in five years' time, the completed project really has to look like that, then the image loses its relevance. What makes it interesting is when the landscape adds its own resistance. For me, designing landscape is like bringing up a child: of course, it has to obey you a little bit, but afterwards, it also has to become itself. That's why these renderings where you don't know whether it's a photo or reality… there's no point to them. It's pointless if there's no, sense of becoming when you build a project. You don't go to see a movie if you already know how it ends.[24]

SNAPSHOTS AND ATLASES: PHOTOGRAPHIC FICTIONS IN THE LANDSCAPE PROJECT

In the Bureau Bas Smets exhibitions held in Charleroi and Bordeaux in 2014, the agency's work was presented in the form of "photographic walls" made up of hundreds of shots taken by the landscaper on his iPhone and assembled into a regular grid to form a monumental mosaic **| FIG. 6 and 7 |**. Embedded in this device, which he calls an "atlas", the aim of the photographs is less to document the project than to "fictionalize" it and affirm the inevitable disconnect between image and reality.

Smets prefers to photograph his work himself, rather than entrust the task to a professional, including when preparing for an exhibition. These "snapshots", as he calls them, "are really photos taken from my viewpoint, never using zoom effects. It's good old 50 mm: reality as seen on the ground." The styles of specialist photographers strike him as having "too many connotations, given the architects they work with," but this is not the main reason why he chooses not to use their services: it is also a way of asserting the specificity of the landscape project, which differs from the architectural project by its horizontal breadth and its uncertain boundaries in time and space. "It's very difficult to show landscape with an image, as all my architect friends do," Smets explains. "They have their favorite photographers, and the photo is a work of art that reveals the building. We [landscape architects] can't do that, because when our project is completed, it isn't beautiful. That takes five years, or ten, or twenty. So we propose 24 photos per project, and this set of 24 photos gives an idea of the reality, or of what we wanted to do. And this set of 24 photos creates a walk-through experience. The problem with landscape is that it needs movement. It isn't just about the optimal perspective; you have to move around, and it's impossible to show that with a single photo."[25] The aesthetics of the "snapshot" are, therefore, deliberately embraced: assembled into photographic walls, with no privileged moments or viewpoints of the project, but rather an accumulation of fragments, the snapshots resonate with Smets's thinking on landscape in progress.

This "other way of thinking" – defined, according to Smets, by the representation of the project in the field of landscape architecture – engages structurally with movement in space and change over time: in the case of the Tour & Taxis park, for example, he mentions "a very beautiful photo taken by the project manager when the gravel was being sorted at the site | **FIG. 5** |. There were three very high hills: one that was black, one that was yellow, and the last, which was slightly green, as there were three different soil compositions. It's a magnificent photo. Today, those hills can longer be seen, obviously, because it was just a phase. [...] The snapshots of the transformation of the site are like the photo album of a person over a period of several years: the poses aren't always the same, but it gives you an idea of their different centers of interest." Countering the idea that photography can encapsulate a project "transparently", Bas Smets's snapshots are fragments extracted at different stages in the execution of a landscape project, understood as a process with undefined boundaries.

This poetic, diffuse and fragmentary quality of photography, induced by the inherent instability of landscape, is further underlined by the choice of shots displayed on the photographic walls at Bureau Bas Smets: they show, for example, the same open space (the landscape around the Château de Padiès at Lempaut, France) under different lighting conditions, at different seasons, and from different angles | **FIG. 7** |. But far from striving for comprehensiveness or clarity – those tasks are devolved to the text and to other forms of representation such as plans and sections – the photographs play on repetitions and slight variances, focussing on the range of different ambiances, the contrast between close-ups and panoramic views, or variations on a theme: plants, geometry, colors, etc.: "From a distance, you can see the seasons. Here, for example, you can see a series under the snow, which makes for a white patch. From a distance, it's a sort of color pixel, which turns out to be a photo as you move closer. Using these snapshots, we have car-

23
"From the outset, people made use of the worksite. First on the foundations, then on the ground cover. So people experienced the worksite. There wasn't a before and an after, there was always a during." Bas Smets in an interview with Marie-Madeleine Ozdoba, Brussels, August 20, 2015.

24
Smets's experimental approach is closely tied to the political and institutional context of the project. In the case of the Tour & Taxis park, this was an urban project developed by a group of private owners on a site that was the object of a policy of temporary occupation and sustainable development overseen by a government agency (IBGE). On the subject of militant participatory involvement in landscape projects, see Margaux Vigne, *Entre alternative et modèle: expérimentations institutionnelles, professionnelles et habitantes dans la fabrication des espaces verts*, PhD thesis (forthcoming), ENSA Nantes.

25
Bas Smets in an interview with Marie-Madeleine Ozdoba, Brussels, June 13, 2014. Smets adds: "It isn't that architecture photographers don't know [how to photograph the landscape], it's because I'm trying to define for myself what the landscaping profession is about, and I do it through dialogue – sometimes in agreement, sometimes in opposition – with the architectural profession."

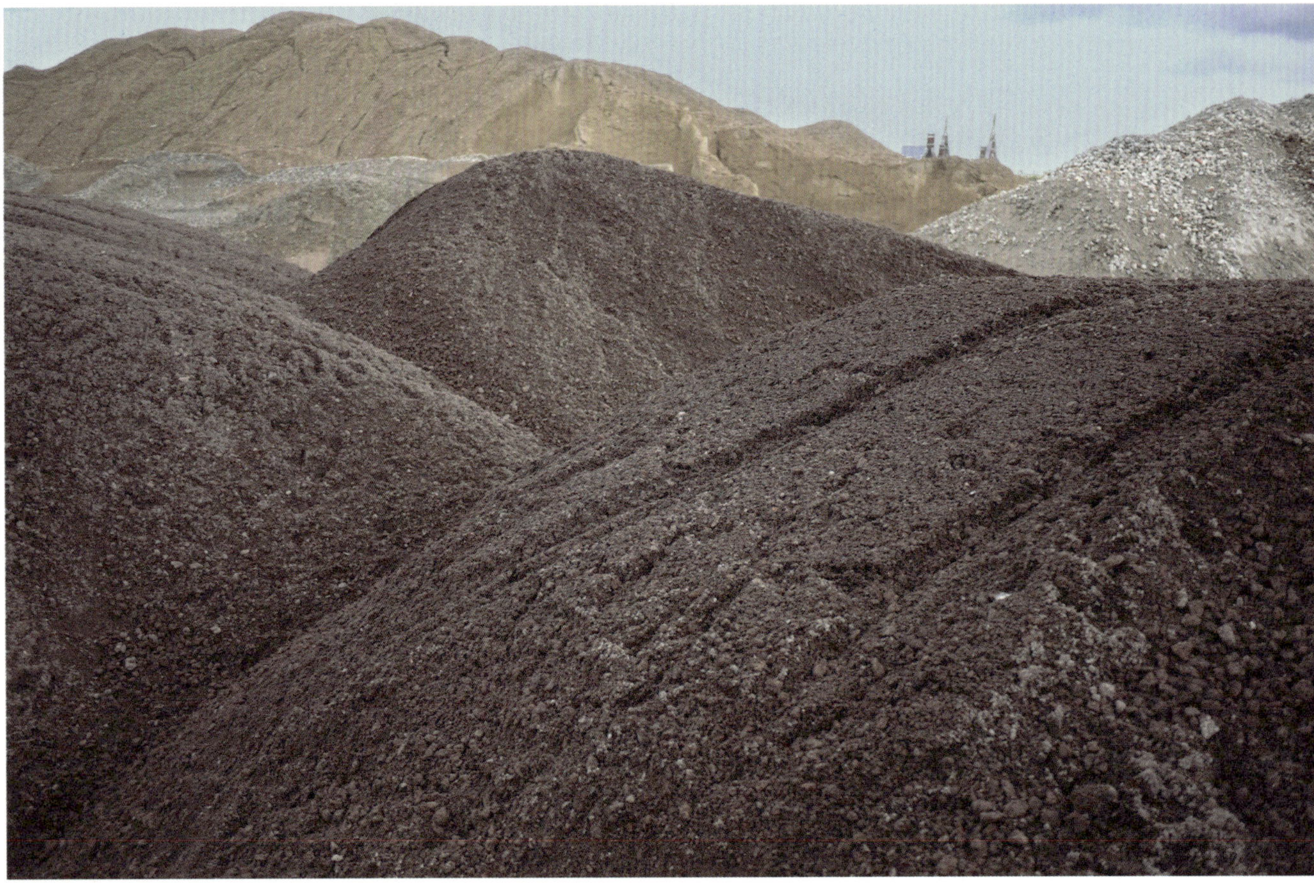

| FIG. 5 |

| FIG. 5 |
Snapshot of the sieving of soil on the site of the Tour & Taxis park.

| FIG. 6 |
Photographic wall in the exhibition *Paysages* by Bureau Bas Smets at the Palais des Beaux-Arts, Charleroi, in 2014.

| FIG. 7 |
Detail of the photographic wall in the exhibition *Paysages* by Bureau Bas Smets at the Palais des Beaux-Arts, Charleroi, in 2014.

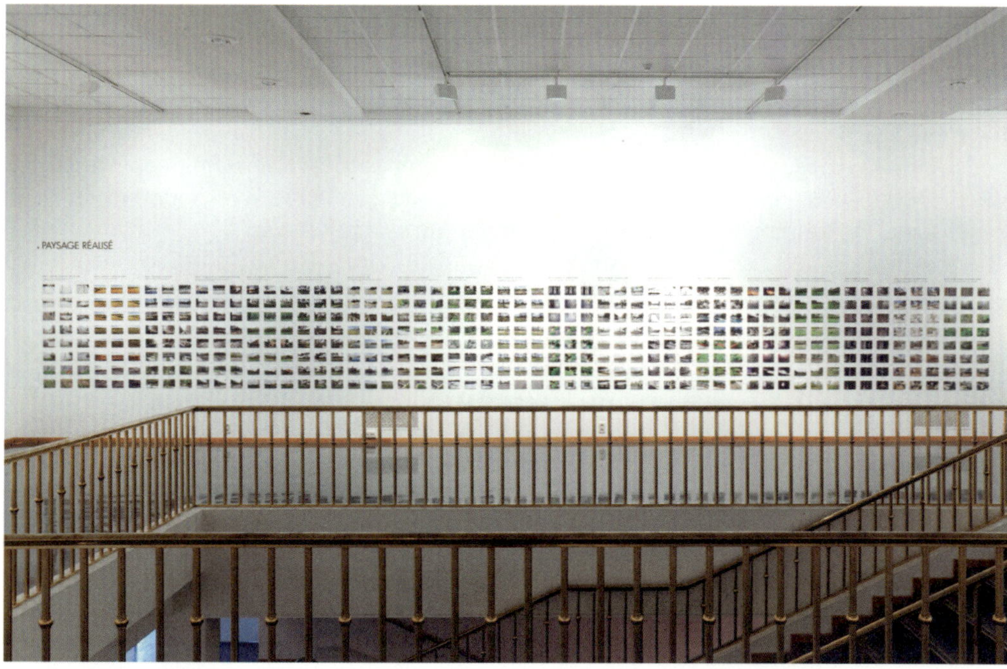

| FIG. 6 |

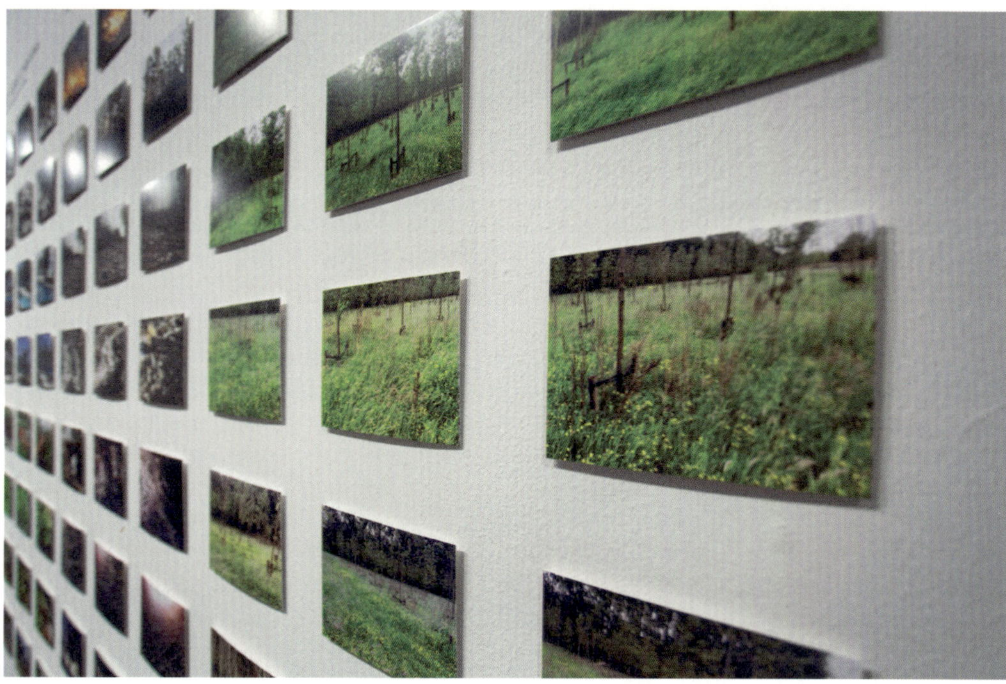

| FIG. 7 |

ried out a major reflection on the colors, without having to send in a great photographer… My dream would be to commission movie-makers to shoot films in the landscape […] so as to have the sequence."[26]

By systematically juxtaposing images, the photographic wall device seeks to encourage transversal navigation between them. Smets cites as a reference Gerhard Richter's *Atlas*, a monumental work commenced in 1962, in which the German painter exposes an immense collection of photographs – found images, family snapshots, even press clippings – grouped together on boards and displayed in a regular grid, which today numbers over 5000 images **| FIG. 8 |**.[27] But beyond what they have in common, it is the inventory of their differences that offers more insight into the specificity of Smets's project: whereas Richter's *Atlas*, which is both personal archive and a work of art, is truly a part of the painter's subjectivity, Smets's snapshots are characterized, conversely, by their fleeting and interchangeable nature, like screen captures.

Before Richter, the atlas device was explored, in the 1920s, by the art historian and anthropologist Aby Warburg: retracing survival, or "afterlife" (*Nachleben*) of visual figures across epochs and civilizations, Warburg linked artifacts from diverse contexts together on photographic plates. Smets's atlas too, like that of Richter or Warburg, employs photography for heuristic ends: each fragment bears clues that are revealed through contact with the others. But Smets's photos are intimately bound up with geographical places. They involve the notion of movement in space, and suggest the existence of a storyline: slight changes of viewpoint reveal what remained hidden in the previous shot… Hints, close-ups, followed by wider framed shots, a succession of seasons, with a new line of questioning, perhaps a last attempt at finding an answer… The people in them come across as enigmatic; what could be going on beneath those calm exteriors?

Following the exhibitions in 2014, the landscape architect explained that the atlas was a stage in, rather than the culmination of, his "continual search for a way to depict landscape": "Maybe here I have finally solved the problem I've had for the last five years, which is 'How to photograph my projects?' […] I contacted a director of photography[28] and asked him to take photos of our sites as if they were sets for something else. Which they are. Because you can't photograph a park; it's not an object." To produce an image from reality, continuing the endless cycle between site, representation and transformation: such is the mission entrusted to this specialist in art direction. His brief from Smets is to develop his own viewpoint on the landscapes, the better to reveal them: "He has an eye. He sees landscape where others don't. I'm really curious to see what he does." And so photography becomes a very conscious fictionalizing of the "realized landscape", shunning the usual delineations between the existing site and the intervention of the landscape architect, preferring instead to develop a subjective way of looking at the landscape: "He told me, 'Give me the list and I'll go and take some photos by myself […]. I don't want to know where the limit is between what you did and what you didn't do, I want to feel it for myself.' And I like that idea, that he decides on the frame, that there might be – in the photo – a part of what we did and a part of what we didn't do. Buildings are finite: 'Here's the building I did; I didn't do the one next to it.' The essential thing about landscapes is that they are 'indefinite'. I think it would be amusing if he took a photo of the existing site, where we hadn't intervened… which, after all, is also a kind of intervention."

For Smets, the continuation of the atlas seems, therefore, to be taking the shape of an interdisciplinary collaboration with a director or photography, for whom a project site is

26
Bas Smets in an interview with Marie-Madeleine Ozdoba, Brussels, June 13, 2014.

27
On Richter's *Atlas*, and on the relationship between painting and photography that it articulates, see Jean-Philippe Antoine, "Photographie, peinture et réel: la question du paysage dans la peinture de Gerhard Richter", *Gerhard Richter*, Dis Voir, Paris, 1995, p. 55–91; Benjamin Buchloh et al., *Photography and Painting in the Work of Gerhard Richter*, Actar, Barcelona, 2000.

28
A director of photography from the movie industry, whose name he did not reveal.

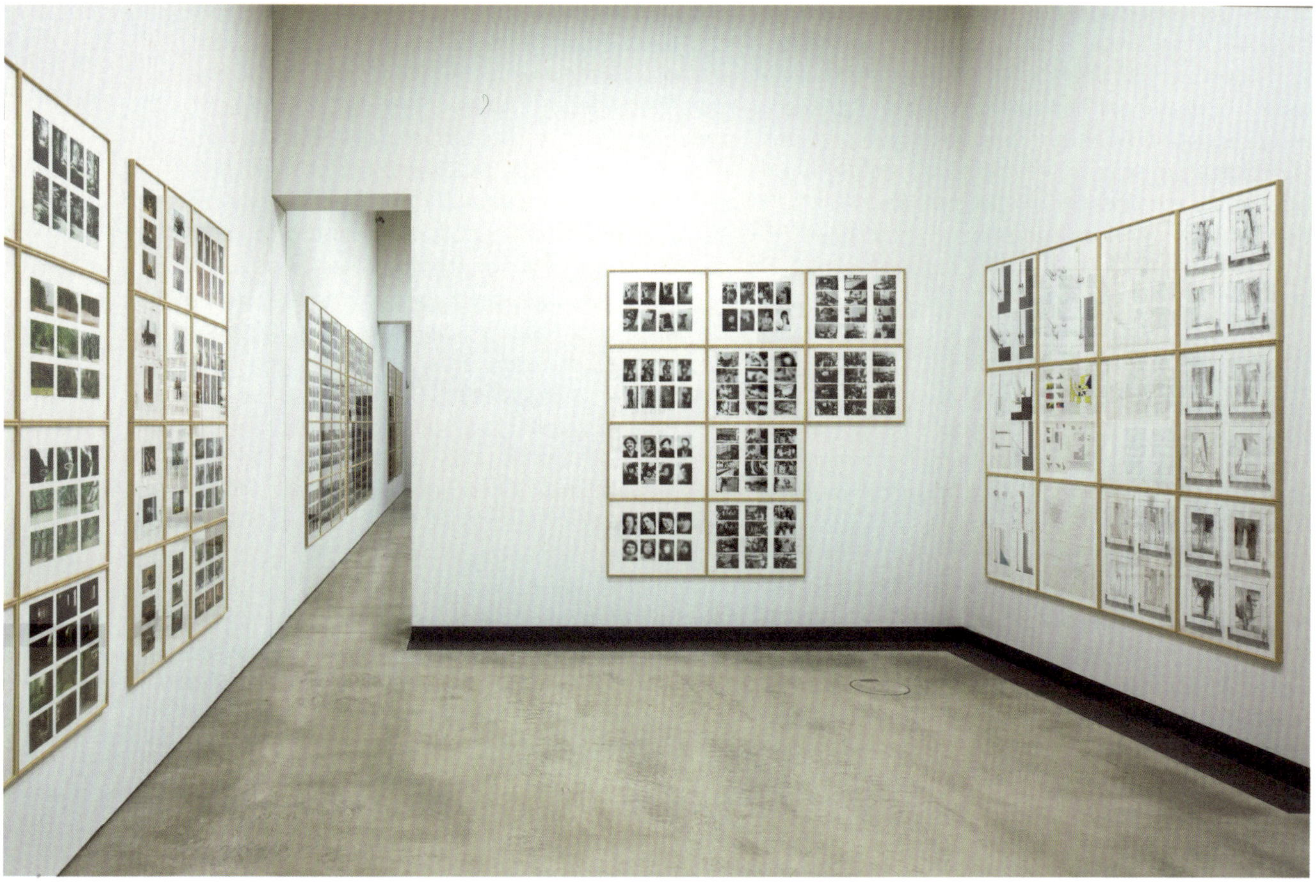

| FIG. 8 |

| FIG. 8 |
Gerhard Richter's *Atlas*, view of the installation, Kunsthalle im Lipsiusbau, Dresden, 2012.

primarily the setting for a fictional work. Not only does it acknowledge the fuzzy limits of landscape, in its horizontal dimension, it deploys them strategically in the service of a discourse about the representation of the project: inasmuch as the landscape project is not something clearly identifiable, in the "center" of the image, the story that is told, or the ambience that is created, truly constitutes its representation in post-photographic mode. This way, the landscape project is genuinely "put to work" in a critique of the photo-realistic representation of the project. The light, the colors, the effects, the framing, the human subjects ... all contribute to create a certain atmosphere, or to present a certain storyline, through which the landscape project as such attains visibility.[29]

Quite differently from the illustrative, or even purely decorative, photographic walls that adorn landscape and architecture exhibitions today, Bas Smets's scenography seeks to examine the relationship between photography and the "realized landscape": the imaginative power of the landscape unleashed by this device takes precedence over the documentation of the photographed sites, becoming the key element of an expressive approach. The landscape architect becomes the inventor of "possible worlds", represented photographically, but not necessarily real. Scenography joins photography as a means of stimulating and enriching the way we look at landscape.

CONTINUOUSLY HABITABLE ZONES: A CINEMATIC LANDSCAPE BETWEEN IMAGE AND REALITY

The film *Continuously Habitable Zones (CHZ)*, on which Bas Smets collaborated in 2011 with the visual artist Philippe Parreno, is his most accomplished challenge to the instrumental use of the photo-realistic image in the landscape project: the landscape architect contributed to the design of an environment in shades of black, realized on a piece of land in Porto for a science fiction script filmed by Parreno, creating a hybrid object – half-film, half-landscape.[30]

In response to a commission from the Daimler Art Collection, the project also involved – in addition to the artist and the landscape architect – a director of photography, Darius Khondji, and a composer, Nicolas Becker. After visiting several sites belonging to Mercedes-Benz in Stuttgart, the project emerged to design a garden out of these physically distant pieces of land, which would be juxtaposed only in the diegetic space of the film. "This is a landscape read as a script for a film, and a film that produces a landscape. We have to imagine this place as a semi-fictional and semi-real object. [...] it is both mythical and real [...]. A place that you can access, but not really."[31] But as the permits for the landscaping work in Stuttgart were not obtained on time, the plants and topographic motifs identified in Stuttgart were assembled into a single "garden" in Portugal, at Vila Nova de Famalicão near Porto, where the five sites were brought together as a single set **| FIG. 9 |**.

In addition to Stuttgart and Porto, which are joined together in filmic space, *CHZ* invokes the imagined spaces of science fiction: the film script makes reference to recent developments in astronomy, based on the notion of *continuously habitable zone* coined by the Chinese astrophysicist Su-Shu Huang in 1959, who posited that life can develop on a planet as a function of its orbit around one or more stars, providing that its orbit is maintained for a minimum period of four to six million years. In 2011, NASA published the interim results of its Kepler mission, which suggested that more than 50 planets outside our solar system are located in such zones, and in April of the same year, a scientist at the University of St Andrews in Scotland published a study claiming that on an Earth-like planet, but with two or three suns, any plants would probably have a blackish appearance.

Starting out from the hypothesis that the exoplanet vegetation would be black, and based on the landscape motifs taken from his survey of the Mercedes-Benz sites in Stuttgart, Smets set out to design a "CHZ" at the Porto site, based on black plants, anthracite soils, eroded surfaces and extruding roots. The film, shot on location, consists of ten scenes that explore this landscape with different cameras (defining various image qualities), with angles ranging from close-ups to panoramas **| FIG. 10 |**.[32] Holes, canyons, and the shimmering heat deform the image; the slow, sinuous traveling shots through the fluctuating vegetation disrupt the sense of scale; crystal clear sounds, incoherent lighting configurations ... all combine to create a mysterious atmosphere. No human observer, the eye of the camera seems to float, dream-like, over a planet inhabited only by climatic phenomena. The wind caresses fields of giant grasses, where from time to time one seems to glimpse the outlines of a path. The curved horizon of the little planet is lit up by two dazzling stars; in the final scene of the traveling shot, they illuminate a dark forest devoid of animal life. "Fashioned from earth, black minerals and vegetation, this real garden tells a topographical story that comes from the world of science fiction."[33]

CHZ unfolds both in physical space – the plot of land where the film was shot – and in the poetic space of the artwork, without it being possible to clearly delimit the two registers. The whole purpose of transforming the landscape, in this instance, is to produce images, reversing the usual logic of the representation as a tool serving the project. "[...] Reality, through its perception, through photos, through drawings, becomes an image; this image is used to transform reality, which in turn produces new images. There is a sort of cycle of reality, perception, reality, perception ... which, I think, is at the heart of every change; it isn't far from the rhythm of the seasons, of life and death. I discovered that by making a film with the artist Philippe Parreno. [...] The idea was 'let's make a landscape that exists only in film.' So I did some landscaping work that he proceeded to film, but in itself, the work didn't amount to a landscape; it's only the film that portrays it as a landscape. And that's when I understood that I do drawings to produce a reality, and he creates a reality in order to produce images."[34] As a result *CHZ* is a hybrid object, between a landscape project and an artwork, which now belongs to several contemporary art collections. For his part, Smets explores its evolution out there, regularly revisiting the Porto site, where he continues to experiment with "ways of seeing". In one such visit, he recently developed a technique that combines a GoPro camera with an amateur drone, in the quest for an image of "uncertain quality"...

The fantastical world of *CHZ* is a borderline case of a landscape project, where the device of film, far from offering some kind of evidence in image form, contributes to the very construction of the project. An image/reality hybrid, *CHZ* makes the point ad absurdum of the impossibility of having a "transparent" image of the project – in that the project, in this particular case, only exists through the image. The purpose of this interdisciplinary post-photographic construct is, ultimately, to act upon the way we look at things and make us more attentive to what the landscape elicits in us, the imaginaries that it evokes, and the stories that could unfold within it.

URBAN IMAGINARIES AND POSSIBLE WORLDS: THE PHOTOGRAPHIC IMAGE AS PROJECT

The notion of the post-photographic image, taken from photographic theory, paves the path for a fresh conception of the photo-realistic representation of landscape projects: emancipated from the instrumental uses that are still largely associated with it in the profession, photography leaves behind the paradigm of the "transparent" image to join the medium of drawing, long used by landscapers for expressive purposes. Bas Smets embeds photo-realistic renderings in the cultural heritage of landscape painting to reveal them as fictions, while he frees photography and cinema from their documentary roles to employ them in the construction of "possible worlds".

Rather than referring to a particular reality that requires faithful documentation, these uses of photo-realistic images by Bureau Bas Smets are an invitation to think about the representation of the landscape project in terms of atmospheres, imagin-

29
In the sketching phase, some landscapers produce representations in which the project as such is not drawn: the atmosphere *makes* the landscape project. One example is the animation for the project that won the Pershing Square contest in Los Angeles, by Agence Ter (2016). On this topic, see Blake Belanger and Ellen Urton, "Situating eidetic photomontage in contemporary landscape architecture", *Landscape Journal*, 33.2, 2014, p. 109–126.

30
On *CHZ*, see Bas Smets, *Landscape Stories*, Bureau Bas Smets, Brussels, 2015. For a detailed description of the project, see Marc Treib, "Landscape for a planet with two dwarf suns", *JoLA – Journal of Landscape Architecture*, no. 3, 2016.

31
Renate Wiehager, "Philippe Parreno, Continuously Habitable Zones: CHZ, 2011. A cinematographic landscape", Daimler AG Corporate Art Department (www.collection.daimler.com).

32
The film uses the "day for night" technique, by which scenes filmed during the day are darkened in post-production to create the illusion that they were shot at night. For the sound, techniques borrowed from entomology and volcanology were used to "record the landscape" (small mikes were buried in the soil or attached to branches); see Renate Wiehager, *op. cit.*

33
Nancy Spector, *Philippe Parreno: CHZ*, Damiani/Beyeler Foundation, Basel/Bologna, 2012.

34
Bas Smets in an interview with Marie-Madeleine Ozdoba, Brussels, June 13, 2014.

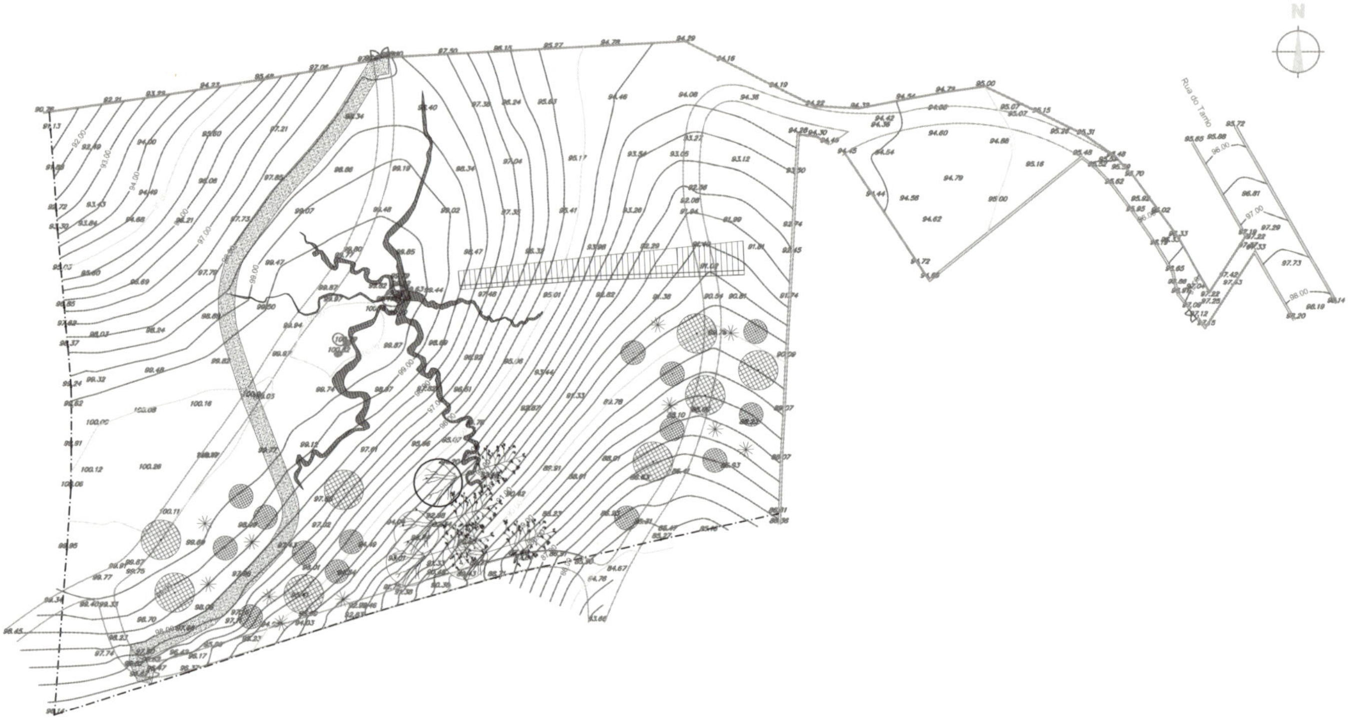

| FIG. 9 |

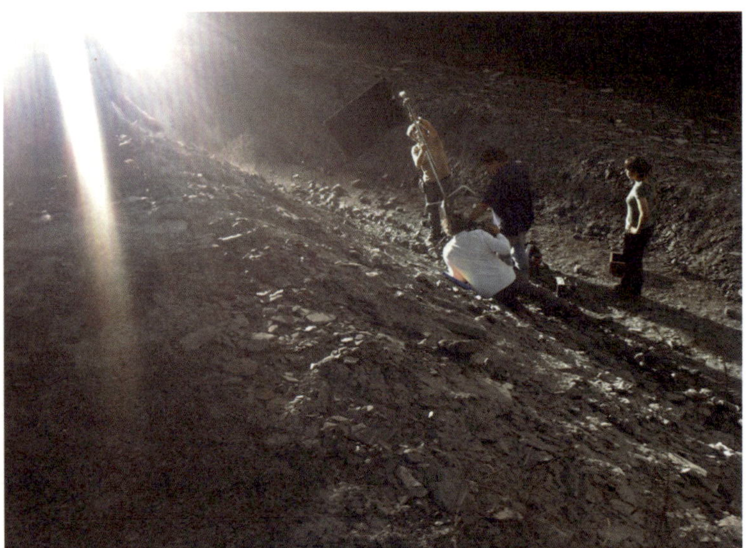

| FIG. 10 |

| FIG. 9 |
Topographic map of Bas Smets's landscape work in Porto.

| FIG. 10 |
Photo of the shooting of *CHZ*, 2011.

aries, or ways of looking. Far removed from "visualization" or "simulation", which imply an expectation of "truth" with regard to photographic and photo-realistic representations of the project, the post-photographic approach productively channels the always uncertain relationship between an image, no matter how realistic, and the realized landscape: the image becomes a space of fiction and experimentation – in other words, a project space – for the landscape architect, whose field of intervention is no longer confined to the transformation of reality.

The post-photographic approach could, in the same way, enrich the creation of urban imaginaries – a field currently marked by the use of stereotyped scenarios and publicity "packaging" – thereby expanding landscape architects' scope of action and placing them at the heart of the production of the "imagined landscape" as part of an interdisciplinary collaboration. Smets's visual practice is a forerunner in this respect.[35]

Finally, if the notion of the post-photographic image, taken from photographic theory, is apt to enrich our thinking about the expressive uses of the photographic medium in the practice of landscape architecture, conversely, the body of photo-realistic images derived from landscape architecture may provide singularly fertile ground for thinking the post-photographic image, "so long as the supposed reality that it reflects is no longer systematically presented as a trace of 'that which has been'."[36]

35
On "fictional urban planning", see Laurent Matthey, "Urbanisme fictionnel. L'action urbaine à l'heure de la société du spectacle", *Métropolitiques*, October 28, 2011, URL: http://www.metropolitiques.eu/Urbanisme-fictionnel-l-action.html. The Bureau Bas Smets exhibition in Charleroi in 2014 was very much part of such an exploration of the urban imaginary, initiated by the municipality (www.charleroi-bouwmeester.be).

36
Philippe Dubois, *op. cit.*

When the Camera Sticks its Lens into the Landscape Project

Gérard Dufresne and Alain Marguerit –
a Thirty-year Collaboration

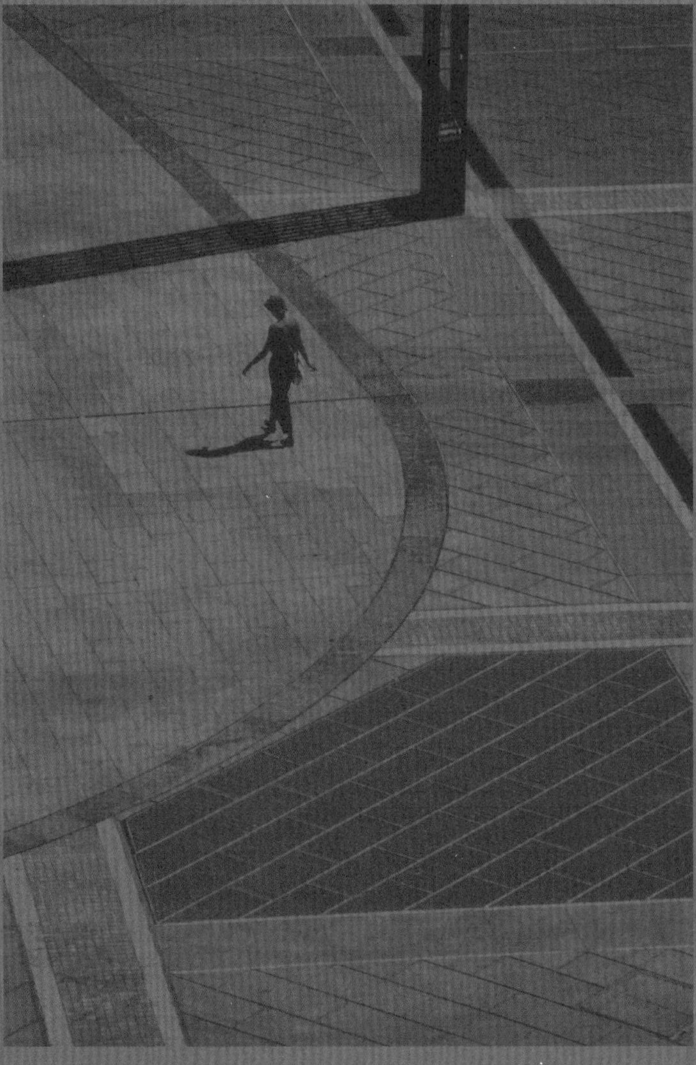

Sonia Keravel

While several academic works have already been written about the history of architectural photography,[1] very little research has yet been done on landscape project photography. No publication treats it as a genre; no book retraces its history. The landscape project – as a transformative action that operates on a territory – may be a fairly narrow field, but it is an extremely rich one for photography, in large part due to its links to regional development. Photography is present at every stage of the landscape project, from design through to execution, and today photographers increasingly work alongside landscape designers. In his article "Photographie, projet de paysage et culture professionnelle", Frédéric Pousin lays down a number of milestones to help us begin to sketch out the history of the genre.[2] He stresses the significance of the post-war reconstruction period, when all publicly funded French worksites were photographed, and pinpoints the 1960s as the moment when a personalized relationship began to develop between designers and photographers. He also underlines the importance of the *Mission photographique de la DATAR* in the 1980s,[3] and that of concomitant or subsequent institutional commissions, such as the Belfort Photographic Mission, the Cross-Channel Photographic Mission, and Jean-François Chevrier's quest to shed new light on the Paris region: "In all of these extensions of the DATAR mission, the intended object is the territory, as a photographic and cultural reality, the product of a history and of human activities, a place of transformation whose understanding is yet to be constructed. But the relationship with development as an action performed on a space, to embed people and their activities in a forward-looking vision,[4] is a horizon that remains unspecified by any discourse."[5]

Landscape project photography has been around at least since the early 20th century – thanks notably to the photographs of the parks of Sceaux, Versailles and Saint-Cloud taken by Eugène Atget[6] – but it has always been a minor genre. Long used as a transparent medium for the sole purpose of registering documents, it has not been an object of study. The reduction of the photograph to the signified that it represents, i.e. the real thing placed in front of the lens, is a problem inherent to the medium itself: "Every photograph is a certificate of presence," wrote Roland Barthes in *Camera Lucida*.[7] Photographs have often, indeed, been used by landscape architects to attest to the existence of a project, long confining the photographer to the role of a simple operator. The "innovative perception" aspect was never given much consideration, and even today remains largely overlooked. And yet we often learn about projects through the eye of a photographer, whose perception is part of the project: is landscape not, at one and the same time, both reality and representation? It is thanks to photography, after all, that different perceptions on landscape projects have emerged over time and have been transmitted, mainly through the collaboration between photographer and landscape designer.

The connection between these two professionals jointly engaged in the transformation of a territory often takes the form of a commission. Duos are formed, developing complex bonds, often interwoven with friendship,[8] which are worthy of investigation. How does the photographer gain a foothold in the designer's work, and at what point does he or she intervene? What do the photographs bring to the landscape architect, and how does the photographic project dialogue with the landscape project? And finally, can one speak, in certain cases, of the landscape project being co-produced?

1
Examples would include the recent study by Giovanni Fanelli, *Histoire de la photographie d'architecture*, Presses polytechniques et universitaires romandes, Lausanne, 2016.

2
Frédéric Pousin, "Photographie, projet de paysage et culture professionnelle", in *La Mission photographique de la DATAR. Nouvelles perspectives critiques*, La documentation française, Paris, 2014, p. 11–127.

3
See Raphaële Bertho, *La Mission photographique de la DATAR. Un laboratoire du paysage contemporain*, La documentation française, Paris, 2013.

4
Pierre Merlin, *L'aménagement du territoire en France*, La documentation française, Paris, 2007.

5
Frédéric Pousin, *op. cit.*, p. 119. Unless otherwise indicated, all translations are our own.

6
See Aurélie Kaminski et al., *Eugène Atget Miroirs Daniel Quesney. Reconstitution photographique/Photographical reconstruction*, ARP Editions, Brussels, 2001.

7
Roland Barthes, *Camera Lucida: Reflections on Photography*, transl. R. Howard, Hill and Wang, New York, NY, 1982, p. 85 (original: *La Chambre claire. Note sur la photographie*, Cahiers du cinéma/Gallimard/Seuil, Paris, 1980).

8
The duo phenomenon is also found in architecture, with such examples as: Le Corbusier and Lucien Hervé; Herman Hertzberger and Johann Van der Keuken; William Diepraam or Violette Cornelius and Aldo Van Eyck; Hélène Binet and Peter Zumthor; Richard Pare and Tadao Ando, etc.

Just as Philippe Bonin has called for the recognition of "interior photography" as a genre in its own right,[9] so recognizing a "landscape project photography" genre would reveal the importance of these images in both the construction and transmission of landscape projects. The history of this genre remains to be written, starting with the constitution of a corpus, which would doubtless raise awareness of the essential role played by photographers. A collection of images exists, but it is dispersed across different agencies and remains unexploited as a research tool. The images should be gathered together – a long-haul task – and analyzed, to see what they tell us about the spaces and uses shown, and indeed about the history of landscape architects, landscape projects and the evolution of perception.[10]

The 30-year (and more) collaboration between the landscape architect Alain Marguerit and the photographer Gérard Dufresne seems to have much to teach us in this respect. It has engendered an extremely varied photographic output, which has never previously been explored. By analyzing three representative case studies – the Place de la Comédie in Montpellier, the La Duchère major urban project in Lyon, and the Lauragais landscape plan – we will get a glimpse of the different roles that photography can play in such a collaboration.

ALAIN MARGUERIT AND GÉRARD DUFRESNE: TWO FRIENDS OF MICHEL CORAJOUD

Anyone familiar with the projects of landscape architects in France will inevitably have seen photographs taken by Gérard Dufresne, whose images have accompanied the careers of numerous professionals. He has photographed projects by Jacques Simon, Michel Corajoud, Jacques Coulon, Alain Marguerit, Gilles Vexlard, Alexandre Chemetoff and many other landscape architects, often graduates of the *École Nationale Supérieure de Paysage* (ENSP) in Versailles. Reflecting the resurgence of that profession, Dufresne's photographs have played a key role in constructing the image of landscape architects. They have been published by the trade press *(Techniques et Architecture, Archivert, Pages Paysages, Garten und Landschaft,* etc.) as well as in books, most notably in one of the first works to be published in the field: *Paysages*, by Linda Leblanc and Jacques Coulon.[11] The Parc de la Villeneuve in Grenoble and the Parc des Coudrays in Trappes – by Michel Corajoud – the Parc Saint-John-Perse in Reims by Jacques Simon **| FIG. 1 |**, and the beach at Saint-Valéry-en-Caux by Jacques Coulon: these pioneering projects were often revealed for the first time through Dufresne's photographic eye and framing.

Throughout the 1980s and 1990s, and on into the present, landscape architects have gradually asserted themselves as "designers whose project approach is part of a culture akin to that of the architect, but with its own distinctive characteristics."[12] The specificity of their approach traces its foundations back to the proud heritage of the art of gardens, but it rests primarily on the ability to act upon the available space and to read the site by understanding its history and morphology. The site is seen as the substrate of the landscape project, which cannot be grasped outside of its context. The landscaping method can then be seen as a form of urban planning based on a reading of the site;[13] it is also anchored in time and enriched by knowledge of the dynamics of landscape management and evolution on every scale.[14] In 1980, Michel Corajoud – then a faculty member of the ENSP in Versailles – was already insisting on the singular position of the landscape architect in the field of planning and development. His argument was structured around the specificities of landscaping: "Landscaping is an art that is rooted in the soil. The art of completing the geometry of substances. The art of the model. Landscaping is the art of arrested motion. Landscaping is the art of preparation. Landscaping is the art of duration. The art of living things.

9
Philippe Bonin, *Images habitées. Photographies et spatialités*, Créaphis, Grane, 2006.

10
I began this research by looking at several photographer/landscape architect partnerships from different generations. The interviews conducted with the landscape architects and photographers are accessible on the ANR *PhotoPaysage* research program website: http://photopaysage.huma-num.fr

11
Linda Leblanc and Jacques Coulon, *Paysages*, Le Moniteur, Paris, 1993.

12
Françoise Dubost, "Les paysagistes et la demande de paysage", in Michel Racine (ed.), *Créateurs de jardins et de paysages en France du XIXe au XXIe siècle*, vol. 2, Actes Sud/ENSP, Arles/Versailles, 2002.

13
Sébastien Marot, "L'alternative du paysage", *Le Visiteur*, no. 1, 1995, p. 54–81. Françoise Fromonot, meanwhile, speaks of "revelatory urban planning": Françoise Fromonot, "Manières de classer l'urbanisme", *Criticat*, no. 8, 2012.

14
On the history of the landscaping profession, see Sonia Keravel, *Passeurs de paysage. Le projet de paysage comme art relationnel*, MétisPresss, Geneva, 2015.

| FIG. 1 |
Gérard Dufresne, Parc Saint-John-Perse, Reims.
Project by Jacques Simon.

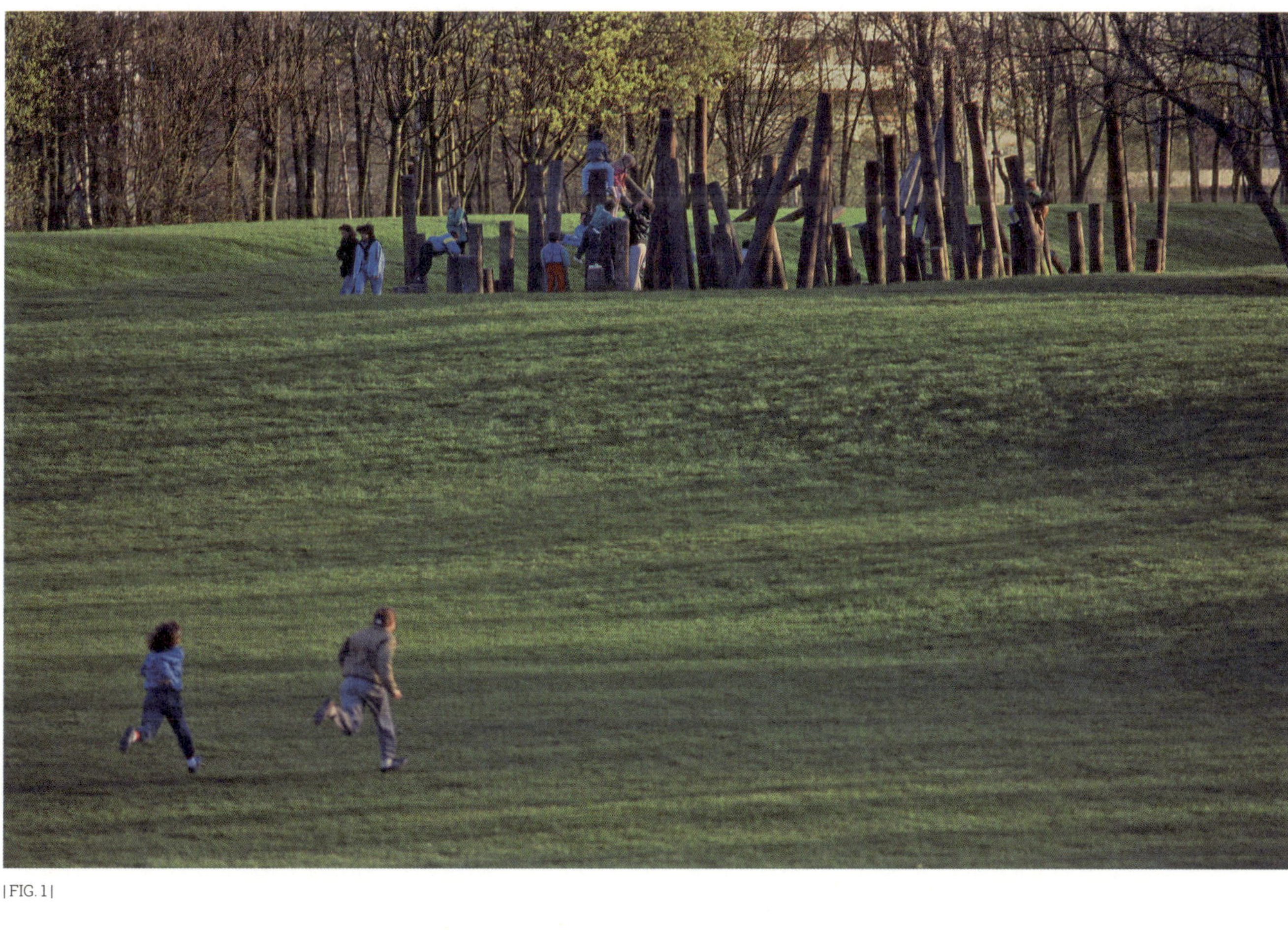

| FIG. 1 |

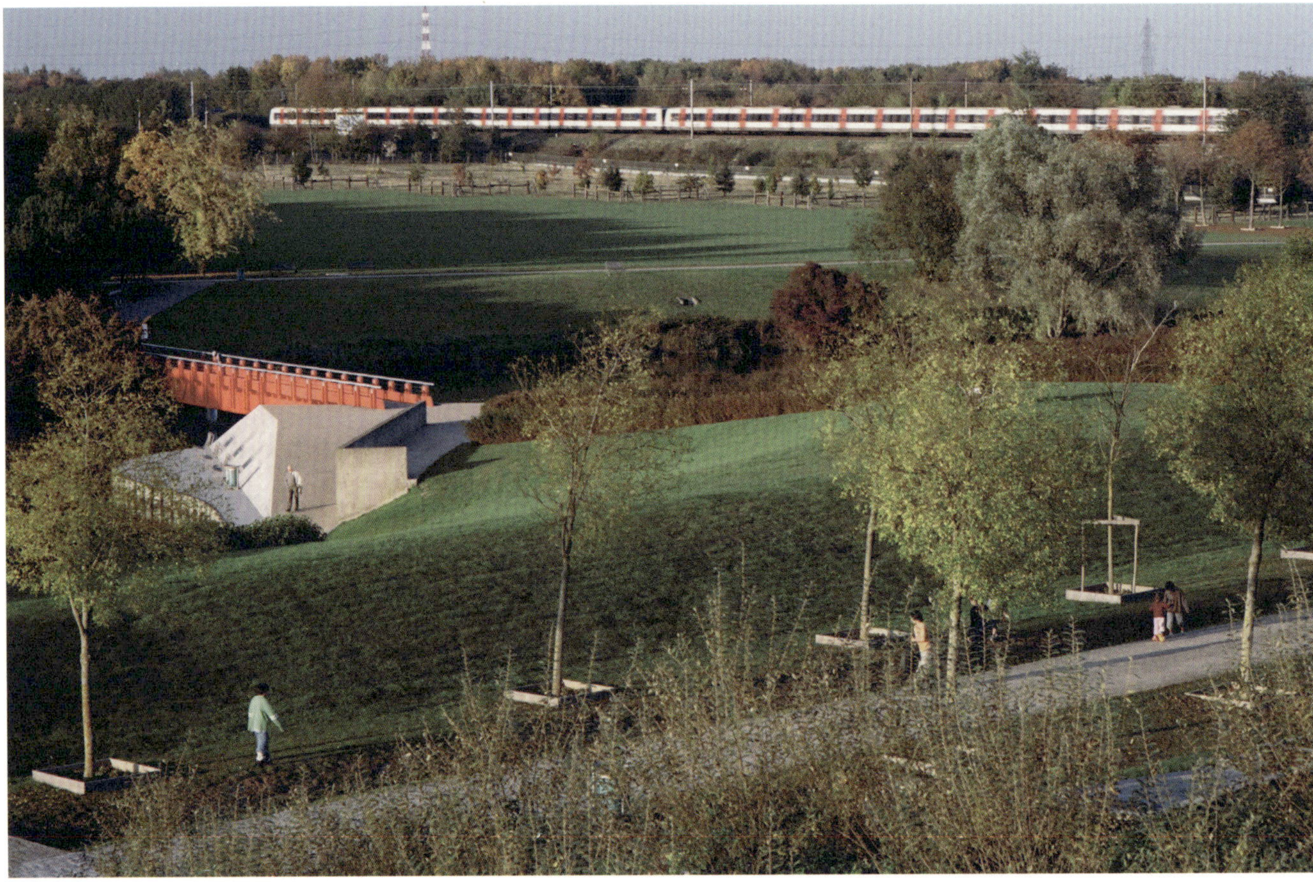

| FIG. 2 |

| FIG. 2 |
Gérard Dufresne, Parc du Sausset, Villepinte. Project by Claire and Michel Corajoud.

| FIG. 3 |
Gérard Dufresne, Parc du Sausset, Villepinte. Project by Claire and Michel Corajoud.

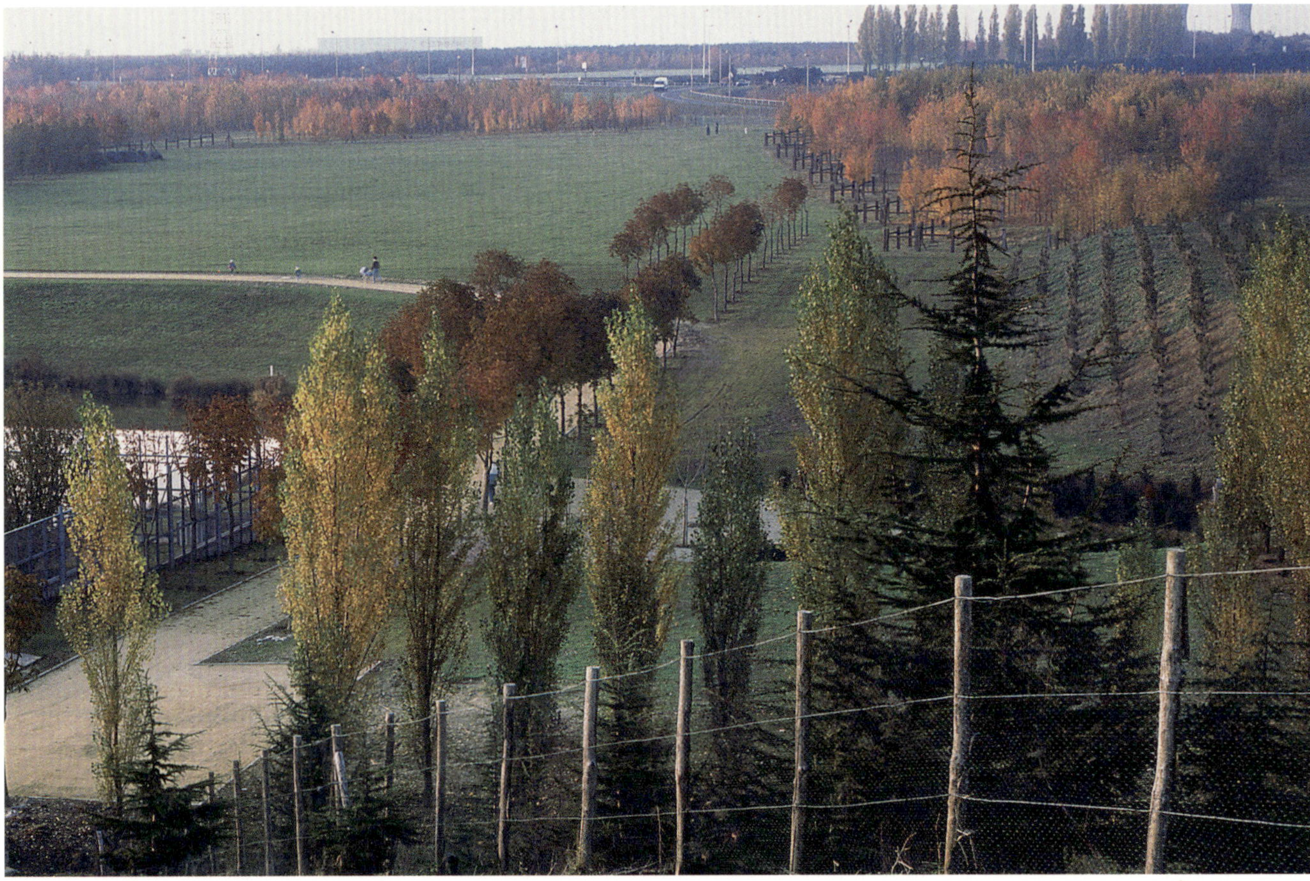

| FIG. 3 |

Landscaping is the art of recovery. The art of landscaping is a profession."[15]

This founding text was published in the review *Espaces verts* alongside one of Dufresne's photographs, a country landscape under the snow: rolling fields, structured by hedges, and whose well-marked furrows, highlighted by the snow, above all reveal a soil that has been "architectured" by farming. This image, later reproduced in other works,[16] perfectly illustrates the affinities that existed at the time between Michel Corajoud and Gérard Dufresne, in particular their shared fascination for the agricultural countryside and the landscapes built and shaped by successive generations of farmers.[17] The two men's worlds of reference appear to be extremely close; it is not always easy to tell which is inspiring the other.

The complicity between the landscape architect and the photographer owes much to their long-standing friendship. They met in 1958, when they were both living in Annecy, through Maurice Littoz-Baritel, a local photographer who was teaching Dufresne the trade. While frequenting the same group of friends, who were intensely active both culturally and politically, they were introduced to the architect Bernard Rousseau, whom they were to meet again in Paris. Even before meeting Michel Corajoud, Dufresne had learned about photography and landscapes in the darkroom of his grandfather Paul Jacquin, a journalist-photographer working in the Drôme and Ardèche area of southeast France. In the 1960s, Dufresne moved to Paris, where he worked for Pictorial Service, developing black and white stills by Cartier-Bresson and other famous photographers. Here, in the capital, he met up again with Michel Corajoud, who put him in contact with the *Atelier d'urbanisme et d'architecture* (AUA), where he met Jacques Simon and produced his first pictures of architecture and landscape projects. He realized that landscape projects had something new to offer, and from the 1980s onward, he elected to work alongside landscape architects.

Gérard Dufresne's images resonated with the language of the landscape designers of the day. They were seeking to break out of their allocated role as gardeners, claiming the status of designers at the urban or even regional scale. The photographer was quick to understand their aims: he often used aerial views, revealing landscape projects in their context. He also showed how they made use of volume, leveling, composition and plant cover, the main tools that designers claimed as their own. For the Parc du Sausset, for example **| FIG. 2 and 3 |**, a vast forested peri-urban park in Villepinte, in the Paris region, by Claire and Michel Corajoud, Dufresne most often took general views that gave an initial impression of the major segments, the overall composition, and the relationship between empty and occupied spaces. Through his photos, he reveals a territory in the process of change, insisting particularly on the presence of infrastructures (the RER urban railway, water towers and electricity pylons) that cut through or border the park and serve as landmarks. In so doing, he illustrates the contemporaneity of landscape projects: they are of their time, not so much picturesque as a form of Land Art. The park is deliberately portrayed as a rural landscape where the landscape designer's task has more to do with forestry or agriculture than horticulture.

In addition to landscape commissions, Gérard Dufresne pursued his work as an author, making him a natural choice to be one of the first recruits of the *Observatoire photographique national du paysage* (OPNP).[18] From 1994 to 1999, he was tasked with documenting Itinerary 7 near Valence, a part of the world close to his heart, as he was born there. He focused in particular on the development of infrastructures, industry and urban growth in this intensive fruit-growing region. This gave him numerous opportunities to photograph the landscape from the TGV high-speed train between Paris and Valence, and from 2005 to 2009 he mounted several exhibitions of photos snapped from the train, entitled *Du train où vont les choses*.[19] **| FIG. 4 |** These images also spawned a book project with Jacques Coulon, as yet unpublished.

Alain Marguerit belongs to a generation of professionals marked by the teaching of Michel Corajoud and Jacques Simon. He is representative of those landscape designers who carved out a place for themselves in the

15
Michel Corajoud, "Le paysage comme condition d'architecture", *Espaces verts*, no. 65, May 1980, p. 60–63; republished in *Le paysage c'est là où le ciel et la terre se touchent*, Actes Sud/ENSP, Arles/Versailles, 2010. See also Michel Corajoud, "Dufresne au naturel", *Zoom*, no. 22, 1974.

16
Notably in Jacques Leenhardt, *Michel Corajoud*, Hartmann, Paris, 2000.

17
One of the references shared by Michel Corajoud and Gérard Dufresne is the paper by Vittorio Gregotti, "La forma del territorio", published in 1965 in no. 87–88 of *Edilizia moderna*, in which Gregotti uses a host of aerial photographs and images of agricultural landscapes, which fired the imagination of the landscape architect and the photographer. Gregotti's phrase: "The origin of architecture is not the primitive hut, but the marking of ground" would be cited on multiple occasions by Michel Corajoud.

18
The *Observatoire photographique national du paysage* (National Photographic Landscape Observatory) or OPNP was founded in 1989 on the principle of using time-lapse photography to monitor changing landscapes at the national scale. A strict nationwide protocol is defined for each observatory set up on a territory. A steering committee, made up of elected representatives, professionals and non-profit associations defines the territory's landscape goals. Thus far, 19 observatories have followed the nationally defined protocol; together, they constitute the OPNP. On this topic, see also Raphaële Bertho's article in this volume, p. 36.

19
Literally "From the train, where things go" but also a pun on a popular saying meaning "The rate things are going". See the article by Anne Demerlé-Got, "Gérard Dufresne. Du train où vont les choses", *Archiscopie*, no. 51, summer 2005, p. 26–27.

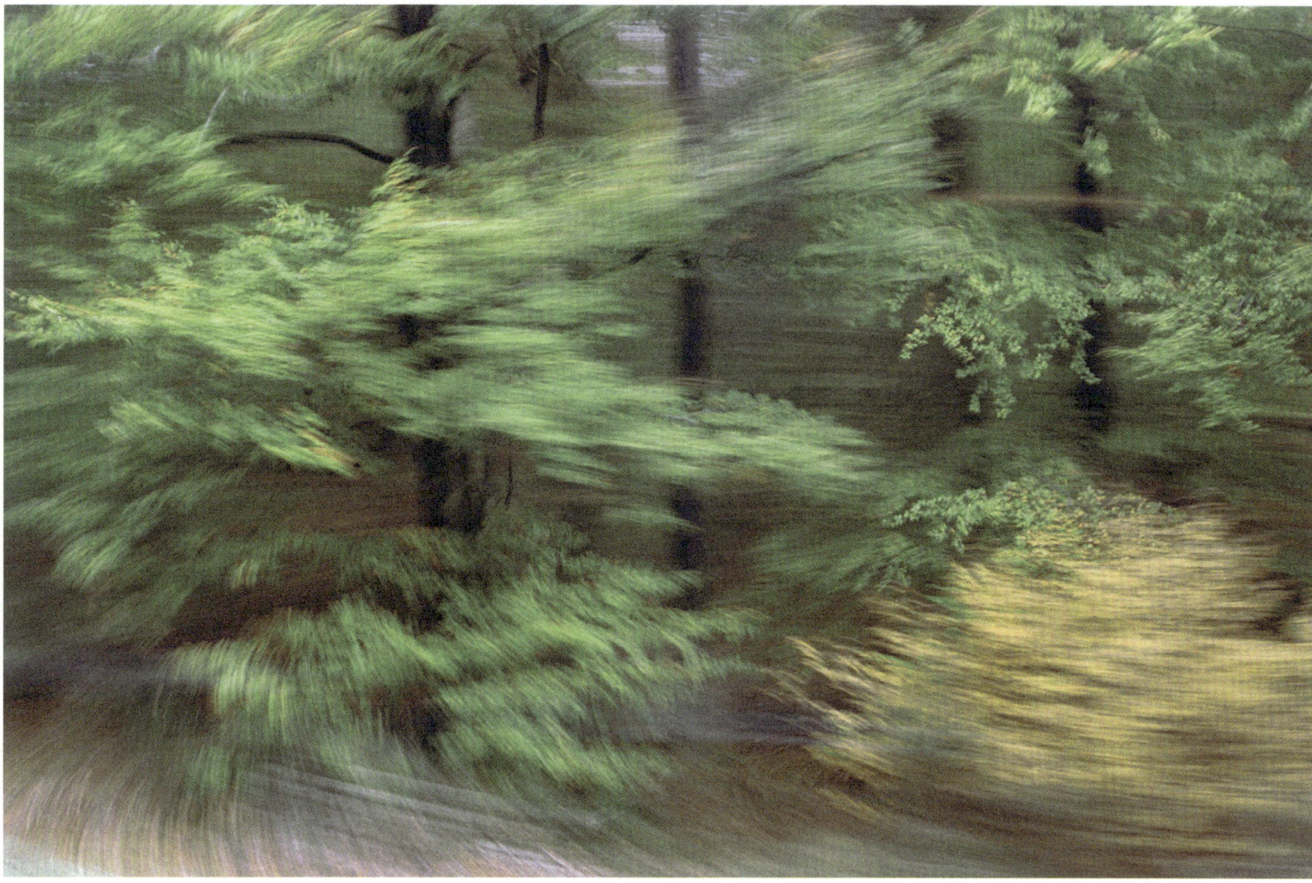

| FIG. 4 |

| FIG. 4 |
Gérard Dufresne, Photograph from the series
Du train où vont les choses.

field of planning and development and who played a part in the construction and invention of a type of urban landscape planning founded on the history and geography of each site. In 1973, after graduating from the landscaping section of the *École Nationale Supérieure d'Horticulture* (ENSH),[20] he set up the Carré Vert agency with Alexandre Chemetoff, Jacques Coulon and Claire Corajoud. The experimental field of landscape designers at that time was that of leftover spaces in large projects or facilities on the edge of towns or cities. These young professionals worked for municipalities in the Paris region, such as Pantin, Saint-Ouen and Marne-la-Vallée.

In 1979, Marguerit decided to base himself in the Mediterranean region. He left Paris and founded – with his wife Sonia Agogué – an agency in Montpellier: the *Atelier des paysages*. Here, he surrounded himself with a team of co-workers from different disciplines and engaged in a series of militant urban projects.[21] He developed an approach to the project as a process with a long timeframe, conducting a continual dialogue with decision-makers, from design through to management oversight. In the 1980s, he switched from project management to urban planning, notably working on several large housing projects in the northern districts of Marseille and for the city authorities of Lyon. The transformation of the center of Vaulx-en-Velin, in the Lyon conurbation, in conjunction with the urban planner Bernard Paris, was awarded the *Prix de l'aménagement urbain* in 1994.[22] In parallel with this urban focus, he began, in the 1990s, to develop a nationwide approach, producing major landscape studies and working as a government landscape advisor. He was also involved, for a period, in the training of future landscape architects, setting up the Mediterranean branch of the Versailles School of Landscape in Marseille.

THE PLACE DE LA COMÉDIE: PORTRAIT OF A PROJECT

The Place de la Comédie was a founding project for the *Atelier des paysages*, and one of Alain Marguerit's first completed works in Montpellier.[23] This urban development set out to transform the area formerly occupied by one of the city gates into a central space, and the project had to reaffirm this new centrality. The landscape architects opted for a clean-lined, unitary approach, covering the car park and the tunnel of the main road that hitherto encumbered the square with a huge "carpet" of stone. The composition of this vast public space – capable of accommodating all sorts of public events – followed a strict layout and zoning plan.

On delivery, Alain Marguerit commissioned Gérard Dufresne, whose work he appreciated, to portray the final project – to produce, in other words, its portrait. Projects often find themselves being associated in this way with a few emblematic pictures: iconic images that play a big part in constructing the identity of a designer and the originality of a work. In this case, how much choice does the photographer have in the matter? Does he have a free hand, or does he have to present a case? Just how specific is the commission, and what exactly does he know about the project before he photographs it?

Gérard Dufresne replies: "Just how much I know about a project before photographing it varies enormously. Most landscape architects don't have much to say; maybe they're saturated with all the work they've put in beforehand, and just trust me to get on with it. They give me, almost secretively, a few drawings and texts, as if they didn't want to constrain me but rather leave me free to discover it for myself, with my interpretation, my imagination. Sometimes they'll insist on particular viewpoints, certain details of the planting, the fittings (ramps, seating, lighting). [...] More often, I'm totally free, and can take shots with my own perceptions and intuitions about the project. It's a commission: obviously I have to bring out the idea behind the project, but I do it without being didactic."[24]

This valuable testimony suggests that the photographer does not generally have to meet any specific expectations. He has *carte blanche*: his freedom of perception is untrammeled.

The most famous photo of the Place de la Comédie is doubtless the one that shows a woman, from behind, walking alone over a vast stretch of stone pavement **| FIG. 5 |**. It has been used on the cover of several national and international magazines, often printed full-page; it has also been used in many books. What does it tell us about the project? Above all, this photographic icon expresses a moment of exception; it captures the fleeting moment when the woman is crossing the square, projecting her shadow onto the ground. Presumably taken with a zoom lens from an apartment building, the photo does not show the horizon: the framing concentrates on the interplay of elements in the layout. This fragmentary view of the project pushes the viewer to imagine what lies outside the frame, suggesting that it must be a very large space.

By Dufresne's own admission, "the key thing is to come up with 'powerful images', but it's interesting to skew it, to get people to discover the project from a different angle by being, basically, less explicit and more poetic. Even bringing in some enigmatic elements that might intrigue people and make them wonder." Which is precisely what he achieves with this tightly framed image.

The photograph depicts the ground just as a painting would, playing with the lines, colors and textures of the shadows and various materials. It is highly constructed: the darker line to the top right lends it an impetus that is echoed by the movement of the woman in the middle and by the red ochre arc. Its composition satisfies the canonical rules of balance and proportion; it obeys conventions and follows widely shared – and therefore easily understood – codes.

Careful observation of this image shows, therefore, to what extent landscape project photography is a cultural construction, as Dufresne confirms: "The landscape is not just a visual reality that I record, it is, above all, a representation shaped by my experience, my relationship to the world, my culture."[25]

Alain Marguerit speaks of certain photos by Gérard Dufresne that he found particularly striking: "Gérard's first images of la Comédie and Miramas are powerful images; they took me by surprise. Some of them are remarkable for their graphic aspect: you can see the project, but the image goes beyond that, through its composition, and through the presence and position of the figures."[26] So it is not merely a record, a showcase for the project, or a marketing story that Marguerit is seeking, but rather someone else's perception of project, that of an artist, an author, capable of creating a new narrative.

Hélène Binet, who has worked as a photographer for architects Peter Zumthor and Zaha Hadid, clearly understood what designers were looking for: "Photography is so realistic, it's hard work bringing it to a different level. We want to see something other than reality."[27] And indeed, in the field of landscaping, as in architecture, what is asked of the photographer is to move towards another reality, to bring the project a new, poetic dimension; to that end, reducing the information, restricting the work to fragments or instants, not showing everything – much as Dufresne did for the Place de la Comédie – is often a very promising route. The landscape architect is looking for an image that connects to the dreams that originally spawned the project. The interpretation of the finished project by the photographer breathes the magic back into it, enabling it to be rediscovered. Dufresne is adamant that the photos of a project do more than simply illustrate, document and publicize it: "Landscape architecs are eager to see the photographer's angle, to reobserve and sometimes rediscover the work they have orchestrated, and how it is appropriated by the public. I am very much external to the design and at the same time involved in the commission; I am a privileged witness, a 'singular visitor', the author of an account that forces the landscape architect to confront his ideas about his own work."[28]

20 Prior to 1976, when the ENSP was created in Versailles, landscape architects were trained in the landscaping section of the ENSH.

21 See the chapter on Alain Marguerit in Ariella Masboungi (ed.), *Penser la ville par le paysage*, coll. "Projet urbain ", Éditions de La Villette, Paris, 2002.

22 The transformation of Vaulx-en-Velin town center also earned him the *Trophée de l'aménagement urbain* in 2007.

23 The Place de la Comédie project was carried out in association with landscape architects Gilles Vexlard and Laurence Vacherot; the client, Ville de Montpellier; architects Bernard Paris and Joan Casanelles; plastic artists Jean-Marc Bourry and Alain Goetschy; lighting consultant, ECA; structural design office, Arcora.

24 Gérard Dufresne in an interview with Marie-Hélène Loze and Sonia Keravel, April 2016.

25 *Idem.*

26 Alain Marguerit in an interview with Marie-Hélène Loze and Sonia Keravel, November 2016.

27 Hélène Binet, "Composing Space", lecture at the Harvard Graduate School of Design, March 2012.

28 Gérard Dufresne in an interview with Marie-Hélène Loze and Sonia Keravel, April 2016.

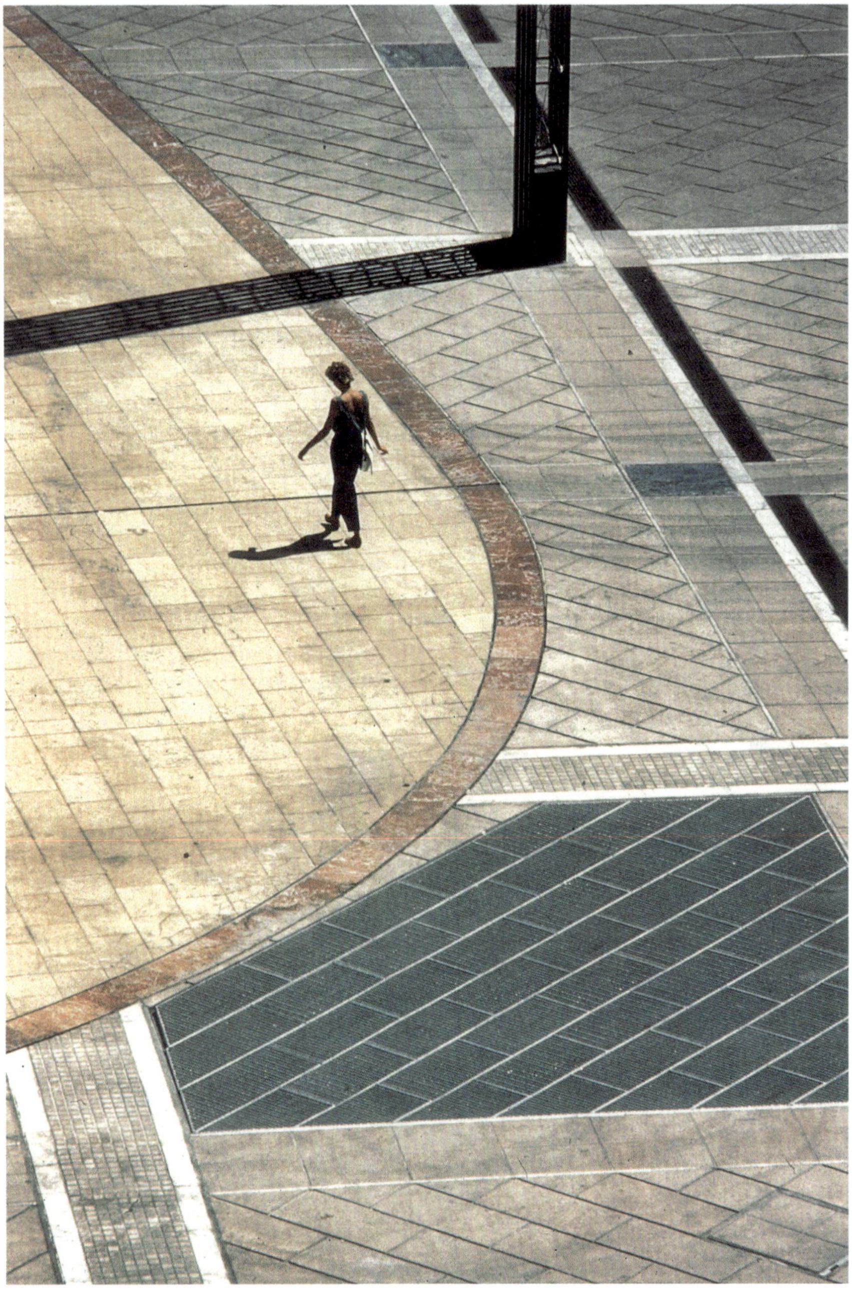

| FIG. 5 |

| FIG. 5 |
Gérard Dufresne, Place de la Comédie, Montpellier. Project by Alain Marguerit, in association with Gilles Vexlard and Laurence Vacherot.

LA DUCHÈRE: WHEN THE CAMERA CAPTURES THE LONG TIME OF THE PROJECT

Photographing the project on delivery is not the only way for the photographer to collaborate with the landscape architect. Alain Marguerit claims, even, that photographs of the site before work begins are of greater interest to him than those of the finished project. For him, the "before" picture makes the viewer fully aware of the time that has elapsed and of the magnitude of the transformations: "Photography facilitates the work of memory. It enables us to see how time constantly modifies space. It allows us to go back in history and show the different times of the project: it's an extraordinary tool. When people see things side by side, it becomes clear to them."[29]

Alain Marguerit and Gérard Dufresne have experimented with photographic time-series in several projects, and notably in monitoring the development of the public spaces at La Duchère in Lyon. The idea is not a new one; it was explored for scientific and political purposes as early as the 19th century, and was taken up by the *Observatoire photographique national du paysage* (OPNP) to record changes to the landscape in accordance with a strict protocol.[30] These series measure the transformation of the site, making it possible to retrace the steps and retrieve the memory of the place.

In the year 2000, all the public agencies of the Lyon metropolitan area decided to join forces around a Major Urban Project to upgrade the district of La Duchère. A landscape competition was organized, and was won by Alain Marguerit.[31] The brief was to embed the district in its territory and to give it a central focus. La Duchère enjoys a privileged location, looking out over the plain of the Saône from the edge of the Western Lyon plateau. The goal is to revitalize it by creating new dwellings that will gradually supplant the existing mid-rise apartment blocks. The project, which began in 2001, is not yet complete.

Faced with the "long time" so characteristic of urban planning projects, Alain Marguerit asked Gérard Dufresne to follow up the works with his camera. Rather than accept the duration of the works as a long period of waiting, the landscape architect wanted to show that the worksite is a constantly evolving landscape, and wanted these changes to be seen. The photographer started work as soon as the ZAC (*zone d'aménagement concerté*, joint development zone) was created.[32] He agreed with the designer on a systematic monitoring approach, following a protocol inspired by his experience of working for the OPNP in Valence. Here also, Dufresne decided to work using time-lapse: he suggested selecting 40 viewpoints, defined jointly with the designer, to be photographed every year. To determine the right locations, they would need to anticipatefuture transformations, and know where to position the camera to reveal insights aboutthe worksite. To begin with, Marguerit planned for a ten-year time series and hoped to persuade the actors of the Major Urban Project and the developer-contractor (SERL) of the value of the mission, but in this he failed: "The Major Urban Project wanted the city's official photographer, who takes good photos; but she takes 'THE photo', not the photo as part of an approach."[33] He therefore took it upon himself to commission Dufresne for the time-series, which was ultimately produced over four years: 2005, 2007, 2008 and 2009.

Of all the pictures shot by Gérard Dufresne, the panoramic views from the "Barre des 200" (the highest apartment block in the district) are perhaps the most interesting | **FIG. 6** |. Taken from a high floor, they offer an all-encompassing vista that makes this stretch of land easier to understand, representing it in all its complexity and showing the project in its context. The series of time-lapse panoramas highlight what changes from one photo to the next: what appears, and what disappears. They record the steps in the making of the district by breaking down the different times in its development. The most visible transformation is without doubt the demolition of the apartment blocks, which were still there in 2005, the subsequent opening out of the view over the territory in 2007 and then, in 2009, the new apartment blocks which, instead of blocking the view, accompany the sense of openness by espousing the topography. These pictures also show the construction of a street, with the layout of the new street blocks, a square, and a number of facilities (a school, a covered market, sports fields).

But beyond the spectacle of demolitions and reconstructions, these photographs reveal the

29 Alain Marguerit in an Interview with Marie-Hélène Loze and Sonia Keravel, November 2016.

30 See note 18.

31 Alain Marguerit's agency, associated with Atelier Bernard Paris (architecture & urban planning), Pascal Gontier (HEQ architect), and Philippe Masse, ETC (traffic flow design), was commissioned by Lyon urban community for two projects in La Duchère: the urban project, with the rehabilitation of the district's public spaces, and the development of the public spaces in the zone.

32 Work began on the La Duchère ZAC (demolitions, streets and squares) in 2005.

33 Alain Marguerit in an interview with Marie-Hélène Loze and Sonia Keravel, November 2016.

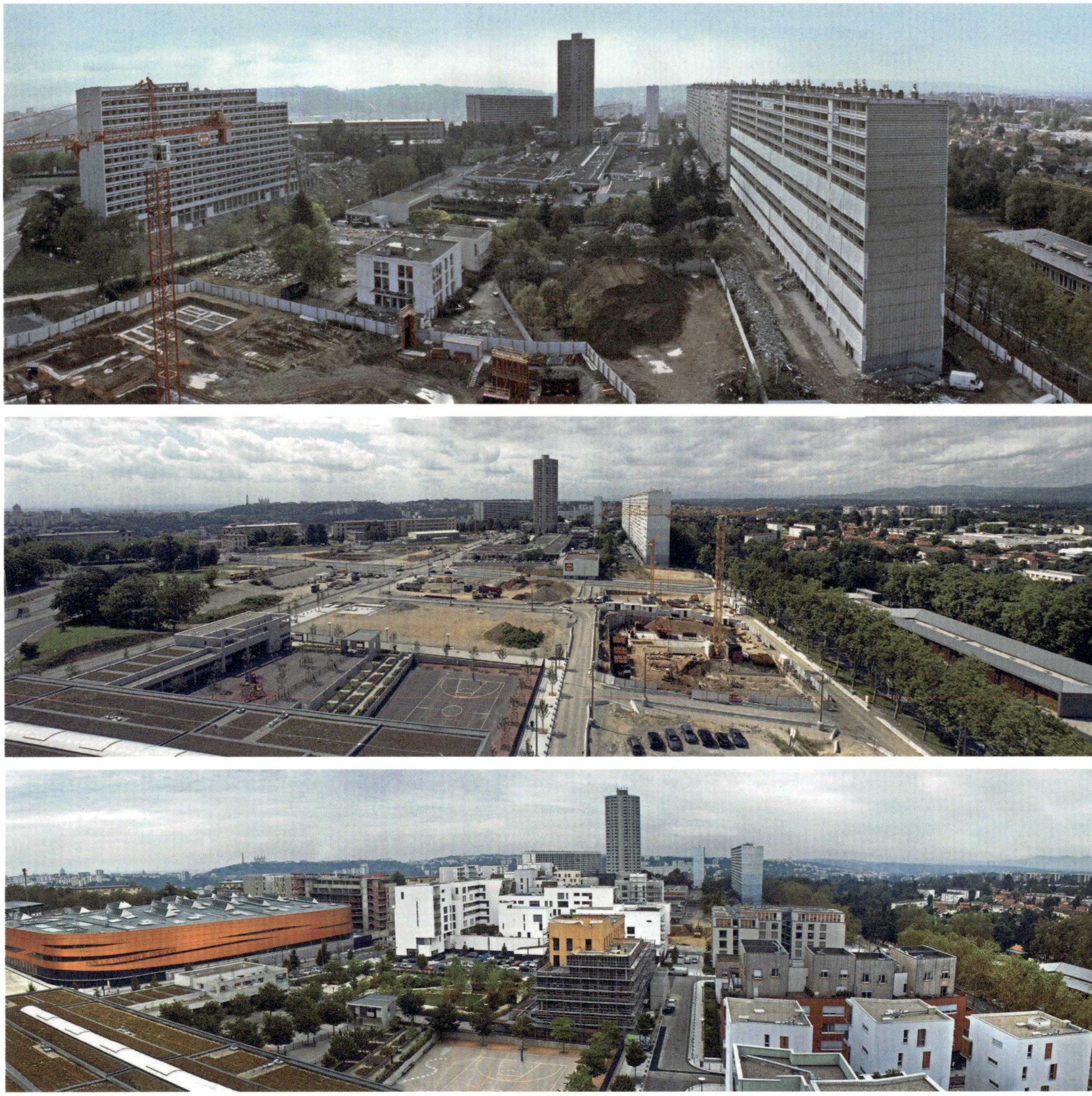

| FIG. 6 |

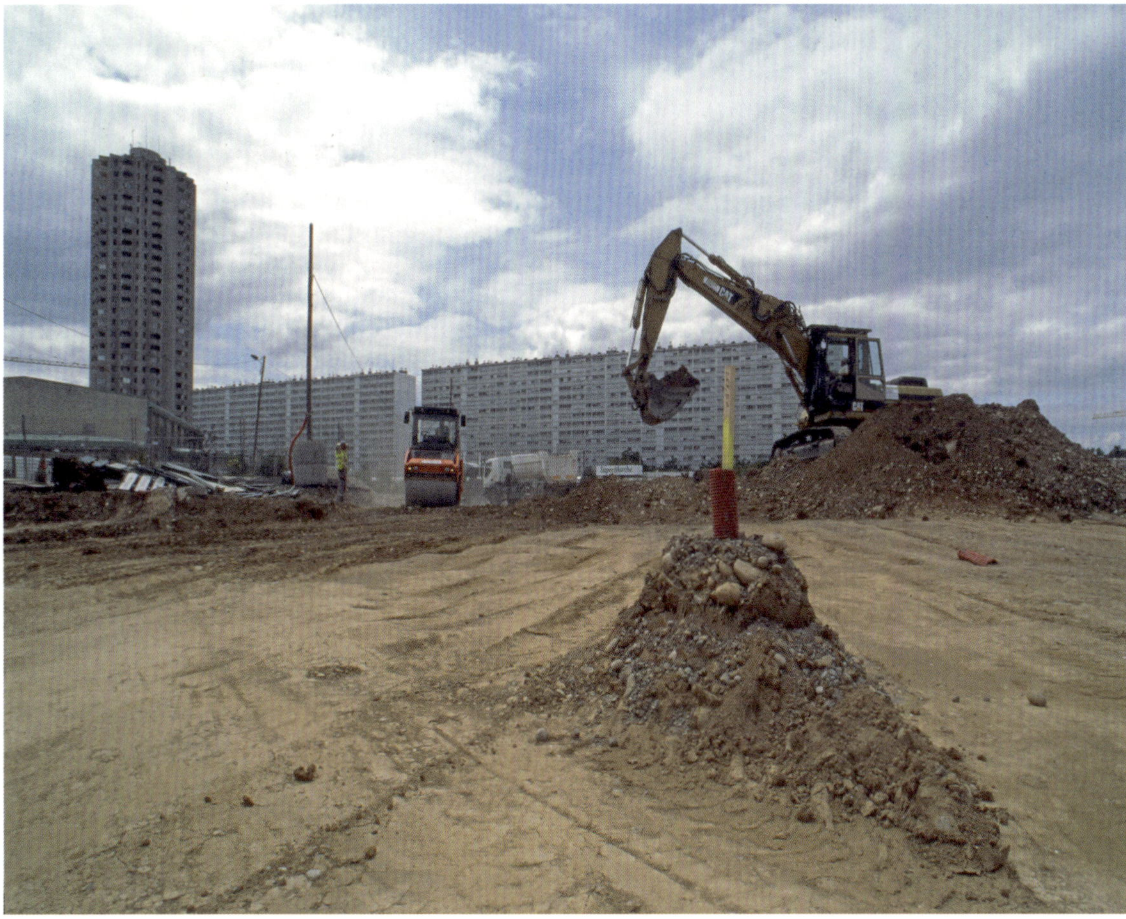

| FIG. 7 |

| FIG. 6 |
Gérard Dufresne, The La Duchère district of Lyon seen from the "Barre des 200" in 2005, 2007 and 2009.

| FIG. 7 |
Gérard Dufresne, The La Duchère district of Lyon in 2007.

ephemeral landscapes formed by the storage of materials, the cuts and fills, the construction equipment in action, the digging out of foundations and the planting of greenery, where fragments of rebuilt and inhabited city coexist beside vast worksites. These panoramic series offer powerful, informationally dense images; they record change, but above all, they depict it from a viewpoint that allows us to understand the intentions of the designers.

In addition to the time-lapse work, Dufresne experimented with other ways of portraying this lived-in worksite: he photographed the inhabitants of these ephemeral landscapes. These photos, taken at eye level, no longer depict the project as such, but rather share moments of life in this in-between space: machines in activity on the worksite **| FIG. 7 |**; a child running through gravel next to a freshly laid out square; a couple with a stroller walking along the edges; lampposts, power poles and temporary signs; piles of backfill; constantly changing pathways; and passers-by who nonetheless navigate their way around and continue to inhabit the district.

Together with the time-lapse series, these scenes from everyday life construct a landscape that grows out of the multiplicity of representations. Each in its own way, these photographs help create a memory for the future: a memory of the project, by depicting the gradual emergence of a district; of the place, as the pictures also freeze in time the former configurations of the territory; of the techniques, by showing how the site was physically transformed; and, finally, of the uses to which it was put. By giving the place temporal substance, these series of photographs show more than just the finished project: they show a process, a philosophy in action. Though the photos were not taken over the ten years of the project that Marguerit originally advocated, they nonetheless record and transmit the history of the landscape at La Duchère.

THE LAURAGAIS: FIRST IMPRESSIONS OF A TERRITORY

In parallel with his urban development and renewal projects, Alain Marguerit develops his ideas on a territorial scale in large landscaping studies and in particular, landscape plans. Here again, he calls upon Gérard Dufresne. For the Lauragais landscape plan, implemented in 2005 on a territory of 130 municipalities in Haute-Garonne, he commissioned the photographer upstream of the study. Dufresne was given *carte blanche*, with a brief to bring back his first impressions of the Lauragais.

A landscape plan is a diagnostic analysis of the current state of a territory, drawing on a range of different thematic approaches (geomorphology, hydrography, agriculture, urban planning, infrastructures) and, primarily, on current thinking about the emergence of new landscape challenges. The role of the landscape architect is to guide and accompany the evolution of the landscapes involved and put forward a project that is negotiated and shared by all the actors in the territory. For the Lauragais, the idea was to display the work of Gérard Dufresne at the outset of the study in order to elicit a response from the different parties and get the project underway. This choice reflects the importance Marguerit places on photos: for him, it goes without saying that they will orient the debate and, indeed, his own viewpoint on the territory.

Dufresne's pictures **| FIG. 8, 9 and 10 |** show an opulent, cultivated part of France with very picturesque landscapes. The views, relatively wide-angled, reveal the characteristic slopes of the Lauragais: rolling hills, punctuated by tall trees, reminiscent of Tuscany. The horizon line is often high, with the ground occupying almost the entire picture: taking their rhythm from the succession of designs formed by farm hedges, the photographs are centered on the earth, yellow ochre or deep black, often bathed in warm light. All of them show the marks of furrows, underlining the geometry and the microtopographies of a landscape shaped by agriculture. For those familiar with Dufresne's work, they recall his early pictures, used by Michel Corajoud, but also his personal work, particularly his work on landscapes seen from the TGV express train. To find the sensitivity and the eye of the photographer again in these images is not in itself surprising, since the brief he received from Marguerit was, explicitly, to immortalize his first contact with the site and capture his first impressions. It is an exercise in perception, a photographic project framed within a landscape project.

In this case, the landscape architect sent the photographer to obtain first-hand experience of

| FIG. 8, 9, 10 |
Gérard Dufresne, Photographs of the Lauragais, 2003.

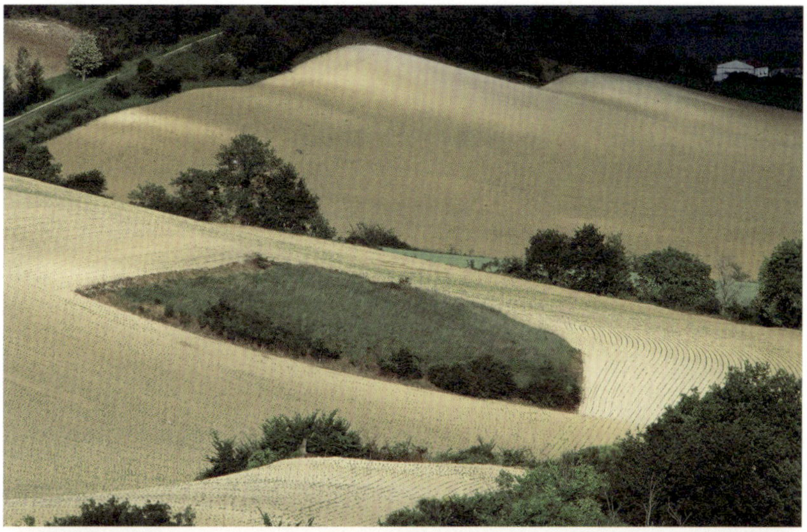

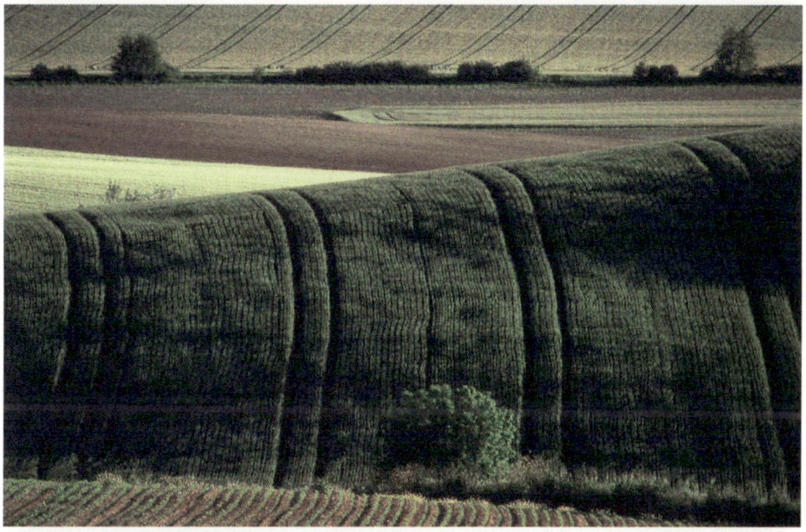

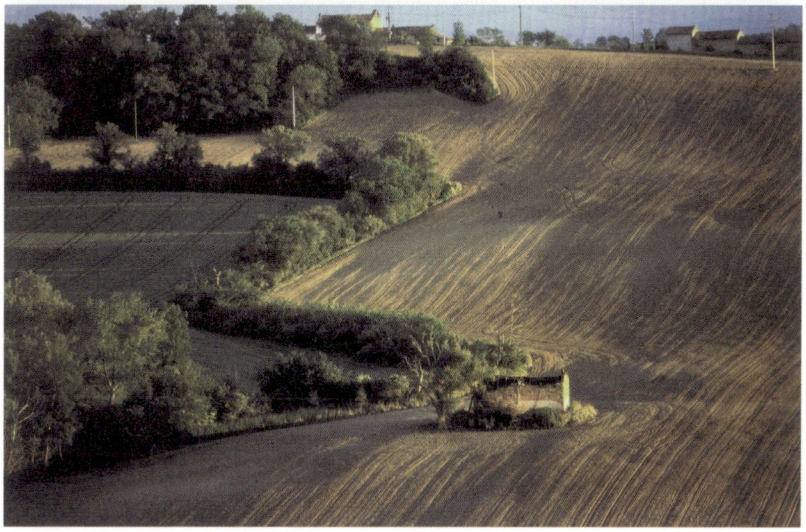

| FIG. 8, 9, 10 |

the site, explore the locations, get a feel for the landscape and bring back images of it in order to provoke discussion among those involved in the project. In so doing, he delegated a large part of the project to the photographer. "For the Lauragais," Marguerit relates, "we started by projecting 20 or so photos and of course, everyone was awestruck. The photographer's images quickly caught people's attention and as I commented on them, I was making the clients of the study aware of the complexity of the territory and of human action on the landscape. Commenting on the images enabled me to focus people's ideas on the landscape they wanted to see, and to steer the debate, for example, onto intensive agriculture and implied spaces like runoff ditches..."[34] Daring to initiate a study in such a way, and immersing the actors of the project in the landscape is an unusual move on the part of a designer. "The image is important. What images do the actors have? They are often mental images. What is their long-term vision? The answer depends on each person's logic. When everyone has their own particular vision, you end up with a bit of everything, and you have to find some way of bringing it all together. The photos helped us by demonstrating the strength and quality of these landscapes."[35] Marguerit's goal, in using these images, is therefore eminently political: it is about achieving convergence between the different actors' representations. The landscape architect uses the photographs primarily as a mediation tool.

But he also uses them to support his own reading of the landscape. These very strong images help him develop his ideas, make choices, and even visualize maps consistent with these initial pictures. The agency's book is quite telling in this respect: it shows maps side by side with sketches and photos, developing the same reading of the landscape, with obvious graphical correspondences. The Lauragais landscape plan is, in this respect, a very fine example of hybridized practices, where the photographic project informs and inflects the landscape project and, conversely, where the landscape architect's reading of the site has clearly influenced the pictures taken by the photographer. Could this, then, be called a coproduction? That would be to ignore that the landscape architect is, in this case, the sole commissioning agent. The photographic dimension of the landscaping plan was Alain Marguerit's initiative; it did not stem from a request by the end client. To speak of a coproduction, one would have to imagine commissions being awarded jointly to a landscape architect and a photographer.

THE MULTIPLE ROLES OF PHOTOGRAPHY IN THE LANDSCAPE PROJECT

Project photography is too often reduced to a beautiful image designed to showcase and promote an operation. This brief investigation of the partnership between Alain Marguerit and Gérard Dufresne shows that the role of photography in a landscape project is infinitely richer than that, and that it fulfills a specific function for each project.

In the case of the Place de la Comédie, the commission, though not expressly stipulated by the landscape architect, was for creative photography that would develop the audience's sensitivity to the quality of the project. Dufresne's pictures performed a documentary function as well as an artistic one: two dimensions which – as Michel Poivert, pointing to example of Italian 19th-century painters, reminds us – are not necessarily antithetical, but are in fact part of a tradition of historically rooted descriptive art.[36]

The urban project at La Duchère gave rise to a series of pictures from fixed viewpoints in accordance with a strategy embedded in time. They are not, however, simply a record: they also reflect the choices and perceptions of a creative photographer. In *Les raisons du paysage*, Augustin Berque compares a photograph of Le Tréport taken by Gabriele Basilico for the DATAR photographic mission to one taken by a tourist: "The photograph is not only of incomparably greater breadth and acuity; it is immediately obvious that the landscape in it is much more strongly structured and characterized. At every step in the production of the work, the artist has labored to ensure that rather than an insignificant tourist snapshot, we find ourselves looking at a real landscape: something that moves us, because certain motifs, which the artist has managed to bring to the fore, resonate with our own sensitivities."[37] Likewise, it can be said of Dufresne's images of La Duchère that they move us, and give us keys with which to read its urban landscape.

Finally, for the Lauragais landscape plan, Marguerit brought the photographer in upstream of his study. Dufresne's pictures served to stimulate the project, acting as catalysts to reveal the different mental representations that the project actors held of the same territory. But they were also a source of inspiration for the designer, as the photographer's perception of the terrain (his take on the topography, construction lines, relation to the horizon, expanse of land, etc.) here clearly influenced the landscape architect's viewpoint.

From one commission or project to the next, photography plays a different role, and the photographer takes a different creative approach. These depend greatly on the timeframe of the missions and the point at which they intervene in the project process. They may be designed to enhance the project, but also to shed light on the designers' approach. While they play a key part in constructing and transmitting the poetic dimension of the project, they are also an aid for mediation, and a way of documenting the memory and history of a site.

Some pictures are demonstrative: they present the qualities of the project, clarify it, and provide keys for understanding it, as for example at La Duchère. Other photographs ask questions. The images of the Lauragais fulfill this role: they offer a subjective vision of the territory in order to trigger discussion. The pictures of the Place de la Comédie also ask questions in their own way: by showing only fragments of the project, they leave the viewer with something of a puzzle to solve. The collaboration between Alain Marguerit and Gérard Dufresne has changed over time. In the 1980s, the landscape architect would call the photographer in at the end of a project to "immortalize" it. Beginning in the 1990s, however, he experimented with other forms of collaboration: firstly over longer timeframes, then far upstream of the project. This development reflects the landscape architect's growing interest in photography within the project approach: the designer is looking for images that will stimulate his own thinking, challenge his contribution, while at the same time conveying an argument, a critical and constructive vision. Surveys of other landscape architect/photographer dyads often reveal a similar evolution and, in every case, they show that the photographers' images are an integral part of, and intrinsically bound up with, landscape projects.

"There is always a subjective aspect in landscape art, something in the picture that tells us as much about who is behind the camera as about what is in front of it," wrote Robert Adams in 1981.[38] And indeed, landscape project photographs tell us as much about the photographer as about the actual project. The photographer is not a simple operator. The photographer's work generates a discourse, a line of thought, helping to construct the project by bringing a viewpoint that is a source of enrichment not only for the designer-project manager, but also for the client, the administrators, and the public at large. The photographer is therefore very much one of the actors in the landscape project. One who is too often silent, and whose role deserves to be given greater prominence.

---

* The author extends her heartfelt thanks to Marie-Hélène Loze for her assistance, and to Gérard Dufresne and Alain Marguerit for their readiness to help, and the information they so kindly made available.

34
Alain Marguerit in an interview with Marie-Hélène Loze and Sonia Keravel, November 2016.

35
Idem.

36
"From the Italian veduta artists to 19th-century paintings, this documentary aspect of the work, sometimes stipulated in the commission (Joseph Vernet), is part of the history of art. When we demonstrate this, we demonstrate that the documentary function is not antithetical to art, that there is precedent and therefore legitimacy for including the photographic landscape in the tradition of a historically rooted descriptive art," writes Michel Poivert, drawing on arguments developed by Jean-François Chevrier. See Michel Poivert, *La Photographie contemporaine*, Flammarion, Paris, 2010, p. 125.

37
Augustin Berque, *Les Raisons du paysage. De la Chine antique aux environnements de synthèse*, Hazan, Paris, 1995, p. 17.

38
Robert Adams, *Beauty in Photography*, Aperture (1981) 1989, p. 15.

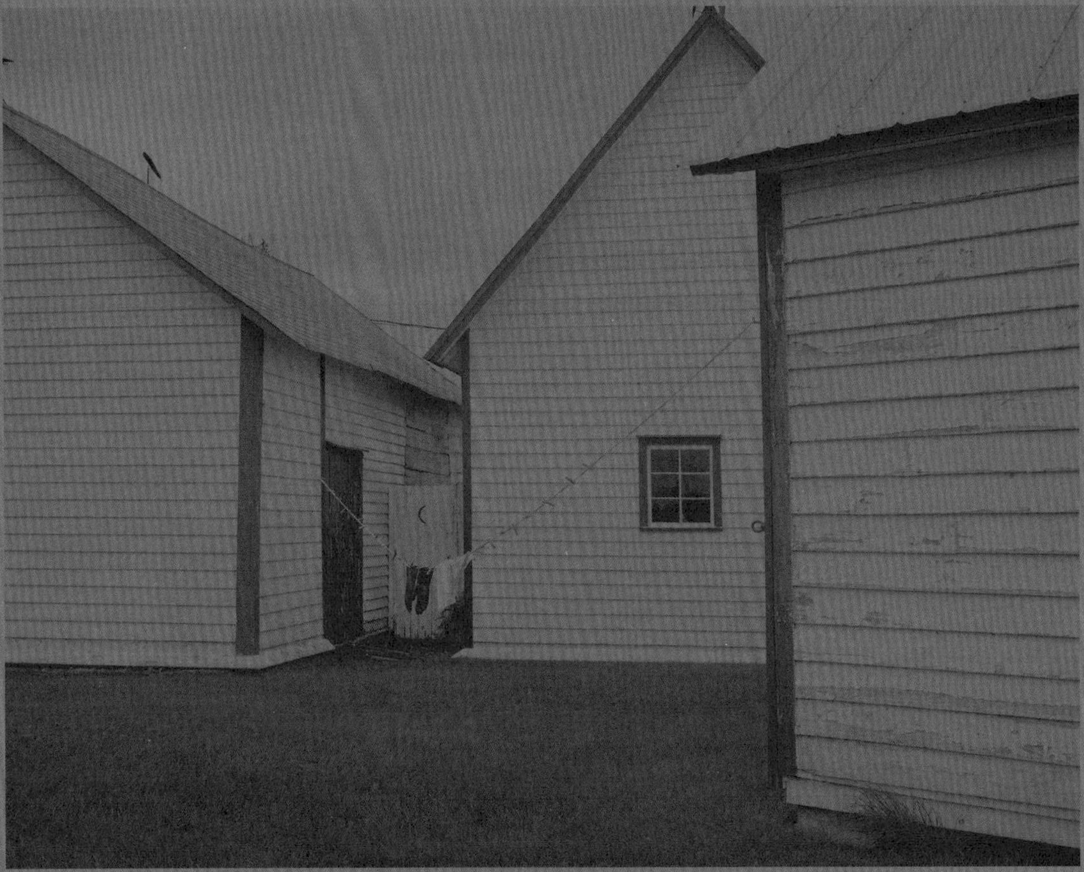

Après Strand, an Anatomy of Bertrand Carrière's Photographic Project

Franck Michel

GENESIS OF THE PHOTOGRAPHIC PROJECT

Québecois photographer Bertrand Carrière began working in the early 1980s. At that time his approach to photography took inspiration from the American documentary photograph tradition and from Québecois direct cinema. Later on he developed an intimist approach, over the years compiling a highly sensitive poetic inventory of everyday life. His photographs of places, objects and those dear to him evoke not only solitude, absence, the unexpected, but also happiness, gentleness and tenderness. They speak to our relationship with the world, with time, with creation and with others. Carrière regularly exhibits in Québec, Canada and Europe. His work has also been the subject of a dozen books.

At the same time as this first-person approach, he had for fifteen years or so been interested in places of remembrance and in marks of the passage of time embedded in the landscape.[1] He devoted several projects to traces of the First World War in Belgium and northern France, looking to reignite the memory of regions which had been historically and socially affected. Regarding his *Caux* series, Carrière explains: "Along this coastline I searched for deaf and silent aspects of this History. In this way, through what was visible, I wanted to bring out that which is embedded in this region and above all awaken that which is dramatically absent."[2] This type of project requires meticulous investigative work and a keen awareness of the past and present. It was on the strength of this experiential background and this dual approach that Bertrand Carrière began the *Après Strand* project.

Après Strand is an encounter with a major figure in the history of photography, that of Paul Strand, and with a historically situated perspective on a region dear to Bertrand Carrière. It tells us about the close and complex relationship that existed between a photographer and the region he chose to examine. His apprehension and appropriation of this region, his journey through this space and his attitude towards its inhabitants formed the basis of his photographic approach. Yet his photographic project cannot be reduced to this human and geographical experience: it is also a journey into the historical depths of the region, into its photographic references and into the historicity of perspectives. What roads should then be followed, what studies should be carried out and what stance should be taken? Bertrand Carrière set out on the trail of his predecessor, choosing to reproduce some of the latter's photographs, but without reducing his project to a token gesture that has become a symbol for certain photographers. Indeed, above and beyond the photo shooting and its vagaries, the photographic project was also deployed in strategies developed to share, exhibit and publish. *Après Strand* was also conceived as a project to exhibit in several places: the choices and constraints of exhibition, but also of its reception, contributed to the complexity of the project. Finally, the publication of a catalogue accompanied, prolonged and promoted the exhibition, whilst at the same time constituting a milestone in the artist's written and published work.

While watching John Walker's film, *Strand, Under the Dark Cloth*,[3] on the life of the famous American photographer, Carrière discovered the photos that the latter had taken in the Gaspé region of Québec in the 1930s. Fascinated by these exceptional pictures – unjustly unknown to the general public – he decided to follow in the master's footsteps. This decision was based both on his desire to photograph Québec after several years of projects abroad and by his interest in the history of the 20th century and of photography. He thus set out to discover a region for which he felt great fondness, whilst at the same time continuing his exploration of landscape as a place of remembrance. *Après Strand* was also part of an approach that the artist had initiated with his previous project, *Lieux mêmes*, where he had followed in the footsteps of an unknown photographer of the First World War in northern France and Flanders.

Carrière stayed in the Gaspésie throughout the summers of 2010 and 2011. With copies of Strand's photographs in hand as his only clues, he attempted to detect the mutations that this remarkable land had undergone over the previous

1 Here we mainly refer to the *Jubilee* (2002), *Caux* (2004), *Ce qui demeure* (2005–2006) and *Lieux mêmes* (2005–2006) projects, and to the following publications: *Bertrand Carrière. Lieux mêmes*, coll. "L'instant décisif", L'instant même, Québec, 2010, 120 p. and *Dieppe, paysages et installations*, Les 400 coups, Montreal, 2006, 126 p.

2 Extract from: http://www.bertrandcarriere.com/caux/

3 *Strand, Under the Dark Cloth* by John Walker, Canada, 1990, 81 minutes.

80 years and to rediscover the spirit that had inspired Strand during his Gaspesian journeys. Over the twelve weeks of his two visits, Carrière traveled through Gaspésie, from village to village, talking with its inhabitants, with his predecessor's pictures forever in his mind. Little by little, his exploration of the region and the testimonies he collected – patiently documented in notes and photographs – he was able to reconstruct Paul Strand's account of his travels **| FIG. 1 |**. The *Après Strand* project is a photographic project, but it is also the experience of an encounter with a region and with the people who live there.

A vast peninsula located in east-central Québec, Gaspésie is surrounded by the waters of the Saint Lawrence River to the north, by the Gulf of Saint Lawrence to the east, and by Chaleur Bay to the south. A mere 80,000 inhabitants are spread over a territory of 30,300 square kilometers. The center is mountainous and for the most part wild. Regional development was based around fishing, an industry that is now in rapid decline. Former fishing villages are dotted along the main road that runs around the peninsula.

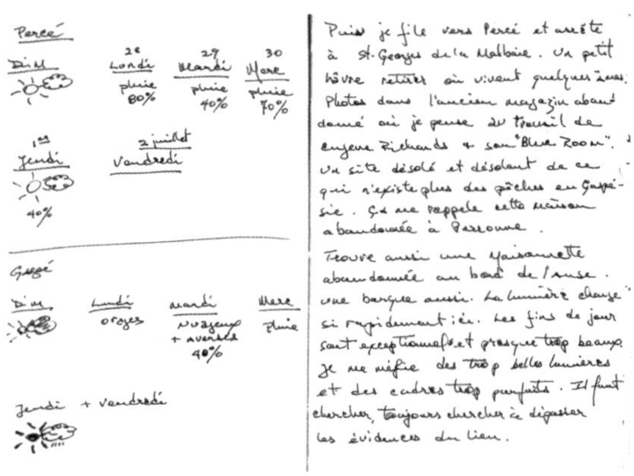

| FIG. 1 | Bertrand Carrière, notebooks, Gaspésie, 2010.

Historically marked by the presence of Native Americans, early colonists and generations of fishermen, the region has a strong identity and the inhabitants have a deep feeling of belonging. This very sparsely populated land, hostile and isolated, with its harsh living conditions and magnificent scenery, has fascinated and continues to fascinate travelers, tourists and artists from Québec and abroad as it has done for more than a century. As early as 1870, Montreal photographer William Notman spent time in the region, since then followed by painters, writers and photographers. Faced with this photogenic scenery begging to be photographed, one of Carrière's first challenges was to avoid the picture-postcard and the commonplace, and instead capture the essence of a region whose economic orientations have sometimes led to choices that have had catastrophic impacts on its landscapes.[4]

Bertrand Carrière's intentions were thus embedded in a historical continuity and in the need to document a territory undergoing profound transformation. During the summer of 2009 he came to the *Musée régional de Rimouski*, which I was running at the time, to propose his ambitious project. Located on the outskirts of the Gaspesian peninsula, in a small town of 40,000 inhabitants, this museum, essentially dedicated to contemporary art, seemed perfectly suited to his needs. Finding the proposition to be both fascinating and convincing, the Rimouski institution decided to join the adventure and promised to support the artist in his preparations, to organize an exhibition and to publish a catalogue. The *Après Strand* project was born.[5]

Après Strand is made up of three temporal phases that are both distinct and complementary: the photographic phase (traveling through the region and shooting), the exhibition phase (sharing) and the publishing phase (the trace), to which must be added the history phase (Paul Strand and the Gaspésie). Of these aspects, exhibition would seem to be both the culmination of the project and a constraint. The artist had promised to deliver, by a precise date, a corpus of photos sufficient for an exhibition and a book. He had two years to achieve this, taking into account the risks and uncertainties of such an exploration. He also made a commitment to a landscape, to an audience and to a slice of photographic history he intended to rediscover.

PAUL STRAND AND THE GASPÉSIE: PHOTOGRAPHY SERVING THE LANDSCAPE

Paul Strand, a leading light of photographic Modernism, traveled the Gaspesian peninsula in 1929 and in 1936, bringing back a large quantity of pictures little known to the general public. Whilst it is easy to make the link between his fascination for small communities and his interest in the Gaspésie, we know little about Strand's reasons for making these two trips, 1500 kilometers from New York, on board a Ford Model T. He had most probably heard about the region from friends and acquaintances in New England and was attracted by the notion of discovering a territory that was isolated from the industrial world and where modernity was apparently yet to arrive.

Although they were very short, these two episodes in Québec marked a decisive turning point in his work. Until then he had been interested in city life and in the emergence of industrial society; but during his first stay in Québec he became fascinated with the problems posed by the photographic representation of landscape, the vision of which he would ultimately overhaul. "Their importance is that they were the first, more systematic, conscious efforts to organize a landscape and its elements, all its elements. It was quite well recognized at the time that something new in landscape and in photography had evolved as far as my work was concerned."[6]

Strand's approach signaled a break away from the sublime that was so dear to the American landscape photography tradition of the 19th century; the latter stemmed, in part, from the major photographic missions that magnified the immensity of the American territory with overt spiritualism. Here there was no deified nature, no grandiloquence, but instead a methodical viewpoint that explored the organization of space through its planes and its volumes. Strand's landscapes, direct and frontal, demonstrate clarity, extreme precision and perfect technical mastery. At the time, Strand was trying to solve the problem of unifying the various elements that made up a landscape: "The landscape problem is the unity of whatever is included. In a landscape you usually have foreground, middle ground, distance and sky. All these have to be related. This is very difficult to do, of course... Anyway, I became conscious of the need to master this problem."[7] This modernist vision was strongly influenced by his friend and mentor, the photographer Alfred Stieglitz, with whom in 1917 he founded the *straight photography* movement. In opposition to the pictorialism that was very much in vogue at the time, this movement advocated using the specificities of the photographic medium and of its presumed objectivity, banishing all manipulation.

Although Strand had been one of the most ardent supporters of this approach in his work during the 1920s, his attitude towards the Gaspesian landscape does not appear to have been quite so radical, particularly during his second visit. It oscillated between his Modernist vision and a certain classicism, as can be seen, for example, in the notable differences between *Village, Gaspé, 1936* | FIG. 2 | and *Beach, Percé, Gaspé, 1929* | FIG. 3 |. In the former, the very precise composition and framing of the buildings highlight the play on volume, line and successive planes, demonstrating concerns that are essentially of a formal nature. In the latter, the human figure makes its appearance: a group of men are pulling a fishing boat up onto the sand, with Cap Barré in the background. Whilst here, too, Strand takes great care with his composition, he focuses more on the subject – dramatized by the imposing presence of the cloud-filled sky and the rocky cape – than on the form. The stylistic exercise gives way to a photographic style of far greater subjectivity, social, and open to the world.

During this period Stand considered himself to be a socially committed artist on a quest to capture "The essential character of a place and its people."[8] During his second stay, in 1936, in addition to landscape and architecture photos, he shot several portraits, mainly of fishermen, which humanized his approach and completed

4
As an example, consider the vast gaping wound in the landscape that is the recent Port-Daniel cement plant, built in one of the peninsula's most beautiful bays, the ecological impacts of which have proved to be disastrous.

5
I myself had a dual role in this project: that of curator of the exhibition and, as director of the *Musée régional de Rimouski*, that of project manager.

6
Paul Strand, transcription of an interview with Milton Brown and Walter Rosemblum, for *Archives of American Art, The Smithsonian Institution*, November 1971, p. 21 cited in *Paul Strand, Sixty years of photographs*, New York Aperture Foundation, New York, 2010 (1st edition 1976), p. 151.

7
Idem., p. 24. According to Strand, one of the few artists to have succeeded in this stylistic and technical exercise is Cézanne, "Because not only is every element in the picture unified but there is also unity in depth."

8
Paul Strand, *op. cit.*, p. 25.

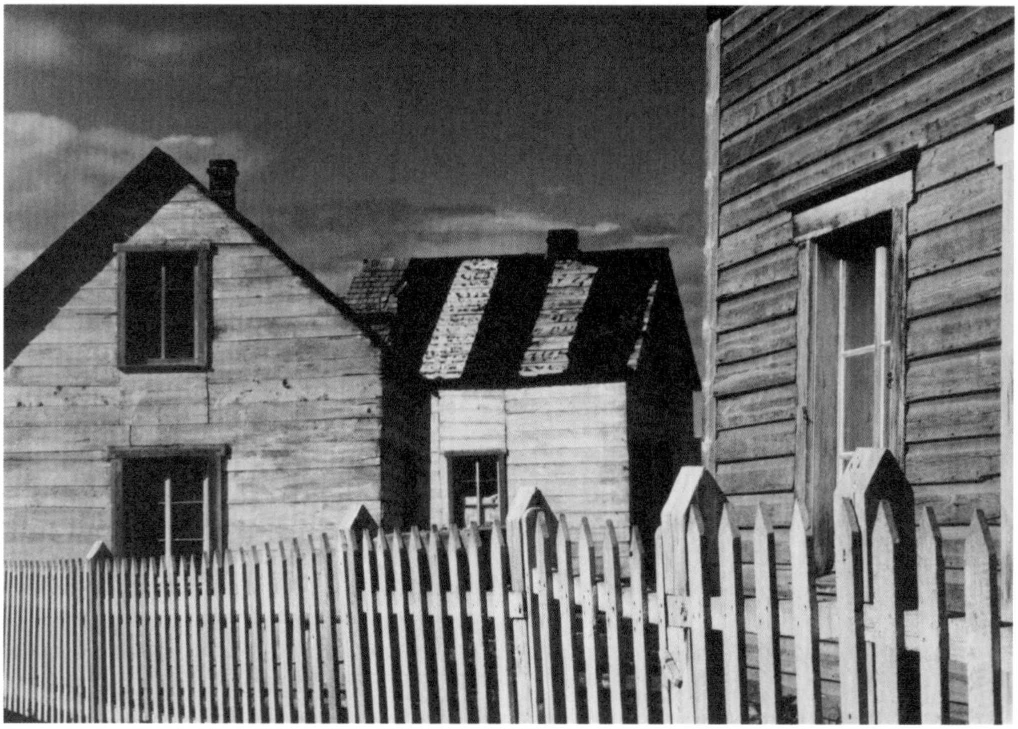

| FIG. 2 |

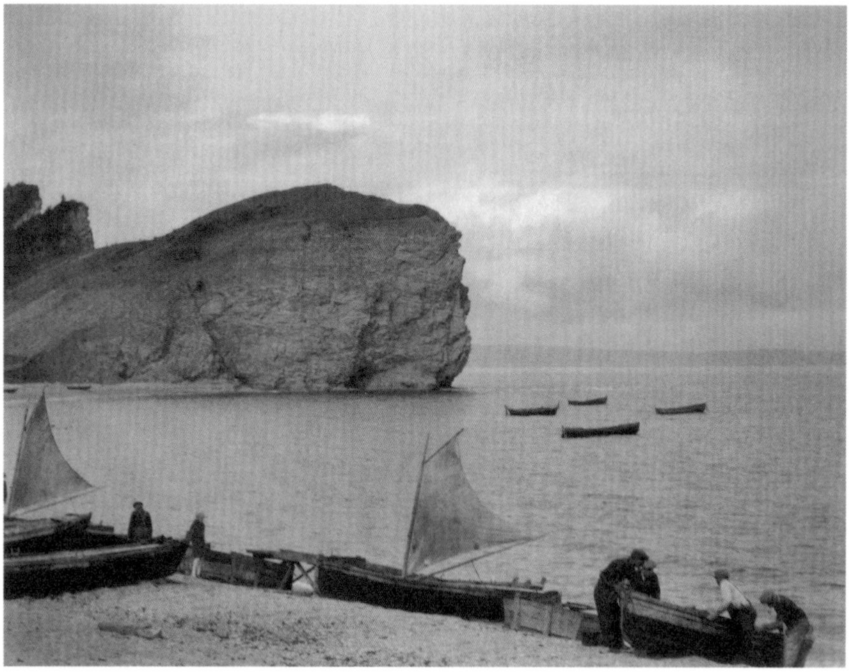

| FIG. 3 |

| FIG. 2 |
Paul Strand, *Village, Gaspé*, 1936, Philadelphia Museum of Art.

| FIG. 3 |
Paul Strand, *Beach, Percé, Gaspé*, 1929.

his photographic documentation of the Gaspesian community.[9] This same approach, combining landscapes, architecture and portraits, would henceforth characterize his work as a whole.

BERTRAND CARRIÈRE'S LANDSCAPE STORIES

During the summer of 2010, Bertrand Carrière set out on his first six-week exploration of the Gaspésie, equipped with a traditional medium-format camera and a digital camera. He returned the following summer. As he had very little information on Strand's photographs, aside from the photos themselves, a few vague titles, and some short extracts from interviews, he was obliged to do some real investigative work on site. This investigation brought him into contact with the locals to glean information that might guide his research. Unlike his previous projects, essentially composed of landscapes, he chose to take a humanistic approach and shot several portraits. Following a tradition rooted in the recent history of Québec's documentary photography, he photographed his subjects in their immediate environment – workshop, lounge, place of work, bedroom, veranda, etc. – using wide and often frontal angles **| FIG. 4 |**.[10]

In the photos he took on the peninsula, made the Strandian vision of photography and of the landscape his own. Making a conscious effort not to copy, he allowed himself to soak up this vision, adding a layer of interpretation, that of time and of landscape memory. His earlier projects had demonstrated his fascination for the stories embedded in the landscapes and their remaining traces. Eighty years later, his interest in Paul Strand's photographs is part of this same sensitivity. Like Strand, he is interested in humanized landscapes and in vernacular architecture: modest homes, barns, huts, fences, wayside crosses, and roads **| FIG. 5 |**. During his chance encounters with local people, he showed them copies of Strand's photos, asked questions about a given place, building or person, so as to orientate his project.

In his book *Discovering the Vernacular Landscape*, American landscape historian John Brinckerhoff Jackson defines vernacular landscapes as "usually small, irregular in shape, subject to rapid change in use, in ownership, in dimensions; that the houses, even the villages themselves, grow, shrink, change morphology, change location; that there is always a vast amount of 'common land' – waste, pasturage, forest, area where natural resources are exploited in a piecemeal manner [...]."[11] Elsewhere he states: "A landscape is not a fragment of attractive natural scenery it is what is produced when society sets out to modify its environment in order to survive."[12] This definition characterizes the organization of the Gaspé region and part of its habitat, shaped over time by a vital need to adapt to climatic, geographical and socioeconomic conditions. Strand, and later on Carrière, was able to perfectly capture this ordinary aspect of Gaspesian landscapes and architecture **| FIG. 6 |**.

This is also what led Carrière to take an interest in the place names. The Gaspésie has a wide variety of toponyms, many of which are Native American names: Miguasha, Escouminac, Chics-Chocs, Pasbébiac, Shigawake, Marsoui, and others that relate to history or geography: Pointe-à-la-Frégate, Anse-aux-Gascons, Petite-Vallée, Cannes-de-Roches, Barachois, Bonaventure, etc. Fascinated by the diversity and poetry of these

9
According to Nancy Newhall, the 1936 photographs were "incomparably warmer and more powerful than the first. The Gaspé is no longer remote, under huge skies: children smile, a hardy old fisherman stands behind chicken wire in his barn doorway. The white picket fence, no longer a challenging abstraction, recurs among the clapboarded, gabled houses, 'like a musical figure'." Nancy Newhall, *Paul Strand Photographs 1915–1945*, Museum of Modern Art, New York, 1945, p. 7, cited by Alexander Reford, "La Gaspésie de Paul Strand", *Après Strand, Bertrand Carrière, Musée régional de Rimouski*, Rimouski, 2012, p. 12.

10
Here we refer, among other things, to commissions from the *Office national du film* (ONF), which sent photographers and filmmakers to document the rural habitat in the 1960s and 1970s. The figurehead of this movement was undoubtedly the photographer Gabor Szilasi, several of whose projects on rural Québec, particularly that on the Charlevoix region (1970), have become cornerstones of Québec's photographic history.

11
John Brinckerhoff Jackson, *Discovering the Vernacular Landscape*, Yale University Press, New Haven, CT, London, 1984, p. 151. On this subject see also Jordi Ballesta, "Le vernaculaire selon John. Quatre étapes dans la définition d'une notion centrale dans l'œuvre de J.B. Jackson", in "John Brinckerhoff Jackson", *Les Carnets du paysage*, no. 30, Actes Sud/ *École Nationale Supérieure de Paysage*, Arles, Versailles, 2016, p. 31–45.

12
Handwritten notes by John Brinckerhoff Jackson, from "Alphabetized notebook pre-1960", archive MSS 633 (JBJ Papers Collection (B3F7), Center for Southwest Research Special Collections, University Libraries, University of New Mexico, reproduced in *Les carnets du paysage*, *op. cit.*, p. 74.

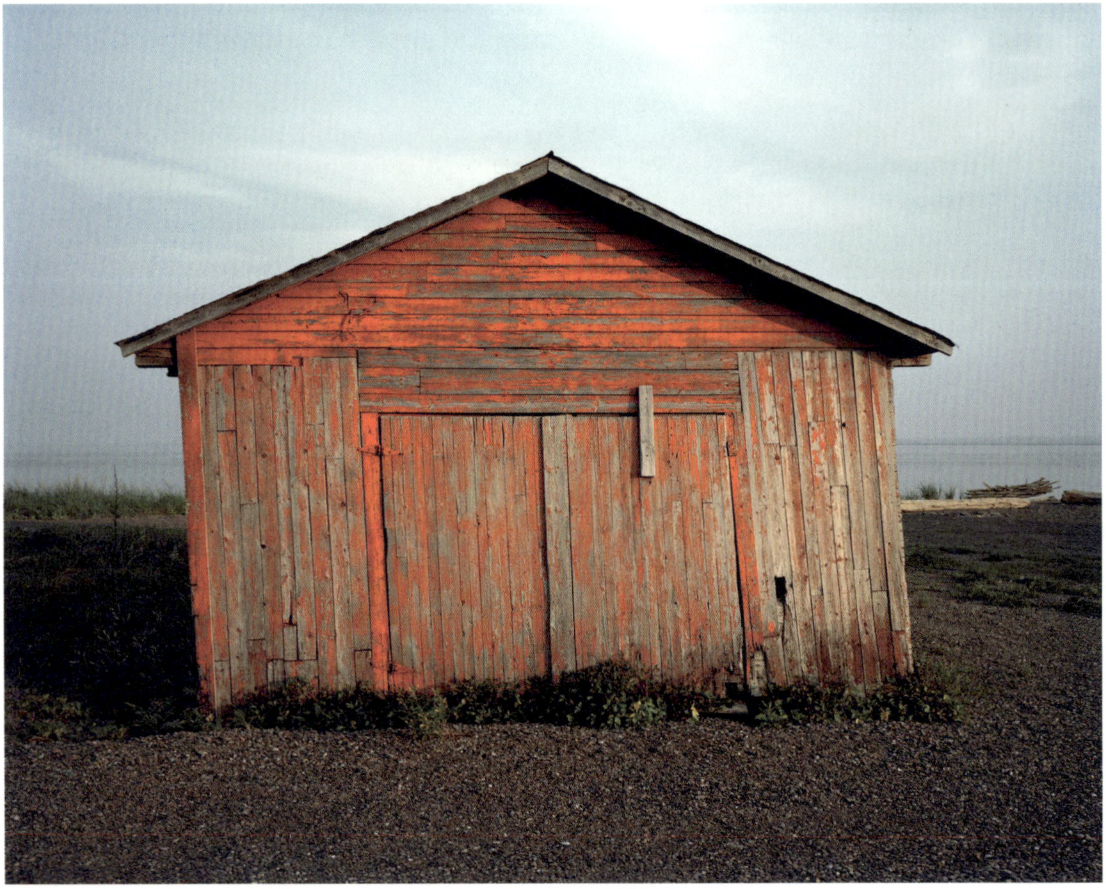

| FIG. 5 |

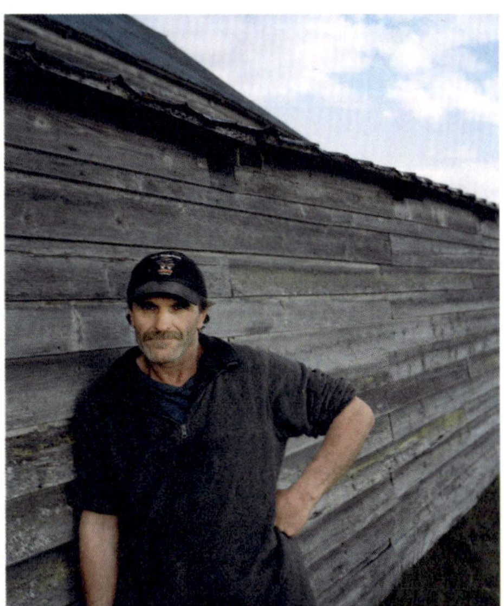

| FIG. 4 |

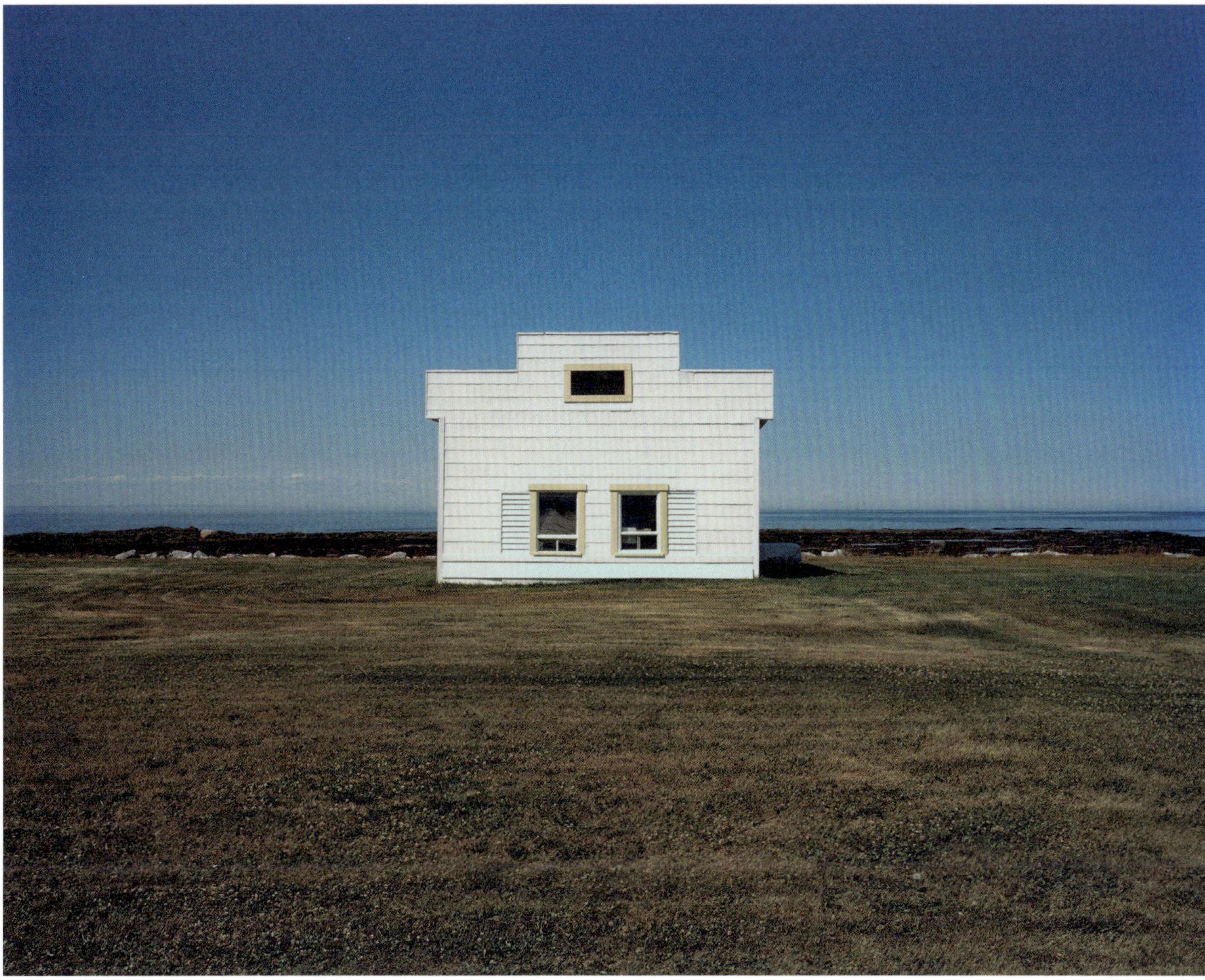

| FIG. 6 |

| FIG. 4 |
Bertrand Carrière, *David Bond, Cap-Saint-Pierre, Gaspésie,* Québec, 2010.

| FIG. 5 |
Bertrand Carrière, *Cabin, Rivière-au-Renard, Gaspésie, Québec,* 2010.

| FIG. 6 |
Bertrand Carrière, *Sainte-Anne-des-Monts, Gaspésie*, Québec, 2010.

names, he wanted to include them in the exhibition. A hundred or so names were thus placed on a board at the entrance to the exhibition and on the first page of the catalogue.

STRAND'S LEGACY

The majority of Carrière's photographs bear no direct relation to those by Strand. They have their own identity. In this respect, the decision not to use the same format (a Mamiya 6 × 7 cm instead of Strand's Graflex 4 × 5 inch) and above all to use color rather than black and white allowed him to avoid a certain amount of nostalgia, whilst at the same time updating his discourse and clearly distancing it from that of his predecessor. From the master's teachings, he retained his great feel for light and, of course, the absolute key to the Strandian vision: frontality. In certain pictures he nevertheless plays with explicit reference, thus allowing his project to root itself in history, as for example with *Coin-du-Banc, Gaspésie, Québec, 2010* | **FIG. 7** | which conjures up *Village, Gaspé, 1936* | **FIG. 2** |. In both cases, the very precise composition and framing of the buildings highlight the play on volume, line and successive planes. The viewpoint and choice of subject demonstrate concerns that are purely formal. For Carrière, this stylistic exercise paid true homage to Strand's modernism.

The final picture of the exhibition was a portrait of the grandson of Hilaire Coton, a fisherman photographed by Strand in 1936, whom Carrière had managed to find | **FIG. 8** |. Simply entitled *Old Fisherman, Gaspé, 1936*, Strand's photograph is undoubtedly the best known of his Gaspesian corpus | **FIG. 9** |. This portrait loaded with humanism symbolizes the pride of the Gaspesian people, as does Carrière's photo 80 years later. The two pictures also illustrate the huge respect shown by the photographers, in their vision of the Gaspésie, towards the people who shaped this land, and how they bring alive these communities who are struggling against a harsh nature and often difficult socioeconomic conditions. Like Strand, Carrière is fascinated by the little stories to be found in all of these communities. Whether it be a red hut on the shore, a huge abandoned house that seems to emerge from a cotton wool sky, or a field where a white horse grazes, these landscapes enclose the memories of those who inhabited them. They tell their stories. And in photographing them, Carrière offers us scattered fragments, like the tiny moments that constitute a narrative, that of his view of the Gaspésie today.

This sensitivity makes him attentive to the symbols found in the landscape. Next to the omnipresence of the sea, it is undoubtedly the cross that is most recurrent symbol of the Gaspesian landscape. Already present in Strand's pictures, the cross appears in many of Carrière's photos: wayside crosses, sailors' cemeteries, roadside altars | **FIG. 10** |. This motif is also to be found in the inescapable presence of power poles and in the road junctions, melting into the sea on the horizon.

The cross is a strong historical symbol, because it is at the far point of the Gaspésie that, on July 24, 1934, Jacques Cartier planted a cross to claim possession of the territory in the name of France. Indeed, Carrière remembers that an illustration showing Jacques Cartier erecting a cross, surrounded by a group of admiring Indians, decorated one of his childhood history books. Another sign of the importance of the cross in Gaspesian history: during a trip to the Gaspésie in 1932, American painter Georgia O'Keeffe, married to photographer Alfred Stieglitz, painted a landscape that showed a white wooden cross on the edge of a cape. Carrière searched for this cross throughout his travels, not finding it until the very last day, in Rivière-à-Claude. This highly evocative photograph was the last to be shown in the exhibition; it also appears on the last page of the catalogue.

"ROUTE 132"

The Gaspesian peninsula is ringed by a single 850 kilometer road, commonly referred to as "the 132", around which the territory's town and country planning was organized. Although it only appears in three pictures, the majority of Carrière's photographs were taken from this road. It acts as a guide, establishing a link between photographer and landscape; it gives direction to wanderings, makes photography possible and generates encounters. Over time, Carrière developed a certain intimacy with "the 132". Day after day he traveled the road, moving onwards, turning back: "Roads do not simply lead to places, they are places."[13] It became his strongest ally, but also his greatest constraint. When Paul Strand traveled in the Gaspésie, the road had just been made suitable for vehicles, thus making it easier for him to roam the peninsula, and it undoubtedly influenced his documentation of the region. As Jackson declared: "Roads transformed not only the way people traveled, but also the manner in which they perceived the world"[14] (our translation). This marked the beginning of automobile tourism | FIG. 11 |.

His car played a key role in Carrière's travels. It was a means of transport, a refuge and a workshop, and it was through its windows that he framed his first photos. His vision was thus reliant on both the car and its corollary, the road. The way the region was planned, dependent on this unique road, and the choice of means of transport with which to explore it, both shaped and restricted his photo shoots. His perception and representation of the Gaspesian territory would have been very different if he had chosen to cover it on foot, walking through the Gaspésie National Park (a vast mountainous natural reserve at the heart of the peninsula) and along the International Appalachian Trail. But Carrière made a conscious choice to focus on the humanized rather than wild landscapes, as had Strand before him.

EXHIBITION AND PUBLICATION

Carrière returned from his first trip to the Gaspésie with more than 200 photos. An initial assessment allowed him to pick out the successes and failures, so that he could set out the following year with precise objectives in mind. At the end of the two trips he had a collection of several hundred film and digital photographs. After a preselection by the artist, the curator's work began. We worked together to try to select some 70 photos – just film – out of the small format prints. From this corpus we trimmed the selection down to approximately 40 pictures, which was still too many for the contemporary art room at the *Musée régional de Rimouski*. To avoid having to discard any more photos and thus risk losing all meaning, we decided to split the exhibition into two and to present the second part at another venue, the Villa Esteban. Located in the Reford Gardens, this heritage building, built in 1887 and extended in 1926, regularly organizes visual art exhibitions. The splendid historical gardens that surround it – very popular with tourists en route to the Gaspésie – were created by Elsie Reford in 1926, shortly before Paul Strand's first in stay in the Gaspésie.[15] During the first half of the 20th century, the village of Métis was a major holiday destination for the English-speaking aristocracy from Québec, Canada, the eastern United States and even from Britain. They came by boat, train or car. The reputation of this part of the Gaspésie among the English-speaking elite of the time might also explain Strand's interest in the region.

The two venues are very different, from both architectural and visitor standpoints. The *Musée régional de Rimouski* is known for its contemporary art exhibitions which are sometimes cutting-edge, attracting visitors who are already art-aware.

13
John Brinckerhoff Jackson, *A Sense of Place, A Sense of Time*, Yale University Press, New Haven, CT, 1994, p. 190; cited by Gilles A. Tiberghien in Francesco Careri, *Walkscapes, la marche comme pratique esthétique*, Jacqueline Chambon, Paris, 2013, p. 11.

14
John Brinckerhoff Jackson, "By Way of Conclusion: How to Study the Landscape", *The Necessity for Ruins*, Amherst: The University of Massachusetts Press, 1980, p. 113–126. See also Gilles A. Tiberghien, "Jackson: chemins et routes", in "John Brinckerhoff Jackson", *Les Carnets du paysage, op. cit.*, p. 31–45.

15
On the history of the *Jardins du Métis* (Reford Gardens), see the website: http://www.jardinsdemetis.com/francais/jardins/villa-estevan.php.

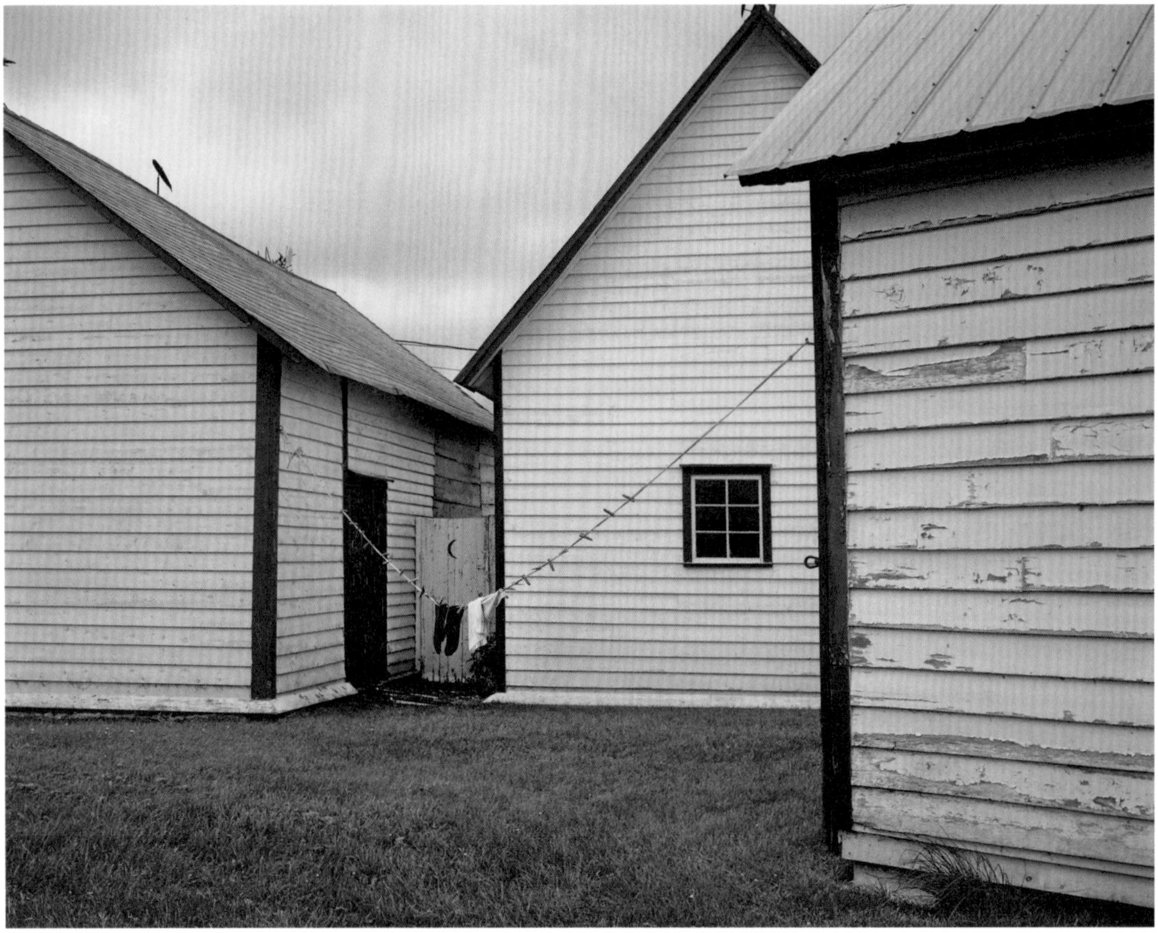

| FIG. 7 |

| FIG. 7 |
Bertrand Carrière, *Coin-du-Banc, Gaspésie*, Québec, 2010.

| FIG. 8 |
Bertrand Carrière, *Hilaire Cotton, Rivière-au-Renard, Gaspésie*, Québec, 2010.

| FIG. 9 |
Paul Strand, *Old Fisherman, Gaspé* (Hilaire Cotton, 1865–1959), 1936.

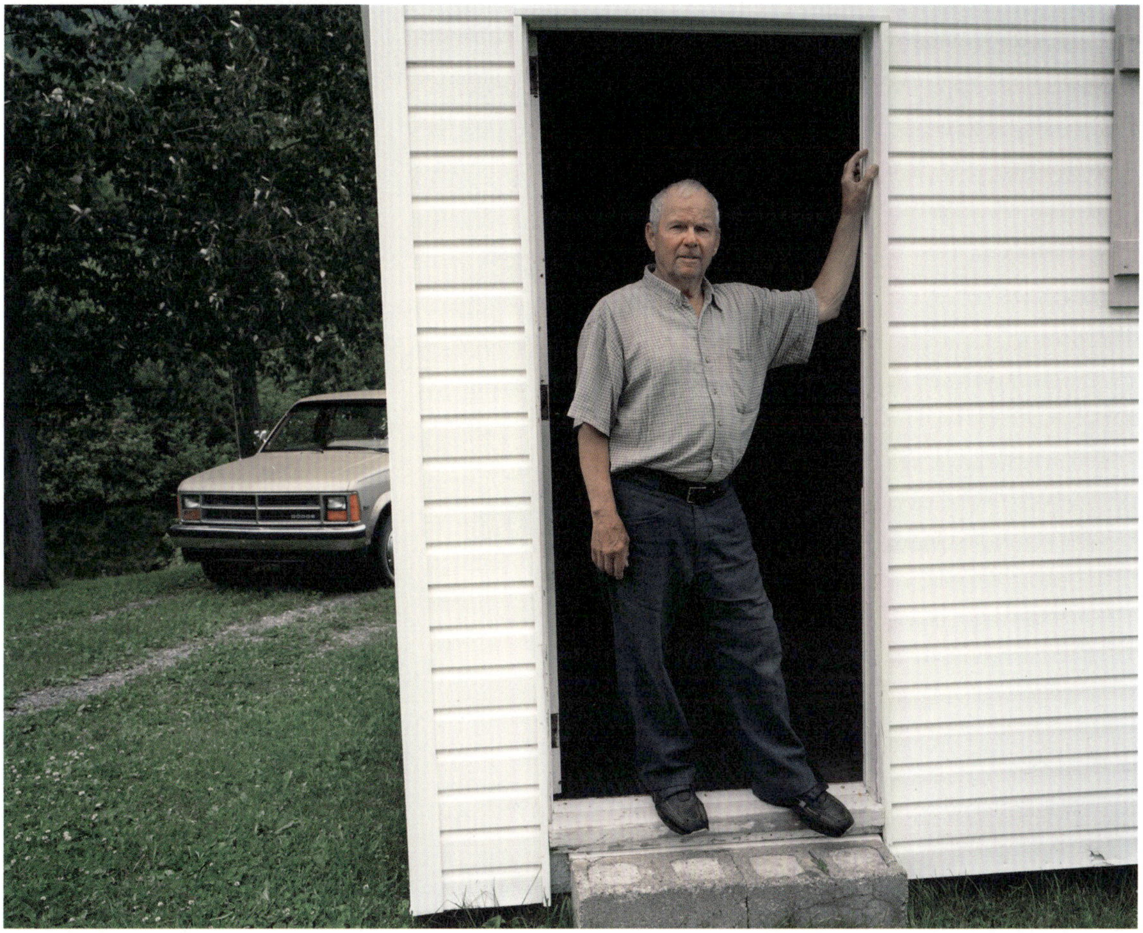

| FIG. 8 |

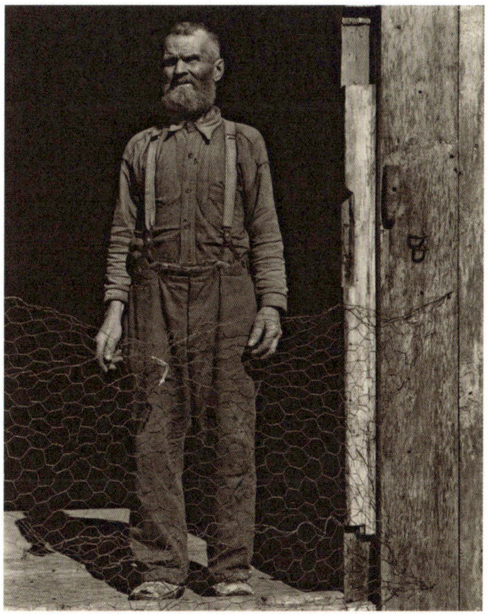

| FIG. 9 |

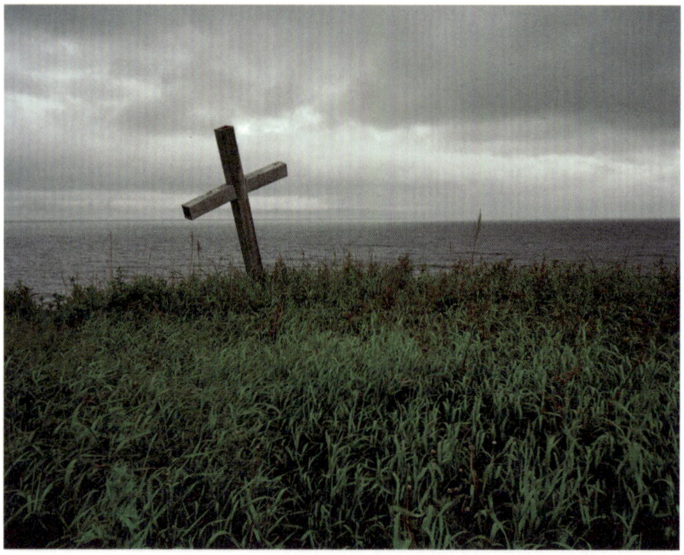

| FIG. 10 |

| FIG. 10 |
Bertrand Carrière, *Croix, Rivière-au-Renard, Gaspésie,* Québec, 2010.

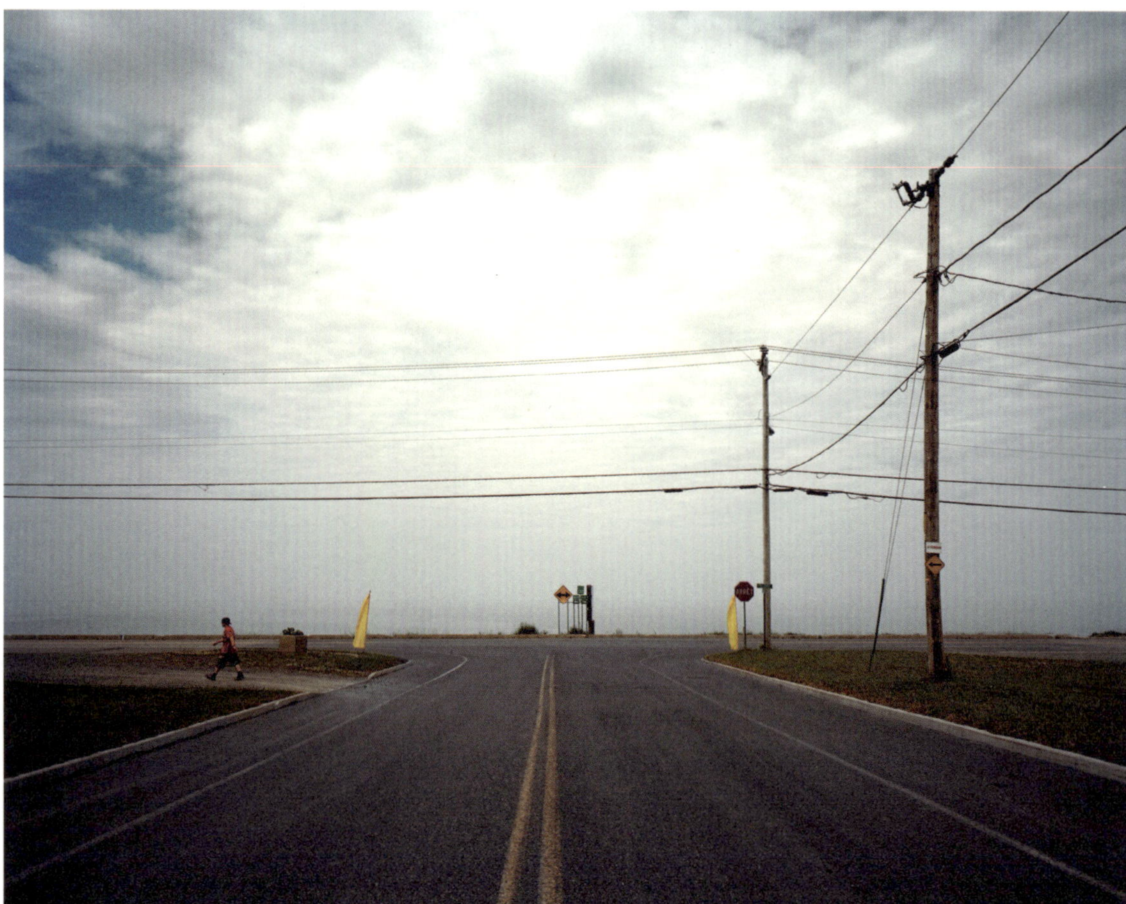

| FIG. 11 |

| FIG. 11 |
Bertrand Carrière, *Mont-Saint-Pierre, Gaspésie,* Québec, 2010.

Villa Esteban, on the other hand, organizes exhibitions that are generally more accessible, attracting a wider public of tourists and families who mainly come to enjoy the historical gardens and the festival's contemporary gardens.[16] We had to take these two realities into account when making the final photo selection, whilst at the same time making sure we did not fall into the clientelism trap. The specificities of each venue therefore influenced the way the photographs were divided. Without going so far as to favor the idyllic vision of the Gaspésie that the public tend to hold, the photos shown in Métis were more accessible and less serious than those at the museum, but nevertheless preserved the essence of the project. For the museum exhibition we opted for a linear mode of presentation. The 36 large-format photos spread throughout the room created a fictitious panorama that evoked "route 132", which had been such a determining factor in Carrière's project **| FIG. 12 |**.

As for Paul Strand's pictures, they had very rarely been shown to the public, and as far as we are aware, never in Québec. The National Gallery of Canada has a certain number of photographs from the Gaspesian corpus, so we initiated steps for permission to exhibit them alongside those of Carrière. Unfortunately, the *Musée régional de Rimouski* was unable to meet the very strict loan conditions that the National Gallery of Canada imposes for such valuable vintage prints. This was a bitter disappointment, as the Rimouski institution is the only place in eastern Québec likely to exhibit this type of work. If we did not succeed this time round, Strand's photos would never be shown in their land of origin and would remain hidden away in the museum's vaults in Ottawa without Gaspesians even being aware of their existence. We had to find an alternative solution. We obtained the rights to copy the pictures, so that we could arrange them, accompanied by explanatory texts, on panels displayed in the final section of the exhibition. This compromise gave visitors the opportunity to come into contact with Strand's work and integrate it into their understanding of the exhibition.

In two of the three small-format photographs at the end of the exhibition, Carrière was trying to use the same viewpoint that Strand had chosen **| FIG. 13 and 14 |**. This strategy, known as "rephotography", involves returning to the same spot used for a shot previously taken by another photographer and attempting to reproduce as precisely as possible the same view and lighting. A comparison of the two photos then reveals the transformation that the landscape has undergone over time. "Rephotography" has become a veritable genre in the history of 20th-century photography.[17] One of the best-known rephotography projects is the *Rephotographic Survey Project*, which took place at the end of the 1970s. Directed by photographer Mark Klett and bringing together photographers Ellen Manchester and JoAnn Verburg, the project aimed to track down and rephotograph 120 sites documented by photographic missions in the western United States at the end of the 19th century.[18] Many other initiatives of this type saw the light of day, including landscape photography observatories in France and Belgium[19] and the *Re: Collecting Landscapes* project.[20]

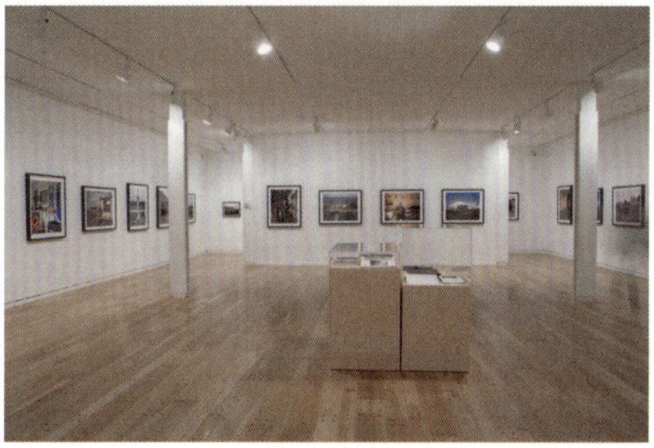

| FIG. 12 | View of the exhibition, *Musée régional de Rimouski*, Québec

The *Après Strand* book shows three pairs of photos, the agreed conditions for reproduction having made it possible for Strand's and Carrière's photos to be placed side by side. Although this was an important part of Carrière's approach, he used it only sparingly, rephotography in the strict sense not being the main aim of the project as a whole. However, as Bernard Lamarche points out in the exhibition catalogue, by following in the footsteps of another photographer, Carrière is

16
An imposing site adjacent to the historical gardens is dedicated to the International Garden Festival, a renowned annual event that brings together architects, landscapers and international artists for the creation of ephemeral gardens.

17
See the catalogue of the *Sur l'espace, la mémoire et la métaphore : Le paysage dans la reprise photographique* exhibition, Martha Langford, Vox Populi, Montréal, 1997.

18
See Mark Klett et al., *Second View: The Rephotographic Survey Project*, University of New Mexico Press, Albuquerque, 1984.

19
Launched in 1994, the *Observatoire national photographique du paysage* set itself the task of monitoring and orienting the evolution of lanscapes. In its initial programme it set out to create an archive of photographic series that would make it possible to analyze the mechanisms and factors affecting landscape transformation. See Raphaële Bertho's article in this volume, p. 36.

20
See http://www.architectuur.ugent.be/2015/02/re-collecting-landscapes/.

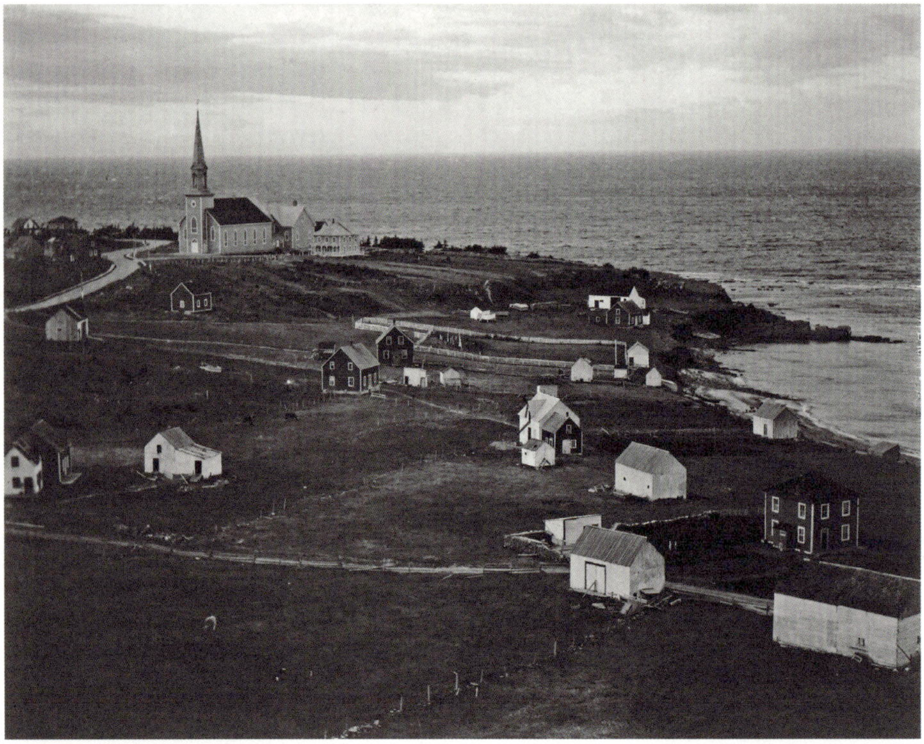

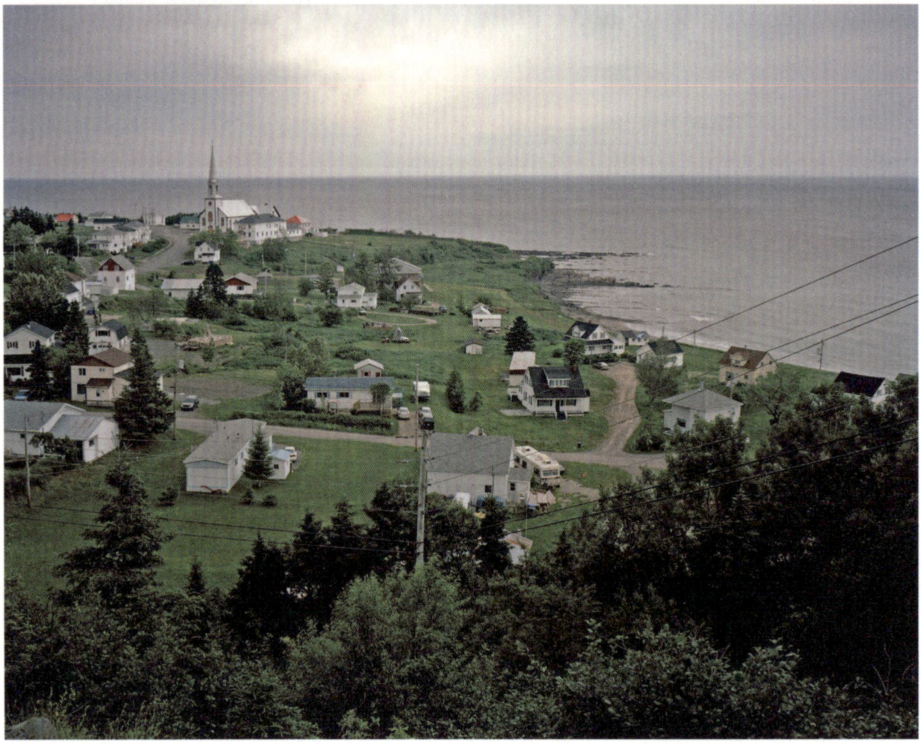

| FIG. 13 and 14 |

| FIG. 13 |
Paul Strand, *Fishing Village, Gulf of St. Lawrence, Gaspé*, 1929.

| FIG. 14 |
Bertrand Carrière, *Saint-Maurice-de-L'Échouerie, Gaspésie, Québec*, 2010.

"certainly adopting a 'rephotographic' approach" in a broader sense.[21]

We were also authorized to reproduce some of Paul Strand's landmark photographs in the catalogue. In addition to these pictures and all of Carrière's, the catalogue contains texts from three authors: Bernard Lamarche, art historian and at that time curator of contemporary art at the *Musée régional de Rimouski*, Alexander Reford, historian and director of the Reford Gardens, and myself. Alexander Reford's text historically contextualizes Strand's two visits to the Gaspésie at the beginning of the 20th century and situates this work within the American photographer's overall *oeuvre*. work as a whole. Bernard Lamarche sketches a brief history of rephotography projects and analyzes Carrière's approach from this standpoint. My contribution focuses mainly on what Strand's vision brings to that of Carrière and on the two photographers' relationships with the Gaspesian landscapes. These three texts provide both a global overview and keys to interpretation that allow for different levels of reading; they allow us to better grasp the different facets of the project and to understand how it is rooted in the history of photography. It is both a book of pictures and a work of critical analysis, aimed just as much at specialists as at amateurs or tourists who want a book of photographs that offers a different vision of the Gaspésie. Carrière has developed a passion for publishing books; he believes that publication is at least as important as exhibition. The majority of his projects have resulted in a published work, something that is rare in Québec's photographic milieu. It was clear from the outset that *Après Strand* had to be a publication that went beyond being a mere catalogue, to become an object in its own right. Complementary to the exhibition, it documents it and constitutes a tangible and lasting trace whilst at the same time feeding the artist's critical fortune **| FIG. 15 |**.[22]

DEALING WITH PERCEPTIONS

The exhibition was simultaneously presented at both venues over the course of summer 2011.[23] It was a resounding success, receiving excellent media coverage, and the majority of visitors' comments were positive. We were nevertheless aware that today's Gaspesian reality, as presented in unvarnished form by Bertrand Carrière, might offend the susceptibility of certain visitors. Indeed, when it was presented in Rimouski, the exhibition provoked very negative comments from certain Gaspesians who felt that Carrière's photographs offered a degrading image of their region. Yet his pictures never portray squalor, they never accuse or denigrate. Nor do they attempt to embellish; they are simply borne by the conscientious viewpoint of a photographer who has infinite respect for this land and for its inhabitants.

Considerable efforts have been made over recent years to change people's perceptions of the Gaspésie, one of the most "devitalized" regions of Québec, focusing on the beauty of its wild and maritime landscapes, on certain iconic spots such as Pierced Rock, and on the friendly welcome proffered by its inhabitants.[24] There is tourism, but poverty too is ever-present. With the decline of the fishing and forestry industries, many people feel that tourism is only way forward. For Québec, the Gaspésie, remote and austere, remains a politically, economically and socially

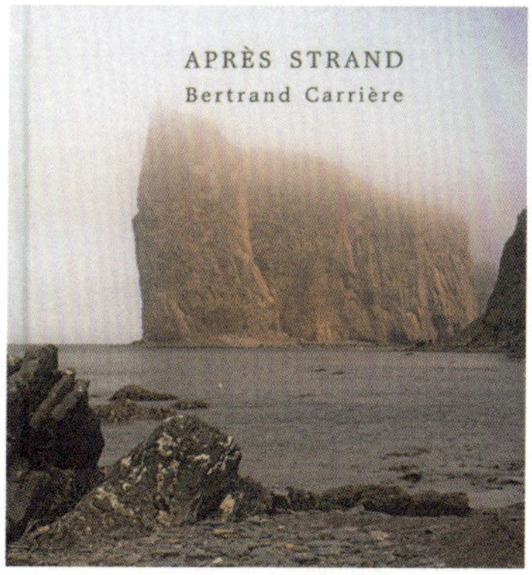

| FIG. 15 | Cover of the *Après Strand, Bertrand Carrière* catalogue, *Musée régional de Rimouski*, Québec, 2012.

21 Bernard Lamarche, "Considérations rephotographiques", *Après Strand, Bertrand Carrière,* exhibition catalogue, *Musée régional de Rimouski*, Rimouski, 2012, p. 61–63.

22 The catalogue was extremely successful as soon as it was published: indeed, it remains the best-selling catalogue in the museum's recent history; astonishingly, it also topped one of the leading Québec newspaper's list of coffee-table books to give at Christmas!

23 *Musée régional de Rimouski*, Rimouski, and *Villa Esteban des Jardins de Métis*, Grand-Métis, Québec, June 19– October 2, 2011.

24 The 2016 tourism campaign, with its "Gaspésie, I love you" slogan, focused its message on a region that is "unique", "lively", "welcoming" and "epicurean"; see https://www.tourisme-Gaspésie.com/

delicate subject, which makes Gaspesians highly sensitive to what is said about their region.

In the months and years that followed its presentation at the *Musée régional de Rimouski*, the *Après Strand* exhibition traveled throughout Québec and Ontario.[25] For each presentation, a new choice of photographs, determined by the artist and the curator, was required, to meet the physical specificities of the venue concerned. Only at the *Maison de la culture Frontenac* in Montreal was it possible to show the exhibition in its entirety. In 2014, a very limited selection of just a few photos was presented in Toronto at the Stephen Bulger gallery, representing Bertrand Carrière. The challenge was twofold: to make a very narrow selection that would attract potential buyers, and to allow people to gain a proper understanding of the project.

The final presentation took place during the summer of 2015 at the *Musée de la Gaspésie* in Gaspé. Given the size of the room, only three-quarters of the exhibition could be shown, but for Carrière it was vital that the exhibition be seen in the very region where the project had taken place. Whilst we unfortunately have no information on how the exhibition was received at the various venues, we can assume that opinions were certainly not the same in downtown Montreal, at a museum in a region far from Québec, or in a private gallery at the heart of a fashionable district of Toronto.

If Carrière's vision upset certain people, it is because it brought to light – and this is one of its strengths – the difference that exists between an image that is invented and promoted by the tourist industry, and reality. With the former being superposed onto the latter and thus blurring it. It is true that the Gaspésie is bursting with wonderful and unique landscapes, but its inhabitants are often living in conditions of extreme poverty: an aspect of the region that it is preferable to hide, so as not to put tourists off, and one that Carrière chose to simply portray, without making any judgement. This does not mean that his perception was neutral. It is his perception of Strand's work, but it also bears the stamp of his own photographic culture and of his earlier projects. Like all of Carrière's work, *Après Strand* is in part autobiographical, an account of his intimate experience of the region. The different ways in which the exhibition was presented, and the publication that accompanied it, on each occasion reshaped the account of the experience. These forms of sharing confirm the fact that one's view of a region is always multifold and ever-changing.

EPILOGUE

The *Après Strand* project allowed us to discover the forgotten pictures of a key figure of 19th-century photography and a contemporary photographer's viewpoint of modern-day Gaspésie. Like those by Strand, Carrière's photos seem to be inhabited by slowness. They bear witness to the stretching of time and landscape that makes the Gaspésie so unique, so beautiful, yet so harsh.

Bertrand Carrière's dual stance, that of historian-ethnologist and that of photographer, shaped his vision of the landscape. His perception, like that of any photographer, is multidimensional, made up of experiences, and knowledge, and of the determining choice of viewpoint. It will nevertheless always serve a visual discourse. During his visits to the Gaspésie, his travels were constantly guided by his search for the places photographed by Strand. Even though he kept his distance, these were what delineated his movements and more often than not motivated his shots. So the objective of his photographic project was by no means to constitute an exhaustive documentation of the region. It was fragmentary and subjective, and he accepted full responsibility for this choice. And one of his greatest merits, due to his historical roots and the strength of his photographs, was that he shone a spotlight on the layers of meaning and history of these fabulous landscapes | **FIG 16** |.

For Bertrand Carrière, this demanding experience profoundly changed his perception of the Gaspésie and of its communities: from a vacation destination for family and friends, it became a subject for photographic and historical study and exploration. It was also an opportunity to create links between his European projects and this return to Québec. For the time being, Carrière is not envisaging any other project of this type, but he does not exclude the possibility of one day returning to photograph the Gaspésie or to show as yet unseen photos collected during his Gaspesian travels. Be that as it may, this privileged encounter with a founding figure of modern photography, and with the humanized landscapes of a region that is from many points of view exceptional, undoubtedly had an impact on his current approach to photography.

Après Strand shows how the unique viewpoint of an artistic photographic project actively helps feed our thinking, broaden our understanding of the world and critically examine a region. Through publication and his various exhibitions, Carrière was calling for a debate on the current situation and its challenges. We are asked to think about the historicity of the perceptions of a region and about the interpretations that they propose. As we have seen, the perception of a photographic approach can sometimes lead to controversy. It has to be said that Québec unfortunately lags far behind other countries when it comes to the use and recognition of photography as a tool for observing and understanding a country. The rare initiatives that have emerged in this respect have stemmed from artistic milieus and not from any real commitment from public authorities. Since the completion of Carrière's project, the *Rencontres photographiques de la Gaspésie* has become a leading photographic event in Québec. These exhibitions, which bring together artists from Québec and abroad, have led to numerous regional projects, including a photographic mission that took place in 2016. It would of course be good if this initiative could be extended to Québec as a whole. Landscape observatories and missions have proved their worth in many countries, including France. Québec would have everything to gain by using the thoughtful and sensitive viewpoints of photographers to document and understand its vast territory and monitor transformations to its landscapes.

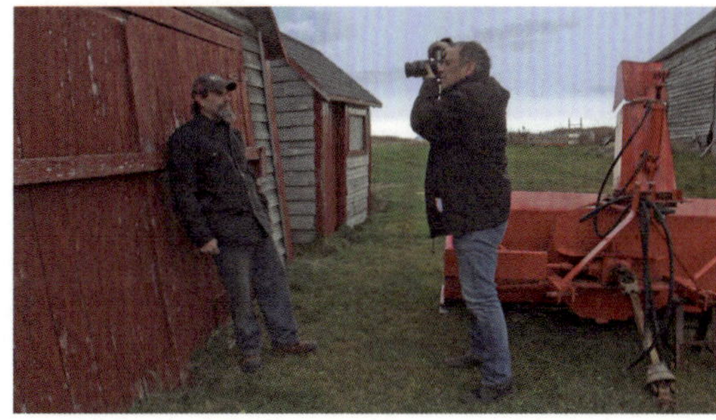

| FIG. 16 | Roger Lemoyne, Bertrand Carrière, Gaspésie, Québec, 2010.

25 *Vu Photo, Centre de diffusion et de production de la photographie*, Québec, October 14 – November 13, 2011; *Maison de la Culture Frontenac*, Montreal, Québec, October 18 – November 25, 2012 ; Stephen Bulger Gallery, Toronto, Ontario, April 6 –May 4, 2013 ; *Musée de la Gaspésie*, Gaspé, Québec, August 21 – November 1, 2015.

Photographers' Conversation

Alexandre Petzold, Édith Roux,
Geoffroy Mathieu and Bertrand Stofleth,
photographers, Pascale Hannetel,
Valérie Kauffmann and Catherine Mosbach,
landscape architects, with Marie-Hélène Loze,
Raphaële Bertho, Sonia Keravel,
Cristina Ros and Frédéric Pousin

Exhibiting, Publishing, Communicating on the Landscape Project through Photography

Frédéric Pousin

Nowadays, landscape photographers develop their work whilst at the same time taking an active part in public debate through exhibition, publication, public speaking, lectures and conferences. Landscape projects are exhibited and debated in the public arena in accordance with consultation procedures, or in spaces designed for the dissemination and valorization of the landscape culture, more often than not in the shape of exhibitions, brochures and various digital supports.

Like publications, exhibitions relate to situations which, in reality, are very different. When they are shown in galleries, contemporary art collections or museums, they are embedded in the field of art and are directed at art lovers. In events such as the Arles photography festival or in institutions with a pedagogical mission, such as the *Cité de l'architecture et du patrimoine* or the CAUEs (urban and environmental architecture committees), they target as many people as possible. These various venues offer specific spaces that depend on the scenographic modes, codes and visitors. The choice of venue is in itself a way of taking part in public debate. The same goes for publications, where the choice of publisher and collection steers the project towards a specific type of book and readership. A book of photography is not an art book or a book on human sciences, even though the latter attach considerable importance to photography. Finally, more than the other forms of communication mentioned above, the conference medium is inseparable from its audience and from the objectives in hand. Lectures often consist of the explicitation of an approach for educational purposes. They might also aim to propagate ideas or ways of doing things, so as to establish the existence of a field of activity, that of landscape design or photography. As is the case with exhibitions, the venue chosen for the conference is not without significance and the latter very often accompanies the exhibition.

The purpose of this round table was to bring photographers and landscape architects together, to explore the way an exhibition, publication or conference project is chosen. We invited three photographers and three landscape architects to think about each of these modes of presentation.

The photographers were asked to present a significant production which had allowed them to experience photography's impact on landscape transformation, and which had also helped them to evolve their approach. Their attention was drawn to picture selection, choice of format and the forms created through image association.

The landscape architects were asked about the role that photography plays in the exhibitions and publication of their projects, and about their experiences as conference speakers. The institutional viewpoint, that of the Essonne CAUE, responsible for developing a landscape policy at *département* level, rounded off the testimonials of two landscape agencies. These various testimonials illustrate what actors expect from photography, the different uses they make of it and the diversity of the commissions that are placed.

The role of the researchers in this round table was to broaden the debate so as to identify the multiple uses of photography and its malleability as a medium. The idea was to use case studies to gain a better understanding of what is at stake when transforming a landscape and to underline the fecundity of existing and future collaborations. Many themes ran through the contributions made and debated during the discussions. Firstly, photography's relationship with the landscape project, with the observation that it identifies several different instances, from the definition of the site through to management of the completed projects. Secondly, because photography makes it possible to document these moments of transformation, there is invariably the temptation to archive the pictures. What is shown or hidden touches just as much upon the expression of the project itself as upon the issue of what is off-frame in photography. Furthermore, the photographic image being inherently fixed, it faces the challenge of representing the movement that makes up the landscape. Finally, the collaboration between the various landscape actors concerns landscape architects just as much as it does photographers, whose approaches echo the demands for mediation that characterize contemporary society.

It is therefore by constructing the encounter of several discourses on both the landscape project and the photographic project that this round table examined, through their characteristics and implications, the different levers – exhibitions, publications and conferences – that help to put landscape forward for discussion.

ALEXANDRE PETZOLD

Alexandre Petzold is a photographer with a government-approved (DPLG) degree in landscape design from the *École Nationale Supérieure de Paysage* in Versailles. His work invariably relates to landscape or gardens. Here he presents three examples of his work:

– Photographs taken for landscape designer Béatrice Fauny in the context of landscape studies to define the scope for the classification of two sites: Chaumont-sur-Loire and Saint-Benoît-sur-Loire.

– Photographs from completed or ongoing projects commissioned by the TER agency (cofounded by Henri Bava, Michel Hoessler and Olivier Philippe and employing 50 landscape designers, architects and engineers of different nationalities in Paris and Karlsruhe).

– Non-commissioned photographs of work by Japanese market gardener Asafumi Yamashita, which led to the publication of a book *(Nō Dō. L'Homme qui écoute les légumes,* Actes Sud, Arles, 2016).

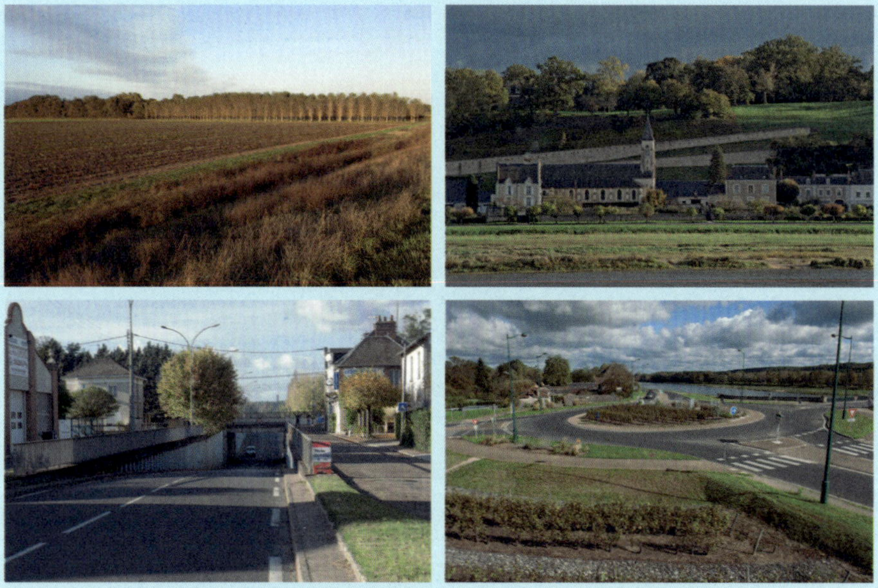

|1|

| ALEXANDRE PETZOLD |

Let's begin with the photographs taken in the context of landscape studies on the perimeter for the classification of Chaumont-sur-Loire and Saint-Benoît-sur-Loire. The landscape designer in charge of this study, Béatrice Fauny, asked me to join the team created to respond to the invitation to tender, even though no photographer was included in the specifications.
Before my mission began, she sent me a series of frames she had taken on-site and that she wanted me to reproduce.
But out in the field I had the opportunity to suggest other viewpoints that were in keeping with the study.
Ultimately, my job was to "give concrete expression" to her analysis of the landscape. It might seem somewhat simplistic, but the photographic commission was essentially one of confirming the landscape designer's opinion.

| SONIA KERAVEL |

If Béatrice Fauny gave you the job, wasn't it so that your photographs would help her to think, to shift her professional viewpoint, by offering an alternative interpretation of the site?

| ALEXANDRE PETZOLD |

We went back and forth between what she had imagined, what she had seen from her side and what I saw from mine. That was how the final document was constructed, at least in part. For example, my photos helped her to think about the definition of the scope. My objective was for the photographs to serve the study.

| GEOFFROY MATHIEU |

In studies like this, does working on the landscape interest you more than the landscape itself? Does photography have a utilitarian function?

| ALEXANDRE PETZOLD |

When I take a photograph as part of a commission, I always ask myself whether it will be able to serve an opinion or make visible an aspect that is not necessarily visible to a decision-maker or to a local actor. How might I approach issues of landscape evolution, which are sometimes complex and which don't always lean towards a harmonious development of the territory?
In effect, it is an almost functional use of photography. With a photo, I put my finger on specific things that I want to make visible and comprehensible. There is an educational aspect to my work.

| PASCALE HANNETEL |

In commissions where analysis is required, it is important to have pictures that are sufficiently powerful and explicit to express an idea. The aim is to examine, to produce a vision and to prove that it is true. When you analyze a site, you go too fast. You have an idea, you know more or less what you want to show, but it's hard to find the right viewpoint that will truly illustrate what you're trying to show. That's important if you want to convince others. When you have to define the perimeter of a site there comes a time when there can be no more debate. When you talk about a project, you need to get to what's essential, what's fundamental.

| SONIA KERAVEL |

Let's move on to the photographs of projects you work on for the TER agency. These photos are shown in the press, in monographs. They quickly become icons for the project and feed the imaginary of the professionals; whence the importance of the pictures selected for publication, their format and their layout. How are these images chosen? How do you deliver them to the designers? Presenting a project via a selection of photos is an art in itself ...

| ALEXANDRE PETZOLD |

Back in the days of film photography, when I handed in my ektachromes, I was already working in a specific order: I told my story, how I had perceived what I had shot. I appropriated the project, with a beginning and an end. I also introduced a hierarchy into the story I told, in line with the shades of color and light. Nowadays, with digital photography, I use the same procedure. At first you tend to have wide-angle views that allow you to get into the site, to understand it, to see how it fits into a broader context. Then you gradually move around and finally you focus on the details. It's easier for the person placing the commission. When he or she has to make a choice, they can go straight to the detail. So I do a lot of work on selecting the photos and putting them in order.

| SONIA KERAVEL |

The *Peuple de l'herbe* park project (see the portfolio, pages 210–217) is somewhat different, because in that case you've been following the entire project, which is coming to an end. This work hasn't yet been showcased to any great extent. Are you considering a different form of dissemination than classic articles?

| II |

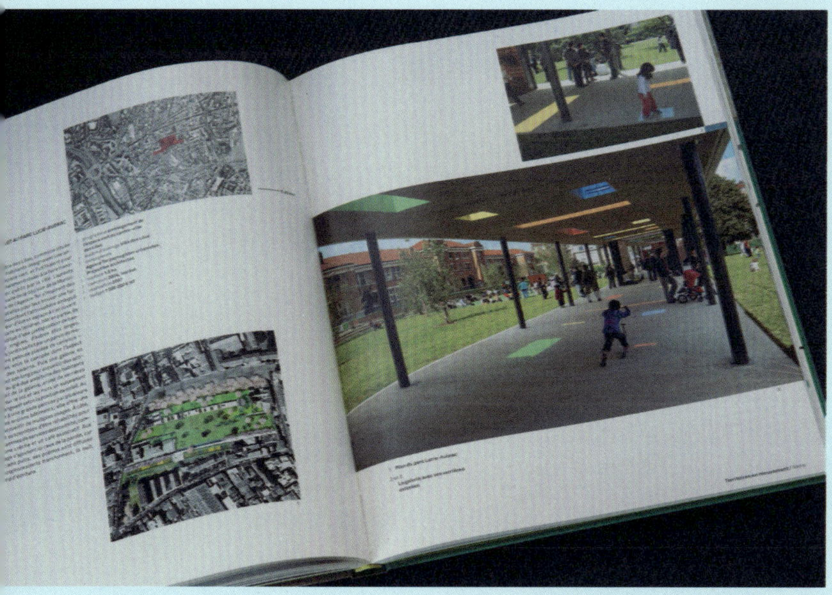

| I |

Recognized landscapes
Poplar grove as seen from the D952 road at Les Grillons, Onzain (45), October 28, 2012.
Chaumont-sur-Loire as seen from the D952 at La Gaillardière, Onzain (45), October 28, 2012.

Concealed landscapes
D1 underpass of the French railway (axis Onzain/Chaumont-sur-Loire), Onzain (45), October 28, 2012.
Roundabout at the junction of the D1 and D952 roads, Onzain (45), October 27, 2012.

| II |

Parc Lucie Aubrac, Les Lilas (93), extract from TER's monograph *Territoires. Révéler la ville par le paysage*, Birkhäuser, Basel, 2009.

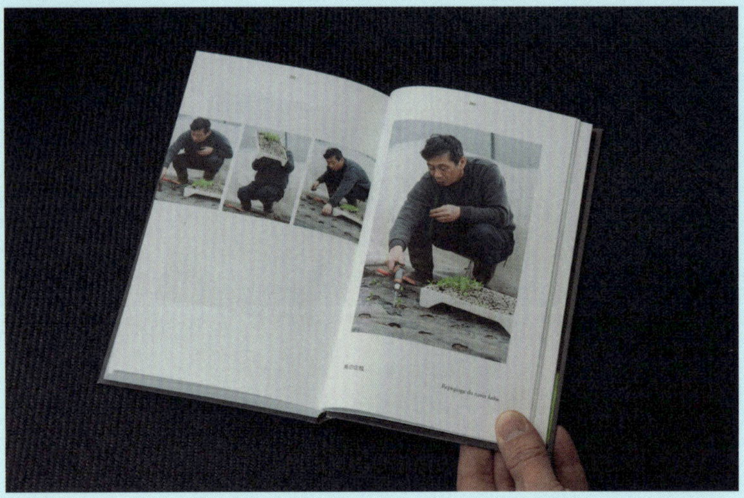

| III |

| III |
Extract from: *Nō Dō. L'homme qui écoute les légumes*, Actes Sud, Arles, 2016.

| ALEXANDRE PETZOLD |
It's a very recent work, I completed it at the end of 2016. My idea was for the agency to have a memorandum of the project and I worked to achieve that. I gave them a folder with all of the photographs presented in sets and, more importantly, organized by park sector. The idea is always to give the commissioning party an operational tool. The day I need a particular picture taken in a specific part of the park, I can find the photo in less than a minute. Next, how to disseminate the work? I haven't thought about that yet because it's too recent. We might tell the story of the project in an exhibition, but a book might be good too, or both. For the time being, the aim was to deliver an operational document.

| SONIA KERAVEL |
You're interested in manufacturing places and in what you need to do to complete a project – this can be seen in the way you followed this project but also in your work on Mr. Yamashita, which is a type of landscape project in the broader sense.

| ALEXANDRE PETZOLD |
That was a personal initiative. I worked for several years on the holding of a Japanese market gardener Asafumi Yamashita. We made a book together, *L'Homme qui écoute les légumes*. The idea behind the book was to use photos to describe life on the holding, by presenting the different families of vegetable, from seed to harvest. I frequently used triptychs to deconstruct a gesture or to underline the diversity and quality of the vegetables. The idea was to describe series of gestures in three pictures. The strength of the book is that Mr. Yamashita wanted to write. He created short texts that summarized his thoughts and his life trajectory. They are little background stories that allow you to understand his almost ritual approach to market gardening.

| FRÉDÉRIC POUSIN |
What strikes me is the high level of coherency between your different photographic works, due to the importance that you attach to the manufacture of the project and the landscape. This latest work, somewhat different in that it relates to a gardener, plunges us into the creation of living things, from the sowing through to the fully grown vegetable.

| PASCALE HANNETEL |
What I find interesting is the search for a form and not just a picture. The triptych also introduces the notion of movement, which is hard to get across in a landscape. Landscape photography is often highly static – there's something missing. The assembly you have created makes it possible to talk about movement, about the location. It's hard to find the right format. It's a bit like *haikus*, there's an essential aspect to these triptychs.

| SONIA KERAVEL |
I'd also mention your book on the king's vegetable garden (*Le Potager du Roi. Dialogue avec La Quintinie*, Éditions Artlys, Paris, 2017): you examine the life of the gardeners to demonstrate how a place is made, how it lives.

| ALEXANDRE PETZOLD |
With Antoine Jacobsohn, who was in charge of the *Potager du Roi*, our starting point was a common observation: here is a place where the gardeners are at the heart of the project. But at the same time we wanted to show that this site is a piece of heritage that is constantly evolving. It is not frozen in the past. It's a book in the same vein as my previous work. This is the direction I wish to take. I truly want human beings to be at the heart of my personal work.

Pascale Hannetel, a graduate of the *École Nationale Supérieure de Paysage* in Versailles, is a state-registered landscape architect and a government landscaping consultant. Since 2005 she has also been a member of UNESCO's committee of experts on French world heritage sites. She co-founded the HYL agency in 1997 with architect Arnaud Yver. The agency brings together fifteen architects, urbanists, landscape designers and engineers.
Pascale Hannetel chose to comment on three sets of photographs:
The first set was taken from a conference in Rome on the theme of "landscapes and infrastructures", which presented projects relating to water management.
The second was made up of extracts from an article on the Mont-Saint-Michel's public access infrastructures for Italian review Paysage.
The third concerns Bois-Badeau park in Brétigny sur Orge (Essonne *département*). It is taken from a park management document that is intended to be just as much an observatory of landscape evolutions in the park as a tool of communication.

| PASCALE HANNETEL |

For me, photography is both a design tool and a communication tool. It allows me to conceptualize the site, move forward with the project and then relate it and make it understood. At the start, I often begin with an embedding and manipulation of the ground plan in the aerial photograph, which is a remarkable medium for the scale of a landscape project. This perception is then intersected with ground-level viewpoints which give it another materiality: in my opinion, "seen from the sky and seen from the ground" are iterative project approaches. For the Mont-Saint-Michel visitor reception infrastructures, the search for mimicry with the polder landscapes fed off the complementarity of these viewpoints: "seen from the sky" to espouse the main outlines and milieus, "seen from the ground" to understand its horizontality, its broad horizons and its small amplitudes.

| ÉDITH ROUX |

It's the scale that interests you.

| PASCALE HANNETEL |

It's the scale and its variations in perception depending on the viewpoint but also on movement that interests me. The way that groups of people move into a location and position themselves in the space and transform it, also speaks to its scale in terms of accommodating different uses.

| PIERRE ENJELVIN |

How do you use these aerial views? We've discussed the distancing that they imply. But even at ground level you can gain distance ...

| I |

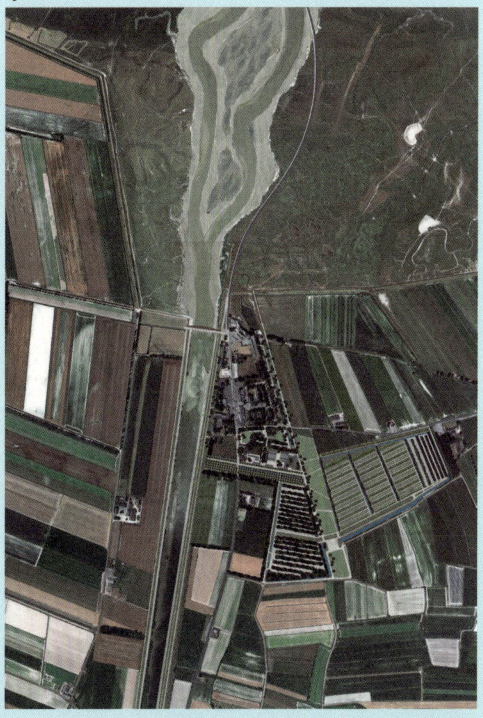

| I |
HYL, 2001, project site plan embedded in the aerial photo. Competition, winning project.

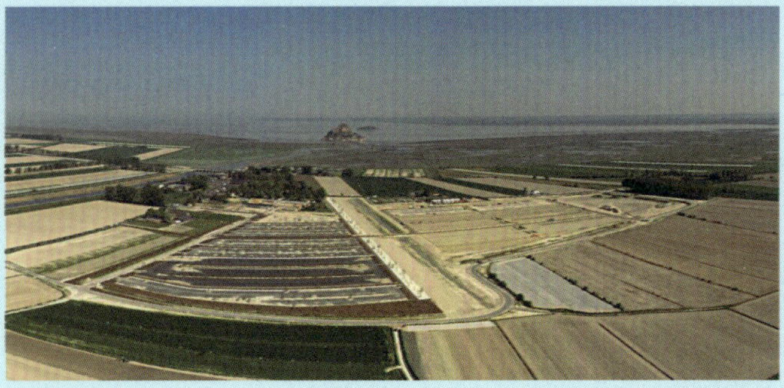

| II |

| PASCALE HANNETEL |
It seems to me that to develop a landscape project and to be able to consider its modification on a given scale, you need to detach yourself from its formal and material reality in order to conceptualize it. Such distancing was even more important at the Mont-Saint-Michel site, where the reality of the mount is ever-changing and impossible to grasp: you never know if it is far, near, small, large, or if it is hovering! In this polder landscape where very small amplitudes (1.8 meters) are interwoven with huge horizons, I wouldn't have been able to plan this project without aerial photography.

| PIERRE ENJELVIN |
Because your projects are aimed at users, wouldn't a map or plan be just as useful as an aerial view for dealing with this question of scale?

| PASCALE HANNETEL |
Both are necessary. There's got to be a toing and froing between a cross-section, a map and an aerial photograph. It is of course very difficult to transform a location without having a level of abstraction that lets you detach yourself from what it is to begin with – though without betraying it. For me, it is in this distancing process that the seeds of a landscape project are to be found. Aerial photography has the scale of a map but also provides very accurate information on the materiality of the land and vegetation. The depth of this information allows you to make the "sensitive" abstraction that is required to undertake the project work. So it's a design tool that is very complete and also highly effective when it comes to verifying the appropriateness of the work after the project has been finished.

| MARIE-HÉLÈNE LOZE |
During your lectures on the hydraulic challenges of a flood zone, do you show powerful works of construction, supporting walls, or instead pictures of quiet and peaceful parks?

| PASCALE HANNETEL |
I tend to want to evoke three states that illustrate a single reality: when the water is calm under the sun; when the water overflows in a turmoil; and after the ebb, when everything has calmed down and dried out.
For me, this way of showing the amplitude of a location that is subject to such vagaries and their ephemeralities is essential ... It is nevertheless difficult for photography to render the movement that is inherent to this rapid dynamic. Just like the ebb and flow of the tides, or the skies above dams, in my projects I try to capture these moments of landscape and emotion.
There are also those photographs that are never shown and about which I have asked myself many questions. Everything seems relatively simple when it's all over, but everything required so much work and, in most projects, a great deal of moved earth or consolidation. The photographs you don't show are photographs of building sites: they allow you to understand the extent of the works.

| III |

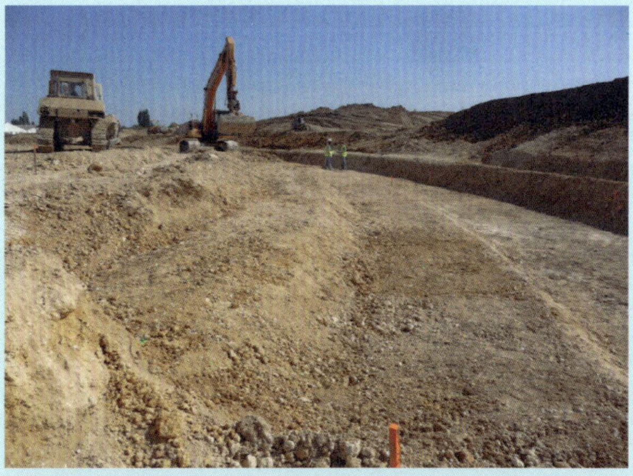

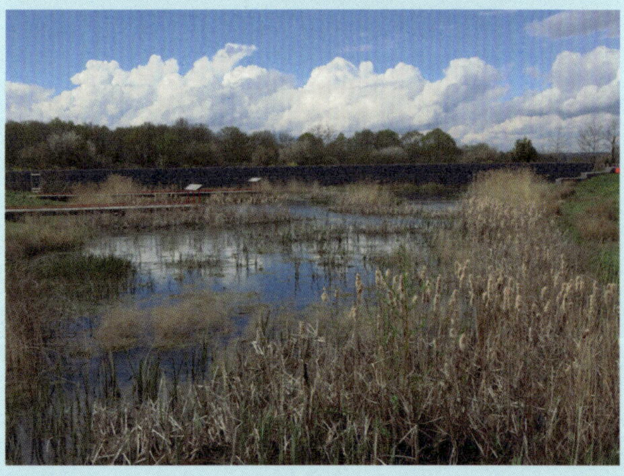

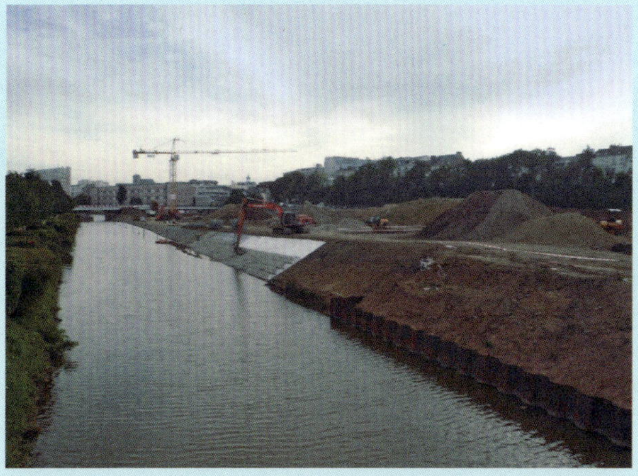

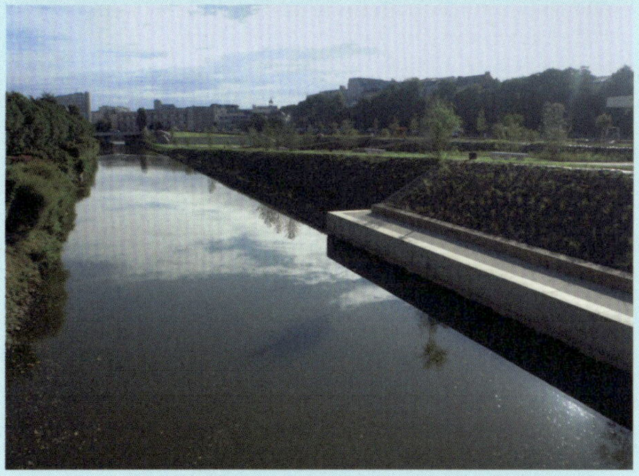

|IV|

|II|
2011, Earthworks at the parking lot, Mont-Saint-Michel.

|III|
Brétigny-sur-Orge, Parc du Bois Badeau, basin earthworks in 2012, and the 2016 site.

|IV|
Ile aux Planches park in Le Mans, 2007–2008.

|V|
Parc du Bois Badeau, extract from Logbook 2: Plants.

Photographs chosen to communicate on projects tend to focus on the slick, finished aspects and leave little room for the rough stages of the work.
Regarding the project on the Mont-Saint-Michel's public access infrastructures, its successful integration required very major earthworks that profoundly transformed the ground whilst at the same time preserving the horizontal lines and wide horizons. This raw, preformed state is not easy to see. The land has not yet healed.

On the last photographs, that of the Bois Badeau park pond site and that of the canal in Ile aux Planches park, in its preparatory phase the ground is still a shapeless mush. In most projects there is a big difference between the quantity of turned over earth and the final perception which gives the impression that only light work has been done on the initial site. If one doesn't know and if they are not shown, transformations become imperceptible, as if the project had always been there.

For the *Parc de Bois Badeau* project, we created a park management logbook. At the time, we were wondering how to reconcile this work with our communication objectives, because maintenance, unfortunately, is never valorized.

We divided the logbook into four sections:
– The first introduces the park and explains the principles and reasons for this or that layout.
– The second sets out the different milieus, itemized by typology (forested areas, humid zones, lawns, and areas defined by their plant species). The photographs make it possible to talk about each milieu and about its plants when they are fully grown.
– The third list the plants found in the park. They are all photographed and named. Indeed, we found that the gardeners were not always very familiar with the plants and over the first few seasons they destroyed many interesting varieties!
– The last was designed as a park observatory. The idea was to make the most of the regular visits needed to program management activities, to take "control" photographs. Always taken from the same spots, they keep track of evolutions and constitute a sort of "Park Album".

|V|

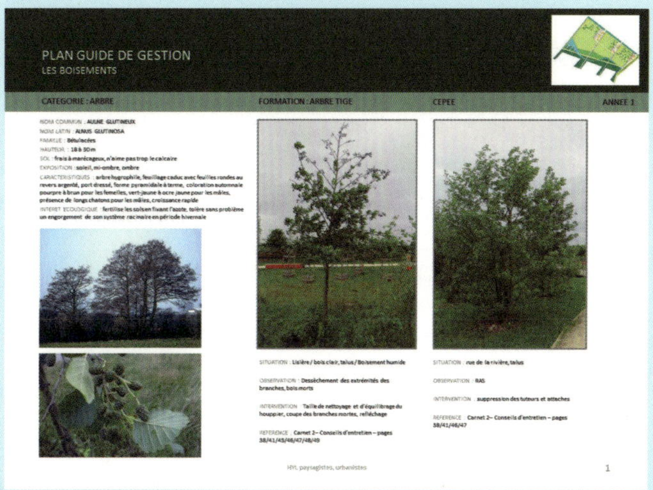
PLAN GUIDE DE GESTION
LES BOISEMENTS

CATEGORIE : ARBRE — FORMATION : ARBRE TIGE — CEPEE — ANNEE 1

NOM COMMUN : AULNE GLUTINEUX
NOM LATIN : ALNUS GLUTINOSA
FAMILLE : Bétulacées
HAUTEUR : 18 à 30m
SOL : frais à marécageux, n'aime pas trop le calcaire
EXPOSITION : soleil, mi-ombre, ombre
CARACTERISTIQUES : arbre hygrophile, feuillage caduc avec feuilles rondes au revers argenté, port dressé, forme pyramidale à terme, coloration automnale pourpre à brun pour les femelles, vert-jaune à ocre jaune pour les mâles, présence de longs chatons pour les mâles, croissance rapide
INTERET ECOLOGIQUE : fertilise les sols en fixant l'azote, tolère sans problème un engorgement de son système racinaire en période hivernale

SITUATION : Lisière / bois clair, talus / Boisement humide
OBSERVATION : Dessèchement des extrémités des branches, bois morts
INTERVENTION : Taille de nettoyage et d'équilibrage du houppier, coupe des branches mortes, reffléchage
REFERENCE : Carnet 2 – Conseils d'entretien – pages 38/41/45/46/47/48/49

SITUATION : rue de la rivière, talus
OBSERVATION : RAS
INTERVENTION : suppression des tuteurs et attaches
REFERENCE : Carnet 2 – Conseils d'entretien – pages 38/41/46/47

HYL paysagistes, urbanistes — 1

| MARIE-HÉLÈNE LOZE |
Is it usual for the agency to come up with this sort of management tool?

| PASCALE HANNETEL |
More and more often, landscape projects are management projects, because milieus are so fragile that if they are not cared for, they disappear within a few years. The way you shape a place is totally linked to how you manage it. So when you deliver a park or a landscape, it is absolutely vital to provide a user manual, or at least a reminder of the common objectives that underpin the management priorities.
This is an issue we've encountered in all of our projects. We have tried to make this job of management more attractive, and to valorize maintenance operations, including in relation to communication. Municipalities communicate to show the results, but all of the background work is glossed over. We don't take photos of the gardeners cutting the grass – we show children playing instead!

| MARIE-HÉLÈNE LOZE |
Do you use outside photographers or do you photograph your own projects as you go along?

| PASCALE HANNETEL |
For a while we worked with Gérard Dufresne, a photographer whose work I really liked. We had wonderful photos of spaces with beautiful landscape moments and beautiful respiration Then we tried working with another photographer, but he didn't have the same sensitivity.

| ÉDITH ROUX |
Could you clarify exactly what you mean by "the same sensitivity"? Is it in terms of choice of viewpoints?

| PASCALE HANNETEL |
A long time ago Gérard Dufresne took photos of several of our projects. We talked, we explained the project, every time we launched photo or reportage campaigns ...
When we commission photographs, we tend to set out our point of view, to underline what interests us and explain what we are looking for. We nevertheless like to discover something more than that, a photographic vision that goes beyond the subject, that offers a viewpoint we would not have imagined.

I remember a photograph that Gérard Dufresne took of retention basins. A tiny stream of water crosses three basins with a sort of large square that I'd never seen in that way before, except from above. He had climbed on top of the highway embankment to get a bird's eye view. It was a unique manner of relating the project. We want to be amazed, overwhelmed.
He had also photographed simple earthworks and connections to what was already there, that formed a sort of wonderful pleat: he had managed to take some superb photos of this. I would never have imagined having such beautiful photos. My business card shows one of Gérard Dufresne's photographs.

| ÉDITH ROUX |
In this relationship with the photographer, do you give priority to a neutral, distant viewpoints, or instead to subjective viewpoints linked to a certain temporality?

| PASCALE HANNETEL |
At a given moment in time, a photograph is also a stage production where the characters show the scale of the project.
What is interesting is the relationship between the human scale and the project, between the crowd and the desert; the object is precisely this dialogue between a place and what happens. We simply recount what led us to do it, what we like, what we missed, what we succeeded in doing. We also want to see how the people, the water, the elements play with that.

| VI |

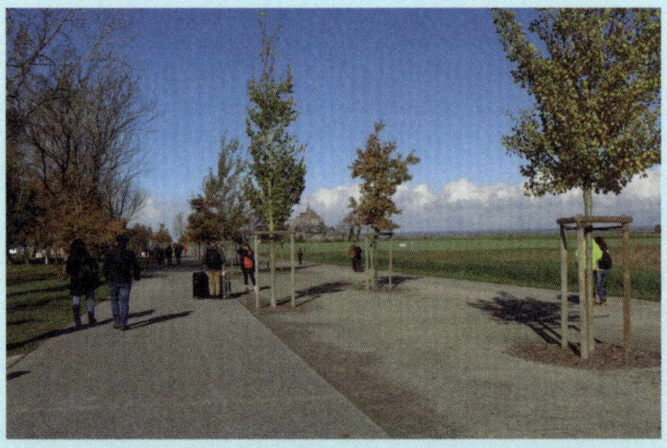

| VI |
Mont-Saint-Michel, Allée du marais blanc, November 2014.

Photographer and video maker Édith Roux lives and works in Paris. She is a graduate of the *École Nationale Supérieure de la Photographie* in Arles. Her work often reveals concerns of a sociopolitical nature, dealing with matters relating to the environment and to urban change. In addition to her personal work, she also accepts certain public commissions, as can be seen from those of the *Observatoire photographique national de paysage's* mission on the Hainaut cross-border nature park (between 2009 and 2011) and her work on the *Conservatoire du littoral* for the French Ministry of the Environment (in 2013). Here she spoke about her *Dreamscape* project, which gave rise to several exhibitions (Le Quartier art center in Quimper in 2005, the *Passages en ville* festival in Biarritz in 2006, the *Urbi et orbi* festival in Sedan in 2006, the QPN festival at *Lieu unique* in Nantes in 2008), to a book, and to several conferences (*Salon du Livre* in 2004 with Arnaud Bizalion, *Maison du geste de l'image* with Michel Poivert in 2012).

| ÉDITH ROUX |

Dreamscape **is a contraction of *dream* and *landscape*. The title is a verbal construction just as the work is a montage of pictures of architecture and landscape. When I arrived in Shanghai, I was struck by all the bills and posters on the walls that hid the building sites. These pictures convey a certain idea of the beautiful landscape, they aren't rooted in any territorial specificity, they come from all over the place and are pretty much exoticized. I wanted to connect them to the promoters' pictures, which relate to different architectural styles in a copy-paste fashion. I combined these two types of picture to make a long 23 meter frieze, where the wall acts as a visual link between the pictures.**
This work led to a *leporello*, i.e. a book that folds out like an accordion. The text is in French, English and Chinese. The book is illustrative of the work itself, because it reproduces the visual continuity found in the work. I was interested in the relationship between architecture and image, because these architectures are not rooted in a cultural reality, they are simply pictures. The device itself is also an illusion, because at first glance one might think that the landscape photographs are real landscapes. In reality they are pictures of pictures, and we can think about the function of these relatively stereotyped and decontextualized landscapes. Maybe their purpose is to project the urbanite into a promising universe.

| FRÉDÉRIC POUSIN |

What did you want to put forward for debate through the *Dreamscape* project?

| ÉDITH ROUX |

It's first and foremost a debate on the transformation of society in China. These urban mutations began in the 1990s. What interested me was the way they reveal a transformation and societal evolution in Shanghai and in other cities. When I arrived in Shanghai, I had no preconceived ideas about what I would find. I was struck by the solid walls that enclosed the building sites. That goes back to the latent architecture that is going to rise up behind the site. In the construction of the images, you find the architecture that we present as already completed, the wall and the building site hidden between the two. So there is also a question concerning the future of this city.

| RAPHAËLE BERTHO |

In this installation, as in the book, the montage problem is clear. It introduces a certain rhythm that, in the cinema, might be fast-paced. The pictures can no longer be separated, the montage becomes the work in itself. The idea of picture continuity goes further than just your photographic work: it even governs the presentation of your website.

| ÉDITH ROUX |

Yes, indeed, the frieze really is a whole, something to be grasped in its entirety. Exhibition curators have sometimes asked me to present just one part of it, but for me that's impossible.

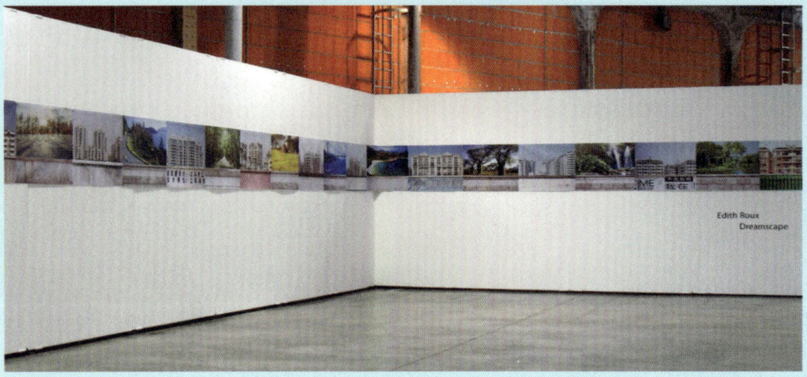

|I|

|I|
Dreamscape, exhibition at *Lieu unique*, Nantes, 2008.

|II|
Landscape variations, Haveluy, Chemin d'Hélesmes, photographic landscape observatory of the cross-border natural reserve situated in the Hainaut province, 2009/2010/2011/2014.

| FRÉDÉRIC POUSIN |
From the point of view of spectator immersion, does this frieze work as a panorama when it is hung like that on picture rails or in a room?

| ÉDITH ROUX |
The intention is to be immersed in this visual device, but at the same time such immersion is impossible. The viewer is encapsulated but cannot see the details. So he has to move closer in order to see them, and seeing what happens between the pictures is just as important as the picture itself; that's the principle of montage. Except that here, the device invites the viewer's body to move along the pictures in an attempt to understand the work.

| PASCALE HANNETEL |
Your installations really do produce an impression of space. The device very much creates the feeling of entering these landscapes and these pathways. I'm amazed by the extreme effectiveness of the walk. When you talk about the difficulty of encapsulating the landscape, I get the impression that your devices, although they are static, perfectly render this manner of grasping the different scales or pathways.

| FRÉDÉRIC POUSIN |
You used this panoramic device for the *Observatoire photographique national du paysage's* Hainaut cross-border nature park. What inspired you to use the panorama?

| ÉDITH ROUX |
This device gained in importance at the time of the *Observatoire du paysage* mission that took place from 2009 to 2011 and in 2014. The Hainaut cross-border nature park is a French-Belgian park. When choosing certain viewpoints, it was important to me to encompass a broad section of the territory. I didn't want to do panoramas in the traditional sense of the term, but rather to stay in a more human dimension, to adopt a vision closer to the eye, whence the idea of fragmenting this portion of the territory. Also, the viewer is encouraged to mentally reconstitute it himself, to make the effort to reconstruct the image.

| FRÉDÉRIC POUSIN |
As we are talking about panoramas, I'd like to mention the work you've done for the *Conservatoire du littoral*, particularly the panorama of the Baie de Cavalaire, next to Saint-Tropez, seen from the sea. It is divided into regular sections and there is one photograph, one picture missing; this interferes with the viewer's reconstruction of the landscape. Can you tell us some more about this?

| ÉDITH ROUX |
How do we display images in space? It's an important question, especially in the work for the *Conservatoire du littoral*. As for the view of the Baie de Cavalaire, the commission concerned the Corniche des Maures, which is an area protected by the *Conservatoire*. I thought it was interesting to choose a viewpoint from the sea. Part of it is protected, but the polyptych also shows the unprotected part, which is highly urbanized. The viewpoint from the sea is a constantly moving viewpoint that is nevertheless stabilized by the horizon, which forms a continuous line between the pictures. When reading the polyptych, there's one image missing. The white wall of the exhibition venue appears in its place. It's a way of taking the exhibition space into account in one's understanding of the work and of making the viewer active in the process of mentally reconstituting the polyptych. The missing picture is still shown, but elsewhere in the exhibition space, or even outside that space, like in my exhibition during the *Mois de la photographie* in 2014.

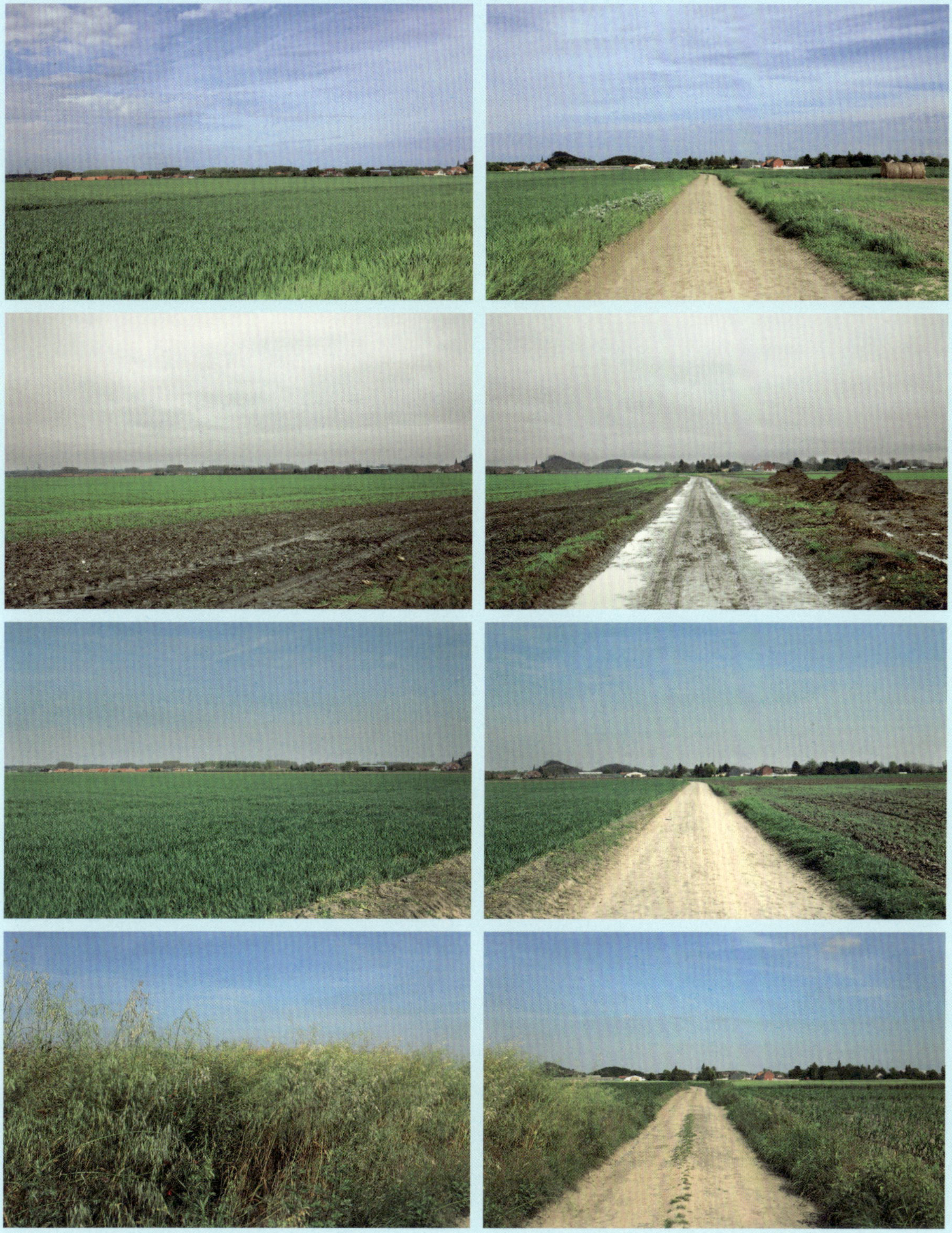

|II|

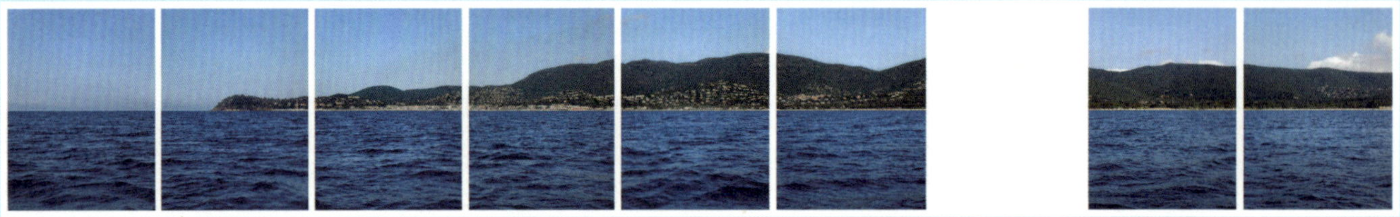

| III |

| MARIE-HÉLÈNE LOZE |
I have the impression that your work asks an open question, with numerous possible interpretations. Do you have an idea of what the visitors perceived? Was it very different from what you were suggesting?

| ÉDITH ROUX |
I position myself as a photographer, or in any case as an artist. I want to take pictures that ask questions, visual propositions that cause viewers to project their own questions. Of course I have an intention when I do this work, but I like to leave the interpretation of the pictures relatively open. Your remark echoes my concerns.

| FRÉDÉRIC POUSIN |
When you present your work at conferences, do you build your presentation around the work and pictures that you are presenting, or do you first construct your presentation and then add a visual?

| ÉDITH ROUX |
The presentation issue is a pertinent one, because I often wonder how an artist should speak of his or her work. In my projects I develop a highly intuitive visual language, based on questions and on ways of representing… I don't think with words, but with pictures. Then I have to translate this thought with words, conceptualize it. For example, the question of fragmentation first came to me in the form of images. So then I thought: in what way might this be interesting? The desire to verbalize is first of all for myself, which might take time; it sometimes happens that I don't immediately understand why I took this or that picture. This verbalization is necessary: it enables me to communicate better on the work, in a language we all share. But I find that it can also be too simplistic. It's one way of approaching the work, but it's not the only way. I want – I don't know if I achieve this – to not wrap my work up too much in a discourse, so that what is shown is more powerful than discourse or the spoken word.

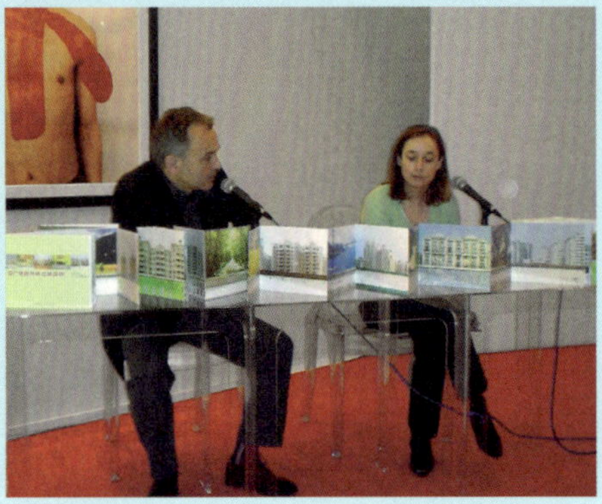

| IV |

| III |
Seuil. Corniche des Maures, 2013. http://www.edithroux.fr/commissions/cdl/indexFR.php

| IV |
Arnaud Bizalion and Édith Roux at the *Salon du livre*, behind the *Dreamscape* leporello, Paris, 2004.

VALÉRIE KAUFFMANN

Valérie Kauffmann is an architect, urban planner and landscape designer. In 1999 she joined the CAUE team in the Essonne region, where she develops landscape policy and works on the representation of local landscapes. Since 2009 she has been assistant director of CAUE 91, whose team includes two other landscapers. At the round table she presented three types of work that are representative of her work within the organization:
– An exhibition at the *Maison de la banlieue et de l'architecture* in Athis-Mons in 2007, entitled *Tout sauf d'éternité, ou les mutations de paysages de banlieue en Essonne,* showing the importance of landscape in regional planning.
– The *Images d'avenir en Essonne* exhibition, produced by CAUE 91 in 2014, An exhibition displaying the results of a photographic survey involving 15 actors in 6 key territories (Plateau de Saclay, Triangle vert, the Essonne lakes, Vallée de l'Orge, Plateau de Vert-le-Grand, Pôle d'Orly).
– Various examples of pictures shown during a conference at the *Institut de géographie* during a seminar entitled "*Espaces publics locaux et identité métropolitaine*" (Local public spaces and metropolitan identity) in 2014.

| VALÉRIE KAUFFMANN |

The Essonne is a young French *département* created in 1968. It has a major problem of representation and of establishing the reality of the region, which is however extremely rich. We have made several attempts to find the most pertinent and effective tools to deal with an issue that is difficult, complex and which apparently inspires little interest among our elected officials: the landscape.
With the *Tout sauf d'éternité* exhibition, we wanted to show the complexity and richness of this region, with pictures that would shake up the viewer, and throw a spotlight onto the hidden landscapes, contrasts and paradoxes that make the Essonne what it is. We also wanted to break away from the simplistic representations of an urban north and a rural south. The idea was to show that each area has peri-urban characteristics, mixing together the rural and the urban, even in the north of the region. So our discourse was intentionally complex.
For this exhibition we made considerable use of photographs. We took some ourselves and we borrowed several others from our partners; we added diagrams and maps. In some ways it was a case of proving our point and of collecting "evidence".
We chose a different approach for the *Images d'avenir en Essonne* exhibition in 2014. We wanted to ask the actors about their region. Generally speaking, we have been using photography far more since Clément Briandet – a landscape architect who is very enthusiastic about photography – joined CAUE 91. For this particular exhibition he ran the study with photographer Pierre Enjelvin. His approach showed me the extent to which photography was useful and how it could lead to more in-depth and more open debates than we were used to.
The idea was for the study to rely on photography, to use it as a medium. The project related to six areas located between open spaces and urban spaces that were evolving and which were likely to be very rapidly transformed.
The exhibition was to a great extent made up of picture boards relating to each of the areas, showing photographs that had been selected by our partners. We added comments. Sometimes a gray rectangle took the place of a picture. This expressed the fact that the partners had no opinion on the subject. The exhibition showed us that this was often the case.
It taught us that we had to work on what people knew about the areas and create a debate on how these territories were interpreted.
I had no preconceived ideas about the mediation; I simply see that when we work with photography, something speaks to people and they are prepared to grab hold of it. Prior to that we had done quite a few workshops using drawings, but it wasn't so easy, people aren't used to expressing themselves through drawing.

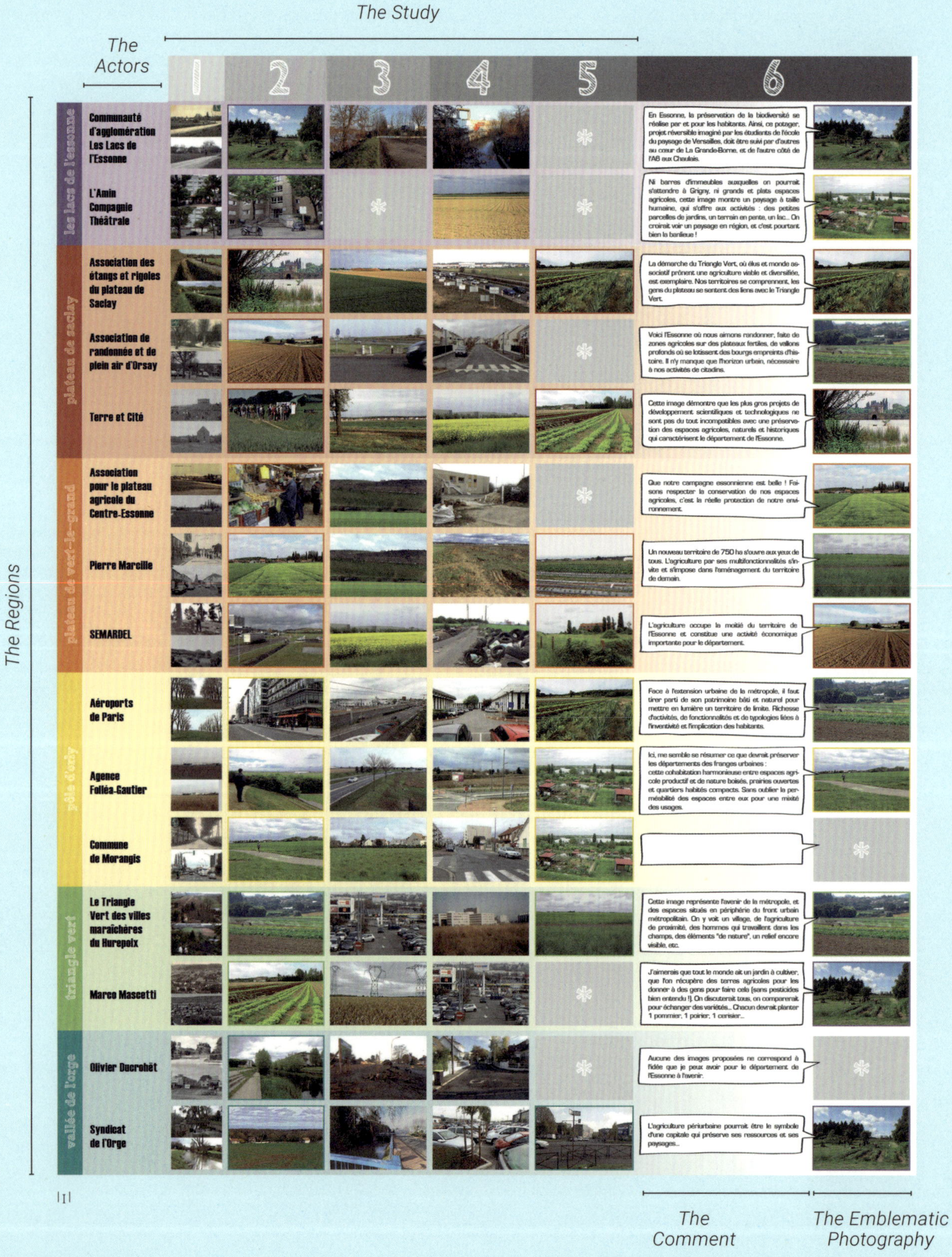
The Study
The Actors
1
2
3
4
5
6
The Regions
les lacs de l'essonne
Communauté d'agglomération Les Lacs de l'Essonne
En Essonne, la préservation de la biodiversité se réalise par et pour les habitants. Ainsi, ce potager, projet réversible imaginé par les étudiants de l'école du paysage de Versailles, doit être suivi par d'autres au cœur de La Grande-Borne, et de l'autre côté de l'A6 aux Chaulais.
L'Amin Compagnie Théâtrale
Ni barres d'immeubles auxquelles on pourrait s'attendre à Grigny, ni grands et plats espaces agricoles, cette image montre un paysage à taille humaine, qui s'offre aux activités : des petites parcelles de jardins, un terrain en pente, un lac... On croirait voir un paysage en région, et c'est pourtant bien la banlieue !
plateau de saclay
Association des étangs et rigoles du plateau de Saclay
La démarche du Triangle Vert, où élus et monde associatif prônent une agriculture viable et diversifiée, est exemplaire. Nos territoires se comprennent, les gens du plateau se sentent des liens avec le Triangle Vert.
Association de randonnée et de plein air d'Orsay
Voici l'Essonne où nous aimons randonner, faite de zones agricoles sur des plateaux fertiles, de vallons profonds où se lotissent des bourgs empreints d'histoire. Il n'y manque que l'horizon urbain, nécessaire à nos activités de citadins.
Terre et Cité
Cette image démontre que les plus gros projets de développement scientifiques et technologiques ne sont pas du tout incompatibles avec une préservation des espaces agricoles, naturels et historiques qui caractérisent le département de l'Essonne.
plateau de vert-le-grand
Association pour le plateau agricole du Centre-Essonne
Que notre campagne essonnienne est belle ! Faisons respecter la conservation de nos espaces agricoles, c'est la réelle protection de notre environnement.
Pierre Marcille
Un nouveau territoire de 750 ha s'ouvre aux yeux de tous. L'agriculture par ses multifonctionnalités s'invite et s'impose dans l'aménagement du territoire de demain.
SEMARDEL
L'agriculture occupe la moitié du territoire de l'Essonne et constitue une activité économique importante pour le département.
pôle d'orly
Aéroports de Paris
Face à l'extension urbaine de la métropole, il faut tirer parti de son patrimoine bâti et naturel pour mettre en lumière un territoire de limite. Richesse d'activités, de fonctionnalités et de typologies liées à l'inventivité et l'implication des habitants.
Agence Folléa-Gautier
Ici, me semble se résumer ce que devrait préserver les départements des franges urbaines :
cette cohabitation harmonieuse entre espaces agricole productif et de nature boisés, prairies ouvertes et quartiers habités compacts. Sans oublier la perméabilité des espaces entre eux pour une mixité des usages.
Commune de Morangis
triangle vert
Le Triangle Vert des villes maraîchères du Hurepoix
Cette image représente l'avenir de la métropole, et des espaces situés en périphérie du front urbain métropolitain. On y voit un village, de l'agriculture de proximité, des hommes qui travaillent dans les champs, des éléments "de nature", un relief encore visible, etc.
Marco Mascetti
J'aimerais que tout le monde ait un jardin à cultiver, que l'on récupère des terres agricoles pour les donner à des gens pour faire cela (sans pesticides bien entendu !). On discuterait tous, on comparerait pour échanger des variétés... Chacun devrait planter 1 pommier, 1 poirier, 1 cerisier...
vallée de l'orge
Olivier Ducrohët
Aucune des images proposées ne correspond à l'idée que je peux avoir pour le département de l'Essonne à l'avenir.
Syndicat de l'Orge
L'agriculture périurbaine pourrait être le symbole d'une capitale qui préserve ses ressources et ses paysages...
|1|
The Comment
The Emblematic Photography

| I |
A picture board through which to project oneself, to imagine a desirable future and to characterize the territory in relation to the metropolis. *Images d'avenir en Essonne* exhibition, photographs by Pierre Enjelvin, 2014. each protagonist was asked to chose a symbolic photograph (likely to be reproduced on a document introducing the Parisian conurbation) through a selection from the enquiry's "images-answers".

| II |
Photos with which to create a narrative about our peri-urban region, in response to a given question. Photos to challenge preconceptions, to deconstruct imaginaries and to allow other possibles to be invented. Residential street in Grigny, 2014.

| SONIA KERAVEL |
How was the exhibition received?

| PIERRE ENJELVIN |
I attended a workshop where we had set up a mechanism that combined people's perspectives with the spoken word. We asked participants three questions: which picture do you like best? Which one shocks you the most? Which is the perfect picture that you might use in your everyday work? We also asked them to add comments next to the photos. We wanted to see if the comments were similar, if opinions were shared.

| SONIA KERAVEL |
I see that in the cases you have presented, the photographs are almost always accompanied by a text, albeit very short (captions, questions, little bubbles). Do comments help one to read or question the picture?

| VALÉRIE KAUFFMANN |
There are two systems: in *Images d'avenir,* the comments are words from out in the field, from people we met. When I put pictures on the screen for elected officials, I like to create a narrative. I've realized that they have a limited attention span. You have to grab their attention very quickly, and if they remember just one sentence or idea, that's already something of a plus. You have to find the format that will most effectively speak to them. Full-page picture captions are quite effective in that respect.

| A PERSON IN THE ROOM |
In what you have shown, the relationship between words and picture is an interesting one. It's close to a certain form of contemporary photography, and that gives it tremendous power. The picture conveys a sort of iconic representation and the words do the exact opposite, while nevertheless remaining just as valid as the picture. This tension challenges people's perceptions and representations of their everyday space. The photograph is not aesthetic, but it provides a shortcut to meaning.

| VALÉRIE KAUFFMANN |
I use these photos to construct a narrative. The pictures are linked to one another and I don't spend much time on each individual one. This is how I tell the story of the Essonne. When I'm with elected officials, I project a single full-page picture, with few words, but words that ask questions. It's very useful for deconstructing imaginaries, shifting perspective, encouraging questions and nourishing a more in-depth debate.

| II |

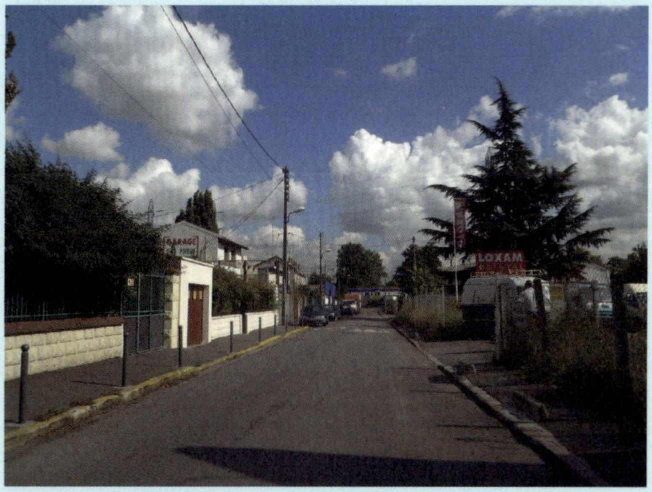

| SONIA KERAVEL |

These somewhat provocative photographs that you use with elected officials, do you also use them in other contexts, as educational tools or to create awareness? Do you use them differently, depending on the audience?

| VALÉRIE KAUFFMANN |

It depends more on the questions I'm asked than on the audience. But in all cases it's important to shift perception. When we began our work, a very beautiful book of photos was published on the Essonne seen from the sky. They were wonderful pictures, which now constitute the "official" representation of the *département*. At the CAUE, we have a different approach: when we take a photo of the river, we will include the adjacent traffic circle. It's a question of encouraging people to pay attention to their planning. For example, it is absolutely our role to say: "Be careful, a house is a small building, but if you put it in the wrong place, it can ruin the entire landscape."

| FRÉDÉRIC POUSIN |

Is a photograph that challenges perception necessarily a beautiful photograph? What is its intrinsic quality? Is it that it represents an object that interests you or does it have its own inherent qualities, which might be contained within the picture but maybe also in the photographer's approach?

| VALÉRIE KAUFFMANN |

A beautiful photograph is one that has something to say and which at the same time – I don't know if we can use the term aesthetic – catches the eye. Photographs of a series are chosen because they represent exactly what we want to say and express complexity in the best possible way.

When a photograph is powerful, things are immediately expressed and constructed.

We had a truly wonderful experience in one rapidly changing agri-urban territory. In the *Triangle vert*, the project manager was also a photographer, and the quality of her work made it much easier to discuss issues with our partners during the study phase.

| GEOFFROY MATHIEU |

The beautiful picture issue has come to the fore in debates, with regard to the effectiveness of the representation. It's complicated, because it's not easy to say why one photograph is better than another.

| VALÉRIE KAUFFMANN |

I'm not a photographer by any means. I sometimes choose the viewpoint, but it's not necessarily me who takes the photograph. When I choose the pictures, it's with the narrative in mind, they illustrate what's being said: the photograph must contain enough messages, complexity or questions for the viewer to draw something from it – and each individual will draw something different, depending on the situation.

I use this road photo in the following way: I say that on the right there's the Seine and on the left there are the Essonne lakes, i.e. the most beautiful landscape in the region. None of the people who use the N7 road every day at this spot are aware that they are driving between such magnificent landscapes. That's the issue I want to bring before elected officials, the general public, technicians, etc. Photography provides a useful support.

| III |

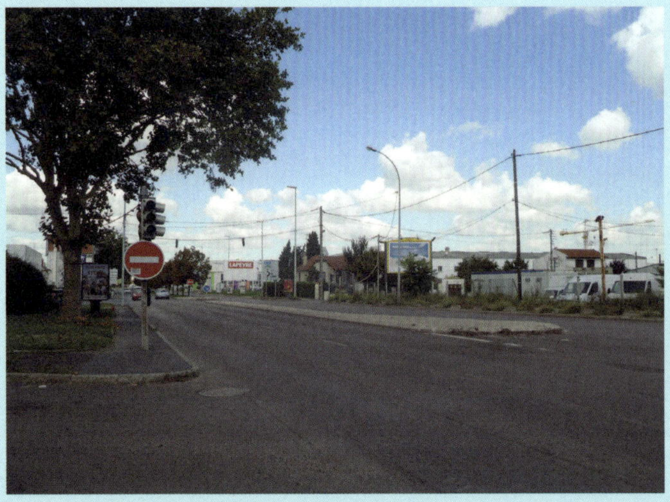

| III |
Full-page pictures to convince people: the Nationale 7 road in Viry-Châtillon, 2013. Presentation at the *Institut de géographie, "Espaces publics locaux et identité métropolitaine"*, 2014.

Geoffroy Mathieu is a photographer who graduated from the *École Nationale de la Photographie* in Arles in 1999. The photographer Bertrand Stofleth also graduated from the *École Nationale de la Photographie* in Arles, in 2002, after taking a university course in the history of art.
Together they have created several landscape photography observatories. In this round table, the discussion turned around a photographic project conducted in the metropolis of Marseille; *Paysages usagés* took the form of a landscape photography observatory within the context of a public commission cofinanced by the CNAP and Marseille-Provence 2013.
The idea was to follow the GR2013 hiking trail, which has since then been officially recognized by the French hiking federation (FFRP). This 365 kilometer trail crosses almost all of the metropolis' 38 municipalities. The photographers' work thus constitutes an archive of the metropolitan landscape, set up before the institutional body was created. Along with several other artists, they defined a path in the form of an infinity symbol, with its crossover point at the Aix TGV station, on the Arbois plateau, and organized around the metropolis' two huge open spaces: the Étang de Berre lagoon and the Massif de l'Étoile mountain range. A guidebook was published at a later date.

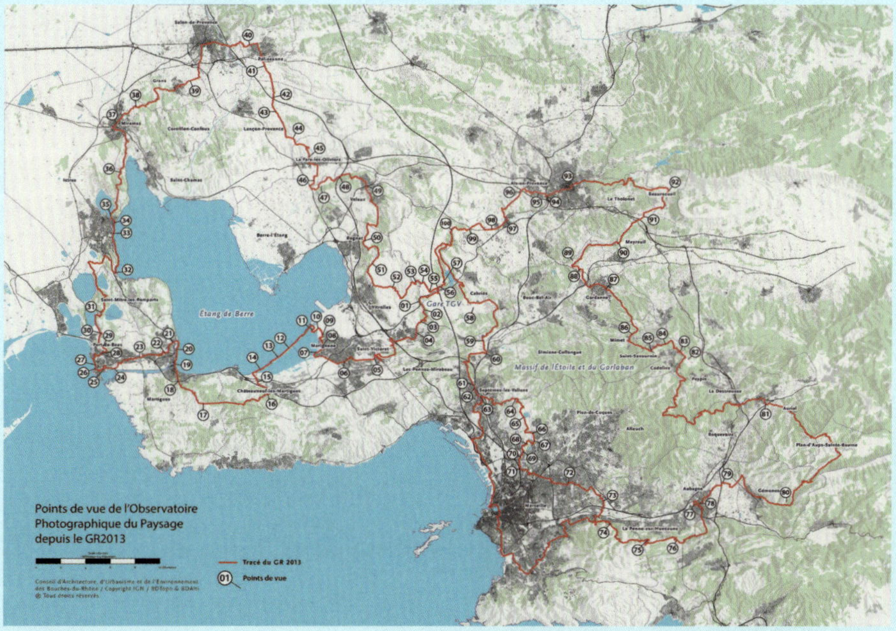

|1|

| GEOFFROY MATHIEU |
We suggested making a series of photographs all along this trail, which we would then activate in accordance with the type of protocol used by landscape photography observatories, i.e. on the principle of itineraries methodically defining viewpoints to be regularly repeated over time.
We identified and numbered 100 viewpoints, approximately 3.5 kilometers apart from one another. They all say something about the region and were chosen for their representativeness. The entrance into the town of Marignane is not necessarily the viewpoint that makes the most sense, but it is representative of a recurring situation. In the same way, we chose certain natural spaces for their vegetation. The project as a whole must be perceived on the basis of the full corpus of 100 viewpoints. It produces a form of intelligence on the region's past, present and future landscape issues.

| BERTRAND STOFLETH |

We brought together 70 people to have recurring shoots with us and to monitor these landscapes over time. We didn't want subjects that would simply be perceived as isolated artistic acts. From the outset, as agreed with the steering committee, we chose to include what we called "adopters", i.e. people who committed free of charge to take repeat photographs from a viewpoint over a ten-year period. They have become the depositories and monitors of the original photographs, producing diachronic sequences of them. It was also a way of rooting the project within the region, of making it an object that resonates with all possible interlocutors.

| RAPHAËLE BERTHO |

Who are these adopters? How do they approach a project that is already ongoing? Is it through networking? Are they local inhabitants?

| GEOFFROY MATHIEU |

There was no selection process, people came forward spontaneously. But in practice, they had to have a little bit of experience with photography, in order to cope with the constraints of repeat photography, and have a few technical accessories, such as a tripod. Generally speaking, the participants lived in the region, and the majority were landscape designers, architects and photographers …

| BERTRAND STOFLETH |

Of the 100 photos, 30 were bought by regional contemporary art archives (FRACs) and 70 were adopted. Right from the start we said that we wanted to show this collective work in various forms: in a format sufficient for the picture to be seen and for it to make sense hanging from the rails of a gallery or an exhibition venue, but also placed on the mantelpiece – or wherever – in a private home. We also laid out the terms of the exchange: the work (here I'm referring to the original photograph, protected back and front by acrylic glass) becomes your property, you are its depository. You commit to taking one photograph per year from the same spot and sending it to us.

| RAPHAËLE BERTHO |

We know the modality for photographic work: an author produces a work which is the end product. This project almost systematically deconstructs that principle: you work in tandem, you bring adopters into the project and you reexamine spaces of mediation …

| GEOFFROY MATHIEU |

This work has only been shown once in its entirety, as part of the *Le sentier et le palais* inaugural exhibition, during the Marseille-Provence event in 2013. The 100 pictures were hung together for the first and last time.

| II |

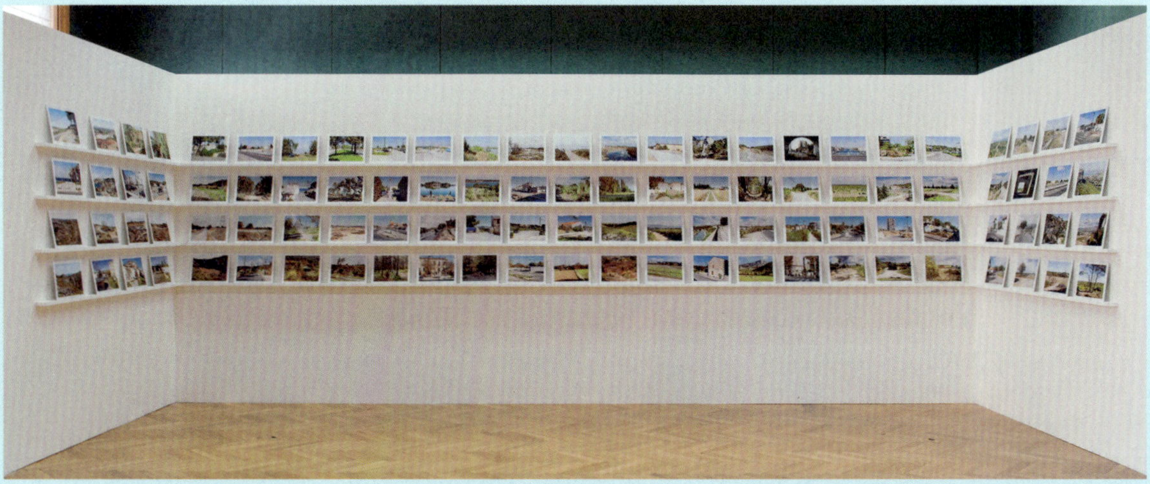

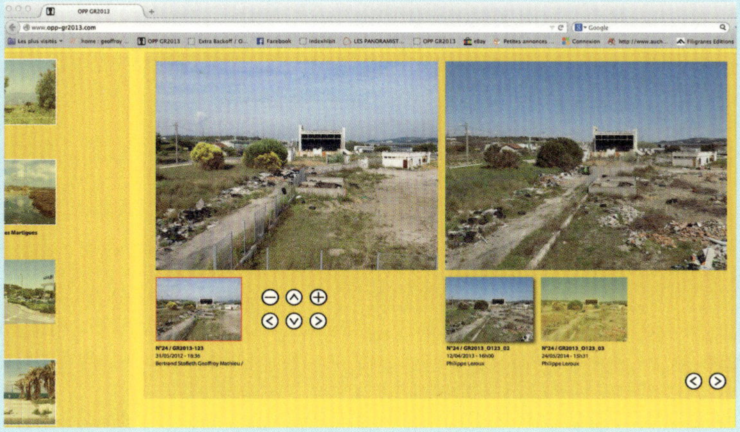

| III |

| I |
Map indicating the various observation sites of the photographic landscape observatory, from the long hiking trail 2013.

| II |
Inaugural *Le sentier et le palais* exhibition, CCI Palais de la Bourse, Marseille, 2013. Exhibition photography showing 100 viewpoints created for *Paysages usagés,* landscape photography observatory from the GR2013.

| III |
Screenshot of the "extrazoom" module allowing the targeted close-up comparison of a specific zone of the picture over a period of years (www.opp-gr2013.com).

| IV |
Paysages usagés, Geoffroy Mathieu & Bertrand Stofleth, Éditions Wildproject, 100 postcards and a geographical map in a cardboard box, Marseille, March 2013.

| RAPHAËLE BERTHO |
In 2014, some of these pictures (the 30 that you repeat each year) were shown again as part of the *France(s) Territoire Liquide* project, in two exhibitions linked to the CNAP, and then in 2015 at the museum of contemporary art in Palma, in Majorca, and at MuCEM in the *J'aime les panoramas* exhibition.
In your project, it is the photographers themselves who laid down the rules and directives and who went off to find funding. So these exhibitions do not relate to Marseille but to the status of the commission work. It's no longer a question of region but of the way of creating this other work or object – you are shattering the principle.

| GEOFFROY MATHIEU |
The first exhibition took place at the mail sorting facility in Lille. We only showed the 30 photos that we repeat annually, but we added the map of the 100 viewpoints so that people understood they only represented a fragment. We printed a certain number of viewpoints as diptychs to illustrate the principle behind the observatory – i.e. that of recurring shoots.

| RAPHAËLE BERTHO |
People can handle your photos at exhibitions …

| GEOFFROY MATHIEU |
They are placed on shelves in such a way that you can turn them over and see the reverse side of the photograph. What's important is that the object is fully autonomous, in other words that you have both the picture and the way it was taken. The front of the picture provides the information needed to ensure that it can be repeated. Such elements are part of the constraints of a landscape photography observatory and generally remain confined to a technical space reserved for the photographers in charge of the recurring shoots.

| BERTRAND STOFLETH |
The website is really the heart of the project. It is continuously updated; the adopters send us their pictures and we add them to the site. The artistic object gains momentum and comes to life. The site provides one entry per picture and one entry per map, outlining the cone of vision. The system for high-definition viewing of the pictures allows you to zoom in on the same spot on two adjacent pictures. You can see the differences and the micro-details.

| RAPHAËLE BERTHO |
You also did a book on this experience, published in 2013. Once again, this book is not a … Its form allows people to appropriate the pictures.

| BERTRAND STOFLETH |
We wanted to perpetuate the experience and at the same time democratize the photos. At the time we were thinking about the contemporary picturesque, about new landscapes that forge the identity of the Marseille-Provence region. And postcards seemed to us to be the most common way to represent a territory. We looked at a great many pictures taken in the 1920s and 1930s, series that show 10 viewpoints of Lourdes, 20 viewpoints of Nice and its rocky inlets, etc. Over time they became icons and created new representa-

| IV |

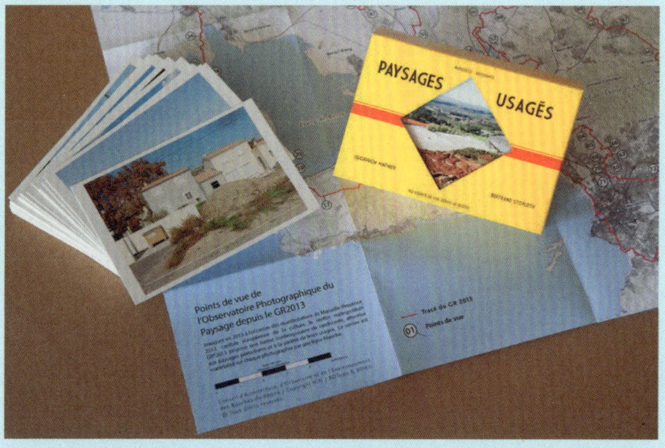

tions of their regions – if you go to X spot, this is what you should visit. That is exactly what we are trying to do with these 100 viewpoints. Except that instead of having very precise landmarks, showing sorts of cultural monoliths like the Bonne Mère, Sainte-Baume, etc., we created a box in which these 100 photographs are like postcards.

| PASCALE HANNETEL |
I think this is an extraordinary project. The GR lives and has roots. You were talking about the contemporary picturesque and that speaks to me; think that the postcard is an interesting way of sharing a representation.

| GEOFFROY MATHIEU |
This project also allowed us to propose a public debate on the pictures and a participatory element within the process as a whole. The encounter was facilitated by its integration into the Marseille 2013 operation and that caught people's interest. Our view is that the purpose of an observatory is to generate discussions about landscape, through photography. And we have seen that as a support for debate, photography works pretty well.

| BERTRAND STOFLETH |
A steering committee was set up, with artists, people involved in the invention of the trail, architects and landscape designers, members of the CAUE and people from the city. They participated in the final selection of the pictures and the adopters ware able to talk to them about how the operation would move forward and about the issues that had arisen in a metropolitan region already undergoing exploration and development. The project continues to live today. We regularly invite local actors to come and see how it is evolving. Every year we organize a picnic with our community of adopters, and we look for new forms of mediation and exchange, such as conferences and screenings.

| GEOFFROY MATHIEU |
At public events we also ask the adopters to talk about their pictures. We project series of photos, they talk about their relationship with the series, why they chose that particular viewpoint or did not stick to it, etc. We encourage them to investigate the adopted landscape in order to enrich our understanding of this region.

| SONIA KERAVEL |
The transformations of the region that are recorded in these pictures, even though it is artistic work, do they resonate with the developers? Do they appropriate the work and use it to feed their projects?

| GEOFFROY MATHIEU |
We visited two local schools and we were invited to take part in seminars to discuss the metropolis. The metropolitan planning department contacted us, they wanted to become custodians of the collection, or be able to use it.

| V |

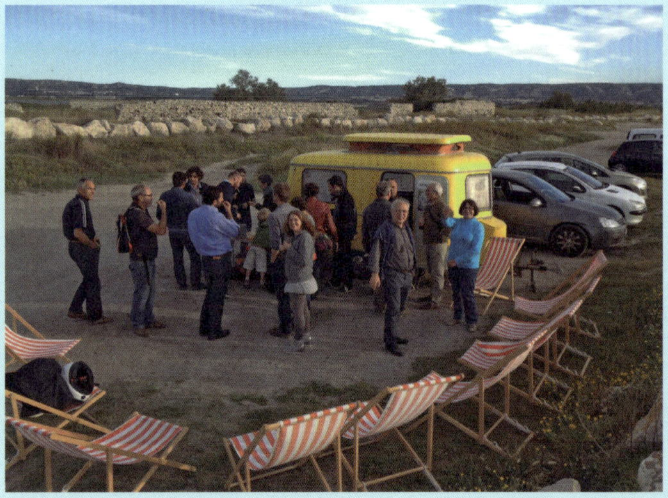

| V |
The GR2013 caravan photographed during the first meeting of adopters, Le Jaï, municipality of Marignane, 2014.

| VI |
Étang de l'Olivier, Istres, 11:35, November 2, 2012. *Paysages usagés*, landscape photography observatory from the GR2013, 2012–2022.

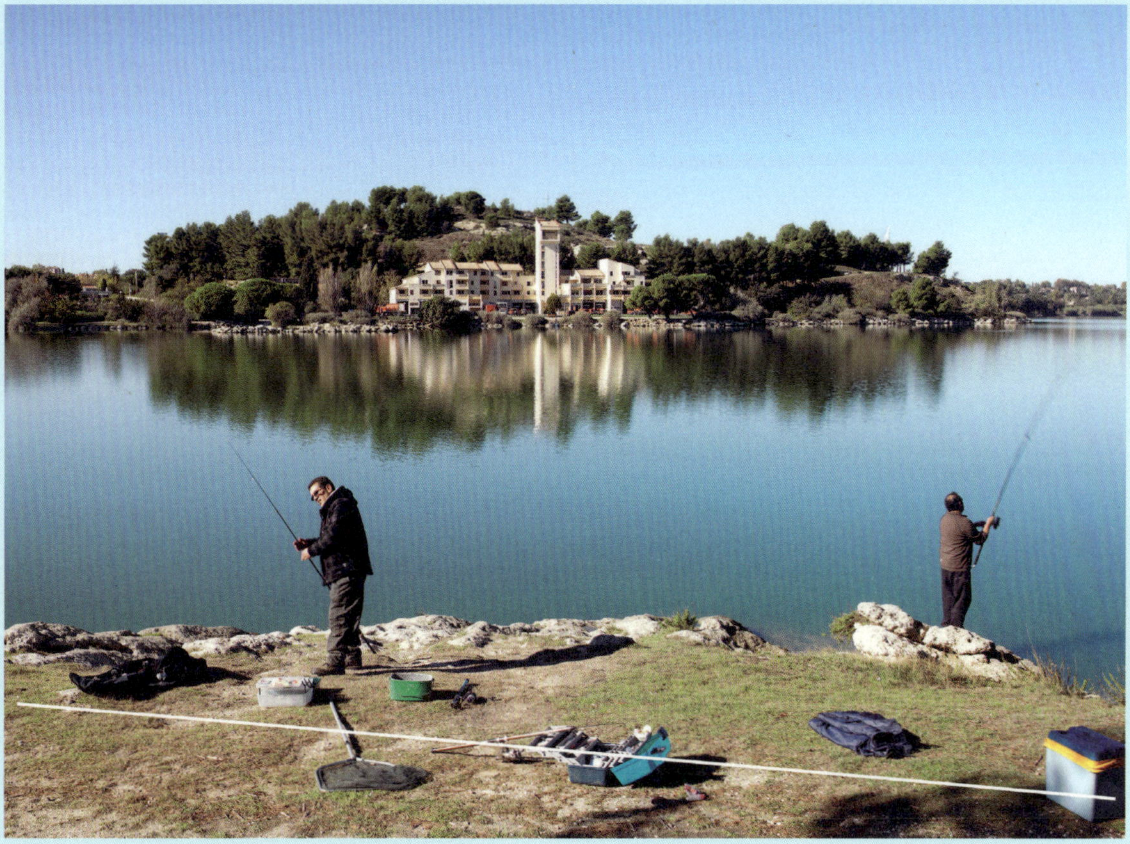

| VI |

| PASCALE HANNETEL |
I think the principle of sharing a vision is an interesting one. It goes against the current craze, where pictures are always pretty much the same, a few minor differences aside.

| GEOFFROY MATHIEU |
We want to offer an imagery that runs counter to the institutional representation of territories, which is based on fantasy. We want to produce pictures that are powerful and, we hope, aesthetic enough for the public to consider them beautiful.

| RAPHAËLE BERTHO |
So there's the idea of being behind the scenes while avoiding any banality of representation?

| BERTRAND STOFLETH |
It's not really behind the scenes; it's what can't be found in the "official" aesthetic canon. We were nevertheless careful to integrate a few canons into the 100 pictures, not to turn our back on them as if they didn't exist. They certainly do exist but they only represent a tiny part of the region. What is essential usually remains hidden and under-represented.

Catherine Mosbach studied at the *École Nationale Supérieure de Paysage* in Versailles, graduating in 1986. In 1987 she created the *Pages Paysages* journal with Marc Claramunt, Pascale Jacotot and Vincent Tricaud. In 1990 at the *École des Hautes Études en Sciences Sociales* she defended her postgraduate thesis (DEA), jointly supervised by Jacques Revel, Louis Marin and Jacques Cloarec. She is self-employed.
She presented a series of five recent photographs of the Bordeaux botanical garden (2000–2007), compiled with architect Françoise-Hélène Jourda. She then showed us two pictures of the more recent development of the Louvre-Lens (2005–2014), carried out with the Sanaa agency.

| I |

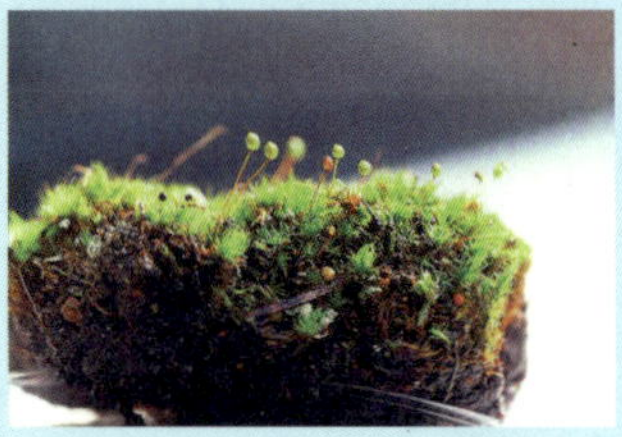

| CATHERINE MOSBACH |
The first picture, a photograph by Claude Figureau, botanist and researcher, was at the origin of the concept behind the *Galerie des Milieux* in the Bordeaux garden. It was a photo-manifesto that had a major impact on how we worked later on. It announces and introduces the other two pictures which speak to the manufacturing and construction process and illustrate the different stages.
I wouldn't know how to do my job without photos. I know that some landscape designers and architects do without, because they are fascinated by an idea or a concept. But for me it's a tool for thinking that's just as important as a text, just as much – if not more – a tool for reflection as a tool for communication.
I use photography in the same way I use drawing. I think as I draw, and I am unable to think about a project without drawing.

| II | III |

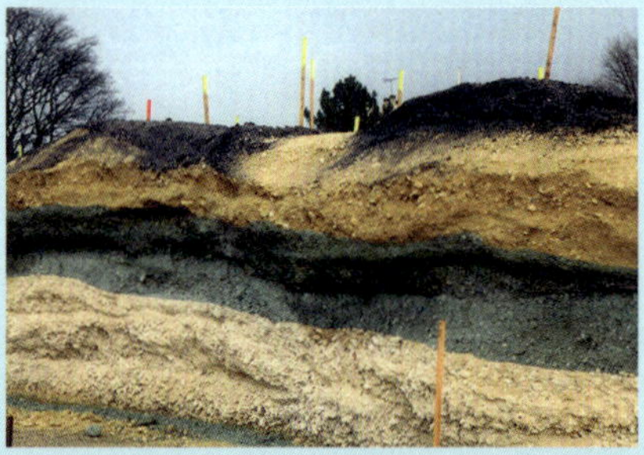

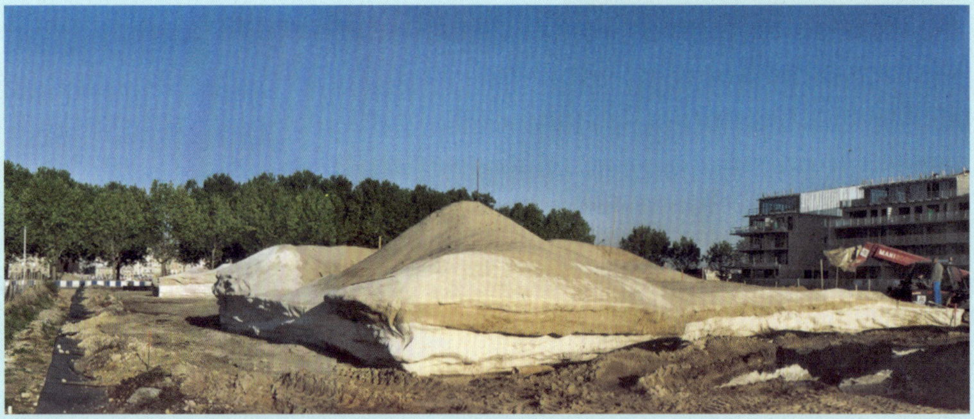

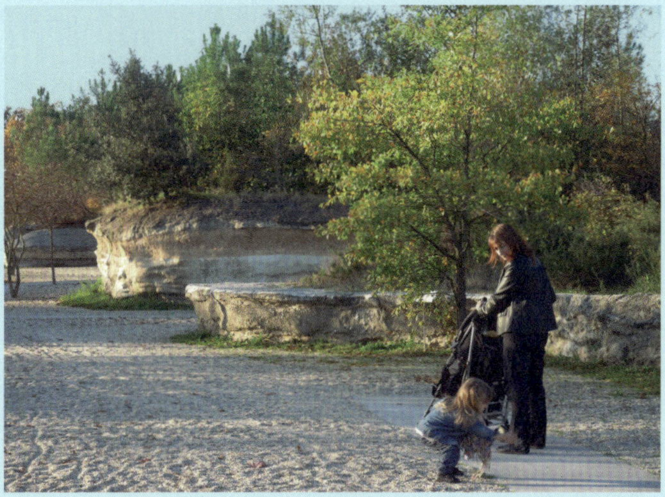

| IV |

| I |
Claude Figureau, mosses.

| II AND III |
Catherine Mosbach,
Gallery of Environments under construction.
Bordeaux's Botanical Garden, 2001.

| IV |
Catherine Mosbach, tailings heaps at
Loos-en-Gohelle, 2006.

| CRISTINA ROS |
Do you know what you are looking for when you take a photograph? Or do you interpret it later on, when you see it?

| CATHERINE MOSBACH |
To take a photo I need to be moved. Then I look at the picture I've taken. Because you can't store everything like you can with a universal bank, I forget the photo. I think it's a shame to forget, but it allows you to be receptive towards new things. When I have to explain myself or convince other people during the project process, I search my photo bank to find pictures that echo the response I want to give. So I need these pictures.

| SONIA KERAVEL |
Pascale Hannetel has shown us some aerial photographs. You have chosen not to. Yet I believe you do use them. Can you tell us how you use them?

| CATHERINE MOSBACH |
I haven't used any vertical photos here because the point of the round table wasn't to explain a project. In fact I differentiate between two types of aerial photograph: vertical ones and oblique ones, which relate to what you see when the plane flies low and you cross the landscape. Vertical photography has been important to me, it's allowed me to understand what makes a project pertinent, at the scale of a building, a landscape and a region.

| PASCALE HANNETEL |
The question of scale is vital when developing a landscape project and in this picture of the Bordeaux botanical garden it's difficult to estimate the size of the trees. Why did you decide to show the garden ten years after it had been delivered? And why didn't you show it at a five-year stage? Ten years, that corresponds to the greatest transformation of the site to date.
But even then the trees are not yet tall and that begs the question of the shrub stratum and of tree development. At five years, it's a totally different scale.

| CATHERINE MOSBACH |
Of course there are pictures for all of the stages, but time was limited, my selection was purely pragmatic.
The question of scale has always fascinated me because it's an issue inherent to our profession. We all treat it differently. I was surprised by the "joyful chaos" aspect of the park, something I'd never imagined. We know what we want to control, but with total control you lose the resources that a certain amount of freedom allows.

| PASCALE HANNETEL |
In this work on scale, I like the way things shift or flip over at a given point in time. On some projects, I end up with the opposite of what had been considered at the start. With landscape projects there's a part that gets away from you …

| CATHERINE MOSBACH |
Pictures allow you to record these moments better than the written or spoken word. We do what we can to play around with scale. We all have our clues or our crutches. The way a picture should be taken raises this question.

| FRÉDÉRIC POUSIN |
When you showed the Bordeaux botanical garden at the MoMA exhibition, why did you make a video and how was it constructed?

| CATHERINE MOSBACH |
Every time you put yourself forward for an award or present a project, you need a video. In my opinion this is not necessarily a positive thing. A film in no way has the same information content as a photograph or a set of photographs, especially as for this type of communication with the public we believe that after two and a half minutes one's concentration drops and that this has to be the maximum duration. It's totally alien to the way we think.
The editing of *Choreography in five movements* for MoMA was a homespun piece of handiwork. I felt it was essential to show how the garden was made. In 2005 it was just three years after the opening and what we were able to show didn't correspond to the desired public image. *Choreography in five movements* was a sort of timeline at time T. The first sequence was devoted entirely to the building phase, but I contaminated it with pictures taken five years later; so 20 percent of the photos were from a later date.
To cut a long story short, it was a case of showing where we came from and where we were heading. The way you evolve from a place obviously depends on how it was built.
From a conceptual standpoint, I felt it was vital and interesting to have this dual perception, of what came before and what came after. The notion of recording is an accurate term. A picture really is a very important marker, a marker of understanding, of knowledge and of sensitivity of course, but also of evolution and life. In my opinion fixed time makes no sense, not for a landscape in any case. Even for people it makes no sense. Our human survival instincts mean that we constantly hang on to whatever we feel to be stable. People aren't comfortable seeing the different phases of life come and then disappear.
Photography records data that allow us to understand a situation, to anticipate upstream and to project ourselves downstream. These are real-time recordings of how our work as landscape designers was constructed. They are almost as essential as drawing and in any case more essential than words.
The series allows us to stand back from the installation and from the actual fabrication of the spaces. Ten years on, this is what is happening at the space you saw earlier. Our mission, as landscape architects, at conferences, is to help people understand our design and building tools.
In the following series, we can clearly see the installation that is at the origin of the transformation and continued formation of things,

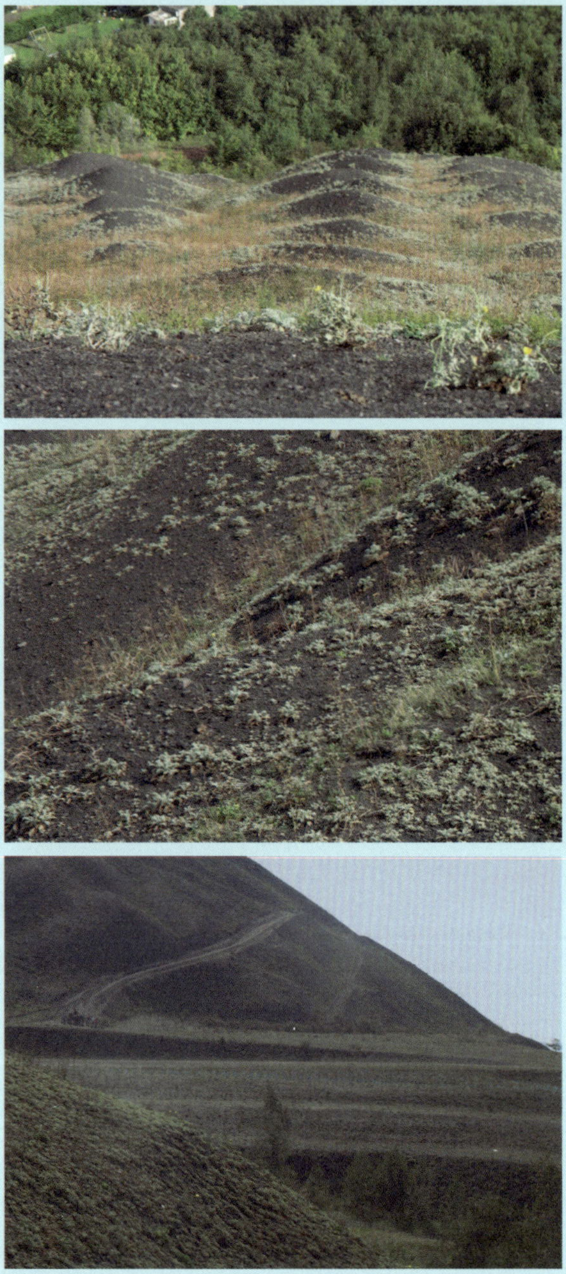

| V |

| V |
Catherine Mosbach, slag heaps at Loos-en-Gohelle, 2006.

| VI |
Iwan Baan, *Depuis le puits,* Louvre Lens, December 2012.

of what once more thrusts up out of the ground. To be more specific, not everything that appeared in terms of shrub stratum was necessarily expected; some seeds were in the ground or were carried there by chance, there were surprises.

The use of iconic, perennial and irreversible pictures means nothing in landscaping. It's as if you thought your face was enduring and irreversible, it's futile. When you take photos of family and friends over ten or twenty years, it's very disturbing to see that they are not at all the same. Whilst we can understand this where a person is concerned, it's harder for a landscape. So I think that this ability to record is wonderful. It helps us remember the intermediate stages. As for accepting the fact that it changes all the time, that's another matter. Today it's a building, but maybe tomorrow it'll be a landscape. You need to wait a bit. I'm in no hurry. As landscape designers, we've been trained not to rush. Pictures in the mind are very precious when it comes to fixing these moments of change and uncertainty. I think that is something beautiful.

| CRISTINA ROS |

Did Iwan Baan's photograph, taken at the inauguration of the Louvre-Lens museum, teach you anything about your project?

| CATHERINE MOSBACH |

This photograph of the Louvre-Lens by Iwan Baan came from a commission placed by the architects for immediate release at the opening of the museum. The inauguration took place in 2012. It is the question that this photo raises that interests me. The program is a museum, so a building. The building is at the center of a large plot of land (25 hectares) and this project was chosen because it articulates architecture with a landscape. I'm fascinated by the contradictory relationship between an extremely precious and evanescent object, the harshness and abrupt nature of the ground – which is the physical reality of the land reserved for the installation – and the fragility of the trees in the foreground. These are the three concrete parameters for the completion of the object. I know that politicians and operators tend to want finished, iconic pictures, i.e. ones where you can take ownership of what it represents. Of course, what I'm showing you is the exact opposite. This is the paradox of showing something precious within something that is very harsh. You dare show the naked earth, the poor soil, the damaged trees. Everyone was of course shocked by these embankments, and that remains true today.

| VI |

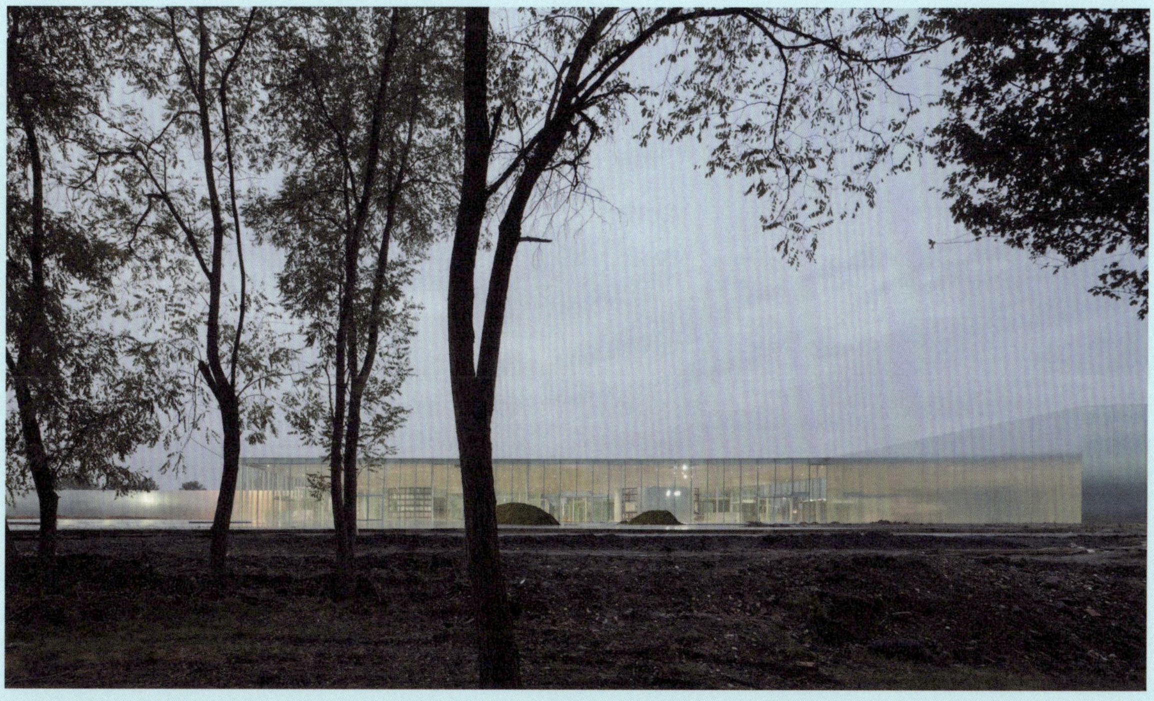

Biographies

RAPHAËLE BERTHO

Raphaële Bertho is a historian of photography and Associate Professor in Arts at Tours François Rabelais University. Her research activity focuses on the institutional, artistic, professional and vernacular uses of photography and visual representation of regions since 1945. In 2013, she published *La Mission photographique de la DATAR, Un laboratoire du paysage contemporain* (La Documentation française). In 2017 she curated two exhibitions : *Dans l'atelier de la Mission* at the *Rencontres internationales de la photographie d'Arles* and *Paysages français: une aventure photographique (1984–2017)* at the *Bibliothèque nationale de France*. She is a member of the *PhotoPaysage* research team.

TIM DAVIS

Tim Davis is a historian for the U.S. National Park Service. His research, teaching and professional activities focus on documenting and preserving cultural landscapes and illuminating the ways in which they shape and reflect historical processes, social practices, ideological frameworks and individual experiences. He has contributed to numerous scholarly journals and anthologies and is the author of *National Park Roads: A Legacy in the American Landscape* (University of Virginia Press, 2016) and coeditor of *National Park Roads: Drawings from the Historic American Engineering Record* (Johns Hopkins University Press, 2004).

PASCALE HANNETEL

Pascale Hannetel is a landscape architect, graduated from the *École Nationale Supérieure de Paysage* (ENSP) in Versailles (1983). Since 1994 she has served as consultant landscape architect in local or regional authorities (Calvados, Cher, Corse du Sud). Since 2005 she has been designated as a member of the expert committee for French property of UNESCO world heritage. In 1997 she cofounded HYL agency, with Arnaud Yver (architect). The HYL team consists of some fifteen employees and is resolutely multidisciplinary (architecture, landscape architecture, urban design, engineering). Among its recent projects, the reconfiguration of the surrounding area of the castle Ladoucette in Drancy (France).

DEBORA HUNTER

Debora Hunter was born in Chicago in 1950 and drew up in architectural rich Oak Park, Illinois. She studied visual sociology with Howard S. Becker at Northwestern University and received a MFA from Rhode Island School of Design. She is Professor Emerita, Southern Methodist University, Dallas, Texas. Hunter has exhibited her photographs at the Museum of Modern Art, Art Institute of Chicago, Dallas Museum of Art, Amon Carter Museum and Museum of Contemporary Photography Chicago. Early photographic projects explored the potency of interior spaces upon the individual. Since 2004 she has documented houses of various architectural styles and conditions within in the majestic landscape of Taos, New Mexico. Her website is **www.deborahunter.com.**

VALÉRIE KAUFFMANN

Valérie Kauffmann is an architect and landscape designer. She has collaborated with architectural agencies such as HYL and Antoine Grumbach & Associates for ten years. In 1999 she joined the CAUE 91 team, where she develops landscape policies and carries out works on representations of local andregional landscape. When the team incorporated three other landscape designers, she was designated Assistant Director of the CAUE 91. She also currently teaches at the *École Nationale Supérieure de Paysage* (ENSP) in Versailles, as Assistant Professor in Thierry Laverne's studio.

SONIA KERAVEL

Sonia Keravel is a landscape architect. She received a doctoral degree in geography from *École des Hautes Études en Sciences Sociales* (EHESS). She is an assistant professor at the *École Nationale Supérieure de Paysage* (ENSP) in Versailles where she teaches design, criticism and history of landscape architecture. She currently carries out research work on reception of landscape projects. Since 2013, she has been collaborating with the ANR program PhotoPaysage and focused her research on collaboration between landscape architects and photographers. She is the author of *Passeurs de paysages. Le projet de paysage comme art relationnel*, Métis Presses 2015.

MARIE-HÉLÈNE LOZE

Marie-Hélène Loze is a landscape architect, who graduated from the *École Nationale Supérieure de Paysage* (ENSP) in Versailles. She collaborated with several landscape architecture agencies (Allain Provost, Robert Berthet, Michel Corajoud). She subsequently developed professional skills in graphic communication and worked as a consultant in various private and state institutions. She currently teaches landscape design at ENSP and collaborates with the ANR program PhotoPaysage.

GEOFFROY MATHIEU

Geoffroy Mathieu, born in 1972, lives and works in Marseille. He is graduated from the *École Nationale Supérieure de la Photographie* in Arles. His photography investigates mutating landscapes, rural territories, and Mediterraneen metropolis. He is author of: *Dos à la mer, promenade en Méditerranée urbaine* (Filigranes, 2009) and *Geum Urbanum* (Filigranes, 2013). Since 2012, with the photographer Bertrand Stofleth, he has set up a landscape photographic observatory (*Paysages usagés*) along the GR 2013 hiking trail in the suburban area of Marseille (sponsored by the *Centre National des Arts Plastiques* and Marseille 2013 European Capital of Culture). Since 2016 he has carried out a documentary series on objects, gestures, and agricultural landscapes in suburban Paris, sponsored by the CNAP.
www.geoffroymathieu.com

FRANCK MICHEL

Franck Michel lives in Québec (Canada). For more than 25 years he has been involved in the visual arts community, curated more than 15 exhibitions and edited several books about representation of landscape in contemporary photography. From 1999 to 2008 he served as the head of the *Centre Est-Nord-Est* in Saint-Jean-Port-Joli (Québec) and from 2008 to 2014 as the director of the *Musée régional de Rimouski* (Québec). In 2015 he received a research grant from the Canada Council for the Arts for carrying out research on walking as creative process in contemporary landscape photography. In 2016 and 2017 he curated the 8th and 9th photo meetings in Kamouraska (Québec). He is currently the head of Culture Montérégie (Québec).

CATHERINE MOSBACH

Catherine Mosbach is a landscape architect, who graduated from *École Nationale Supérieure de Paysage* (ENSP) in Versailles in 1986. She first studied natural and life sciences at Louis Pasteur University, Strasbourg. In 1990 she received a postgraduate degree in history and civilizations from *École des Hautes Études en Sciences Sociales* (EHESS) in Paris. She was visiting Professor at Penn Design University, Philadelphia in 2003–2006, and at Harvard Graduate School of Design, Cambridge, in 2017. Her recent publications include: *Soil, air, water under photons* (with A. Daval) www.projetsdepaysage.fr, 2016; "Delta, or the Transgression of Lines", *Pamphlet 20: Delta Dialogues*, Christophe Girot, Susann Ahn, Isabelle Fehlmann, Lara Mehling (eds.), gta Publishers, ETH Zurich, Switzerland, 2017; "Design of Biosphere", *Stream 04: The paradoxes of the Living*, Philippe Chiambaretta (ed.), Paris, 2017.

BRUNO NOTTEBOOM

Bruno Notteboom studied civil engineering-architecture at Ghent University and urban planning at KU Leuven. He obtained his doctoral degree in urban and regional planning at the Department of Architecture & Urban Planning, Ghent University in 2009 with a thesis on the relationship between urban planning and landscape iconography in Belgium. He was an assistant professor at Ghent University and the University of Antwerp, and a visiting scholar at UC Berkeley before joining the Department of Architecture of KU Leuven as Associate Professor in Urban and Rural Landscapes in 2017. Notteboom's current research focuses on landscape design in a context of urbanization and shifting disciplinary alignments, from a historical and a contemporary perspective. He is an editor of *OASE. Journal for Architecture* and *Journal of Landscape Architecture*.

LAURIE OLIN

Laurie Olin, landscape architect, educator and author. Laurie Olin guided such signature projects of OLIN Studio – the LA practice which he founded in 1976 – as the National Gallery of Art Sculpture Garden in Washington, DC; The Getty Center in Los Angeles; and Bryant Park in New York City. Professor of Practice at the University of Pennsylvania, he is also the former chair of the Landscape Architecture Department at Harvard University.

MARIE-MADELEINE OZDOBA

Marie-Madeleine Ozdoba is a PhD candidate in visual culture studies at the *École des Hautes Études en Sciences Sociales* (EHESS) in Paris. She graduated in Architecture from the Vienna University of Technology and in Art Theory from Goldsmiths, University of London, and practiced in the fields of architecture and urban planning in Vienna, London and Paris. Her research explores the cultural dimensions of architectural visualization. Marie-Madeleine Ozdoba has received research grants from the Getty Foundation, the University of Chicago, the Austrian Academy of Sciences, and the British Arts and Humanities Research Board.

ALEXANDRE PETZOLD

Alexandre Petzold has been working as a photographer since 1998. He graduated from the *École Nationale Supérieure de Paysage* (ENSP) in Versailles and worked as a landscape architect in local authorities (CAUE 80). He is currently commissioned by public institutions as well as landscape architects and agencies. In 2004, the Rhône-Alpes Regional Department for the Environment (DIREN) assigned to him the mission of creating a landscape photographic observatory in the Ardèche area. From 2013 to 2016 he had been commissioned by the TER Agency for the photographic survey of the construction site of the *Parc du peuple de l'herbe* in the Paris region (Yvelines). Most of his books deal with gardens. Some of them such as *L'homme qui écoute les légumes. Nō Dō* (Actes Sud, 2016) and *Le Potager du Roi. Dialogues avec La Quintinie* (Artlys, 2017) show the relationship between people and the environment.
http://alexandrepetzold.com

FRÉDÉRIC POUSIN

Frédéric Pousin is an architect and Research Director at the CNRS (National Centre for Scientific Research). He has taught in various schools of Architecture and Universities in France and recently at the *École Nationale Supérieure de Paysage* (ENSP) in Versailles, where he headed research. He has been working extensively on urban landscape and the epistemological value of visuality in landscape architecture and urbanism. He currently heads the ANR program *PhotoPaysage*. Recent publications include: "Putting the Narrative in the Image. The Editorial Work of Landscape Architect Jacques Simon" (with Denis Delbaere), *OASE 98*, 2017, *Seeing from above: the aerial view in visual culture*, (with Mark Dorrian) I.B. Tauris, 2013; "Urban Cuttings: Sections and Crossings", in *Landscape, Vision, Motion*, (C. Girot, F. Truninger, eds.), Jovis Verlag, Berlin, 2012; "Aerial Views and the Future of Metropolitan Paris", *New Geographies 4, Scales of the Earth*, Puritan Press, Harvard, 2011.

CRISTINA ROS-BALLESTER

Cristina Ros-Ballester is an architect, who graduated from the school of architecture of Barcelona (Spain). She obtained a Master's degree in theory of landscape design from the *École Nationale Supérieure de Paysage* (ENSP) in Versailles. She has worked as project collaborator in several landscape architecture agencies in France: Agence TN+, d'Ici-là, Catherine Mosbach. She currently collaborates with the ANR program *PhotoPaysage*.

ÉDITH ROUX

Édith Roux works and lives in Paris. She is a photographer and video maker, who graduated from the *École Nationale Supérieure de la Photographie* in Arles, with a particular interest in sociopolitics, environment, and urban mutations. Parallel to her personal work she has been commissioned by public institutions: Scarpe-Escaut Nature Park has entrusted her with a mission of landscape photographic observatory consisting of four rephotographing campaigns from 2009 to 2011 and 2014. In 2013 she was commissioned by the Coastline Protection Agency for a series entitled *Corniche des Maures*. Some of her personal works, such as *Dreamscape, Euroland* and *Les Dépossédés* have been published as books. Her photographs now belong to private and public prestigious collections such as *Fonds National d'Art contemporain*, FRAC Bretagne, BnF, *Maison européenne de la photographie.*
http://www.edithroux.fr/

BERTRAND STOFLETH

Bertrand Stofleth lives and works in Lyon, France. He studied art history and the performing arts in Lyon, then photography at the *École Nationale Supérieure de la Photographie* in Arles, from which he graduated in 2002. His photography explores modes of occupying territory, along with uses and representations of landscapes. *Belvédère series* is a memoir based on geographical reconstruction. The photographic observations he has carried out in several regional nature reserves since 2005, then in urban settings since 2011, examine territorial transformations over time. *Rhodanie,* 2007–2015, is a documentary series whose iconography of the everyday illustrates different ways in which a fluvial environment has been set up and utilized. He currently works with the photographer Geoffroy Mathieu on *Paysages usagés*, a photographic landscape observatory along the GR2013 hiking trail, sponsored by the *Centre National des Arts Plastiques* and Marseille 2013 European Capital of Culture. He also currently works on *Aeropolis*, a project dealing with airports and their connections to the cities (CNAP and Atelier Medicis 2016–2017).
http://www.bertrandstofleth.com/stofleth.php

CHRIS WILSON

Chris Wilson is J. B. Jackson Chair of Cultural Landscape Studies at the University of New Mexico School of Architecture and Planning, Albuquerque, USA. He is author of *The Myth of Santa Fe: Creating a Modern Regional Traditions* (1997), *Facing Southwest: The Life and Houses of John Gaw Meem* (2001), and "Une vie sur le chemin de l'étranger," *Les Carnets du paysage* (2016, translated by Jean-Marc Besse); coauthor of *La Tierra Amarilla: Its History, Architecture and Cultural Landscape* (1991), and *The Plazas of New Mexico* (2011); and coeditor of *Everyday America: Cultural Landscape Studies After J. B. Jackson* (2003), and *Drawn to Landscape: The Pioneering Work of J. B. Jackson* (2015). He has served as president of the Vernacular Architecture Forum, and on the editorial board of its journal, *Buildings and Landscapes*. He is currently writing a field guild to the historic and contemporary, mixed-use and multi-family building types of North America.

Credits

TIMOTHY DAVIS
[PAGES 14–35]
Page 14 and figure 1 : NARA Still Pictures Branch
Figures 2, 3, 5 to 10: NPS Historic Photograph Collection
Figure 4: Author's collection
Figures 11 and 12: National Park Service Collection, Still Pictures Branch, National Archives and Records Administration

RAPHAËLE BERTHO
[PAGES 36–51]
Page 36 and figure 6: Stéphane Duroy/Bureau audiovisuel du Ministère de l'Agriculture et de la Pêche, France
Figure 1: rights reserved
Figure 2: Daniel Quesney
Figure 3: Alain Ceccarolli/*Mission photographique du Conservatoire du littoral*, France
Figure 4: Jean-Louis Garnell/*Mission photographique de la DATAR/Direction des Routes du Ministère de l'Équipement*, France
Figure 5: Éric Bénard/*Direction des Routes du Ministère de l'Équipement*, France

CHRIS WILSON
[PAGES 52–71]
Page 52 and figure 9: UNM Art Museum 82.136.18
Figure 1: F. Douglas Adams Collection
Figure 2: Helen Lefkowitz Horowitz Collection
Figure 3: Prints and Photographs Collection, Library of Congress, Washington, DC, LC-DIG-fsa-8b29228
Figure 4: "Jackson Graphics Portfolio", Jackson Textual Materials Collection, Center for Southwest Research, University of New Mexico Libraries, MSS 866 BC © UNM School of Architecture and Planning
Figure 5: J. B. Jackson Pictorial Materials Collection, Center for Southwest Research, University of New Mexico Libraries, PICT 866-6-P-03. © UNM School of Architecture and Planning
Figure 6: J. B. Jackson Pictorial Materials Collection, Center for Southwest Research, University of New Mexico Libraries, PICT 866-2-H-01. © UNM School of Architecture and Planning
Figure 7: J. B. Jackson Pictorial Materials Collection, Center for Southwest Research, University of New Mexico Libraries, PICT 866-4-I-03. © UNM School of Architecture and Planning
Figure 8: J. B. Jackson Pictorial Materials Collection, Center for Southwest Research, University of New Mexico Libraries, PICT 866-3-F-04. © UNM School of Architecture and Planning
Figure 10: J. B. Jackson Pictorial Materials Collection, Center for Southwest Research, University of New Mexico Libraries, PICT 866-1-Q2-12. © UNM School of Architecture and Planning

BRUNO NOTTEBOOM
[PAGES 72–87]
Page 72 and figures 1 to 11: *Landscape* magazine

LAURIE OLIN
[PAGES 88–99]
Page 88 and figure 10: illustration from Elizabeth Kassler, *Modern Gardens and the Landscape*, Museum of Modern Art, New York, 1964
Figure 1: Garrett Eckbo, *Landscapes for Living*, University of Massachussets Press, 1950, pages 106–107
Figures 2 and 3: Laurie Olin
Figure 4: Alan Ward
Figure 5: Ezra Stoller, published in Elizabeth Kassler, *Modern Gardens in the Landscape*, Museum of Modern Art, 1964
Figure 6: Ian McHarg, *Design with Nature*, 1969
Figures 7 to 9: University of Pennsylvania School of Design Architectural Archive

FRÉDÉRIC POUSIN
[PAGES 100–117]
Page 100 and figures 1, 4 to 11: Gilles Clément
Figure 2: Sandra Parvu
Figure 3: *Collège de France*, Paris

MARIE-MADELEINE OZDOBA
[PAGES 118–135]
Page 118 and figures 1, 2, 5, 9 and 10: Bureau Bas Smets
Figure 3: Marie-Madeleine Ozdoba
Figure 4: Philadelphia Museum of Art, Gift of Mrs. Gordon A. Hardwick and Mrs. W. Newbold Ely in memory of Mr. and Mrs. Roland L. Taylor, 1944-9-2
Figures 6 and 7: Marie-Noëlle Dailly
Figure 8: David Brandt/Gerhard Richter 2017 (26102017)

SONIA KERAVEL
[PAGES 136–153]
Page 136 and figures 1 to 10: Gérard Dufresne

FRANCK MICHEL
[PAGES 154–171]
Page 154 and figures 1, 4 to 8, 10, 11, 14: Bertrand Carrière
Figures 2, 3, 9, 13: Aperture Foundation, Inc., Paul Strand Archive
Figures 12 and 15: *Musée régional de Rimouski, Québec*
Figure 16: Roger Lemoyne

ROUND TABLES
[PAGES 173–199]
Pages 176–178, figures 1 to 3: Alexandre Petzold
Page 179–182, figures 1 to 6: agence HYL
Pages 183–186, figures 1, 2 and 3: Édith Roux, figure 4: rights reserved
Pages 187–190, figures 1, 2 and 3: CAUE de l'Essonne
Pages 191–195, figures 1 to 6: Geoffroy Mathieu and Bertrand Stofleth
Pages 196–199, figure 1: Claude Figureau, *Pages Paysages, no. 7, 1998-1999,* figures 2, 3, 4, 5: Catherine Mosbach, figure 6: Iwan Baan

PORTFOLIOS
[PAGES 209–255]
p. 211–217: Alexandre Petzold
p. 219–227: Édith Roux
p. 229–237: Geoffroy Mathieu
p. 239–245: Bertrand Stofleth
p. 247–255: Debora Hunter

Photographers' portfolios

Alexandre Petzold

Édith Roux

Geoffroy Mathieu

Bertrand Stofleth

Debora Hunter

For a period of more than three years I observed the metamorphosis of a 110 hectare site located in a meander of the Seine, in Carrières-sous-Poissy, in the Yvelines.
At the end of 2012, my attention was drawn to banners giving concrete form to pathways on a wasteland that I could see from my home. I realized that my everyday landscape was going to rapidly change and I wanted to record the transformation. An internet search informed me that there was an ongoing park project, run by the Ter agency. I know these landscape architects well and I was able to convince them to give me a photographic mission with the objective of constituting a record of the creation of the Peuple de l'Herbe park.
Ter's main wish was for me to organize recurring shoots so as to show how the different phases of project evolution. That aside, I was free to work as I thought fit.
When I work on this type of project, I proceed as follows: I start by roaming the area without any photography equipment, to try to understand it and also to consider the challenges of the planned landscaping work. This observation is a mixture of sensitive feelings and analytical approach. I then develop work hypotheses which will later on infuse the nature of my pictures. Also, sometimes the photography project feeds off unforeseen events that allow me to tell the story in a different way. Perfect examples of this are the flood on June 4, 2016, and the sudden appearance of a backhoe loader that looked like a somewhat clumsy bumblebee.

| P. 211 & p. 212–13 (top) |: *La danse du bourdon* series, March 11, 2014.
| P. 212–213 (bottom) |: Flooding of the Seine, June 4, 2016, as seen from the heights of Villennes-sur-Seine.
| P. 214 & 215 | Build-up of temporary pools, March 18 and November 26, 2015.
| P. 216 & 217 | June 24, 2017, inauguration day.

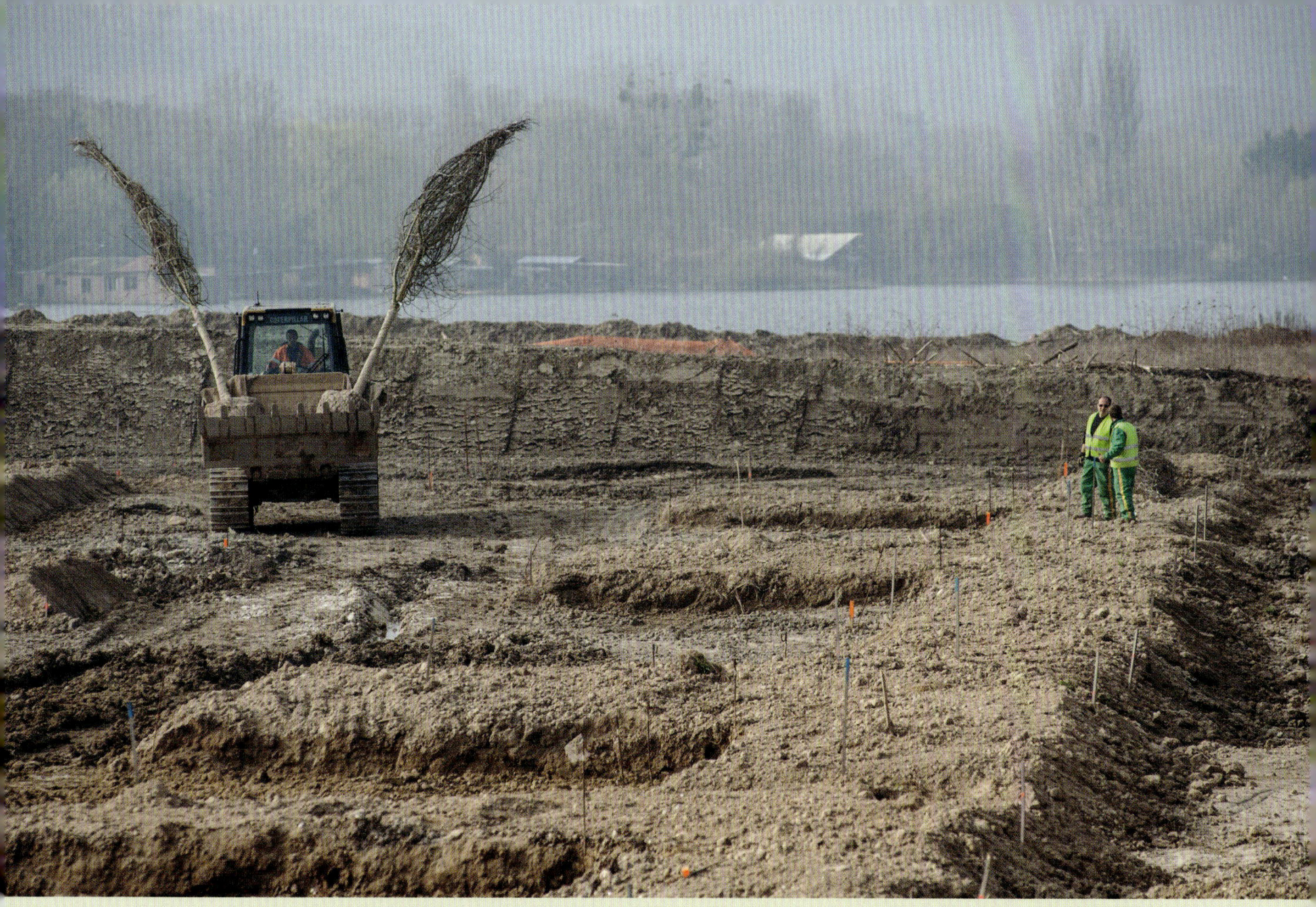

Alexandre Petzold

THE PEUPLE DE L'HERBE PARK

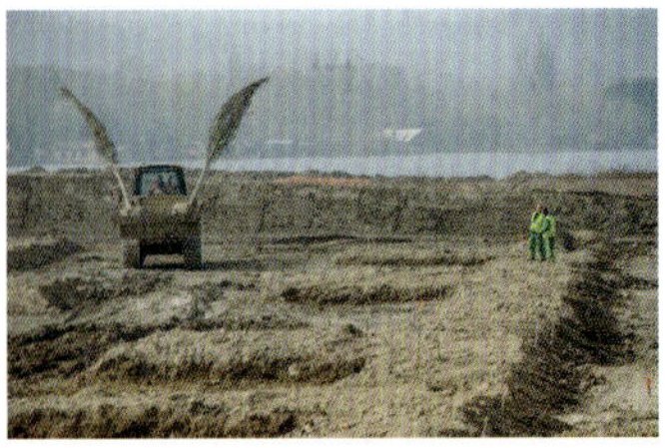
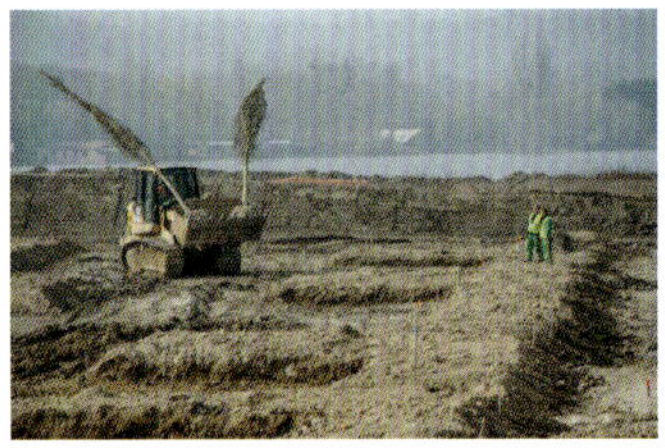
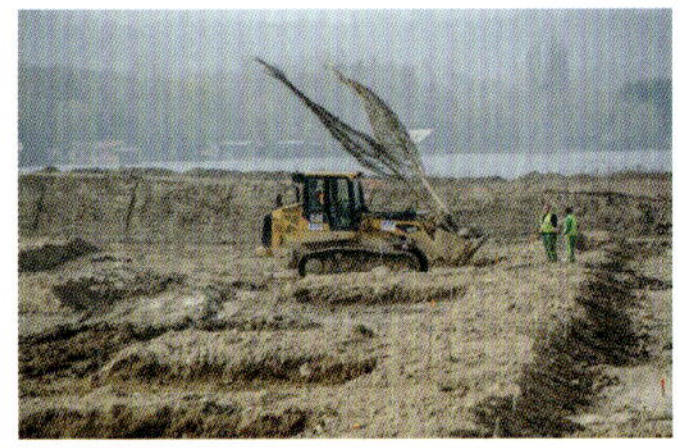
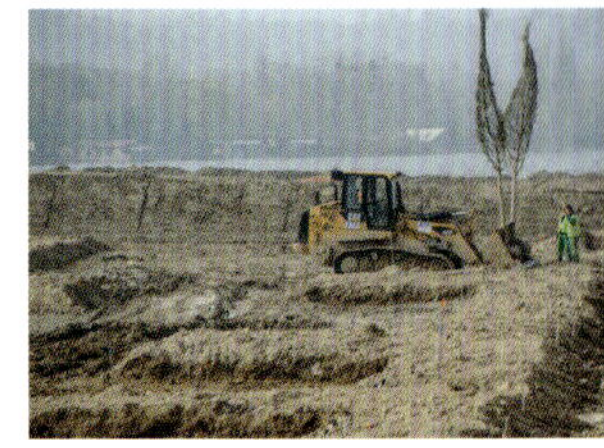

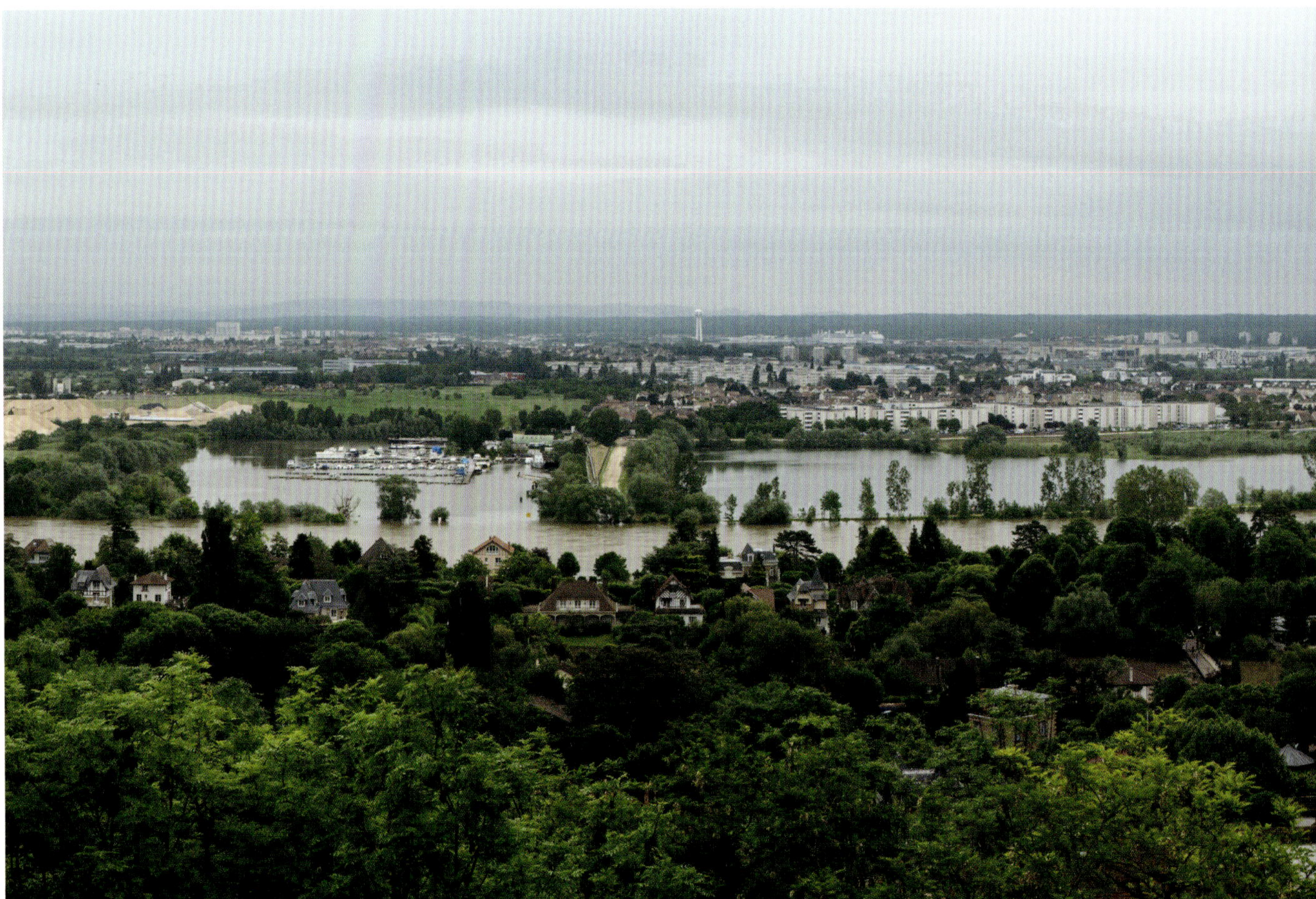

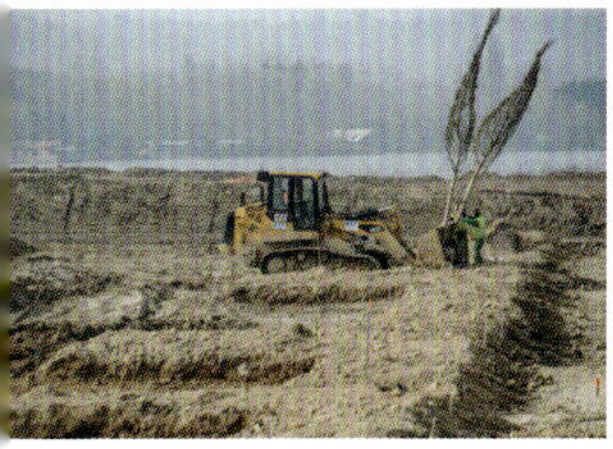

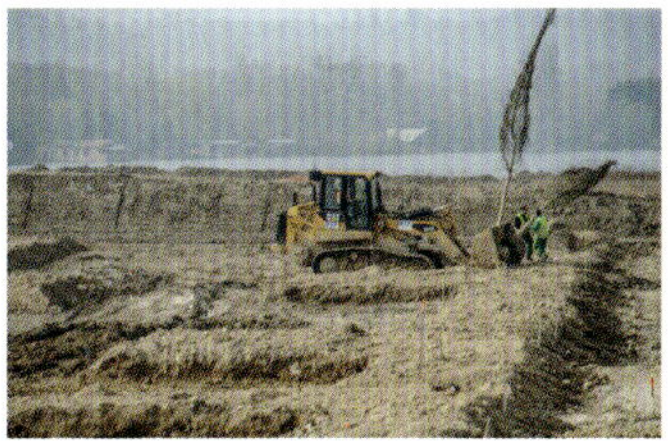

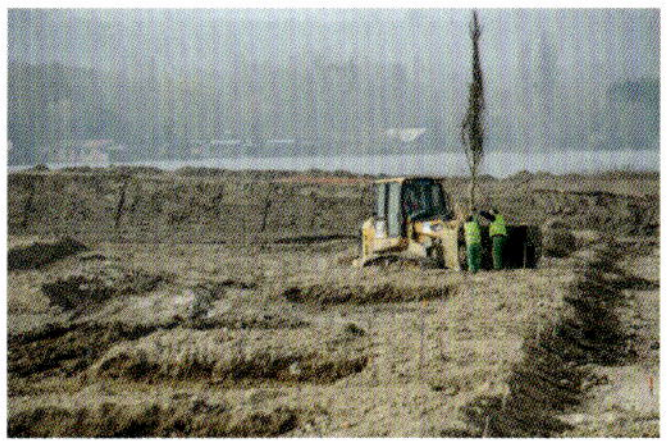

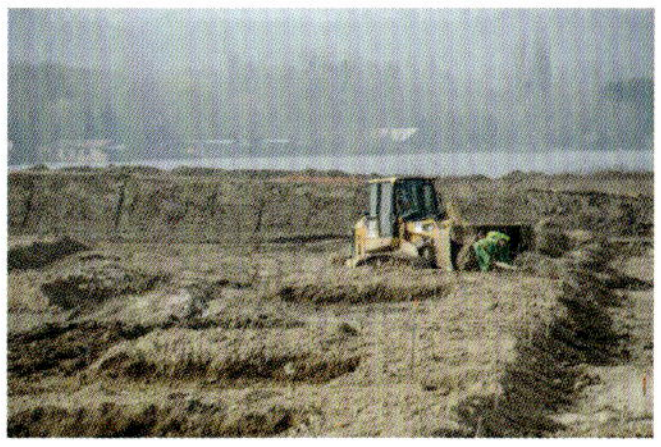

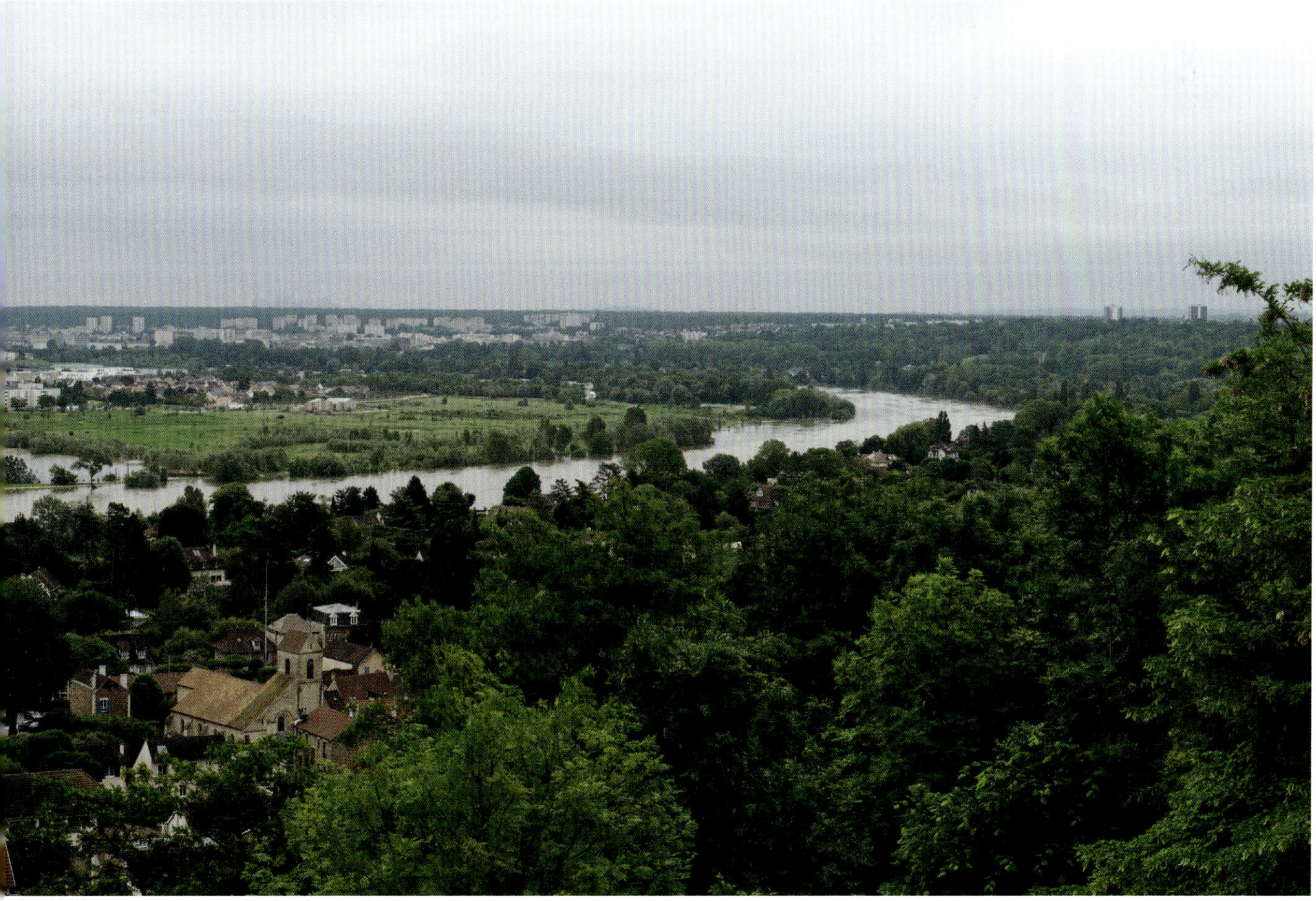

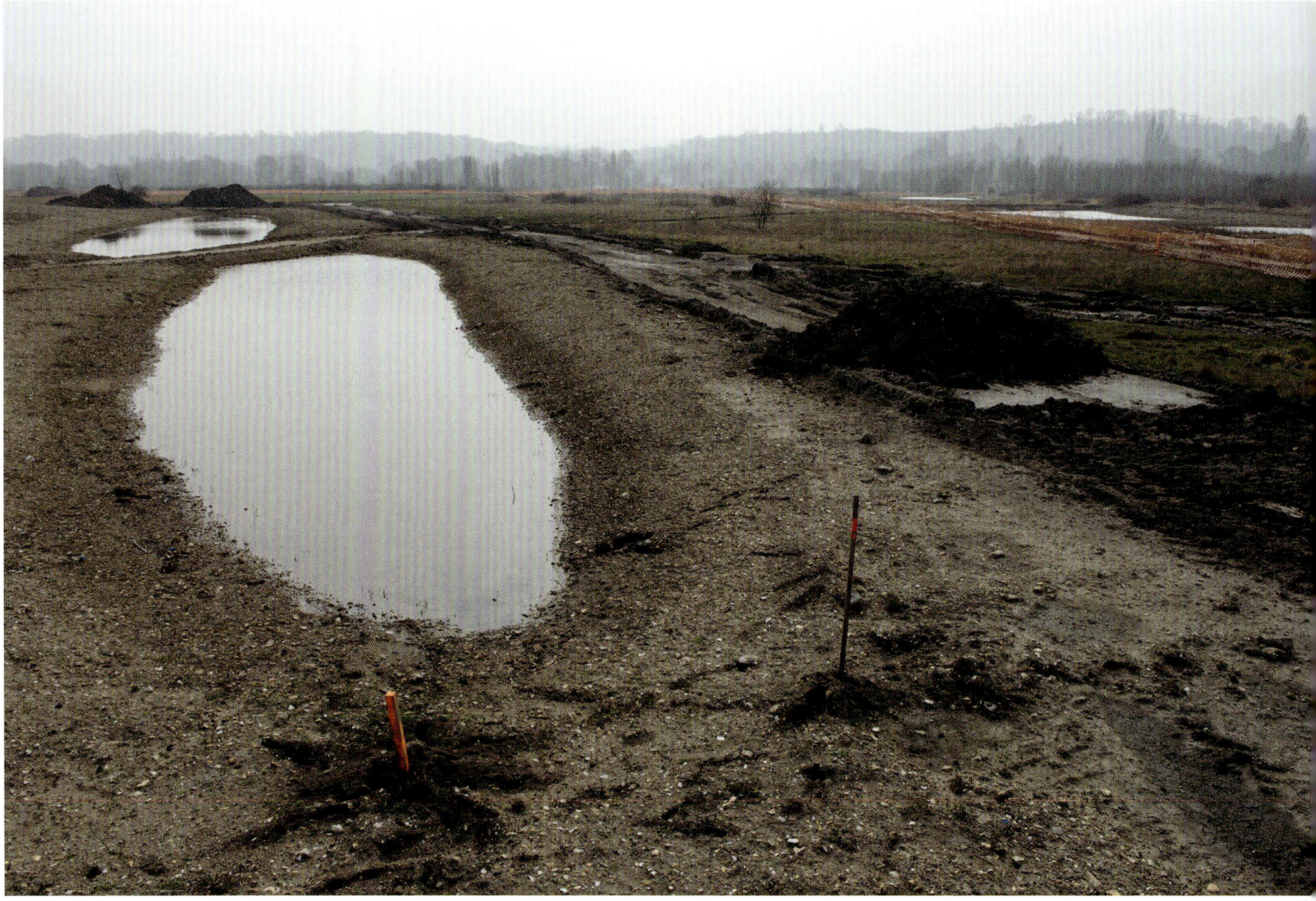

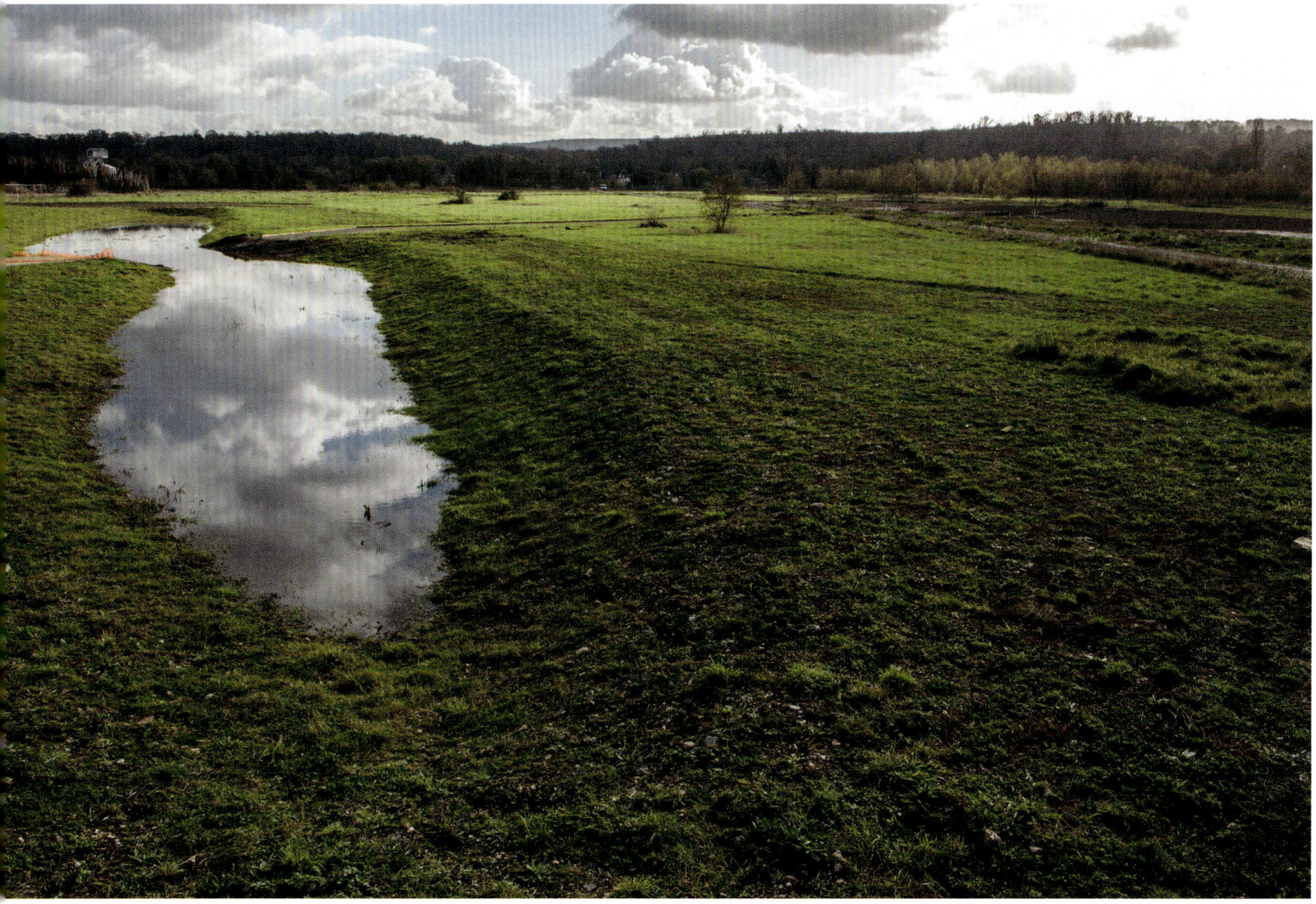

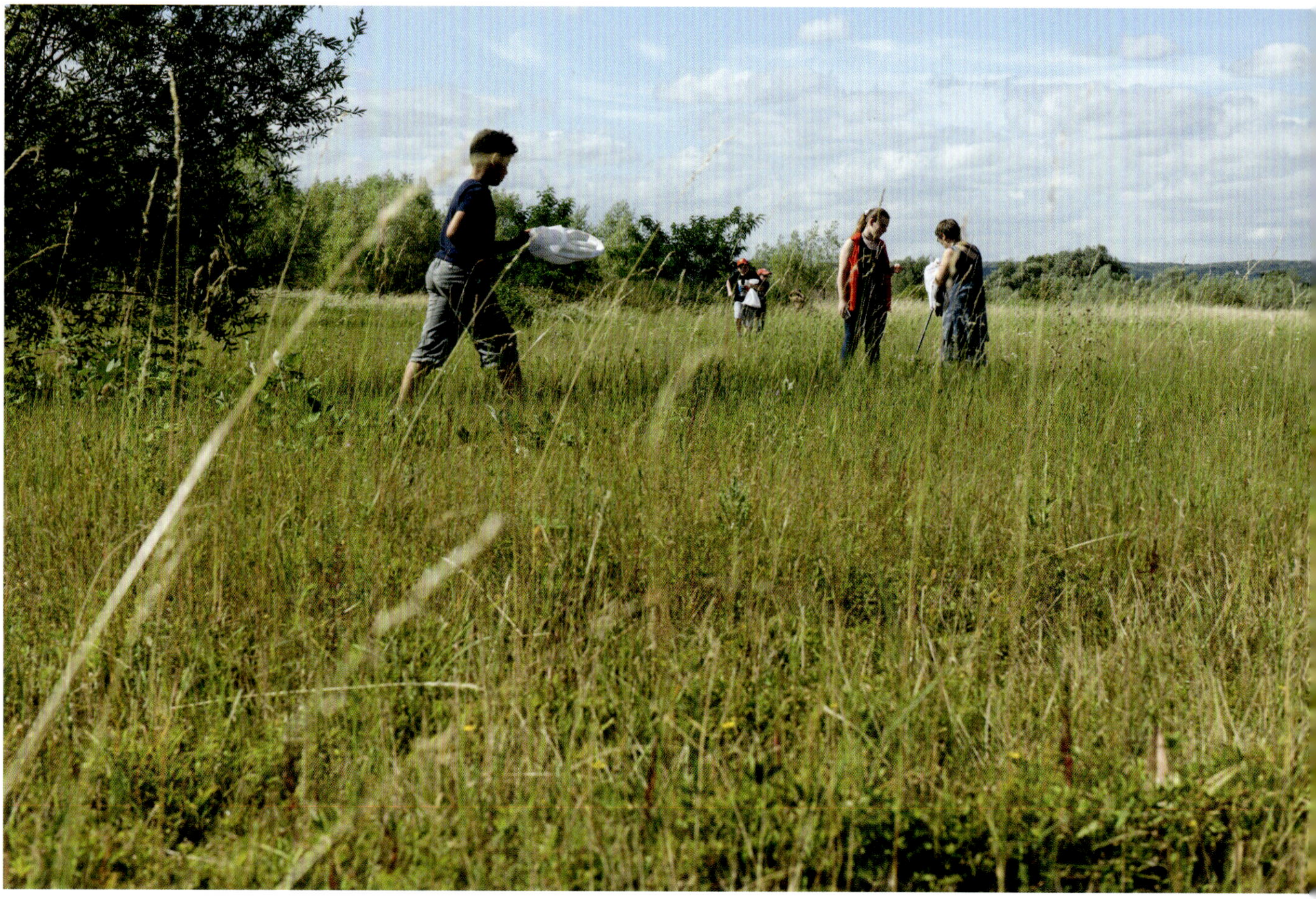

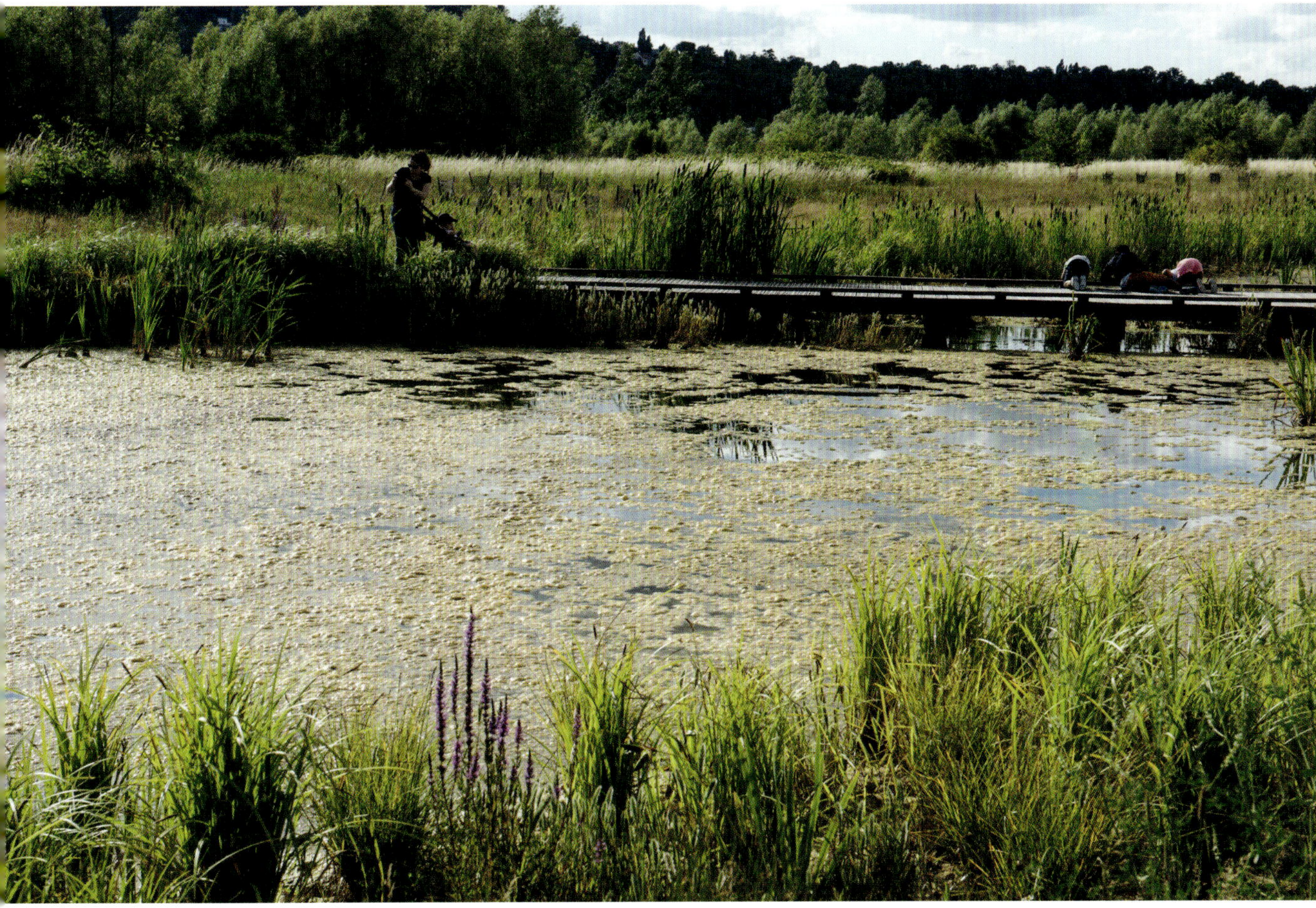

Euroland is a photographic series on peri-urban landscapes in Europe, created in 2000 and culminating in a publication in 2005.[1] The pictures are constructed as a reflection upon the evolution of urban development on the outskirts of European cities. The project showcases wasteland vegetation, with the latter's presence in the foreground of the photographs catching our eye.

This work caught the attention of the editorial staff at Italian journal *Lotus,* who gave me a commission for Scalo Farini in Milan.[2] Scalo Farini is a freight station in a fast-changing district in the center of Milan. This zone of approximately 60,000 square meters will be the object of a landscaping and architectural project. The aim of the commission was to photograph Scalo Farini in its current state of abandon and to reveal its riches and particularities. The photographic representation of the zone showcases the richness and diversity of its vegetation, particularly when it comes to the captioned pictures of plants, presented in the form of an inexhaustible photographic herbarium.

The zone is also a refuge for migrants, who find room for shelter among its architectural remains. Akim, a Tunisian migrant, is pictured in the middle of the wasteland. His presence reminds us of the human dimension inherent to the development of any landscaping project. In the same way, the photo of Angela, a Columbian student in Milan, transports us to somewhere imaginary. The young woman appears in a cinematographic light, as if she is rising up from the depths of the earth towards a place that is giving way to nature's diversity, to a respect for fragility, to the unpredictable and to the imagination. Will this visual proposition, which of course contains its share of utopia, become part of the Scalo Farini landscape project?

1 *Euroland,* texts by Gilles Clément and Guy Tortosa, Jean-Michel Place/Sujet-Objet, Paris, 2005.

2 "Meteo Milano, Scalo Farini", *Lotus*, Milan, 2016, p. 6–25.

| P. 219 | Untitled, *Euroland* series, 2000.
| P. 220 (top) | Untitled, *Euroland* series, 2000.
| P. 221 (top) | Untitled, *Euroland* series, 2000.
| P. 220–221 (bottom) | Scalo Farini, Milan, 2016.
| P. 222–223 | Scalo Farini, Milan, 2016.
| P. 224 | Scalo Farini, Milan, 2016 (Oenothera sp., Artemisia sp., Conysa canadensis, Setaria italica, Glaucium flavum, Phytolacca americana, Conysa canadensis, Cinopodium vulgare, Buddleja davidii).
| P. 225 | Scalo Farini, Milan, 2016.
| P. 226 | Scalo Farini, Milan, 2016.
| P. 227 (top) | Scalo Farini, Milan, with Akim, 2016.
| P. 227 (bottom) | Scalo Farini, Milan, with Angela, 2016.

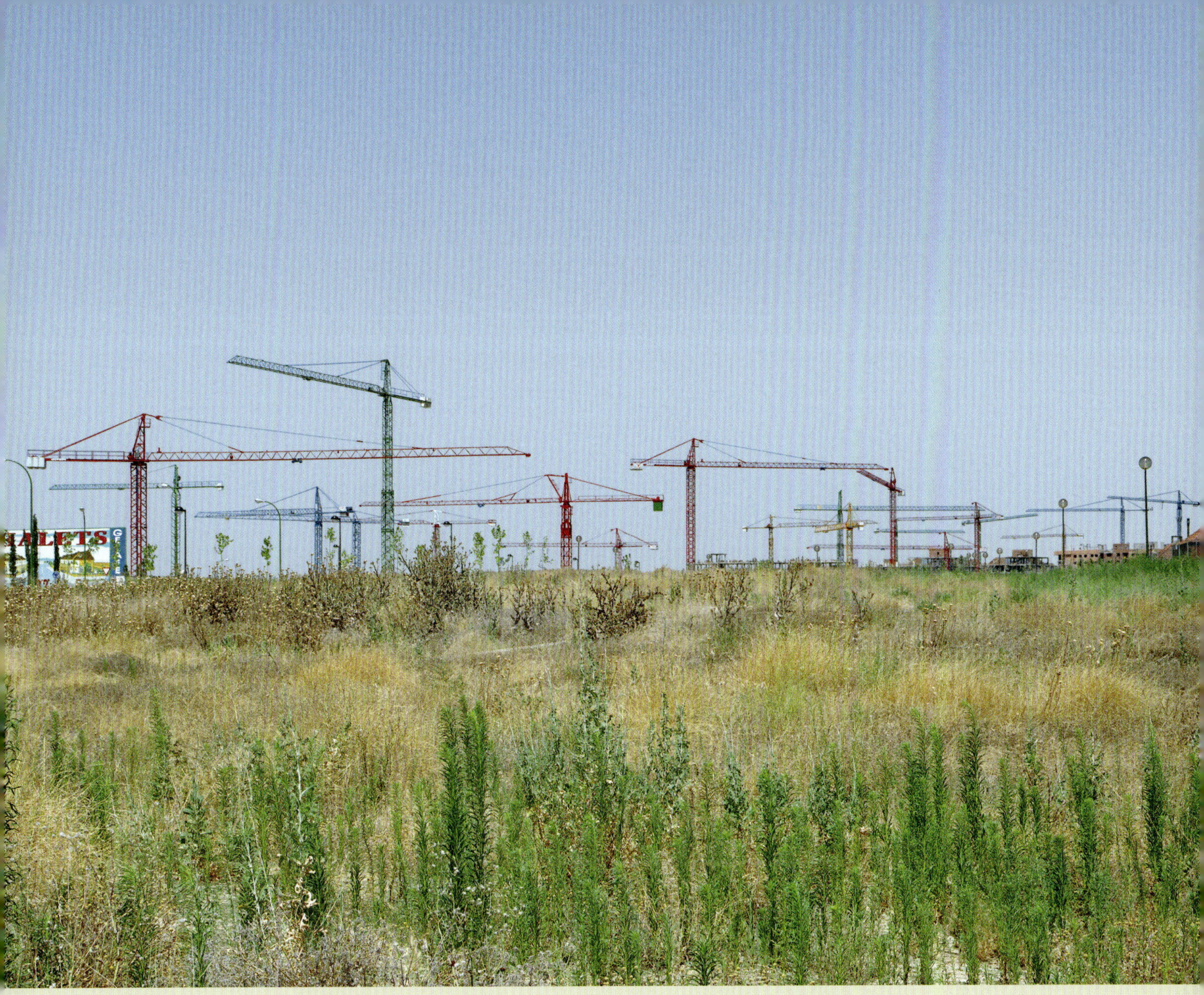

Édith
Roux

SCALO FARINI

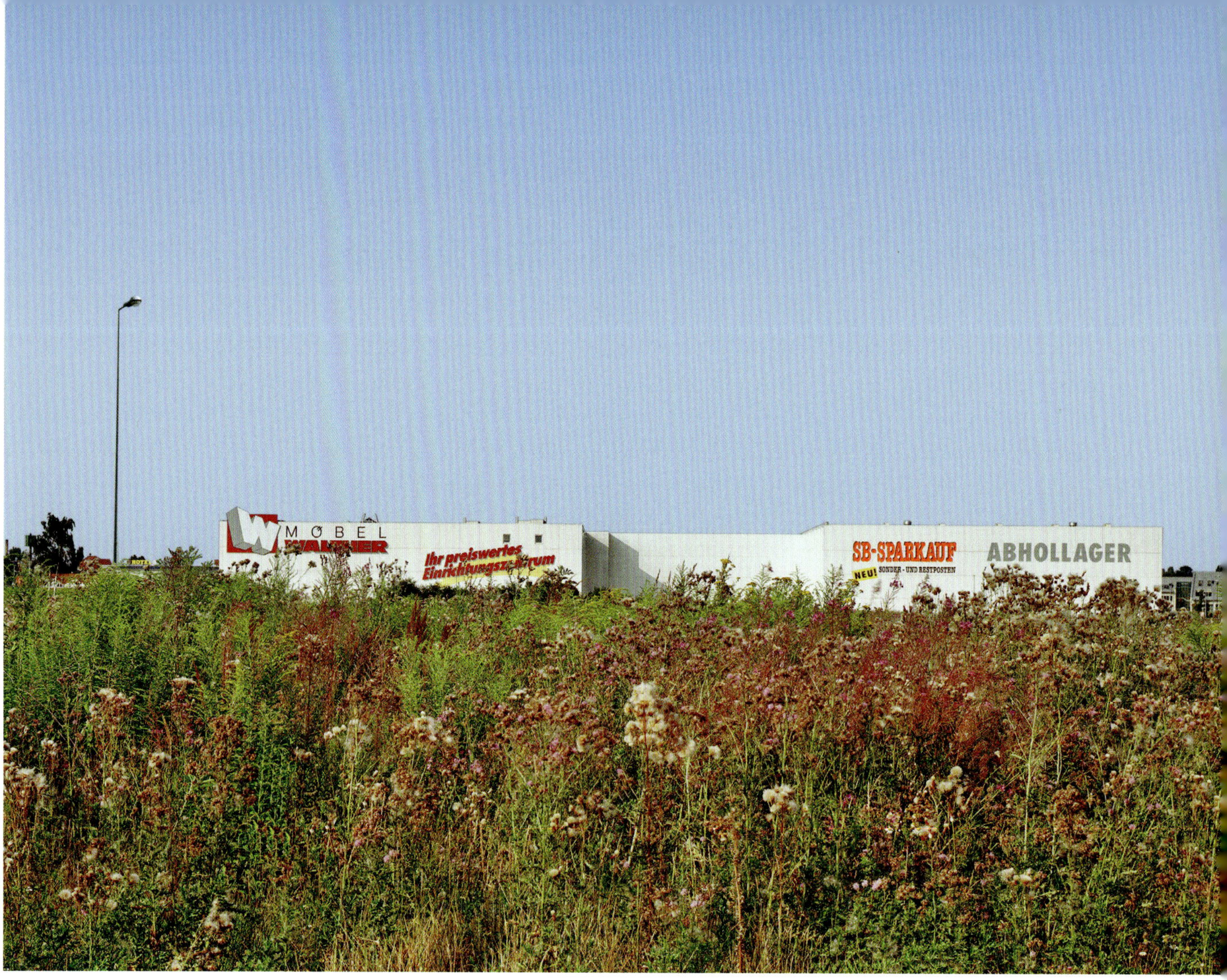
MØBEL
Ihr preiswertes
SB-SPARKAUF
NEU! SONDER - UND RESTPOSTEN
ABHOLLAGER

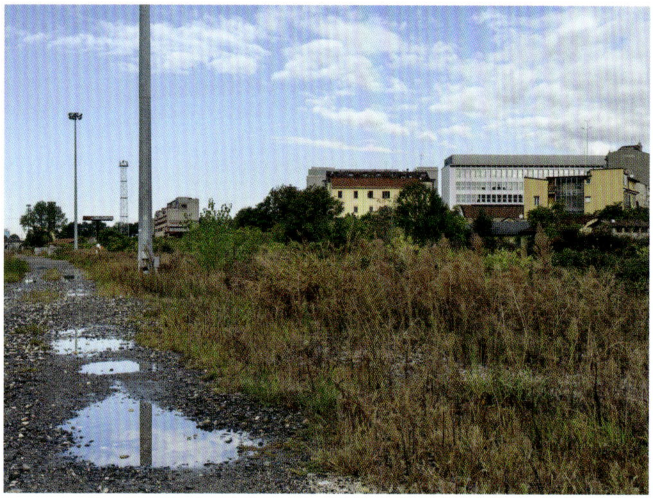

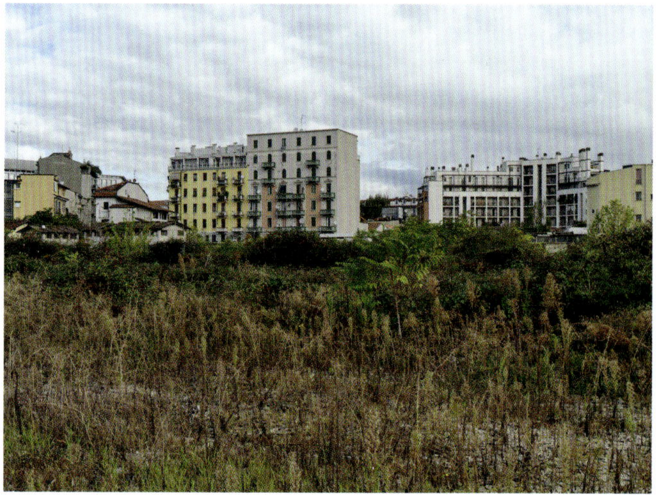

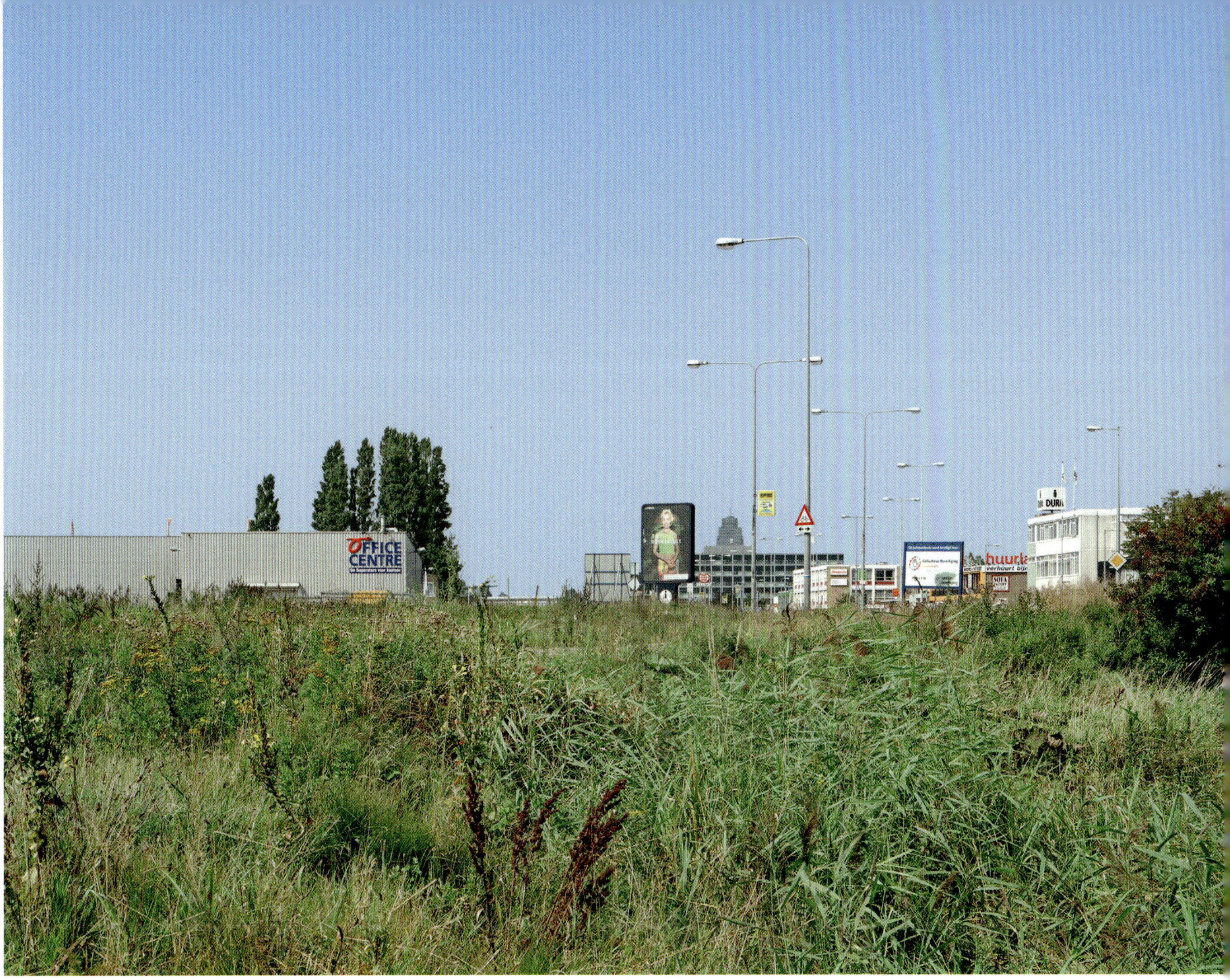
OFFICE
CENTRE

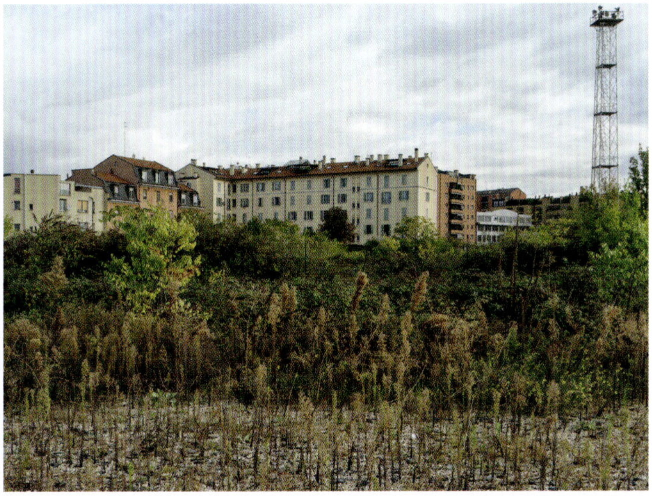

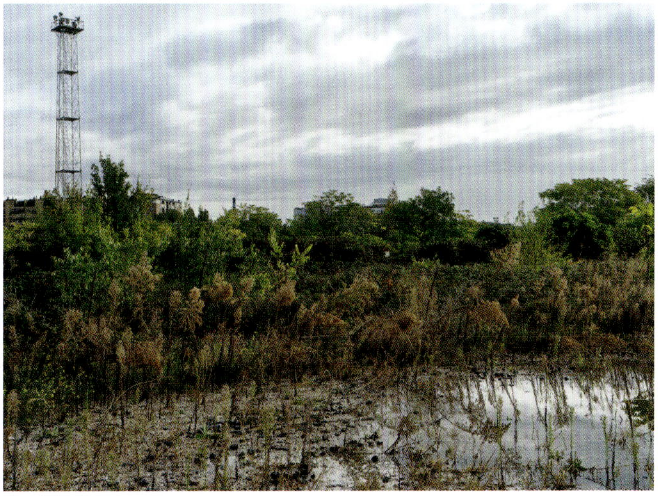

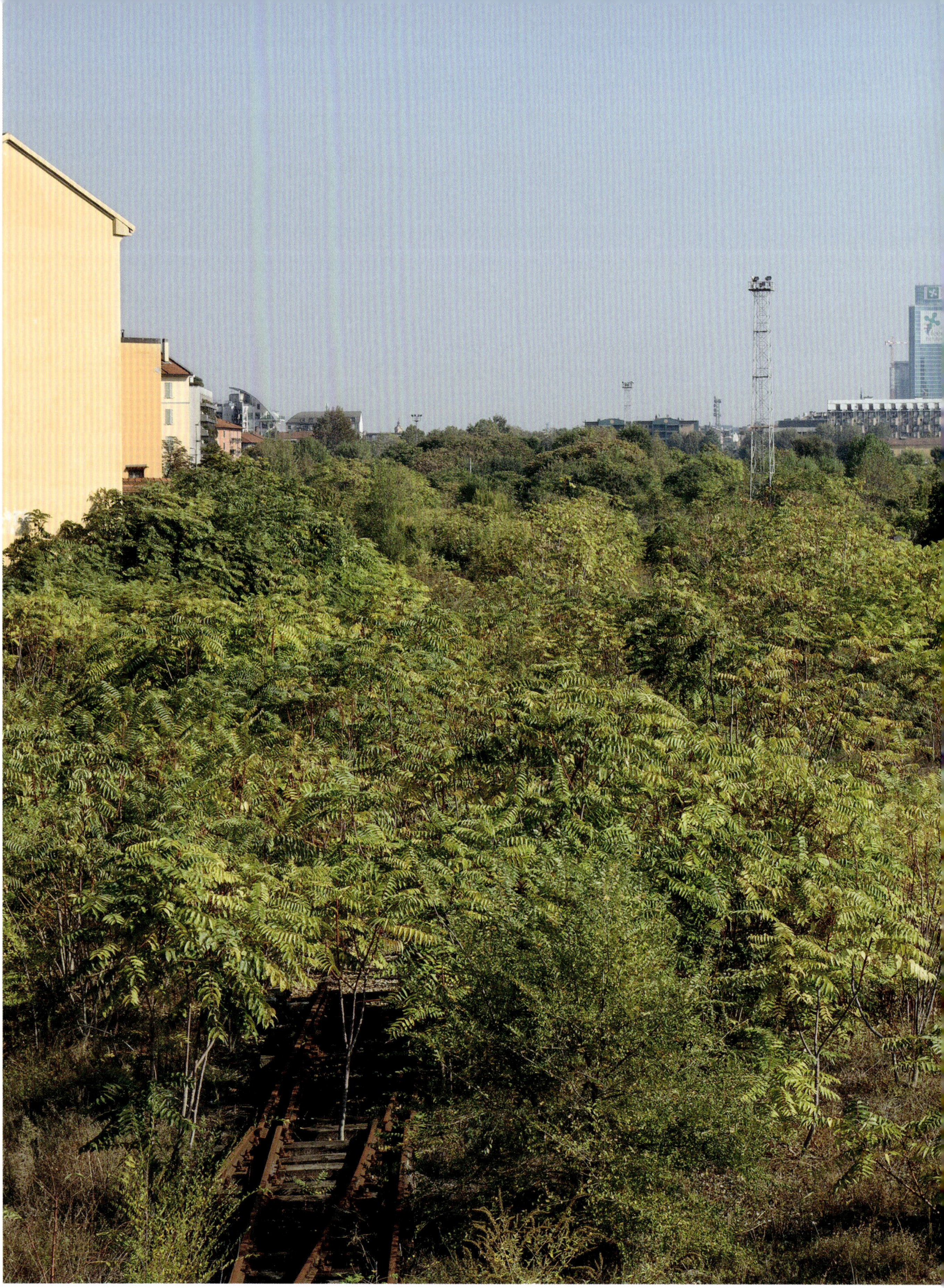

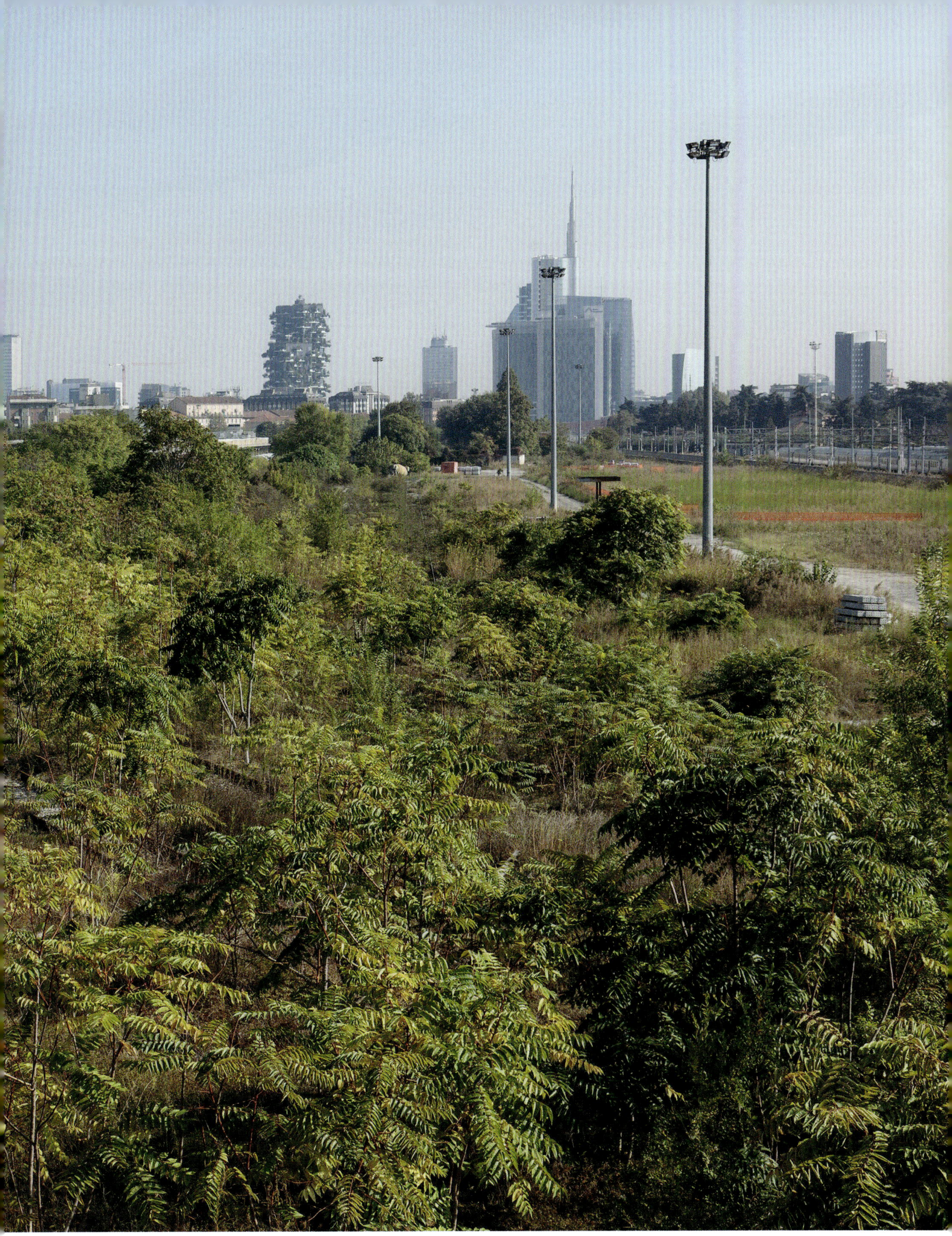

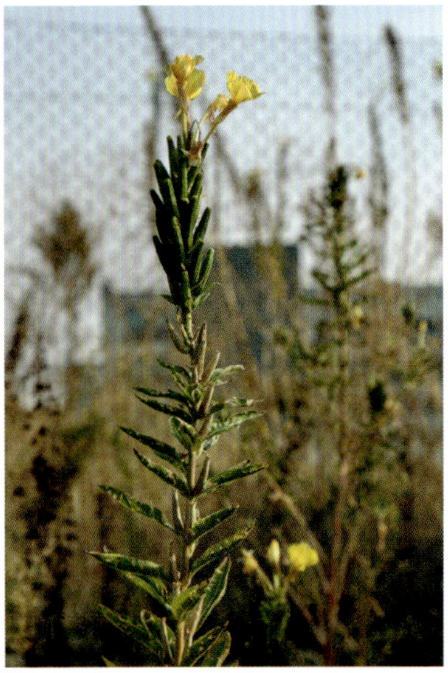
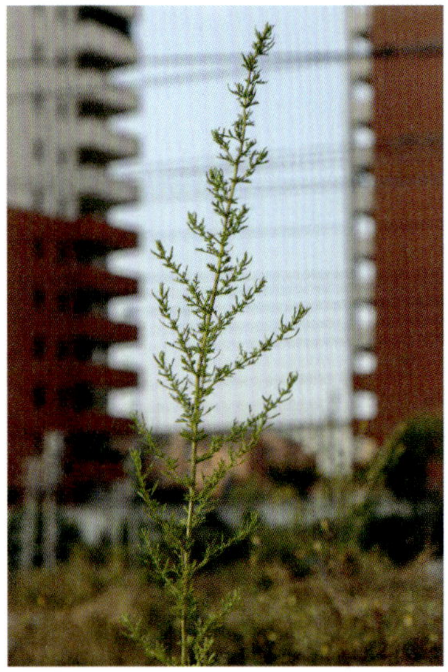
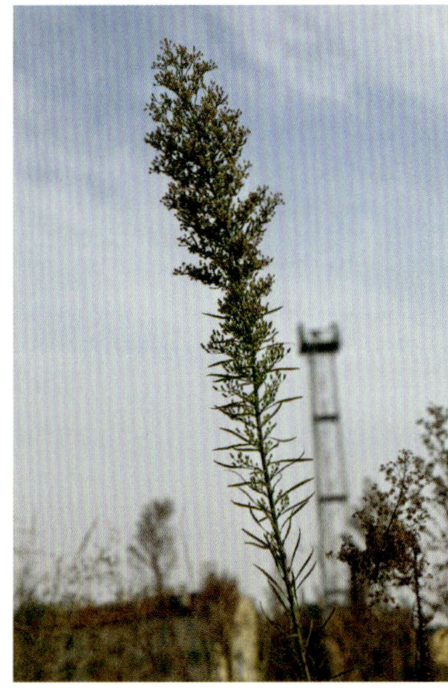
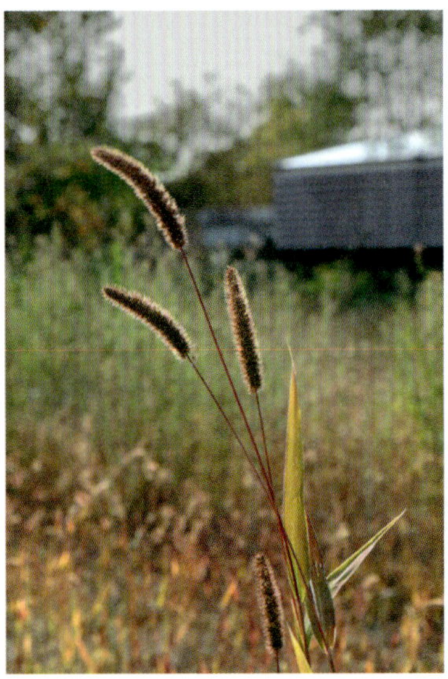
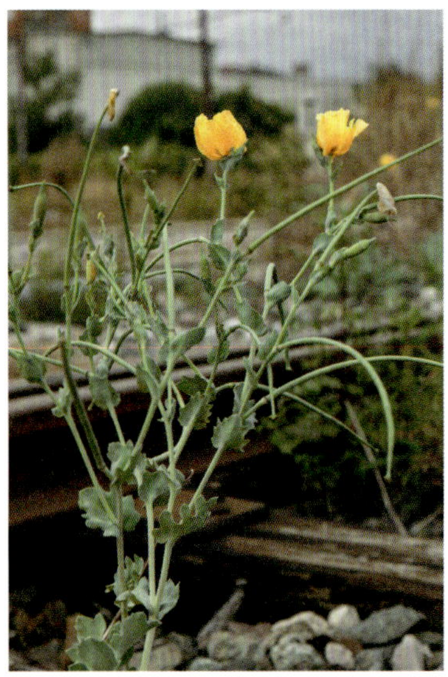
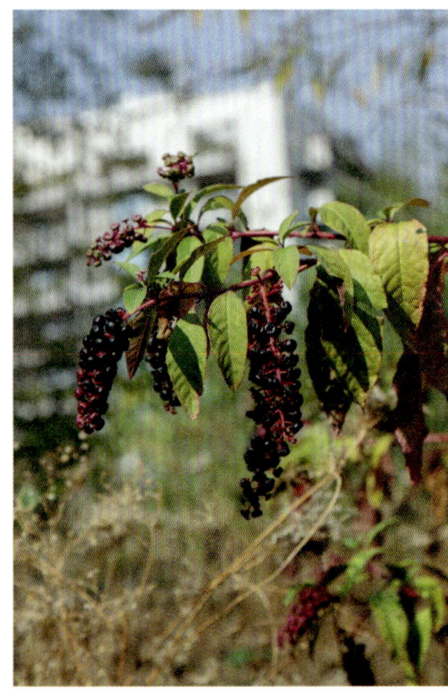
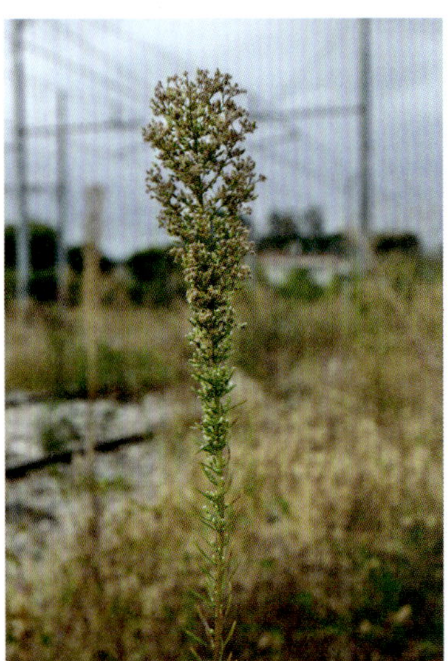
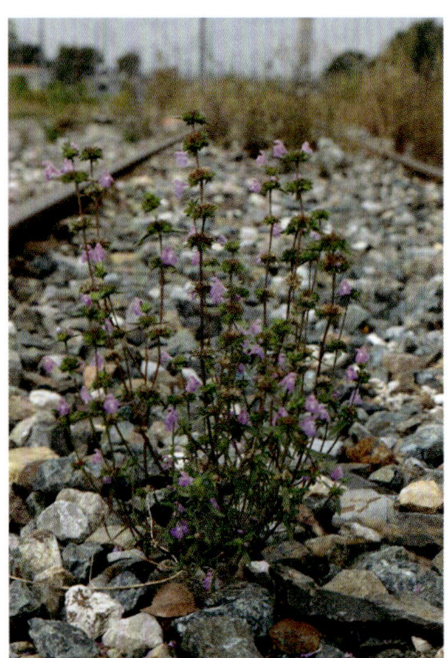
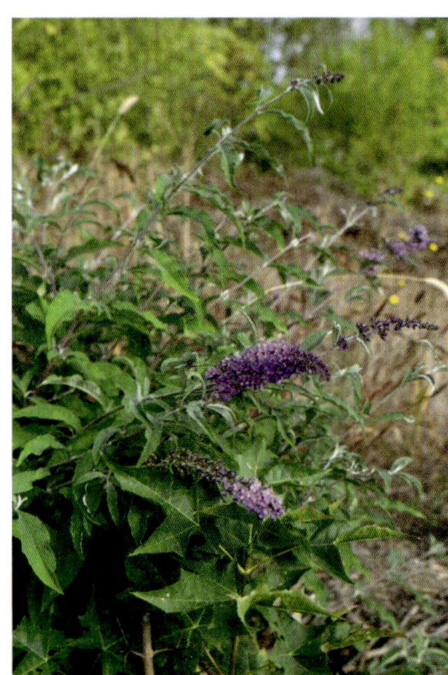

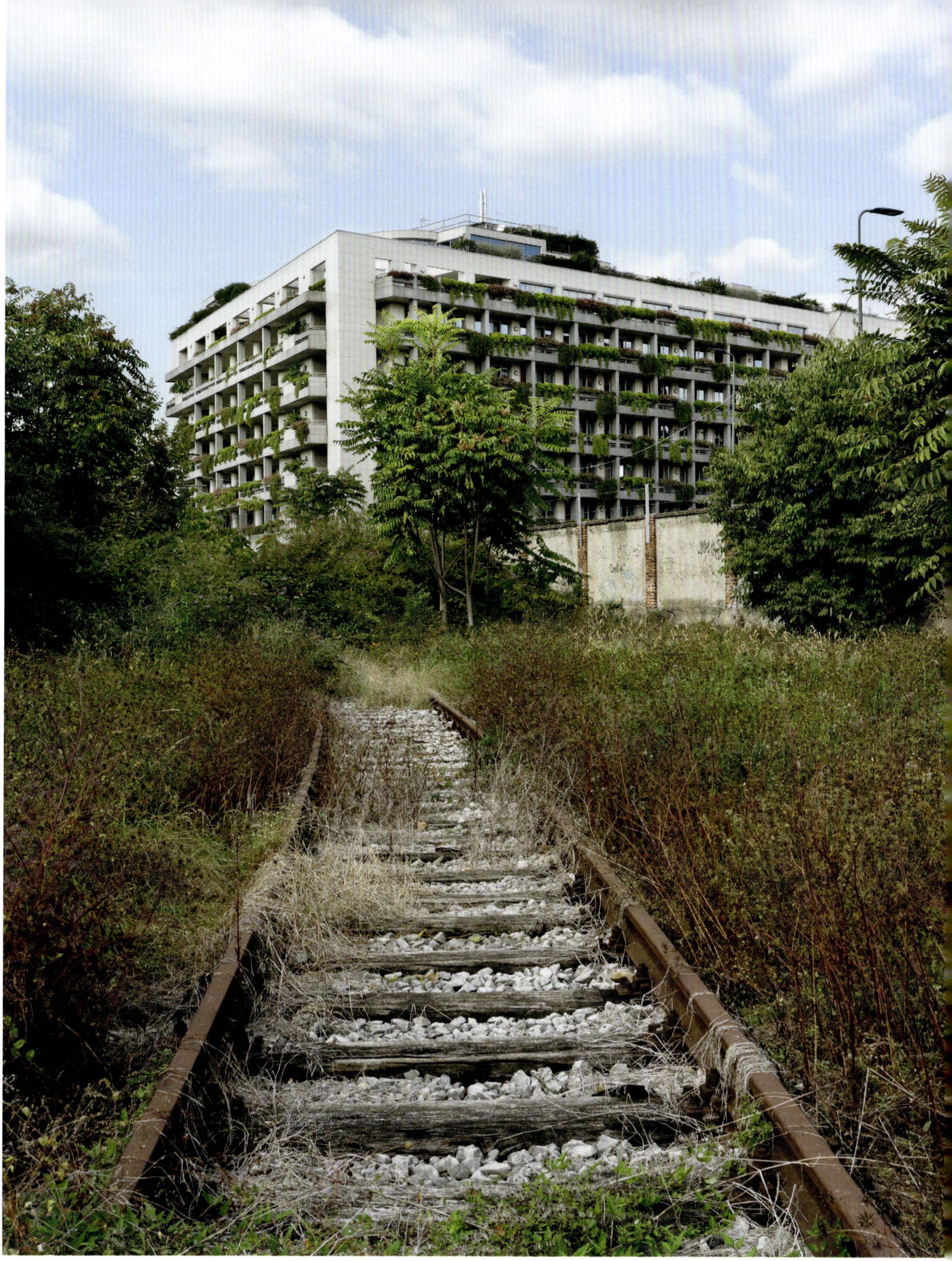

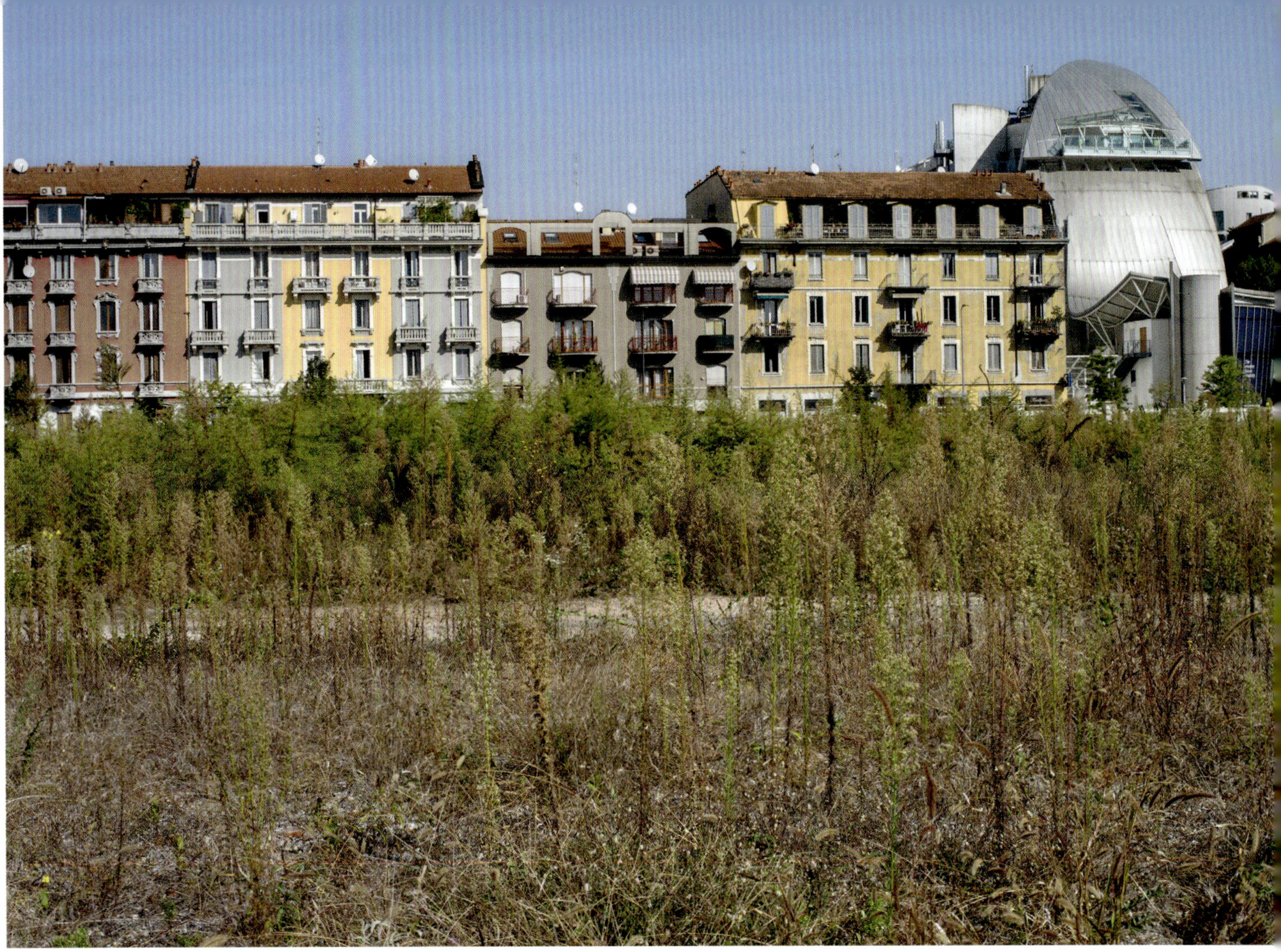

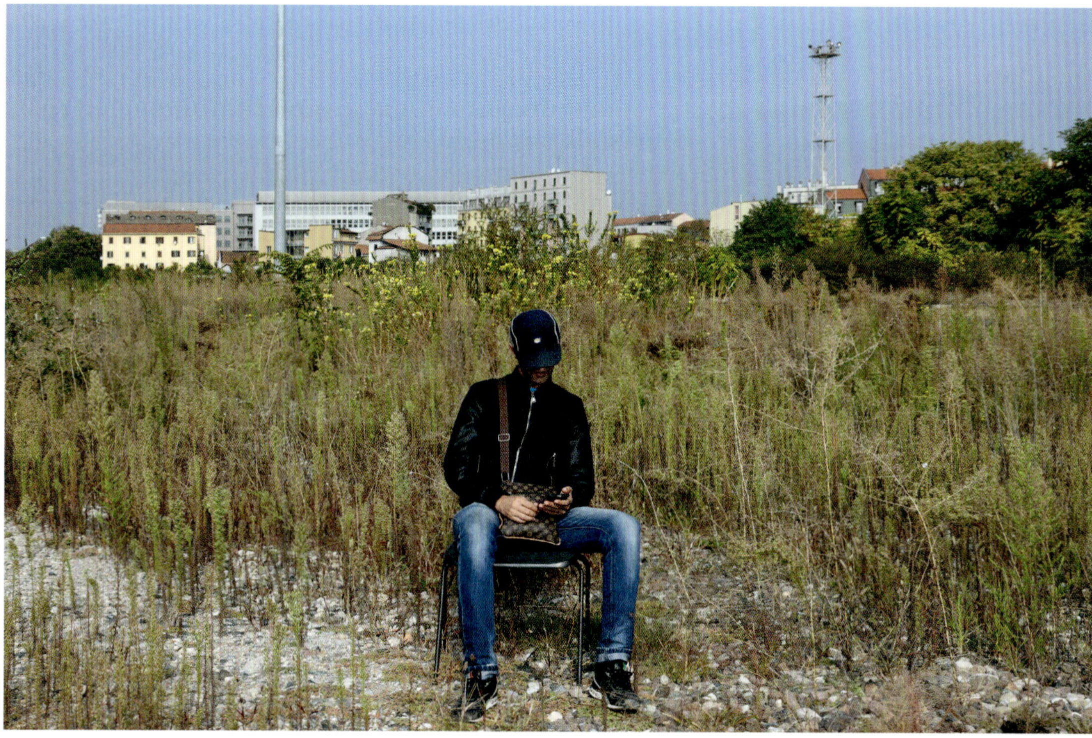

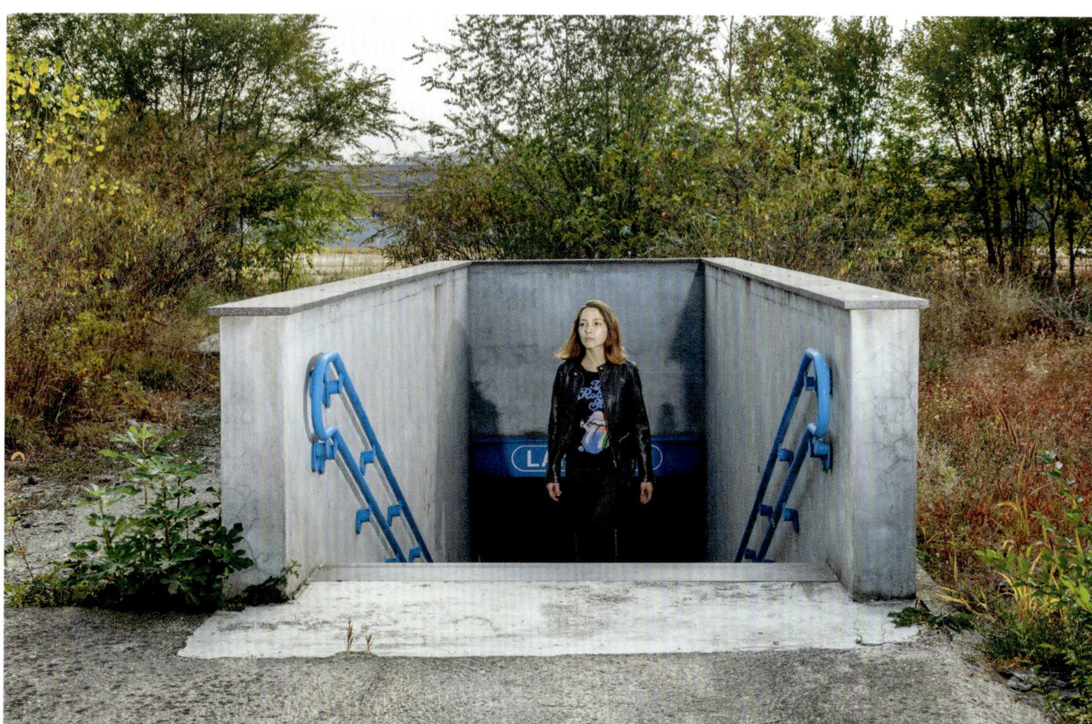

For more than half a century the countryside has been suffering from "hyper-landscaping", with its landscapes being forced to conform to our cultural representation of the rural environment. Although the illusion is sometimes preserved, with some village or small corner of countryside still being able to move us, it is now heavily subsidized, far less diverse and productive, and does not offer a way of living different from that of globalized urban life, the "rural community" being on the road to extinction.
Whilst this situation is especially keen in rural areas, circumstances differ closer to towns, where one encounters "the monster". Those who produce and/or experiment accept the fact that if they are to survive, they must integrate urban reality into their urban farming practices, their production and their distribution. Those who develop the land, design the interfaces, roadways and thoroughfares to allow the urban and the agricultural to exist side by side, have the task of inventing a new type of town that includes an element of rurality.
All of these situations lead to new ways of inhabiting space and, in so doing, create new landscapes. One of the objectives of the *Le principe de ruralité* project, which began in 2015, is to offer a representation of farming landscapes within the Paris conglomeration by examining all forms of production (intensive, family, associative, experimental, social, etc.) so as to document ways of producing, distributing or consuming, and to showcase new forms of rurality. These pictures are designed to become part of the task of bringing cultural representations up to date, this being the driving force behind our landscaping projects.

| P. 229 | Roof of the Aubervilliers Fashion Center, run by Topager, May 2017.
| P. 230 | Horse-drawn plowing, Association Clinamene, Université de Villetaneuse, April 2015.
| P. 231 | Organic Gardens for professional insertion, Association Aurore, Cité Basse in Sevran, June 2016.
| P. 232 | AgroParisTech's vegetable garden, Paris, 5th arr., July 2017.
| P. 233 | Association Clinamen's sheep, La Courneuve, July 2017.
| P. 234 | (top): Fruit and vegetable picking day at Viltain Farm, Jouy-en-Josas, October 2016.
| P. 234 | (bottom): Inhabitants cultivating a plot of land, Sartrouville, May 2015.
| P. 235 | Family gardens in Pantin-Aubervilliers, Cité des Courtillières, Pantin, November 2016.
| P. 236 | Kersanté farmlands, Saint-Denis, June 2016.
| P. 237 | Field of lettuce, chemin des Champs-Pirouys, Montesson, July 2015.

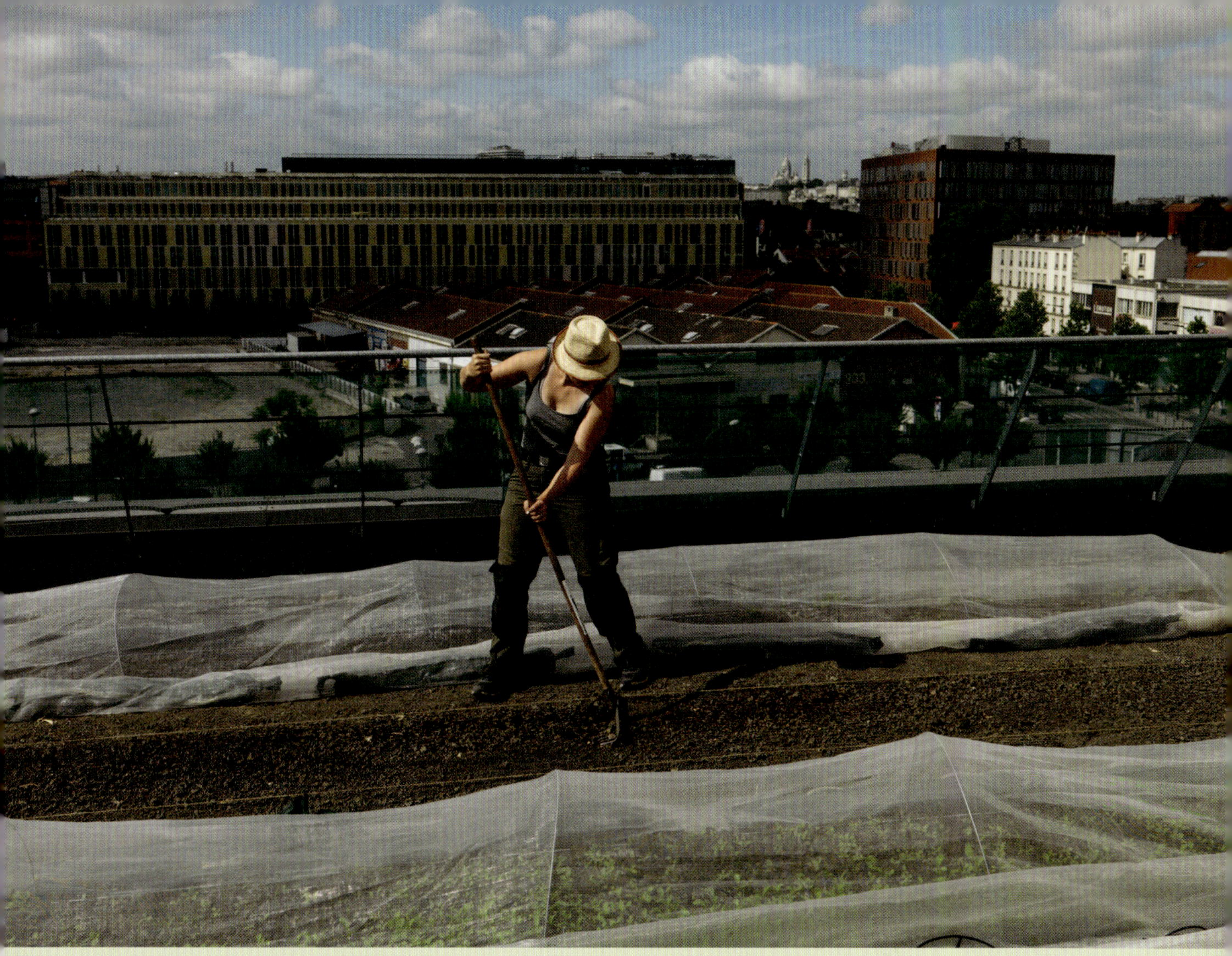

Geoffroy Mathieu

THE PRINCIPLE OF RURALITY

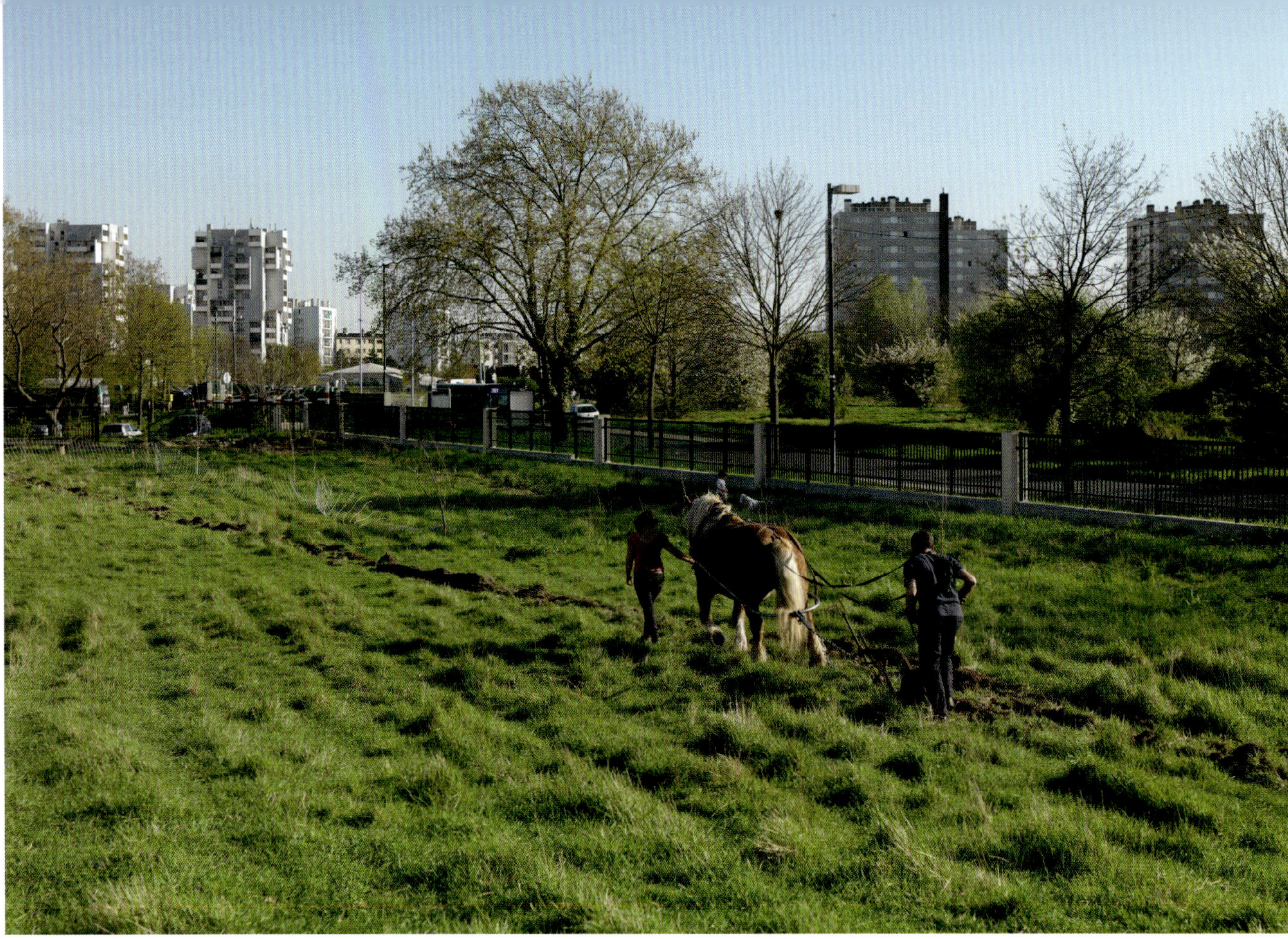

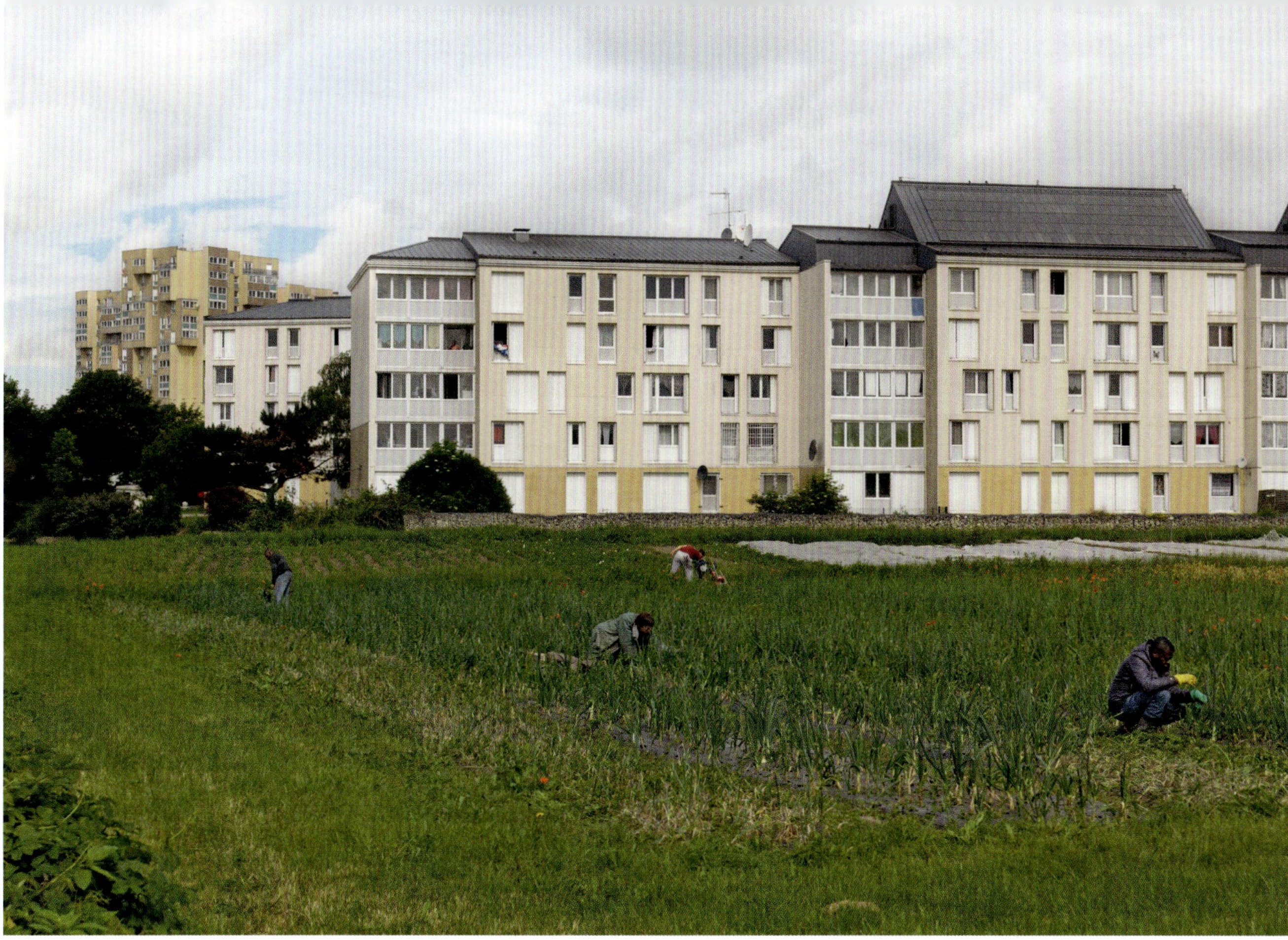

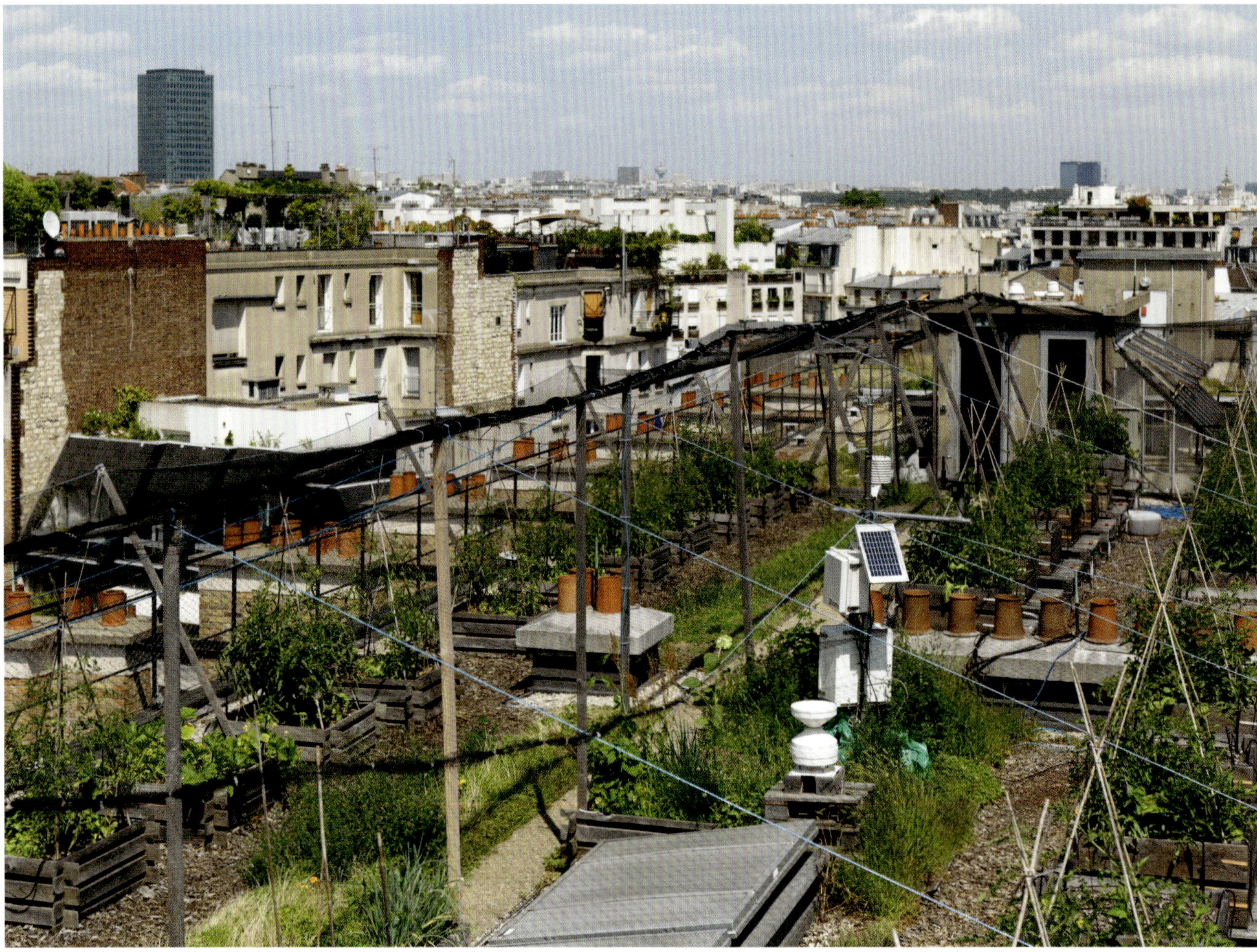

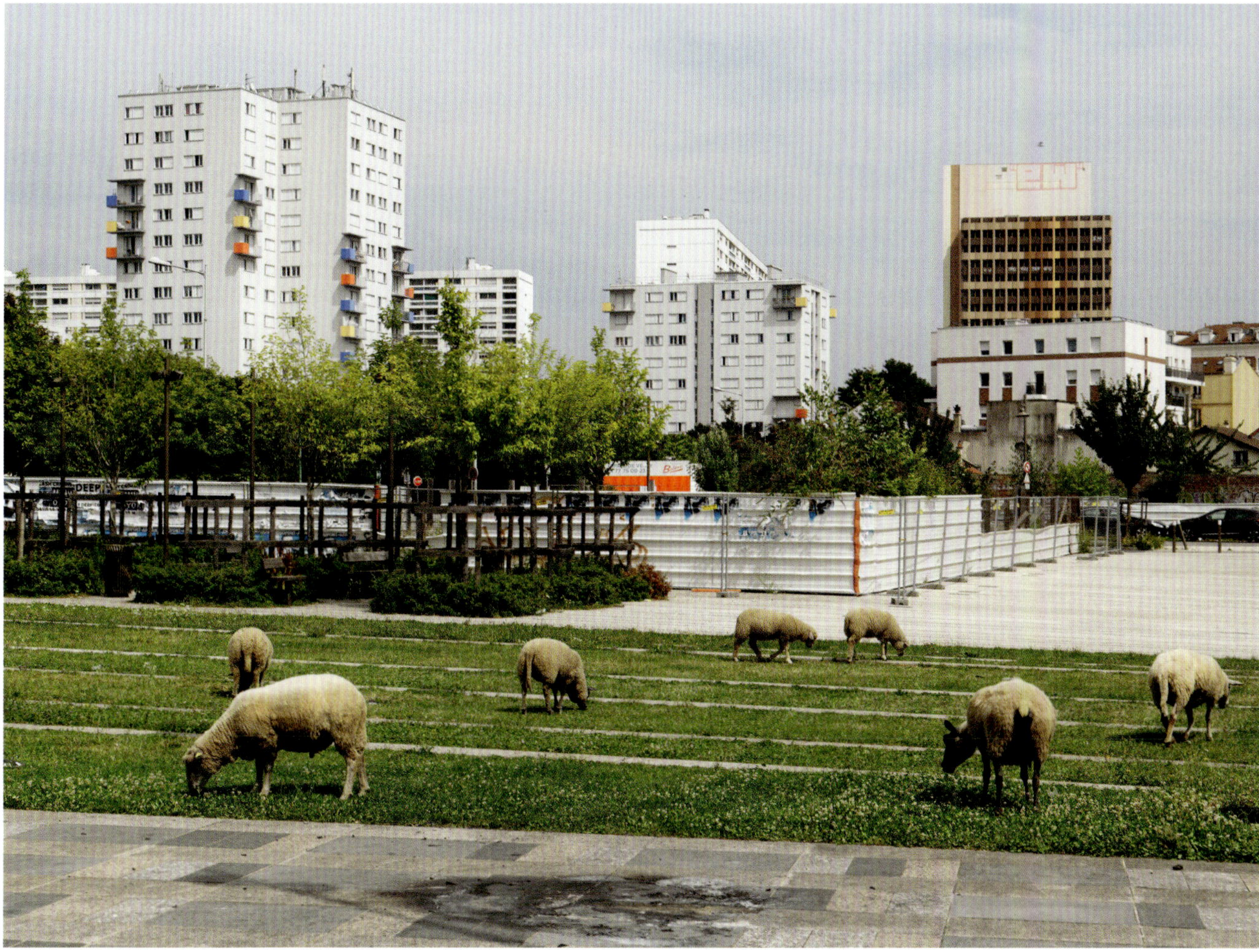

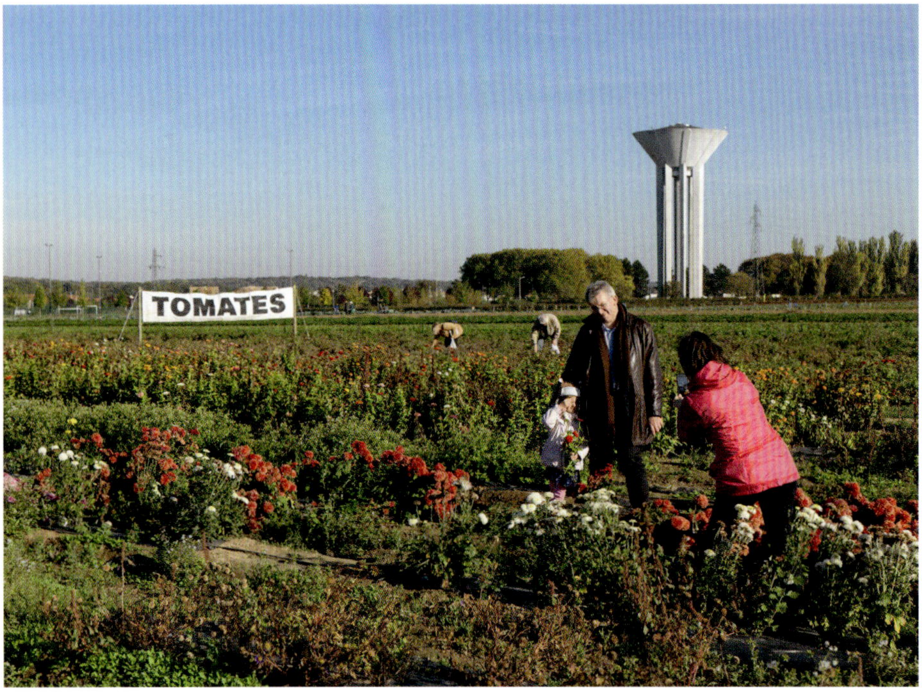
TOMATES

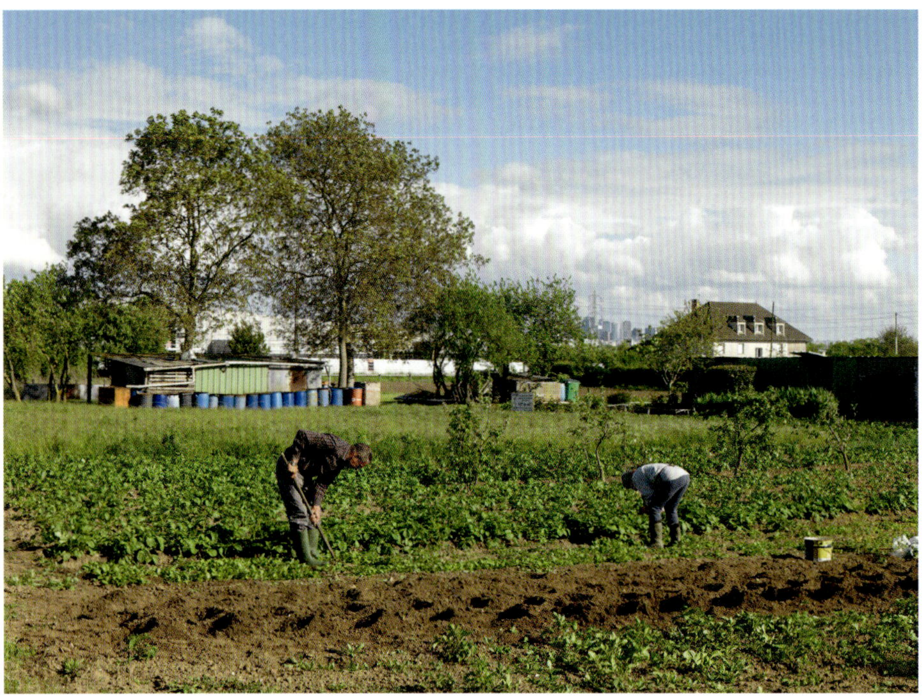

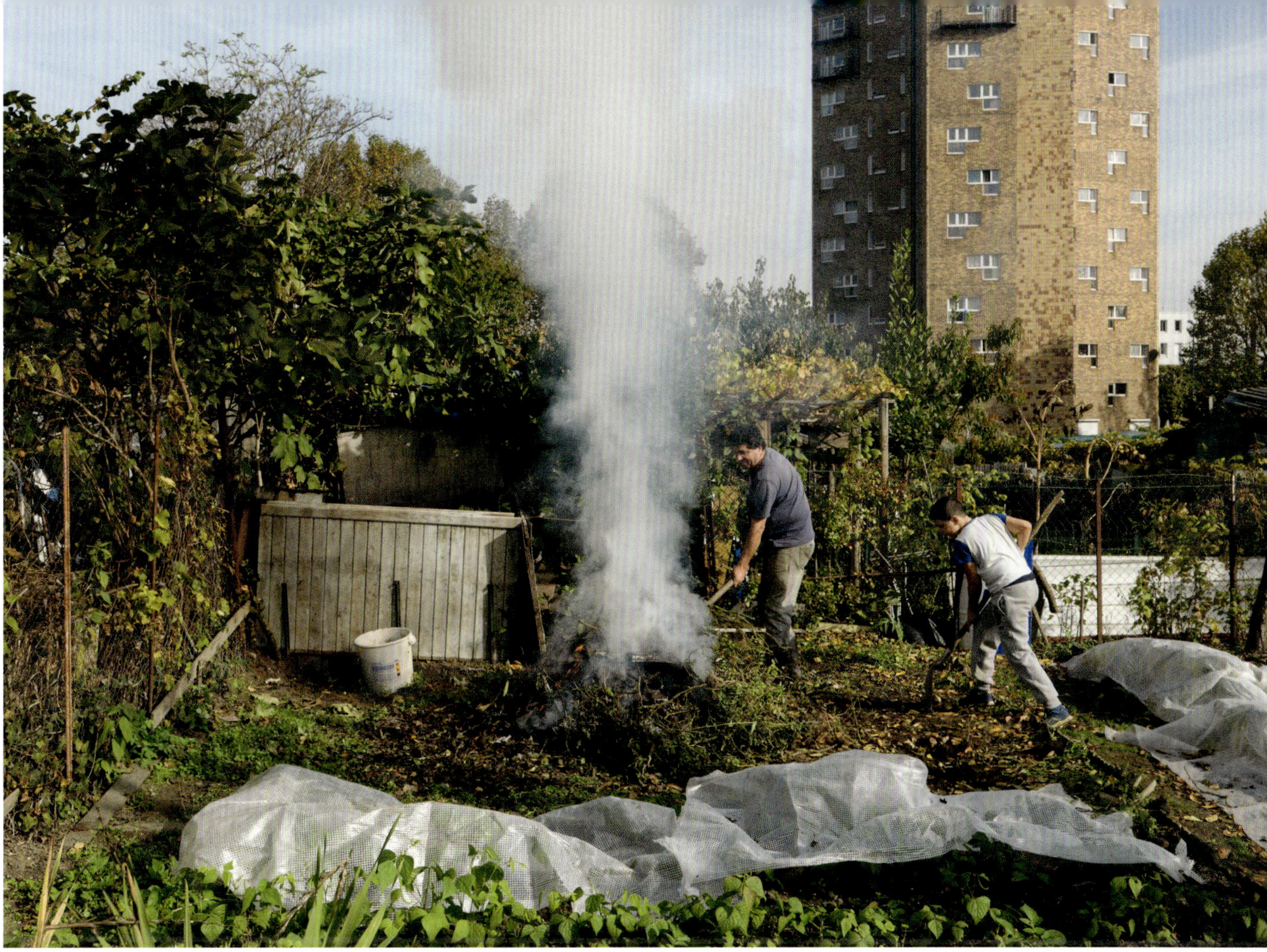

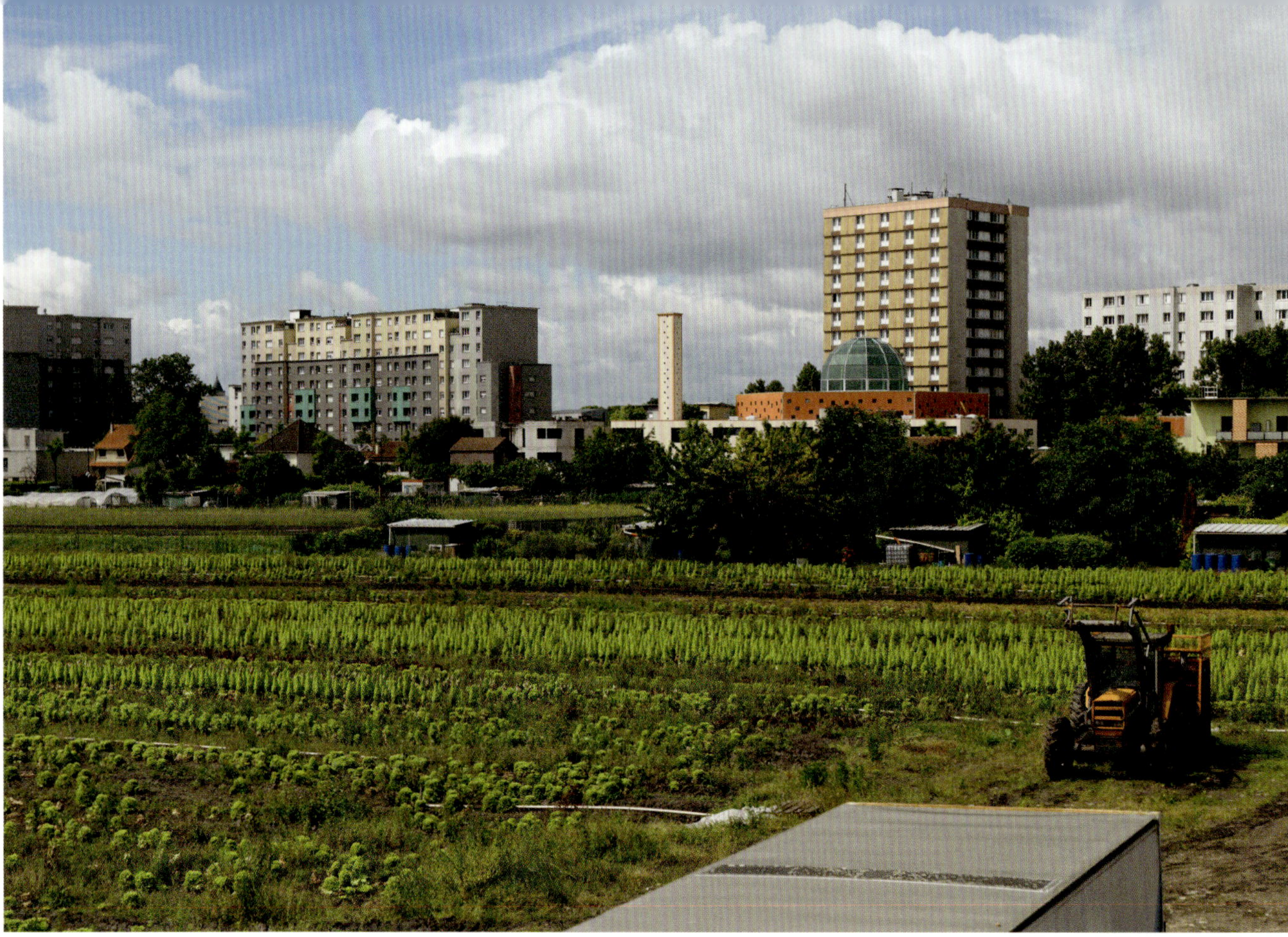

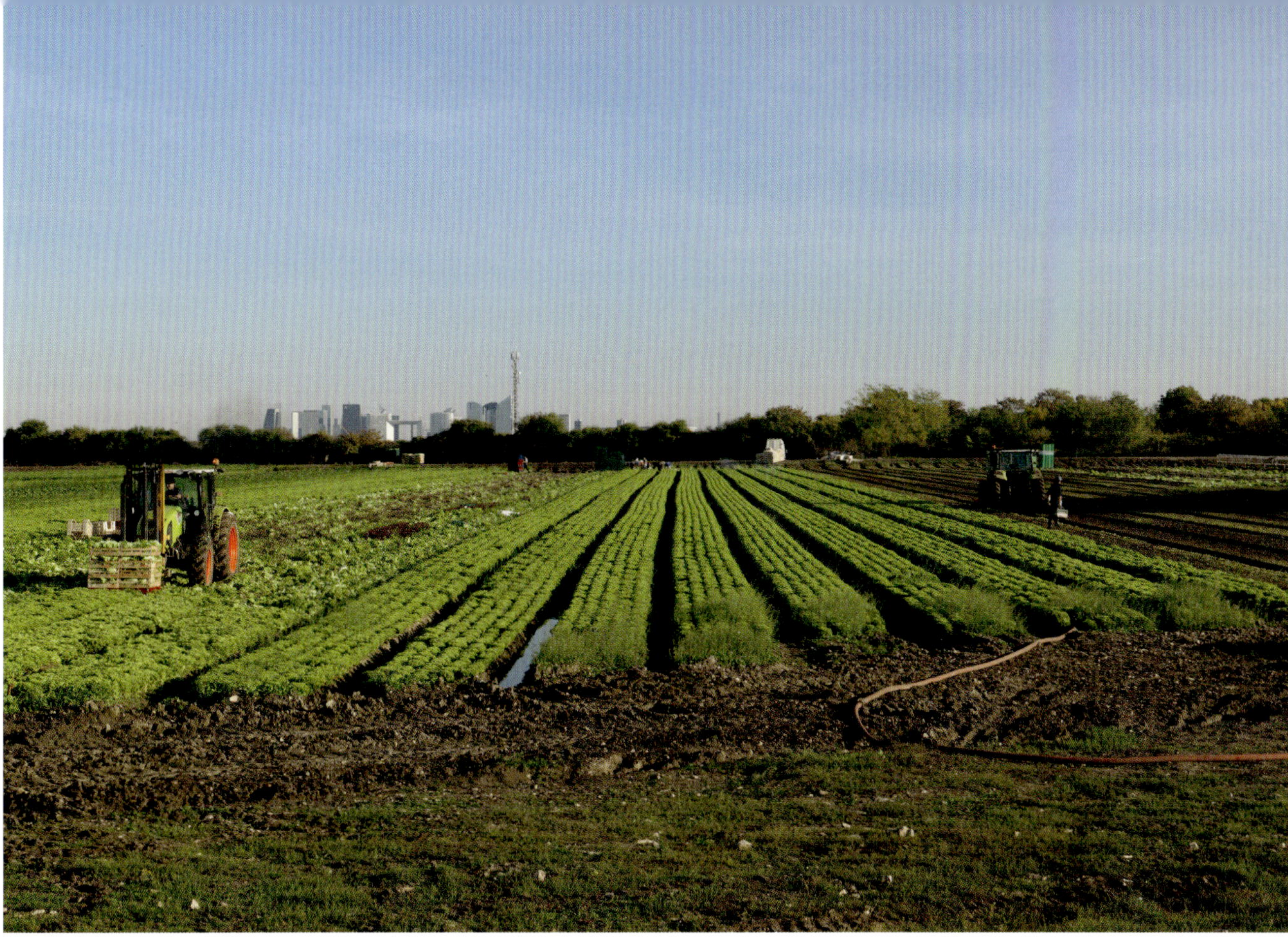

The *Rhodanie* documentary project began in an autonomous fashion, from a reflection on contemporary representations of unremarkable natural and man-made spaces. Here the river is seen as a place where one can quietly observe the encounter between nature and culture, the wild and the tamed. From its source to its mouth, and through the richness of the lands it traverses (towns, countryside, flat farmlands, natural reserves, etc.), it allows one to consider the various questions and delicate balances that exist between these two extremities.

Given that we are more familiar with photographic journeys through peri-urban spaces, the decision to begin with a visual exploration of peri-fluvial territories proved to be a useful way of revealing the different levels of interpretation of landscape and of its mutations: cultural (mythologies, local stories and preexisting visual representations), physical landscaping, political or economic issues.

The encounter with projects to transform the landscape can also be seen in the various reappropriations of use observed within the photographs. Among other things, they highlight several forms of resilience proper to natural milieus and to those who use these riverbanks, following specific events or accidents (floods, drownings, dam construction, dike building, etc.).

With the *Rhodanie* project, we find this dual notion, that of portraying these landscapes and their related practices, and of understanding and representing them in an attempt to show how the seeing is organized*.

* See *Rhodanie*, bilingual monograph, Actes Sud, Arles, 2015, 160 p., and *Rhodanie, paysages déclassés, de Pont-Saint-Esprit à la mer Méditerranée*, Éditions 205, Lyon, 2013.

| P. 239 | Décines-Charpieux, the Jonage canal at Le Grand Large, the Herbens spillway and the canal towpath, 2009.
| P. 240 | Alps, Saint-Gotthard Massif, Rhône Glacier, 2013.
| P. 241 | Leuk, ring road, cross and belvedere overlooking Finges forest, 2013.
| P. 242 | Bollène, Donzère-Mondragon diversion canal, Lez spillway, 2011.
| P. 243 | Île de la Barthelasse north of Avignon, Parc des Libertés. Backwater following hydroelectric development work, 2011.
| P. 244 | Codolet, flood protection dikes, cofferdam and drainage pumps, 2011.
| P. 245 | Arles, Ségonnaux, sheds and homes built between river and dikes, 2011.

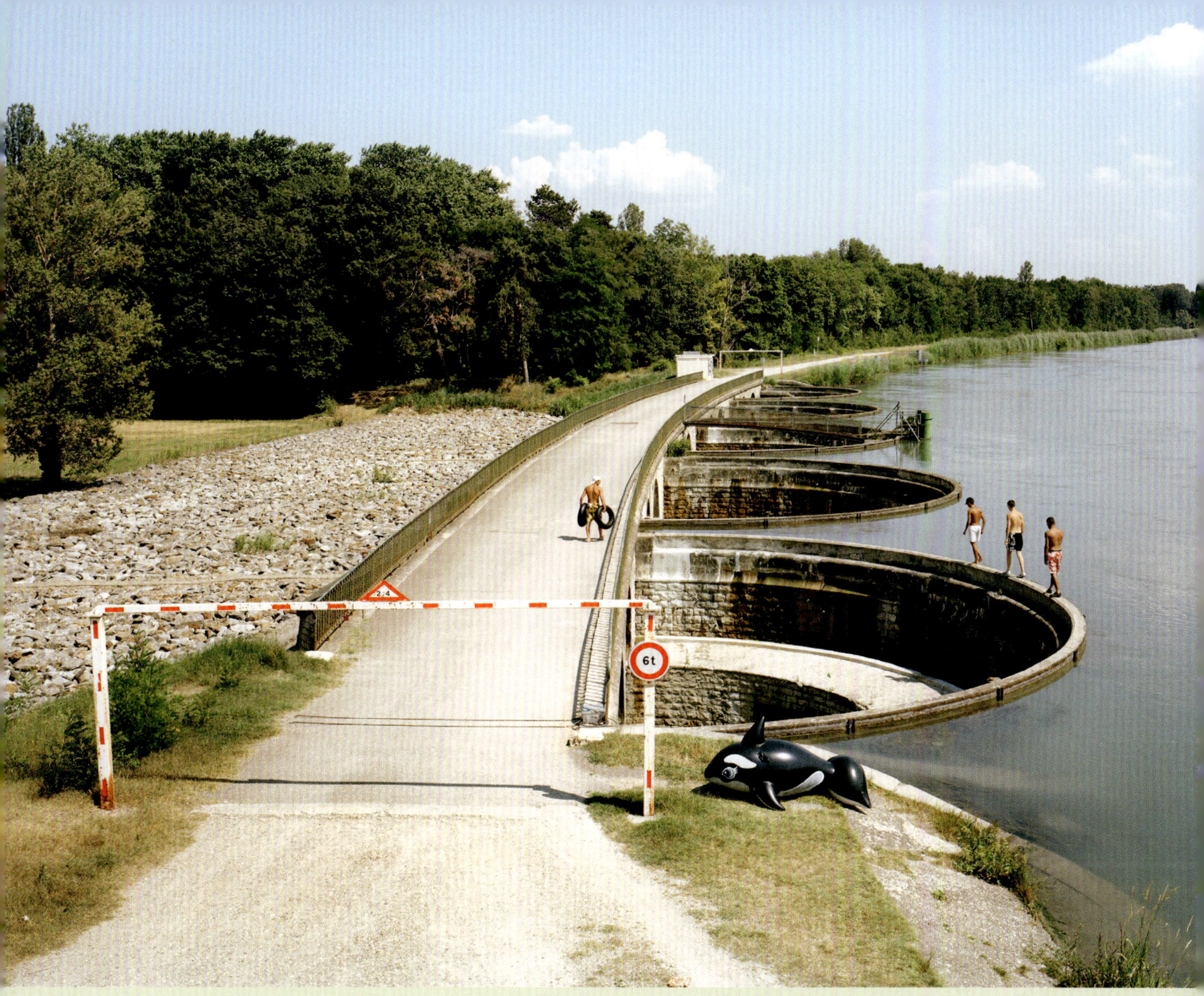

Bertrand Stofleth

RHODANIE

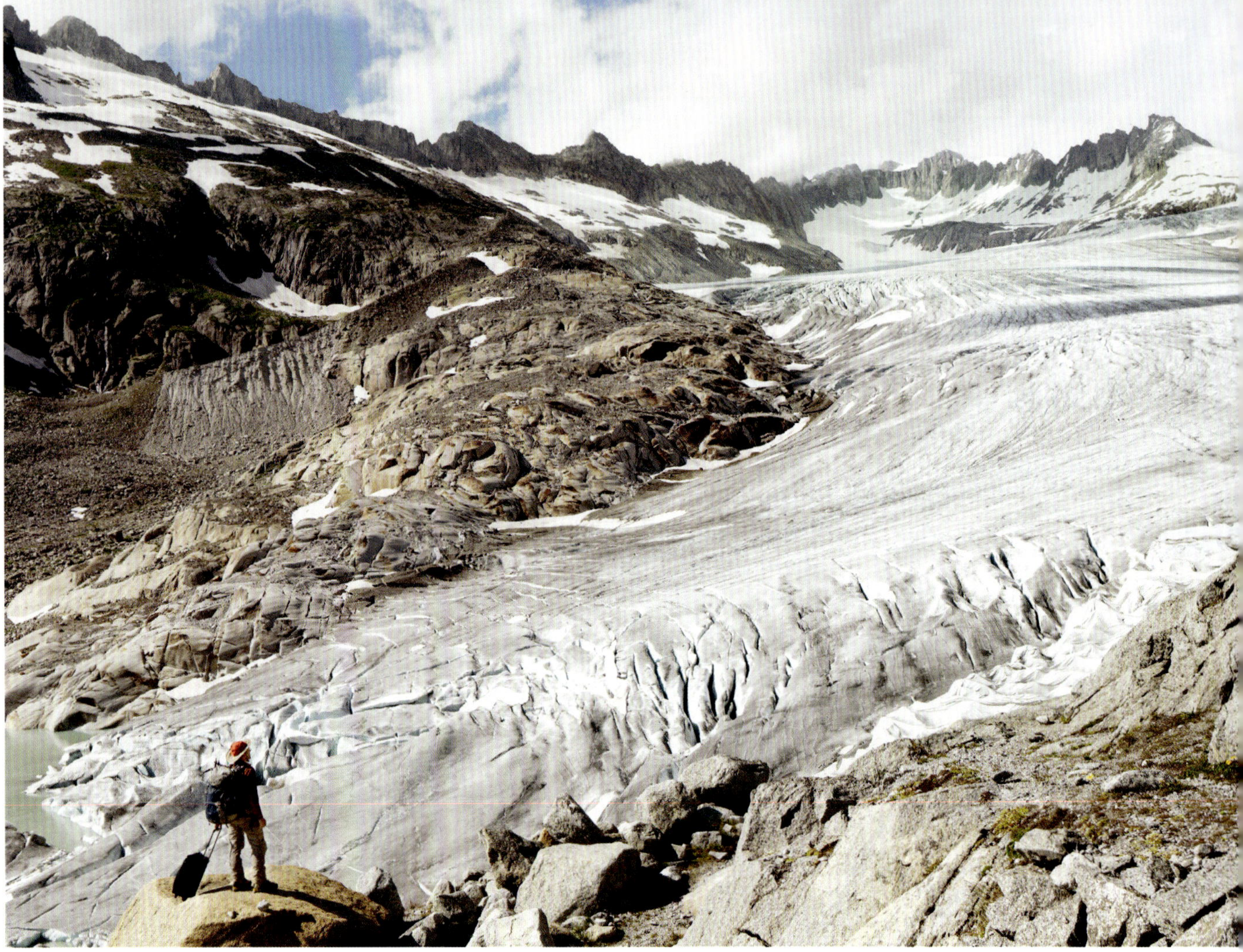

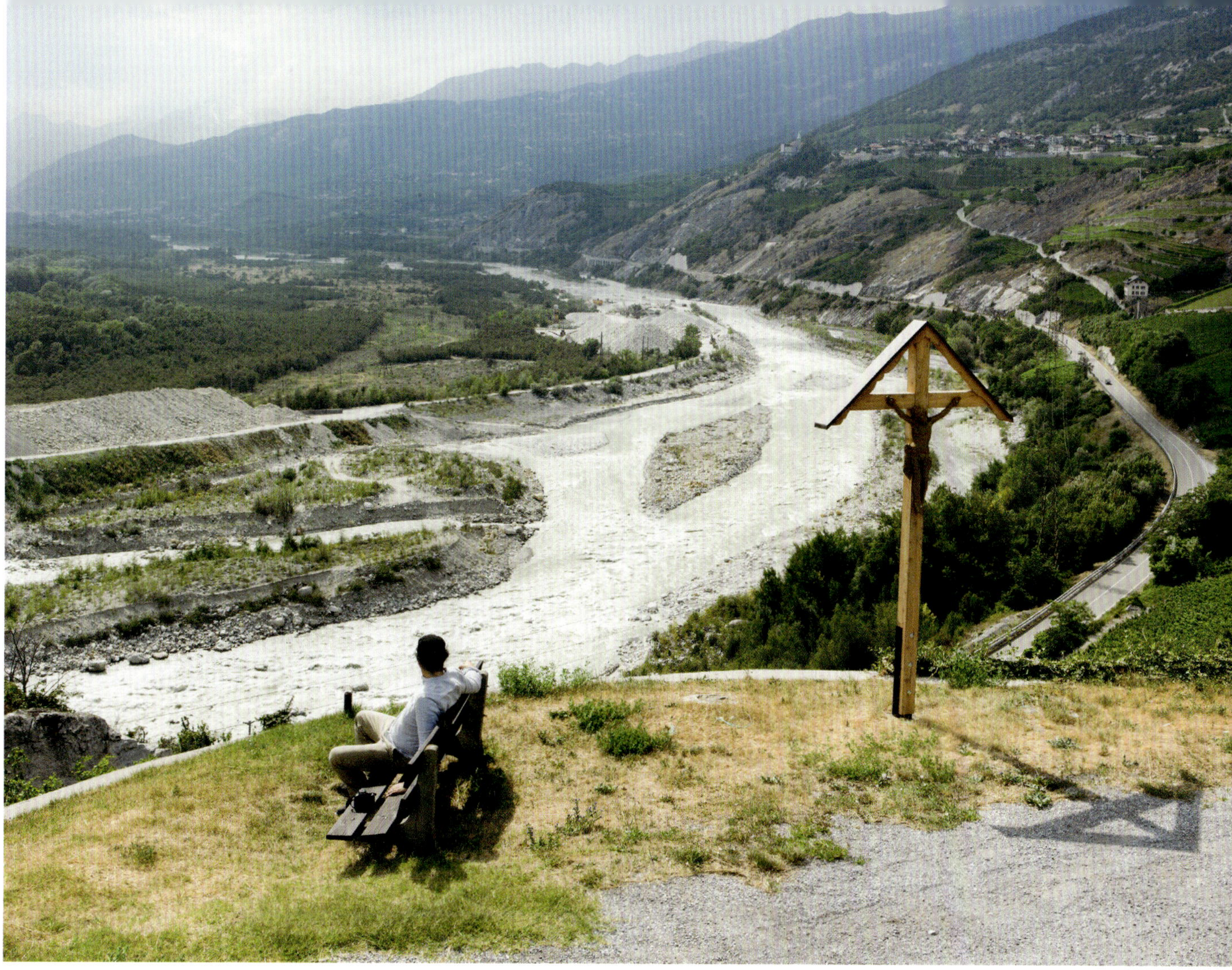

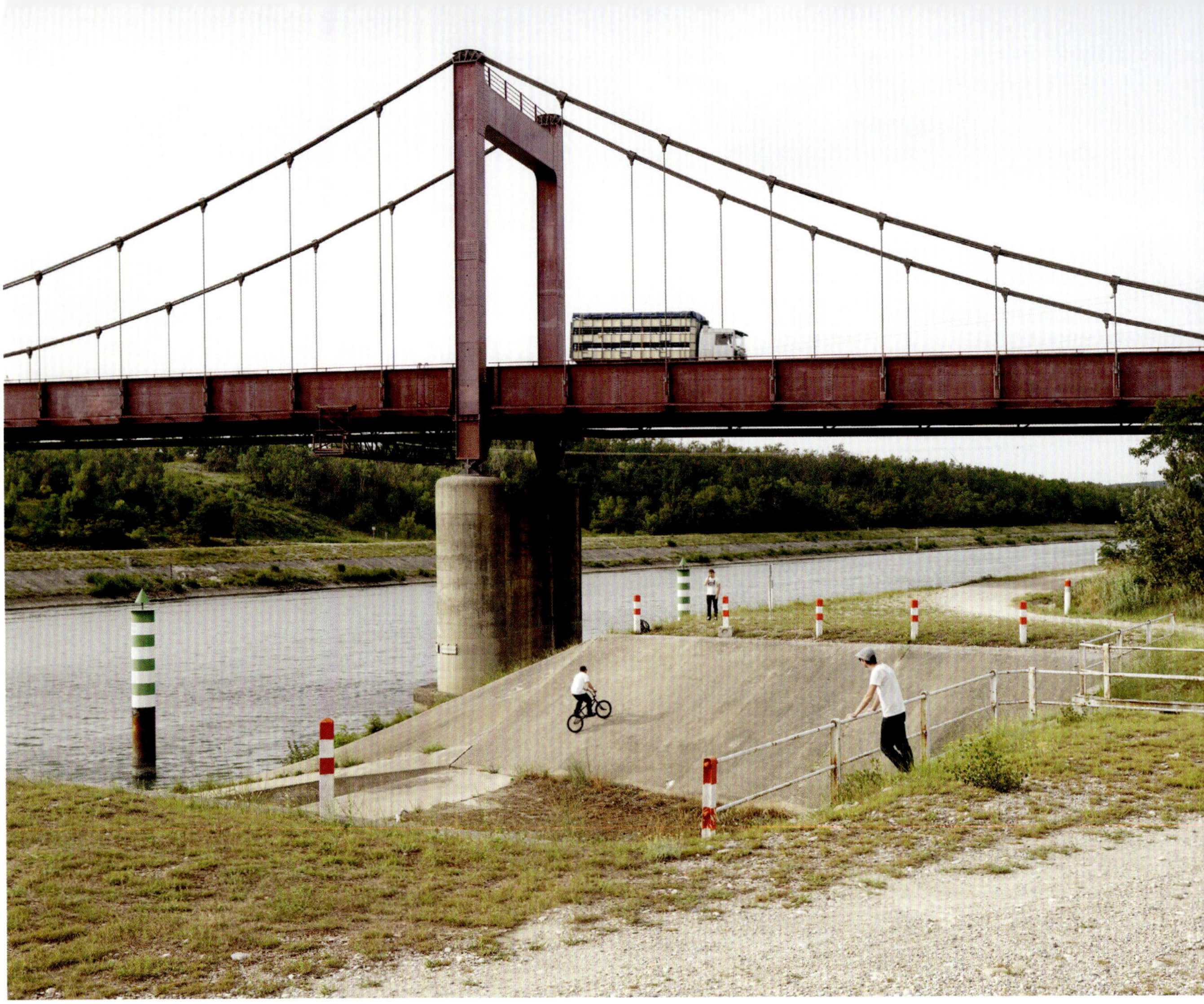

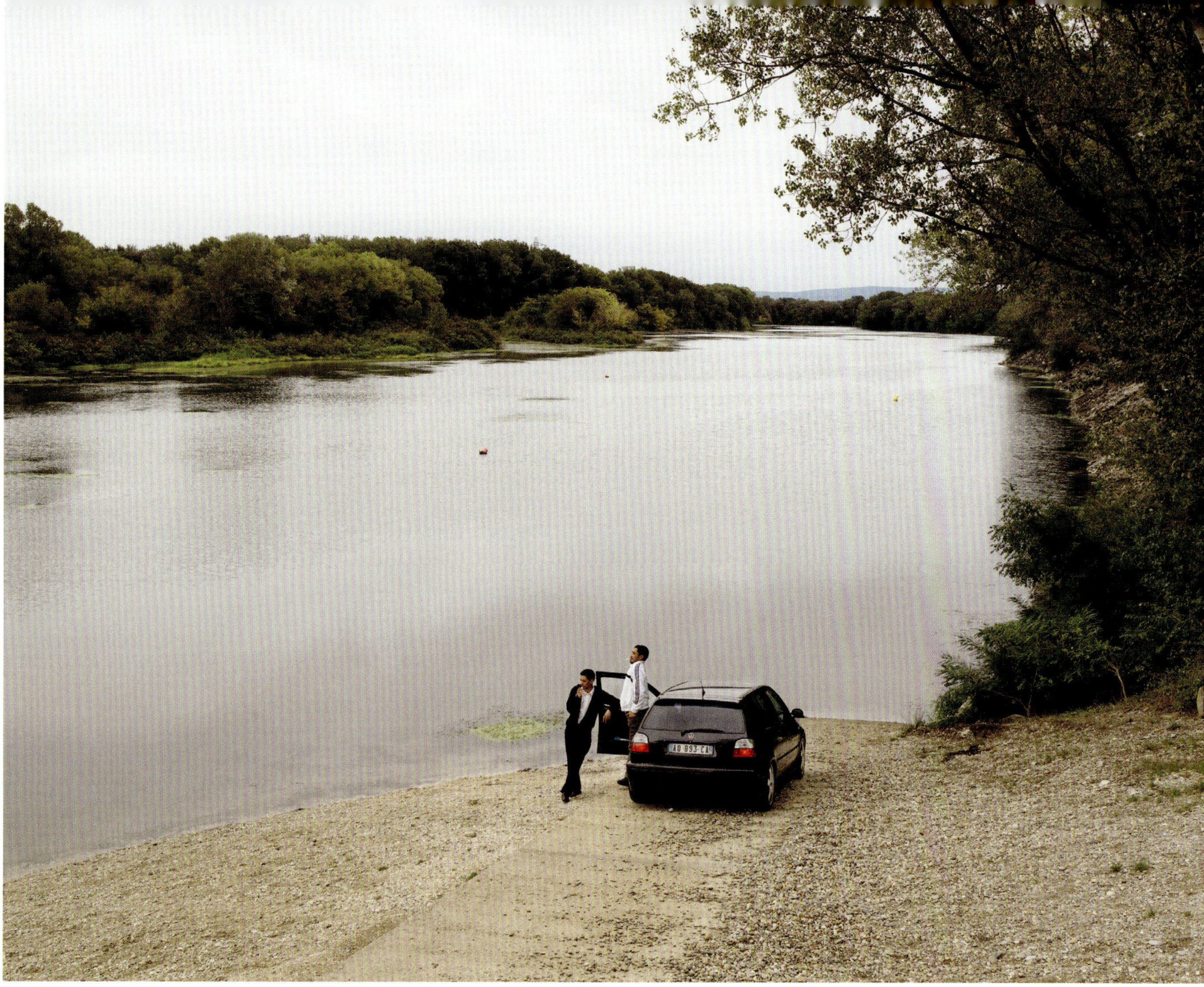

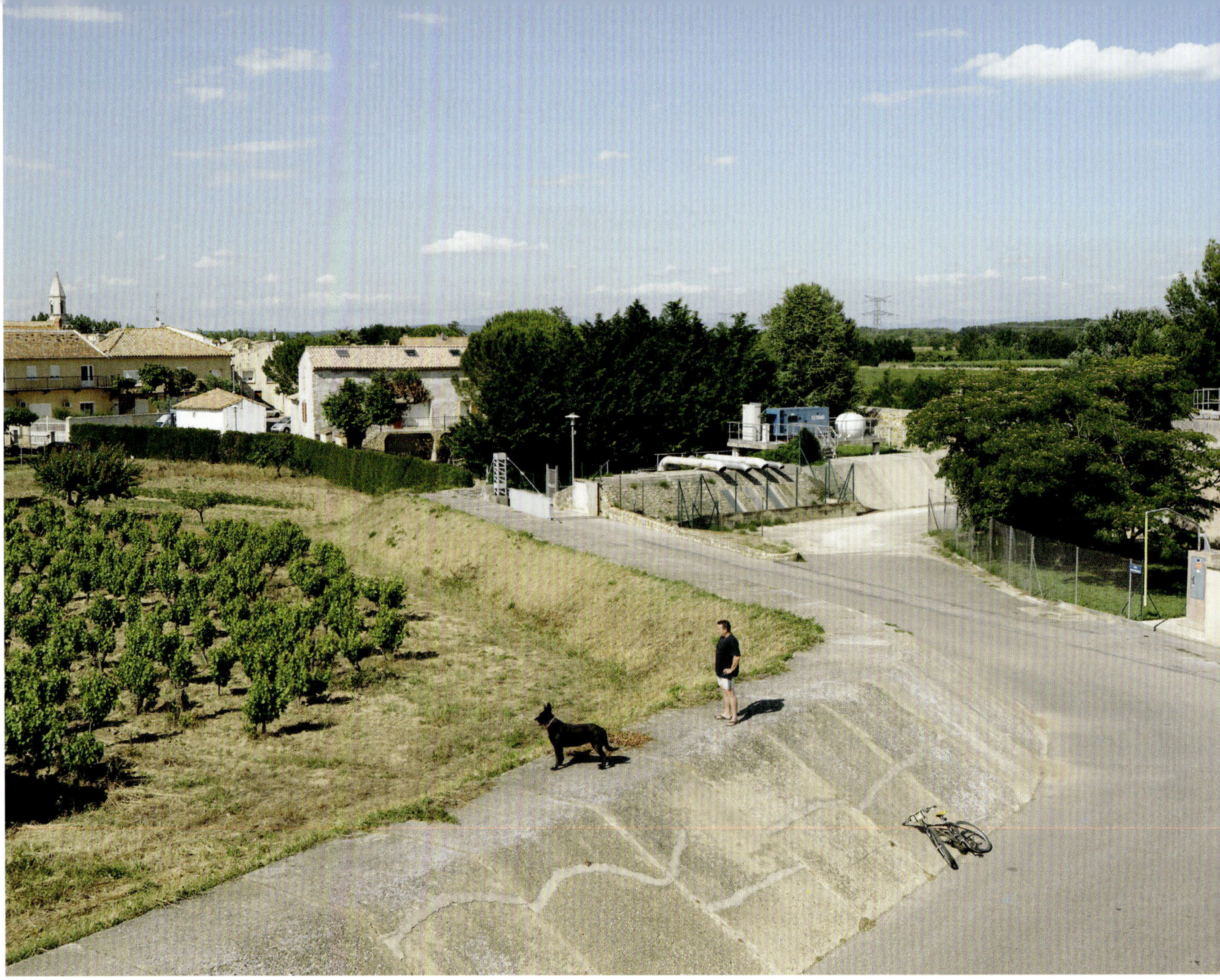

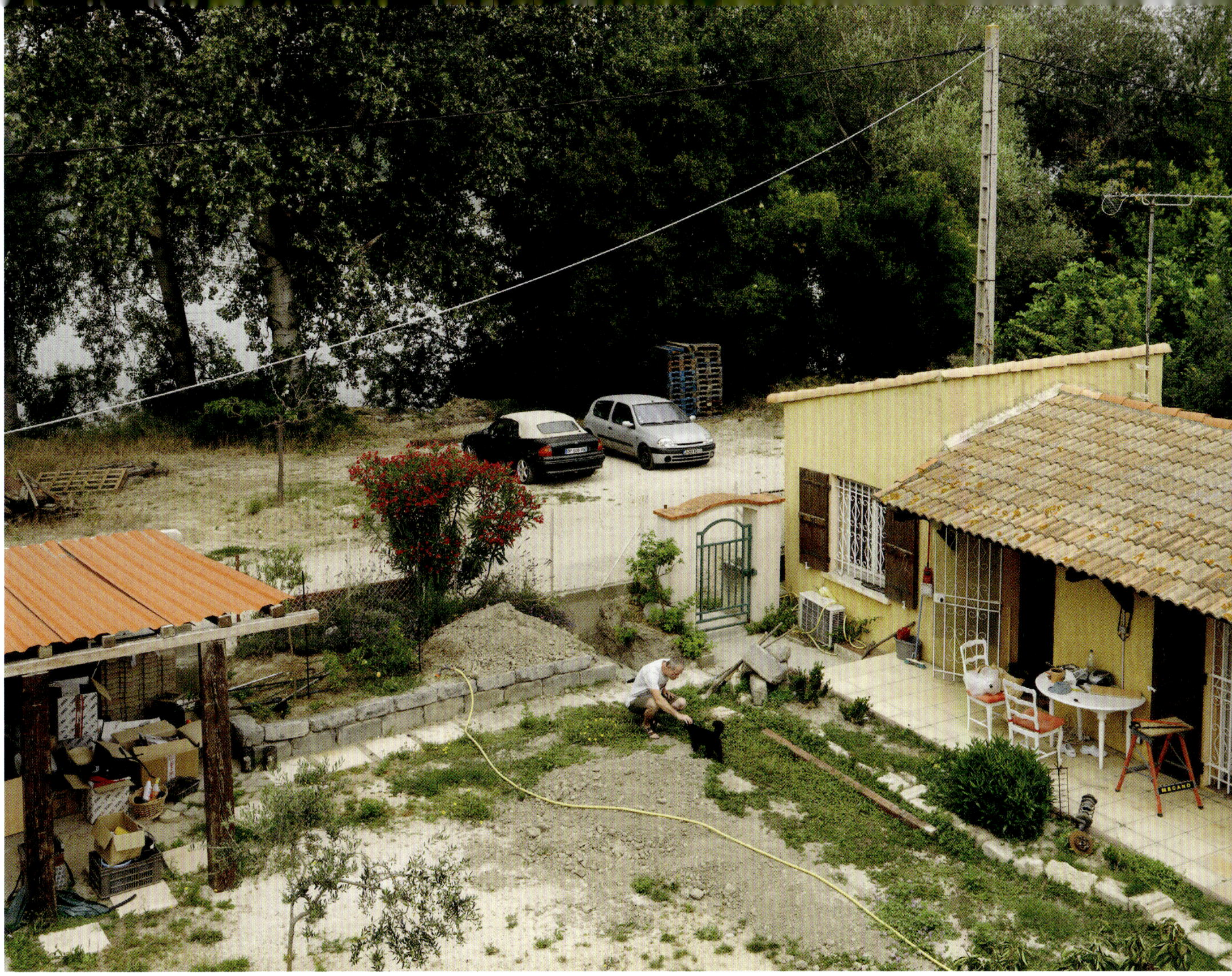
MECANO

The Taos Valley in Northern New Mexico occupies a unique place in American landscape, history and contemporary culture. Ancient geological forces formed a valley bordered by majestic Sangre de Cristo Mountains, the powerful Rio Grande River and sweeping cinematic skies. Living together amid this great natural beauty are Native American Pueblo people, descendants of the Colonial Spanish, and more recently an influx of Anglo baby boomer retirees. Each group, with their own cultural values and traditions, shapes this shared physical environment. These photographs reference the production, consumption, preservation and destruction of material culture within this sparsely populated desert landscape. They are selected from an ongoing documentary of Taos begun in 2004.

www.deborahunter.com

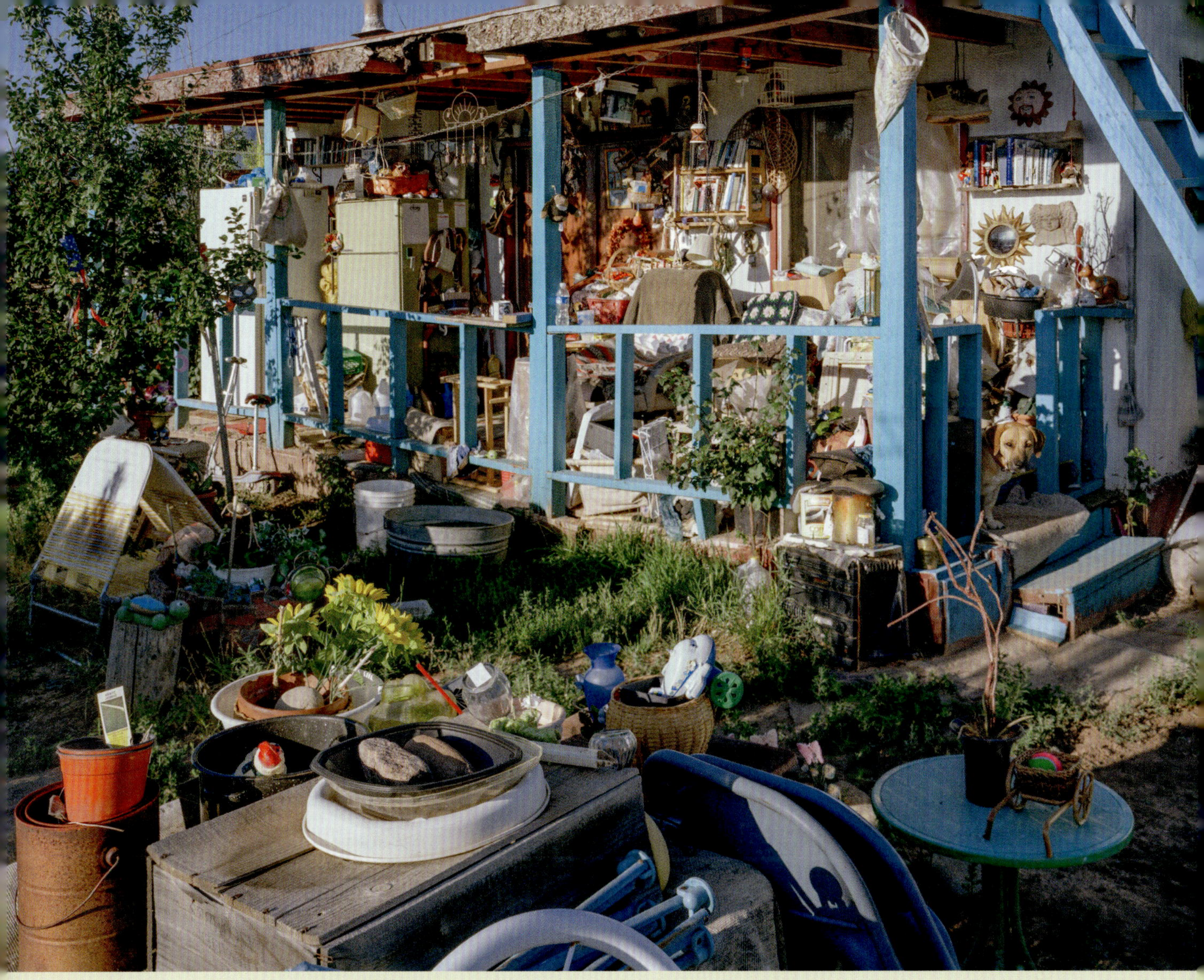

Debora Hunter

HOLDING ON AND LETTING GO:
MATERIAL CULTURE AT WORK IN TAOS, NEW MEXICO

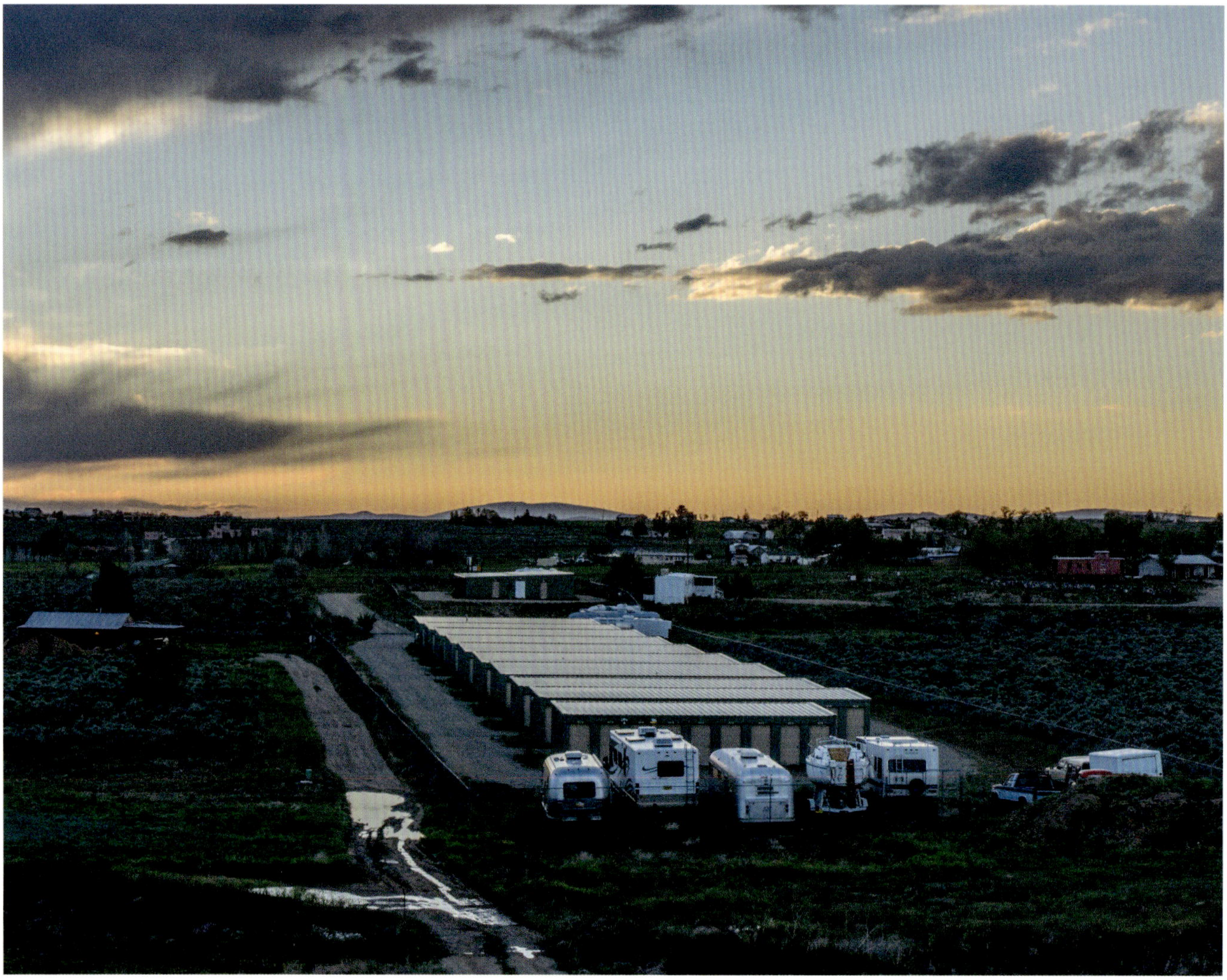

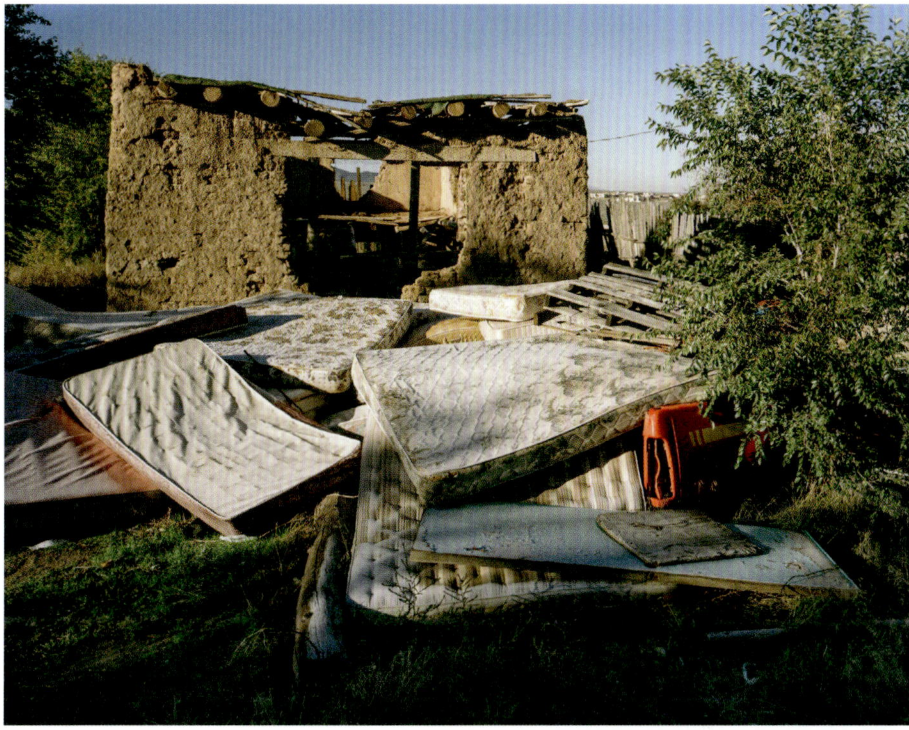

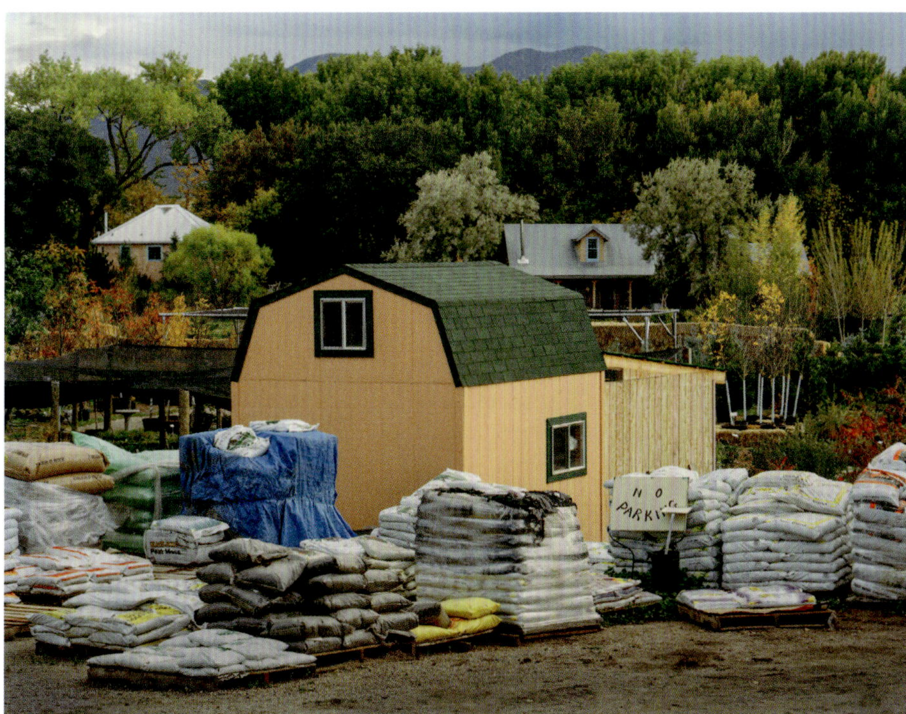

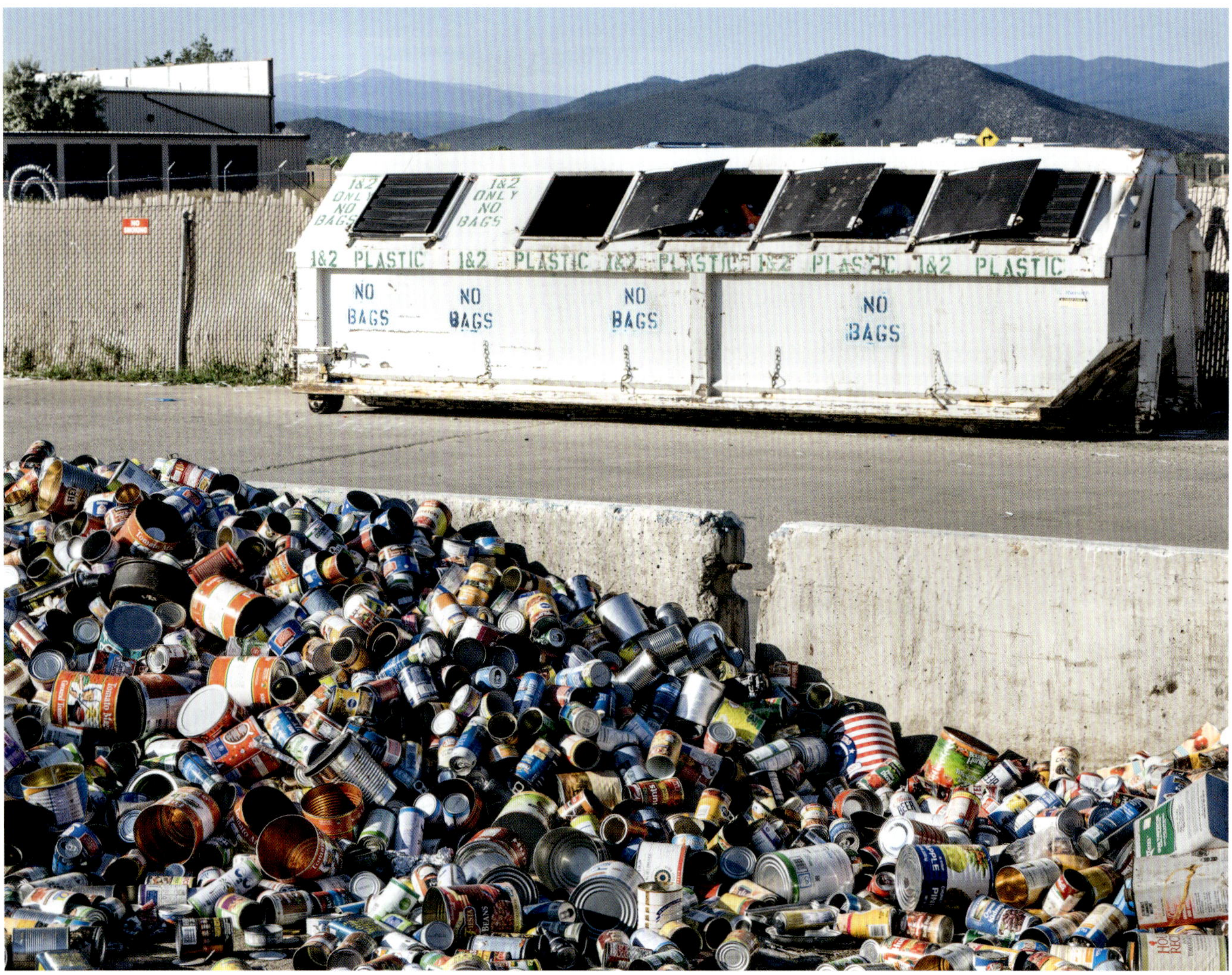
1&2 ONLY NO BAGS
1&2 PLASTIC
NO BAGS

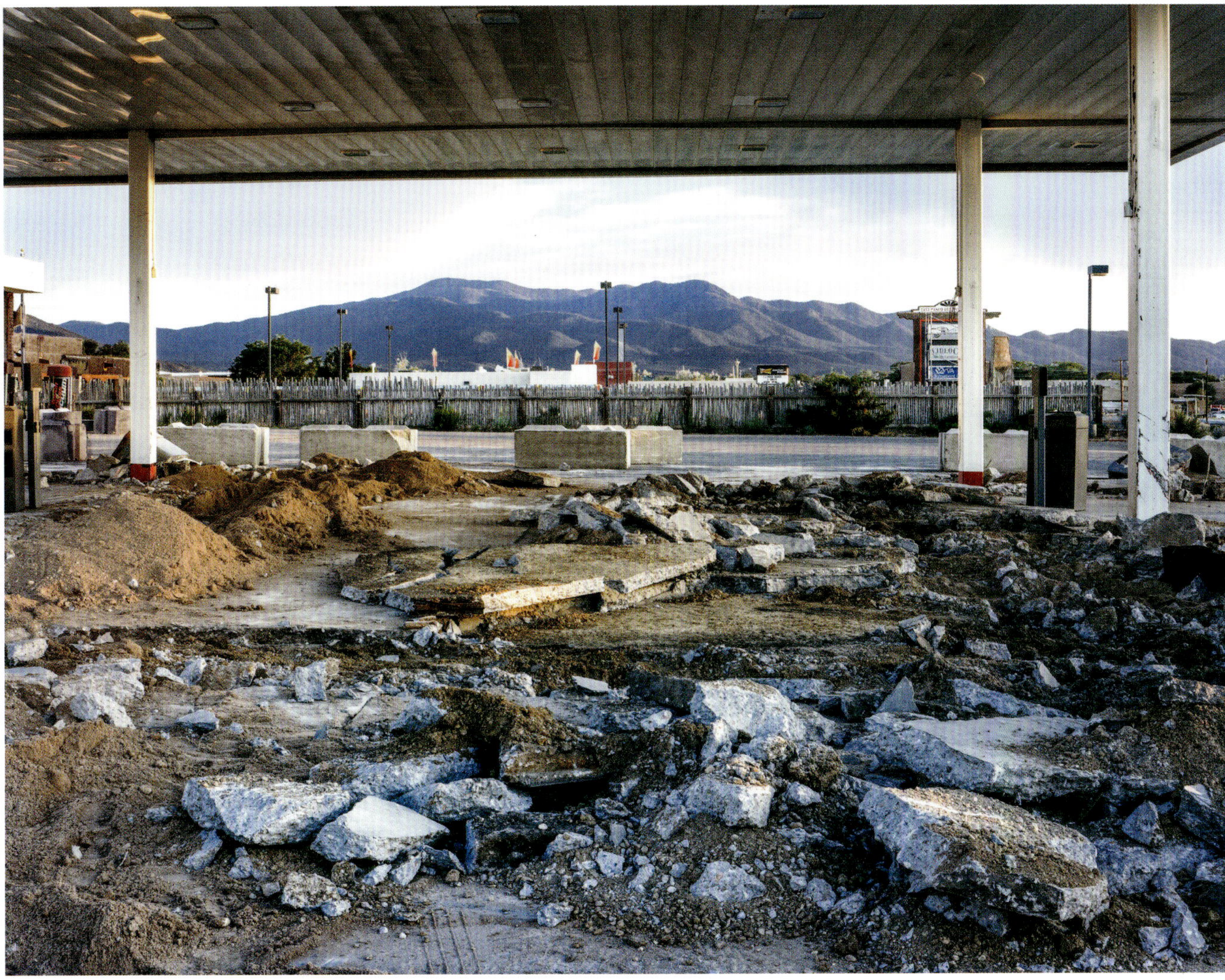

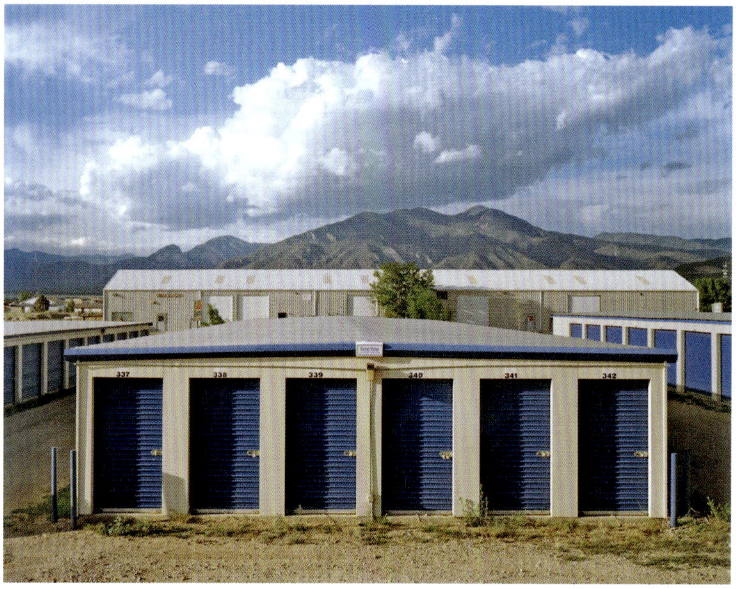
337
338
339
340
341
342

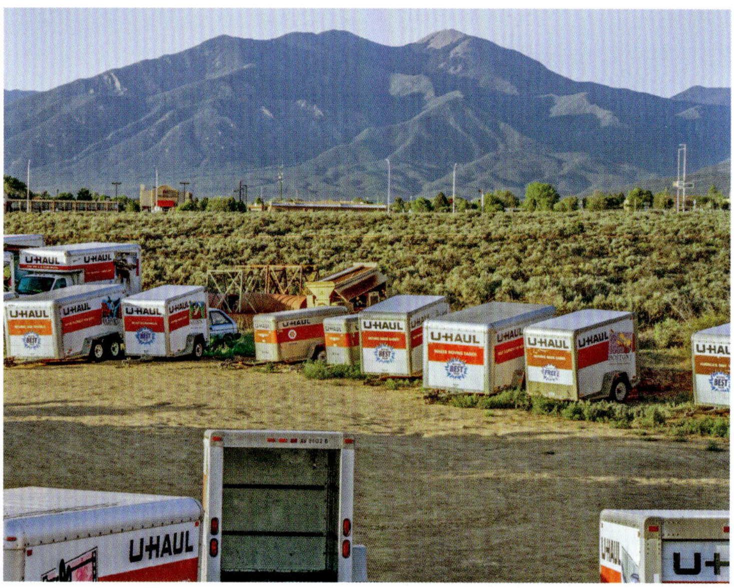
U-HAUL
U-HAUL
U-HAUL
U-HAUL
U-HAUL
U-HAUL
U-HAUL
U-HAUL

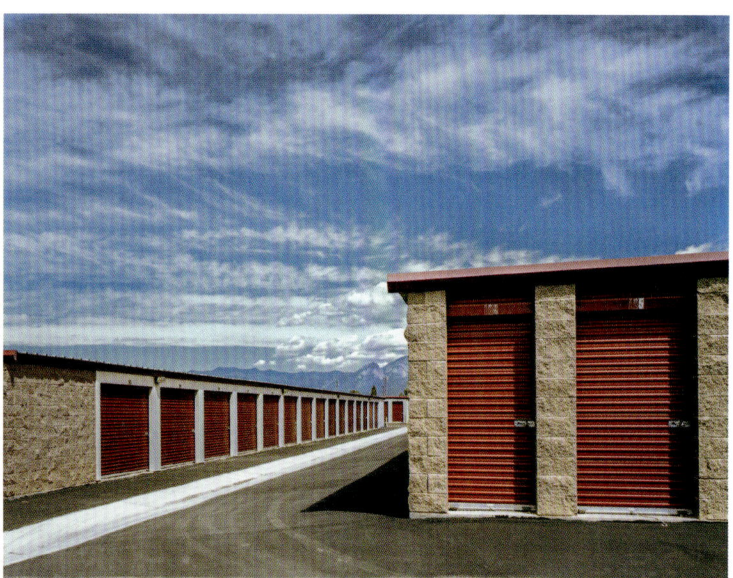

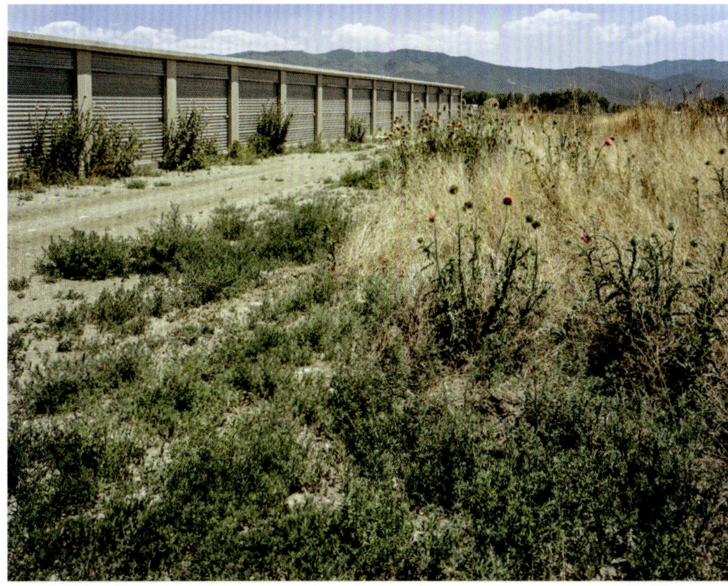

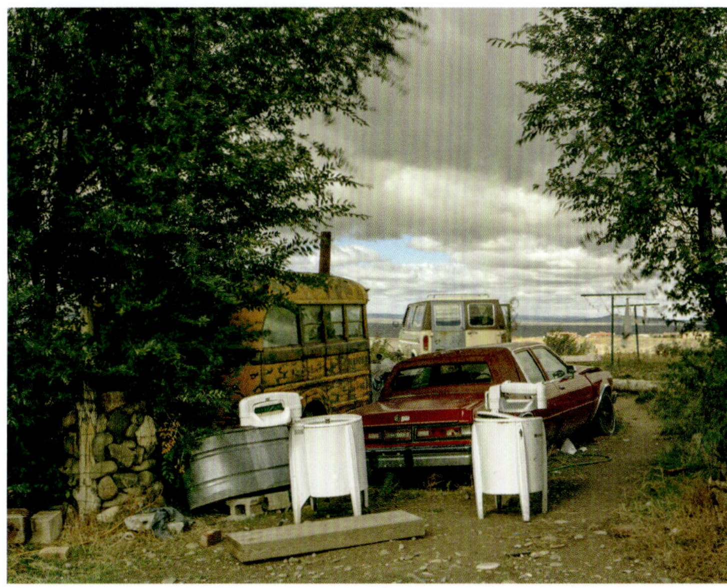

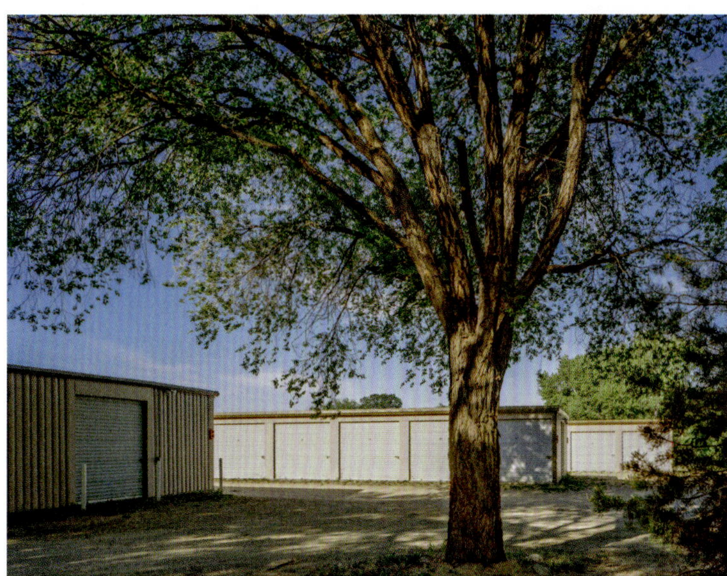

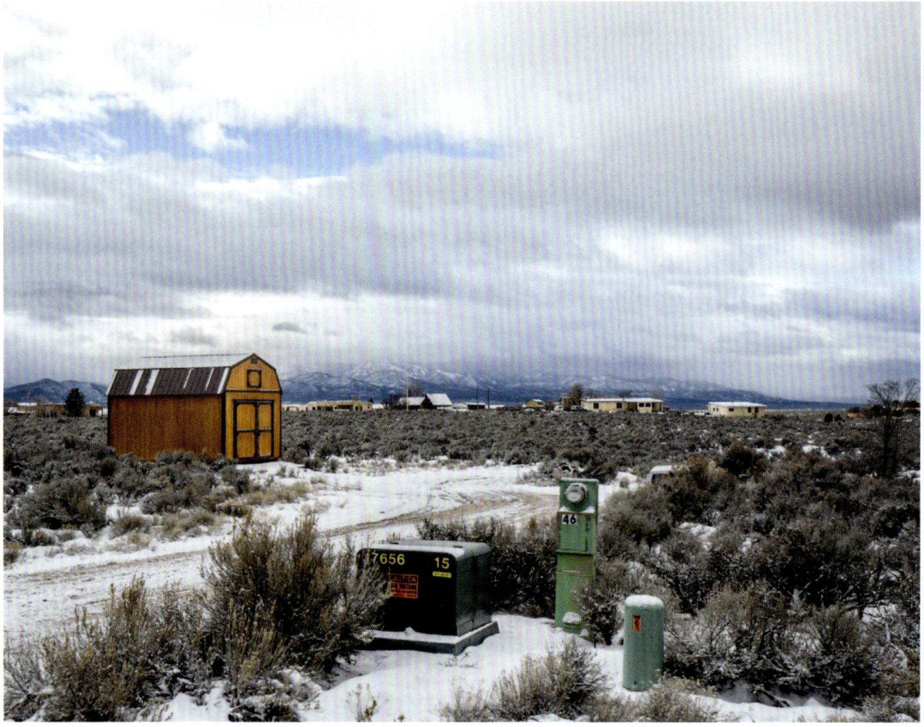
7656 15
46

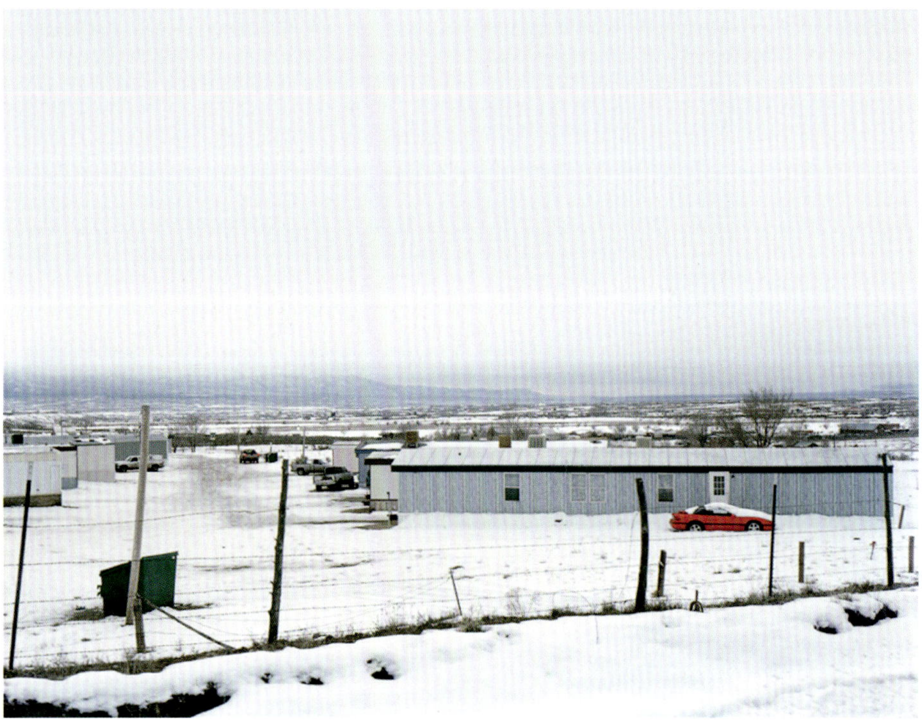

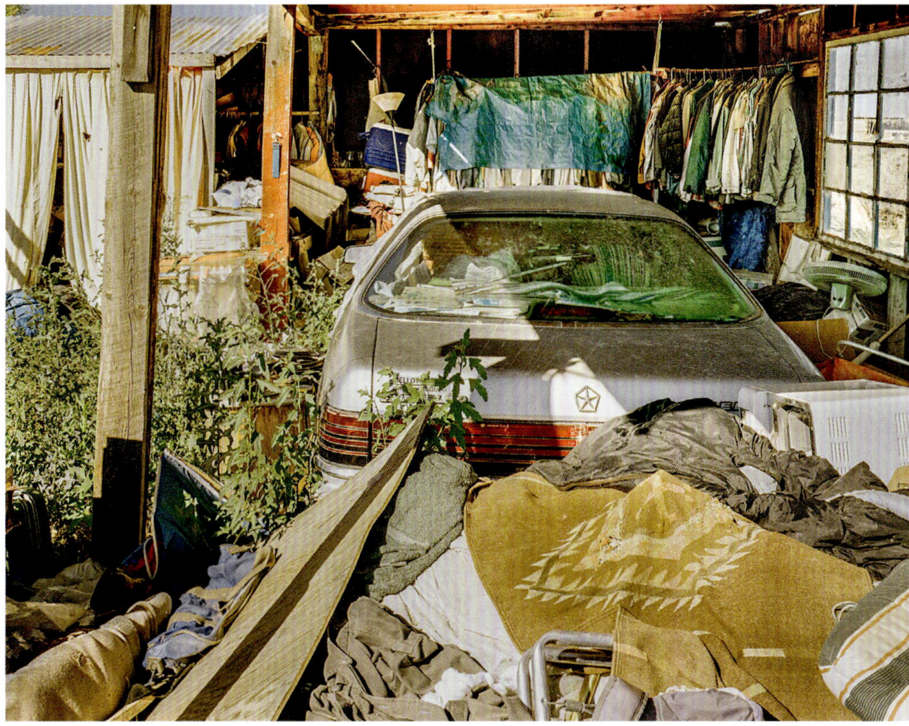

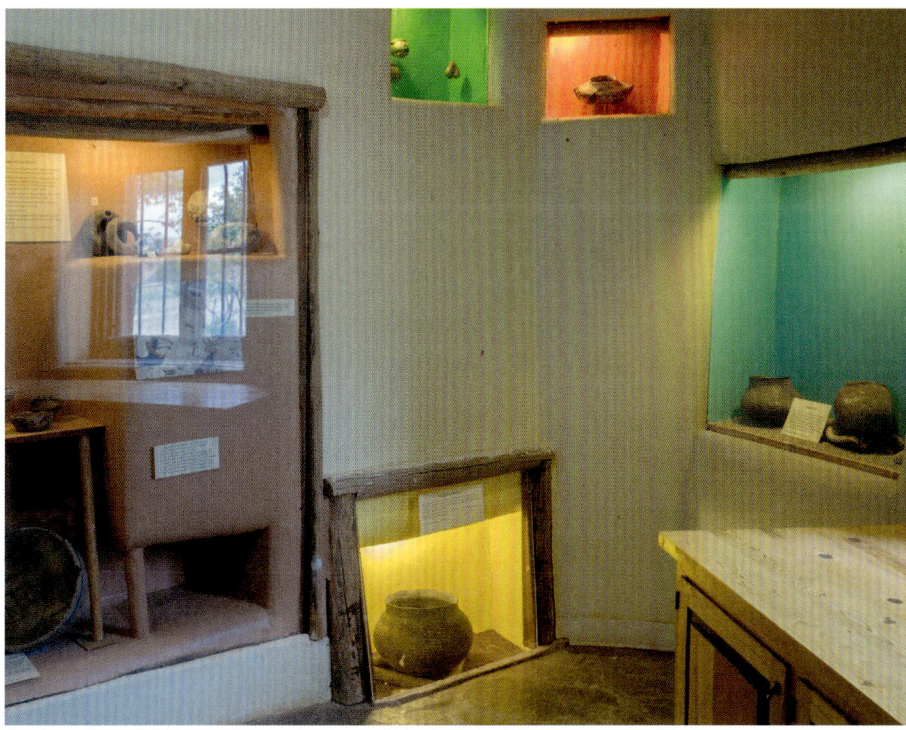

Layout
Michelines/Line Célo and Clémence Michon, Paris

Cover design and typesetting
hawemannundmosch, Berlin

Cover illustration
Gérard Dufresne

Copy editing
Françoise Arnold and Valérie Thouard, Paris

Project management
Henriette Mueller-Stahl, Berlin

Translation from French
Chris Hinton and Nicolas Carter, Great Missenden

Production
Heike Strempel, Berlin

Lithography
SNEL, Vottem

Paper
Arcoprint milk 1,5 Vol., 120 g/m²
Magno Volume, 135 g/m²

Printing
optimal media GmbH, Röbel/Müritz

Library of Congress Control Number: 2019936657

Bibliographic information published by the German National Library
The German National Library lists this publication in the Deutsche Nationalbibliografie; detailed bibliographic data are available on the Internet at http://dnb.dnb.de.

ISBN 978-3-0356-1826-6
e-ISBN (PDF) 978-3-0356-1837-2

9 8 7 6 5 4 3 2 1 www.birkhauser.com

ANR · AUSser umr 3329 du cnrs · cnrs
paris-belleville école nationale supérieure d'architecture · larep laboratoire de recherche en paysage · école nationale supérieure de paysage Versailles Marseille